WORLD TRADE ORGANIZATION

# Dispute Settlement Reports

1998
Volume VII

Pages 2753-3324

CAMBRIDGE
UNIVERSITY PRESS

PUBLISHED BY THE PRESS SYNDICATE OF THE UNIVERSITY OF CAMBRIDGE
The Pitt Building, Trumpington Street, Cambridge, United Kingdom

CAMBRIDGE UNIVERSITY PRESS
The Edinburgh Building, Cambridge CB2 2RU, UK
40 West 20th Street, New York, NY 10011–4211, USA
10 Stamford Road, Oakleigh, VIC 3166, Australia
Ruiz de Alarcón 13, 28014 Madrid, Spain
Rock House, The Waterfront, Cape Town 8001, South Africa

http://www.cambridge.org



Printed in the United Kingdom at the University Press, Cambridge

French edition and Spanish edition paperbacks of this title are both available directly from WTO Publications, World Trade Organization, Centre William Rappard, 154 rue de Lausanne, CH-1211 Geneva 21, Switzerland http://www.wto.org

ISBN 0 521 80098 6 hardback
ISBN 0 521 80503 1 paperback

**THE WTO DISPUTE SETTLEMENT REPORTS**

The *Dispute Settlement Reports* of the World Trade Organization (the "WTO") include panel and Appellate Body reports, as well as arbitration awards, in disputes concerning the rights and obligations of WTO Members under the provisions of the *Marrakesh Agreement Establishing the World Trade Organization*. The *Dispute Settlement Reports* are available in English, French and Spanish.

*This volume may be cited as DSR 1998:VII*

# TABLE OF CONTENTS

# UNITED STATES - IMPORT PROHIBITION OF CERTAIN SHRIMP AND SHRIMP PRODUCTS

**Report of the Appellate Body**
WT/DS58/AB/R

*Adopted by the Dispute Settlement Body on 6 November 1998*

| | |
|---|---|
| United States, *Appellant*<br>India, Malaysia, Pakistan, Thailand, *Appellees*<br>Australia, Ecuador, the European Communities, Hong Kong, China, Mexico and Nigeria, *Third Participants* | Present:<br>Feliciano, Presiding Member<br>Bacchus, Member<br>Lacarte-Muró, Member |

**TABLE OF CONTENTS**

## I. INTRODUCTION : STATEMENT OF THE APPEAL

1. This is an appeal by the United States from certain issues of law and legal interpretations in the Panel Report, *United States - Import Prohibition of Certain Shrimp and Shrimp Products*.[1] Following a joint request for consultations by India, Malaysia, Pakistan and Thailand on 8 October 1996[2], Malaysia and Thailand requested in a communication dated 9 January 1997[3], and Pakistan asked in a communication dated 30 January 1997[4], that the Dispute Settlement Body (the "DSB") establish a panel to examine their complaint regarding a prohibition imposed by the United States on the importation of certain shrimp and shrimp products by Section

[1] WT/DS58/R, 15 May 1998.

[2] WT/DS58/1, 14 October 1996.

[3] WT/DS58/6, 10 January 1997.

[4] WT/DS58/7, 7 February 1997.

609 of Public Law 101-162[5] ("Section 609") and associated regulations and judicial rulings. On 25 February 1997, the DSB established two panels in accordance with these requests and agreed that these panels would be consolidated into a single Panel, pursuant to Article 9 of the *Understanding on Rules and Procedures Governing the Settlement of Disputes* (the "DSU"), with standard terms of reference.[6] On 10 April 1997, the DSB established another panel with standard terms of reference in accordance with a request made by India in a communication dated 25 February 1997[7], and agreed that this third panel, too, would be merged into the earlier Panel established on 25 February 1997.[8] The Report rendered by the consolidated Panel was circulated to the Members of the World Trade Organization (the "WTO") on 15 May 1998.

2. The relevant factual and regulatory aspects of this dispute are set out in the Panel Report, in particular at paragraphs 2.1-2.16. Here, we outline the United States measure at stake before the Panel and in these appellate proceedings. The United States issued regulations in 1987 pursuant to the Endangered Species Act of 1973[9] requiring all United States shrimp trawl vessels to use approved Turtle Excluder Devices ("TEDs") or tow-time restrictions in specified areas where there was a significant mortality of sea turtles in shrimp harvesting.[10] These regulations, which became fully effective in 1990, were modified so as to require the use of approved TEDs at all times and in all areas where there is a likelihood that shrimp trawling will interact with sea turtles, with certain limited exceptions.

3. Section 609 was enacted on 21 November 1989. Section 609(a) calls upon the United States Secretary of State, in consultation with the Secretary of Commerce, *inter alia*, to "initiate negotiations as soon as possible for the development of bilateral or multilateral agreements with other nations for the protection and conservation of ... sea turtles" and to "initiate negotiations as soon as possible with all foreign governments which are engaged in, or which have persons or companies engaged in, commercial fishing operations which, as determined by the Secretary of Commerce, may affect adversely such species of sea turtles, for the purpose of entering into bilateral and multilateral treaties with such countries to protect such species of sea turtles; ... ." Section 609(b)(1) imposed, not later than 1 May 1991, an import ban on shrimp harvested with commercial fishing technology which may adversely affect sea turtles. Section 609(b)(2) provides that the import ban on shrimp will not apply to harvesting nations that are certified. Two kinds of annual certifications are required for harvesting nations, details of which were further elaborated in regulatory guidelines in 1991, 1993 and 1996[11]: First, certification shall be granted to countries with a

---

5 16 United States Code (U.S.C.) §1537.

6 WT/DSB/M/29, 26 March 1997.

7 WT/DS58/8, 4 March 1997.

8 WT/DSB/M/31, 12 May 1997.

9 Public Law 93-205, 16 U.S.C. 1531 *et seq.*

10 52 Fed. Reg. 24244, 29 June 1987 (the "1987 Regulations"). Five species of sea turtles fell under the regulations: loggerhead (*Caretta caretta*), Kemp's ridley (*Lepidochelys kempi*), green (*Chelonia mydas*), leatherback (*Dermochelys coriacea*) and hawksbill (*Eretmochelys imbricata*).

11 Hereinafter referred to as the "1991 Guidelines" (56 Federal Register 1051, 10 January 1991), the "1993 Guidelines" (58 Federal Register 9015, 18 February 1993) and the "1996 Guidelines" (61 Federal Register 17342, 19 April 1996), respectively.

fishing environment which does not pose a threat of the incidental taking of sea turtles in the course of shrimp harvesting.[12] According to the 1996 Guidelines, the Department of State "shall certify any harvesting nation meeting the following criteria without the need for action on the part of the government of the harvesting nation: (a) Any harvesting nation without any of the relevant species of sea turtles occurring in waters subject to its jurisdiction; (b) Any harvesting nation that harvests shrimp exclusively by means that do not pose a threat to sea turtles, *e.g.*, any nation that harvests shrimp exclusively by artisanal means; or (c) Any nation whose commercial shrimp trawling operations take place exclusively in waters subject to its jurisdiction in which sea turtles do not occur."[13]

4. Second, certification shall be granted to harvesting nations that provide documentary evidence of the adoption of a regulatory program governing the incidental taking of sea turtles in the course of shrimp trawling that is comparable to the United States program *and* where the average rate of incidental taking of sea turtles by their vessels is comparable to that of United States vessels.[14] According to the 1996 Guidelines, the Department of State assesses the regulatory program of the harvesting nation and certification shall be made if the program includes: (i) the required use of TEDs that are "comparable in effectiveness to those used in the United States. Any exceptions to this requirement must be comparable to those of the United States program ... "; and (ii) "a credible enforcement effort that includes monitoring for compliance and appropriate sanctions."[15] The regulatory program may be in the form of regulations, or may, in certain circumstances, take the form of a voluntary arrangement between industry and government.[16] Other measures that the harvesting nation undertakes for the protection of sea turtles will also be taken into account in making the comparability determination.[17] The average incidental take rate "will be deemed comparable if the harvesting nation requires the use of TEDs in a manner comparable to that of the U.S. program ... ."[18]

5. The 1996 Guidelines provide that all shrimp imported into the United States must be accompanied by a Shrimp Exporter's Declaration form attesting that the shrimp was harvested either in the waters of a nation currently certified under Section 609 or "under conditions that do not adversely affect sea turtles", that is: (a) "Shrimp harvested in an aquaculture facility in which the shrimp spend at least 30 days in ponds prior to being harvested"; (b) "Shrimp harvested by commercial shrimp trawl vessels using TEDs comparable in effectiveness to those required in the United States"; (c) "Shrimp harvested exclusively by means that do not involve the retrieval of fishing nets by mechanical devices or by vessels using gear that, in accordance with the U.S. program ... , would not require TEDs"; and (d) "Species of shrimp, such as the pandalid species, harvested in areas where sea turtles do not occur."[19] On

---

12 Section 609(b)(2)(C).
13 1996 Guidelines, p. 17343.
14 Section 609(b)(2)(A) and (B).
15 1996 Guidelines, p. 17344.
16 *Ibid.*
17 *Ibid.*
18 *Ibid.*
19 1996 Guidelines, p. 17343.

8 October 1996, the United States Court of International Trade ruled that the 1996 Guidelines were in violation of Section 609 in allowing the import of shrimp from non-certified countries if accompanied by a Shrimp Exporter's Declaration form attesting that they were caught with commercial fishing technology that did not adversely affect sea turtles.[20] A 25 November 1996 ruling of the United States Court of International Trade clarified that shrimp harvested by manual methods which did not harm sea turtles could still be imported from non-certified countries.[21] On 4 June 1998, the United States Court of Appeals for the Federal Circuit vacated the decisions of the United States Court of International Trade of 8 October and 25 November 1996.[22] In practice, however, exemption from the import ban for TED-caught shrimp from non-certified countries remained unavailable while this dispute was before the Panel and before us.[23]

6. The 1991 Guidelines limited the geographical scope of the import ban imposed by Section 609 to countries in the wider Caribbean/western Atlantic region[24], and granted these countries a three-year phase-in period. The 1993 Guidelines maintained this geographical limitation. On 29 December 1995, the United States Court of International Trade held that the 1991 and 1993 Guidelines violated Section 609 by limiting its geographical scope to shrimp harvested in the wider Caribbean/western Atlantic region, and directed the Department of State to extend the ban worldwide not later than 1 May 1996.[25] On 10 April 1996, the United States Court of International Trade refused a subsequent request by the Department of State to postpone the 1 May 1996 deadline.[26] On 19 April 1996, the United States issued the 1996 Guidelines, extending Section 609 to shrimp harvested in *all* foreign countries effective 1 May 1996.

7. In the Panel Report, the Panel reached the following conclusions:

> In the light of the findings above, we conclude that the import ban on shrimp and shrimp products as applied by the United States on the basis of Section 609 of Public Law 101-162 is not consistent with Article XI:1 of GATT 1994, and cannot be justified under Article XX of GATT 1994.[27]

and made this recommendation:

> The Panel *recommends* that the Dispute Settlement Body request the United States to bring this measure into conformity with its obligations under the WTO Agreement.[28]

8. On 13 July 1998, the United States notified the DSB of its decision to appeal certain issues of law covered in the Panel Report and certain legal interpretations

---

20 *Earth Island Institute v. Warren Christopher*, 942 Fed. Supp. 597 (CIT 1996).

21 *Earth Island Institute v. Warren Christopher*, 948 Fed. Supp. 1062 (CIT 1996).

22 1998 U.S. App. Lexis 11789.

23 Response by the United States to questioning at the oral hearing.

24 Specifically, Mexico, Belize, Guatemala, Honduras, Nicaragua, Costa Rica, Panama, Colombia, Venezuela, Trinidad and Tobago, Guyana, Suriname, French Guyana and Brazil.

25 *Earth Island Institute v. Warren Christopher*, 913 Fed. Supp. 559 (CIT 1995).

26 *Earth Island Institute v. Warren Christopher*, 922 Fed. Supp. 616 (CIT 1996).

27 Panel Report, para. 8.1.

28 Panel Report, para. 8.2.

developed by the Panel, pursuant to paragraph 4 of Article 16 of the DSU, and filed a notice of appeal[29] with the Appellate Body pursuant to Rule 20 of the *Working Procedures for Appellate Review*. On 23 July 1998, the United States filed an appellant's submission.[30] On 7 August 1998, India, Pakistan and Thailand ("Joint Appellees") filed a joint appellees' submission and Malaysia filed a separate appellee's submission.[31] On the same day, Australia, Ecuador, the European Communities, Hong Kong, China, and Nigeria each filed separate third participants' submissions.[32] At the invitation of the Appellate Body, the United States, India, Pakistan, Thailand and Malaysia filed additional submissions on certain issues arising under Article XX(b) and Article XX(g) of the GATT 1994 on 17 August 1998. The oral hearing in the appeal was held on 19-20 August 1998. The participants and third participants presented oral arguments and responded to questions put to them by the Members of the Division hearing the appeal.

## II. ARGUMENTS OF THE PARTICIPANTS AND THIRD PARTICIPANTS

### A. *Claims of Error by the United States - Appellant*

#### 1. *Non-requested Information from Non-governmental Organizations*

9. The United States claims that the Panel erred in finding that it could not accept non-requested submissions from non-governmental organizations. According to the United States, there is nothing in the DSU that prohibits panels from considering information just because the information was unsolicited. The language of Article 13.2 of the DSU is broadly drafted to provide a panel with discretion in choosing its sources of information. When a non-governmental organization makes a submission to a panel, Article 13.2 of the DSU authorizes the panel to "seek" such information. To find otherwise would unnecessarily limit the discretion that the DSU affords panels in choosing the sources of information to consider.

#### 2. *Article XX of the GATT 1994*

10. In the view of the United States, the Panel erred in finding that Section 609 was outside the scope of Article XX. The United States stresses that under the Panel's factual findings and undisputed facts on the record, Section 609 is within the scope of the Article XX chapeau and Article XX(g) and, in the alternative, Article XX(b), of the GATT 1994. The Panel was also incorrect in finding that Section 609 constitutes "unjustifiable discrimination between countries where the same conditions prevail". The Panel interprets the chapeau of Article XX as requiring panels to determine whether a measure constitutes a "threat to the multilateral trading system". This interpretation of Article XX has no basis in the text of the GATT 1994, has

---

29 WT/DS58/11, 13 July 1998.

30 Pursuant to Rule 21(1) of the *Working Procedures for Appellate Review*.

31 Pursuant to Rule 22(1) of the *Working Procedures for Appellate Review*.

32 Pursuant to Rule 24 of the *Working Procedures for Appellate Review*.

never been adopted by any previous panel or Appellate Body Report, and would impermissibly diminish the rights that WTO Members reserved under Article XX.

11. The United States contends that the Panel's findings are not based on the ordinary meaning and context of the term "unjustifiable discrimination". That term raises the issue of whether a particular discrimination is "justifiable". During the Panel proceeding, the United States presented the rationale of Section 609 for restricting imports of shrimp from some countries and not from others: sea turtles are threatened with extinction worldwide; most nations, including the appellees, recognize the importance of conserving sea turtles; and shrimp trawling without the use of TEDs contributes greatly to the endangerment of sea turtles. In these circumstances, it is reasonable and justifiable for Section 609 to differentiate between countries whose shrimp industries operate without TEDs, and thereby endanger sea turtles, and those countries whose shrimp industries do employ TEDs in the course of harvesting shrimp.

12. The Panel, the United States believes, did not address the rationale of the United States for differentiating between shrimp harvesting countries. Rather, the Panel asked a different question: would the United States measure and similar measures taken by other countries "undermine the multilateral trading system"? The distinction between "unjustifiable discrimination" - the actual term used in the GATT 1994 - and the Panel's "threat to the multilateral trading system" test is crucial, in the view of the United States, and is posed sharply in paragraph 7.61 of the Panel Report, where the Panel states: "even though the situation of turtles is a serious one, we consider that the United States adopted measures which, irrespective of their environmental purpose, were clearly a threat to the multilateral trading system ... ." An environmental purpose is fundamental to the application of Article XX, and such a purpose cannot be ignored, especially since the preamble to the *Marrakesh Agreement Establishing the World Trade Organization*[33] (the "*WTO Agreement*") acknowledges that the rules of trade should be "in accordance with the objective of sustainable development", and should seek to "protect and preserve the environment". Moreover, Article XX neither defines nor mentions the "multilateral trading system", nor conditions a Member's right to adopt a trade-restricting measure on the basis of hypothetical effects on that system.

13. In adopting its "threat to the multilateral trading system" analysis, the Panel fails to apply the ordinary meaning of the text: whether a justification can be presented for applying a measure in a manner which constitutes discrimination. Instead, the Panel expands the ordinary meaning of the text to encompass a much broader and more subjective inquiry. As a result, the Panel would add an entirely new obligation under Article XX of the GATT 1994: namely that Members may not adopt measures that would result in certain effects on the trading system. Under the ordinary meaning of the text, there is sufficient justification for an environmental conservation measure if a conservation purpose justifies a difference in treatment between Members. Further inquiry into effects on the trading system is uncalled for and incorrect.

14. In the view of the United States, the Panel also fails to take account of the context of the term "unjustifiable discrimination". The language of the Article XX

[33] Done at Marrakesh, 15 April 1994.

chapeau indicates that the chapeau was intended to prevent the abusive application of the exceptions for protectionist or other discriminatory aims. This is consistent with the approach of the Appellate Body in *United States - Standards for Reformulated and Conventional Gasoline*[34] ("*United States - Gasoline*") and with the preparatory work of the GATT 1947. In context, an alleged "discrimination between countries where the same conditions prevail" is not "unjustifiable" where the policy goal of the Article XX exception being applied provides a rationale for the justification.

15. In the context of the GATT/WTO dispute settlement system, measures within the scope of Article XX can be expected to result in reduced market access or discriminatory treatment. To interpret the prohibition of "unjustifiable discrimination" in the Article XX chapeau as excluding measures which result in "reduced market access" or "discriminatory treatment" would, in effect, erase Article XX from the GATT 1994. The Panel's "threat to the multilateral trading system" analysis erroneously confuses the question of whether a measure reduces market access with the further and separate question arising under the chapeau as to whether that measure is nevertheless "justifiable" under one of the general exceptions in Article XX. The proper inquiry under the Article XX chapeau is whether a non-protectionist rationale, such as a rationale based on the policy goal of the applicable Article XX exception, could justify any discrimination resulting from the measure. Here, any "discrimination" resulting from the measure is based on, and in support of, the goal of sea turtle conservation.

16. The United States also argues that the Panel incorrectly applies the object and purpose of the *WTO Agreement* in interpreting Article XX of the GATT 1994. It is legal error to jump from the observation that the GATT 1994 is a trade agreement to the conclusion that trade concerns must prevail over all other concerns in all situations arising under GATT rules. The very language of Article XX indicates that the state interests protected in that article are, in a sense, "pre-eminent" to the GATT's goals of promoting market access.

17. Furthermore, the Panel failed to recognize that most treaties have no single, undiluted object and purpose but rather a variety of different, and possibly conflicting, objects and purposes. This is certainly true of the *WTO Agreement*. Thus, while the first clause of the preamble to the *WTO Agreement* calls for the expansion of trade in goods and services, this same clause also recognizes that international trade and economic relations under the *WTO Agreement* should allow for "optimal use of the world's resources in accordance with the objective of sustainable development", and should seek "to protect and preserve the environment". The Panel in effect took a one-sided view of the object and purpose of the *WTO Agreement* when it fashioned a new test not found in the text of the Agreement.

18. The additional bases, the United States continues, invoked by the Panel to support its "threat to the multilateral trading system" analysis - i.e. the protection of expectations of Members as to the competitive relationship between their products and the products of other Members; the application of the international law principle

---

[34] Adopted 20 May 1996, WT/DS2/AB/R.

according to which international agreements must be applied in good faith; and the *Belgian Family Allowances*[35] panel report - are without merit.

19. The United States submits that Section 609 does not threaten the multilateral trading system. The Panel did not find Section 609 to be an *actual* threat to the multilateral trading system. Rather, the Panel found that if other countries in other circumstances were to adopt the same type of measure here adopted by the United States *potentially* a threat to the system might arise. The United States urges that in engaging in hypothetical speculations regarding the effects of other measures which might be adopted in differing situations, while ignoring the compelling circumstances of this case, the Panel violated the Appellate Body's prescription in *United States - Gasoline*[36] that Article XX must be applied on a "case-by-case basis", with careful scrutiny of the specific facts of the case at hand. The Panel's "threat to the multilateral trading system" analysis adds a new obligation under Article XX of the GATT 1994 and is inconsistent with the proper role of the Panel under the DSU, in particular Articles 3.2 and 19.2 thereof.

20. To the United States, Section 609 reasonably differentiates between countries on the basis of the risk posed to endangered sea turtles by their shrimp trawling industries. Considering the aim of the Article XX chapeau to prevent abuse of the Article XX exceptions, an evaluation of whether a measure constitutes "unjustifiable discrimination where the same conditions prevail" should take account of whether the differing treatment between countries relates to the policy goal of the applicable Article XX exception. If a measure differentiates between countries on a basis "legitimately connected" with the policy of an Article XX exception, rather than for protectionist reasons, that measure does not amount to an abuse of the applicable Article XX exception.

21. The contention of the United States is that its measure does not treat differently those countries whose shrimp trawling industries pose similar risks to sea turtles. Only nations with shrimp trawling industries that harvest shrimp in waters where there is a likelihood of intercepting sea turtles, and that employ mechanical equipment which harms sea turtles, are subject to the import restrictions. The Panel properly recognized that certain naturally-occurring conditions relating to sea turtle conservation (namely, whether sea turtles and shrimp occur concurrently in a Member's waters) and at least certain conditions relating to how shrimp are caught (namely, whether shrimp nets are retrieved mechanically or by hand) are relevant factors in applying the Article XX chapeau. However, the Panel found that another condition relating to how shrimp are caught - namely, whether a country requires its shrimp fishermen to use TEDs - did not provide a basis under the chapeau for treating countries differently. Differing treatment based on whether a country had adopted a TEDs requirement was, in the Panel's view, "unjustifiable".

22. The United States believes that the analysis employed by the Appellate Body in *United States - Gasoline*[37] leads to the conclusion that Section 609 does not constitute "unjustifiable discrimination". Section 609 is applied narrowly and fairly. The United States does not apply sea turtle conservation rules differently to United States

35 Adopted 7 November 1952, BISD 1S/59.

36 Adopted 20 May 1996, WT/DS2/AB/R.

37 Adopted 20 May 1996, WT/DS2/AB/R.

and foreign shrimp fishermen. Moreover, the United States has taken steps to assist foreign shrimp fishermen in adopting conservation measures and has undertaken efforts to transfer TED technology to governments and industries in other countries, including the appellees. In addition, Section 609 is limited in coverage and focuses on sea turtle conservation.

23. During the Panel proceeding, the United States presented "compelling evidence", reaffirmed by five independent experts, that Section 609 was a *bona fide* conservation measure under Article XX, imbued with the purpose of conserving a species facing the threat of extinction. To uphold the findings of the Panel would impermissibly change the basic terms of the bargain agreed to by WTO Members in agreeing to the GATT 1994. Further, to condone the Panel's adoption of a vague and subjective "threat to the multilateral trading system" test would fundamentally alter the intended role of panels under the DSU, and could call into question the legitimacy of the WTO dispute settlement process.

24. The United States states that neither it nor the appellees have appealed the decisions of the Panel to address first the Article XX chapeau and not to reach the issues regarding Article XX(b) and Article XX(g). Because the Panel made no findings regarding the applicability of Article XX(b) and XX(g), there are no findings in respect thereof that could even be the subject of appeal. Accordingly, issues regarding the applicability of Article XX(b) and Article XX(g) are not initially presented to the Appellate Body. However, the United States concurs with Joint Appellees that the Appellate Body may address Article XX(b) or Article XX(g) if it finds that Section 609 meets the criteria of the Article XX chapeau. In that case, the United States asserts that Article XX(g) should be applied first as it is the "most pertinent" of the Article XX exceptions, and that issues relating to Article XX(b) need be reached only if Article XX(g) were found to be inapplicable. The United States incorporates by reference and briefly summarizes the submissions that it made to the Panel regarding Article XX(b) and Article XX(g).

25. The essential claim of the United States is that Section 609 meets each element required under Article XX(g). Sea turtles are important natural resources. They are also an exhaustible natural resource since all species of sea turtles, including those found in the appellees' waters, face the danger of extinction. All species of sea turtles have been included in Appendix I of the Convention on International Trade in Endangered Species of Wild Flora and Fauna[38] (the "CITES") since 1975, and other international agreements also recognize the endangered status of sea turtles.[39] In paragraph 7.58 of the Panel Report, the Panel noted: "The endangered nature of the species of sea turtles mentioned in [CITES] Annex I as well as the need to protect them are consequently not contested by the parties to the dispute."

26. The United States maintains Section 609 "relates to" the conservation of sea turtles. A "substantial relationship" exists between Section 609 and the conservation

[38] Done at Washington, 3 March 1973, 993 U.N.T.S. 243, 12 International Legal Materials 1085.

[39] The United States states that all species of sea turtle except the flatback are listed in Appendices I and II of the Convention on the Conservation of Migratory Species of Wild Animals, done at Bonn, 23 June 1979, 19 International Legal Materials 15; and in Appendix II of the Protocol concerning Specially Protected Areas and Wildlife to the Convention for the Protection and Development of the Marine Environment of the Wider Caribbean Region, 29 March 1983, T.I.A.S. No. 11085.

of sea turtles. Shrimp trawl nets are a major cause of human-induced sea turtle deaths, and TEDs are highly effective in preventing such mortality. The Panel noted that "TEDs, when properly installed and used and adapted to the local area, would be an effective tool for the preservation of sea turtles."[40] By encouraging the use of TEDs, Section 609 promotes sea turtle conservation.

27. The United States contends that Section 609 is also "made effective in conjunction with restrictions on domestic production or consumption" within the meaning of Article XX(g). The United States requires its shrimp trawl vessels that operate in waters where there is a likelihood of intercepting sea turtles to use TEDs at all times, and Section 609 applies comparable standards to imported shrimp. Section 609 is also "even-handed": it allows any nation to be certified - and thus avoid any restriction on shrimp exports to the United States - if it meets criteria for sea turtle conservation in the course of shrimp harvesting that are comparable to criteria applicable in the United States. With respect to nations whose shrimp trawl vessels operate in waters where there is a likelihood of intercepting sea turtles, Section 609 provides for certification where those nations adopt TEDs-use requirements comparable to those in effect in the United States.

28. The United States submits, moreover, that Section 609 is a measure "necessary to protect human, animal or plant life or health" within the meaning of Article XX(b). Section 609 is intended to protect and conserve the life and health of sea turtles, by requiring that shrimp imported into the United States shall not have been harvested in a manner harmful to sea turtles. Section 609 is "necessary" in two different senses. First, efforts to reduce sea turtle mortality are "necessary" because all species of sea turtles are threatened with extinction. Second, Section 609 relating to the use of TEDs is "necessary" because other measures to protect sea turtles are not sufficient to allow sea turtles to move back from the brink of extinction.

## *B. India, Pakistan and Thailand - Joint Appellees*

### *1. Non-requested Information from Non-governmental Organizations*

29. Joint Appellees submit that the Panel's ruling rejecting non-requested information is correct and should be upheld. According to Joint Appellees, the United States misinterprets Article 13 of the DSU in arguing that nothing in the DSU prohibits panels from considering information merely because the information was unsolicited. The Panel correctly noted that, "pursuant to Article 13 of the DSU, the initiative to seek information and to select the source of information rests with the Panel."[41] It is evident from Article 13 that Members have chosen to establish a formalized system for the collection of information, which gives a panel discretion to determine the information it needs to resolve a dispute. Panels have no obligation to consider unsolicited information, and the United States is wrong to argue that they do.

[40] The United States refers to Panel Report, para. 7.60, footnote 674.

[41] Joint Appellees refer to Panel Report, para. 7.8.

30. According to Joint Appellees, when a panel does seek information from an individual or body within a Member's jurisdiction, that panel has an obligation to inform the authorities of that Member. This demonstrates that a panel retains control over the information sought, and also that the panel is required to keep the Members informed of its activities. The process accepted by the Members necessarily implies three steps: a panel's decision to seek technical advice; the notification to a Member that such advice is being sought within its jurisdiction; and the consideration of the requested advice. In the view of Joint Appellees, the interpretation offered by the United States would eliminate the first two of these three steps, thereby depriving a panel of its right to decide whether it needs supplemental information, and what type of information it should seek; as well as depriving Members of their right to know that information is being sought from within their jurisdiction.

31. Joint Appellees point to Appendix 3 of the DSU, which sets out Working Procedures for panels, and especially paragraphs 4 and 6 thereof, which limit the right to present panels with written submissions to parties and third parties. Thus, Joint Appellees argue, Members that are not parties or third parties cannot avail themselves of the right to present written submissions. It would be unreasonable, in the view of Joint Appellees, to interpret the DSU as granting the right to submit an unsolicited written submission to a non-Member, when many Members do not enjoy a similar right.

32. Joint Appellees maintain that, if carried to its logical conclusion, the appellant's argument could result in panels being deluged with unsolicited information from around the world. Such information might be strongly biased, if nationals from Members involved in a dispute could provide unsolicited information. They argue that this would not improve the dispute settlement mechanism, and would only increase the administrative tasks of the already overburdened Secretariat.

33. Joint Appellees argue as well that parties to a panel proceeding might feel obliged to respond to all unsolicited submissions - just in case one of the unsolicited submissions catches the attention of a panel member. Due process requires that a party know what submissions a panel intends to consider, and that all parties be given an opportunity to respond to all submissions. Finally, because Article 12.6 of the DSU requires that second written submissions of the parties be submitted simultaneously, if a party is permitted to append *amicus curiae* briefs to its second submission, other parties can be deprived of their right to respond and be heard.

### 2. *Article XX of the GATT 1994*

34. Joint Appellees maintain that the Panel's ruling on the chapeau of Article XX is correct and should be upheld by the Appellate Body. They underline that the appellant does not appeal either the Panel's conclusion that Section 609 violated Article XI:1 of the GATT 1994, or the Panel's decision to address the chapeau of Article XX before addressing sub-paragraph (b) or (g) of that Article. Nor does the United States dispute that it bears the burden of proving that its measure is within Article XX. The United States takes issue with the Panel's alleged application of the chapeau to protect against a "threat to the multilateral trading system", submitting that the Panel developed a new chapeau "interpretation", "analysis" or "test" to invalidate Section 609, thus impermissibly diminishing the rights of WTO Members. According to Joint Appellees, the appellant's argument is baseless and results from a

mischaracterization of the Panel's decision. The Panel did not invent a new "interpretation", "analysis" or "test", nor did it simply interpret "unjustifiable" to mean "a threat to the multilateral trading system". Instead, the Panel rendered a well-reasoned decision fully supported by the *WTO Agreement*, past GATT/WTO practice, and the accepted rules of interpretation set forth in the Vienna Convention on the Law of Treaties[42] (the "Vienna Convention").

35. Joint Appellees argue that the flaw in Section 609, and in the appellant's argument, is the appellant's failure to accept that conditioning access to markets for a given product upon the adoption of certain policies by exporting Members, can violate the *WTO Agreement*. A Member must seek multilateral solutions to trade-related environmental problems. The threat to the multilateral trade system cited by the Panel is unrelated to the appellant's support for TEDs or turtle conservation. The threat is much simpler: the United States has abused Article XX by unilaterally developing a trade policy, and unilaterally imposing this policy through a trade embargo, as opposed to proceeding down the multilateral path. The multilateral trade system is based on multilateral cooperation. If every WTO Member were free to pursue its own trade policy solutions to what it perceives to be environmental concerns, the multilateral trade system would cease to exist. By preventing the abuse of Article XX, the chapeau protects against threats to the multilateral trading system. The prevention of abuse and the prevention of threats to the multilateral trading system are therefore inextricably linked to the object, purpose and goals of Article XX of the GATT 1994.

36. Joint Appellees submit that on the basis of its interpretation of the term "unjustifiable" in the chapeau and in light of the object and purpose of Article XX of the GATT 1994 and the object and purpose of the *WTO Agreement*, the Panel concluded that the chapeau of Article XX permits Members to derogate from GATT provisions, but prohibits derogations which would constitute abuse of the exceptions contained in Article XX, thereby undermining the WTO multilateral trading system. According to Joint Appellees, what the appellant claims to be a new "test" for justifiability is nothing more than a restatement of the principle that the chapeau's object and purpose is to prevent the abuse of the Article XX exceptions, specifying more clearly what may result from such abuse. In the light of recent and past GATT/WTO practice, in particular the panel report in *United States - Restrictions on Imports of Tuna*[43], the Panel correctly interpreted the chapeau, identifying its object and purpose as the prevention of abuse of the Article XX exceptions, and associating the prevention of such abuse with the preservation of the multilateral trading system.

37. In the view of Joint Appellees, the Panel's decision mirrors the Appellate Body's reasoning in *United States - Gasoline*[44] and is therefore correct. The Appellate Body made three pronouncements in *United States - Gasoline* that influenced the Panel's ruling: first, that the chapeau, by its express terms, addresses, not so much the questioned measure or its specific contents as such, but rather the manner in which the measure is applied[45]; second, that it is, accordingly, important to underscore that the purpose and object of the introductory clauses of Article XX is gener-

[42] Done at Vienna, 23 May 1969, 1155 U.N.T.S. 33; 8 International Legal Materials 679.

[43] Unadopted, DS29/R, 16 June 1994, para 5.26.

[44] Adopted 20 May 1996, WT/DS2/AB/R.

[45] *United States - Gasoline*, adopted 20 May 1996, WT/DS2/AB/R, DSR 1996:I, page 20.

ally the prevention of abuse of the exceptions of Article XX[46]; and, third, that the Appellate Body cautioned against the application of Article XX exceptions so as to "frustrate or defeat" legal obligations of the holder of rights under the GATT 1994.[47]

38. Joint Appellees state that, in examining Section 609, the Panel paid particular attention to the manner in which the embargo is applied, and the Panel noted that the appellant conditioned market access on the adoption by exporting Members of conservation policies comparable to its own. The Panel also found that the United States did not enter into negotiations before it imposed its import ban. The Panel concluded that Section 609 abused Article XX and posed a threat to the multilateral trading system. The Panel equated the prevention of the abuse of Article XX with the avoidance of measures that would "frustrate or defeat the purposes and objects of the General Agreement and the WTO Agreement or its legal obligations under the substantive rules of GATT by abusing the exception contained in Article XX."[48] The Panel buttressed its conclusion by referring to the related principles of good faith and *pacta sunt servanda*, and by citing the *Belgian Family Allowances*[49] panel report.

39. Should the Appellate Body decide to reverse the Panel's findings with respect to the chapeau of Article XX, Joint Appellees request that the Appellate Body rule that Section 609 is "applied in a manner which would constitute a means of arbitrary or unjustifiable discrimination between countries where the same conditions prevail, or a disguised restriction on international trade" in violation of the chapeau of Article XX. Consistently with its decision in *United States - Gasoline*[50], the Appellate Body should examine the manner in which Section 609 has been applied, and decide whether an Article XX exception is being abused so as to frustrate or defeat the substantive rights of the appellees under the GATT 1994.

40. Joint Appellees submit that, even leaving aside the "threat to the multilateral trading system" language of the Panel, there is "compelling evidence" in the record that the appellant abused Article XX and its exceptions. Joint Appellees maintain that this abuse takes several forms, each instance "grave", and, by itself, adequate to support a finding that Section 609 has been applied in an abusive manner so as to frustrate the substantive rights of the appellees under the *WTO Agreement*.

41. First, Section 609 was applied without a serious attempt to reach a cooperative multilateral solution with Joint Appellees. The importance of multilateralism should be clear to the United States because it is an integral provision of Section 609, has been emphasized at numerous GATT and WTO meetings, is reflected in Article 23.1 of the DSU and in Principle 12 of the Rio Declaration on Environment and Development[51], and was underscored by the Appellate Body in *United States - Gasoline*.[52] The chapeau violation that the United States committed in *United States - Gasoline* is, Joint Appellees believe, the same violation committed by the United States in this dispute.

---

46 *United States - Gasoline*, adopted 20 May 1996, WT/DS2/AB/R, DSR 1996:I, page 20.

47 *Ibid.*

48 Joint Appellees refer to Panel Report, para 7.40.

49 Adopted 7 November 1952, BISD 1S/59.

50 Adopted 20 May 1996, WT/DS2/AB/R.

51 UN Doc. A/CONF. 151/5/Rev.1, 13 June 1992, 31 International Legal Materials 874.

52 Adopted 20 May 1996, WT/DS2/AB/R, DSR 1996:I, pp. 23-24.

42. Second, the United States discriminated impermissibly among exporting countries, and between exporting countries and the United States in, *inter alia*, the following ways: (a) "[t]he Panel found that the Appellant negotiated an agreement to protect and conserve sea turtles with some WTO Members, but did not propose the negotiation of such an agreement with the ... Appellees until after having concluded its negotiations with the other Members. The Panel also found that Section 609 was already in effect against the Appellees by the time such negotiations were proposed"; (b) "[p]hase-in periods for the use of TEDs differed depending on the countries involved. 'Initially affected countries' had a three year phase-in period, while 'newly affected nations' were given four months or less to change shrimp harvesting practices"; and (c) Section 609 "discriminates between products based on non-product-related processes and production methods."

43. Third, Joint Appellees contend that the appellant's argument misconstrues key portions of the chapeau and of the Panel Report. The appellant's starting-point is that the Panel's findings are not based on the ordinary meaning of the phrase "unjustifiable discrimination" in the context in which it appears. The appellant also suggests that the only object and purpose of the chapeau is the prevention of "indirect protection". This interpretation is contradicted by recent WTO practice. The Appellate Body Report in *United States - Gasoline*[53] stands for the proposition that "unjustifiable discrimination" has a meaning larger than "indirect protection". The appellant, in effect, suggests that justifiability should be determined by reference to the specific Article XX exception invoked. If discrimination were to be justified merely on the basis of the policy goals of the particular exception invoked, all trade measures that meet the requirements of an Article XX exception would, *ipso facto,* satisfy the requirements of the chapeau. The chapeau would be rendered meaningless - in violation of the commonly accepted rule of treaty interpretation which requires that meaning and effect be given to all treaty terms. The principles enunciated in the Appellate Body Report in *United States - Gasoline* would also become null.

44. Joint Appellees argue that both the Appellate Body in *United States - Gasoline*[54] and the Panel in the present case, recognized that the Article XX chapeau must be interpreted in light of the object and purpose of the *WTO Agreement.* This does not mean re-incorporating substantive GATT provisions into the analysis through the chapeau; it means instead examining a proposed Article XX derogation from the perspective of the broader policy goals of the *WTO Agreement.* The Panel identified two such goals: endeavouring to find cooperative solutions to trade problems; and preventing the risk that a multiplicity of conflicting trade requirements, each justified by reference to Article XX, could emerge. Section 609 jeopardizes both goals and poses a threat to the multilateral trading system.

45. Should the Appellate Body decide to reverse the Panel's legal findings with respect to the chapeau of Article XX and rule that Section 609 meets the requirements of the chapeau, Joint Appellees request that the Appellate Body make legal findings on Article XX(b) and Article XX(g) of the GATT 1994. They incorporate by reference their submissions to the Panel with respect to the interpretation of Article

---

53 Adopted 20 May 1996, WT/DS2/AB/R.

54 *Ibid.*

XX(b) and Article XX(g), while noting at the same time that there are persuasive reasons for following the interpretative approach adopted by the Panel in examining the chapeau first. Not only does the concept of judicial economy favour such an analysis, but also none of the participants has questioned the Panel's interpretative approach in their submissions (although, Joint Appellees note, one third participant, Australia, did comment with disapproval on this approach).

### *C. Malaysia - Appellee*

#### *1. Non-requested Information from Non-governmental Organizations*

46. Malaysia submits that the Panel ruled correctly on this issue and that its ruling should be upheld as there is nothing in the DSU that *permits* the admission of unsolicited briefs from non-governmental organizations. Malaysia does not agree with the United States that there is nothing in the DSU *prohibiting* panels from considering information just because the information was offered unsolicited. Under Article 13 of the DSU, the prerequisite for invocation of that provision is that a panel must "seek" information. In the view of Malaysia, the Panel correctly noted that the initiative to seek information and to select the source of information rests with the Panel. The Panel could not consider unsolicited information. In the alternative, should the Appellate Body accept the United States argument that panels may accept *amicus curia* briefs, it must be left to the complete discretion of panel members whether or not to read them. A panel's decision not to read the briefs cannot constitute a procedural mistake and cannot influence the outcome of a panel report.

#### *2. Article XX of the GATT 1994*

47. Malaysia maintains that the Panel's decision concerning Article XX of the GATT 1994 represents a balanced view of the requirements of the provisions of the *WTO Agreement*, rules of treaty interpretation and GATT practice. The appellant misconceives the Panel's findings: the Panel did not in any way allude to the supremacy of trade concerns over non-trade concerns, and did not fail to recognize that most treaties have no single, undiluted object and purpose but a variety of different objects and purposes. The Panel in fact alluded to the first, second and third paragraphs of the preamble to the *WTO Agreement*, which make reference to different objects and purposes. Moreover, in Malaysia's view, the appellant misapplies the principle in *India - Patent Protection for Pharmaceutical and Agricultural Chemical Products*[55] to the facts of this case, and misconstrues the Panel's application of the *Belgian Family Allowances*[56] panel report.

48. To Malaysia, the Panel's "threat to the multilateral trading system" analysis does not constitute a new test, but is in fact a restatement of the approach taken by the Panel that Members are not allowed to resort to measures that would undermine the multilateral trading system and thus abuse the exceptions contained in Article XX. The Panel itself states that its findings are the result of the application of the

[55] Adopted 16 January 1998, WT/DS50/AB/R.

[56] Adopted 7 November 1952, BISD 1S/59.

interpretative methods required by Article 3.2 of the DSU and that its process of interpretation does not add to Members' obligations in contravention of Article 3.2 of the DSU.

49. It was also noted by Malaysia that the Panel found on the facts that the import ban is applied even on TED-caught shrimp, as long as the country has not been certified; certification is only granted if comprehensive requirements regarding the use of TEDs by fishing vessels are applied by the exporting country concerned or if shrimp trawling operations of the exporting country take place exclusively in waters in which sea turtles do not occur. On the basis of these findings, the Panel concluded that the United States measure constitutes unjustifiable discrimination between countries where the same conditions prevail.

50. Malaysia believes that the Panel relied in large measure on the Appellate Body Report in *United States - Gasoline*.[57] Although the requirement of use of TEDs is applied to both United States and foreign shrimp trawlers, Malaysia contends that Section 609 violates the chapeau prohibition of "unjustifiable discrimination between countries where the same conditions prevail": not all species of sea turtles covered by Section 609 and found in Malaysia and the United States are alike - Kemp's ridley and loggerhead turtles, which occur in the United States, are absent or occur only in negligible numbers in Malaysian waters; the habitats of these turtles do not coincide with areas of shrimp trawling operations in Malaysia; certain countries which have been exempted from TED requirements are harvesting sea turtles commercially and exploiting the eggs; and the time given to countries to comply with the requirements of Section 609 varied.

51. In response to the appellant's statement that it has taken steps to assist foreign shrimp fishermen in adopting turtle conservation measures, Malaysia states that there has been no transfer of TEDs technology to the government and industries in Malaysia, apart from participation by Malaysia in one regional workshop.

52. Malaysia's submissions on legal issues arising under Article XX(b) and Article XX(g) have been addressed by the Panel, at paragraphs 3.213, 3.218-3.221, 3.231, 3.233, 3.236, 3.240, 3.247, 3.257, 3.266, 3.271-3.275, 3.286-3.288 and 3.293 of the Panel Report.

### *D. Arguments of Third Participants*

#### *1. Australia*

53. Australia states that with respect to unsolicited submissions to the Panel by non-governmental organizations, the United States appears to suggest that the Panel's legal interpretation of the provisions of the DSU would limit the discretion the DSU affords to panels in choosing the sources of information they should consider. However, in the view of Australia, nothing in the Panel Report suggests that the Panel saw any legal obstacles to its requesting information from the non-governmental sources, if it had so wished. The decision of the Panel not to seek such information would appear to reflect the exercise of its discretion as provided by the DSU, and was not the result of any perceived legal obstacles. Australia notes that the United

[57] Adopted 20 May 1996, WT/DS2/AB/R.

States has not claimed that the Panel's exercise of its discretion in this matter was inappropriate or involved an error in law.

54. Australia believes that the Panel correctly found that Section 609 constitutes "unjustifiable discrimination between countries where the same conditions prevail". However, Australia supports the appeal by the United States of the Panel's finding that Section 609 "is not within the scope of measures permitted under the chapeau of Article XX." Australia submits that the Appellate Body should complete the analysis under Article XX and find that the United States has not demonstrated that its measure is in conformity with Article XX, including the provisions of the chapeau. Australia's concerns are that the United States has sought to impose a unilaterally determined conservation measure through restrictions on trade, and has not explored the scope for working cooperatively with other countries to identify internationally shared concerns about sea turtle conservation issues and consider ways to address these concerns. Therefore, the United States has imposed Section 609 in a manner that constitutes unjustifiable discrimination between countries where the same conditions prevail and also a disguised restriction on international trade.

55. Australia agrees with the United States that the Panel failed to interpret the terms of the chapeau of Article XX requiring that measures not be applied in a manner which would constitute "a means of arbitrary or unjustifiable discrimination between countries where the same conditions prevail" in accordance with customary rules of interpretation of public international law, in particular, with its ordinary meaning and in context.

56. In Australia's view, the Panel's decision to examine first whether Section 609 met the requirements of the chapeau before considering whether it met the requirements of any of the paragraphs of Article XX may not necessarily have been an error in law, but contributed to the Panel's errors in its examination of Section 609 under Article XX. Australia argues that it is preferable to begin examination of the legal issues raised by Article XX by considering the policy objective of the measure, and the connection between the policy objective and the measure, before turning to the chapeau. This approach would enable the examination of all aspects of the case that may be relevant in determining whether a particular measure meets the requirements of the chapeau. There is nothing in the wording of Article XX, read in its context and in the light of the object and purposes of the GATT 1994 and the *WTO Agreement*, to suggest that it is intended to exclude particular classes or types of measures from its coverage. The Panel erred in law in conducting this generalized inquiry. By its terms, Article XX would seem capable of application only on a case-by-case basis.

57. Article XX contains a series of tests designed to ensure that its provisions cannot be abused. There must be a presumption that a measure which meets the requirements of Article XX will not "undermine the WTO multilateral trading system." According to Australia, there is no textual basis for interpreting "unjustifiable discrimination" in such a broad manner that it becomes an independent test of this issue. Under the Panel's interpretation, the chapeau of Article XX could serve to nullify the effects of the paragraphs of that Article, rather than acting as a safeguard against their abuse.

58. Australia agrees with the United States that the Panel's interpretation of "unjustifiable discrimination" is based on an incorrect interpretation and application of the object and purpose of the *WTO Agreement* in construing the GATT 1994. The Panel has projected a view of the relationship between the objectives of the WTO

multilateral trading system and environmental considerations which is at odds with the Ministerial Decision on Trade and Environment.[58]

59. At the same time, to Australia, the alternative interpretation of "unjustifiable discrimination" put forward by the United States - i.e. that discrimination is not "unjustifiable" where the policy goal of the Article XX exemption being applied provides a rationale for the justification - is in error. This interpretation would weaken the important safeguard represented by the chapeau of Article XX of avoiding the abuse or illegitimate use of the Article XX exceptions. This interpretation confuses the tests applied under the two tiers of Article XX, fails to give effect to all the terms of the treaty and is not based on the ordinary meaning of "unjustifiable discrimination" in its context and in the light of the object and purpose of the *WTO Agreement* and the GATT 1994.

60. Australia maintains that Section 609 is applied by the United States in a manner constituting an unjustifiable discrimination and a disguised restriction on international trade. Australia observes that the only justification the United States appears to offer for Section 609 is that it is required to enforce a unilaterally determined conservation measure. However, Australia argues that the United States has not demonstrated that it has adequately explored means of addressing its concerns about shrimp harvesting practices and turtle conservation in other countries through cooperation with the governments concerned.

61. It is the view of Australia that Section 609 does not reasonably and properly differentiate between countries based on the risks posed to sea turtles in the exporting country's shrimp fishery. The Panel focused on exports of wild shrimp, and it is misleading to suggest that the Panel drew conclusions about whether the same conditions prevailed in certain other circumstances with respect to shrimp not subject to the import prohibition. Furthermore, the United States has provided no evidence that it took into account the views of other countries about sea turtle conservation issues within their jurisdictions, or their respective national programs, in making its determination of "countries where the same conditions prevail". In particular, the United States has provided no evidence that it considered the possibility that other Members may have had sea turtle conservation programs in place which differed from that of the United States but which were comparable and appropriate for their circumstances. Australia argues that the United States refused to certify Australia under Section 609 even though Australia's sea turtle conservation regime "extends well beyond protecting turtles from shrimping nets and ... includes cooperative programs with the shrimp industry to limit turtle bycatch."

62. In Australia's view, the legal obligations of the United States under the chapeau of Article XX required the United States to explore adequately means of mitigating the discriminatory and trade restrictive application of its measure. In particular, given the transboundary and global character of the environmental concern involved in this dispute, the United States should have consulted with affected Members to see whether the discrimination imposed by the measure in dispute could have been avoided, whether the restrictions on trade were required, whether alternative

58 Adopted by Ministers at the Meeting of the Trade Negotiations Committee at Marrakesh, 14 April 1994.

approaches were available, and whether the incidence of any trade measures could have been reduced.

### 2. *Ecuador*

63. Ecuador endorses the Panel's finding that Section 609 is inconsistent with Article XI:1 of the GATT 1994 and cannot be justified under Article XX of the GATT 1994. Ecuador is participating as a third party in this case in order to defend basic principles, such as the principle reaffirming that relations among states should be established on the basis of international law - since it is unacceptable that one state impose its domestic policy objectives upon other states - as well as the observance of more specific principles and aspects set forth in the agreements governing the multilateral trading system. These include non-discrimination in national treatment, the protection of the environment and the implementation of environmental policy.

64. According to Ecuador, this dispute does not concern the desirability of implementing some kind of conservation policy, to which Ecuador attaches the utmost importance, but rather the manner in which such a policy should be implemented. It is unacceptable that internal legislation is applied in an arbitrary manner, creating a high degree of uncertainty, and consequently prejudice, in a sector that is central to Ecuador's national economy. Ecuador endorses the Panel's view that Members are free to establish their own environmental policies in a manner consistent with their WTO obligations.

### 3. *European Communities*

65. With respect to unsolicited submissions to a panel by non-governmental organizations, the European Communities asserts that Article 13 of the DSU clearly gives a panel the "pro-active discretion" to "seek" certain information that the panel believes may be relevant to the case at hand. In addition, non-governmental organizations are free to publish their views so that their opinion is heard by the general public, which could include the parties to a dispute, the WTO Secretariat or the members of a panel. However, the European Communities "wonders whether the text of the DSU could be interpreted so widely" as to give non-governmental organizations the right to file submissions directly to a panel.

66. The European Communities contends that Article 13 of the DSU "does not oblige panels to 'accept' non-requested information which was not 'sought' for the purposes of a dispute settlement procedure." Panels should therefore reject submissions from non-governmental organizations when the panel itself had not requested such submissions. However, in the view of the European Communities, if a panel were interested in the information contained in an *amicus curiae* brief from a non-governmental organization, it would have the right to request and receive (to "seek") exactly the same information as had first been sent to it in an unsolicited manner. The European Communities agrees with the Panel that a Member, party to a dispute, is free to put forward as part of its own submission, a submission of a non-governmental organization that it considers relevant. The European Communities notes that its comments are based on the current language of Article 13 of the DSU.

67. The European Communities states further that the issues at stake in this dispute concern principles to which it attaches great importance, such as respect for the

environment and the functioning of the multilateral trading system. The European Communities is bound by the text of the Treaty Establishing the European Community[59] to ensure a harmonious and balanced development of economic activities with respect for the environment. The principle of sustainable development, also laid down in the first paragraph of the preamble to the *WTO Agreement*, as well as the precautionary principle, play an important role in the implementation of all EC policies. The EC position is mirrored in public international law by statements of the International Court of Justice, stressing the significance of respect for the environment.[60]

68. The European Communities is convinced that international cooperation is the most effective means to address global and transboundary environmental problems, rather than unilateral measures which may be less environmentally effective and more trade disruptive. Economic performance and environmental performance are not necessarily incompatible. The European Communities asserts that "[w]hile countries have the sovereign right to design and implement their own environmental policies through the measures they consider appropriate to protect their domestic environment - including the life and health of humans, animals and plants - all countries have a responsibility to contribute to the solution of international environmental problems." Thus, the European Communities considers that, "in general, the most effective means to attain the shared objectives relating to the conservation of global resources is by proceeding through the process of international co-operation."

69. To the European Communities, the approach to Article XX developed by previous panels and followed by the Appellate Body in *United States - Gasoline*[61] - that is, first examining whether a measure falls under one of the exceptions set out in paragraphs (a) to (j) of Article XX and, then, making an inquiry under the chapeau - makes logical sense and could reasonably have been applied by the Panel in this case.

70. The European Communities agrees with the United States that it would be wrong for trade concerns to prevail over all other concerns in all situations under WTO rules. Article XX should not be construed so that trade concerns always prevail over the non-trade concerns reflected in that Article, including environmental concerns and those related to health and other legitimate policy objectives. It is up to panels and the Appellate Body to judge each case on its own merits, taking into account Members' rights and obligations.

71. The European Communities also agrees with the United States that the adoption of the Panel's "test" - namely, whether a measure is of a type that would threaten the security and predictability of the multilateral trading system - would make trade concerns paramount to all other concerns and is thus inconsistent with the object and purpose of the *WTO Agreement*.

72. In the view of the European Communities, certain species, in particular migratory species, may require application of protective measures beyond usual territorial boundaries. Sea turtles should be considered a globally shared environmental

---

59 Done at Rome, 25 March 1957, as amended.

60 The European Communities refers to: *Legality of the Threat or Use of Nuclear Weapons*, Advisory Opinion, (1996), *I.C.J Rep*. pp. 241-242, para. 29; *Case Concerning the Gabcikovo-Nagymoros Project*, (1998) 37 International Legal Materials 162, para. 140.

61 Adopted 20 May 1996, WT/DS2/AB/R.

resource because they are included in Annex I of CITES and are a species protected under the Convention on the Conservation of Migratory Species of Wild Animals.[62] The appropriate way for Members concerned with the preservation of globally shared environmental resources to ensure such preservation is through internationally agreed solutions. Measures taken pursuant to such multilateral agreements would in general be allowed under the chapeau of Article XX.

73. However, the European Communities would not want to exclude the possibility, as a last resort, for a WTO Member, on its own, to take a "reasonable" measure with the aim of protecting and preserving a particular global environmental resource. However, such a measure would only be justified under exceptional circumstances and if consistent with general principles of public international law on "prescriptive jurisdiction". The Member would have to demonstrate that its environmentally protective measure was "reasonable", that is, no more trade restrictive than required to protect the globally shared environmental resource. Such a measure should be directly connected to the environmental objective and not go beyond what was required to limit the environmental damage. Finally, in such a case, the Member should have made genuine efforts to enter into cooperative environmental agreements with other Members. This is consistent with Principle 12 of the Rio Declaration on Environment and Development.

74. Given the Panel's factual finding that the United States did not enter into negotiations with the appellees before it imposed the import ban, the European Communities concludes that the United States has not demonstrated that a negotiated solution in respect of measures to protect sea turtles could not be found.

### 4. *Hong Kong, China*

75. Hong Kong, China states that it would be a "serious misunderstanding of the role of the WTO" if the multilateral trading system were viewed as impervious to environmental concerns. The WTO system does not, and should not, impede the adoption of non-arbitrary and justifiable measures to protect the environment. Hong Kong, China fully shares the Panel's concern that the chapeau of Article XX should not be interpreted in a way that will threaten the security and predictability of trade relations under the *WTO Agreement*. With reference to the Appellate Body Report in *United States - Gasoline*[63], Hong Kong, China contends that an examination under the chapeau should focus on the manner in which the measure is applied, and answer the key question of whether the manner of application constitutes an abuse of the exceptions. Questions pertaining to the policy objective of the measure concerned should be set aside in examining the consistency of a measure with the chapeau.

76. Hong Kong, China argues that in line with the views of the Appellate Body in *United States - Gasoline*[64], Article XX should not be read to establish an unqualified deviation from the GATT principle of non-discrimination. Taken together, the three elements of the chapeau of Article XX impose an obligation not to discriminate based on the origin of the product. With respect to "non-discrimination", the standard

[62] Done at Bonn, 23 June 1979, 19 International Legal Materials 15.
[63] Adopted 20 May 1996, WT/DS2/AB/R, DSR 1996:I, page 20.
[64] *Ibid.*

of obligation imposed by the chapeau is different from that imposed by Articles I and III of the GATT 1994, which is based on a strict interpretation of the concept of "like products". The chapeau of Article XX requires governments that intervene in order to achieve one of the objectives laid down in the sub-paragraphs of Article XX to ensure that the competitive conditions resulting from their intervention do not *de jure* or *de facto* favour their domestic products, nor the products of a certain specific origin. There should be no ambiguity about the exact content of the level of protection and the competitive conditions established as a result of government intervention. In the view of Hong Kong, China, a legal finding of inconsistency of a measure with the chapeau of Article XX is predicated on a factual finding that a particular measure does not respect the principle of non-discrimination. If this requirement is satisfied, a panel then can proceed to examine whether the requirements laid down in a sub-paragraph of Article XX have been satisfied as well.

77. Hong Kong, China contends that Section 609 violates the chapeau of Article XX to the extent that, after the October 1996 ruling of the United States Court of International Trade, shrimp caught by fishermen in uncertified countries are subject to the import ban even if they were caught with nets that are equipped with TEDs. The resulting competitive conditions show that Section 609 does not meet the requirement of no arbitrary or unjustifiable discrimination between countries where the same conditions prevail. In addition, the 1993 Guidelines removed the possibility available to foreign producers to use any form of fishing other than TEDs in shrimp harvesting to avoid the incidental taking of sea turtles. This would be consistent with the Article XX chapeau only if the use of TEDs is proven to be the sole means by which the stated objective can be achieved. Otherwise, it must be acknowledged that other means may exist whose effectiveness can be demonstrated to be comparable to TEDs, and the United States must give the same treatment to shrimp harvested with measures that exporters could demonstrate are comparable in effectiveness to TEDs. Failure to do so renders Section 609 a means of arbitrary and unjustifiable discrimination between countries where the same conditions prevail. If the Appellate Body finds it necessary to examine the measure in question under sub-paragraphs (b) and (g) of Article XX, Hong Kong, China invites the Appellate Body to consider its arguments submitted to the Panel and reflected in the Panel Report, in particular, at paragraphs 4.44 and 4.45.

### *5. Nigeria*

78. Nigeria confirms its views expressed in paragraph 4.53 of the Panel Report and requests the Appellate Body to uphold the Panel's decision. Nigeria shares the concern about the conservation and protection of sea turtles but, however, objects to the methods and measures for doing so. Nigeria's position is defined by paragraphs 169 and 171 of the Report (1996) of the Committee on Trade and Environment.[65]

---

[65] Nigeria refers to WT/CTE/1, 12 November 1996. Paragraph 169 of the Report states: "WTO Member governments are committed not to introduce WTO-inconsistent or protectionist trade restrictions or countervailing measures in an attempt to offset any real or perceived adverse domestic economic or competitiveness effects of applying environmental policies; not only would this undermine the open, equitable and non-discriminatory nature of the multilateral trading system, it would

## III. PROCEDURAL MATTERS AND RULINGS

### A. *Admissibility of the Briefs by Non-governmental Organizations Appended to the United States Appellant's Submission*

79. The United States attached to its appellant's submission, filed on 23 July 1998, three Exhibits, containing comments by, or "*amicus curiae* briefs" submitted by, the following three groups of non-governmental organizations[66]: 1. the Earth Island Institute; the Humane Society of the United States; and the Sierra Club; 2. the Center for International Environmental Law ("CIEL"); the Centre for Marine Conservation; the Environmental Foundation Ltd.; the Mangrove Action Project; the Philippine Ecological Network; Red Nacional de Accion Ecologica; and Sobrevivencia; and 3. the Worldwide Fund for Nature and the Foundation for International Environmental Law and Development. On 3 August 1998, CIEL *et al.* submitted a slightly revised version of their brief.

80. In their joint appellees' submission, filed on 7 August 1998, Joint Appellees object to these briefs appended to the appellant's submission, and request that the Appellate Body not consider these briefs. Joint Appellees argue that the appellant's submission, including its three Exhibits, is not in conformity with the stipulation in Article 17.6 of the DSU that an appeal "shall be limited to issues of law covered in

---

also prove counterproductive to meeting environmental objectives and promoting sustainable development. Equally, and bearing in mind the fact that governments have the right to establish their national environmental standards in accordance with their respective environmental and developmental conditions, needs and priorities, WTO Members note that it would be inappropriate for them to relax their existing national environmental standards or their enforcement in order to promote their trade. The CTE notes the statement in the 1995 Report on Trade and Environment to the OECD Council at Ministerial Level that there has been no evidence of a systematic relationship between existing environmental policies and competitiveness impacts, nor of countries deliberately resorting to low environmental standards to gain competitive advantages. The CTE welcomes similar policy statements made in other inter-governmental fora."

Paragraph 171 of the Report states: "The CTE notes that governments have endorsed in the results of the 1992 U.N. Conference on Environment and Development their commitment to Principle 12 of the *Rio Declaration* that "Unilateral actions to deal with environmental challenges outside the jurisdiction of the importing country should be avoided. Environmental measures addressing transboundary or global problems should, as far as possible, be based on an international consensus." There is a clear complementarity between this approach and the work of the WTO in seeking cooperative multilateral solutions to trade concerns. The CTE endorses and supports multilateral solutions based on international cooperation and consensus as the best and most effective way for governments to tackle environmental problems of a transboundary or global nature. WTO Agreements and multilateral environmental agreements (MEAs) are representative of efforts of the international community to pursue shared goals, and in the development of a mutually supportive relationship between them due respect must be afforded to both."

[66] In respect of these Exhibits, the United States stated the following: "Encouraging the use of TEDs in order to promote sea turtle conservation is a matter of great importance to a number of nongovernmental environmental organizations. Three groups of these organizations - each with specialized expertise in conservation of sea turtles and other endangered species - have prepared submissions reflecting their respective independent views with respect to the use of TEDs and other issues. The United States is submitting these materials to the Appellate Body for its information attached hereto as U.S. Appellant Exhibits 1-3." United States appellant's submission, para. 2, footnote 1.

the panel report and legal interpretations developed by the panel", nor with Rule 21(2) of the *Working Procedures for Appellate Review*. They ask the Appellate Body to reject as irrelevant the factual assertions made in certain paragraphs of the appellant's submission, as well as the factual information presented in the Exhibits. In their view, because of the incorporation of unauthorized material through the attachment of the Exhibits, the appellant's submission could no longer be considered a "precise statement" as required by Rule 21(2) of the *Working Procedures for Appellate Review*. Rather, a number of the factual and legal assertions contained in the Exhibits go beyond the position taken by the appellant, resulting in confusion concerning the exact nature and linkage between the appeal and the three Exhibits.

81. Joint Appellees state further that the submission of Exhibits that present the views of non-governmental organizations, as opposed to the views of the appellant Member, is not contemplated in, or authorized by, the DSU or the *Working Procedures for Appellate Review*. Such submissions were not in conformity with Article 17.4 of the DSU, nor with Rule 28(1) of the *Working Procedures for Appellate Review*, which vests the discretion to request additional submissions with the Appellate Body. According to Joint Appellees, the decision of the appellant to attach the Exhibits to its submission gives rise both to contradictions and internal inconsistencies, and raises serious procedural and systemic problems. Joint Appellees maintain that by virtue of their incorporation into the appellant's submission, these pleadings are no longer "*amicus curiae* briefs", but instead have become a portion of the appellant's submission, and thus have also become what would appear to be the official United States position.

82. In its appellee's submission, also filed on 7 August 1998, Malaysia similarly urges the Appellate Body to rule that the three Exhibits appended to the United States appellant's submission are inadmissible in this appeal. Malaysia refers to its argument before the Panel that briefs from non-governmental organizations do not fall within Article 13 of the DSU. In addition, according to Malaysia, admission of the Exhibits would not be consonant with Article 17.6 of the DSU, or with Rule 21(2) of the *Working Procedures for Appellate Review*, as the United States appellant's submission and Exhibit 2 contain statements of facts. Moreover, Article 17.4 of the DSU only grants the right to make written and oral submissions to third parties. Articles 11 and 17.12 of the DSU are significant and serve to safeguard the admissibility of evidence before the Appellate Body. In the alternative, in the event the Appellate Body ruled that Exhibits 1-3 of the appellant's submission should be admitted, Malaysia submits rebuttals to each of the Exhibits.

83. On 11 August 1998, we issued a ruling on this preliminary procedural matter addressed to the participants and third participants, as follows:

> We have decided to accept for consideration, insofar as they may be pertinent, the legal arguments made by the various non-governmental organizations in the three briefs attached as exhibits to the appellant's submission of the United States, as well as the revised version of the brief by the Center for International Environmental Law *et al.*, which was submitted to us on 3 August 1998. The reasons for our ruling will be given in the Appellate Body Report.

84. In the same ruling, we addressed the following questions to the appellant, the United States:

> to what extent do you agree with or adopt any one or more of the legal arguments set out in the three briefs prepared by the non-governmental organizations and appended as exhibits to your appellant's submission? In particular, do you adopt the legal arguments stated therein relating to paragraphs (b) and (g) and the chapeau of Article XX of the GATT 1994?

85. We asked the United States to respond in writing to these questions by 13 August 1998, and offered an opportunity to the appellees and the third participants to respond, by 17 August 1998, to the answer filed by the United States concerning which aspects of these briefs it accepted and endorsed as part of its appeal as well as to the legal arguments made in the briefs by the non-governmental organizations. We noted at the time that Malaysia had already done the latter in Exhibits 1 through 3 attached to its appellee's submission.

86. On 13 August 1998, the United States replied as follows:

> The main U.S. submission reflects the views of the United States on the legal issues in this appeal. As explained in our appellant's submission, the three submissions prepared by non-governmental organizations reflect the independent views of those organizations .... These non-governmental organizations have a great interest, and specialized expertise, in sea turtle conservation and related matters. It is appropriate therefore that the Appellate Body be informed of those organizations' views. The United States is not adopting these views as separate matters to which the Appellate Body must respond.
>
> The United States agrees with the legal arguments in the submissions of the non-governmental organizations to the extent those arguments concur with the U.S. arguments set out in our main submission … .

87. On 17 August 1998, Joint Appellees filed a joint response, and Malaysia filed a separate one, to the matters raised in the reply of the United States, as well as in the Exhibits. Without prejudice to their view that the receipt and consideration by the Appellate Body of the briefs of non-governmental organizations attached to the appellant's submission is not authorized by the DSU or the *Working Procedures for Appellate Review*, Joint Appellees responded to certain legal arguments made in the briefs. Malaysia incorporated by reference its rebuttals to the briefs contained in its appellee's submission of 7 August 1998, and made certain additional comments in respect of each of the briefs. Also, on 17 August 1998, Hong Kong, China and Mexico filed statements in respect of the same matters. Hong Kong, China stated that the reply by the United States was unclear and that it was not possible, at that stage, to comment further on the legal arguments. For its part, Mexico stated that if the Appellate Body were to make use of arguments which are outside the terms of Article 17.6 of the DSU and which are not clearly and explicitly attributable to a Member that is a party to the dispute, the Appellate Body would exceed its powers under the DSU.

88. The admissibility of the briefs by certain non-governmental organizations which have been appended to the appellant's submission of the United States is a legal question raised by the appellees. This is a legal issue which does not relate to a finding of law made, or a legal interpretation developed, by the Panel in the Panel Report. For this reason, it has seemed appropriate to us to deal with this issue sepa-

rately from the issues raised by the appellant and addressed in the succeeding portions of this Appellate Body Report.

89. We consider that the attaching of a brief or other material to the submission of either appellant or appellee, no matter how or where such material may have originated, renders that material at least *prima facie* an integral part of that participant's submission. On the one hand, it is of course for a participant in an appeal to determine for itself what to include in its submission. On the other hand, a participant filing a submission is properly regarded as assuming responsibility for the contents of that submission, including any annexes or other attachments.

90. In the present appeal, the United States has made it clear that its views "on the legal issues in this appeal" are found in "the main U.S. submission." The United States has confirmed its agreement with the legal arguments in the attached submissions of the non-governmental organizations, to the extent that those arguments "concur with the U.S. arguments set out in [its] main submission."

91. We admit, therefore, the briefs attached to the appellant's submission of the United States as part of that appellant's submission. At the same time, considering that the United States has itself accepted the briefs in a tentative and qualified manner only, we focus in the succeeding sections below on the legal arguments in the main U.S. appellant's submission.

### *B. Sufficiency of the Notice of Appeal*

92. In their joint appellee's submission, filed on 7 August 1998, Joint Appellees contend that the notice of appeal by the United States is defective in form and that the action is, therefore, not properly before the Appellate Body. They contend that the appellant's notice of appeal is both vague and cursory, and is, accordingly, not in compliance with the procedural requirements set forth in Rule 20(2)(d) of the *Working Procedures for Appellate Review*. It is also not a proper "submission" filed "within the required time periods" pursuant to Rule 29 of the *Working Procedures for Appellate Review*. As a result, it is argued, the United States' appeal should be dismissed by the Appellate Body on this ground alone. The appellant's notice of appeal does not identify any legal errors in a manner sufficient for the appellees to develop a defence, and this, in the appellees' view, made it impossible for them to discern the issues that were going to be the subject of the appeal until the appellant filed its written submission 10 days later. This reduced the time available for all appellees to draft their responsive submissions from 25 days to 15 days.

93. According to Joint Appellees, vague notices of appeal should not be tolerated for at least two reasons. First, considerations of fundamental fairness and good faith mandate that the appellant should not be permitted to gain a tactical advantage through its failure to fulfil the requirements of the *Working Procedures for Appellate Review*. Second, carefully considered and well-drafted submissions benefit the decision-making process of the Appellate Body.

94. The United States in turn submits that the notice of appeal provided just the type of "*brief* statement of the nature of the appeal, including the allegations of error in the issues of law covered in the panel report and legal interpretations developed by the panel" (emphasis in the original) called for in Rule 20(2)(d) of the *Working Procedures for Appellate Review*. First, the notice of appeal explained that the United States was appealing from the findings on issues of law and related legal interpreta-

tions leading to the panel's conclusion that the United States measure was outside the scope of the Article XX chapeau. Second, the notice of appeal stated that the United States was appealing the Panel's procedural finding that the Panel lacked discretion to accept materials received from non-governmental sources. The appellees did not explain what additional information they believed should have been included in the notice of appeal. Furthermore, according to the United States, the appellees' allegation of prejudice was unfounded. The appellees well knew the basic argument that the United States would present to support its claim of legal error. Indeed, the appellees themselves had pointed out that the United States appeal rests solely on one leg, that is, that the Panel created a "threat to the multilateral trading system" test, and that the United States already raised this same issue at the interim review stage. In short, the appeal did not result in any unfair surprise to the appellees.

95. Rule 20(2) of the *Working Procedures for Appellate Review* provides, in relevant part:

> (2) A Notice of Appeal shall include the following information:
>
> ...
>
> (d) a *brief statement of the nature of the appeal, including the allegations of errors* in the issues of law covered in the panel report and legal interpretations developed by the panel.(emphasis added)

The *Working Procedures for Appellate Review* enjoin the appellant to be *brief* in its notice of appeal in setting out "the nature of the appeal, including the allegations of errors". We believe that, in principle, the "nature of the appeal" and "the allegations of errors" are sufficiently set out where the notice of appeal adequately identifies the findings or legal interpretations of the Panel which are being appealed as erroneous. The notice of appeal is not expected to contain the reasons why the appellant regards those findings or interpretations as erroneous. The notice of appeal is not designed to be a summary or outline of the arguments to be made by the appellant. The legal arguments in support of the allegations of error are, of course, to be set out and developed in the appellant's submission.

96. In this instance, the notice of appeal does communicate the decision by the United States to appeal certain legal issues covered and certain legal interpretations developed in the Panel Report. The notice then refers to the two allegedly erroneous findings of the Panel being appealed from - the finding that the United States measure at issue is not within the scope of measures permitted under the chapeau of Article XX; and the finding that accepting non-requested information from non-governmental sources is incompatible with the DSU. The notice did not cite the numbered paragraphs of the Panel Report containing the above findings, but Joint Appellees do not assert that that is necessary. The references in the notice of appeal to these two findings of the Panel are terse[67], but there is no mistaking which findings or interpretations of the Panel the Appellate Body is asked to review. We accordingly hold that the notice of appeal by the United States meets the requirements

[67] The interpretation of the Panel concerning non-requested information, and its finding on the inconsistency of Section 609 with Article XX of the GATT 1994, are themselves cast in fairly terse language; Panel Report, paras. 7.8, fourth sentence, 7.49 and 7.62.

of Rule 20(2)(d) of the *Working Procedures for Appellate Review*, and deny the request of Joint Appellees to dismiss the entire appeal summarily on the sole ground of insufficiency of the notice of appeal.

97. It remains only to recall that the right of a party to appeal from legal findings and legal interpretations reached by a panel in a dispute settlement proceeding is an important new right established in the DSU resulting from the Uruguay Round. We believe that the provisions of Rule 20(2) and other Rules of the *Working Procedures for Appellate Review* are most appropriately read so as to give full meaning and effect to the right of appeal and to give a party which regards itself aggrieved by some legal finding or interpretation in a panel report a real and effective opportunity to demonstrate the error in such finding or interpretation. It is scarcely necessary to add that an appellee is, of course, always entitled to its full measure of due process. In the present appeal, perhaps the best indication that that full measure of due process was not in any degree impaired by the notice of appeal filed by the United States, is the developed and substantial nature of the appellees' submissions.

## IV. ISSUES RAISED IN THIS APPEAL

98. The issues raised in this appeal by the appellant, the United States, are the following:

(a) whether the Panel erred in finding that accepting non-requested information from non-governmental sources would be incompatible with the provisions of the DSU as currently applied; and

(b) whether the Panel erred in finding that the measure at issue constitutes unjustifiable discrimination between countries where the same conditions prevail and thus is not within the scope of measures permitted under Article XX of the GATT 1994.

## V. PANEL PROCEEDINGS AND NON-REQUESTED INFORMATION

99. In the course of the proceedings before the Panel, on 28 July 1997, the Panel received a brief from the Center for Marine Conservation ("CMC") and the Center for International Environmental Law ("CIEL"). Both are non-governmental organizations. On 16 September 1997, the Panel received another brief, this time from the World Wide Fund for Nature. The Panel acknowledged receipt of the two briefs, which the non-governmental organizations also sent directly to the parties to this dispute. The complaining parties - India, Malaysia, Pakistan and Thailand - requested the Panel not to consider the contents of the briefs in dealing with the dispute. In contrast, the United States urged the Panel to avail itself of any relevant information in the two briefs, as well as in any other similar communications.[68] The Panel disposed of this matter in the following manner:

> *We had not requested such information* as was contained in the above-mentioned documents. We note that, pursuant to Article 13 of the DSU, the initiative to seek information and to select the source of in-

[68] Panel Report, para. 3.129

> formation rests with the Panel. In any other situations, only parties and third parties are allowed to submit information directly to the Panel. *Accepting non-requested information from non-governmental sources would be, in our opinion, incompatible with the provisions of the DSU as currently applied. We therefore informed the parties that we did not intend to take these documents into consideration.* We observed, moreover, that it was usual practice for parties to put forward whatever documents they considered relevant to support their case and that, *if any party in the present dispute wanted to put forward these documents, or parts of them, as part of their own submissions to the Panel, they were free to do so. If this were the case, the other parties would have two weeks to respond to the additional material.* We noted that the United States availed themselves of this opportunity by designating Section III of the document submitted by the Center for Marine Conservation and the Center for International Environmental Law as an annex to its second submission to the Panel.[69](emphasis added)

100. We note that the Panel did two things. First, the Panel declared a legal interpretation of certain provisions of the DSU: i.e., that accepting non-requested information from non-governmental sources would be "incompatible with the provisions of the DSU as currently applied." Evidently as a result of this legal interpretation, the Panel announced that it would not take the briefs submitted by non-governmental organizations into consideration. Second, the Panel nevertheless allowed any party to the dispute to put forward the briefs, or any part thereof, as part of its own submissions to the Panel, giving the other party or parties, in such case, two additional weeks to respond to the additional material. The United States appeals from this legal interpretation of the Panel.

101. It may be well to stress at the outset that access to the dispute settlement process of the WTO is limited to Members of the WTO. This access is not available, under the *WTO Agreement* and the covered agreements as they currently exist, to individuals or international organizations, whether governmental or non-governmental. Only Members may become parties to a dispute of which a panel may be seized, and only Members "having a substantial interest in a matter before a panel" may become third parties in the proceedings before that panel.[70] Thus, under the DSU, only Members who are parties to a dispute, or who have notified their interest in becoming third parties in such a dispute to the DSB, have a *legal right* to make submissions to, and have a *legal right* to have those submissions considered by, a panel.[71] Correlatively, a panel is *obliged* in law to accept and give due consideration only to submissions made by the parties and the third parties in a panel proceeding. These are basic legal propositions; they do not, however, dispose of the

---

[69] Panel Report, para. 7.8.

[70] See Articles 4, 6, 9 and 10 of the DSU.

[71] Articles 10 and 12, and Appendix 3 of the DSU. We note that Article 17.4 of the DSU limits the right to appeal a panel report to parties to a dispute, and permits third parties which have notified the DSB of their substantial interest in the matter to make written submissions to, and be given an opportunity to be heard by, the Appellate Body.

issue here presented by the appellant's first claim of error. We believe this interpretative issue is most appropriately addressed by examining what a panel is *authorized* to do under the DSU.

102. Article 13 of the DSU reads as follows:

> Article 13
>
> *Right to Seek Information*
>
> 1. *Each panel shall have the right to seek information and technical advice from any individual or body which it deems appropriate.* However, before a panel seeks such information or advice from any individual or body within the jurisdiction of a Member it shall inform the authorities of that Member. *A Member should respond promptly and fully to any request by a panel for such information as the panel considers necessary and appropriate.* Confidential information which is provided shall not be revealed without formal authorization from the individual, body, or authorities of the Member providing the information.
>
> 2. *Panels may seek information from any relevant source* and may consult experts to obtain their opinion on certain aspects of the matter. With respect to a factual issue concerning a scientific or other technical matter raised by a party to a dispute, a panel may request an advisory report in writing from an expert review group. Rules for the establishment of such a group and its procedures are set forth in Appendix 4.(emphasis added)

103. In *EC Measures Affecting Meat and Meat Products (Hormones)*, we observed that Article 13 of the DSU[72] "enable[s] panels to seek information and advice as they deem appropriate in a particular case."[73] Also, in *Argentina - Measures Affecting Imports of Footwear, Textiles, Apparel and Other Items*, we ruled that:

> Pursuant to Article 13.2 of the DSU, a panel may seek information from any relevant source and may consult experts to obtain their opinions on certain aspects of the matter at issue. *This is a grant of discretionary authority: a panel is not duty-bound to seek information in each and every case or to consult particular experts under this provision.* We recall our statement in *EC Measures Concerning Meat and Meat Products (Hormones)* that Article 13 of the DSU enables a panel to seek information and technical advice as it deems appropriate in a particular case, and that the DSU leaves "to the sound discretion of a panel the determination of whether the establishment of an expert review group is necessary or appropriate." *Just as a panel has the discretion to determine how to seek expert advice, so also does a panel have the discretion to determine whether to seek information or expert advice at all.*

---

[72] As well as Article 11.2 of the *Agreement on the Application of Sanitary and Phytosanitary Measures*.

[73] Adopted 13 February 1998, WT/DS26/AB/R, WT/DS48/AB/R, para. 147.

...

> In this case, we find that the *Panel acted within the bounds of its discretionary authority under Articles 11 and 13 of the DSU in deciding not to seek information from, nor to consult with, the IMF.*[74] (emphasis added)

104. The comprehensive nature of the authority of a panel to "seek" information and technical advice from "any individual or body" it may consider appropriate, or from "any relevant source", should be underscored. This authority embraces more than merely the choice and evaluation of the *source* of the information or advice which it may seek. A panel's authority includes the authority to decide *not to seek* such information or advice at all. We consider that a panel also has the authority to *accept or reject* any information or advice which it may have sought and received, or to *make some other appropriate disposition* thereof. It is particularly within the province and the authority of a panel to determine *the need for information and advice* in a specific case, to ascertain the *acceptability* and *relevancy* of information or advice received, and to decide *what weight to ascribe to that information or advice* or to conclude that no weight at all should be given to what has been received.

105. It is also pertinent to note that Article 12.1 of the DSU authorizes panels to depart from, or to add to, the Working Procedures set forth in Appendix 3 of the DSU, and in effect to develop their own Working Procedures, after consultation with the parties to the dispute. Article 12.2 goes on to direct that "[p]anel procedures should provide *sufficient flexibility* so as to *ensure high-quality panel reports* while *not unduly delaying the panel process.*"(emphasis added)

106. The thrust of Articles 12 and 13, taken together, is that the DSU accords to a panel established by the DSB, and engaged in a dispute settlement proceeding, ample and extensive authority to undertake and to control the process by which it informs itself both of the relevant facts of the dispute and of the legal norms and principles applicable to such facts. That authority, and the breadth thereof, is indispensably necessary to enable a panel to discharge its duty imposed by Article 11 of the DSU to "make an objective assessment of the matter before it, including an *objective assessment of the facts of the case* and the *applicability of and conformity with the relevant covered agreements* … ." (emphasis added)

107. Against this context of broad authority vested in panels by the DSU, and given the object and purpose of the Panel's mandate as revealed in Article 11, we do not believe that the word "seek" must necessarily be read, as apparently the Panel read it, in too literal a manner. That the Panel's reading of the word "seek" is unnecessarily formal and technical in nature becomes clear should an "individual or body" first ask a panel for permission to file a statement or a brief. In such an event, a panel may decline to grant the leave requested. If, in the exercise of its sound discretion in a particular case, a panel concludes *inter alia* that it could do so without "unduly delaying the panel process", it could grant permission to file a statement or a brief, subject to such conditions as it deems appropriate. The exercise of the panel's discretion could, of course, and perhaps should, include consultation with the parties to the

[74] Adopted 22 April 1998, WT/DS56/AB/R, paras. 84-86.

dispute. In this kind of situation, for all practical and pertinent purposes, the distinction between "requested" and "non-requested" information vanishes.

108. In the present context, authority to *seek* information is not properly equated with a *prohibition* on accepting information which has been submitted without having been requested by a panel. A panel has the discretionary authority either to accept and consider or to reject information and advice submitted to it, *whether requested by a panel or not*. The fact that a panel may *motu proprio* have initiated the request for information does not, by itself, bind the panel to accept and consider the information which is actually submitted. The amplitude of the authority vested in panels to shape the processes of fact-finding and legal interpretation makes clear that a panel will *not* be deluged, as it were, with non-requested material, *unless that panel allows itself to be so deluged.*

109. Moreover, acceptance and rejection of the information and advice of the kind here submitted to the Panel need not exhaust the universe of possible appropriate dispositions thereof. In the present case, the Panel did not reject the information outright. The Panel suggested instead, that, if any of the parties wanted "to put forward these documents, or parts of them, as part of their own submissions to the Panel, they were free to do so." [75] In response, the United States then designated Section III of the document submitted by CIEL/CMC as an annex to its second submission to the Panel, and the Panel gave the appellees two weeks to respond. We believe that this practical disposition of the matter by the Panel in this dispute may be detached, as it were, from the legal interpretation adopted by the Panel of the word "seek" in Article 13.1 of the DSU. When so viewed, we conclude that the actual disposition of these briefs by the Panel does not constitute either legal error or abuse of its discretionary authority in respect of this matter. The Panel was, accordingly, entitled to treat and take into consideration the section of the brief that the United States appended to its second submission to the Panel, just like any other part of the United States pleading.

110. We find, and so hold, that the Panel erred in its legal interpretation that accepting non-requested information from non-governmental sources is incompatible with the provisions of the DSU. At the same time, we consider that the Panel acted within the scope of its authority under Articles 12 and 13 of the DSU in allowing any party to the dispute to attach the briefs by non-governmental organizations, or any portion thereof, to its own submissions.

## VI. APPRAISING SECTION 609 UNDER ARTICLE XX OF THE GATT 1994

111. We turn to the second issue raised by the appellant, the United States, which is whether the Panel erred in finding that the measure at issue[76] constitutes unjustifiable discrimination between countries where the same conditions prevail and, thus, is not within the scope of measures permitted under Article XX of the GATT 1994.

---

[75] Panel Report, para. 7.8.

[76] The United States measure at issue is referred to in this Report as "Section 609" or "the measure". By these terms, we mean Section 609 and the 1996 Guidelines.

### A. *The Panel's Findings and Interpretative Analysis*

112. The Panel's findings, from which the United States appeals, and the gist of its supporting reasoning, are set forth below *in extenso*:

> ... [W]e are of the opinion that the *chapeau* [of] *Article XX*, interpreted within its context and in the light of the object and purpose of GATT and of the WTO Agreement, *only allows Members to derogate from GATT provisions so long as, in doing so, they do not undermine the WTO multilateral trading system*, thus also abusing the exceptions contained in Article XX. Such undermining and abuse would occur when a Member jeopardizes the operation of the WTO Agreement in such a way that guaranteed market access and nondiscriminatory treatment within a multilateral framework would no longer be possible. ... We are of the view that a *type of measure adopted by a Member* which, on its own, may appear to have a relatively minor impact on the multilateral trading system, *may* nonetheless *raise a serious threat to that system if similar measures are adopted by the same or other Members*. Thus, by allowing such type of measures even though their individual impact may not appear to be such as to threaten the multilateral trading system, one would affect the security and predictability of the multilateral trading system. We consequently find that when considering a measure under Article XX, we must determine not only whether the measure *on its own* undermines the WTO multilateral trading system, but also whether *such type of measure*, if it were to be adopted by other Members, would threaten the security and predictability of the multilateral trading system.[77]
>
> In our view, if an interpretation of the chapeau of Article XX were to be followed which would allow a Member *to adopt measures conditioning access to its market for a given product upon the adoption by the exporting Members of certain policies, including conservation policies*, GATT 1994 and the WTO Agreement could no longer serve as a multilateral framework for trade among Members as security and predictability of trade relations under those agreements would be threatened. This follows because, if one WTO Member were allowed to adopt such measures, then other Members would also have the right to adopt similar measures on the same subject but with differing, or even conflicting, requirements. ... Market access for goods could become subject to an increasing number of conflicting policy requirements for the same product and this would rapidly lead to the end of the WTO multilateral trading system.[78]
>
> ... Section 609, as applied, is a measure conditioning access to the US market for a given product on the adoption by exporting Members of conservation policies that the United States considers to be compara-

[77] Panel Report, para. 7.44.

[78] Panel Report, para. 7.45.

ble to its own in terms of regulatory programmes and incidental taking.[79]

... it appears to us that, in light of the context of the term "unjustifiable" and the object and purpose of the WTO Agreement, *the US measure at issue constitutes unjustifiable discrimination* between countries where the same conditions prevail and thus is not within the scope of measures permitted under Article XX.[80]

...

We therefore find that the *US measure* at issue is *not within the scope of measures permitted under the chapeau of Article XX*.[81](emphasis added)

113. Article XX of the GATT 1994 reads, in its relevant parts:

Article XX

*General Exceptions*

Subject to the requirement that such measures are not applied in a manner which would constitute a means of arbitrary or unjustifiable discrimination between countries where the same conditions prevail, or a disguised restriction on international trade, nothing in this Agreement shall be construed to prevent the adoption or enforcement by any Member of measures:

...

(*b*) necessary to protect human, animal or plant life or health;

...

(*g*) relating to the conservation of exhaustible natural resources if such measures are made effective in conjunction with restrictions on domestic production or consumption;

114. The Panel did not follow all of the steps of applying the "customary rules of interpretation of public international law" as required by Article 3.2 of the DSU. As we have emphasized numerous times[82], these rules call for an examination of the ordinary meaning of the words of a treaty, read in their context, and in the light of the object and purpose of the treaty involved. A treaty interpreter must begin with, and focus upon, the text of the particular provision to be interpreted. It is in the words constituting that provision, read in their context, that the object and purpose of the

---

79 Panel Report, para. 7.48.

80 Panel Report, para. 7.49.

81 Panel Report, para. 7.62.

82 See, for example, the Appellate Body Reports in: *United States - Gasoline*, adopted 20 May 1996, WT/DS2/AB/R, p. 17; *Japan - Taxes on Alcoholic Beverages*, adopted 1 November 1996, WT/DS8/AB/R, WT/DS10/AB/R, WT/DS11/AB/R, DSR 1996:I, pp. 104-106; *India - Patent Protection for Pharmaceutical and Agricultural Chemical Products*, adopted 16 January 1998, WT/DS50/AB/R, paras. 45-46; *Argentina - Measures Affecting Imports of Footwear, Textiles, Apparel and Other Items*, adopted 13 February 1998, WT/DS56/AB/R, para. 47; and *European Communities - Customs Classification of Certain Computer Equipment*, adopted 22 June 1998, WT/DS62/AB/R, WT/DS67/AB/R, WT/DS68/AB/R, para. 85.

states parties to the treaty must first be sought. Where the meaning imparted by the text itself is equivocal or inconclusive, or where confirmation of the correctness of the reading of the text itself is desired, light from the object and purpose of the treaty as a whole may usefully be sought.[83]

115. In the present case, the Panel did not expressly examine the ordinary meaning of the words of Article XX. The Panel disregarded the fact that the introductory clauses of Article XX speak of the "manner" in which measures sought to be justified are "applied". In *United States - Gasoline*, we pointed out that the chapeau of Article XX "by its express terms addresses, not so much the questioned measure or its specific contents as such, *but rather the manner in which that measure is applied.*"[84](emphasis added) The Panel did not inquire specifically into how the *application* of Section 609 constitutes "a means of arbitrary or unjustifiable discrimination between countries where the same conditions prevail, or a disguised restriction on international trade." What the Panel did, in purporting to examine the consistency of the measure with the chapeau of Article XX, was to focus repeatedly on the *design of the measure itself*. For instance, the Panel stressed that it was addressing "a particular situation where a Member has taken unilateral measures which, *by their nature*, could put the multilateral trading system at risk." [85](emphasis added)

116. The general design of a measure, as distinguished from its application, is, however, to be examined in the course of determining whether that measure falls within one or another of the paragraphs of Article XX following the chapeau. The Panel failed to scrutinize the *immediate* context of the chapeau: i.e., paragraphs (a) to (j) of Article XX. Moreover, the Panel did not look into the object and purpose of the *chapeau of Article XX*. Rather, the Panel looked into the object and purpose of the *whole of the GATT 1994 and the WTO Agreement*, which object and purpose it described in an overly broad manner. Thus, the Panel arrived at the very broad formulation that measures which "undermine the WTO multilateral trading system"[86] must be regarded as "not within the scope of measures permitted under the chapeau of Article XX."[87] Maintaining, rather than undermining, the multilateral trading system is necessarily a fundamental and pervasive premise underlying the *WTO Agreement*; but it is not a right or an obligation, nor is it an interpretative rule which can be employed in the appraisal of a given measure under the chapeau of Article XX. In *United States - Gasoline*, we stated that it is "important to underscore that the purpose and object of the introductory clauses of Article XX is generally the prevention of '*abuse of the exceptions of* [*Article XX*]'."[88](emphasis added) The Panel did not

---

83 I. Sinclair, *The Vienna Convention on the Law of Treaties*, 2nd ed. (Manchester University Press, 1984), DSR 1996:I, page 20.

84 Adopted 20 May 1996, WT/DS2/AB/R, p. 22.

85 Panel Report, para. 7.60. The Panel also stated, in paras. 7.33-7.34 of the Panel Report:

> ... Pursuant to the chapeau of Article XX, a measure may discriminate, but not in an 'arbitrary' or 'unjustifiable' manner.
>
> We therefore move to consider *whether the US measure* conditioning market access on the adoption of certain conservation policies by the exporting Member *could be considered as 'unjustifiable' discrimination* ... .(emphasis added)

86 See, for example, Panel Report, para. 7.44.

87 Panel Report, para. 7.62.

88 Adopted 20 May 1996, WT/DS2/AB/R, DSR 1996:I, page 20.

attempt to inquire into how the measure at stake was being *applied in such a manner* as to constitute *abuse or misuse of a given kind of exception.*

117. The above flaws in the Panel's analysis and findings flow almost naturally from the fact that the Panel disregarded the sequence of steps essential for carrying out such an analysis. The Panel defined its approach as first "determin[ing] whether the measure at issue satisfies the conditions contained in the chapeau."[89] If the Panel found that to be the case, it said that it "shall then examine whether the US measure is covered by the terms of Article XX(b) or (g)." [90] The Panel attempted to justify its interpretative approach in the following manner:

> As mentioned by the Appellate Body in its report in the *Gasoline* case, in order for the justification of Article XX to be extended to a given measure, it must not only come under one or another of the particular exceptions - paragraphs (a) to (j) - listed under Article XX; it must also satisfy the requirements imposed by the opening clause of Article XX. We note that panels have in the past considered the specific paragraphs of Article XX before reviewing the applicability of the conditions contained in the chapeau. However, *as the conditions contained in the introductory provision apply to any of the paragraphs of Article XX, it seems equally appropriate to analyze first the introductory provision of Article XX.*[91](emphasis added)

...

118. In *United States - Gasoline*, we enunciated the appropriate method for applying Article XX of the GATT 1994:

> In order that the justifying protection of Article XX may be extended to it, the measure at issue must not only come under one or another of the particular exceptions - paragraphs (a) to (j) - listed under Article XX; it must also satisfy the requirements imposed by the opening clauses of Article XX. *The analysis is,* in other words, *two-tiered: first, provisional justification by reason of characterization of the measure under XX(g); second, further appraisal of the same measure under the introductory clauses of Article XX.*[92](emphasis added)

119. The sequence of steps indicated above in the analysis of a claim of justification under Article XX reflects, not inadvertence or random choice, but rather the fundamental structure and logic of Article XX. The Panel appears to suggest, albeit indirectly, that following the indicated sequence of steps, or the inverse thereof, does not make any difference. To the Panel, reversing the sequence set out in *United States - Gasoline* "seems equally appropriate."[93] We do not agree.

120. The task of interpreting the chapeau so as to prevent the abuse or misuse of the specific exemptions provided for in Article XX is rendered very difficult, if indeed it remains possible at all, where the interpreter (like the Panel in this case) has

---

89 Panel Report, para. 7.29.

90 *Ibid.*

91 Panel Report, para. 7.28.

92 Adopted 20 May 1996, WT/DS2/AB/R, DSR 1996:I, page 20.

93 Panel Report, para 7.28.

not first identified and examined the specific exception threatened with abuse. The standards established in the chapeau are, moreover, necessarily broad in scope and reach: the prohibition of the *application* of a measure "in a manner which would constitute a means of *arbitrary* or *unjustifiable discrimination* between countries where the same conditions prevail" or "a *disguised restriction* on international trade."(emphasis added) When applied in a particular case, the actual contours and contents of these standards will vary as the kind of measure under examination varies. What is appropriately characterizable as "arbitrary discrimination" or "unjustifiable discrimination", or as a "disguised restriction on international trade" in respect of one category of measures, need not be so with respect to another group or type of measures. The standard of "arbitrary discrimination", for example, under the chapeau may be different for a measure that purports to be necessary to protect public morals than for one relating to the products of prison labour.

121. The consequences of the interpretative approach adopted by the Panel are apparent in its findings. The Panel formulated a broad standard and a test for appraising measures sought to be justified under the chapeau; it is a standard or a test that finds no basis either in the text of the chapeau or in that of either of the two specific exceptions claimed by the United States. The Panel, in effect, constructed an *a priori* test that purports to define a category of measures which, *ratione materiae*, fall outside the justifying protection of Article XX's chapeau.[94] In the present case, the Panel found that the United States measure at stake fell within that class of excluded measures because Section 609 conditions access to the domestic shrimp market of the United States on the adoption by exporting countries of certain conservation policies prescribed by the United States. It appears to us, however, that conditioning access to a Member's domestic market on whether exporting Members comply with, or adopt, a policy or policies unilaterally prescribed by the importing Member may, to some degree, be a common aspect of measures falling within the scope of one or another of the exceptions (a) to (j) of Article XX. Paragraphs (a) to (j) comprise measures that are recognized as *exceptions to substantive obligations* established in the GATT 1994, because the domestic policies embodied in such measures have been recognized as important and legitimate in character. It is not necessary to assume that requiring from exporting countries compliance with, or adoption of, certain policies (although covered in principle by one or another of the exceptions) prescribed by the importing country, renders a measure *a priori* incapable of justification under Article XX. Such an interpretation renders most, if not all, of the specific exceptions of Article XX inutile, a result abhorrent to the principles of interpretation we are bound to apply.

122. We hold that the findings of the Panel quoted in paragraph 112 above, and the interpretative analysis embodied therein, constitute error in legal interpretation and accordingly reverse them.

123. Having reversed the Panel's legal conclusion that the United States measure at issue "is not within the scope of measures permitted under the chapeau of Article XX" [95], we believe that it is our duty and our responsibility to complete the legal

94 See, for example, Panel Report, para. 7.50.
95 Panel Report, para. 7.62.

analysis in this case in order to determine whether Section 609 qualifies for justification under Article XX. In doing this, we are fully aware of our jurisdiction and mandate under Article 17 of the DSU. We have found ourselves in similar situations on a number of occasions. Most recently, in *European Communities - Measures Affecting the Importation of Certain Poultry Products,* we stated:

> In certain appeals, ... the reversal of a panel's finding on a legal issue may require us to make a finding on a legal issue which was not addressed by the panel.[96]

In that case, having reversed the panel's finding on Article 5.1(b) of the *Agreement on Agriculture*, we completed the legal analysis by making a finding on the consistency of the measure at issue with Article 5.5 of the *Agreement on Agriculture.* Similarly, in *Canada - Certain Measures Concerning Periodicals*[97], having reversed the panel's findings on the issue of "like products" under the first sentence of Article III:2 of the GATT 1994, we examined the consistency of the measure with the second sentence of Article III:2. And, in *United States - Gasoline*[98], having reversed the panel's findings on the first part of Article XX(g) of the GATT 1994, we completed the analysis of the terms of Article XX(g), and then examined the application of the measure at issue in that case under the chapeau of Article XX.

124. As in those previous cases, we believe it is our responsibility here to examine the claim by the United States for justification of Section 609 under Article XX in order properly to resolve this dispute between the parties. We do this, in part, recognizing that Article 3.7 of the DSU emphasizes that: "The aim of the dispute settlement mechanism is to secure a positive solution to a dispute." Fortunately, in the present case, as in the mentioned previous cases, we believe that the facts on the record of the panel proceedings permit us to undertake the completion of the analysis required to resolve this dispute.

### *B. Article XX(g): Provisional Justification of Section 609*

125. In claiming justification for its measure, the United States primarily invokes Article XX(g). Justification under Article XX(b) is claimed only in the alternative; that is, the United States suggests that we should look at Article XX(b) only if we find that Section 609 does not fall within the ambit of Article XX(g).[99] We proceed, therefore, to the first tier of the analysis of Section 609 and to our consideration of whether it may be characterized as provisionally justified under the terms of Article XX(g).

126. Paragraph (g) of Article XX covers measures:

> relating to the conservation of exhaustible natural resources if such measures are made effective in conjunction with restrictions on domestic production or consumption;

96 Adopted 23 July 1998, WT/DS69/AB/R, para. 156.
97 Adopted 30 July 1997, WT/DS31/AB/R, DSR 1997:I, pp. 468-469.
98 Adopted 20 May 1996, WT/DS2/AB/R, DSR 1996:I, page.17 ff.
99 Additional submission of the United States, dated 17 August, 1998, para. 5.

### 1. "*Exhaustible Natural Resources*"

127. We begin with the threshold question of whether Section 609 is a measure concerned with the conservation of "exhaustible natural resources" within the meaning of Article XX(g). The Panel, of course, with its "chapeau-down" approach, did not make a finding on whether the sea turtles that Section 609 is designed to conserve constitute "exhaustible natural resources" for purposes of Article XX(g). In the proceedings before the Panel, however, the parties to the dispute argued this issue vigorously and extensively. India, Pakistan and Thailand contended that a "reasonable interpretation" of the term "exhaustible" is that the term refers to "finite resources such as minerals, rather than biological or renewable resources."[100] In their view, such finite resources were exhaustible "because there was a limited supply which could and would be depleted unit for unit as the resources were consumed."[101] Moreover, they argued, if "all" natural resources were considered to be exhaustible, the term "exhaustible" would become superfluous.[102] They also referred to the drafting history of Article XX(g), and, in particular, to the mention of minerals, such as manganese, in the context of arguments made by some delegations that "export restrictions" should be permitted for the preservation of scarce natural resources.[103] For its part, Malaysia added that sea turtles, being living creatures, could only be considered under Article XX(b), since Article XX(g) was meant for "nonliving exhaustible natural resources".[104] It followed, according to Malaysia, that the United States cannot invoke both the Article XX(b) and the Article XX(g) exceptions simultaneously.[105]

128. We are not convinced by these arguments. Textually, Article XX(g) is *not* limited to the conservation of "mineral" or "non-living" natural resources. The complainants' principal argument is rooted in the notion that "living" natural resources are "renewable" and therefore cannot be "exhaustible" natural resources. We do not believe that "exhaustible" natural resources and "renewable" natural resources are mutually exclusive. One lesson that modern biological sciences teach us is that living species, though in principle, capable of reproduction and, in that sense, "renewable", are in certain circumstances indeed susceptible of depletion, exhaustion and extinction, frequently because of human activities. Living resources are just as "finite" as petroleum, iron ore and other non-living resources.[106]

129. The words of Article XX(g), "exhaustible natural resources", were actually crafted more than 50 years ago. They must be read by a treaty interpreter in the light of contemporary concerns of the community of nations about the protection and con-

---

[100] Panel Report, para. 3.237.

[101] *Ibid.*

[102] *Ibid.*

[103] Panel Report, para 3.238. India, Pakistan and Thailand referred, *inter alia*, to E/PC/T/C.II/QR/PV/5, 18 November 1946, p. 79.

[104] Panel Report, para. 3.240.

[105] *Ibid.*

[106] We note, for example, that the World Commission on Environment and Development stated: "The planet's species are under stress. There is growing scientific consensus that species are disappearing at rates never before witnessed on the planet … ." World Commission on Environment and Development, *Our Common Future* (Oxford University Press, 1987), p. 13.

servation of the environment. While Article XX was not modified in the Uruguay Round, the preamble attached to the *WTO Agreement* shows that the signatories to that Agreement were, in 1994, fully aware of the importance and legitimacy of environmental protection as a goal of national and international policy. The preamble of the *WTO Agreement* - which informs not only the GATT 1994, but also the other covered agreements - explicitly acknowledges "the objective of *sustainable development*[107]":

> The *Parties* to this Agreement,
>
> *Recognizing* that their relations in the field of trade and economic endeavour should be conducted *with a view to raising standards of living, ensuring full employment and a large and steadily growing volume of real income and effective demand, and expanding the production of and trade in goods and services,* while allowing for the optimal use of the world's resources in accordance with the *objective of sustainable development, seeking both to protect and preserve the environment and to enhance the means for doing so* in a manner consistent with their respective needs and concerns at different levels of economic development, ...[108](emphasis added)

130. From the perspective embodied in the preamble of the *WTO Agreement*, we note that the generic term "natural resources" in Article XX(g) is not "static" in its content or reference but is rather "by definition, evolutionary".[109] It is, therefore, pertinent to note that modern international conventions and declarations make frequent references to natural resources as embracing both living and non-living resources. For instance, the 1982 United Nations Convention on the Law of the Sea[110]

---

[107] This concept has been generally accepted as integrating economic and social development and environmental protection See e.g., G. Handl, "Sustainable Development: General Rules versus Specific Obligations", in *Sustainable Development and International Law* (ed. W. Lang, 1995), p. 35; World Commission on Environment and Development, *Our Common Future* (Oxford University Press, 1987), p. 43.

[108] Preamble of the *WTO Agreement*.

[109] See *Namibia (Legal Consequences) Advisory Opinion* (1971) I.C.J. Rep., p. 31. The International Court of Justice stated that where concepts embodied in a treaty are "by definition, evolutionary", their "interpretation cannot remain unaffected by the subsequent development of law ... . Moreover, an international instrument has to be interpreted and applied within the framework of the entire legal system prevailing at the time of the interpretation." See also *Aegean Sea Continental Shelf Case*, (1978) I.C.J. Rep., p. 3; Jennings and Watts (eds.), *Oppenheim's International Law*, 9th ed., Vol. I (Longman's, 1992), p. 1282 and E. Jimenez de Arechaga, "International Law in the Past Third of a Century", (1978-I) 159 *Recueil des Cours* 1, p. 49.

[110] Done at Montego Bay, 10 December 1982, UN Doc. A/CONF.62/122; 21 International Legal Materials 1261. We note that India, Malaysia and Pakistan have ratified the UNCLOS. Thailand has signed, but not ratified the Convention, and the United States has not signed the Convention. In the oral hearing, the United States stated: "... we have not ratified this Convention although, with respect to fisheries law, for the most part we do believe that UNCLOS reflects international customary law." Also see, for example, W. Burke, *The New International Law of Fisheries* (Clarendon Press, 1994), p. 40:

> [the] coastal state sovereign rights over fisheries in a 200-mile zone are now considered part of customary international law. The evidence of state practice supporting this derives not only from the large number of coastal states claiming an

("UNCLOS"), in defining the jurisdictional rights of coastal states in their exclusive economic zones, provides:

Article 56

*Rights, jurisdiction and duties of the coastal State in the exclusive economic zone*

1. In the exclusive economic zone, the coastal State has:

(a) sovereign rights for the purpose of exploring and exploiting, conserving and managing the *natural resources, whether living or non-living*, of the waters superjacent to the sea-bed and of the sea-bed and its subsoil, ...(emphasis added)

The UNCLOS also repeatedly refers in Articles 61 and 62 to "living resources" in specifying rights and duties of states in their exclusive economic zones. The Convention on Biological Diversity[111] uses the concept of "biological resources". Agenda 21[112] speaks most broadly of "natural resources" and goes into detailed statements about "marine living resources". In addition, the Resolution on Assistance to Developing Countries, adopted in conjunction with the Convention on the Conservation of Migratory Species of Wild Animals, recites:

> Conscious that an important element of development lies in the conservation and management of *living natural resources* and that migratory species constitute a significant part of these resources; ...[113](emphasis added)

131. Given the recent acknowledgement by the international community of the importance of concerted bilateral or multilateral action to protect living natural resources, and recalling the explicit recognition by WTO Members of the objective of sustainable development in the preamble of the *WTO Agreement*, we believe it is too late in the day to suppose that Article XX(g) of the GATT 1994 may be read as referring only to the conservation of exhaustible mineral or other non-living natural re-

EEZ [exclusive economic zone] in which such rights are advanced, but also from the fact that many of those states not claiming an EEZ assert rights not appreciably different than those in an EEZ. The provision for sovereign rights of the coastal state in [Article 56.1(a) of] the 1982 Convention is also a part of this evidence, but has particular weight because of the uniformity of state practice outside the Convention.

[111] Done at Rio de Janeiro, 5 June 1992, UNEP/Bio.Div./N7-INC5/4; 31 International Legal Materials 818. We note that India, Malaysia and Pakistan have ratified the Convention on Biological Diversity, and that Thailand and the United States have signed but not ratified the Convention.

[112] Adopted by the United Nations Conference on Environment and Development, 14 June 1992, UN Doc. A/CONF. 151/26/Rev.1. See, for example, para. 17.70, ff.

[113] Final Act of the Conference to Conclude a Convention on the Conservation of Migratory Species of Wild Animals, done at Bonn, 23 June 1979, 19 International Legal Materials 11, p. 15. We note that India and Pakistan have ratified the Convention on the Conservation of Migratory Species of Wild Animals, but that Malaysia, Thailand and the United States are not parties to the Convention.

sources. [114] Moreover, two adopted GATT 1947 panel reports previously found fish to be an "exhaustible natural resource" within the meaning of Article XX(g). [115] We hold that, in line with the principle of effectiveness in treaty interpretation[116], measures to conserve exhaustible natural resources, whether *living* or *non-living*, may fall within Article XX(g).

132. We turn next to the issue of whether the living natural resources sought to be conserved by the measure are "exhaustible" under Article XX(g). That this element is present in respect of the five species of sea turtles here involved appears to be conceded by all the participants and third participants in this case. The exhaustibility of sea turtles would in fact have been very difficult to controvert since all of the seven recognized species of sea turtles are today listed in Appendix 1 of the Convention on International Trade in Endangered Species of Wild Fauna and Flora ("CITES"). The list in Appendix 1 includes "all species *threatened with extinction* which are or may be affected by trade."[117](emphasis added)

133. Finally, we observe that sea turtles are highly migratory animals, passing in and out of waters subject to the rights of jurisdiction of various coastal states and the high seas. In the Panel Report, the Panel said:

> ... Information brought to the attention of the Panel, including documented statements from the experts, tends to *confirm the fact that sea turtles, in certain circumstances of their lives, migrate through the waters of several countries and the high sea.* ...[118] (emphasis added)

The sea turtle species here at stake, i.e., covered by Section 609, are all known to occur in waters over which the United States exercises jurisdiction.[119] Of course, it is

---

[114] Furthermore, the drafting history does not demonstrate an intent on the part of the framers of the GATT 1947 *to exclude* "living" natural resources from the scope of application of Article XX(g).

[115] *United States - Prohibition of Imports of Tuna and Tuna Products from Canada*, adopted 22 February 1982, BISD 29S/91, para. 4.9; *Canada - Measures Affecting Exports of Unprocessed Herring and Salmon*, adopted 22 March 1988, BISD 35S/98, para. 4.4.

[116] See the following Appellate Body Reports: *United States - Gasoline*, adopted 20 May 1996, WT/DS52/AB/R, DSR 1996:I, page 21; *Japan - Taxes on Alcoholic Beverages*, adopted 1 November 1996, WT/DS8/AB/R, WT/DS10/AB/R, WT/DS11/AB/R, DSR 1996:I, page 104; and *United States - Restrictions on Imports of Cotton and Man-made Fibre Underwear*, adopted 25 February 1997, WT/DS24/AB/R, DSR 1997:I, page 22. See also Jennings and Watts (eds.), *Oppenheim's International Law*, 9th ed., Vol. I (Longman's, 1992), pp. 1280-1281; M.S. McDougal, H.D. Lasswell and J. Miller, *The Interpretation of International Agreements and World Public Order: Principles of Content and Procedure* (New Haven/Martinus Nijhoff, 1994), p. 184; I. Sinclair, *The Vienna Convention on the Law of Treaties*, 2nd ed. (Manchester University Press, 1984), p. 118; D. Carreau, *Droit International* (Editions A. Pedone, 1994), para. 369; P. Daillier and A. Pellet, *Droit International Public*, 5th ed. (L.G.D.J., 1994), para. 172; L.A. Podesta Costa and J.M. Ruda, *Derecho Internacional Público* (Tipografica Editora Argentina, 1985), pp. 109-110 and M. Diez de Velasco, *Instituciones de Derecho Internacional Público*, 11th ed. (Tecnos, 1997), p. 169.

[117] CITES, Article II.1.

[118] Panel Report, para. 7.53.

[119] See Panel Report, para. 2.6. The 1987 Regulations, 52 Fed. Reg. 24244, 29 June 1987, identified five species of sea turtles as occurring within the areas concerned and thus falling under the regulations: loggerhead (*Caretta caretta*), Kemp's ridley (*Lepidochelys kempi*), green (*Chelonia mydas*), leatherback (*Dermochelys coriacea*) and hawksbill (*Eretmochelys imbricata*). Section 609 refers to "those species of sea turtles the conservation of which is the subject of regulations promulgated by the Secretary of Commerce on 29 June, 1987."

not claimed that *all* populations of these species migrate to, or traverse, at one time or another, waters subject to United States jurisdiction. Neither the appellant nor any of the appellees claims any rights of exclusive ownership over the sea turtles, at least not while they are swimming freely in their natural habitat - the oceans. We do not pass upon the question of whether there is an implied jurisdictional limitation in Article XX(g), and if so, the nature or extent of that limitation. We note only that in the specific circumstances of the case before us, there is a sufficient nexus between the migratory and endangered marine populations involved and the United States for purposes of Article XX(g).

134. For all the foregoing reasons, we find that the sea turtles here involved constitute "exhaustible natural resources" for purposes of Article XX(g) of the GATT 1994.

### 2. *"Relating to the Conservation of [Exhaustible Natural Resources]"*

135. Article XX(g) requires that the measure sought to be justified be one which "relat[es] to" the conservation of exhaustible natural resources. In making this determination, the treaty interpreter essentially looks into the relationship between the measure at stake and the legitimate policy of conserving exhaustible natural resources. It is well to bear in mind that the policy of protecting and conserving the endangered sea turtles here involved is shared by all participants and third participants in this appeal, indeed, by the vast majority of the nations of the world.[120] None of the parties to this dispute question the genuineness of the commitment of the others to that policy.[121]

136. In *United States - Gasoline*, we inquired into the relationship between the baseline establishment rules of the United States Environmental Protection Agency (the "EPA") and the conservation of natural resources for the purposes of Article XX(g). There, we answered in the affirmative the question posed before the panel of whether the baseline establishment rules were "primarily aimed at" the conservation of clean air.[122] We held that:

> ... The baseline establishment rules whether individual or statutory, were designed to permit scrutiny and monitoring of the level of compliance of refiners, importers and blenders with the "non-degradation" requirements. Without baselines of some kind, such scrutiny would not be possible and the Gasoline Rule's objective of stabilizing and preventing further deterioration of the level of air pollution prevailing in 1990, would be substantially frustrated. ... We consider that, given that substantial relationship, the baseline establishment rules cannot be regarded as merely incidentally or inadvertently aimed at the conservation of clean air in the United States for the purposes of Article XX(g).[123]

[120] There are currently 144 states parties to CITES.

[121] We note that all of the participants in this appeal are parties to CITES.

[122] Adopted 20 May 1996, WT/DS2/AB/R, DSR 1996:I, page 17.

[123] *Ibid*.

The substantial relationship we found there between the EPA baseline establishment rules and the conservation of clean air in the United States was a close and genuine relationship of ends and means.

137. In the present case, we must examine the relationship between the general structure and design of the measure here at stake, Section 609, and the policy goal it purports to serve, that is, the conservation of sea turtles.

138. Section 609(b)(1) imposes an import ban on shrimp that have been harvested with commercial fishing technology which may adversely affect sea turtles. This provision is designed to influence countries to adopt national regulatory programs requiring the use of TEDs by their shrimp fishermen. In this connection, it is important to note that the general structure and design of Section 609 *cum* implementing guidelines is fairly narrowly focused. There are two basic exemptions from the import ban, both of which relate clearly and directly to the policy goal of conserving sea turtles. First, Section 609, as elaborated in the 1996 Guidelines, excludes from the import ban shrimp harvested "under conditions that do not adversely affect sea turtles". Thus, the measure, by its terms, excludes from the import ban: aquaculture shrimp; shrimp species (such as *pandalid* shrimp) harvested in water areas where sea turtles do not normally occur; and shrimp harvested exclusively by artisanal methods, even from non-certified countries.[124] The harvesting of such shrimp clearly does not affect sea turtles. Second, under Section 609(b)(2), the measure exempts from the import ban shrimp caught in waters subject to the jurisdiction of certified countries.

139. There are two types of certification for countries under Section 609(b)(2). First, under Section 609(b)(2)(C), a country may be certified as having a fishing environment that does not pose a threat of incidental taking of sea turtles in the course of commercial shrimp trawl harvesting. There is no risk, or only a negligible risk, that sea turtles will be harmed by shrimp trawling in such an environment.

140. The second type of certification is provided by Section 609(b)(2)(A) and (B). Under these provisions, as further elaborated in the 1996 Guidelines, a country wishing to export shrimp to the United States is required to adopt a regulatory program that is comparable to that of the United States program and to have a rate of incidental take of sea turtles that is comparable to the average rate of United States' vessels. This is, essentially, a requirement that a country adopt a regulatory program requiring the use of TEDs by commercial shrimp trawling vessels in areas where there is a likelihood of intercepting sea turtles.[125] This requirement is, in our view, directly connected with the policy of conservation of sea turtles. It is undisputed among the participants, and recognized by the experts consulted by the Panel[126], that the harvesting of shrimp by commercial shrimp trawling vessels with mechanical retrieval devices in waters where shrimp and sea turtles coincide is a significant cause of sea turtle mortality. Moreover, the Panel did "not question ... the fact generally acknowledged by the experts that TEDs, when properly installed and adapted to the local area, would be an effective tool for the preservation of sea turtles."[127]

---

124 See the 1996 Guidelines, p. 17343.

125 See the 1996 Guidelines, p. 17343.

126 For example, Panel Report, paras. 5.91-5.118.

127 Panel Report, para. 7.60, footnote 674.

141. In its general design and structure, therefore, Section 609 is not a simple, blanket prohibition of the importation of shrimp imposed without regard to the consequences (or lack thereof) of the mode of harvesting employed upon the incidental capture and mortality of sea turtles. Focusing on the design of the measure here at stake[128], it appears to us that Section 609, *cum* implementing guidelines, is not disproportionately wide in its scope and reach in relation to the policy objective of protection and conservation of sea turtle species. The means are, in principle, reasonably related to the ends. The means and ends relationship between Section 609 and the legitimate policy of conserving an exhaustible, and, in fact, endangered species, is observably a close and real one, a relationship that is every bit as substantial as that which we found in *United States - Gasoline* between the EPA baseline establishment rules and the conservation of clean air in the United States.

142. In our view, therefore, Section 609 is a measure "relating to" the conservation of an exhaustible natural resource within the meaning of Article XX(g) of the GATT 1994.

### 3. *"If Such Measures are Made Effective in Conjunction with Restrictions on Domestic Production or Consumption"*

143. In *United States - Gasoline*, we held that the above-captioned clause of Article XX(g),

> ... is appropriately read as a requirement that the measures concerned impose restrictions, not just in respect of imported gasoline but also with respect to domestic gasoline. The clause is a requirement of *even-handedness* in the imposition of restrictions, in the name of conservation, upon the production or consumption of exhaustible natural resources.[129]

In this case, we need to examine whether the restrictions imposed by Section 609 with respect to imported shrimp are also imposed in respect of shrimp caught by United States shrimp trawl vessels.

144. We earlier noted that Section 609, enacted in 1989, addresses the mode of harvesting of imported shrimp only. However, two years earlier, in 1987, the United States issued regulations pursuant to the Endangered Species Act requiring all United States shrimp trawl vessels to use approved TEDs, or to restrict the duration of tow-times, in specified areas where there was significant incidental mortality of sea turtles in shrimp trawls.[130] These regulations became fully effective in 1990 and were later modified. They now require United States shrimp trawlers to use approved TEDs "in areas and at times when there is a likelihood of intercepting sea turtles" [131], with certain limited exceptions.[132] Penalties for violation of the Endangered Species Act, or

[128] We focus on the *application* of the measure below, in Section VI.C of this Report.

[129] Adopted 20 May 1996, WT/DS2/AB/R, DSR 1996:I, page 19.

[130] 52 Fed. Reg. 24244, 29 June 1987.

[131] See the 1996 Guidelines, p. 17343.

[132] According to the 1996 Guidelines, p. 17343, the exceptions are: vessels equipped exclusively with certain special types of gear; vessels whose nets are retrieved exclusively by manual rather than mechanical means; and, in exceptional circumstances, where the National Marine Fisheries Service

the regulations issued thereunder, include civil and criminal sanctions.[133] The United States government currently relies on monetary sanctions and civil penalties for enforcement.[134] The government has the ability to seize shrimp catch from trawl vessels fishing in United States waters and has done so in cases of egregious violations.[135] We believe that, in principle, Section 609 is an even-handed measure.

145. Accordingly, we hold that Section 609 is a measure made effective in conjunction with the restrictions on domestic harvesting of shrimp, as required by Article XX(g).

### *C. The Introductory Clauses of Article XX: Characterizing Section 609 under the Chapeau's Standards*

146. As noted earlier, the United States invokes Article XX(b) only if and to the extent that we hold that Section 609 falls outside the scope of Article XX(g). Having found that Section 609 does come within the terms of Article XX(g), it is not, therefore, necessary to analyze the measure in terms of Article XX(b).

147. Although provisionally justified under Article XX(g), Section 609, if it is ultimately to be justified as an exception under Article XX, must also satisfy the requirements of the introductory clauses - the "chapeau" - of Article XX, that is,

> Article XX
>
> *General Exceptions*
>
> Subject to the requirement that such measures are *not applied in a manner which would constitute a means of arbitrary or unjustifiable discrimination between countries where the same conditions prevail, or a disguised restriction on international trade*, nothing in this Agreement shall be construed to prevent the adoption or enforcement by any Member of measures: (emphasis added)

We turn, hence, to the task of appraising Section 609, and specifically the manner in which it is applied under the chapeau of Article XX; that is, to the second part of the two-tier analysis required under Article XX.

#### *1. General Considerations*

148. We begin by noting one of the principal arguments made by the United States in its appellant's submission. The United States argues:

> In context, *an alleged "discrimination between countries where the same conditions prevail" is not "unjustifiable" where the policy goal of the Article XX exception being applied provides a rationale for the justification*. If, for example, a measure is adopted for the purpose of conserving an exhaustible natural resource under Article XX(g), it is

determines that the use of TEDs would be impracticable because of special environmental conditions, vessels are permitted to restrict tow-times instead of using TEDs.

[133] Endangered Species Act, Section 11.

[134] Statement by the United States at the oral hearing.

[135] Statement by the United States at the oral hearing.

> relevant whether the conservation goal justifies the discrimination. In this way, the Article XX chapeau guards against the misuse of the Article XX exceptions for the purpose of achieving indirect protection.[136]
>
> ...
>
> [A]n evaluation of whether a measure constitutes "unjustifiable discrimination [between countries] where the same conditions prevail" should take account of *whether differing treatment between countries relates to the policy goal of the applicable Article XX exception. If a measure differentiates between countries based on a rationale legitimately connected with the policy of an Article XX exception*, rather than for protectionist reasons, *the measure does not amount to an abuse of the applicable Article XX exception.*[137] (emphasis added)

149. We believe this argument must be rejected. The policy goal of a measure at issue cannot provide its rationale or justification under the standards of the chapeau of Article XX. The legitimacy of the declared policy objective of the measure, and the relationship of that objective with the measure itself and its general design and structure, are examined under Article XX(g), and the treaty interpreter may then and there declare the measure inconsistent with Article XX(g). If the measure is not held provisionally justified under Article XX(g), it cannot be ultimately justified under the chapeau of Article XX. On the other hand, it does not follow from the fact that a measure falls within the terms of Article XX(g) that that measure also will necessarily comply with the requirements of the chapeau. To accept the argument of the United States would be to disregard the standards established by the chapeau.

150. We commence the second tier of our analysis with an examination of the ordinary meaning of the words of the chapeau. The precise language of the chapeau requires that a measure not be applied in a manner which would constitute a means of "arbitrary or unjustifiable discrimination between countries where the same conditions prevail" or a "disguised restriction on international trade." There are three standards contained in the chapeau: first, arbitrary discrimination between countries where the same conditions prevail; second, unjustifiable discrimination between countries where the same conditions prevail; and third, a disguised restriction on international trade. In order for a measure to be applied in a manner which would constitute "arbitrary or unjustifiable discrimination between countries where the same conditions prevail", three elements must exist. First, the application of the measure must result in *discrimination.* As we stated in *United States - Gasoline*, the nature and quality of this discrimination is different from the discrimination in the treatment of products which was already found to be inconsistent with one of the substantive obligations of the GATT 1994, such as Articles I, III or XI.[138] Second, the discrimination must be *arbitrary* or *unjustifiable* in character. We will examine this element of *arbitrariness* or *unjustifiability* in detail below. Third, this discrimi-

---

[136] United States appellant's submission, para. 28.

[137] United States appellant's submission, para. 53.

[138] In *United States - Gasoline*, adopted 20 May 1996, WT/DS2/AB/R, DSR 1996:I, page 21, we stated: "The provisions of the chapeau cannot logically refer to the same standard(s) by which a violation of a substantive rule has been determined to have occurred."

nation must occur *between countries where the same conditions prevail.* In *United States - Gasoline*, we accepted the assumption of the participants in that appeal that such discrimination could occur not only between different exporting Members, but also between exporting Members and the importing Member concerned.[139] Thus, the standards embodied in the language of the chapeau are not only different from the requirements of Article XX(g); they are also different from the standard used in determining that Section 609 is violative of the substantive rules of Article XI:1 of the GATT 1994.

151. In *United States - Gasoline*, we stated that "the purpose and object of the introductory clauses of Article XX is generally the prevention of 'abuse of the exceptions of [Article XX]'."[140] We went on to say that:

> ... The chapeau is animated by the principle that while the exceptions of Article XX may be invoked as a matter of legal right, they should not be so applied as to frustrate or defeat the legal obligations of the holder of the right under the substantive rules of the *General Agreement*. If those exceptions are not to be abused or misused, in other words, the measures falling within the particular exceptions must be applied reasonably, with due regard both to the legal duties of the party claiming the exception and the legal rights of the other parties concerned.[141]

152. At the end of the Uruguay Round, negotiators fashioned an appropriate preamble for the new *WTO Agreement,* which strengthened the multilateral trading system by establishing an international organization, *inter alia,* to facilitate the implementation, administration and operation, and to further the objectives, of that Agreement and the other agreements resulting from that Round.[142] In recognition of the importance of continuity with the previous GATT system, negotiators used the preamble of the GATT 1947 as the template for the preamble of the new *WTO Agreement*. Those negotiators evidently believed, however, that the objective of "full use of the resources of the world" set forth in the preamble of the GATT 1947 was no longer appropriate to the world trading system of the 1990's. As a result, they decided to qualify the original objectives of the GATT 1947 with the following words:

> ... while allowing for the optimal use of the world's resources in accordance with the objective of sustainable development, seeking both to protect and preserve the environment and to enhance the means for doing so in a manner consistent with their respective needs and concerns at different levels of economic development, ...[143]

---

[139] In *United States - Gasoline*, adopted 20 May 1996, WT/DS2/AB/R, DSR 1996:I, page 21, we stated: "The provisions of the chapeau cannot logically refer to the same standard(s) by which a violation of a substantive rule has been determined to have occurred."

[140] *Ibid.*, p. 20.

[141] *Ibid.*

[142] *WTO Agreement*, Article III:1.

[143] Preamble of the *WTO Agreement*, first paragraph.

153. We note once more[144] that this language demonstrates a recognition by WTO negotiators that optimal use of the world's resources should be made in accordance with the objective of sustainable development. As this preambular language reflects the intentions of negotiators of the *WTO Agreement*, we believe it must add colour, texture and shading to our interpretation of the agreements annexed to the *WTO Agreement*, in this case, the GATT 1994. We have already observed that Article XX(g) of the GATT 1994 is appropriately read with the perspective embodied in the above preamble.[145]

154. We also note that since this preambular language was negotiated, certain other developments have occurred which help to elucidate the objectives of WTO Members with respect to the relationship between trade and the environment. The most significant, in our view, was the Decision of Ministers at Marrakesh to establish a permanent Committee on Trade and Environment (the "CTE"). In their Decision on Trade and Environment, Ministers expressed their intentions, in part, as follows:

> … *Considering* that there should not be, nor need be, any policy contradiction between upholding and safeguarding an open, non-discriminatory and equitable multilateral trading system on the one hand, and acting for the protection of the environment, and the promotion of sustainable development on the other, …[146]

In this Decision, Ministers took "note" of the Rio Declaration on Environment and Development [147], Agenda 21[148], and "its follow-up in the GATT, as reflected in the statement of the Council of Representatives to the CONTRACTING PARTIES at their 48th Session in 1992 … ."[149] We further note that this Decision also set out the following terms of reference for the CTE:

> (a) to identify the relationship between trade measures and environmental measures, in order to promote sustainable development;
>
> (b) to make appropriate recommendations on whether any modifications of the provisions of the multilateral trading system are

---

144 *Supra*, para. 129.

145 *Supra*, para. 131.

146 Preamble of the Decision on Trade and Environment.

147 We note that Principle 3 of the Rio Declaration on Environment and Development states: "The right to development must be fulfilled so as to equitably meet developmental and environmental needs of present and future generations." Principle 4 of the Rio Declaration on Environment and Development states that: "In order to achieve sustainable development, environmental protection shall constitute an integral part of the development process and cannot be considered in isolation from it."

148 Agenda 21 is replete with references to the shared view that economic development and the preservation and protection should be mutually supportive. For example, paragraph 2.3(b) of Agenda 21 states: "The international economy should provide a supportive international climate for achieving environment and development goals by … [m]aking trade and environment mutually supportive … ." Similarly, paragraph 2.9(d) states that an "objective" of governments should be: "To promote and support policies, domestic and international, that make economic growth and environmental protection mutually supportive."

149 Preamble of the Decision on Trade and Environment.

required, compatible with the open, equitable and non-discriminatory nature of the system, as regards, in particular:

- the need for rules to enhance positive interaction between trade and environmental measures, for the promotion of sustainable development, with special consideration to the needs of developing countries, in particular those of the least developed among them; and
- the avoidance of protectionist trade measures, and the adherence to effective multilateral disciplines to ensure responsiveness of the multilateral trading system to environmental objectives set forth in Agenda 21 and the Rio Declaration, in particular Principle 12; and
- surveillance of trade measures used for environmental purposes, of trade-related aspects of environmental measures which have significant trade affects, and of effective implementation of the multilateral disciplines governing those measures.[150]

155. With these instructions, the General Council of the WTO established the CTE in 1995, and the CTE began its important work. Pending any specific recommendations by the CTE to WTO Members on the issues raised in its terms of reference, and in the absence up to now of any agreed amendments or modifications to the substantive provisions of the GATT 1994 and the *WTO Agreement* generally, we must fulfill our responsibility in this specific case, which is to interpret the existing language of the chapeau of Article XX by examining its ordinary meaning, in light of its context and object and purpose in order to determine whether the United States measure at issue qualifies for justification under Article XX. It is proper for us to take into account, as part of the context of the chapeau, the specific language of the preamble to the *WTO Agreement*, which, we have said, gives colour, texture and shading to the rights and obligations of Members under the *WTO Agreement*, generally, and under the GATT 1994, in particular.

156. Turning then to the chapeau of Article XX, we consider that it embodies the recognition on the part of WTO Members of the need to maintain a balance of rights and obligations between the right of a Member to invoke one or another of the exceptions of Article XX, specified in paragraphs (a) to (j), on the one hand, and the substantive rights of the other Members under the GATT 1994, on the other hand. Exercise by one Member of its right to invoke an exception, such as Article XX(g), if abused or misused, will, to that extent, erode or render naught the substantive treaty rights in, for example, Article XI:1, of other Members. Similarly, because the GATT 1994 itself makes available the exceptions of Article XX, in recognition of the legitimate nature of the policies and interests there embodied, the right to invoke one of those exceptions is not to be rendered illusory. The same concept may be expressed from a slightly different angle of vision, thus, a balance must be struck between the *right* of a Member to invoke an exception under Article XX and the *duty*

[150] Decision on Trade and Environment.

of that same Member to respect the treaty rights of the other Members. To permit one Member to abuse or misuse its right to invoke an exception would be effectively to allow that Member to degrade its own treaty obligations as well as to devalue the treaty rights of other Members. If the abuse or misuse is sufficiently grave or extensive, the Member, in effect, reduces its treaty obligation to a merely facultative one and dissolves its juridical character, and, in so doing, negates altogether the treaty rights of other Members. The chapeau was installed at the head of the list of "General Exceptions" in Article XX to prevent such far-reaching consequences.

157. In our view, the language of the chapeau makes clear that each of the exceptions in paragraphs (a) to (j) of Article XX is a *limited and conditional* exception from the substantive obligations contained in the other provisions of the GATT 1994, that is to say, the ultimate availability of the exception is subject to the compliance by the invoking Member with the requirements of the chapeau.[151] This interpretation of the chapeau is confirmed by its negotiating history.[152] The language initially proposed by the United States in 1946 for the chapeau of what would later become Article XX was unqualified and unconditional.[153] Several proposals were made during the First Session of the Preparatory Committee of the United Nations Conference on Trade and Employment in 1946 suggesting modifications.[154] In November 1946, the United Kingdom proposed that "in order to prevent abuse of the exceptions of Article 32 [which would subsequently become Article XX]", the chapeau of this provision should be qualified.[155] This proposal was generally accepted, subject to later review

---

[151] This view is consistent with the approach taken by the panel in *United States - Section 337 of the United States Tariff Act of 1930,* which stated:

> Article XX is entitled "General Exceptions" and ... the central phrase in the introductory clause reads: "nothing in this Agreement shall be construed to prevent the adoption or enforcement ... of measures...". Article XX(d) thus provides *a limited and conditional exception from obligations under other provisions.*[151] (emphasis added) Adopted 7 November 1989, BISD 365/345, para. 5.9.

[152] Article 32 of the Vienna Convention permits recourse to "supplementary means of interpretation, including the preparatory work of the treaty and the circumstances of its conclusion, in order to confirm the meaning resulting from the application of article 31, or to determine the meaning when interpretation according to article 31: (a) leaves the meaning ambiguous or obscure; or (b) leads to a result which is manifestly absurd or unreasonable." Here, we refer to the negotiating history of Article XX to confirm the interpretation of the chapeau we have reached from applying Article 31 of the Vienna Convention.

[153] The chapeau of Article 32 of the United States Draft Charter for an International Trade Organization, which formed the basis for discussions at the First Session of the Preparatory Committee of the United Nations Conference on Trade and Employment in late 1946, read, in relevant part:

> Nothing in Chapter IV of this Charter shall be construed to prevent the adoption or enforcement by any member of measures: ...

[154] For example, the Netherlands, Belgium and Luxembourg stated that the exceptions should be qualified in some way:

> Indirect protection is an undesirable and dangerous phenomenon. ... Many times, the stipulations to 'protect animal or plant life or health' are misused for indirect protection. It is recommended to insert a clause which prohibits expressly to direct such measures that they constitute an indirect protection or, in general, to use these measures to attain results, which are irreconsiliable [*sic*] with the aim of chapters IV, V and VI. E/PC/T/C.II/32, 30 October 1946

[155] The United Kingdom's proposed text for the chapeau read:

of its precise wording. Thus, the negotiating history of Article XX confirms that the paragraphs of Article XX set forth *limited and conditional* exceptions from the obligations of the substantive provisions of the GATT. Any measure, to qualify finally for exception, must also satisfy the requirements of the chapeau. This is a fundamental part of the balance of rights and obligations struck by the original framers of the GATT 1947.

158. The chapeau of Article XX is, in fact, but one expression of the principle of good faith. This principle, at once a general principle of law and a general principle of international law, controls the exercise of rights by states. One application of this general principle, the application widely known as the doctrine of *abus de droit*, prohibits the abusive exercise of a state's rights and enjoins that whenever the assertion of a right "impinges on the field covered by [a] treaty obligation, it must be exercised bona fide, that is to say, reasonably."[156] An abusive exercise by a Member of its own treaty right thus results in a breach of the treaty rights of the other Members and, as well, a violation of the treaty obligation of the Member so acting. Having said this, our task here is to interpret the language of the chapeau, seeking additional interpretative guidance, as appropriate, from the general principles of international law.[157]

159. The task of interpreting and applying the chapeau is, hence, essentially the delicate one of locating and marking out a line of equilibrium between the right of a Member to invoke an exception under Article XX and the rights of the other Members under varying substantive provisions (e.g., Article XI) of the GATT 1994, so that neither of the competing rights will cancel out the other and thereby distort and nullify or impair the balance of rights and obligations constructed by the Members themselves in that Agreement. The location of the line of equilibrium, as expressed

---

> The undertaking in Chapter IV of this Charter relating to import and export restrictions shall not be construed to prevent the adoption or enforcement by any member of measures for the following purposes, provided that they are not applied in such a manner as to constitute a means of arbitrary discrimination between countries where the same conditions prevail, or a disguised restriction on international trade.
> E/PC/T/C.II/50, pp. 7 and 9; E/PC/T/C.II/54/Rev.1, 28 November 1946, p. 36.

[156] B. Cheng, *General Principles of Law as applied by International Courts and Tribunals* (Stevens and Sons, Ltd., 1953), Chapter 4, in particular, p. 125 elaborates:

> ... A reasonable and bona fide exercise of a right in such a case is one which is appropriate and necessary for the purpose of the right (*i.e.*, in furtherance of the interests which the right is intended to protect). It should at the same time be *fair and equitable as between the parties* and not one which is calculated to procure for one of them an unfair advantage in the light of the obligation assumed. A reasonable exercise of the right is regarded as compatible with the obligation. But the exercise of the right in such a manner as to prejudice the interests of the other contracting party arising out of the treaty is unreasonable and is considered as inconsistent with the bona fide execution of the treaty obligation, and a breach of the treaty. ...(emphasis added)

Also see, for example, Jennings and Watts (eds.), *Oppenheim's International Law*, 9th ed, Vol. I (Longman's, 1992), pp. 407-410, *Border and Transborder Armed Actions Case*, (1988) I.C.J. Rep. 105; *Rights of Nationals of the United States in Morocco Case*, (1952) I.C.J. Rep. 176; *Anglo-Norwegian Fisheries Case*, (1951) I.C.J. Rep. 142.

[157] Vienna Convention, Article 31(3)(c).

in the chapeau, is not fixed and unchanging; the line moves as the kind and the shape of the measures at stake vary and as the facts making up specific cases differ.

160. With these general considerations in mind, we address now the issue of whether the *application* of the United States measure, although the measure itself falls within the terms of Article XX(g), nevertheless constitutes "a means of arbitrary or unjustifiable discrimination between countries where the same conditions prevail" or "a disguised restriction on international trade". We address, in other words, whether the application of this measure constitutes an abuse or misuse of the provisional justification made available by Article XX(g). We note, preliminarily, that the application of a measure may be characterized as amounting to an abuse or misuse of an exception of Article XX not only when the detailed operating provisions of the measure prescribe the arbitrary or unjustifiable activity, but also where a measure, otherwise fair and just on its face, is actually applied in an arbitrary or unjustifiable manner. The standards of the chapeau, in our view, project both substantive and procedural requirements.

### 2. *"Unjustifiable Discrimination"*

161. We scrutinize first whether Section 609 has been applied in a manner constituting "unjustifiable discrimination between countries where the same conditions prevail". Perhaps the most conspicuous flaw in this measure's application relates to its intended and actual coercive effect on the specific policy decisions made by foreign governments, Members of the WTO. Section 609, in its application, is, in effect, an economic embargo which requires *all other exporting Members*, if they wish to exercise their GATT rights, to adopt *essentially the same* policy (together with an approved enforcement program) as that applied to, and enforced on, United States domestic shrimp trawlers. As enacted by the Congress of the United States, the *statutory* provisions of Section 609(b)(2)(A) and (B) do not, in themselves, *require* that other WTO Members adopt *essentially the same* policies and enforcement practices as the United States. Viewed alone, the statute appears to permit a degree of discretion or flexibility in how the standards for determining comparability might be applied, in practice, to other countries.[158] However, any flexibility that may have been intended by Congress when it enacted the statutory provision has been effectively eliminated in the implementation of that policy through the 1996 Guidelines promulgated by the Department of State and through the practice of the administrators in making certification determinations.

162. According to the 1996 Guidelines, certification "shall be made" under Section 609(b)(2)(A) and (B) if an exporting country's program includes a requirement that

---

[158] Pursuant to Section 609(b)(2), a harvesting nation may be certified, and thus exempted from the import ban, if:

> (A) the government of the harvesting nation has provided documentary evidence of the adoption of a program governing the incidental taking of such sea turtles in the course of such harvesting that is comparable to that of the United States; and
>
> (B) the average rate of that incidental taking by vessels of the harvesting nation is comparable to the average rate of incidental taking of sea turtles by United States vessels in the course of such harvesting…

all commercial shrimp trawl vessels operating in waters in which there is a likelihood of intercepting sea turtles use, at all times, TEDs comparable in effectiveness to those used in the United States.[159] Under these Guidelines, any exceptions to the requirement of the use of TEDs must be comparable to those of the United States program.[160] Furthermore, the harvesting country must have in place a "credible enforcement effort".[161] The language in the 1996 Guidelines is mandatory: certification "shall be made" if these conditions are fulfilled. However, we understand that these rules are also applied in an *exclusive* manner. That is, the 1996 Guidelines specify the *only* way that a harvesting country's regulatory program can be deemed "comparable" to the United States' program, and, therefore, they define the *only* way that a harvesting nation can be certified under Section 609(b)(2)(A) and (B). Although the 1996 Guidelines state that, in making a comparability determination, the Department of State "shall also take into account other measures the harvesting nation undertakes to protect sea turtles"[162], in practice, the competent government officials only look to see whether there is a regulatory program requiring the use of TEDs or one that comes within one of the extremely limited exceptions available to United States shrimp trawl vessels.[163]

163. The actual *application* of the measure, through the implementation of the 1996 Guidelines and the regulatory practice of administrators, *requires* other WTO Members to adopt a regulatory program that is not merely *comparable*, but rather *essentially the same*, as that applied to the United States shrimp trawl vessels. Thus, the effect of the application of Section 609 is to establish a rigid and unbending standard by which United States officials determine whether or not countries will be certified, thus granting or refusing other countries the right to export shrimp to the United States. Other specific policies and measures that an exporting country may have adopted for the protection and conservation of sea turtles are not taken into account, in practice, by the administrators making the comparability determination.[164]

164. We understand that the United States also applies a uniform standard throughout its territory, regardless of the particular conditions existing in certain parts of the country. The United States requires the use of approved TEDs at all times by domestic, commercial shrimp trawl vessels operating in waters where there is any likelihood that they may interact with sea turtles, regardless of the actual incidence of sea turtles in those waters, the species of those sea turtles, or other differences or disparities that may exist in different parts of the United States. It may be quite acceptable for a government, in adopting and implementing a domestic policy, to adopt

159 1996 Guidelines, p. 17344.

160 As already noted, these exceptions are extremely limited and currently include only: vessels equipped exclusively with certain special types of gear; vessels whose nets are retrieved exclusively by manual rather than mechanical means; and, in exceptional circumstances, where the National Marine Fisheries Services determines that the use of TEDs would be impracticable because of special environmental conditions, vessels are permitted to restrict tow-times instead of using TEDs. See the 1996 Guidelines, p. 17343. In the oral hearing, the United States informed us that the exception for restricted tow-times is no longer available.

161 1996 Guidelines, p. 17344.

162 *Ibid.*

163 Statements by the United States at the oral hearing.

164 Statement by the United States at the oral hearing.

a single standard applicable to all its citizens throughout that country. However, it is not acceptable, in international trade relations, for one WTO Member to use an economic embargo to *require* other Members to adopt essentially the same comprehensive regulatory program, to achieve a certain policy goal, as that in force within that Member's territory, *without* taking into consideration different conditions which may occur in the territories of those other Members.

165. Furthermore, when this dispute was before the Panel and before us, the United States did not permit imports of shrimp harvested by commercial shrimp trawl vessels using TEDs comparable in effectiveness to those required in the United States if those shrimp originated in waters of countries not certified under Section 609. In other words, *shrimp caught using methods identical to those employed in the United States* have been excluded from the United States market solely because they have been caught in waters of *countries that have not been certified by the United States*. The resulting situation is difficult to reconcile with the declared policy objective of protecting and conserving sea turtles. This suggests to us that this measure, in its application, is more concerned with effectively influencing WTO Members to adopt essentially the same comprehensive regulatory regime as that applied by the United States to its domestic shrimp trawlers, even though many of those Members may be differently situated. We believe that discrimination results not only when countries in which the same conditions prevail are differently treated, but also when the application of the measure at issue does not allow for any inquiry into the appropriateness of the regulatory program for the conditions prevailing in those exporting countries.

166. Another aspect of the application of Section 609 that bears heavily in any appraisal of justifiable or unjustifiable discrimination is the failure of the United States to engage the appellees, as well as other Members exporting shrimp to the United States, in serious, across-the-board negotiations with the objective of concluding bilateral or multilateral agreements for the protection and conservation of sea turtles, before enforcing the import prohibition against the shrimp exports of those other Members. The relevant factual finding of the Panel reads:

> ... However, *we have no evidence that the United States actually undertook negotiations on an agreement on sea turtle conservation techniques which would have included the complainants before the imposition of the import ban as a result of the CIT judgement*. From the replies of the parties to our question on this subject, in particular that of the United States, we understand that the United States did not propose the negotiation of an agreement to any of the complainants until after the conclusion of negotiations on the Inter-American Convention for the Protection and Conservation of Sea Turtles, in September 1996, i.e. well after the deadline for the imposition of the import ban of 1 May 1996. Even then, it seems that the efforts made merely consisted of an exchange of documents. We therefore conclude that, in spite of the possibility offered by its legislation, the United States did not enter into negotiations before it imposed the import ban. As we consider that the measures sought by the United States were of the type that would normally require international cooperation, we do not find it necessary to examine whether parties entered into negotiations in good faith and whether the United States, absent any result,

would have been entitled to adopt unilateral measures.[165](emphasis added)

167. *A propos* this failure to have prior consistent recourse to diplomacy as an instrument of environmental protection policy, which produces discriminatory impacts on countries exporting shrimp to the United States with which no international agreements are reached or even seriously attempted, a number of points must be made. First, the Congress of the United States expressly recognized the importance of securing international agreements for the protection and conservation of the sea turtle species in enacting this law. Section 609(a) *directs* the Secretary of State to:

> (1) *initiate negotiations as soon as possible for the development of bilateral or multilateral agreements with other nations* for the protection and conservation of such species of sea turtles;
>
> (2) *initiate negotiations as soon as possible* with all foreign governments which are engaged in, or which have persons or companies engaged in, commercial fishing operations which, as determined by the Secretary of Commerce, may affect adversely such species of sea turtles, *for the purpose of entering into bilateral and multilateral treaties with such countries to protect such species of sea turtles*;
>
> (3) *encourage such other agreements* to promote the purposes of this section *with other nations* for the protection of specific ocean and land regions which are of special significance to the health and stability of such species of sea turtles;
>
> (4) *initiate the amendment of any existing international treaty* for the protection and conservation of such species of sea turtles to which the United States is a party *in order to make such treaty consistent with the purposes and policies of this section*; and
>
> (5) provide to the Congress by not later than one year after the date of enactment of this section: ...
>
> (C) a full report on:
>
> (i) the results of his efforts under this section; ... (emphasis added)

Apart from the negotiation of the Inter-American Convention for the Protection and Conservation of Sea Turtles[166] (the "Inter-American Convention") which concluded in 1996, the record before the Panel does not indicate any serious, substantial efforts to carry out these express directions of Congress.[167]

168. Second, the protection and conservation of highly migratory species of sea turtles, that is, the very policy objective of the measure, demands concerted and cooperative efforts on the part of the many countries whose waters are traversed in the course of recurrent sea turtle migrations. The need for, and the appropriateness of, such efforts have been recognized in the WTO itself as well as in a significant number of other international instruments and declarations. As stated earlier, the Decision

165 Panel Report, para. 7.56.

166 First written submission of the United States to the Panel, Exhibit AA.

167 Panel Report, para. 7.56.

on Trade and Environment, which provided for the establishment of the CTE and set out its terms of reference, refers to both the Rio Declaration on Environment and Development and Agenda 21.[168] Of particular relevance is Principle 12 of the Rio Declaration on Environment and Development, which states, in part:

> Unilateral actions to deal with environmental challenges outside the jurisdiction of the importing country should be avoided. *Environmental measures addressing transboundary or global environmental problems should, as far as possible, be based on international consensus.*(emphasis added)

In almost identical language, paragraph 2.22(i) of Agenda 21 provides:

> Governments should encourage GATT, UNCTAD and other relevant international and regional economic institutions to examine, in accordance with their respective mandates and competences, the following propositions and principles: …
>
> (i) Avoid unilateral action to deal with environmental challenges outside the jurisdiction of the importing country. *Environmental measures addressing transborder problems should, as far as possible, be based on an international consensus.*(emphasis added)

Moreover, we note that Article 5 of the Convention on Biological Diversity states:

> … each contracting party shall, as far as possible and as appropriate, cooperate with other contracting parties directly or, where appropriate, through competent international organizations, in respect of areas beyond national jurisdiction and on other matters of mutual interest, for the conservation and sustainable use of biological diversity.

The Convention on the Conservation of Migratory Species of Wild Animals, which classifies the relevant species of sea turtles in its Annex I as "Endangered Migratory Species", states:

> The contracting parties [are] convinced that conservation and effective management of migratory species of wild animals requires the concerted action of all States within the national boundaries of which such species spend any part of their life cycle.

Furthermore, we note that WTO Members in the Report of the CTE, forming part of the Report of the General Council to Ministers on the occasion of the Singapore Ministerial Conference, endorsed and supported:

> … *multilateral solutions based on international cooperation and consensus as the best and most effective way for governments to tackle environmental problems of a transboundary or global nature.* WTO Agreements and multilateral environmental agreements (MEAs) are representative of efforts of the international community to pursue *shared goals*, and in the development of a mutually supportive rela-

[168] See Decision on Trade and Environment, preamble and para. 2(b). See *Supra*, para. 154.

tionship between them, *due respect must be afforded to both.* [169] (emphasis added)

169. Third, the United States did negotiate and conclude one regional international agreement for the protection and conservation of sea turtles: The Inter-American Convention. This Convention was opened for signature on 1 December 1996 and has been signed by five countries[170], in addition to the United States, and four of these countries are currently certified under Section 609.[171] This Convention has not yet been ratified by any of its signatories. The Inter-American Convention provides that each party shall take "appropriate and necessary measures" for the protection, conservation and recovery of sea turtle populations and their habitats within such party's land territory and in maritime areas with respect to which it exercises sovereign rights or jurisdiction.[172] Such measures include, notably,

> [t]he reduction, to the greatest extent practicable, of the incidental capture, retention, harm or mortality of sea turtles in the course of fishing activities, through the appropriate regulation of such activities, as well as the development, improvement and use of appropriate gear, devices or techniques, including the use of turtle excluder devices (TEDs) pursuant to the provisions of Annex III [of the Convention].[173]

Article XV of the Inter-American Convention also provides, in part:

## Article XV

*Trade Measures*

> 1. *In implementing this Convention, the Parties shall act in accordance with the provisions of the Agreement establishing the World Trade Organization* (WTO), as adopted at Marrakesh in 1994, including its annexes.
>
> 2. In particular, and *with respect to the subject-matter of this Convention, the Parties shall act in accordance with the provisions of* the Agreement on Technical Barriers to Trade contained in Annex 1 of the WTO Agreement, as well as *Article XI of the General Agreement on Tariffs and Trade of 1994.* ...(emphasis added)

170. The juxtaposition of (a) the *consensual* undertakings to put in place regulations providing for, *inter alia*, use of TEDs *jointly determined* to be suitable for a particular party's maritime areas, with (b) the reaffirmation of the parties' obligations

[169] Report (1996) of the Committee on Trade and Environment, WT/CTE/1, 12 November 1996, para. 171, Section VII of the Report of the General Council to the 1996 Ministerial Conference, WT/MIN(96)/2, 26 November 1996.

[170] Brazil, Costa Rica, Mexico, Nicaragua and Venezuela.

[171] As of 1 January 1998, Brazil was among those countries certified as having adopted programs to reduce the incidental capture of sea turtles in shrimp fisheries comparable to the United States' program. See Panel Report, para. 2.16. However, according to information provided by the United States at the oral hearing, Brazil is not currently certified under Section 609.

[172] Inter-American Convention, Article IV.1.

[173] Inter-American Convention, Article IV.2(h).

under the *WTO Agreement*, including the *Agreement on Technical Barriers to Trade* and Article XI of the GATT 1994, suggests that the parties to the Inter-American Convention together marked out the equilibrium line to which we referred earlier. The Inter-American Convention demonstrates the conviction of its signatories, including the United States, that consensual and multilateral procedures are available and feasible for the establishment of programs for the conservation of sea turtles. Moreover, the Inter-American Convention emphasizes the continuing validity and significance of Article XI of the GATT 1994, and of the obligations of the *WTO Agreement* generally, in maintaining the balance of rights and obligations under the *WTO Agreement* among the signatories of that Convention.

171. The Inter-American Convention thus provides convincing demonstration that an alternative course of action was reasonably open to the United States for securing the legitimate policy goal of its measure, a course of action other than the unilateral and non-consensual procedures of the import prohibition under Section 609. It is relevant to observe that an import prohibition is, ordinarily, the heaviest "weapon" in a Member's armoury of trade measures. The record does not, however, show that serious efforts were made by the United States to negotiate similar agreements with any other country or group of countries before (and, as far as the record shows, after) Section 609 was enforced on a world-wide basis on 1 May 1996. Finally, the record also does not show that the appellant, the United States, attempted to have recourse to such international mechanisms as exist to achieve cooperative efforts to protect and conserve sea turtles[174] before imposing the import ban.

172. Clearly, the United States negotiated seriously with some, but not with other Members (including the appellees), that export shrimp to the United States. The effect is plainly discriminatory and, in our view, unjustifiable. The unjustifiable nature of this discrimination emerges clearly when we consider the cumulative effects of the failure of the United States to pursue negotiations for establishing consensual means of protection and conservation of the living marine resources here involved, notwithstanding the explicit statutory direction in Section 609 itself to initiate negotiations as soon as possible for the development of bilateral and multilateral agreements.[175] The principal consequence of this failure may be seen in the resulting unilateralism evident in the application of Section 609. As we have emphasized earlier, the policies relating to the necessity for use of particular kinds of TEDs in various maritime areas, and the operating details of these policies, are all shaped by the Department of State, without the participation of the exporting Members. The system and processes of certification are established and administered by the United States agencies alone. The decision-making involved in the grant, denial or withdrawal of certification to the exporting Members, is, accordingly, also unilateral. The unilateral character of the application of Section 609 heightens the disruptive and discriminatory influence of the import prohibition and underscores its unjustifiability.

---

[174] While the United States is a party to CITES, it did not make any attempt to raise the issue of sea turtle mortality due to shrimp trawling in the CITES Standing Committee as a subject requiring concerted action by states. In this context, we note that the United States, for example, has not signed the Convention on the Conservation of Migratory Species of Wild Animals or UNCLOS, and has not ratified the Convention on Biological Diversity.

[175] Section 609(a).

173. The application of Section 609, through the implementing guidelines together with administrative practice, also resulted in other differential treatment among various countries desiring certification. Under the 1991 and 1993 Guidelines, to be certifiable, fourteen countries in the wider Caribbean/western Atlantic region had to commit themselves to require the use of TEDs on all commercial shrimp trawling vessels by 1 May 1994. These fourteen countries had a "phase-in" period of three years during which their respective shrimp trawling sectors could adjust to the requirement of the use of TEDs. With respect to all other countries exporting shrimp to the United States (including the appellees, India, Malaysia, Pakistan and Thailand), on 29 December 1995, the United States Court of International Trade directed the Department of State to apply the import ban on a world-wide basis not later than 1 May 1996.[176] On 19 April 1996, the 1996 Guidelines were issued by the Department of State bringing shrimp harvested in *all* foreign countries within the scope of Section 609, effective 1 May 1996. Thus, all countries that were not among the fourteen in the wider Caribbean/western Atlantic region had only four months to implement the requirement of compulsory use of TEDs. We acknowledge that the greatly differing periods for putting into operation the requirement for use of TEDs resulted from decisions of the Court of International Trade. Even so, this does not relieve the United States of the legal consequences of the discriminatory impact of the decisions of that Court. The United States, like all other Members of the WTO and of the general community of states, bears responsibility for acts of all its departments of government, including its judiciary.[177]

174. The length of the "phase-in" period is not inconsequential for exporting countries desiring certification. That period relates directly to the onerousness of the burdens of complying with the requisites of certification and the practical feasibility of locating and developing alternative export markets for shrimp. The shorter that period, the heavier the burdens of compliance, particularly where an applicant has a large number of trawler vessels, and the greater the difficulties of re-orienting the harvesting country's shrimp exports. The shorter that period, in net effect, the heavier the influence of the import ban. The United States sought to explain the marked difference between "phase-in" periods granted to the fourteen wider Caribbean/western Atlantic countries and those allowed the rest of the shrimp exporting countries. The United States asserted that the longer time-period was justified by the then undeveloped character of TED technology, while the shorter period was later made possible by the improvements in that technology. This explanation is less than persuasive, for it does not address the administrative and financial costs and the difficulties of governments in putting together and enacting the necessary regulatory programs and "credible enforcement effort", and in implementing the compulsory use of TEDs on hundreds, if not thousands, of shrimp trawl vessels.[178]

---

[176] *Earth Island Institute* v. *Warren Christopher*, 913 F. Supp. 559 (CIT 1995).

[177] See *United States - Gasoline*, adopted 20 May 1996, WT/DS2/AB/R, DSR 1996:I, page 26. Also see, for example, Jennings and Watts (eds.), *Oppenheim's International Law*, 9th ed., Vol. I (Longman's 1992), p. 545; and I. Brownlie, *Principles of Public International Law*, 4th ed. (Clarendon Press, 1990), p. 450.

[178] For example, at the oral hearing, India stated that its "number of mechanized nets is estimated at about 47,000. Most of these are mechanized vessels ... ."

175. Differing treatment of different countries desiring certification is also observable in the differences in the levels of effort made by the United States in transferring the required TED technology to specific countries. Far greater efforts to transfer that technology successfully were made to certain exporting countries - basically the fourteen wider Caribbean/western Atlantic countries cited earlier - than to other exporting countries, including the appellees.[179] The level of these efforts is probably related to the length of the "phase-in" periods granted - the longer the "phase-in" period, the higher the possible level of efforts at technology transfer. Because compliance with the requirements of certification realistically assumes successful TED technology transfer, low or merely nominal efforts at achieving that transfer will, in all probability, result in fewer countries being able to satisfy the certification requirements under Section 609, within the very limited "phase-in" periods allowed them.

176. When the foregoing differences in the means of application of Section 609 to various shrimp exporting countries are considered in their cumulative effect, we find, and so hold, that those differences in treatment constitute "unjustifiable discrimination" between exporting countries desiring certification in order to gain access to the United States shrimp market within the meaning of the chapeau of Article XX.

### *3. "Arbitrary Discrimination"*

177. We next consider whether Section 609 has been applied in a manner constituting "arbitrary discrimination between countries where the same conditions prevail". We have already observed that Section 609, in its application, imposes a single, rigid and unbending requirement that countries applying for certification under Section 609(b)(2)(A) and (B) adopt a comprehensive regulatory program that is essentially the same as the United States' program, without inquiring into the appropriateness of that program for the conditions prevailing in the exporting countries.[180] Furthermore, there is little or no flexibility in how officials make the determination for certification pursuant to these provisions.[181] In our view, this rigidity and inflexibility also constitute "arbitrary discrimination" within the meaning of the chapeau.

178. Moreover, the description of the administration of Section 609 provided by the United States in the course of these proceedings highlights certain problematic aspects of the certification processes applied under Section 609(b). With respect to the first type of certification, under Section 609(b)(2)(A) and (B), the 1996 Guidelines set out certain elements of the procedures for acquiring certification, including the requirement to submit documentary evidence of the regulatory program adopted

[179] Response by the United States to questioning by the Panel; statements by the United States at the oral hearing.

[180] *Supra*, paras. 161-164.

[181] In the oral hearing, the United States stated that "as a policy matter, the United States government believes that all governments should require the use of turtle excluder devices on all shrimp trawler boats that operate in areas where there is a likelihood of intercepting sea turtles" and that "when it comes to shrimp trawling, we know of only one way of effectively protecting sea turtles, and that is through TEDs."

by the applicant country. This certification process also generally includes a visit by United States officials to the applicant country.[182]

179. With respect to certifications under Section 609(b)(2)(C), the 1996 Guidelines state that the Department of State "shall certify" any harvesting nation under Section 609(b)(2)(C) if it meets the criteria in the 1996 Guidelines "without the need for action on the part of the government of the harvesting nation ... ."[183] Nevertheless, the United States informed us that, in all cases where a country has not previously been certified under Section 609, it waits for an application to be made before making a determination on certification.[184] In the case of certifications under Section 609(b)(2)(C), there appear to be certain opportunities for the submission of written evidence, such as scientific documentation, in the course of the certification process.[185]

180. However, with respect to neither type of certification under Section 609(b)(2) is there a transparent, predictable certification process that is followed by the competent United States government officials. The certification processes under Section 609 consist principally of administrative *ex parte* inquiry or verification by staff of the Office of Marine Conservation in the Department of State with staff of the United States National Marine Fisheries Service.[186] With respect to both types of certification, there is no formal opportunity for an applicant country to be heard, or to respond to any arguments that may be made against it, in the course of the certification process before a decision to grant or to deny certification is made. Moreover, no formal written, reasoned decision, whether of acceptance or rejection, is rendered on applications for either type of certification, whether under Section 609(b)(2)(A) and (B) or under Section 609(b)(2)(C).[187] Countries which are granted certification are included in a list of approved applications published in the Federal Register; however, they are not notified specifically. Countries whose applications are denied[188] also do not receive notice of such denial (other than by omission from the list of approved applications) or of the reasons for the denial.[189] No procedure for review of, or appeal from, a denial of an application is provided.[190]

181. The certification processes followed by the United States thus appear to be singularly informal and casual, and to be conducted in a manner such that these processes could result in the negation of rights of Members. There appears to be no way that exporting Members can be certain whether the terms of Section 609, in particular, the 1996 Guidelines, are being applied in a fair and just manner by the appropriate governmental agencies of the United States. It appears to us that, effectively, exporting Members applying for certification whose applications are rejected are de-

---

[182] Statement by the United States at the oral hearing.

[183] 1996 Guidelines, p. 17343.

[184] Statement by the United States at the oral hearing.

[185] Statement by the United States at the oral hearing.

[186] Statement by the United States at the oral hearing.

[187] Statement by the United States at the oral hearing.

[188] We were advised at the oral hearing by the United States that these include: Australia, Pakistan and Tunisia.

[189] Statement by the United States at the oral hearing.

[190] Statement by the United States at the oral hearing.

nied basic fairness and due process, and are discriminated against, *vis-à-vis* those Members which are granted certification.

182. The provisions of Article X:3[191] of the GATT 1994 bear upon this matter. In our view, Section 609 falls within the "laws, regulations, judicial decisions and administrative rulings of general application" described in Article X:1. Inasmuch as there are due process requirements generally for measures that are otherwise imposed in compliance with WTO obligations, it is only reasonable that rigorous compliance with the fundamental requirements of due process should be required in the application and administration of a measure which purports to be an exception to the treaty obligations of the Member imposing the measure and which effectively results in a suspension *pro hac vice* of the treaty rights of other Members.

183. It is also clear to us that Article X:3 of the GATT 1994 establishes certain minimum standards for transparency and procedural fairness in the administration of trade regulations which, in our view, are not met here. The non-transparent and *ex parte* nature of the internal governmental procedures applied by the competent officials in the Office of Marine Conservation, the Department of State, and the United States National Marine Fisheries Service throughout the certification processes under Section 609, as well as the fact that countries whose applications are denied do not receive formal notice of such denial, nor of the reasons for the denial, and the fact, too, that there is no formal legal procedure for review of, or appeal from, a denial of an application, are all contrary to the spirit, if not the letter, of Article X:3 of the GATT 1994.

184. We find, accordingly, that the United States measure is applied in a manner which amounts to a means not just of "unjustifiable discrimination", but also of "arbitrary discrimination" between countries where the same conditions prevail, contrary to the requirements of the chapeau of Article XX. The measure, therefore, is not entitled to the justifying protection of Article XX of the GATT 1994. Having made this finding, it is not necessary for us to examine also whether the United States measure is applied in a manner that constitutes a "disguised restriction on international trade" under the chapeau of Article XX.

185. In reaching these conclusions, we wish to underscore what we have *not* decided in this appeal. We have *not* decided that the protection and preservation of the environment is of no significance to the Members of the WTO. Clearly, it is. We have *not* decided that the sovereign nations that are Members of the WTO cannot adopt effective measures to protect endangered species, such as sea turtles. Clearly, they can and should. And we have *not* decided that sovereign states should not act together bilaterally, plurilaterally or multilaterally, either within the WTO or in other

[191] Article X:3 states, in part:

> (a) Each Member shall administer in a uniform, impartial and reasonable manner all its laws, regulations, decisions and rulings of the kind described in paragraph 1 of this Article.
>
> (b) Each Member shall maintain, or institute as soon as practicable, judicial, arbitral or administrative tribunals or procedures for the purpose, inter alia, of the prompt review and correction of administrative action relating to customs matters … .

international fora, to protect endangered species or to otherwise protect the environment. Clearly, they should and do.

186. What we *have* decided in this appeal is simply this: although the measure of the United States in dispute in this appeal serves an environmental objective that is recognized as legitimate under paragraph (g) of Article XX of the GATT 1994, this measure has been applied by the United States in a manner which constitutes arbitrary and unjustifiable discrimination between Members of the WTO, contrary to the requirements of the chapeau of Article XX. For all of the specific reasons outlined in this Report, this measure does not qualify for the exemption that Article XX of the GATT 1994 affords to measures which serve certain recognized, legitimate environmental purposes but which, at the same time, are not applied in a manner that constitutes a means of arbitrary or unjustifiable discrimination between countries where the same conditions prevail or a disguised restriction on international trade. As we emphasized in *United States - Gasoline*, WTO Members are free to adopt their own policies aimed at protecting the environment as long as, in so doing, they fulfill their obligations and respect the rights of other Members under the *WTO Agreement*.[192]

## VII. FINDINGS AND CONCLUSIONS

187. For the reasons set out in this Report, the Appellate Body:

(a) reverses the Panel's finding that accepting non-requested information from non-governmental sources is incompatible with the provisions of the DSU;

(b) reverses the Panel's finding that the United States measure at issue is not within the scope of measures permitted under the chapeau of Article XX of the GATT 1994, and

(c) concludes that the United States measure, while qualifying for provisional justification under Article XX(g), fails to meet the requirements of the chapeau of Article XX, and, therefore, is not justified under Article XX of the GATT 1994.

188. The Appellate Body *recommends* that the DSB request the United States to bring its measure found in the Panel Report to be inconsistent with Article XI of the GATT 1994, and found in this Report to be not justified under Article XX of the GATT 1994, into conformity with the obligations of the United States under that Agreement.

[192] Adopted 20 May 1996, WT/DS2/AB/R, DSR 1996:I, page 28.

# UNITED STATES - IMPORT PROHIBITION OF CERTAIN SHRIMP AND SHRIMP PRODUCTS

## Report of the Panel

WT/DS58/R

*Adopted by the Dispute Settlement Body on 6 November 1998 as Modified by the Appellate Body Report*

## TABLE OF CONTENTS

## I. INTRODUCTION

1.1. In a letter dated 8 October 1996, India, Malaysia, Pakistan and Thailand, acting jointly, requested consultations with the United States pursuant to Article 4 of the Understanding on Rules and Procedures Governing the Settlement of Disputes ("DSU") and Article XXII:1 of the General Agreement on Tariffs and Trade 1994 ("GATT 1994") regarding the ban imposed upon importation of certain shrimp and shrimp products from the respective countries by the United States under Section 609 of U.S. Public Law 101-162[1] ("Section 609") and the "Revised Notice of Guidelines for Determining Comparability of Foreign Programs for the Protection of Turtles in Shrimp Trawl Fishing Operations"[2] (WT/DS58/1). Consultations were held on 19 November 1996 without resulting in a satisfactory solution of the matter.

1.2. In a communication dated 9 January 1997, Malaysia and Thailand requested the Dispute Settlement Body ("DSB") to establish a panel to examine, under Article XXIII:2 of GATT 1994 and Article 6 of the DSU, the partial embargo on the importation of certain shrimp and shrimp products implemented through a series of actions, including enactment of Section 609, promulgation of regulations and issuance of judicial decisions interpreting the law and regulations (WT/DS58/6). In a communication dated 30 January 1997, Pakistan made the same request to the DSB (WT/DS58/7). On 25 February 1997, the DSB established a panel pursuant to the request of Malaysia and Thailand. At the same meeting, the DSB established a panel in

---

1 Codified at 16 U.S.C. 1537 note, amending the Endangered Species Act of 1973, 16 U.S.C. § 1531 *et seq.*

2 61 Fed. Reg. 17342, (19 April 1996).

accordance with the request made by Pakistan. The DSB also agreed that the two panels would be consolidated into a single panel, pursuant to Article 9 of the DSU, with standard terms of reference (WT/DSB/M/29).

1.3. In a communication dated 25 February 1997, India requested the DSB to establish a panel pursuant to Article XXIII of GATT 1994 and 6 of the DSU (WT/DS58/8). At its meeting on 10 April 1997, the DSB established a panel in accordance with the request made by India. The DSB also agreed that this Panel would be consolidated with the Panel already established at the request of Malaysia, Thailand and Pakistan on 25 February 1997, pursuant to Article 9 of the DSU (WT/DSB/M/31).

1.4. The parties to the dispute agreed that the Panel should have standard terms of reference (Article 7 of the DSU):

> "To examine, in the light of the relevant provisions of the covered agreements cited by Malaysia and Thailand in document WT/DS58/6, Pakistan in document WT/DS58/7 and India in document WT/DS58/8, the matter referred to the DSB by Malaysia, Thailand, Pakistan and India in these documents and to make such findings as will assist the DSB in making the recommendations or in giving the rulings provided for in those agreements."

1.5. On 15 April 1997, the parties to the dispute agreed on the following composition of the Panel (WT/DS58/9):

| | |
|---|---|
| Chairman: | Mr. Michael Cartland |
| Members: | Mr. Carlos Cozendey |
| | Mr. Kilian Delbrück |

1.6. Australia, Colombia, Costa Rica, Ecuador, El Salvador, the European Communities, Guatemala, Hong Kong (since 1 July 1997, "Hong Kong, China"), Japan, Mexico, Nigeria, the Philippines, Senegal, Singapore, Sri Lanka and Venezuela reserved their third-party rights in accordance with Article 10 of the DSU.

1.7. The Panel met with the parties to the dispute on 17-19 June 1997 and on 15-16 September 1997. It met with the interested third parties on 19 June 1997.

1.8. In a communication dated 22 September 1997, the Chairman of the Panel informed the DSB that the Panel would not be able to issue its report within six months. The reasons for that delay are stated in document WT/DS58/10.

1.9. A meeting with scientific experts selected by the Panel, at which the parties were present, was held on 21 and 22 January 1998.

1.10. The Panel issued its interim report to the parties on 2 March 1998. The Panel issued its final report to the parties on 6 April 1998.

## II. FACTUAL ASPECTS

### *1. Basic Facts About Sea Turtles*

2.1. Seven species of sea turtles are currently recognized: the green turtle (*Chelonia mydas*), loggerhead (*Caretta caretta*), flatback (*Natator depressus*), hawksbill (*Eretmochelys imbricata*), leatherback (*Dermochelys coriacea*), olive ridley (*Lepidochelys olivacea*), and Kemp's ridley (*Lepidochelys kempi*).

2.2. Most species of sea turtles are distributed around the globe, in subtropical or tropical areas. Sea turtles spend their lives at sea, where they migrate between their foraging and their nesting grounds, but reproduce on land. Adult females nest in multi-year cycles, coming ashore to lay clutches of about 100 eggs in nests they dig on the beach. After about 50 to 60 days of incubation, the hatchlings dig their way out of the nest and head for the sea. Few survive and reach the age of reproduction (10-50 years, depending on the species). While maturing, they move through a variety of habitats. Little is known about the existence of sea turtles at seas.

2.3. Sea turtles have been adversely affected by human activity, either directly (sea turtles have been exploited for their meat, shells and eggs), or indirectly (incidental captures in fisheries, destruction of their habitats, pollution of the oceans). Presently, all species of sea turtles are included in Appendix I of the 1973 Convention on International Trade in Endangered Species ("CITES"). All species except the Australian flatback are listed in Appendices I and II of the 1979 Convention on Migratory Species of Wild Animals ("CMS") and appear in the IUCN Red List as endangered or vulnerable.

### 2. *The US Endangered Species Act (ESA) and Related Legislation*

2.4. All sea turtles that occur in US waters are listed as endangered or threatened species under the Endangered Species Act of 1973 ("ESA"). The ESA prohibits take of endangered sea turtles within the United States, within the US territorial sea, and the high seas, except as authorized by the Secretary of Commerce (for sea turtles in marine waters) or the Secretary of the Interior (for sea turtles on land).

2.5. Research programmes in the Gulf of Mexico and the Atlantic Ocean off the southeastern United States led to the conclusion that incidental capture and drowning of sea turtles by shrimp trawlers was the most significant source of mortality for sea turtles.[3] Within the context of a programme aiming at reducing the mortality of sea turtles in shrimp trawls, the National Marine Fisheries Service ("NMFS") developed turtle excluder devices ("TEDs"). A TED is grid trapdoor installed inside a trawling net that allows shrimp to pass to the back of the net while directing sea turtles and other unintentionally caught large objects out of the net. In 1983, NMFS began a formal programme to encourage shrimp fishermen to use TEDs voluntarily, so as to reduce the incidental catch and mortality of sea turtles associated with shrimp trawling. As part of the voluntary TED programme, NMFS delivered TEDs to volunteer shrimp fishermen and showed them how to properly install and use the TEDs. However, this voluntary programme did not turn out to be successful because an insufficient number of fishermen used TEDs on a regular basis.

2.6. In 1987, the United States issued regulations, pursuant to the ESA, whereby all shrimp trawlers were required to use TEDs or tow time[4] restrictions in specified areas

---

[3] National Research Council, National Academy of Sciences, (1990), *Decline of the Sea Turtles: Causes and Prevention*, Washington D.C.

[4] Tow time is the interval from trawl doors entering the water to trawl doors being removed from the water. Tow times were restricted to 90 minutes or less, period of time which is determined to result in fewer drowning of sea turtles in shrimp trawls. Tow time restrictions were an alternative to TEDs in some areas and for some categories of shrimp trawlers.

where there was a significant mortality of sea turtles in shrimp trawls. In offshore waters, all shrimp trawlers 25 feet and longer were required to use qualified TEDs and all shrimp trawlers smaller than 25 feet were required to restrict tow times to 90 minutes or less, or the use TEDs. In inshore waters, all shrimp trawlers were required to restrict tow times to 90 minutes or less. The rules, which became fully effective in 1990, further set forth specifications for TEDs, areas and seasons for which TEDs and/or tow times were required. They were subsequently modified so as to require the use of TEDs at all times and places where shrimp trawl fishing interacts in a significant way with sea turtles. Five species of sea turtles were identified as living in the areas concerned and, thus, falling under the regulations: loggerhead (*Caretta caretta*), Kemp's ridley (*Lepidochelys kempi*), green (*Chelonia mydas*), leatherback (*Dermochelys coriacea*) and hawksbill (*Eretmochelys imbricata*).[5]

2.7. In 1989, the United States enacted Section 609 of Public Law 101-102[6] ("Section 609", see Annex I). Section 609 calls upon the US Secretary of State, in consultation with the US Secretary of Commerce, *inter alia*, to initiate negotiations for the development of bilateral or multilateral agreements for the protection and conservation of sea turtles, in particular with foreign governments of countries which are engaged in commercial fishing operations likely to affect adversely sea turtles. Section 609 further provides that shrimp harvested with technology that may adversely affect certain sea turtles may not be imported into the United States, unless the President certified to Congress by 1 May 1991, and annually thereafter, that the harvesting nation has a regulatory programme and an incidental take rate comparable to that of the United States, or that the particular fishing environment of the harvesting nation does not pose a threat to sea turtles.

2.8. In 1991, the United States issued guidelines ("1991 Guidelines") for assessing the comparability of foreign regulatory programmes with the US programme. To be found comparable a foreign nation's programme had to include, *inter alia*, a commitment to require all shrimp trawl vessels to use TEDs at all times (or reduce tow times for vessels under 25 feet), or, alternatively, a commitment to engage in a statistically reliable and verifiable scientific programme to reduce the mortality of sea turtles associated with shrimp fishing. Foreign nations were given three years for the complete phase-in of a comparable programme. The 1991 Guidelines also determined that the scope of Section 609 was limited to the wider Caribbean/western Atlantic region, and more specifically to the following countries: Mexico, Belize, Guatemala, Honduras, Nicaragua, Costa Rica, Panama, Colombia, Venezuela, Trinidad and Tobago, Guyana, Suriname, French Guyana, and Brazil. It was also determined that the import restriction did not apply to aquaculture shrimp, whose harvesting does not adversely affect sea turtles.[7]

2.9. In 1993, the United States issued revised guidelines ("1993 Guidelines") providing that, to receive a certification in 1993, affected nations (those determined in the 1991 Guidelines) had to maintain their commitment to require TEDs on all commercial shrimp trawl vessels by 1 May 1994, and be able to demonstrate the use of

5 52 Fed. Reg. 24244 (29 June 1987).

6 Section 609 of Public Law 101-102, codified at 16 United States Code (U.S.C.) § 1537.

7 56 Federal Register 1051 (10 January 1991).

TEDs on a significant number of shrimp trawl vessels by 1 May 1993.[8] To receive certification in 1994 and in subsequent years, affected nations were required to use TEDs on all their shrimp trawl vessels, subject to a limited number of exemptions.[9] The 1993 Guidelines eliminated the second option for certification which was contained in the 1991 Guidelines, i.e. the commitment to engage in a scientific programme to reduce the mortality of sea turtles in shrimp trawling.

2.10. In December 1995, the US Court of International Trade ("CIT") found that the 1991 and 1993 Guidelines were contrary to law in limiting the geographical scope of Section 609 to shrimp harvested in the wider Caribbean/western Atlantic region and directed the Department of State "to prohibit not later than May 1, 1996 the importation of shrimp or products of shrimp wherever harvested in the wild with commercial fishing technology which may affect adversely those species of sea turtles the conservation of which is the subject of regulations promulgated by the Secretary of Commerce ... ".[10] The Department of State requested the CIT to modify its judgement by allowing a one-year extension for the worldwide enforcement of Section 609. In its request, the States Department argued, *inter alia*, that many of the major shrimp exporting nations would likely be unable to implement a comparable programme by 1 May 1996. The CIT refused the requested extension and confirmed the 1 May 1996 deadline.[11]

2.11. In April 1996, the Department of State published revised guidelines ("1996 Guidelines") to comply with the CIT order of December 1995.[12] The new guidelines extended Section 609 to shrimp harvested in all foreign nations. The Department of State further determined that, as of 1 May 1996, all shipments of shrimp and shrimp products into the United States were to be accompanied by a declaration ("Shrimp Exporter's Declaration form") attesting that the shrimp or shrimp product in question was harvested "either under conditions that do not adversely affect sea turtles ... or in waters subject to the jurisdiction of a nation currently certified pursuant to Section 609".

2.12. The 1996 Guidelines define "shrimp or shrimp products harvested in conditions that does not affect sea turtles" to include: "(a) Shrimp harvested in an aquaculture facility ... ; (b) Shrimp harvested by commercial shrimp trawl vessels using TEDs comparable in effectiveness to those required in the United States; (c) Shrimp harvested exclusively by means that do not involve the retrieval of fishing nets by mechanical devices or by vessels using gear that, in accordance with the US programme ... would not require TEDs; (d) Species of shrimp, such as the pandalid species, harvested in areas in which sea turtles do not occur".

2.13. The 1996 Guidelines further determine the criteria for certifying a harvesting nation whose particular fishing environment "does not pose a threat of incidental taking of sea turtles in the course of commercial shrimp trawl harvesting" (Section 609

---

8 58 Federal Register 9015 (18 February 1993).

9 In particular, vessels whose nets are retrieved exclusively by manual rather than mechanical means are not required to use TEDs, because it is considered that the lack of a mechanical retrieval system necessarily restricts tow times to a short duration, thereby limiting the threats of incidental drowning of sea turtles.

10 *Earth Island Institute* v. *Warren Christopher*, 913 F. supp. 559 (CIT 1995).

11 *Earth Island Institute* v. *Warren Christopher*, 922 Fed. Supp. 616 (CIT 1996).

12 61 Fed. Reg. 17342 (19 April 1996).

(b)(2)(C)) as follows: "(a) Any harvesting nation without any of the relevant species of sea turtles occurring in waters subject to its jurisdiction; (b) Any harvesting nation that harvests shrimp exclusively by means that do not pose a threat to sea turtles, e.g. any nation that harvests shrimp exclusively by artisanal means; (c) Any nation whose commercial shrimp trawling operations take place exclusively in waters subject to its jurisdiction in which sea turtles do not occur".

2.14. The 1996 Guidelines also provide that "other certifications" can be granted by 1 May 1996, and annually thereafter, to other harvesting nations "only if the government of that nation has provided documentary evidence of the adoption of a regulatory program governing the incidental taking of sea turtles in the course of commercial shrimp trawl harvesting that is comparable to that of the United States and if the average take rate of that incidental taking by vessels of the harvesting nation is comparable to the average take rate of incidental taking of sea turtles by United States vessels in the course of such harvesting." For the purpose of these "other certifications", a regulatory programme shall include, *inter alia*, "a requirement that all commercial shrimp trawl vessels operating in waters in which there is a likelihood of intercepting sea turtles use TEDs at all times. TEDs must be comparable in effectiveness to those used in the United States ...". Moreover, the average incidental take rate "will be deemed comparable if the harvesting nation requires the use of TEDs in a manner comparable to that of the US program ...". The 1996 Guidelines contain additional considerations to be taken into account in determining the comparability of foreign programmes, such as "other measures the harvesting nation undertakes to protect sea turtles, including national programs to protect nesting beaches and other habitats, prohibitions on the directed take of sea turtles, national enforcement and compliance programs, and participation in any international agreement for the protection and conservation of sea turtles."

2.15. In October 1996, the CIT ruled that the embargo on shrimp and shrimp products enacted by Section 609 applied to all "shrimp or shrimp products harvested in the wild by citizens or vessels of nations which have not been certified". The Court found that the 1996 Guidelines were contrary to Section 609 when allowing, with a Shrimp Exporter's Declaration form, imports of shrimp from non-certified countries, if the shrimp was harvested with commercial fishing technology that did not adversely affect sea turtles.[13] The CIT later clarified that shrimp harvested by manual methods, which did not harm sea turtles, could continue to be imported even from countries which had not been certified under Section 609. The CIT also refused to postpone the worldwide enforcement of Section 609.[14]

2.16. As of 1 January 1998, the following 19 countries had been certified as having adopted programmes to reduce the incidental capture of sea turtles in shrimp fisheries comparable to the US programme: Belize, Brazil, Colombia, Costa Rica, Ecuador, El Salvador, Fiji, Guatemala, Guyana, Honduras, Indonesia, Mexico, Nicaragua, Nigeria, Panama, the People's Republic of China, Thailand, Trinidad and Tobago, and Venezuela. The following 16 nations have been certified as having shrimp fisheries in

---

[13] *Earth Island Institute* v. *Warren Christopher*, 942 Fed. Supp. 597 (CIT 1996). The US Administration has appealed this ruling to the US Court of Appeals for the Federal Circuit.

[14] *Earth Island Institute* v. *Warren Christopher*, 948 Fed. Supp. 1062 (CIT 1996).

only cold waters where there was essentially no risk of taking sea turtles: Argentina, Belgium, Canada, Chile, Denmark, Finland, Germany, Iceland, Ireland, the Netherlands, New Zealand, Norway, Russia, Sweden, the United Kingdom and Uruguay. The following 8 countries have been certified on grounds that their fishermen only harvested shrimp using manual rather than mechanical means to retrieve nets: the Bahamas, Brunei, the Dominican Republic, Haiti, Jamaica, Oman, Peru and Sri Lanka.

## III. MAIN ARGUMENTS

### A. *General*

3.1. India, Malaysia, Pakistan and Thailand requested the Panel to find that Section 609 of US Public Law 101-162 ("Section 609") and its implementing measures:

(a) were contrary to Articles, XI:1 and XIII:1 of GATT 1994;

(b) were not covered by the exceptions under Article XX(b) and (g) of GATT 1994;

(c) nullified or impaired benefits accruing to India, Malaysia, Pakistan and Thailand within the meaning of Article XXIII:1(a) of GATT 1994.

India, Pakistan and Thailand additionally requested the Panel to find that Section 609 was contrary to Article I:1 of GATT 1994.

3.2. Accordingly, India requested the Panel to recommend that the United States remove its embargo immediately in order to comply with its obligations under the General Agreement on Tariffs and Trade. Malaysia, Pakistan and Thailand requested the Panel to recommend that the United States take all necessary steps to bring Section 609 and its implementing measures into conformity with its obligations under the General Agreement on Tariffs and Trade.

3.3. The United States requested the Panel to find that Section 609 and its implementing measures fell within the scope of Article XX, paragraphs (b) and (g) of GATT 1994.

### B. *Conservation and Management of Sea Turtles*

#### 1. *Sea Turtle Conservation*

3.4. **India** submitted it had a well-established history of protecting endangered species, including sea turtles. For many centuries, the essential harmony between the environment and man had been a central precept in Indian society, based on the fact that the continued replenishment of environmental resources was crucial for the very livelihood of a vast majority of Indians. The objectives of environmental protection were therefore deeply ingrained in Indians. Environmental resources had traditionally been safeguarded by their close association with the teachings of India's major religions. For example, the turtle itself was considered by many Indians to be an incarnation of the Divine. Fishermen were particularly careful not to catch turtles in their nets while fishing. As early as 1972, India had enacted the Wildlife Protection Act that imposed penalties for the capture, destruction or trade in endangered species, including certain sea turtles. Such measures had been extremely successful in ensuring the survival of endangered species. For example, the nesting population of olive ridley had increased over the past ten years in the Gahirmatha region, off India's Orissa coast, and every year approximately 600,000 olive ridley sea turtles nested in this area. The local government had banned fishing and shrimping within a radius of 20 kilometres around Gahirmatha to protect these turtles. In addition, 65,000 hectares in the Bhitarkanika and Gahirmatha regions had been declared a sea turtle sanctuary.[15] Other state governments had issued public notices reminding fishermen and others that catching or endangering sea turtles was illegal. Not only was the Government of India establishing programmes to ensure the preservation of sea turtles, but the Government had also established programmes to ensure that the laws were enforced. For example, the Indian Coast Guard, Forest Department and Fisheries Department assisted the Wild Life Protection Department officials in monitoring the annual nesting period in the Orissa Coast.

3.5. India further submitted that many other governmental institutes and departments, as well as non-governmental organizations, continued to implement projects and conduct studies for the conservation and preservation of sea turtles. The Central Marine Fisheries Research Institute in India monitored olive ridley turtles nesting in some regions during 1978 and 1986, and conducted an exhaustive study on the nesting population. The Institute also operated a hatchery for sea turtles in Madras, from which hatchlings were released at sea. The Institute was currently conducting a study on incidental catches of sea turtles during fishing in India. As part of India's ongoing efforts regarding the most efficient method of protecting sea turtles in its territory, two training programmes with shrimpers had been organized to discuss the fabrication and installation of TEDs. An Indian organization, CIFNET, even fabricated TEDs indigenously. Moreover, India was an active party of the CITES and had, accordingly, prohibited trade in endangered sea turtles. However, India could not find any provision in CITES which called for an import restriction on shrimp and shrimp products in order to protect and conserve sea turtles, nor could it find in CITES any reference to the TEDs as a "multilateral environmental standard" to be used for the protection and conservation of sea turtles. India did not accept the US assertion that the use of TEDs was the only way to keep sea turtles species found in India's territorial waters from becoming extinct; conservation programmes such as the ones undertaken by India were also essential for conserving sea turtles.

3.6. The protection of sea turtles was a challenging task being shared by a large number of countries in a variety of ways. The use of TEDs was not the only way to keep sea turtle species found in India's territorial waters from becoming extinct; conservation programmes such as the ones undertaken by India were also essential in furthering the goal of sea turtle protection. While India shared the US concern over the plight of sea turtles and considered it important to ensure their survival, the importance of this goal did not justify the United States taking unilateral actions that infringed upon India' sovereign right to formulate its own environmental and conservation policies. India considered that since it had adequate measures in place to protect and preserve endangered species of sea turtles, there was no need for the United States to impose its own agenda on third parties through the use of far-reaching, extraterritorial measures

---

[15] Ordered pursuant to Orissa Government Notification No. 7FY-SE(H)49/95-60-FARD, dated 1 January 1996.

such as the one imposed by Section 609. This action constituted an unacceptable interference in policies within India's sovereign jurisdiction.

3.7. **Malaysia** submitted that none of the Malaysian fishermen used TEDs. A significant amount of wild harvested shrimps were caught using traditional mechanisms (such as hand retrieval nets) which would not in anyway cause incidental catches of turtles. In Sabah and Sarawak in particular, shrimps were caught in locations that were far from turtle nesting grounds. Sabah and Sarawak had turtle protection laws, and fishing trawlers were not allowed to operate within designated areas where turtles mated and nested. In the East Coast of Peninsular Malaysia, the turtle nesting season occurred between April and October while the shrimp trawling season was from November to February. Along the west coast of Peninsular Malaysia, there was no shrimp trawling except along the Perak coast near Sigari which was a very limited area. Sarawak had been carrying out research on marine turtles particularly around the Turtle Islands since the 1930s. Studies done over the last 20 years had revealed a cyclical pattern of a good year followed by a poor year. Conservation efforts in Sarawak had begun in the early 1950s. It had been established by DNA fingerprinting that green turtles in Sarawak were distinct populations that did not mix with those of other countries implying that the conservation programme had managed to contribute to the survival of the turtle population. Moreover, the active enforcement of fishery laws by the Department of Fisheries had successfully kept the trawlers away from the coastal and Turtle Island waters and the existing trawling operations had been successfully kept away from the migration routes of these turtles. While recognizing that the use of TEDs was a step in contributing to the conservation of turtles, Malaysia considered that it was just one of the many accepted methods for the conservation of turtles. The use of TED alone could not absolutely ensure the survival of turtles.

3.8. Malaysia had a comprehensive legal framework on the conservation and management of marine turtles which were under the jurisdiction of 13 individual states. The states' legislation on turtle protection had been enacted in 1932 and prohibited, *inter alia*, the capture, killing, injuring, possession or sale of turtles, collection of eggs, disturbing turtles during laying eggs, and provided for the establishment of turtle sanctuaries. Subsidiary legislation had also been enacted, such as the Customs (Prohibition of Export/Import) Orders of 1988, enforced specifically to ban the exports and imports of turtle eggs to and from all countries. At the federal level, the Fisheries Act 1985 prohibited the capture of marine turtles by any type of fishing methods. Enforcement of existing legislation within 2 nautical miles of marine parks would provide protection to nesting turtles in the area. An Order made under the Act in 1990 prohibited the use of driftnet with mesh sizes exceeding 25.4 cm in order to reduce turtle mortality.

3.9. Olive ridley, leatherback, hawksbill and green turtle were the four species of sea turtles found in Malaysia; the last three of them were at issue in this dispute. Malaysia had always been actively engaged in turtle conservation programmes aiming at reducing mortalities both on nesting beaches and at sea. They had been in place for more than 20 years and efforts were continuously undertaken to develop more effective conservation measures and improve upon existing ones. Organizations actively involved in the conservation of turtles included the Fisheries Department, local universities, NGOs (e.g. WWF and the Malaysian Society of Marine Sciences) and corporate bodies (as sponsors of conservation projects).[16] The conservation programmes included the following:

(a) Protection of turtle eggs by incubation programmes, involving *in situ* methods or protected beach hatcheries, and banning the commercial harvest and sale of eggs in certain areas (e.g. Sabah Turtle Islands and leatherbacks eggs in Terengganu). In other areas where the nesting beaches were extensive, turtle egg collection was licensed to the local inhabitants from whom the eggs were purchased for incubation in protected beach hatcheries. Efforts were continuously made to increase the proportion of eggs bought from licensed egg collectors for incubation. In Pulau Redang, where the nesting beaches were less extensive, *in situ* egg incubation was carried out by the Fisheries Department and turtle conservation biologists from the local university; this conservation programme aimed at incubating at least 70 per cent of the total egg production in the island, which was the most important nesting site for green turtles in Peninsular Malaysia.[17] Another example was seen in the Sarawak green turtle population, whose annual nesting density had declined from 1945 to the early 1960s, period during which fish and shrimp trawling did not exist. The decline had been attributed to over-exploitation of eggs. In the last thirty years (1960s to 1990s), conservation programmes in Sarawak concentrating on egg protection, at the exclusion of TEDs, allowed the nesting population to remain constant within the range of annual fluctuation characteristic with green turtle population. Therefore, in the case of the Sarawak population of green turtles, even in the absence of TEDs, the population had remained constant over a long period and had been sustained.

(b) Establishment of turtle sanctuaries/state parks in recognized turtle nesting areas to protect the nesting sites. This ensured that commercial development did not encroach upon the nesting beaches. Therefore the nesting beaches could remain pristine and not be subject to detrimental factors like beach lighting which adversely affected nesting turtles and hatchling orientation to the sea. The Turtle Island of Sabah was constituted as a State Park in 1984, after the Sabah State Government had compulsorily acquired the islands from private ownership. In 1988, after 22 years of 100 per cent egg protection, the nesting population of green turtles showed a reversal in its declining trend; nesting density reached a record in 1991. Annual nesting of 8,084 sea turtles in the period 1990-94 represented a threefold increase over annual nesting of 2,633 sea turtles recorded in the 1982-86 period. The Sabah Parks of Malaysia won the 1997 J. Paul Getty Wildlife Conservation Award for having released more than 4 million turtle hatchlings into the wild over the last 15 years and helped designate, together with the Philippines, the nine islands of the Turtle Islands Protected Heritage (TIPHA) as a single unit. This showed that a dedicated conservation programme concentrating mainly on egg protection could result in population recovery, and that Malaysia's domestic legislation was comprehensive

[16] E.H. Chan and H.C. Liew, (1991), *Sea Turtles*, The State of Nature Conservation in Malaysia, Malaysian Nature Society (R. Kiew ed.), pp. 120-134.

[17] E.H. Chan and H.C. Liew, (1995), *In-situ Incubation of Green Turtle Eggs in Pulau Redang, Malaysia: Hope After Decades of Egg Exploitation*, Proceedings of the International Congress of Chelonian Conservation, 6-10 July 1995, Gonfaron, France, pp. 68-71.

enough for the protection and conservation of turtles, and further sought to prevent the national and international trade of sea turtles.

(c) Measures to protect sea turtles in their marine habitat during the nesting season. In marine parks where key nesting sites of green turtles occurred, fishing activities within a radius of two nautical miles surrounding the island or island groups was prohibited. Malaysian scientists had discovered that these measures were effective in protecting the turtles during the internesting periods since the turtles had been found not to venture beyond one nautical mile of the shoreline.[18] In 1991, an offshore sanctuary had been established in the Rantau Abang area - gazetted as Rantau Abang Fisheries Prohibited Area - to provide protection to leatherback turtles. Its boundaries had been determined by a scientific study using radio-telemetry techniques and conducted by local scientists in collaboration with US counterparts.[19] Fishing gear known to be detrimental to turtles, such as driftnets, trawlnets and fish traps had been banned in the restricted zone during the nesting season.[20] Finally, the use of large mesh driftnets along coastal areas had been banned across the nation to reduce the mortality of turtles in these areas.

(d) Because sea turtles were highly migratory going beyond the national boundaries of countries, Malaysia recognized that an effective management and conservation of turtles required the concerted and combined efforts of countries in the region concerned. Malaysia had cooperated with the Philippines in the launching of the Turtle Island Heritage Protected Area in 1996, to develop uniform conservation measures for the turtles on the islands. The same year, Malaysia hosted the first South East Asia Fisheries Development Centre (SEAFDEC) workshop on marine turtle research and conservation. Bilateral and regional turtle conservation programmes were currently being developed through the ASEAN Working Group for Nature Conservation. Malaysia was also a party to CITES and, accordingly, regulated strictly the import and export of marine turtles and their products. Its domestic legislation made an offence for any person to fish for, disturb, harass, catch or take any turtle. The law also applied to the Exclusive Economic Zone.

(e) Research programmes were undertaken by local universities and the Fisheries Department to provide scientific information for further development and enhancement of conservation programmes. For example, after the discovery that high incubation temperatures of beach hatcheries for leatherback turtles were producing biased sex ratios, the conservation programme had been modified and adjusted to incubate a proportion of the eggs under cooler temperatures so as to produce a balanced sex ratio output. The radio-tracking on leatherback turtles had been another

---

[18] H.C. Liew and E.H. Chan, (1992), *Biotelemetry of Green Turtles (Chelonia Mydas) in Pulau Redang, Malaysia, During the Internesting Period*, Biotelemetry XII, 31 August-5 September, pp. 157-163.

[19] E.H. Chan, S.A. Eckert, H.C. Liew and K.L. Eckert, (1990), *Locating the Internesting Habitats of Leatherback sea turtles (Dermochelys Coriacea) in Malaysian Waters Using Radio Telemetry*, Biotelemetry XI, 29 August-4 September, Japan, pp. 133-138.

[20] E.H. Chan and H.C. Liew, (1995), *An Offshore Sanctuary for the Leatherback Turtles in Rantau Abang, Malaysia*, in J.I. Richardson and T.H. Richardson (compilers), Proceedings of the 12th Annual Workshop on Sea Turtle Biology and Conservation, NOAA Technical Memo. NMFS-SEFSC-361, pp. 18-20.

study translated into conservation action, resulting in the establishment of the off-shore sanctuary in Rantau Abang.[21] To date, over 200 papers had been written on Malaysian sea turtles.[22] In 1984, Universiti Pertanian Malaysia, Kuala Terengganu (now Universiti Kolej, Universiti Putra Malaysia, Terengganu) had initiated a sea turtle research and conservation programme which had expanded to cover all aspects of the biology and ecology of sea turtles. Conservation and educational projects were also conducted. For example, the University maintained a longterm green and hawksbill turtle conservation project in Chagar Hutang, the major nesting beach for green turtles in Pulau Redang, Terengganu.[23] The conservation project protected turtle eggs through *in situ* incubation, and also included a tagging and nesting research programme.

(f) Public educational programmes on sea turtles. They included travelling exhibitions, production of educational kits, brochures and videos, as well as turtle camps for children. For instance, a turtle camp called "Kem Si Penyu" was organized: children from the Redang Village were brought to the beach to watch nesting turtles, listen to turtle stories, and attend fun art sessions facilitated by local artists. It was hoped that the children would develop a feeling of love for turtles.[24]

3.10. Malaysia considered that its commitment was evident by the actions taken both domestically and internationally in order to protect these endangered species from extinction. Conservation efforts were better achieved through bilateral or multilateral agreements rather than resorting to trade sanctions under the WTO.

3.11. **Pakistan** submitted that it shared the United States' concerns over the plight of sea turtles. However, the US requirement that TEDs be installed on Pakistan's commercial fishing vessels not only violated US obligations under the GATT, but was completely unnecessary given Pakistan's long history of protecting endangered species, including sea turtles. Pakistan stated that its culture embraced a traditional belief that it was sinful to kill sea turtles. In 1950, Pakistan had passed legislation to protect sea turtles by enacting the Imports and Exports (Control) Act (amended on 13 August 1996), which made it illegal to export protected species, including sea turtles and sea turtle by-products from Pakistan. In addition to laws protecting sea turtles, various public and private organizations in Pakistan were engaged in sea turtle protection programmes. Since 1979, Pakistan's Sindh Wildlife Department was engaged in sea turtle conservation programmes in conjunction with WWF and IUCN. The main objective of this programme was to protect sea turtles from extinction. In this regard, this programme had established enclosures on beaches to protect sea turtles and their

---

[21] E.H. Chan and H.C. Liew, (1995), *An Offshore Sanctuary for the Leatherback Turtles in Rantau Abang, Malaysia*, in J.I. Richardson and T.H. Richardson (compilers), Proceedings of the 12th Annual Workshop on Sea Turtle Biology and Conservation, NOAA Technical Memo. NMFS-SEFSC-361, pp. 18-20.

[22] E.H. Chan (compiler), (1996), *A Bibliography of Malaysian Sea Turtles and Terrapins*, SEATRU (Sea Turtle Research Unit), Universiti Kolej, Universiti Putra Malaysia, Terengganu.

[23] E.H. Chan and H.C. Liew, (1995), *In-situ Incubation of Green Turtle Eggs in Pulau Redang, Malaysia: Hope After Decades of Egg Exploitation*, Proceedings of the International Congress of Chelonian Conservation, 6-10 July 1995, Gonfaron, France, pp. 68-71.

[24] The range of research and conservation projects conducted in the Universiti Kolej is described on the SEATRU website at URL<http://www.upmt.edu.my/seatru/>.

eggs from predators and poachers. The Sindh Wildlife Department had also engaged in turtle conservation training programmes designed to teach the public about the importance of protecting sea turtles. This programme had proven to be extremely effective in preserving and protecting sea turtles. It was estimated that between October 1979 and December 1995 more than 1.5 million sea turtle eggs had been protected and thousands of hatchlings had been released safely to the sea. The government of Pakistan was also instrumental in ensuring that sea turtle protection laws were enforced.

3.12 Pakistan considered that the protection of sea turtles was a challenging task tackled by a large number of countries in a variety of ways. Pakistan did not accept the US assertion that the use of TEDs was the only way to prevent the extinction of sea turtles and considered the US action to be an unacceptable interference in policies within Pakistan's sovereign jurisdiction. Programmes such as the ones undertaken by Pakistan were also essential in furthering the goal of sea turtle protection. Pakistan argued that, since it had adequate measures in place to protect and preserve endangered species of sea turtles, there was no need for the United States to impose its own agenda on third parties through the use of far-reaching, extra-territorial measures such as the one imposed by Section 609.

3.13 **Thailand** submitted that it had a long history of taking action to protect the four species of sea turtles (leatherback, green, hawksbill and olive ridley) within its jurisdiction. The Thai culture embraced a traditional belief that it was sinful to kill sea turtles. As early as 1947, the Fisheries Act had been passed prohibiting the catching, harvesting or harming of any sea turtle. This Act also specified that any accidentally caught turtles had to be released into the sea immediately. Further, the Act prohibited the collection or harm of sea turtle eggs on any beach in Thailand. In 1980, pursuant to authority granted under the Export and Import Act of 1979, the Ministry of Commerce had prohibited the exportation of the carcasses of six species of turtles, including the four species of sea turtles present in Thai waters, unless an export license was granted. In 1981, Thailand had further prohibited exports of the five species of live sea turtles (the four previously mentioned, plus olive ridley), unless an export license was granted. So far, no export licenses had been granted. Furthermore, in 1993 the Department of Fisheries had enacted a decree that imposed a prohibition on the importation of protected species of sea turtles.

3.14. In 1983, Thailand had ratified CITES, pursuant to which it had passed the Wildlife Preservation and Protection Act in 1992. Five species of sea turtles were among the protected wild animals listed in this legislation. The legislation prohibited the importation, exportation, and transitory movement of listed wild animals, or carcasses thereof, and subjected violators to severe penalties, including imprisonment and monetary fines. Three branches of the Government of Thailand were responsible for sea turtle restoration programmes: the Department of Fisheries, the Department of Forestry, and the Royal Thai Navy. The Department of Fisheries administered the Phuket Marine Biological Center, which run several conservation programmes. Sea turtle eggs were collected from nesting beaches and were taken to the center to be incubated. Additional sea turtle egg collection programmes were run by 5 Marine Fisheries Development Centers and 13 Coastal Aquaculture Development Centers within the Department of Fisheries. The goal of the restoration programmes administered by these institutions was to cultivate and release 5,000 baby sea turtles a year. In addition to these legislative initiatives, several conservation programmes had been adopted in Thailand. Since 1979, Her Royal Highness Queen Sirikit personally patronized the "Queen's Project on Sea Turtle Conservation". Her Majesty's patronage included the donation of private property to the Thai Department of Fisheries for use as a research station for sea turtle conservation. There were also several private conservation initiatives, including programmes administered by the Magic Eyes Foundation and the Siam Commercial Bank, which raised money to support efforts to rear and release baby sea turtles.

3.15. Thailand said it had also engaged in many educational projects aimed at protecting the natural habitat of sea turtles. Further, programmes involving hatching, nursing and releasing sea turtles to the sea had been initiated. In addition, approximately 20 research studies had been conducted since 1973 in order to learn more about indigenous sea turtles and to assist in formulation of policies to ensure their survival.[25] Significantly, during the course of a night trawled monitoring survey conducted from 1967 to 1996, there had been no observed incidental sea turtle kills in connection with shrimping.[26] The reason for this was that sea turtles inhabited coral reefs and sea grass beds within three kilometres of the shoreline where shrimp trawling was prohibited. While there had been a general decline in the population of nesting sea turtles in Thailand from 1950 to 1985, Thailand's conservation programme had ensured the survival of a sufficient stock of sea turtles to protect against their extinction. The measures that had achieved this result included a combination of strong protection for nesting beaches and the incubation and release programme. Thus, Thailand had found that measures other than the use of TEDs could be made effective in preserving sea turtles in Thai waters.

3.16 At the regional level, there had also been efforts initiated within ASEAN to reach a multilateral agreement on sea turtle conservation efforts. During the fifth meeting of the ASEAN Sectoral Working Group on Fisheries, held on 13-14 March 1997, Thailand had suggested that an agreement be negotiated within ASEAN with respect to sea turtles. The meeting had agreed to authorize Thailand to draft a Memorandum of Understanding ("MOU") setting forth the steps that could be taken jointly for the protection and conservation of sea turtles. In the Special Senior Officials meeting of the ASEAN, in May 1997, Ministers on Agriculture and Forestry had approved a draft MOU submitted by Thailand for consideration and agreed that the MOU would be finalized at the forthcoming meeting of the ASEAN Ministers on Agriculture and Forestry, in September 1997. The MOU committed its signatories to the protection, conservation, replenishment and recovery of sea turtles and of their habitats based upon the best available scientific evidence. The MOU also established a Technical Expert Working Group to prepare an ASEAN programme for Sea Turtle Conservation and Protection, coordinated by Malaysia. It also established mutual recognition of each nation's laws and regulations on this subject and called for

---

25 *Sea Turtle Conservation in Thailand*, (1996), Department of Fisheries, Ministry of Agriculture and Cooperatives, Thailand.

26 *The Night-Trawled Monitoring Surveys During 1967-1996*, (1997), Marine Fisheries Division, Department of Fisheries.

harmonization of such laws and for the sympathetic consideration of such new laws that might be proposed by the working group.

3.17. The **United States** explained that since the 1970s, all species of sea turtles that occurred in waters subject to US jurisdiction had been listed as either endangered or threatened under the US Endangered Species Act of 1973 ("ESA"). In addition to requiring the use of TEDs since 1990, the United States had taken a wide variety of other steps to halt the decline and aid in the recovery of sea turtles. The US Federal Government had acquired some high density nesting beaches of loggerhead turtles and had placed them within the Archie Carr National Wildlife Refuge in Florida. One of the two largest loggerhead rookeries in the world was concentrated along the Atlantic beaches of central and southern Florida. A number of state and federal laws had been passed to protect the beach and dune habitat of nesting sea turtles, including the Coastal Barrier Resources Act of 1982 (Federal), Coastal Areas Management Act of 1974 (North Carolina), Beachfront Management Act of 1990 (South Carolina), Shore Assistance Act of 1979 (Georgia) and Coastal Zone Protection Act of 1985 (Florida). Progress was also being made by many states, counties and towns in preventing disorientation and misorientation of hatchlings caused by beach lighting. Finally, the United States had established and maintained the world's most long-standing beach management programme to reduce out-of-balance depredation and destruction of nests by natural predators, such as raccoons and feral predators.

3.18. The United States had also actively supported international efforts to protect sea turtles. The United States was a party to CITES and had, accordingly, prohibited international trade in sea turtles, their eggs, parts and products. The United States had also funded training for sea turtle researchers and beach protection efforts in such countries as Costa Rica, El Salvador and Mexico. Since 1978, the United States worked cooperatively with Mexico to protect the beach at Rancho Nuevo, Mexico, the principal nesting beach of Kemp's ridley sea turtles, and had provided financial support for the protection of other nesting beaches throughout Mexico. Since the early 1990s, the United States also gave financial assistance to trainees from Latin American who attended the Caribbean Conservation Corporation's sea turtle training programme in Tortuguero, Costa Rica. The United States had provided significant financial support for the sea turtle conservation programmes of the IUCN (World Conservation Union) and for a wide range of comparable initiatives. Some of these efforts had begun to yield encouraging results. For loggerhead sea turtles, for instance, the combined strategy of requiring TEDs and protecting nesting beaches had led to a noticeable increase in at least some subpopulations. For instance, adult loggerheads of the South Florida Subpopulation (the largest loggerhead nesting assemblage in the Atlantic and one of the two largest in the world) was showing significant increases in recent years, indicating that the population was recovering.[27] The US-Mexican joint effort undertaken at Rancho Nuevo had led to encouraging increases in the number of Kemp's ridley nests.[28]

[27] Report of the Marine Turtle Expert Working Group, (1996), *Status of the Loggerhead Turtle Population (Caretta caretta) in the Western North Atlantic*, pp. 13-14.

[28] Report of the Marine Turtle Expert Working Group, (1996), *Kemp's Ridley Sea (Lepidochelys kempii) Turtle Status Report*, pp. 3-4.

3.19. The United States considered that the incidental mortality of sea turtles in shrimp trawl nets constituted the largest cause of human-induced sea turtle mortality. Other measures to protect sea turtles did not address this problem and had not succeeded on their own. The United States Government required shrimp trawl vessels that operated in waters subject to US jurisdiction in which there was a likelihood of intercepting sea turtles to use TEDs at all times. Any effective programme to allow the recovery of these endangered species had to include the required use of TEDs by shrimp trawl vessels that operated in areas and at times where there was a likelihood of intercepting sea turtles. Other measures to protect sea turtles, including the protection of nesting beaches, bans on the harvest of sea turtle eggs, and "headstarting"[29] baby sea turtles, had proven ineffective in increasing the number of large juvenile and adult sea turtles. Increasing the numbers of large juvenile and adult sea turtles was necessary because they were responsible for the greatest contribution to the growth of sea turtle populations - the reproductive value[30] of a large juvenile or adult sea turtle was 584 times that of a hatchling sea turtle.[31] Of the measures available to protect sea turtles, only the required use of TEDs effectively protected large juvenile and adult sea turtles, and was, therefore, of exponentially greater value to sea turtle populations overall. Even if the other measures could achieve a 100 per cent survival rate for baby sea turtles in their first year, scientific models showed that they were unlikely to have a significant effect on sea turtle populations due to the extremely high mortality of sea turtles before they reached breeding age[32]; scientists currently estimated that it took between 1,000 and 10,000 eggs to produce a single adult female.

3.20. The United States argued that, while the measures adopted by the complainants to protect sea turtles were laudable (although, with the exception of Thailand, none required the use of TEDs), they had not prevented drastic declines in sea turtle populations in the waters of these countries. For example, the leatherback sea turtle population in Terengganu, Malaysia had experienced a 95 per cent decline in the number of nesting turtles since 1956.[33] The number of eggs laid by green, olive ridley and hawksbill sea turtles in Terengganu had also declined an estimated 52-85 per cent since the late 1950s.[34] Sea turtle populations in the Gulf of Thailand had been seriously depleted.[35] Comparable declines throughout that region of the world were well-

---

[29] "Headstarting" is a technique where sea turtle eggs are taken from the wild and incubated. The hatchlings are raised in captivity, usually for approximately one year, then released into the wild.

[30] The "reproductive value" is the relative contribution of an individual of a given age to the growth rate of the population. (National Research Council, National Academy of Sciences, (1990), *Decline of the Sea Turtles: Causes and Prevention*, Washington D.C., p. 49).

[31] National Research Council, National Academy of Sciences (1990), *Decline of Sea Turtles: Causes and Prevention*, p. 70; S. Heppel, et. al., *Population Model Analysis for the Loggerhead Sea Turtle (Caretta caretta) in Queensland*, (1996), Wildlife Research, No. 23, p. 143.

[32] S. Heppel, et. al., (1996), *Population Model Analysis for the Loggerhead Sea Turtle (Caretta caretta) in Queensland*, Wildlife Research No. 23, p. 563.

[33] C.J. Limpus, (1993), *Current Declines in Southeast Asian Turtle Populations*, in Proceedings of the Thirteenth Annual Symposium of Sea Turtle Biology and Conservation, p. 89.

[34] J.A. Mortimer, (1990), *Marine Turtle Conservation in Malaysia*, in Proceedings of the Tenth Annual Symposium of Sea Turtle Biology and Conservation, p. 21.

[35] N.V.C. Polunin and N.S. Nuitja, (rev'd ed. 1995), *Sea Turtle Populations of Indonesia and Thailand*, in K.A. Bjorndal, Biology and Conservation of Sea Turtles, p. 359.

documented.[36] As explained above, even if the other measures taken by the complainants to protect sea turtles were effectively enforced[37], without the required use of TEDs, they would be insufficient to allow sea turtle populations in that region of the world to recover. Actually, none of these measures had prevented the drastic declines of sea turtles in the complainants' waters. Their conservation measures had not been shown to have any significant effect on the number of sea turtles that survived to adulthood and reproduced.

3.21. The United States submitted that scientists recognized the limitations of measures such as nest protection and "head-starting" that only protected sea turtle eggs and hatchlings. A recent study commissioned by Thailand's Office of Natural Resource Conservation noted the "generally accepted scientific opinion that head-starting is not a valid conservation method (at the very least, its value has yet to be demonstrated)".[38] Similarly, IUCN (World Conservation Union) found that the "conservation of eggs and hatchlings, without concurrent conservation of the older life stages, may be of limited value".[39] Finally, Dr. Deborah Crouse, a conservation biologist with special expertise in sea turtle biology, had found as the result of her doctoral research on loggerhead sea turtles that "nest protection, by itself, was not sufficient to stop the decline of threatened loggerhead sea turtle populations, much less to recover them while human-induced mortality (due to drowning in shrimp trawls) of juveniles and adult turtles continued unabated".[40]

3.22. According to the United States, such measures were of some value when taken in conjunction with other measures that protected older sea turtles, such as the required use of TEDs. However, certain nations, and in particular India, Malaysia and Pakistan, had not yet adopted effective measures to protect older sea turtles. One reason the governments maintained such measures could be that the measures protecting eggs and hatchlings appeared, on first blush, to produce impressive results. Consider, for example, the hatchery programme that Malaysia maintained. According to a scientific analysis of this programme: "between 1961 and 1986, an average of about 33,000 eggs were incubated each year with a 50 per cent rate of hatching success. This seems like a large number of hatchlings. But, if current estimates are correct that 1,000 to 10,000 eggs are needed to produce a single adult female, then the hatchery programme

---

[36] IUCN (World Conservation Union), (1997), *A Marine Turtle Conservation Strategy and Action Plan for the Northern Indian Ocean.*

[37] The United States observed that the degree of enforcement of existing sea turtle conservation measures in South Asia was called into question. Despite bans on the harvesting of sea turtle eggs, for example, "near-total egg harvest still characterizes the green turtle nesting populations of Indonesia, Thailand and Terengganu, Malaysia". C.J. Limpus, (rev'd ed. 1995), *Global Overview of the Status of Marine Turtles: A 1995 Viewpoint*, in K.A. Bjorndal, Biology and Conservation of Sea Turtles, p. 606; C.S. Kar and S. Bhaskar, *(1995), Status of Sea Turtles in the Eastern Indian Ocean*, in K.A. Bjorndal, Biology and Conservation of Sea Turtles, p. 365.

[38] S. Settle, (1995), *Status of Nesting Populations of Sea Turtles in Thailand and Their Conservation*, in Marine Turtle Newsletter, No. 68, p. 10.

[39] IUCN (World Conservation Union), (1995), A Global Strategy for the Conservation of Marine Turtles, p. 2. The United States noted that IUCN's finding was based on scientific population modelling. *Ibid.*

[40] Statement of Deborah Crouse, Ph.D., 23 July 1997, paragraph 3, document submitted to the Panel by the United States.

would only have produced about 3 to 34 new adult females each year. Considering that 33,000 eggs represents fewer than 2 per cent of the eggs laid annually in the late 1950s, perhaps we should not be too surprised to note a population decline of more than 98 per cent".[41] The example of Malaysia's programme showed the inherent flaw in any sea turtle conservation programme that relied solely on measures to protect eggs and hatchlings. Where older sea turtles were subject to high rates of mortality, including in shrimp trawl fisheries, the protection of eggs and hatchlings alone was very unlikely to allow decimated populations of sea turtles to recover. Indeed, "it is not clear whether egg protection efforts will ultimately prevent marine turtle extinction".[42]

3.23. The United States asserted that prohibitions on the intentional killing of sea turtles, which the complainants had put in place, had not succeeded. These measures, which were in place for many years, had not prevented the decimation of sea turtle populations in South Asia or permitted their recovery, even in areas where the prohibitions had been effectively enforced. For example, a recent report on *The Status of Marine Turtles in Thailand* noted that: "The populations of green and hawksbill turtles [nesting at Khram Island in the Gulf of Thailand] have declined significantly, even though their nesting areas are controlled by the Thai navy since [a] long time ago. As the area is completely protected, very few fishermen or poachers can enter the island. Thus the reduction of the number of sea turtle nests [is] caused by heavy fishing activities in the Gulf areas".[43] In short, despite complainants' claims to the contrary, most populations of sea turtles that spent at least some portion of their lives in waters subject to their jurisdiction were still declining, and shrimp trawl fishing remained a primary (and easily avoidable) reason for these declines.[44] While the complainants reported that they had taken some measures to protect sea turtles, "the efforts of these protection measures will be negated and wasted if young turtles are released into waters

---

[41] J.A. Mortimer, (1990), *Marine Turtle Conservation in Malaysia*, in Proceedings of the Tenth Annual Symposium of Sea Turtle Biology and Conservation, p. 21. The United States noted that this article also detailed a number of grave difficulties with sea turtle hatchery programmes that impeded their effectiveness. Other studies noted the extensive problems of hatchery programmes: *Country Report for Malaysia*, presented at the Northern Indian Ocean Sea Turtle Workshop and Strategic Planning Session, 13-18 January 1997, in Bhubaneswar, Orissa, India, p. 4 ("Poor hatchling success may result from poor handling and hatchery management techniques. Personnel running the hatcheries sometimes do not receive sufficient training or understand the technical requirements for improved hatchling success"); Statement of Deborah Crouse, Ph.D., 23 July 1997, paragraph 12, document submitted to the Panel by the United States ("These programmes have been costly, fraught with logistic problems, and are still considered highly experimental").

[42] D.T. Crouse, et. al., (1987), *A Stage-Based Model for Loggerhead Sea Turtles and Implications for Conservation*, Ecology, Vol. 68, No. 5, pp. 1412-23. The United States noted that there was also a real question about the ability of some nations to enforce rules to protect sea turtle eggs on nesting beaches. According to one report, "near-total egg harvest still characterizes the green turtle nesting populations of ... Thailand and Terengganu in Malaysia. ... A large proportion of [hawksbill turtle] eggs appear to be harvested in Malaysia (Terengganu) [and] Thailand." C.J. Limpus, (rev'd ed. 1995), *Global Overview of the Status of Marine Turtles: A 1995 Viewpoint*, in Biology and Conservation of Sea Turtles, K.A. Bjorndal ed., p. 606.

[43] S. Chantrapoornsyl, (1997), *Status of Marine Turtles in Thailand*, Phuket Marine Biological Center, p. 1.

[44] Statement of Deborah Crouse, Ph.D., 23 July 1997, paragraphs 6-8, document submitted by the United States to the Panel.

where trawlers operate without TEDs. In such waters, many will be captured and drowned each year and few will survive the two decades or more they will require to mature and reproduce".[45]

3.24. Regarding Malaysia, the United States argued that, whatever measures Malaysia had taken, all four species were endangered in Malaysia.[46] Moreover, Malaysia neglected to mention the populations of sea turtles that nested in Terengganu and elsewhere in Malaysia, particularly the populations of leatherback sea turtles. Numerous scientific reports documented the disastrous declines of these sea turtles. Calculated on the basis of egg production data supplied by the Terengganu State Fisheries department, the population of leatherbacks nesting there had suffered "a greater than 95 per cent decline in nesting turtles over 40 years since 1956".[47] In terms of the number of egg clutches laid by female leatherbacks in Terengganu, the decline was just as precipitous: "In the late 1950s, an estimated 2,000 female leatherbacks laid about 10,000 egg clutches annually. Since then, the population has declined steadily and catastrophically. During the 1989 season, fewer than 200 egg clutches were laid".[48] The most recent available data, supplied in the *Country Report for Malaysia* cited above, confirmed that these trends had continued. The report noted that, in the 1950's, this population had been celebrated as the only remaining leatherback population of importance in the world". However, the numbers of these sea turtles "have declined significantly with present nestings representing only 2 per cent of numbers then ... The Terengganu leatherback population may be lost within a decade or two".[49] Unfortunately, the same trends were present in other species of sea turtles that nested in Terengganu. The olive ridleys that nested there had declined from "possibly thousands annually" to "approximately 20 per year in the early 1990s".[50] Moreover, the *Country Report for Malaysia* cited above found that the population trends of all the major rookeries of Malaysia "indicated a general declining trend, some to near extinction", including those in Sarawak.[51] The only rookeries reported as not experiencing these declines were those at the Sabah Turtle Islands.

---

45 Statement of Deborah Crouse, Ph.D., 23 July 1997, paragraph 10, document submitted by the United States to the Panel.

46 J.A. Mortimer, (1990), *Marine Turtle Conservation in Malaysia*, in Proceedings of the Tenth Annual Symposium of Sea Turtle Biology and Conservation, p. 21.

47 C.J. Limpus, (1993), *Current Declines in South East Asian Turtle Populations*, in Proceedings of the Thirteenth Annual Symposium of Sea Turtle Biology and Conservation, p. 89.

48 J.A. Mortimer, (1990), *Marine Turtle Conservation in Malaysia*, in Proceedings of the Tenth Annual Symposium of Sea Turtle Biology and Conservation, p. 21.

49 *Country Report for Malaysia*, presented at the Northern Indian Ocean Sea Turtle Workshop and Strategic Planning Session 13-18 January 1997 in Bhubaneswar, Orissa, India, p. 3.

50 C.J. Limpus, *Global Overview of the Status of Marine Turtles: A 1995 Viewpoint, in Biology and Conservation of Sea Turtles*, (1995), Biology and Conservation of Sea Turtles, K.A. Bjorndal, p. 606. The United States noted that another analysis of the data documented that "the numbers [of olive ridley sea turtles] in Terengganu have seriously declined to only 35 nestings in 1995 compared to 293 nestings in 1984". *Country Report for Malaysia* presented at the Northern Indian Ocean Sea Turtle Workshop and Strategic Planning Session, 13-18 January 1997, in Bhubaneswar, Orissa, India, p. 3.

51 *Country Report for Malaysia*, presented at the Northern Indian Ocean Sea Turtle Workshop and Strategic Planning Session, 13-18 January 1997, in Bhubaneswar, Orissa, India, p. 3.

3.25. Third, even the green sea turtle populations of both Sarawak and Sabah were in danger, despite Malaysia's claims to the contrary. Placed in historical context, these areas had suffered a massive reduction in green sea turtle populations: the population of green sea turtles in the Sarawak Turtle Islands had suffered a "greater than 90 per cent decline in egg production", while green sea turtles in the Sabah Turtle Islands had suffered a "50 per cent decline in egg production".[52] This demonstrated what sea turtle biologists were saying for many years, i.e. that the establishment of sanctuaries in limited areas would not protect species that migrated widely. Finally, Malaysia's claims of increases in certain other nesting populations of sea turtles in Sabah and Sarawak were themselves of uncertain value. Malaysia reported these increases only very recently, and these reports covered only a short timeframe. It was not surprising that increases in nestings might be occurring in these limited areas, given that Malaysia had allowed an almost total harvest of sea turtle eggs there until quite recently.[53] Moreover, as noted above, scientists estimated that it took between 1,000 to 10,000 eggs to produce a single nesting female, the reported increase in the number of eggs being laid in Sabah and Sarawak might yield very few mature sea turtles, particularly if mature sea turtles remained subject to incidental mortality in shrimp fisheries in Malaysia. Finally, Dr. Crouse pointed out that the reported increases in egg production in Sabah and Sarawak might be nothing more than an increase in the number of eggs placed in hatcheries as a result of Malaysia's headstarting programme, rather than any increase in the number of sea turtle eggs overall in those areas.[54] A document produced by Malaysia examined the ineffectiveness of sea turtle hatcheries and headstarting, and criticized Malaysia's sea turtle conservation programme for relying almost exclusively on hatcheries.[55]

3.26. Regarding Thailand, the United States argued that scientific evidence did not show that Thailand had ensured "the survival of a sufficient stock of sea turtles to protect against extinction". The study commissioned by Thailand's Office of Natural Resource Conservation reported that all populations of sea turtles nesting in Thailand "are seriously reduced from previous levels".[56] This report merely confirmed earlier observations. A 1995 analysis of the *Global Overview of the Status of Marine Turtles* found, for example, that: "[t]he stock [of olive ridleys] in the Andaman Sea of Thailand

---

[52] C.J. Limpus, *Current Declines in South East Asian Turtle Populations*, (1993), in Proceedings of the Thirteenth Annual Symposium of Sea Turtle Biology and Conservation, p. 89. The United States noted that another scientific analysis documented that "the green turtle populations nesting in Sarawak and Sabah have both declined dramatically during the past five decades". J.A. Mortimer, (1990), *Marine Turtle Conservation in Malaysia*, in Proceedings of the Tenth Annual Symposium of Sea Turtle Biology and Conservation, pp. 21-22.

[53] C.J. Limpus, (1993), *Current Declines in South East Asian Turtle Populations*, in Proceedings of the Thirteenth Annual Symposium of Sea Turtle Biology and Conservation, p. 89; J.A. Mortimer, (1990), *Marine Turtle Conservation in Malaysia* in Proceedings of the Tenth Annual Symposium of Sea Turtle Biology and Conservation, pp. 21-22.

[54] Statement of Deborah Crouse, Ph.D., 23 July 1997, paragraph 8. Document submitted to the Panel by the United States.

[55] E.H. Chan and H.C. Liew, (1996), *Decline of the Leatherback Population in Terengganu, Malaysia, 1956-1995*, Chelonian Conservation and Biology, Vol. 2, No. 2, pp. 196-203.

[56] S. Settle, (1995), *Status of Nesting Populations of Sea Turtles in Thailand and Their Conservation*, in Marine Turtle Newsletter 1995, No. 68, p. 8.

has been decimated to only tens of females nesting annually. ... A similar decimation of the nesting population [of leatherbacks] of the Andaman Sea area of western Thailand apparently occurred".[57] Similarly, the report on the *Status of Marine Turtles in Thailand* cited above not only determined that "populations of the sea turtles in Thailand have been found drastically declined" but also that "the loggerhead turtle is believed [as] being extinct from Thai waters".[58] Another document submitted by Thailand revealed that once five species of sea turtles nested in Thailand's waters, but today only four nested there.[59] Thailand could only point to one small area, Khram Island, in which sea turtles were supposedly well protected; but a document submitted by Thailand showed that sea turtle nestings on Khram Island were decreasing, while shrimp trawling in the area had in fact increased.[60] In the face of such evidence, the United States questioned how Thailand could maintain that, prior to its adoption of a TEDs programme in 1996, sea turtles found in the waters of Thailand were protected from extinction. Regarding the 5'000 baby sea turtles released each year by Thailand, the United States said that, due to the recognized and admitted mortality rate of baby sea turtles, this translated into only 10 sea turtles each year that might live to reach breeding age. Meanwhile, tens of thousands of mature sea turtles died every year in shrimp trawl nets. This explained why the United States disagreed with Thailand's conclusion that a nation "can ensure the survival of a sufficient stock of sea turtles to protect against their extinction" through the adoption of such measures without requiring the use of TEDs.

3.27. **India** disagreed with the US assertion that conservation measures other than TEDs were insufficient on their own to allow endangered sea turtles to recover. India had demonstrated that in the case of Gahirmatha, in the State of Orissa, complete protection of eggs along with prevention of exploitation of adults from the breeding area had led to the stabilization of the olive ridley sea turtle population, and thus its measures were "sufficient" to meet the objectives of conservation and protection of endangered sea turtles. India agreed with the United States that the programmes to protect eggs and hatchlings were, by themselves, insufficient. This was the reason why India had taken leading steps for the protection of the mass nesting areas which meant protection of eggs, hatchlings and adults along with protection of breeding grounds which meant protection of hatchlings, juveniles, sub-adults and adults. This had resulted in the stabilization of the sea turtle population at Gahirmatha as already demonstrated. Similarly, India shared the view that "conservation of eggs and hatchlings, without concurrent conservation of the older life stages, may be of limited value." However, the model of Dr. Deborah Crouse referred to by the United States had been questioned by another leading scientist from the United States who wrote that

---

57 C.J. Limpus, (1995), *Global Overview of the Status of Marine Turtles: A 1995 Viewpoint*, in Biology and Conservation of Sea Turtles, K.A. Bjorndal ed., p. 606.

58 S. Chantrapoornsyl, (1997), *Status of Marine Turtles in Thailand*, Phuket Marine Biological Center, pp. 1-3.

59 B. Phasuk, (1992), *Biology, Culture, Technique and Conservation of Sea Turtle in Thailand.*

60 T. Sujittosakul and S. Senaluk, (1997), *Relation Between Sea Turtle Nesting and Number of Shrimp Trawler Around Kram Island, Cholburi Province*, Technical Paper No. 6, Marine Fisheries Division, Department of Fisheries.

"eggs are important and cannot be ignored in recovery plans", and advocated "full protection in all life stages".[61]

3.28. The claim that certain nations, in particular India, had not yet adopted effective measures to protect older sea turtles was not correct. As already mentioned, India's successful conservation programmes had eliminated commercial exploitation and trade of adult hawksbill, green and olive ridley sea turtles and there was no documented evidence of any commercial exploitation or trade of leatherback and loggerhead sea turtles. India had an excellent record of sea turtle protection. Several international forums had acknowledged India's record of preservation of sea turtles.[62] The Director of the US NMFS had written a letter in April 1997 to the Chief Minister of the Government of the State of Orissa to compliment him for his role in conserving the Bhitarkanika sanctuary and specifically the olive ridley population of Orissa, and to express appreciation for the leadership that India had taken in implementing the successful conservation strategy of sea turtles. The assertion that prohibitions of the intentional killing of sea turtles had not succeeded was not applicable to India. As already mentioned, prohibition of the earlier occurrence of intentional killing and harvesting of reproductively mature individuals to the tune of 50,000 to 80,000 per season in Orissa had led to the stabilization of the world's largest olive ridley population, and India's action had in fact led to the effective protection and conservation of this endangered species of sea turtles. In addition to the long-term programme described above, India added that its 8,000 kilometres coastline was protected by law and an area up to 500 meters from beach was virgin land. The Government of India had not allowed this area to be converted to tourist resorts which would disturb sea turtle populations. There were no water sports which caused considerable mauling of turtles in other parts of the world, the sea was not polluted and relatively free of debris which caused damage to sea turtles populations. The coastal zone regulation did not allow fishing up to 5 kilometres from beach and this had been extended up to 20 kilometres in turtle sensitive areas. Awareness programmes, workshops at national, regional and international levels had been organized to coordinate efforts to protect sea turtles.

3.29. **Malaysia** responded that the claim by the United States that measures to protect older sea turtles were of exponentially greater value to sea turtle populations overall was based purely on empirical data which had been generated from a population model, while the situation in Malaysia, which had showed that these programmes to protect eggs had been sufficient to bring about population recovery, was based on hard data collected over almost 30 years of constant monitoring. Malaysia maintained that the use of TEDs had not been found to be the sole measure necessary for the survival and protection of sea turtles. In the case of the United States, it could have been necessary to use TEDs in tandem with other measures since rates of incidental captures had been found to be exceptionally high. With respect to the alleged dramatic decline of sea turtle populations in Malaysia and other South East Asian countries, Malaysia noted that more

---

[61] J. Mortimer, (1997), *On Importance of Eggs*, Marine Turtle Newsletter, No.76.

[62] IUCN (World Conservation Union), (1995), *A Marine Turtle Conservation Strategy and Action Plan for the Northern Indian Ocean*, and *Integrating Marine Conservation in the Indian Ocean 1996 and Beyond*, Summary and Working Group Reports, 28 November-1 December 1995, Mombasa, Kenya, p. 21.

recent publications than those produced by the United States showed population recoveries in Malaysia, e.g. green and hawksbill turtles of Sabah Turtle Islands[63]: in 1988, after 22 years of egg protection, the nesting population showed a reversal in its declining trends and nesting density reached a record high in 1991. Annual nestings of 8,084 in the period 1990-94 represented a threefold increase over annual nestings of 2,633 recorded in the 1982-86 period.[64] Malaysia further noted that while it was true that turtle populations in Terengganu had declined, it had to be borne in mind that "comparable declines throughout the region of the world were well-documented". Since the time when declines in Terengganu had been highlighted by local sea turtle biologists, the Terengganu State Government had intensified turtle conservation efforts, and was now subscribing to 100 per cent protection of leatherback eggs. However, due to the slow maturation time of sea turtles, the intensification of conservation programmes in Terengganu would not become apparent until about 20 years. Therefore, it was erroneous and premature to say that Malaysia's conservation programmes were not effective. In the Sabah Turtle Islands, for instance, 100 per cent egg protection had started in the 1970s and it was only in 1988 that population recovery began to emerge. Malaysia maintained that the prohibition on the intentional and direct harvest of sea turtles in Malaysia had prevented the total collapse of sea turtle populations.

3.30. Malaysia stressed that the United States had to acknowledge the scientific fact that different nesting populations of a particular species were distinct from each other and could not be treated uniformly. This was the reason why sea turtle conservationists stressed that each nesting population had to be protected in its own right. If one population was decimated, it could not be augmented by individuals from another nesting population. Therefore, when considering the marine turtles of Malaysia, it was appropriate to view the different populations separately and not just consider all the four species uniformly. The conditions of the various sea turtle populations in Malaysia could not be treated or described in an uniform manner. Each nesting population was distinct and subject to different conditions. Firstly, the green and hawksbill population in the Sabah Turtle Islands had recovered to levels which surpassed historical records. This recovery was not short-lived, but had been sustained since 1988, when a reversal in the declining trend had first been manifested. The increases in the populations were valid and definitive data was available. The speculative view of Dr. Crouse that increases in egg production might be nothing more than an increase in the number of eggs placed in hatcheries was without scientific merit and without reference to the data which had been vigilantly collected by the staff of Sabah Park. The recovery of the Sabah Turtle Island sea turtle population was based on the number of nestings per year and not on the number of eggs collected. Secondly, the green turtle population of the Sarawak Turtle Islands had stabilized over the last 30 years. However, comparing current nesting levels with historical records showed a decline which had occurred in the 1950s, i.e. before the introduction of trawling in Sarawak. This decline had been attributed to intensive egg harvest and direct capture of turtles. Thirdly, the green turtle

[63] C.J. Limpus, (1995), *Global Overview of the Status of MarineTurtles*, Biology and Conservation of Sea Turtles, K.A. Bjorndal ed., Smithsonian Institution Press, 2nd edition, pp. 605-609.

[64] E.H. Chan and H.C. Liew, (1996), *A Management Plan for the Green and Hawksbill Turtle Populations of the Sabah Turtle Islands - A Report to Sabah Parks*, Sea Turtle Research Unit (SEATRU), Universiti Kolej, Universiti Putra Malaysia, Terengganu.

population of Redang Island had demonstrated a steady trend over the last ten years; no historical data was available for this population. Fourthly, the leatherback population in Terengganu had declined precipitously, due to intense egg harvest, the intensification of the fishing industry and the high seas driftnet fishery. Fifthly, there was no historical record indicating that olive ridleys nested in the thousands in Malaysia; the precipitous decline of olive ridley nesting in Terengganu, as alleged by the United States, was unfouned. As to the leatherback, the causes of its decline had been the rapid development of the fishing industry in Terengganu in the early 1970s, the introduction of Japanese high seas squid drift net fishery of the North Pacific in 1987, and commercial egg collection.[65] Therefore, except for the case of leatherback, sea turtles in Malaysia had either increased or stabilized for an extended period of time, without using TEDs. The US conclusion that all sea turtles in Malaysia were in dire conditions was erroneous and disregarded data available on the Malaysian sea turtle populations.

3.31. **Thailand** replied that the sources relied upon by the United States in paragraph 3.26 did not show that shrimp trawling was the cause of any perceived decline in sea turtle population. In paragraphs 3.56, 3.57 and 3.75, Thailand provided detailed arguments which refuted the US reading of those sources and which showed that Thailand had implemented sufficient sea turtle conservation programmes.

3.32. The **United States** replied to India that the nesting population at Gahirmatha had fluctuated widely in recent times. Large numbers of olive ridley strandings had occurred. The IUCN had noted with alarm the "significant fishing-related mortality" being sustained by this population, and that such mortality would certainly increase "as fishing activities continue to increase rapidly in the Indian Ocean".[66] In short, the olive ridley population at Gahirmatha was not safe. As to the argument that the olive ridley population nesting at Gahirmatha had "stabilized", the United States noted that there was a big difference between a population that was "recovering" and one that had "stabilized". A population that had been depleted to 1 per cent of its former size might achieve stabilization at that very low level and still be at grave risk of extinction. A population that was recovering was one that had made substantial progress back to its former size. The statement that there were no recovering populations of olive ridleys anywhere had been made on the basis of extensive scientific research by C. J. Limpus, an Australian sea turtle biologist.[67] Regarding India's claim that the population model of Dr. D. Crouse had been questioned by another US leading scientist, the United States noted that the article referred to by India was written in fact by Selina Heppell, and not by Dr. Mortimer. More importantly, the article did not question the model of Dr. Crouse. The principal point of Dr. Heppell's article was that sea turtle eggs were important and could not be ignored in recovery plans, and that when sea turtle populations were at low levels, full protection in all life stages was needed. The article stated, as the United States was explaining throughout this proceeding, that "the reproductive value of eggs and hatchlings is generally much lower than that of large

[65] E.H. Chan and H.C. Liew, (1996), *Decline of the Leatherback Population in Terengganu, Malaysia, 1956-1995*, Chelonian Conservation and Biology, Vol. 2, No. 2, pp. 196-203.

[66] IUCN (World Conservation Union), (1997), *A Marine Turtle Conservation Stragegy and Action Plan for the Northern Indian Ocean*, p. 11.

[67] C.J. Limpus, (1995), *Global Overview of the Status of Marine Turtles: A 1995 Viewpoint*, Biology and Conservation of Sea Turtles, K.A. Bjorndal ed., pp. 605-610.

juveniles, subadults or adults", and thus that "an increase in the annual survival in the first year of life will always have comparatively small impact" on the preservation of sea turtle populations.

3.33. The United States replied to Malaysia that, as egg protection programmes existed in Malaysia since 1966, their effects should be known. In this respect, Malaysia's own exhibit[68] stated that "[a]ssuming a 20-year maturation period for leatherbacks, these hatchlings should already be recruiting into the breeding population. However, persistent population declines indicate no evidence of recruitment. ... The 100 per cent egg incubation practised now cannot significantly rehabilitate the population" unless measure were taken to effectively control fishery-related mortality. Malaysia's own exhibits[69] contradicted Malaysia's arguments regarding the recovery of the sea turtle populations at Sabah Turtle Islands and Sarawak Turtle Islands since they showed that egg protection was not enough and that these populations had not recovered. While the prohibitions on direct exploitation of sea turtles might have avoided a total collapse of Malaysian sea turtle populations, all species of sea turtles in Malaysia remained "vulnerable to extinction"[70] and a number of documents submitted to the Panel confirmed that all sea turtles in Malaysia were in dire conditions.[71] Another document submitted by Malaysia stated that TEDs should be used in Malaysia.[72] Finally, a study submitted by Malaysia[73] showed that trawl nets caught more sea turtles than driftnets,

[68] E.H. Chan and H.C. Liew, (1996), *Decline of the Leatherback Population in Terengganu, Malaysia, 1956-1995*, Chelonian Conservation and Biology, Vol. 2, No. 2, pp. 196-203.

[69] M.S. Suliansa, P. Basintal and N.L. Chan, (1996), *Impacts of Fishery Related Activities on Sea Turtles*, Paper presented at the National Seminar/Workshop on Marine Turtle and Terrapin Management, 22-23 October 1996, Cherating, Malaysia; and E.H. Chan and H.C. Liew, (1996), *Decline of the Leatherback Population in Terengganu, Malaysia, 1956-1995*, Chelonian Conservation and Biology, Vol. 2, No. 2, pp. 196-203.

[70] M.S. Suliansa, P. Basintal and N.L. Chan, (1996), *Impacts of Fishery Related Activities on Sea Turtles*, Paper presented at the National Seminar/Workshop on Marine Turtle and Terrapin Management, 22-23 October 1996, Cherating, Malaysia.

[71] The United States referred to the following documents: M.S. Suliansa, P. Basintal and N.L. Chan, (1996), *Impacts of Fishery Related Activities on Sea Turtles*, Paper presented at the National Seminar/Workshop on Marine Turtle and Terrapin Management, 22-23 October 1996, Cherating, Malaysia; and E.H. Chan and H.C. Liew, (1996), *Decline of the Leatherback Population in Terengganu, Malaysia, 1956-1995*, Chelonian Conservation and Biology, Vol. 2, No. 2, pp. 196-203; J.A. Mortimer, (1990), *Marine Turtle Conservation in Malaysia,* Proceedings of the Tenth Annual Symposium of Sea Turtle Biology and Conservation, p. 12; C.J. Limpus, *Current Declines in South East Asian Turtle Populations,* (1993), Proceedings of the Thirteenth Annual Symposium of Sea Turtle Biology and Conservation, p. 89; H.C. Liew, (1997), *Country Report for Malaysia*,paper presented at the Northern Indian Ocean Sea Turtle Workshop and Strategic Planning Session, Bhubaneswar, Orissa, India, 13-18 January 1997; C.J. Limpus, *Global Overview of the Status of Marine Turtles: A 1995 Viewpoint*, Biology and Conservation of Sea Turtles (K.A. Bjorndal ed., rev'd ed), pp. 605-610.; Statement by D. Crouse, 23 July 1997, paragraph 8.

[72] M.S. Suliansa, P. Basintal and N.L. Chan, (1996), *Impacts of Fishery Related Activities on Sea Turtles*, paper presented at the National Seminar/Workshop on Marine Turtle and Terrapin Management, 22-23 October 1996, Cherating, Malaysia.

[73] K. Bin Ibrahim, (1996), *Country Status Report, Malaysia (Peninsular Malaysia)*, paper presented at the First SEAFDEC Workshop on Marine Turtle Research and Conservation, Kuala Terengganu, Malaysia, 15-18 January 1996, p. 17.

thus contradicting Malaysia's claim that driftnets caused more sea turtle deaths than trawl nets.

3.34. As to whether the Indian olive ridley sea turtle population was "recovering", **India** replied that the US statement based on research done by Dr. C. J. Limpus was irrelevant. First, Dr. Limpus had not done any work on any significant population of olive ridley sea turtles in India, and, second, Australia did not have any record of any important olive ridley sea turtle population of its own which had migrated to Indian waters for Dr. Limpus to make any relevant observation.

3.35. **Malaysia** replied that the United States misquoted scientific information and used conclusions reached by Malaysian scientists on a particular population and superimposed those conclusions on a totally different population of sea turtles. For instance, when questioning the recovery of the sea turtle populations at Sabah and Sarawak Turtle Islands, the United States actually referred to the conclusions of an exhaustive analysis of the leatherback population, which had undergone population decline.[74] These conclusions could not be applied to the Sabah Turtle Islands population which had shown an impressive population recovery, to levels beyond historical levels. The United States also misinterpreted the study on leatherback populations[75]: (i) the statement "[h]owever, persistent population declines indicate no evidence of recruitment" contained in that study was made to prove that the low level of egg protection previously practised (only 5 - 20 per cent of total eggs laid) was insufficient for population recovery; (ii) the statement that "[t]he 100 per cent egg incubation practised now cannot significantly rehabilitate the population" was true because the population had declined to such low levels that 100 per cent actually presented only a small quantum of eggs, and in terms of absolute numbers of eggs, was comparable to the 5-20 per cent egg protection practised previously. Malaysia stressed that the same study did not identify shrimp trawls to be the major cause of the decline of the leatherbacks, and recommended that "fishing gear impacts need to be addressed at both the local and international levels". The statement that all species of sea turtles in Malaysia remained "vulnerable to extinction" was a generalization without any reference to statistics. The document stating that TEDs should be used in Malaysia also stated that "there are no direct observations made to prove that certain fishing gear can induce mortality to sea turtles".[76] Finally, the United States was wrong in referring to the Bin Ibrahim study[77] to show that trawl nets caught more sea turtles than driftnets. This study clearly showed that rates of capture for driftnets (for mesh larger than 18 cm) was 16 turtles per gear, while for trawl nets, it was 5 turtles per gear. In the survey, the number of turtles caught by trawls was shown to be 59, compared to the 33 caught by driftnets. A superficial and unscientific interpretation could lead to the conclusion that

74 E.H. Chan and H.C. Liew, (1996), *Decline of the Leatherback Population in Terengganu, Malaysia, 1956-1995*, Chelonian Conservation and Biology, Vol. 2, No. 2, pp. 196-203.

75 *Ibid.*

76 M.S. Suliansa, P. Basintal and N.L. Chan, (1996), *Impacts of Fishery Related Activities on Sea Turtles*, paper presented at the National Seminar/Workshop on Marine Turtle and Terrapin Management, 22-23 October 1996, Cherating, Malaysia.

77 K. Bin Ibrahim, (1996), *Country Status Report, Malaysia (Peninsular Malaysia)*, paper presented at the First SEAFDEC Workshop on Marine Turtle Research and Conservation, Kuala Terengganu, Malaysia, 15-18 January 1996, p. 17.

trawls caught more turtles than driftnets. Malaysia stressed, however, that this study surveyed 12 trawl nets, but only 2 driftnets. Therefore, in terms of rates of capture, and numbers of units of gear licensed, driftnets undoubtedly posed greater threats to sea turtles. To conclude, all the hard data presented by Malaysia refuted the argument made by the United States that all sea turtles in Malaysia were in dire conditions.

### 2. *Whether Sea Turtles Are a Shared Global Resource*

3.36. The **United States** submitted that sea turtles were a shared global resource. All species of sea turtles except the flatback (which was restricted to waters around Australia) regularly spent all or part of their lives in waters subject to US jurisdiction in the Atlantic and Pacific Oceans and the Caribbean Sea. Sea turtles being highly migratory creatures, moving in and out of a variety of ocean and coastal habitats, the species found in US waters swam across vast expanses of the high seas and through waters under the jurisdiction of many other countries. For example, recent DNA analyses revealed that some leatherback sea turtles in American Samoa were from a Malaysian/Indonesian stock, that loggerhead sea turtles found off the Pacific coast of the United States were known to nest in Japan and Australia and that green sea turtles in US Pacific Island territories might have ranges extending to the South China Sea.[78] Sea turtles served important functions in the ecosystems which they inhabited. For example, the regular presence of green turtles made seagrass beds more productive, caused nutrients to be cycled more rapidly, and gave the grass blades a higher protein content, thus benefiting other species. Furthermore, some populations of sea turtles, whose feeding areas might be hundreds or even thousands of kilometres from their nesting beaches, served an important role in nutrient cycling by transporting massive quantities of nutrients from these feeding grounds to typically more nutrient-poor coastal habitats in the vicinity of nesting beaches. Efforts by one nation to protect sea turtles would not

---

[78] B.W. Bowen, (1995), *Tracking Marine Turtles with Genetic Markers,* BioScience, Vol. 45, p. 528; P.H. Dutton, et. al., (1997), *Genetic Stock ID of Turtles Caught in the Pacific Longline Fishery*, paper presented at the Seventeenth Annual Symposium of Sea Turtle Biology and Conservation. The United States observed that other examples of the highly migratory nature of sea turtles abounded. For example, recent DNA analyses indicated that 57 per cent of sea turtles found in Western Mediterranean waters derived from western Atlantic nesting populations. *Ibid.* Loggerhead sea turtles hatched on the beaches of eastern Florida were swept by ocean currents to the eastern Atlantic Ocean before returning to US coastal waters many years later. US Department of Commerce, et. al., (1993), *Recovery Plan for U.S. Population of Loggerhead Turtle Caretta caretta*, p. 5. Green sea turtles nesting in Florida travelled hundreds of kilometres to their resident foraging areas. B.A. Schroeder, et. al., (1994), *Post-Nesting Movements of Florida Green Turtles: Preliminary Results from Satellite Telemetry*, Proceedings of the Fourteenth Annual Symposium of Sea Turtle Biology and Conservation, p. 90. Hawaiian green sea turtles were long-range migrant breeders that nested primarily at French Frigate Shoals, the approximate midpoint of the Hawaiian Archipelago, which extended 2450 linear kilometres. G.H. Balazs, et. al. *Preliminary Assessment of Habitat Utilization by Hawaiian Green Turtles in the Resident Foraging Pastures* (NOAA Technical Memorandum 1987). Green turtles nesting at Ascension Island spent most of their adult lives at foraging grounds off the coast of Brazil and migrated more than 2,000 km to Ascension to nest. J.A. Mortimer and K.M. Portier, (1989), *Reproductive Homing and Internesting Behavior of the Green Turtle (Chelonia Mydas) at Ascension Island, South Atlantic Ocean.*

succeed unless other nations in whose waters these species also occurred took comparable measures.

3.37. With respect to the US argument that sea turtles were a shared global resource, **India** noted that five species of sea turtles had been recorded in the waters and on the beaches of India, including the green turtle, the olive ridley, the leatherback, the hawksbill and the loggerhead. None of the evidence cited by the United States demonstrated that sea turtles found in the US areas subject to the TEDs requirement migrated to Indian territorial seas or beaches. Further, with respect to the olive ridley, the 1990 report cited by the United States specifically stated that "[t]he olive ridley, although probably the most numerous sea turtle worldwide, is very rare in US waters, and its status and future are not in the main, a direct United States responsibility".[79] The olive ridley population nesting in India's territorial waters, however, had increased substantially over the last ten years. India noted that long term tagging of the Gahirmatha sea turtle population had demonstrated that tagged olive ridley sea turtles frequently visited their nesting beach several times a year, proving that they did not engage in such long distance migration as alleged by the United States. Further, only 2 out of the nearly 20,000 tagged olive ridley sea turtles had been recovered off the coast of Sri Lanka, which was proximate to the Indian coast. No long distance recovery of tagged Gahirmatha sea turtles had been recorded in any other Indian Ocean country. At most, therefore, significant numbers of sea turtles would appear to migrate regionally, but not globally.

3.38. **Malaysia** submitted that there was as yet no data to show that green turtles in the US Pacific had ranges extending to the South China Sea.[80] The definitive data available was: (i) green turtles nesting in Pulau Redang, Terengganu, had been tracked by satellite to feeding grounds occurring off Palawan Island (Philippines), west coast of Sabah, Bangka Island of Sumatra (Indonesia) and Natuna Island of Indonesia[81]; and (ii) green and hawksbill turtles tagged while nesting in the Turtle Islands of Sabah had been recovered in Palau Islands, Sangalalei, Cempadak and Kai Islands (Indonesia) and the

---

79 National Research Council, National Academy of Sciences, (1990), *Decline of the Sea Turtles: Causes and Prevention,* p. 26.

80 In responding to similar arguments contained in Annex JJ of the United States (see below Section III.D), Malaysia noted that a careful examination of Bowen (1995), cited by the United States to show that "DNA analysis demonstrated that some leatherback sea turtles in American Samoa are from Malaysian or Indonesian stock" revealed that this study did not mention DNA studies on leatherback turtles. Bowen had conducted studies on loggerheads, hawksbills and green turtles. Further, Dutton et al. (1997) made no mention of green turtles from the US Pacific Island territories reaching the South China Sea. Dutton et al. (1997) stated in fact that "[a]nalysis of mitochondrial DNA (mtDNA) for green turtles indicates that eastern, western and central Pacific nesting populations are genetically distinct and suggests these regional nesting assemblages represent independent demographic units for management purposes". Dutton et al. (1997) also found that green turtles caught in the Hawaiian longline fishery were from Hawaiian and eastern Pacific rookeries, and none from any of the western Pacific rookeries.

81 H.C. Liew, E.H. Chan, F. Papi and P. Lusch, (1995), *Long distance migration of green turtles from Redang Island, Malaysia: The need for regional cooperation in sea turtle conservation,* in Proceedings of the International Congress of Chelonian Conservation. 6-10 July 1995, Confaron, France, pp. 73-75.

Philippines.[82] There was no documentation showing that turtles which nested in the United States migrated to waters of India, Malaysia, Pakistan and Thailand. So far studies on long-distance migration of turtles showed that, although sea turtles were distributed globally, they migrated only within regions, and not globally.[83] This was the reason why sea turtle treaties and conservation programmes were made between nations on a regional basis and not a global basis. As examples of the regional cooperation, Malaysia mentioned the TIHPA Memorandum of Agreement, which had been concluded between Sabah and the Philippines, the Inter-American Convention and the Regional Marine Turtle Conservation Programme of SREP (South Pacific Regional Environment Programme).[84]

3.39. **Pakistan** observed that two species of sea turtles nested on Pakistani coasts (the green and the olive ridley). As stated by India, the olive ridley's status and future were not a direct US responsibility. Further, none of the sources cited by the United States demonstrated that the green turtle found in waters fished by Pakistani shrimpers migrated to US territorial waters during their life cycles.[85] In fact, the sources cited by the United States concluded that "Florida green turtles make use of the extensive

[82] E.H. Chan and H.C. Liew, (1996), *A management plan for the green and hawksbill turtle populations of the Sabah Turtle Islands: A report to Sabah parks*, SEATRU (Sea Turtle Research Unit), Universiti Kolej, Universiti Putra Malaysia, Terengganu.

[83] Malaysia referred to G.H. Balazs, (1994), *Homeward Bound: Satellite Tracking of Hawaiian Green Turtles from Nesting Beaches to Foraging Pastures*, NOAA Technical Memorandum, NMFS-S-SEFSC-341, pp. 205-208 (Green turtles nesting on East Island of the French Frigate Shoals migrated to foraging areas within the 2,400 km span of the Hawaiian Archipelago. The turtles which were tracked by satellite migrated over distances ranging from 830 to 1260 km. The feeding and nesting grounds as well as migratory pathways were confined within the Hawaiian Archipelago); H.C. Liew, E.H. Chan, P. Luschi and F. Papi, (1995), *Satellite Tracking Data on Malaysian Green Turtle Migration*, 9(6), pp. 239-246 (Satellite tracking had demonstrated that green turtles nesting on Redang Island, off the east coast of Peninsular Malaysia, migrated to feeding grounds bordering the South China Sea); A. Meylan, (1995), *Sea Turtle Migration - Evidence from Tag Return*, Biology and Conservation of Sea Turtles, K.A. Bjorndal ed., pp. 91-100 (This study provided numerous examples of range of sea turtle migrations using tag returns. The migrations were restricted to specific regions); B.W. Bowen, (1995), *Tracking Marine Turtles with Genetic Markers*, BioScience, Vol. 45, No. 8, pp. 528-534 (Studies using genetic markers had shown that juvenile loggerhead turtles which fed in the coastal water of Baja California were derived from nesting grounds in Japan and western Australia. The movements of these turtles were trans-Pacific, but were confined to the Pacific Ocean).

[84] Environment Newsletter, The Quarterly Newsletter of the South Pacific Regional Environment Programme (SREP), No. 40, January/March 1995.

[85] Pakistan explained that the source cited by the United States to support its assertion that "[g]reen sea turtles nesting in Florida travelled hundreds of kilometres to their resident foraging areas" noted only that transmitters had been attached to three green turtles and data collected had shown that one of these turtles had remained "just off-shore the lower Florida Keys" and another had been reported "approximately 40 km west of Key West." The conclusion of the study was that "Florida green turtles make use of the extensive seagrass meadows and coral reefs in the Florida Keys as resident foraging habitats." See B.A. Schroeder et. al., (1994), *Post Nesting Movements of Florida Green Turtles: Preliminary Results from Satellite Telemetry*, Proceedings of the Fourteenth Annual Symposium of Sea Turtle Biology and Conservation, p. 90.

seagrass meadows and coral reefs in the Florida Keys as resident foraging habitats".[86] If sea turtles were as highly migratory as claimed by the United States, the exclusion of certain US shrimp fisheries and the shrimp fisheries of other nations from the TEDs requirement would appear to be unjustified. In that regard, the 1990 report cited by the United States noted that "[i]n US Atlantic waters, green turtles occur around the US Virgin Islands and Puerto Rico and from Texas to Massachusetts".[87] In addition, other turtles which occurred in US waters also occurred in waters north of the Virginia-North Carolina border.[88] Further, the report indicated that US shrimp fishing zones extended along the Atlantic coast, including the area north of the Virginia-North Carolina border to and including parts of the Maine coast.[89] Moreover, the report showed that turtle strandings did occur on beaches adjacent to the fishing zones north of the Virginia-North Carolina border.[90]

3.40. **Thailand** noted that while sea turtles did migrate regionally (e.g. between the United States and the Caribbean), they were not defined as "highly migratory" in the Agreement for the Implementation of the Provisions of the UNCLOS relating to the Conservation and Management of Straddling Fish Stocks and Highly Migratory Fish Stocks ( 1995). Further, it was doubtful that any sea turtle ranged from US territorial waters to Thai territorial waters.[91] In fact, the 1990 report cited by the United States noted that the olive ridley (the most abundant species of sea turtle in Thailand), "is very rare in US waters, and its status and future are not in the main, a direct United States responsibility".[92] Thailand was aware of no record of sea turtles from maritime waters

[86] B.A. Schroeder, et. al., (1994), *Post-Nesting Movements of Florida Green Turtles: Preliminary Results from Satellite Telemetry*, Proceedings of the Fourteenth Annual Symposium of Sea Turtle Biology and Conservation, p. 90.

[87] National Research Council, National Academy of Sciences (US), (1990), *Decline of the Sea Turtles: Causes and Prevention*, p. 23.

[88] Pakistan referred to the study by the National Research Council, National Academy of Sciences, (1990), *Decline of the Sea Turtles: Causes and Prevention*, which indicated that: Kemp's Ridley was found "as far north as Long Island and Vineyard Sound, Massachusetts", p. 23; in the Western Hemisphere, the loggerhead was found as far North as Newfoundland, p. 29; "The leatherback is frequently encountered outside the tropics, even in latitudes approaching polar waters. For example, it is often reported in the waters of New England and the Maritime Provinces of Canada, possibly as far north as Baffin Island", p. 39.

[89] The same study (pp. 53 and 83) noted that brown shrimp were found along the north Atlantic and Gulf coasts from Martha's Vineyard to the Yucatan coast and white shrimp ranged along the Atlantic coast from Fire Island, New York to Saint-Lucie Inlet, Florida.

[90] National Research Council, National Academy of Sciences (US), (1990), *Decline of the Sea Turtle: Causes and Prevention*.

[91] Thailand referred to L. Seachrist, (1994), *Sea Turtles Master Migration with Magnetic Memories*, Science No. 264, pp. 661-62, noting that loggerheads born on beaches along the coasts of North and South America migrated to the Sargosso Sea in the middle of the North Atlantic and then returned to their birth places; B.W. Bowen and J.C. Avise, (1994), *Tracking Turtles Through Time*, Natural History, Vol. 103, No. 12, pp. 36-42, showing that South American green turtles migrated from the South American Coast to Ascension Island and then returned to South America and concluding that "green turtles should not be managed as if they were a single, homogeneous population".

[92] See National Research Council, National Academy of Sciences, (1990), *Decline of the Sea Turtles: Causes and Prevention*, p. 41. Thailand noted that before the US Court of Appeals for the Federal Circuit, the US executive branch noted that five species were the subject of Section 609(a) and (b): the loggerhead, the leatherback, the green, the hawksbill, and the Kemp's ridley.

around the North American continent being found in the waters of Southeast Asia. In fact, a tagging study conducted in Thailand demonstrated that juvenile sea turtles remained close to nesting areas. Most sea turtles tagged and released at 3-6 months were recaptured within 8 months of their initial release.[93] Furthermore, Thailand was aware of no doctrine of international law that would permit the United States to regulate unilaterally the use or conservation of a "shared global resource" without the consent of other nations in whose jurisdiction activities took place that could affect that resource. Certainly, the United States had failed to cite any such doctrine or source of law.

3.41. Thailand noted that the United States appeared to argue that Thailand had incomplete jurisdiction with respect to sea turtles that nested on Thai beaches and swam in Thai waters or, at least, that the United States shared jurisdiction with Thailand over such resources. As set forth in the LOS Convention, however, a coastal State had sovereign rights, including the right to establish conservation measures, with respect to natural resources found in territorial sea, contiguous zone and exclusive economic zone. It was the conservation measures adopted by the coastal State that applied within waters subject to the coastal State's sovereignty, not the conservation measures of a State thousands of miles away. If a resource was truly shared between two or more States, those States had a duty to cooperate to resolve resource management issues, but this did not change the fact that it was the conservation policy of the coastal State that applied in its territorial waters and exclusive economic zone. The fact that sea turtles might be found on the high seas was irrelevant. There had been no showing in this case that the measure in question was tailored to prevent the importation of shrimp caught on the high seas as opposed to shrimp caught in Thailand's territorial waters and exclusive economic zone. Moreover, while it was correct that no one State had jurisdiction over the high seas, international law dictated that management of resources found in the high seas should be resolved through cooperative action by interested States. While the United States might establish fishing regulations with respect to its own nationals and flag vessels which operated on the high seas, there was no basis in international law for the United States to determine unilaterally what conservation policies were to be followed by all other nations on the high seas.

3.42. The **United States** reiterated that the very attempt by the complainants to characterize certain sea turtles as "under their jurisdiction" was inaccurate both as a matter of fact and of international law. The same species of sea turtles occurred in the waters subject to the jurisdiction of many nations, as well as on the high seas, an area in which no nation exercised exclusive jurisdiction but in which all nations had a common interest. Moreover, scientific evidence revealed that sea turtles were highly migratory, i.e. that individual sea turtles often swam thousands of kilometres, across vast expanses of open ocean and across dozens of international boundaries. In that regard, the argument made by the complainants that, because few turtles migrated from US waters to their waters, the United States was not entitled to adopt the measures at issue was irrelevant. Sea turtles were a shared global resource, which could only be effectively protected and conserved if trawling-related mortality was reduced throughout their range, by the combined action of many nations.

---

[93] B. Phasuk, (1992), *Biology, Culture, Technique and Conservation of Sea Turtle in Thailand.*

3.43. **India** submitted that the statement that "the same species of sea turtles occur in the waters subject to the jurisdiction of many nations, as well as on the high seas, an area in which no nation exercises exclusive jurisdiction but in which all nations have a common interest" was incorrect. Long distance global migration of sea turtles inhabiting Indian coastal waters had not been established by scientific studies. In fact, the current approach among the experts in this field appeared to be on regional conservation measures to achieve effective sea turtle conservation.[94]

3.44. **Malaysia** agreed that the same species of sea turtles occurred in waters subject to the jurisdiction of many nations. However, the various populations of the same species which occurred in different regions were distinct populations which did not mix and interbreed with populations occurring in other regions, even though they might be of the same species. For instance, the green turtle populations of Malaysia did not migrate to US waters; therefore, the United States did not have jurisdiction over them, even though the same species might occur in the United States.

3.45. The **United States** noted that IUCN, the "experts in this field" referred to by India, had in fact prepared a Global Strategy for the Protection of Marine Turtles in 1995.[95] IUCN was in the process of developing regional strategies as a means to implement its overall global strategy. The recommendations of the regional strategy papers, including the use of TEDs, were very similar to those found in the global strategy paper. As to the tagging studies referred to by India to support the argument that sea turtles migrated only within confined areas, the United States said that these studies only yielded data if a tagged turtle happened to be found later in its life cycle in another location. In other parts of the world, where satellite tracking had been used, sea turtles could be followed continuously and had been found to migrate thousands of kilometres, as confirmed by DNA analyses.[96] Malaysia admitted that sea turtles had been formerly caught by driftnets on the high seas, which reflected their understanding that sea turtles certainly crossed international boundaries in the course of their lives.

3.46. **India** replied that the reference to the IUCN regional strategy established that even the IUCN had not considered it effective to deal with protection and conservation of endangered sea turtles on a global basis, and had evolved towards regional strategies. This reinforced India's point that sea turtles were not highly migratory. Regarding the migratory behaviour of sea turtles, India noted that the United States did not provide specific scientific data regarding endangered sea turtles found in Indian waters, while making general assertions on this issue.

---

[94] IUCN (World Conservatin Union), (1995), *A Marine Turtle Conservation Strategy and Action Plane for the Western Indian Ocean*, p. 14, and IUCN (World Conservation Union), (1997), *A Marine Turtle Conservation Strategy and Action Plan for the Northern Indian Ocean*, p. 11.

[95] IUCN (World Conservation Union), (1995), *A Global Strategy for the Conservation of Marine Turtles*.

[96] B. W. Bowen and J. C. Avise, (1994), *Tracking Turtles Through Time*, Natural History, Vol. 103, No. 12, p. 36.

### 3. *Role of Shrimp Trawl Fishing in Sea Turtle Extinction*

3.47. The **United States** submitted that, as recently as the 19th century, sea turtles were very abundant, with some populations numbering well into the millions.[97] Today, all species of sea turtles faced the danger of extinction, primarily because of human activities. For example:

- In 1946, an estimated 40,000 female Kemp's ridley sea turtles nested on the beach at Rancho Nuevo, Mexico in a single day. By 1988, only an estimated 650 nested at the same site throughout the entire nesting season.[98]
- A 1996 study of the four major Pacific nesting beaches of leatherback turtles, which sustained as much as half of all global nesting for the species, found that the world's largest population of endangered leatherback turtles had collapsed. The decline at one of the sites had progressed at an annual rate of 23 per cent for the last twelve years.[99]
- Hawksbill populations had shrunk 80 per cent or more in the last three generations.[100]
- The Southeast Asian and Indian Ocean regions had experienced particularly alarming declines in sea turtle populations, even with respect to olive ridley sea turtles, which were the most abundant species.
- In Malaysia, the Terengganu stock of nesting olive ridley turtles had shrunk from possibly thousands annually to approximately 20 each year.[101]
- In Thailand, the number of olive ridley turtles from the Andaman Sea that nested each year was now numbered in the tens.[102]
- Other species had also declined dramatically.[103]

---

[97] IUCN (World Conservation Union), (1995), *A Global Strategy for the Conservation of Marine Turtles*, p. 1.

[98] National Research Council, National Academy of Sciences, (1990), *Decline of the Sea Turtles: Causes and Prevention,* p. 26.

[99] S.A. Eckert, et. al., (1996), *Estimation of the Nesting Population Size of the Leatherback Sea Turtle Demochelys coriacea in the Mexican Pacific.*

[100] B. Groombridge and R. Luxmoore, (1989), *The Green Turtle and Hawksbill (Reptilia cheloniidae): World Status, Exploitation and Trade.*

[101] C.J. Limpus, (1995), *Global Overview of the Status of Marine Turtles: A 1995 Viewpoint,* in Biology and Conservation of Sea Turtles, K.A. Bjorndal ed., pp. 605-610.

[102] *Ibid.*

[103] C.S. Kar and S. Bhaskar, (1995), *Status of Sea Turtles in the Eastern Indian Ocean*, in Biology and Conservation of Sea Turtles, K.A. Bjorndal ed., p. 365. The United States noted that some other examples of precipitous declines of sea turtles populations included a 50-80 per cent decline in nesting loggerhead females at eastern Australian rookeries since the mid-1970s and a significant decline in green turtle populations in Indonesia and French Polynesia. C. Limpus and D. Reimer, (1994), *The Loggerhead Sea Turtle, Caretta caretta, in Queensland: A Population in Decline,* in Proceedings of the Australian Marine Turtle Conservation Workshop, Queensland Department of Environment and Heritage and Australian Nature Conservation Agency, R. James ed., pp. 39-60; C.J. Limpus, (1995), *Global Overview of the Status of Marine Turtles: A 1995 Viewpoint,* in Biology and Conservation of Sea Turtles, K.A. Bjorndal ed., pp. 605-609.

3.48. The United States considered that the international community had responded to the imperiled global status of sea turtles. Since 1975, all species of sea turtles had appeared on Appendix I to the CITES. Similarly, all species except the flatback were listed in Appendices I and II to the CMS and in Appendix II of the Protocol Concerning Specially Protected Areas and Wildlife to the Convention for the Protection and Development of the Marine Environment of the Wider Caribbean Region.[104] Since the 1970s, all species of sea turtles that occurred in waters subject to US jurisdiction had been listed as either endangered or threatened under the US Endangered Species Act of 1973.[105]

3.49. Sea turtles faced a variety of threats in both the marine and nesting environments. However, the incidental capture and drowning of sea turtles in shrimp trawl nets had caused the greatest number of human-induced sea turtle deaths, accounting for more deaths than all other human activities combined.[106] For this reason, the Marine Turtle Specialist Group of the IUCN (World Conservation Union) identified reduction of sea turtle mortality in such trawling operations as a priority action item.[107] The United States submitted that, as early as 1982, it was recognized that "shrimp trawlers were considered to capture and drown more sea turtles worldwide than any other form of incidental capture".[108] Illustrative examples of the effects of trawling on these endangered species included:

- A 1994 survey of India's Orissa coast documented 5,000 dead olive ridley sea turtles and concluded that "these deaths were due to accidental capture in trawl nets".[109] Another study similarly concluded that the drowning of the turtles at Gahirmatha, India, during breeding season due to mechanized boats, including trawlers, had become a "major threat" to these species.[110]
- The drastic decline of sea turtles in waters off Thailand, in both the Andaman Sea and the Gulf of Thailand, had resulted in significant part from heavy fishing activities, including trawling.

[104] Protocol Concerning Specially Protected Areas and Wildlife to the Convention for the Protection and Development of the Marine Environment of the Wider Caribbean Region, 24 March 1983, TIAS No. 11085.

[105] Public Law 93-205, 16 U.S.C. 1531 *et. seq.*

[106] National Research Council, National Academy of Sciences, (1990), *Decline of the Sea Turtles: Causes and Prevention*, Washington D.C., pp. 76 and 145.

[107] IUCN (World Conservation Union) Marine Turtle Specialist Group, (1995), *A Global Strategy for the Conservation of Marine Turtles*, p. 8.

[108] H.O. Hillestad et. al., (1982), *Worldwide Incidental Capture of Sea Turtles*, in Biology and Conservation of Sea Turtles, K.A. Bjorndal, pp. 489-495. The United States noted that the incidental take of sea turtles by shrimp trawl vessels had been the largest source of mortality for the Kemp's ridley, the most critically endangered of all sea turtles, and had contributed to the decline and impeded the recovery of the species. National Research Council, National Academy of Sciences, (1990), *Decline of the Sea Turtles: Causes and Prevention*, p. 76.

[109] B.C. Choudhury, (1997), *Country Report: India - Sea Turtle Status, Conservation and Management in India*, p. 2.

[110] P. Mohanty-Hejmadi, (1994), *Biology of the Olive Ridleys of Gahirmatha, Orissa, India,* in Proceedings of the Fourteenth Annual Symposium of Sea Turtle Biology and Conservation, p. 90.

- In Malaysia, the incidental capture of sea turtles in fishing trawls in Terengganu waters had contributed significantly to a catastrophic decline of what had been once the largest nesting sea turtle population in the Malaysian Peninsula.
- Sea turtle researchers from countries in the Northern Indian Ocean region, including India, Pakistan, Malaysia and Bangladesh, had identified incidental capture in trawl nets and other fishing gear as a significant threat to sea turtle populations in the region.
- An analysis of 25 years of loggerhead sea turtle data from Queensland, Australia concluded that "the [prawn] trawling industry has probably been the major contributor to the decline in eastern Australian population numbers".[111]
- In Croatia, trawlers have been identified as the number one source of incidental take, accounting for 70 per cent of the estimated 2,500 sea turtles captured incidentally in Croatian fisheries each year.[112]

3.50. Data from the United States also vividly demonstrated the threat that sea turtles faced from shrimp trawl nets. Before the late 1980s, when the US government first required shrimp trawl vessels to use TEDs, an estimated 5,000 to 50,000 loggerhead turtles and 500 to 5,000 Kemp's ridley turtles drowned in trawl nets pulled by US shrimp vessels each year. Most of these turtles were juveniles and subadults, the age and size classes most critical to the stability and recovery of sea turtle populations.[113] In general, the accidental capture and drowning of sea turtles during fishing had been the major cause of the continuing decline in the United States of these species, despite improved beach protection throughout the 1970s.

3.51. **India** observed that, while the sources referred to by the United States appeared to indicate that shrimp trawling was a major source of sea turtle mortality in waters in and around the continental United States, the United States did not present any evidence indicating that shrimp trawling was the largest source of sea turtle mortality in India. Indeed, the evidence cited by the United States showed the opposite. Specifically, the study referred to by the United States stated that "[a]t Gahirmatha, although trade in turtles and eggs is not there any more, considerable number of turtles are dying due to fishing activities in this area. Even then, if one considers the number of nesting turtles from year to year, it is reasonable to say that the population nesting at Gahirmatha has not been adversely affected by these activities".[114] The study actually noted that the number of olive ridleys nesting at Gahirmatha had increased substantially over the last

[111] C. Limpus and D. Reimer, (1994), *The Loggerhead Sea Turtle, Caretta caretta, in Queensland: A Population in Decline,* in Proceedings of the Australian Marine Turtle Conservation Workshop, Queensland Department of Environment and Heritage and Australian Nature Conservation Agency, R. James ed., pp. 39-60.

[112] B. Lazar and N. Tvrtkovia, (1997), *Results of Marine Turtles Research and Conservation Program in Croatia*, paper presented at the Seventeenth Annual Symposium of Sea Turtle Biology and Conservation.

[113] D.T. Crouse et. al., (1987), *A Stage-based Population Model for Loggerhead Sea Turtles and Implications for Conservation*, Ecology, Vol. 68, pp. 1412-1423.

[114] P. Mohanty-Hejmadi, (1994), *Biology of the Olive Ridleys of Gahirmatha, Orissa, India,* in Proceedings of the Fourteenth Annual Symposium of Sea Turtle Biology and Conservation, p. 90.

ten years. In 1985, a total of 286,000 turtles nested in three batches of mass nesting. By 1991, that number had increased to more than 600,000 and remained constant. Based on these facts, the report concluded that "the Gahirmatha population has attained a stability as [far as] the number of nesting emergences is concerned". Increase in nestings was the factor which the United States pointed to demonstrate that its conservation efforts had yielded encouraging results. Thus, the report demonstrated that the Indian sea turtle population could be sustained without the TEDs requirement contemplated by the United States. Finally, this report indicated that the olive ridley population in India had achieved stability, suggesting that India's current shrimping practices were in accordance with the concept of sustainable development. India further noted that the second study[115] mentioned by the United States - discussing the death of 5,000 olive ridleys in trawling nets -did not distinguish between shrimp trawls and other trawls, and concerned olive ridleys, a species which was not a direct US responsibility. India further submitted that another document produced by the United States noted that the South African loggerhead population had more than doubled since the early 1960s when strong protective measures had been introduced; on the other hand, the United States indicated that only one African country, Nigeria, required TEDS. Thus, the increase in loggerhead population in South Africa was due to conservation measures other than TEDs. Regarding the United States questioning the degree of enforcement of measures currently in place in India, India noted that the effective enforcement of Indian domestic legislation was a matter for India. Moreover, India noted that the US enforcement record with respect to its TEDs programme had been questioned. A Bangkok Post article[116] noted that the "Humane Society alleges that 41 per cent of Texas shrimpers surveyed had violated US regulation to protect sea turtles." Further, undercover investigators stated that 13 of the 32 vessels checked had disabled their TEDs. In response to claims by the Texas Shrimp Association that the report was a hoax and that the US Coast Guard had reported a 96.9 per cent compliance with the law, the article noted that shrimpers knew when Coast Guard inspectors were coming, but "the society's sleuths kept a lower profile."

3.52. **Malaysia** responded that there was no historical record indicating that olive ridleys had nested in the thousands in Malaysia. Neither was there any historical account of the phenomenon of olive ridley *arribadas*[117] occurring in South East Asia. Malaysia further replied that the US conclusion regarding the responsibility of shrimp trawl nets for sea turtles deaths had been reached by the US Academy of Sciences which had estimated that 55,000 turtles drowned annually in US shrimp trawls.[118] While the United States had found that this was the case for the US populations of sea turtles, the same conclusion could not be applied to all sea turtle populations in the

---

[115] B.C. Choudhury, (1997), *Country Report: India - Sea Turtle Status, Conservation and Management in India*, p. 2.

[116] "Troubled Waters", in *Bangkok Post*, 17 April 1997.

[117] *Note*: some species of sea turtles nest in an aggregated manner, i.e. many females gather in the sea near the nesting beach and then emerge to nest in a loosely synchronized manner over several hours. This phenomenon is known as "arribada". (National Research Council, National Academy of Sciences, (1990), *Decline of the Sea Turtles: Causes and Prevention*, Washington D.C., p. 18).

[118] Weber, M., Crouse, D., Irvin, R. and Iudicello, S., (1995), *Delay and Denial: A Political History of Sea Turtles and Shrimp Fishing*, Center for Marine Conservation, p. 12.

world. Moreover, over 90 per cent of the deaths referred to concerned loggerhead turtles[119] which were not found in Malaysia. In other parts of the world, other causes of mortality could take precedence, e.g. harvesting and consumption of turtle eggs or direct capture of turtles for consumption. Therefore, what might be true for the United States could not be extrapolated to other countries. The statement that shrimp trawlers killed more than other forms of incidental capture[120] did not apply to Asia, but was based on studies made in Australia, South and Central America and North America. The study in question also reported that "very little has been reported on the incidental capture of sea turtles" on African and Indian Ocean waters.[121] Moreover, a later publication identified fishing trawl, and not shrimp trawl, as the highest cause of olive ridley mortality in India.[122]

3.53. Malaysia did not deny that the incidental captures of sea turtles in fishing gear in Terengganu waters had contributed significantly to the decline of sea turtles. A study conducted in 1984 showed that fishing gear (trawlnets, i.e. mainly fish trawls and not shrimp trawls, driftnets and bottom longlines) contributed significantly to the mortality of turtles in the waters of Terengganu.[123] Based on estimates, some 1,164 turtles had been caught by licensed fishing vessels in Terengganu in 1984-1985. In a more recent analysis of the leatherback population decline[124], two periods of markedly sharp declines were identified, i.e. from 1972-1974 and from 1978-1980. The 1972-74 decline was attributed to the rapid development of the fishing industry in Terengganu in the early 70's, while the decline in the latter period, 1978-80 was attributed to the introduction of the Japanese high seas squid driftnet fishery of the North Pacific in 1978. Malaysian gear responsible for turtle mortalities in Terengganu were identified as trawlnets (fish trawls), driftnets (large-meshed nets for capture of rays), and sunken fish traps. In Terengganu, the dramatic decline of leatherback sea turtles was due to a combination of factors, of which commercial egg collection was a major factor. However, in the last 10 years the Terengganu State Government had intensified conservation efforts of sea turtles[125], as described in paragraph 3.29. Malaysia further submitted that of the five species of sea turtles sought to be protected under Section 609, the three species found in US waters which were also found in Malaysia

---

119 T.A. Henwood and W.E. Stuntz, (1987), *Analysis of Sea Turtle Captures and Mortalities During Commercial Shrimp Trawling*, Fishery Bulletin Vol. 85, No. 4, pp. 813-817.

120 H.O. Hillestad et. al., (1982), *Worldwide Incidental Capture of Sea Turtles*, in Biology and Conservation of Sea Turtles, K.A. Bjorndal ed., pp. 489-495.

121 *Ibid.*

122 B. Pandav, B.C. Choudhury, C.S. Kar, (1994), *Olive Ridley Sea Turtle (Lepidochelys olivacea) and its Nesting Habitats along the Orissa Coast, India: A Status Survey*, Wildlife Institute of India. Malaysia also noted that olive ridley did not come under the scope of Section 609.

123 E.H. Chan, H.C. Liew. and A.G. Mazlan, (1988), *The incidental capture of sea turtles in fishing gear in Terengganu, Malaysia*, Biological Conservation, Vol. 43, pp. 1-7. Malaysia noted that Table 2 of this paper very clearly showed that incidental captures occurred from March to September, when fish and not shrimp were targeted, but no reports were made of captures between October to February, i.e. during the shrimping season.

124 E.H. Chan and H.C. Liew, (1996), *Decline of the leatherback population in Terengganu, Malaysia, 1956-1995*, Chelonian Conservation and Biology, Vol.2, No. 2, pp. 196-203.

125 E.H. Chan, (1991), *Sea Turtles*, in The State of Nature Conservation in Malaysia, R. Kiew ed., Malaysian Nature Society, Kuala Lumpur, pp. 120-134.

were the green, leatherback and hawksbill turtles. None of these three species fed on shrimps. Two other species - loggerhead and Kemp's ridley - were found in the United States but not in Malaysia. Both were the major species occurring in the United States and accounted for over 95 per cent of the turtle mortalities in shrimp trawl in the United States[126]; they fed on shrimps, i.e. in areas which were shrimp trawling grounds, thus accounting for their vulnerability in shrimp trawls. The Malaysian species did not have feeding grounds coinciding with shrimping grounds. Thus, unlike the situation in the United States, where shrimp trawl fisheries took place in areas where sea turtles occurred, in Malaysia trawl fishing did not coincide with areas where sea turtles occurred. Malaysia also noted that loggerhead turtles were at risk in the groundfish otter-trawl fishery in the US waters in the Gulf of Maine and the mid-Atlantic Ocean, and queried whether TEDs were required in this particular fishery.

3.54. **Pakistan** argued that, as a member of CITES, it recognized that sea turtles were threatened with extinction. However, the fact that sea turtles were endangered did not justify the US measures at issue. Pakistan was in the best position to determine the measures to be taken to protect sea turtles within Pakistani jurisdiction while taking into consideration the concept of sustainable development and Pakistan's needs and concerns based upon its level of economic development. In Pakistan, 100 per cent of wild harvested shrimp was done using manual means, and not with large or sophisticated nets. Thus, turtles were not in danger of being caught. Pakistan argued that the report cited by the United States concluding that shrimp trawl fishing had caused the "greatest number of human-induced sea turtle deaths"[127] was generally based on studies associated with US sea turtle population. Indeed, the report noted that "by far the most important source of deaths was the incidental capture of turtles (especially loggerheads and Kemp's ridleys) in shrimp trawling". As already noted, the two species common to Pakistan were the green and olive ridley. While this report indicated that shrimp trawling in the United States was a serious threat to US sea turtle populations, the United States provided no evidence concerning the level of incidental capture of sea turtles associated with shrimp trawling in Pakistan. Pakistan did not deny that one of the threats to sea turtles was accidental capture in fishing nets.[128] However, this did not suggest that shrimp trawling was the source of the greatest number of human-induced deaths in Pakistani fisheries. Actually, another report cited by the United States noted, with respect to shrimp trawlers in the African and Indian Ocean waters: "very little has been reported on the incidental capture of sea turtles by trawlers in this area".[129]

3.55. Pakistan noted that a document submitted by the United States included the following as one of the action issues: "[i]ncomplete data on accidental mortality in fishing gear, including trawl nets, long lines, drift nets, purse seines, gill nets, and other fishing methods"; sub-items under this issue included "[a]ssess rates of sea turtle mortality in all types of fishing gear and fishing practices used in the NIO" and

[126] T.A. Henwood and W.E. Stuntz, (1987), *Analysis of Sea Turtle Captures and Mortalities During Commercial Fishing Shrimp Trawling*, in Fishery Bulletin, Vol. 85, No. 4, pp. 813-817.

[127] National Research Council, National Academy of Sciences, (1990), *Decline of the Sea Turtles: Causes and Prevention*, Washington D.C.

[128] WWF-Pakistan and Sindh Wildlife Department, *Marine Turtles of Pakistan*.

[129] H.O. Hillestad et. al., (1982), *Worldwide Incidental Capture of Sea Turtles*, Biology and Conservation of Sea Turtles, K.A. Bjorndal ed., pp. 489-495.

"[i]dentify levels of mortality that sea turtle populations can sustain".[130] These statements made clear that the greatest human-induced cause of sea turtle mortality in the Northern Indian Ocean was unknown. It was then difficult to understand how the US action were in accordance with the preamble of the WTO Agreement when the level of incidental take consistent with the principle of sustainable development was unknown. Pakistan further noted that the statement contained in the same document ("promote use of sea turtle excluder devices (TEDs) from trawl fisheries where necessary"[131]), could hardly be said to be an endorsement of the US position that TEDs must be used by all trawls, except those operating in cold-water shrimp fisheries. Notwithstanding these facts, the United States, through the imposition of its embargo, would have Pakistan direct its limited resources first to the shrimp fishery before determining whether it would be better for the local sea turtle population to direct resources elsewhere. Pakistan also noted that IUCN listed 6 areas in which mortality should be reduced but did not suggest that reduction of mortality due to shrimp trawl had to be given priority over other causes of sea turtle deaths; Pakistan pointed out that IUCN also listed as a priority action item the facilitation of "integrated management through regional and international cooperation and coordination".[132]

3.56. **Thailand** submitted that other forms of fishing and fishing for other species were, in some places, more directly related to incidental sea turtle deaths. For example, the 1990 report cited by the United States, noted that turtle strandings increased in North Carolina when flounder trawling was active.[133] In fact, in implementing regulations requiring the use of TEDs for the Virginia and North Carolina summer flounder bottom trawl fishery, the responsible US government agency noted that "bottom trawl nets fished without TEDs for summer flounder can capture sea turtles at a rate comparable with that of shrimp trawl nets fished without TEDs along the southern US Atlantic coast".[134] The United States apparently based its regulations on threats that existed in and near the United States and then generalized those threats to the rest of the world. However, in Thailand, shrimp trawl fisheries were not the major source of anthropogenic threats to sea turtles. In Australia as well, a 1990 study had concluded that trawl-induced turtle drowning did not represent an immediate problem for turtle populations.[135] More recent studies indicated that trawl-induced mortality of marine turtles in fisheries in Australia, Asia and Oceania was likely to be of less impact on sea

[130] IUCN (World Conservation Union), (1997), *A Marine Turtle Conservation Stragegy and Action Plan for the Northern Indian Ocean*, p. 10.

[131] *Ibid.*, p. 11.

[132] IUCN (World Conservation Union), (1995), *A Global Stategy for the Conservation of Marine Turtles*, pp. 8-9.

[133] National Research Council, National Academy of Sciences, (1990), *Decline of the Sea Turtles: Causes and Prevention,* Washington D.C., p. 76.

[134] Sea Turtle Conservation; Restrictions Applicable to Fishery Activities; Summer Flounder Fishery-Sea Turtle Protection Area, 61 Fed. Reg. 1846 (24 January 1996).

[135] I.R. Pioner, R.C. Buckworth and A.N.M. Harris, (1990), *Incidental Capture and Mortality of Sea Turtles in Australia's Northern Prawn Fishery*, in Australian Journal of Marine and Freshwater Research, Vol. 41, pp. 97-110.

turtle populations than other anthropogenic threats.[136] Thus, it was untrue that application of Section 609 to all shrimp exporting nations was necessary to prevent the extinction of sea turtles or that this measure was closely tailored to local conditions. In fact, this measure ignored significant differences in anthropogenic threats to sea turtles in different regions of the world. The statement that US shrimp fishermen were required to harvest shrimp in a manner that was safe for sea turtles was also incorrect. Presently, US shrimpers were permitted to use soft TEDs even though recent testing by the US government had found such TEDs ineffective at excluding turtles.[137]

3.57. Thailand submitted that, while the United States had demonstrated that shrimp trawling was the greatest human-induced threat to the US sea turtle population, it did not show that shrimp trawling was the greatest human-induced threat to sea turtle populations in other regions of the world, including Thailand and the Australo-Pacific region. With regard to Thailand, the sources cited by the United States generally seemed to concur that egg harvest was or had been the single, greatest human-induced threat to Thailand's sea turtle population. Other threats included loss of nesting beaches to development, marine pollution, and fishing for both fish and shrimp by a variety of means. A 30-year *Night-Trawled Monitoring Surveys* uncovered no evidence of incidental turtle deaths in shrimp trawl fisheries conducted in Thai waters or by Thai vessels.[138] Since the reporting of incidental taking of sea turtles in shrimp trawl operations had become mandatory in Thailand, there had been no reported instances of incidental takings. A report cited by the United States noted that "[t]rawling is concentrated primarily in the relatively shallow waters near shore in both temperate and tropical zones. Many of the most intensively trawled waters are adjacent to major sea turtle nesting beaches or feeding grounds".[139] However, as noted in *Status of Marine Turtles in Thailand*, the Fisheries Act of 1972 prohibited commercial fishing in Thai waters within 3 kilometres of the coastline.[140] Furthermore, most sea turtles in Thailand inhabited coral reefs and grassy areas where trawling operations were impractical. This could be the reason why there was no direct evidence of incidental takings of sea turtles in shrimp trawl operations in Thailand. On information and belief, gill netting near nesting areas, egg poaching, long-line hook fishing and fishing for other fish species had historically constituted more serious anthropogenic threats to sea turtles in Thai waters than shrimp trawl fisheries[141] (gill netting near nesting areas was now banned in

---

[136] Commonwealth Scientific and Industrial Research Organization (CSIRO), Division of Fisheries, (1996), Public Nomination of Prawn Trawling as a Key Threatening Process, Submission to Endangered Species Scientific Committee.

[137] Sea Turtle Conservation; Revisions to Sea Turtle Conservation Requirements; Restrictions to Shrimp Trawling Activities, 61 Fed. Reg. 66, 933 (19 December 1996).

[138] *The Night-Trawled Monitoring Surveys During 1967-1996*, (1997), Marine Fisheries Division, Department of Fisheries.

[139] H.O. Hillestad et. al., (1982), *Worldwide Incidental Capture of Sea Turtles*, in Biology and Conservation of Sea Turtles, K.A. Bjorndal ed., p. 491.

[140] S. Chantrapoornsyl, (1997), *Status of Marine Turtles in Thailand*, Phuket Marine Biological Center, p. 6.

[141] Bhatiyasevi et. al., (1997), *Night Trawled Monitoring Surveys*; S. Chantrapoornsyl, (1997), *Status of Marine Turtles in Thailand*, Phuket Marine Biological Center, p. 6; C. Limpus, (1995), *Global Overview of the Status of Marine Turtles: A 1995 Viewpoint*, Queensland Department of Environment and Heritage. Thailand noted that, although the Chantrapornsyl study stated that

Thailand, egg poaching had been eliminated in sanctuary areas but remained a problem elsewhere). Even the United States appeared to concede that other forms of fishing, besides shrimping, could have been a cause of the decline in turtle populations in Thai waters since the 1950's, when attributing the decline to "heavy fishing activities, including trawling". For instance, a document cited by the United States, which noted declines in the stock of both olive ridleys and leatherbacks in the Andaman Sea area of western Thailand, clearly stated that the observed declines were a result of long-term excessive egg harvest.[142] Another document exhibited by the United States revealed that of the four separate locations studied along Thailand's west coast, trawling was noted as a factor in only one area, and only in conjunction with two other causes of sea turtle mortality: egg collection and gill nets. In the other three areas, the major human-induced threat to sea turtles was egg poaching, with gill nets and long lines identified as the fishing gear which posed additional threats.[143] A third study produced by the United States concluded that declines in sea turtle populations in the areas studied were likely to be due to excessive egg collection and adult mortality in fishing gear, but did not identify shrimp trawls as a primary source of mortality.[144] The US measures, therefore, failed to consider that in other nations sustenance harvesting of eggs and turtles, which was not a factor in the United States, might be the greatest human threat to sea turtle life and longevity.

3.58. Regarding India, the **United States** noted that five different species of sea turtles were reported to nest on Indian beaches. Scientific literature dating back two decades found that for each of these species, "their populations are believed to be declining steadily everywhere".[145] More recently, the Northern Indian Ocean Sea Turtle Workshop, held in Bhubaneswar, India in January 1997, adopted "A Marine Turtle Conservation Strategy and Action Plan for the Northern Indian Ocean". That document, in addition to recommending the use of TEDs in trawl fisheries where necessary[146], confirmed the "alarming decrease" in each of the nesting populations of species of sea turtles in question:

> "Historically, the Northern Indian Ocean (NIO) has supported large populations of sea turtles ... Although the world's largest nesting

trawling was one cause of incidental sea turtle deaths in some identified areas of Thailand, it did not distinguish between shrimp trawling and other forms of fish trawling. The *Night Trawled Monitoring Survey* was the only survey to specifically identify the incidence of sea turtle mortality arising from shrimp trawling and it found none. Moreover, in several areas of Thailand, trawling was not even mentioned by the Chantrapornsyl study as a cause of significant sea turtle mortality. The Limpus study mentionned egg poaching as a the single cause of a significant decline in nesting olive ridley sea turtles in the Andaman Sea.

142 C.J. Limpus, (1995), *Global Overview of the Status of Marine Turtles: A 1995 Viewpoint*, Biology and Conservation of Sea Turtles, K.A Bjorndal ed., pp. 606-609.

143 S. Chantrapoornsyl, (1997), *Status of Marine Turtles in Thailand*, Phuket Marine Biological Center.

144 E. Stuart and M. Carlin, (1994), *Conservation of Sea Turtles at Two National Parks on the Andaman Sea Coast of Thailand*, Marine Turtle Newsletter, No. 67.

145 C.S. Kar and S. Bhaskar (1995), *Status of Sea Turtles in the Eastern Indian Ocean*, in Biology and Conservation of Sea Turtles, K.A. Bjorndal ed., p. 365.

146 IUCN (World Conservation Union), (1997), *A Marine Turtle Conservation Strategy and Action Plan for the Northern Indian Ocean*, p. 11.

population of two species, the loggerheads of Oman and the olive ridleys of Gahirmatha, India, are found in the NIO, once abundant populations of hawksbill, leatherback and green turtles have decreased alarmingly in most areas ... Even the olive ridleys nesting at Gahirmatha are sustaining significant fishing-related mortality, and olive ridleys elsewhere are in serious decline. As fishing activities continue to increase rapidly in the Indian Ocean, these interactions are expected to increase".[147]

3.59. Thus, if current fishing practices and patterns continued, even the olive ridley population nesting at Gahirmatha was not safe. Several scientific reports supported this conclusion. A report prepared by Dr. Mohanty-Hejmadi of Uktal University in Bhubaneswar, India concluded that the drowning of sea turtles at Gahirmatha during breeding season due to mechanized boats, including trawlers, had become a "major threat" to these species.[148] Further evidence of the threat to the olive ridleys of Gahirmatha from trawl fisheries was provided in the *Country Report: India - Sea Turtle Status, Conservation and Management in India*: "[n]ear shore mechanized fishing results in the mortality of [a] large number of sea turtles along the Indian coast. More than 5,000 dead olive ridley sea turtles were counted along the 480 km long Orissa coast during a six month survey in 1994. These deaths were due to accidental capture in trawl nets".[149] Even more troubling scientific evidence had emerged. As stated by an authority on sea turtle biology, ecology, and conservation:

"Female [olive ridley sea turtles] generally emerge on Gahirmatha Beach twice during the nesting season. Recent estimates of the size of this nesting aggregation have been as high as 600,000 turtles. In the most recent nesting season (December 1996 through March 1997), there were no large mass emergences and only an estimated 20,000-40,000 turtles emerged to nest on Gahirmatha.

"A declining trend in the Indian Ocean olive ridley nesting population appears imminent and is likely due to the indirect capture and mortality of turtles in fisheries, particularly the shrimp fishery (bottom trawling from mechanized vessels) ... For the past 10 years, researchers working on the Orissa coast have documented annually hundreds to thousands of turtle corpses stranded on beaches during the reproductive season...

[147] IUCN (World Conservation Union), (1997), *A Marine Turtle Conservation Strategy and Action Plan for the Northern Indian Ocean*, p. 1.

[148] P. Mohanty-Hejmadi, (1994), *Biology of the Olive Ridleys of Gahirmatha, Orissa, India*, in Proceedings of the Fourteenth Annual Symposium of Sea Turtle Biology and Conservation, p. 90. The United States indicated that the same author was one of the principal organizers of the TEDs workshop held in Paradeep and had signed the recommendations adopted at that workshop that "the use of TEDs should be made mandatory and a proper and effective monitoring system developed" in areas where shrimp trawling was permitted (*Recommendations of the Training-Cum Demonstration Workshop on Turtle Excluder Device (TED)*, held at Paradeep, Orissa, 11-14 November 1996.

[149] B.C. Choudhury, (1997), *Country Report: India - Sea Turtle Status, Conservation and Management in India*, p. 2.

"Researchers have noted a temporal and spatial correspondence between shrimp fishing activity and sea turtle strandings, demonstrating a correspondence between the two events.

"If shrimp fishing overlaps with areas in which olive ridley turtles are densely aggregated, thousands of turtles may be captured and killed by only a few vessels in a very short time period. The likelihood of this scenario is increasing as India expands its commercial shrimp fishery by building jetties and harbours for mechanized vessels along its east coast.

"Ironically, one of the ports recently built is located adjacent to Gahirmatha Beach".[150]

3.60. Finally, the 1995 report on the *Global Overview of the Status of Marine Turtles* cited above found that the nesting population of olive ridleys in Orissa had "in recent times been under threat of incidental mortality" particularly from gillnet and trawl fisheries. Moreover, that report concluded, "there are no demonstrated recovering populations" of olive ridleys anywhere, including in India".[151] In short, all species of sea turtles nesting on Indian beaches, including the olive ridley, had declined alarmingly. All species, including the olive ridley population that nested at Gahirmatha were in danger from incidental mortality in shrimp trawl nets; far from improving the protection of this endangered species, India was building fishing ports to support more shrimp trawling without TEDs, including a port adjacent to Gahirmatha Beach. Responsible Indian officials understood the problem and agreed that use of TEDs was the best and only way to conserve sea turtles.[152]

3.61. In an answer to a question by India regarding the effectiveness of TEDs in protecting sea turtles in Indian waters, the United States indicated that it had tested the effectiveness of TEDs in all types of fishing environments and conditions. While there could be some differences in bottom conditions, such as variances in the nature and amount of natural debris, and weather conditions may vary, shrimp trawling was essentially the same throughout the world. The nets were set, trawled along the bottom and hauled in the same manner. All shrimp trawl net were very fine meshed in order to capture and retain small fisheries resources such as shrimp. They all had extremely high catch rates of non-target species, or bycatch, because a shrimp trawl would capture and retain every creature it came into contact with, unless that trawl net was fitted with a TED or other bycatch reduction device. Likewise, interactions between shrimp trawls and sea turtles were the same throughout the world. Sea turtles were found in the same general habitats and fed on the same types of food throughout the world. Their feeding

---

150 Affidavit of Pamela Plotkin, Ph.D., 22 July 1997, document submitted by the United States to the Panel, paragraphs 5-7. The United States noted that Dr. Pamela Plotkin had spent the past 15 years on research focused on the biology, ecology and conservation of sea turtles, and had worked during the last 3 years in India in collaboration with Indian academic, non-governmental and government scientists and with government resource managers responsible for the conservation of sea turtles in Indian waters. *Ibid.*, paragraphs 2-3.

151 C.J. Limpus, (1995), *Global Overview of the Status of Marine Turtles: A 1995 Viewpoint*, in Biology and Conservation of Sea Turtles, K.A. Bjorndal ed., p. 606.

152 Affidavit of Pamela Plotkin, Ph.D., 22 July 1997, document submitted by the United States to the Panel, paragraph 8.

habits and habitats put them in the direct path of shrimp trawls where they were captured. The United States had tested and towed several trawl nets equipped with TEDs when it had conducted training workshops in Cuttack, Orissa, in November 1996 and Kochi, Kerala, in May 1997. These trawl nets had been towed along side "naked nets" or nets not equipped with TEDs to compare shrimp catch and rates of shrimp loss. The TEDs had been found to be as effective as when towed in US waters.

3.62. Regarding Malaysia, the United States submitted that the *Country Report for Malaysia* revealed that, while the peak sea turtle nesting season in Malaysia occurred during August-October in Sabah and during June-July in Terengganu, Sarawak and most of the other states, in fact sea turtle nesting in Malaysia occurred "throughout the year".[153] The same report provided evidence that sea turtles did in fact remain in Malaysian waters after nesting: "observations of green turtles feeding over sea-grass beds have been reported along the west coast of Sabah, near Sandakan and at Sipadan Island, Sabah".[154] The scientific literature identified trawling as a significant source of mortality for sea turtles in Malaysian waters. A document submitted by Malaysia discussed the high rates of incidental sea turtle capture in Malaysia's shrimp fishery.[155] In interviews with Malaysian fishermen on the subject of incidental capture of sea turtles in fishing gear in Terengganu, 68 per cent of the fishermen who used trawl nets had reported incidental captures of sea turtles. The interviewer estimated that Malaysian trawlers had the potential to capture an average of 742 sea turtles per year. Moreover, the sea turtles captured in trawl nets almost always drowned before they could be released. The report summarizing these interviews noted, as the United States had pointed out, that "turtles caught in trawls have very little chance of survival because the nets are dragged for long hours along the sea bottom". The interviews also revealed that the fishermen caught sea turtles at different times of the year, calling into question any purported effectiveness of seasonal prohibitions on trawling that Malaysia claimed to have instituted. Given the precipitous decline in sea turtle populations in Malaysia, this level of incidental take represented a serious threat to the continued existence of sea turtles in Malaysia. Most importantly, these interviews showed that "the incidental capture of sea turtles in fishing gear in Terengganu waters is common, and contributes significantly to the mortality of sea turtles. ... The figures are alarmingly high when compared with the number of nestings recorded for each species, and it can be seen that fishing nets have the potential of quickly decimating the current populations of sea turtles".[156]

---

[153] *Country Report for Malaysia*, presented at the Northern Indian Ocean Sea Turtle Workshop and Strategic Planning Session 13-18 January 1997 in Bhubaneswar, Orissa, India, p. 4.

[154] *Ibid.*, p. 3.

[155] M.S. Suliansa, et. al., (1996), *Impact of Fishery Related Activities on Sea Turtles*, paper presented at the National Seminar/Workshop on Marine Turtle and Terrapin Management, 22-23 October 1996, Cherating, Malaysia.

[156] E.H. Chan et. al, (1988), *The Incidental Capture of Sea Turtles in Fishing Gear in Terengganu, Malaysia*, Biological Conservation, No. 43, pp. 1-7. The United States also referred to J.A. Mortimer, (1990), *Marine Turtle Conservation in Malaysia,* Proceedings of the Tenth Annual Symposium of Sea Turtle Biology and Conservation, p. 21; S.K. Tow and E. Moll, (1995), *Status and Conservation of Estuarine and Sea Turtles in West Malaysian Waters*, Biology and Conservation of Sea Turtles, K.A. Bjorndal ed., pp. 339-347; H.C. Liew, (1997), *Country Report for Malaysia*, paper presented at the Norther Indian Ocean Sea Turtle Workshop and Strategic Planning Session, Bhubans-

3.63. The United States believed, therefore, there was evidence that Malaysia had not, as it claimed, effectively prevented trawling in certain areas during certain periods of the year. A study had found that while fishing activities were reduced between October and February, some prawn trawling occurred during this period. The same study also reported that incidental capture of turtles was reported from March through September with greater numbers occurring April through July, months coinciding with the nesting season.[157] 1992 Malaysia Fisheries Statistics published by the Malaysia Department of Fisheries demonstrated that prawns were landed in Malaysia every month of the year, indicating that there was shrimp trawling year round in Malaysian waters. Even assuming that Malaysia had effectively prevented trawling during certain periods of the year, sea turtles nested throughout the year on Malaysian beaches and on beaches of other countries throughout the region.[158] These sea turtles were subject to incidental mortality in trawl nets whenever they swam in waters near the Malaysian nesting beaches.[159] Finally, sea turtles did not, as Malaysia claimed, immediately leave Malaysian waters after nesting. Rather, many remained in these waters where, again, they were subject to incidental mortality in trawl nets. Other species of sea turtles, besides green sea turtles, which had distinct nesting seasons were also at risk of being accidentally captured in shrimp trawl in Malaysian waters. Coastal waters provided habitat that supported immature sea turtles and even some adults that stayed in waters close to shore and did not migrate back to feeding grounds. Malaysia itself had admitted to estimates of approximately 1,000 annual sea turtles mortalities from incidental capture in fishing gear. Finally, on only the second day of the tests in Malaysia, a TED-equipped trawl captured a "mature hawksbill turtle", demonstrating the likelihood that shrimp trawl nets in Malaysia were capturing sea turtles regularly.[160]

3.64. The United States disagreed with Malaysia's premise that sea turtles were being killed by the nets of fish trawlers as opposed to shrimp trawlers. The trawl gear commonly used to harvest shrimp in the United States and in the complainants' waters - namely otter trawls - also caught different species of fish, other marine life (such as sea turtles), debris and virtually any other matter with which it came in contact. Other types of fishing gear also killed sea turtles, but on a scale that paled in comparison to the incidental mortality of sea turtles in shrimp trawl nets. The US National Academy of

---

eswar, Orissa, India, 13-18 January 1997, p. 5 ("Sightings and strandings of dead turtles along the Malaysian coast still occur, many with clear indications that they had entangled in nets and ropes from fishing gears. Though some stranding records are available, they are generally incomplete and largely underestimate the number of turtles acutally killed in fishing gears").

[157] E.H. Chan, H.C. Liew and A.G. Mazlan, (1987), *The Incidental Capture of Sea Turtles in Fishing Gear in Terengganu, Malaysia,*Fisheries and Marine Science Center, Universiti Pertanian Malaysia.

[158] H.C. Liew, (1997), *Country Report for Malaysia*, paper presented at the Northern Indian Ocean Sea Turtle Workshop and Strategic Planning Session, Bhubanseswar, Orissa, India, 13-18 January 1997, p. 3.

[159] The United States noted that the "time and area closures" Malaysia claimed to have instituted were, in any event, of doubtful utility in protecting sea turtles. See Statement of Deborah Crouse, Ph.D., 23 July 1997, paragraph 14 ("time and area closure are also ineffective since closures only protect the large juvenile or adult turtles while they are in the area enclosed, or during the time when the shrimping is banned and not at other times or places").

[160] *Ibid.*, p. 9.

Sciences comprehensive analysis of the issue had showed that the incidental mortality of sea turtles in shrimp trawl nets was the greatest human-induced threat to sea turtles, greater than all other human-induced causes combined. As early as 1982, it had also been recognized that shrimp trawlers killed more sea turtles than any other form of fishing gear. Regarding Malaysia's claim that sea turtles were not at risk from shrimp trawl in its waters because they did not have species that ate shrimp, the United States noted that olive ridley did eat shrimp. More importantly, this claim revealed a fundamental misunderstanding about the relationship of sea turtles and shrimp fisheries. Sea turtles were caught in shrimp trawl nets because they were found in the same warm water habitats as shrimp, not because they ate shrimp. This was true of all species of sea turtles.

3.65. Regarding Pakistan, the United States responded that the method by which Pakistani fishermen retrieved their shrimp trawl nets did not protect sea turtles. The longer a trawl net remained in the water, the more it would fill and the heavier it would become. Generally speaking, fishermen who pulled in their nets by hand had to do so more frequently than those who used mechanical devices (such as winches) to pull in their nets, because such mechanical devices lent more power. However, where large crews worked together on a single vessel, their combined strength allowed them to tow their nets as long as vessels with mechanical devices for net retrieval. Trawl nets that fishermen retrieved by hand were no different from trawl nets that were retrieved by mechanical means with respect to the likelihood that they would catch sea turtles. However, the longer the nets remained in the water, the more likely it was that sea turtles caught in the nets would drown. A comprehensive study issued by the US National Academy of Sciences had found that "the mortality of sea turtles caught in shrimp trawls increases markedly for tow times greater than 60 minutes".[161] Vessels with small crews who had to pull in their nets by hand at least once per hour could release captured sea turtles before they drowned. Such vessels thus represented a markedly lower threat to sea turtles than either vessels with mechanical devices for net retrieval or vessels with large crews who could retrieve their nets that were towed for more than one hour. Pakistan used shrimp trawl vessels with very large crews that were capable of towing their nets for periods far in excess of one hour. At the Northern Indian Ocean Sea Turtle Workshop in January 1997, Fehmida Firdous, the Project Officer of Pakistan's Sindh Wildlife Department, reported that her country had thousands of vessels trawling with very large nets that remained in the water for 2 hours. These vessels therefore posed as great a danger to sea turtles as vessels with nets that were retrieved by mechanical means. Indeed, Ms. Firdous stated at that Workshop that Pakistani fishermen admitted that sea turtles were caught and drowned in those nets. She identified incidental mortality in shrimp trawl nets as a significant threat to Pakistan's sea turtle populations. The only known way to avoid this danger was through the use of TEDs.

3.66. The United States declared that *The Night-Trawled Monitoring Surveys 1967-1996* referred to by Thailand did not demonstrate that there had been no observed incidental sea turtle captures or mortalities in connection with shrimp trawl fishing in

[161] National Research Council, National Academy of Sciences, (1990), *The Decline of Sea Turtles: Causes and Prevention*, Washington D.C., p. 145.

Thailand. Rather, this document apparently had not been designed to provide the information upon which Thailand relied in this case: it had collected data only on the target catch (shrimp) and the bycatch of other "edible marine resources", including fish, invertebrates and cephalopods. The *Monitoring Surveys* did not provide data on the bycatch of "non-edible marine resources" in shrimp trawling. Since sea turtles were not eaten in Thailand, they would be considered "non-edible marine resources", and thus outside the scope of the surveys.[162] The otter trawls used in Thailand, as described in the *Monitoring Surveys*, were an extremely non-selective type of fishing gear. The mesh of these nets was extraordinarily small, so as to retain animals as small as shrimp. The *Monitoring Surveys* demonstrated just how non-selective this gear was: the bycatch of "trash fish" was reported as 67 per cent of the catch in the Gulf of Thailand and 43 per cent in the Andaman Sea. It was simply inconceivable that such gear would not also catch sea turtles when used at times and in areas where sea turtles occurred. And, in fact, the data showed that sea turtles did occur at the same time and in the same areas as such gear was used by Thai vessels. Available scientific studies showed conclusively that, at least until Thailand adopted a TEDs programme, sea turtles were being drowned in shrimp trawl nets in Thai waters. The *Status of Marine Turtles in Thailand* study found that "the main threat to sea turtles" in the Prathong Island area of Thailand was "the heavy fishing activities, trawling and gill nets".[163] Similarly, the study commissioned by Thailand's Office of Natural Resource Conservation specified that the "indirect take in fishing gear (e.g. trawlers, driftnets, purse seines) also plays a significant role" in the threat to sea turtle survival in Thailand[164], while another scientific analysis reported that the "dramatic decline in the number of turtles nesting" in two national parks in Thailand was due, in part, to "high adult mortality in fishing gear offshore".[165] Perhaps the most revealing evidence, however, was provided by Thai fishermen themselves. Interviews conducted with these fishermen by an independent researcher testified to the "drastic deterioration" of the sea turtle's situation in Thailand and the destruction wrought by trawl vessels: "[t]he large number of trawler boats fishing too close to shore ... sweep away all the marine life of all sizes including sea turtles".[166] During a TEDs training workshop held by the United States Government in Songkla, Thailand, Thai fishermen also admitted to officials of the US National Marine Fisheries Services that they caught sea turtles in their trawl nets. The United States

[162] The United States noted that the "Abstract" to the Monitoring Surveys, which appear in a different type-face from the rest of the study, contained the following final sentence: "Besides, the monitoring surveys at night-time never obtain any sea turtle in the catch". The United States noted that this sentence bore no relationship either to the remainder of the paragraph in which it appeared or to the document as a whole.

[163] S. Chantrapoornsyl, (1997), *Status of Marine Turtles in Thailand*, Phuket Marine Biological Center, p. 5.

[164] S. Settle, (1995), *Status of Nesting Populations of Sea Turtles in Thailand and Their Conservation*, in Marine Turtle Newsletter, No. 68, p. 9.

[165] E. Stuart and M. Cartin, (1995), *Conservation of Sea Turtles at Two National Parks on the Andaman Sea Coast of Thailand*, in Marine Turtle Newsletter, No. 67, p. 6.

[166] G. Hill, (1992), *The Sustainable Sea Turtle*, in Marine Turtle Newsletter, No. 58, p. 3. According to the United States, this publication also made clear that sea turtles were found in the "open sea" in Thailand, thus refuting a claim made by Thailand that sea turtles were found only in "coral reefs and grassy areas."

concluded scientific evidence showed that shrimp trawling killed alarming numbers of sea turtles in the complainants' waters, as it did everywhere that shrimp trawling was conducted without TEDs in areas where sea turtles were found in the shrimp grounds. A document produced by Malaysia confirmed that "worldwide, the shrimp trawling industry seemed to capture more sea turtles than any other commercial fishery. ... Many of the most intensively trawled waters are adjacent to major sea turtle nesting beaches or feeding grounds".[167] In any event, the justification for the US measures at stake did not depend on shrimp trawling being the single greatest cause of sea turtle mortality in the waters of the complainants.

3.67. The United States recognized that trawlers in the summer flounder fishery captured sea turtles at a rate comparable to those in the shrimp fishery (though the overall impact to sea turtles was much less significant as fishing effort in the summer flounder fishery paled in comparison to the shrimp fishery). Because these trawlers could capture sea turtles at a comparable rate to the shrimp fishery, the United States required the use of TEDs in the summer flounder fishery from North Carolina to Southern Virginia and required that observers be placed on these trawlers as far north as New York to ascertain whether TEDs should be required elsewhere in this fishery.

3.68. **India** maintained that at Gahirmatha the nesting population of olive ridley had increased over the past ten years. Although some sea turtles were accidentally drowned by fishing activities in this area, Indian experts had opined that the population nesting at Gahirmatha "has not been affected by these activities".[168] Any US concern for the protection and conservation of this endangered species in India should have taken such expert opinion into account before the imposition of import restrictions. The claim that "the greatest human related cause of sea turtle mortality is drowning in shrimp trawl nets" was true only for the case of the United States, and could not be applied to India and universally to the whole world. Indian scientific studies[169] established that in India, the greatest human related cause of sea turtle mortality was the direct exploitation of adult live olive ridley sea turtles, to the tune of 50,000 to 80,000 every season in the late 1970s and early 1980s from their mating and breeding grounds, i.e. near shore and offshore areas of the Gahirmatha coast. Timely and effective steps taken by India under the Wildlife (Protection) Act 1972, implemented and enforced by the Indian Navy, Indian Coast Guard and the various law enforcing agencies of the concerned State Governments, had largely controlled this greatest human related cause of sea turtle mortality gradually since the mid-1980s.[170] The Gahirmatha sea turtle population represented in total aggregate about 50 per cent of the total world population of olive ridley sea turtles, and numerically about 80 per cent of all sea turtles found in Indian territorial waters. In this context, India took exception to the effort of the United States

---

[167] H.O. Hillestad et. al., (1982), *Worldwide Incidental Capture of Sea Turtles*, Biology and Conservation of Sea Turtles, K.A. Bjorndal ed., p. 491.

[168] P. Mohanty-Hejmadi, (1994), *Biology of the Olive Ridleys of Gahirmatha, Orissa, India,* in Proceedings of the Fourteenth Annual Symposium of Sea Turtle Biology and Conservation, p. 90.

[169] M.C. Dash and C.S Kar, (1990), *The Turtle Paradise - Gahirmatha*, Interprint, chapter 7; C.S. Kar and G.S. Padhi, (1992), *Biology, Life History and Conservation Strategy of the Olive Ridley Sea Turtles in Orissa*, Oriforest, Vol. 1, No. 2, pp. 36-40.

[170] C.S. Kar and G.S. Padhi, (1992), *Biology, Life History and Conservation Strategy of the Olive Ridley Sea Turtles in Orissa*, Oriforest, Vol. 1, No. 2, pp. 36-40.

to imply that India was only focusing its efforts on one species of endangered sea turtle on one beach. Of the five species of endangered sea turtles found in India, no commercial exploitation now existed in Indian territorial waters regarding the leatherback and the loggerhead sea turtles. With regard to the hawksbill sea turtles, trade had been eliminated several years ago. Even juvenile hawksbill turtles were recorded in different areas of the Orissa coast during the last ten years, indicating that feeding and developmental habitats existed for this species in areas of breeding grounds of olive ridleys, which were protected by law. Exploitation of green sea turtles had also been eliminated from the early 1980s. Thus, it would be clear to the Panel why India had chosen to focus on the only species of sea turtle which might appear relevant in this case, namely, the olive ridley sea turtle, which mainly nested on one area, Gahirmatha. Due to the conservation measures in India, two new mass nesting areas of olive ridley sea turtles (Devi and Rushikula rookeries) had been located recently. The breeding grounds in front of these rookeries had also been given legal protection. India's action was in accordance with the sea turtle conservation policy and action projects adopted in the Sea Turtle Conservation Strategy of the World Conference on Sea Turtle Conservation held from 26-30 November 1979 at Washington, D.C.

3.69. India submitted that the literature cited by the United States regarding the populations of sea turtles nesting on Indian beaches related to the situation in the late 1970s and contained no data from the period after 1980. No judgement could be made on population status unless data was obtained for all the species. Since there was no commercial exploitation of turtles in India any more, the populations might have improved instead of declining. The experts who had met at the Northern Indian Ocean Sea Turtle Workshop in January 1997 agreed that there was an urgent need for updating data on sea turtle populations in the Northern Indian Ocean. Further, recognizing the status of sea turtles in Indian coastal waters, the Government of India and concerned State Governments had taken necessary protection and conservation measures for the eggs, hatchlings and adults covering all the stages of the life cycle. As an example, trade in tortoise shell relating to endangered hawksbill sea turtles had been totally stopped and after 1980 there had been no documented evidence of any trade of hawksbill sea turtles from India. The capture, killing and exploitation of green sea turtles in the local markets of Tamil Nadu State in India had been completely stopped, and there was no record of such exploitation after 1980. Since 1975, the protection of sea turtles in Gahirmatha had been extensively documented. Such protection had been extended even to the coastal estuarine tidal mangrove forest eco-systems, which were linked to the food chain of the sea turtles. The effectiveness of India's conservation and protection measures had been proved and acknowledged.

3.70. India disagreed with the concern expressed by the United States regarding the absence of "large mass emergences" at Gahirmatha. The "authority" referred to by the United States had not done any work in India, and since she was not familiar with the mass nesting behaviour of the Gahirmatha population, she would not know that the lack of mass nesting behaviour in some years was a feature of the Gahirmatha olive ridley population. Scientific studies over the last two decades indicated that there had been no mass nestings in earlier years either, such as in 1981-1982 and in 1987-1988. Although the reasons for such behaviour was not yet known, the fact remained that this had not affected the population, as recorded in the literature referred to by the United States itself.[171] India would, therefore, not accept the veracity of the views contained in the affidavit referred to by the United States[172], especially since the authority quoted admitted herself that her views were based on her discussions with Indian sea turtle experts or published material. Further, India was not aware of any work done on Indian sea turtles by the expert referred to by the United States. The material provided by the United States on India was based on speculation by experts who had not done any work on Indian sea turtles. Therefore, such material could not be used as a factual basis for any determination. Moreover, India did not have any exclusive shrimp trawlers, as referred to by the authority quoted by the United States. The fishing vessels used in India for shrimp harvesting were quite different from the exclusive shrimp trawlers used in the United States. Therefore, the possibility of capture and death of thousands of sea turtles by a few vessels was unlikely. The information given by the United States regarding the recent building of a port adjacent to Gahirmatha was incorrect. What was referred to as a port was probably the Tachua Jetty, which had not been commissioned due to objections from Indian sea turtle experts and environmentalists. This demonstrated the importance the Government attached to environmental issues. India disagreed with the reference that there were no demonstrated recovering populations of olive ridleys anywhere, including in India. As demonstrated in a document produced by the United States[173], the olive ridley sea turtle population in Gahirmatha in India had in fact stabilized. India had one of the best records as far as conservation and preservation of all aspects of the life cycle of endangered sea turtles was concerned. In fact, India had taken a leading role in organizing national, regional and international meetings and conferences aimed at the protection and conservation of sea turtles. The affidavit submitted by the United States should not be accepted by the Panel, since there was no record of the competent Indian authorities having agreed that TED was the best and only way to conserve sea turtles. In fact, TEDs had not been sufficiently tested in Indian territorial waters to judge their effectiveness, and it would be incorrect to argue that competent Indian authorities had already agreed that these were the best and only way to conserve sea turtles. The demonstration of TEDs referred to by the United States in paragraphs 3.61 and 3.112 could not be taken as adequate, since the demonstration was at sea, had been limited in duration to a single day, which could not be scientifically used to come to the conclusion reached by the United States that TEDs were found to be as effective as when towed in US waters. On the contrary, it established that: (i) TEDs had to be adapted to Indian conditions; (ii) TEDs needed to be tested for a sufficient length of time in Indian waters before India could make any claims regarding their effectiveness; (iii) TEDs were still at an experimental stage in India.

3.71. India noted that the study prepared by IUCN (World Conservation Union) purporting to show that TEDs were required to protect sea turtles in India had actually been co-sponsored by the US Marine Fisheries Service and had been issued following a

[171] P. Mohanty-Hejmadi, (1994), *Biology of the Olive Ridleys at Gahirmatha, Orissa, India*, Proceedings of the Fourteenth Annual Symposium of Sea Turtle Biology and Conservation, p. 90.

[172] Affidavit of Pamela Plotkin, Ph. D, 22 July 1997, document submitted by the United States to the Panel.

[173] P. Mohanty-Hejmadi, (1994), *Biology of the Olive Ridleys of Gahirmatha, Orissa, India*, Proceedings of the Fourteenth Annual Symposium of Sea Turtle Biology and Conservation, p. 90.

workshop held in India in January 1997, which was more than seven months after the embargo had been imposed. Thus, it was apparent that views presented in this paper and at the workshop had not been relevant to the US decision to impose the embargo and represented nothing more than a *post hoc* rationalization to justify the US measures. India disagreed with the US statement that "that document, in addition to recommending the use of TEDs in trawl fisheries where necessary, confirmed the 'alarming decrease' in each of the nesting species". In this context, India was of the view that the United States had combined two different ideas from two different sections of a document[174], one regarding the recommendations about TEDs, and the other from the introduction, thereby conveying an unfortunate and inappropriate cause-and-effect impression. India noted that under the section "[r]esearch and [m]onitoring" of the IUCN study, 10 issues had been identified, of which the first one was "[i]ncomplete data on turtle nesting and feeding habitats in 9 NIO countries". Similarly, the tenth issue was "[i]ncomplete data on accidental mortality in fishing gear, including trawl nets, long lines, drift nets, purse-seines, gill nets and other fishing methods such as dynamite fishing". It might be noted that there was incomplete data to come to any conclusion about the need for TEDs. Moreover, it was under the tenth issue that 6 recommendations had been adopted. The first recommendation was "[a]ssess mortality of sea turtles interacting with high seas long line fisheries, assess turtle by catch by artisanal fisheries and assess the degree to which trawlers and long liners threaten turtles in an NIO". It was only the fifth recommendation that spoke of promoting the use of TEDs for trawl fisheries where necessary.

3.72. **Malaysia** replied that the portion of the report cited by the United States[175] to argue that nesting of sea turtles in Malaysia occurred "throughout the year" applied only to green turtles and not to all species. Sea turtle nesting in Malaysia being seasonal, Malaysia reiterated that limiting the shrimp trawling season in Terengganu to the months of November to February when turtles had left the Malaysian waters to return home to their distant feeding grounds was effective in protecting sea turtles, as clearly shown in the document cited by the United States.[176] Malaysia also disagreed with the US contention that sea turtles remained in Malaysian coastal waters at the end of the nesting season; it was a basic fact in sea turtle biology that after the completion of the nesting season, turtles performed long-distance migrations to return to distant feeding grounds where they took residence until the next breeding season. The scientific literature cited by the United States to show that trawling was a significant source of mortality for sea turtles was quoted out of context: trawl nets referred to in these studies[177] were mainly fish trawls and not shrimp trawls. This had been confirmed by a

174 IUCN (World Conservation Union), (1997), *A Marine Turtle Conservation Strategy and Action Plan for the Western Indian Ocean*, pp. 1 and 11.

175 H.C. Liew, (1995), *Country Report for Malaysia*, paper presented at the Northern Indian Ocean Workshop and Strategic Planning Session, Bhubaneswar, Orissa, India.

176 E.H.Chan, H.C. Liew and A.G. Mazlan, (1988), *The Incidental Capture of Sea Turtles in Fishing Gear in Terengganu, Malaysia*, Fisheries and Marine Science Center, Universiti Pertanian Malaysia, Table 2.

177 E.H. Chan et. al, (1988), *The Incidental Capture of Sea Turtles in Fishing Gear in Terengganu, Malaysia*, Biological Conservation, No. 43, pp. 1-7; S.K. Tow and E. Moll, (1995), *Status and Conservation of Estuarine and Sea Turtles in West Malaysian Waters*, Biology and Conservation of Sea Turtles, K.A. Bjorndal ed., pp. 339-347.

later survey whose results showed "driftnets, with mesh sizes exceeding 18 cm (or locally known as "pukat pari"), to be most destructive to marine turtles compared to four other types of fishing gears".[178] The 1992 Malaysia Fisheries Statistics referred to by the United States were for the whole of Peninsular Malaysia, i.e. both east and west coast. The study cited[179] addressed incidental captures in Terengganu, located on the east coast of Peninsular Malaysia, where shrimp catch was very seasonal (from October to February) as shown by the 1994 Annual Fisheries Statistics of Malaysia. Data showed that nesting of green turtles, leatherbacks and olive ridleys in Terengganu was very seasonal.[180] The United States had therefore erroneously cited figures for one location and imposed it upon another location where conditions were different. Finally, studies had shown that incidental captures of green turtles in Malaysia in shrimp trawl nets did not occur all year round.[181] Malaysia further submitted that the United States misquoted information from published sources in several occasions. For instance, the study which, according to the United States, discussed the "high rates of incidental sea turtle capture in Malaysia's shrimp trawl fishery"[182] actually showed that in the entire 5 year period, 1991-1996, a total of 37 strandings of turtles had been reported, of which 9 were had been attributed to trawl nets. The author of the paper considered it was a high number. To the United States, where hundreds of turtles stranded every year, 37 strandings over 5 years was also "high". Malaysia was of the view that the term "high" was a relative and subjective matter and pointed out that the United States had given a figure of 30 loggerhead turtles being caught annually in the groundfish otter-trawl fishery in the Gulf of Maine and the Mid-Atlantic Ocean; however, there was no mention of TED requirements in this fishery. The same study stated that "there are no specific studies on incidental capture of sea turtles under the impacts of fishing related activities". Another document which the United States submitted to demonstrate that shrimp trawlers were considered to capture and drown more sea turtles worldwide than any other form of incidental capture[183] came from an analysis of captures which did not cover Asian waters.

3.73. Malaysia also disagreed with the US assertion that coastal waters provided habitat to immature sea turtles, which were then at risk of being incidentally captured in shrimp trawl nets. No data supported such assertion; satellite tracking had demonstrated

---

[178] I. Kamarrudin et. al., (1996), *Status of Nesting Population and Related Research on Marine Turtles in Peninsular Malaysia*, Paper presented at the First SEAFEDC Workshop on Marine Turtle Research and Conservation, 15-18 January 1996, Kuala Terengganu, Malaysia, p. 17.

[179] E.H.Chan, H.C. Liew and A.G. Mazlan, (1988), *The Incidental Capture of Sea Turtles in Fishing Gear in Terengganu, Malaysia*, Fisheries and Marine Science Center, Universiti Pertanian Malaysia.

[180] I. Kamarrudin et. al., (1996), *Status of Nesting Population and Related Research on Marine Turtles in Peninsular Malaysia*, Paper presented at the First SEAFEDC Workshop on Marine Turtle Research and Conservation, 15-18 January 1996, Kuala Terengganu, Malaysia.

[181] *Ibid.*

[182] M.S. Suliansa, et. al., (1996), *Impact of Fishery Related Activities on Sea Turtles*, Paper presented at the National Seminar/Workshop on Marine Turtle and Terrapin Management, 22-23 October 1996, Cherating, Malaysia. The study stated that "mortality of sea turtles is recorded to be high in the Turtle Islands Park of Sabah during the shrimping season from November to April".

[183] H.O. Hillestad et. al., *Worldwide Incidental Capture of Sea Turtles (1982),* Biology and Conservation of Sea Turtles, K.A. Bjorndal ed., pp. 489-495.

that green turtles embarked on long-distance migrations to their feeding grounds once the nesting season was over.[184] Malaysia maintained that loggerheads and Kemp's ridleys were the species most at risk with respect to shrimp trawls since they fed on shrimp and, therefore, lived on shrimping grounds.[185] Contrary to what the United States asserted, all sea turtles did not occupy shrimping grounds. Shrimp trawling had been identified as one of the major threats to the survival of loggerheads and Kemp's ridleys, but there was no mention of shrimp trawling as a major threat for green turtles, hawksbill and leatherbacks.[186] Finally, Malaysia, noted that the capture of a mature hawksbill in a TED equipped trawl, referred to by the United States, occurred during the course of an experiment conducted with the purpose of demonstrating the effectiveness of TEDs for conservation purposes. To this end, the experiment was carried out in Zone A (0-5 nautical miles from the shore), i.e. an area which was off limits to trawling and where the probability of catching sea turtles was higher. However, if the experiment had been conducted in Zone B (5-12 nautical miles from the shore), where trawling was legally permitted, it was highly unlikely that any sea turtle would have been caught. Malaysia maintained that it had taken adequate measures to protect sea turtles from trawling, by prohibiting trawling in certain zones and by establishing offshore refuges for sea turtles where all harmful gear were banned.

3.74. **Pakistan** maintained that Pakistani shrimpers left their nets in the water for a duration of approximately 30 to 60 minutes. These tow times were in line with the tow time restrictions applicable to US shrimpers that did not retrieve their nets by mechanical means. The United States referred to a statement made by Ms. Fehmida Firdous at the Northern Indian Ocean Turtle Workshop to the effect that tow times common in Pakistani shrimp industries were up to two hours. Pakistan noted that, after this statement was made, Ms. Firdous had been asked by the Chairman of Pakistan Sea Food Industries Association to substantiate the basis of her claim. Ms. Firdous advised the Chairman that she had not conducted a study on her own and was unable to provide any other substantiation. Pakistan added that it had a programme to monitor the rate of turtle drowning in connection with shrimp trawl operations. This programme, which was administered by the Sindh Wildlife Department, gave strong incentive to report sea turtle drowning in connection with shrimp trawling. The Sindh Wildlife Department offered a cash reward of Rs. 1000, i.e. almost 50 per cent of average monthly income of a fisherman in Pakistan, to fishermen who gave the tag number of sea turtle caught in the fishing net. Since the programme had started, no fisherman had claimed this reward; thus, the incidental catch rate of sea turtles in shrimp trawling operations was presumed to be *de minimis*.

3.75. **Thailand** maintained it had demonstrated that a combination of strict protection of nesting beaches and an egg retrieval, incubation and release programme had been

---

[184] H.C. Liew, E.H. Chan, F. Papi and P. Luschi, (1995), *Long Distance Migration of Green Turtles from Redang Island, Malaysia: The Need for Regional Cooperation in Sea Turtle Conservation*, Proceedings of the International Congress of Chelonian Conservation, 6-10 July 1995, Confaron, France.

[185] Malaysia referred to the following study: *Kemp's Ridley Sea Turtle (Lepidochelys kempii) Status Report*, (1996), Report of the Marine Turtle Expert Working Group".

[186] National Research Council, Academy of Sciences, (1990), *Decline of the Sea Turtles: Causes and Prevention*, Washington, D.C.

successful in stabilizing nesting sea turtle populations in protected areas. Indeed, as noted in a document submitted by the United States with respect to the Khram Island area, "[t]he fact that the nesting beaches have been protected for more than four decades is the logical reason for the relatively high number of nesting females seen there today".[187] Malaysia had also found that an egg retrieval, incubation and release programme was successful in increasing the number of nesting sea turtles after a 15-year gap during which the green turtles grew to sexual maturity. Indeed, a 1989 study in Malaysia concluded that, "[t]oday the turtle population [in Sarawak sanctuary area] has reached an equilibrium level. It will remain at this level if we continue to hatch and release young turtles at a high rate ...".[188] Regarding the argument made by the United States that the *Monitoring Surveys* were not designed to provide information on incidental catch of inedible species but rather were designed to collect data on the harvesting of shrimp and other edible marine creatures, Thailand stressed that all forms of catch had been recorded on the original study worksheets, edible and inedible. While only the quantities of edible catch had been included in published tables, a note to those tables indicated that the catch of inedible species and things, such as sea cucumbers, jellyfish, sea urchins, sand dollars, corals and sponges, had also been recorded in the study. If sea turtles had been caught, this fact would have been noted under the same methodology. However, the study turned up no incidence of the catch of sea turtles over a thirty-year period. Thus, the United States appeared to have erroneously extrapolated from conditions found along the coast of the United States in demanding that Thailand and other Members, where conditions were quite different, expended scarce resources to install TEDs in shrimp trawl nets. Other alternative means, involving less cost and significantly less disruption to shrimp trawl fisheries, had proven effective in stabilizing sea turtle populations in the area.

3.76. The **United States** considered it had submitted scientific studies to the Panel which did show that shrimp trawling was a significant cause of sea turtle mortality in Indian waters.[189] A document submitted by Malaysia reported more than 5,000 strandings of olive ridley turtles along India's Orissa coast "due to accidental capture in trawl nets".[190] Direct exploitation of sea turtles was perhaps once the largest cause of sea turtle mortality in India and elsewhere in the region, but shrimp trawling was today a significant cause of such mortality in India[191] and in the waters of the other

[187] S. Settle, (1995), *Status of Nesting Populations o f Sea Turtles in Thailand and Their Conservation*, Marine Turtle Newsletter, No. 68.

[188] Leh, (1989), *The Green Turtle, Chelonia Mydas (L.), in Sarawak: Is There a Future?*, Annual Symposium of the Malaysian Society of Marine Science.

[189] B.C. Choudhury, (1997), *Country Report: India - Sea Turtle Status, Conservation and Management in India*, p. 2; P. Mohanty-Hejmade, (1994), *Biology of the Olive Ridleys of Gahirmatha, Orissa, India*, Proceedings of the Fourteenth Annual Symposium of Sea Turtle Biology and Conservation, p. 90; IUCN (World Conservation Union), (1997), *A Marine Turtle Conservation Strategy and Action Plan for the Northern Indian Ocean*, p. 11; Statement of Deborah Crouse, Ph.D. paragraph 8; Affidavit of Pamela Plotkin, Ph. D., 22 July 1997, document submitted to the Panel by the United States, paragraphs 6-10.

[190] B. Pandav, B.C. Choudhury and C.S. Kar, (1994), *Olive Ridley Sea Turtle (Lepydochelys olivacea) and its Nesting Habitats Along the Orissa Coast - A Status Survey*, Wildlife Institute of India, p. 29.

[191] See references indicated in footnote 189.

complainants. The scientific literature submitted by the United States confirmed that each population of sea turtles in India other than the olive ridley at Gahirmatha was in serious decline, and that even that population was in jeopardy. Even several documents submitted by Malaysia criticized the sea turtle protection efforts that governments had taken to date in the region. The trawl gear used in the United States and in India, as well as in the other complainants' countries, were the same basic "otter trawl" design, i.e. a gear allowing a net to be dragged along the sea bottom and captured virtually everything it encountered, including sea turtles. The United States maintained that Dr. Plotkin, whose affidavit was rejected by India, was a true expert in the field of sea turtle conservation and had worked in India for the past 3 years. Dr. Plotkin contradicted several of India's assertions, noting in particular that "[a] declining trend in the Indian olive ridley nesting population appears imminent and is likely due to the indirect capture and mortality of turtles in fisheries, particularly the shrimp fishery (bottom trawling from mechanized vessels)".[192] As to Malaysia's argument that limiting shrimp trawling to certain times of the year prevented incidental mortality of sea turtles, the United States noted that a chart established by the Government of Malaysia and showing landings of "marine fish", including shrimp, by month through 1995, showed that the quantities of shrimp landings varied very little month by month for each shrimp species. This called further into question the seasonal restrictions on shrimping that Malaysia had supposedly introduced.

3.77. **India** replied that the data from Indian sources provided to the Panel showed that shrimp trawling was not a significant cause of sea turtle mortality in Indian waters.[193] Moreover, as India previously pointed out, there was no exclusive shrimp trawling by Indian fishermen, and thus any inferences by the United States linked to "shrimp trawling" would *ipso facto* not be applicable to India. Indian fishermen did not trawl exclusively for shrimp, but for all types of fish. Since the function of trawlers in Indian waters was different, it was logical that the design of Indian trawlers be different from shrimp trawlers used in the United States. Finally, the 5,000 strandings of olive ridley turtles did not occur due to trawl fishing activities, but were due to all types of fishing gear. Further, the figure of 5,000 deaths had to be seen in the context of a sea turtle population of 1.2 million olive ridleys, where direct exploitation of adults to the scale of 50,000 to 80,000 per year had been completely stopped. The effectiveness of India's sea turtle protection and conservation programmes had been acknowledged, *inter alia*, by the Director of National Marine Fisheries Service of the United States, the IUCN Marine Turtle Conservation Strategy and Action Plan for the Northern Indian Ocean, the Mombasa, Kenya Meeting on *Integrating Marine Conservation in the Indian Ocean, 1996 and Beyond.*

3.78. **Malaysia** noted that the chart referred to by the United States to show that shrimp was landed throughout the year contained data for the whole of Malaysia, but not specifically for the east coast of Peninsular Malaysia.

---

[192] Affidavit of Pamela Plotkin, Ph. D., 22 July 1997, document submitted to the Panel by the United States, paragraph 6.

[193] See above paragraph 68, and the references therein.

### 4. *Use of TEDs*

3.79. The **United States** considered that a TED was a simple, cheap and highly effective solution to the problem of sea turtle mortality in shrimp trawl nets. TEDs had been first designed in the United States by the NMFS beginning almost 20 years ago. Since then, TEDs had become more effective and less expensive.[194] They had been developed and manufactured on a commercial basis in a wide variety of nations. TEDs ranged in price from US$75-500. A completely installed TED, i.e. a TED including the basic grid device, all webbing, flaps and flotation devices and which could be installed in the shrimp trawl net with a single simple cut, ranged in price form US$300-400. A TED that was installed by the fisherman cost about US$75-100. TEDs constructed in developing countries with local materials cost a great deal less. During the TED training workshops conducted by the United States in India, Indian participants had estimated the cost of constructing and installing a TED made from local materials as ranging from US$8-12. When the United States provided TEDs training, it included construction of a TED from locally available material as part of that training. TEDs were very easy to install: they were sewn into the trawl net, much the same way fishermen sewed other types of nets. Installation of a TED did not require fishermen to acquire new skills. Once installed, the TED did not affect the way in which the trawl was towed. Therefore, through a minimum of trial and error, shrimp fishermen who were new to TEDs could readily learn to use them properly.

3.80. The US Government had conducted a detailed, comprehensive study, involving thousands of hours spent by neutral observers aboard shrimp trawl vessels. Based on this study and its own exhaustive analysis, the US National Academy of Sciences concluded in 1990 that properly installed TEDs - of the sort required for use in the United States for more than seven years - were a practical and cost-effective way to minimize the unintentional drowning of sea turtles in shrimp trawl nets. Properly installed TEDs approached 97 per cent efficiency in allowing sea turtles to escape from shrimp trawl nets, while limiting shrimp loss rates to 1-3 per cent.[195] TEDs also released debris and other unwanted by-catch from shrimp trawl nets. TEDs were now widely used in shrimp trawl fisheries throughout the Western Hemisphere. More recently, African and Asian countries had begun requiring their use as well. Thailand had instituted a comprehensive TEDs programme in 1996. Also in 1996, a workshop organized by the government of Orissa in India recommended that the use of TEDs "should be made mandatory" throughout that region of the world.[196] Similarly, the

---

[194] The United States noted that since TEDs had been first introduced to the US shrimp fishery in the late 1980s, research and development to improve TED performance has continued. Using SCUBA divers and video cameras attached to shrimp trawl nets under actual working conditions, NMFS gear researchers, working with shrimp fishermen and net manufacturers, had made improvements to TEDs, enhancing performance for both turtle exclusion and shrimp retention. Shrimp fishermen in the United States had contributed to improvement in TED design and techniques for handling TEDs at sea.

[195] National Research Council, National Academy of Sciences, (1990), *Decline of the Sea Turtles: Causes and Prevention,* p. 128. The United States also produced to the Panel a *Statement of Scientists* signed by 74 scientists attesting "to the extraordinary effectiveness of TEDs".

[196] Recommendations of the Training-cum-Demonstration Workshop on Turtle Excluder Device (TED), held at Paradeep, Orissa, from 11-14 November 1996.

Marine Turtle Conservation Strategy and Action Plans developed by IUCN (World Conservation Union) for the Western Indian Ocean, and the Northern Indian Ocean, endorsed the use of TEDs in that region.[197]

3.81. **India** disagreed with the costs of TEDs indicated by the United States (US$75-500), and noted that costs had to be considered in context. While TEDs might be inexpensive by US standards, they were certainly not cheap to owners of fishing vessels in India. The average annual income of fishermen in India was only around US$300. Moreover, the US figure did not include the cost of installation and training, which would make any TEDs programme in India more expensive than projected by the United States. Thus, while TEDs might be cheap by US standards, they could not be considered cheap by Indian fishermen. The cost of a TED depended on its size and model. It was India's understanding that TEDs imported from abroad cost approximately US$200 per piece. Imported TEDs suitable for deep sea fishing vessels ranged in cost from US$500 to US$600 per piece. India questioned the cost indicated by the United States for TEDs made with local materials (US$8-12). The design of Indian trawlers was very different from US trawlers; therefore, NMFS gear specialists had found, during the preparation of the 1996 Orissa workshop that only one out of seven models of TED ("Georgia Jumper") was suitable. At the November 1996 workshop, the gear specialists had demonstrated the fabrication, installation and one time fishing in the sea. The TED was constructed from locally available steel rods but the floats, trimmings and angle meter had been brought from the United States. The cost of the steel rods alone was about US$60. With respect to other costs, India did not have relevant data regarding loss of shrimp/fish associated with the use of TEDs. Further, India did not have any information concerning the costs associated with training fishermen to use TEDs properly.

3.82. Another practical issue associated with Indian fisheries, which did not appear to be present in US fisheries, was that other fish caught in nets during trawling, in particular some large fish, were also sought for commercial purposes by Indian fishermen. However, such fish could pass through the grid of a TED and thus escape from the net. This resulted in an increase in catch loss, and corresponding increase in costs for Indian fishermen, which had not been taken into account by the United States in promulgating its TEDs requirements. Fishing methods in India and the United States were completely different and the United States had not so far demonstrated that TEDs could retain large fish in fishing trawl nets. At the Paradeep workshop, US experts had realized that enlarging the distance between the TED grills to retain large fish would result in entangling the heads of turtles within the grills, and thus, in human-induced mortality of sea turtles in TEDs. This practical problem had been noted by participants at the Cochin Workshop, including the US experts present, but no suggestions were provided concerning how to solve it. According to Indian experts, the effectiveness of the TED in Indian waters could only be ascertained after a detailed study covering a reasonable length of time. Issues such as the behaviour of certain models of TEDs and of the TED-equipped net while trawling, the loss of catch (shrimp and fish) while using

[197] IUCN (World Conservation Union), (1995), *A Marine Turtle Conservation Strategy and Action Plan for the Western Indian Ocean*, p. 14, and IUCN (World Conservation Union), (1997), *A Marine Turtle Conservation Strategy and Action Plan for the Northern Indian Ocean*, p. 11.

TEDs, and the effectiveness of the various models under Indian conditions, had to be studied in detail for sufficiently long periods before the Government of India could decide on the suitability of the TEDs in Indian waters. Indian fishermen were apprehensive about the effect of TEDs on different target fish. In the United States, specific TEDs were designed for different types of fishing and, hence, in India only one TED would not be suitable for all types of fishing. The fabrication, installation and monitoring in mass scale had to be organized; the escape opening dimensions had to be determined (for example, it was different in the Gulf of Mexico and in the Atlantic). Therefore, TED technology transfer to suit local fishing was a long process and could not be implemented immediately. India also pointed out that it was still in the process of examining whether and where TEDs should be used to reduce incidental deaths of sea turtles. India stressed, however, that its sea turtles populations were not in danger, even without the use of TEDs.

3.83. With respect to whether TEDs were "simple" and "highly effective", India adopted Thailand's arguments (see paragraph 3.86). Regarding the TEDs workshop conducted in Orissa, in November 1996, i.e. after the embargo on Indian shrimp had been imposed, India noted that the participants at this conference, including US representatives from NMFS, expressed "deep concern at the ban imposed by the US Government on shrimp imports".[198] India also noted that a notice published by the Sea Turtle Restoration Project of Earth Island Institute specifically addressed US enforcement problems. The notice stated: "citing the federal government's apparent inability to end the drowning deaths of thousands of endangered sea turtles every year in US waters, a coalition of over 45 environmental and animal protection organizations and concerned businesses has launched a consumer-powered campaign to end the slaughter". The notice further stated that, despite laws requiring US shrimpers to use TEDs, "in 1995 over 2,000 sea turtles washed up dead on US beaches. These high numbers support the widely-held belief that many US shrimpers, particularly in the Gulf of Mexico, are disabling their TEDs because they fear a reduced catch".[199]

3.84. **Malaysia** disagreed with the claim made by the United States that drowning of sea turtles in shrimp trawls could be virtually eliminated through the use of TEDs and noted that even in the United States the mandatory use of TEDs since 1992 had not resulted in the elimination of mortalities. For example, turtle stranding in the United States in May 1996 had been reported to be more than twice the five year historic average in several zones, while in 1993-94 Kemp's ridley mortalities had reached a record high.[200] Malaysia also considered that, contrary to what was asserted by the United States, the use of TEDs was not necessarily "widely used in shrimp trawls throughout the Western Hemisphere". Even in the United States, there had been non-compliance among local shrimpers. In 1994, large numbers of dead turtles had been

---

198 *Recommendations of the Training-cum-Demonstration Workshop on Turtle Excluder Device (TED)*, held ad Paradeep, Orissa, from 11-14 November 1996, p. 7.

199 Earth Island Institute, *Sea Turtle Restoration Project - First Dolphin-Safe Tuna, now Sea Turtle-Safe Shrimp?*, on http://www.earthisland.org/ei/strp/first.html, on 7 July 1997.

200 D. Crouse, *Action alert!!*, Center for Marine Conservation, 20 May 1996. A release to multiple recipients of list CTURTLE<CTURTLE@NERVM.NERDC.UFL.EDU>; and D. Crouse, *U.S. TEDS still in limbo - believe it or not!!*, 14 October 1996, Center for Marine Conservation. A release to multiple recipients of list CTURTLE <CTURTLE@NERVM.NERDC.UFL.EDU>.

washed ashore on Texas beaches, which was attributed to failures of NMFS to enforce the TED regulations. Many shrimpers had been found to have disabled or misinstalled TEDs in their nets.[201] As to the cost of TEDs, Malaysia said that a SEAFDEC-developed TED adapted to Malaysian trawls and its installation was between Ringgit 90 to 120. The practical aspects of using TEDs in Malaysia were: (i) the joint efforts under SEAFDEC resulted in further work[202] at localizing the SEAFDEC developed TED to Malaysian conditions and the introduction of the TED in an official launch in Sigari, Perak; (ii) practical difficulties were envisaged in the enforcement of the use of TEDs because local fishermen contended that in their fishing experience for shrimps, they rarely caught sea turtles; (iii) the reluctance of fishermen to volunteer information on the number of turtles caught.

3.85. **Pakistan** noted that on average Pakistani fishermen earned the equivalent of approximately US$600-700 per year. The United States had indicated that TEDs ranged in price from US$75-500. Even ignoring additional costs such as training and loss of catch, the United States estimate amounted to approximately 10 to 70 per cent of a Pakistani shrimper's annual income. Thus, while TEDs might be considered to be cheap for US shrimpers, they were not cheap for Pakistani shrimpers. Indeed, conditioning importation of shrimp upon the purchase of such expensive equipment was inconsistent with the language of the preamble of the WTO Agreement, which required Members to enhance the means for protecting and preserving the environment in a manner consistent with the Member's respective needs and concerns at different levels of economic development. Pakistan further noted that even in the United States, where shrimpers had been working with TEDs for more than ten years, improper use of TEDs had been proven to cause a high level of mortality among sea turtles. With regard to whether TEDs were a "simple" and "highly effective" solution, Pakistan adopted the arguments made by Thailand (see paragraph 3.86).

3.86. **Thailand** noted that while the cost of a single TED was relatively modest (the cost of the TED itself, plus installation, was US$100 per vessel), the consequential costs of TEDs use in Thailand had been enormous, principally in lost shrimp catch, estimated at 30-40 per cent. Thailand estimated that the cost of TEDs purchase, installation, training and use (including lost catch to date) amounted to US$3,200 per vessel.[203] This cost would rise as TEDs use and corresponding loss of catch continued. Thailand argued that it was also inaccurate to suggest that TEDs were universally 97 per cent effective in preventing sea turtle deaths or that shrimpers could easily learn how to use this device. As recently as 1994, after several years of use in the United States, there were high numbers of dead sea turtles stranded along the coasts of Texas, Louisiana, Georgia and northeastern Florida. NMFS had found that the major cause of the

---

[201] M. Weber, D. Crouse, R. Irvin and S. Iudicello, (1995), *Delay and Denial: A Political History of Sea Turtles and Shrimp Fishing*, Center for Marine Conservation, p. 12.

[202] A. Ali, S.S. Sayed Alwi and S. Ananpongsuk, *Experiments on the use of Turtle Exclider Devices (TEDs) in Malaysian waters*, paper presented at the regional workshop on Responsible Fishing, 24-27 June 1997, Bangkok, Thailand.

[203] K. Kwanming, (1997), *Impacts of Shrimp Trawl Fishing from TTFD Installation*, Fisheries Economic Division, Department of Fisheries.

strandings was the improper use of TEDs by shrimpers in the Gulf of Mexico.[204] Additionally, high numbers of strandings occurred in various locations during 1995 and 1996. NMFS stated that "[a]mong the identified causes of the continued strandings have been the improper use of TEDs and the use of inefficient TEDs by shrimp fishermen".[205] These findings belied US claims that through a minimum of trial and error, shrimp fishermen who were new to TEDs could readily learn to use them properly. In addition, the NMFS had determined that approval of the Morrision, Parrish, Andrews, and Taylor soft TEDs should be removed because those TEDs were ineffective.[206] NMFS noted that proper installation of soft TEDs was extremely difficult, that problems inherent in using soft webbing material as a turtle excluder device were serious and widespread and that the "Andrews soft TED, as presently designed, is ineffective at excluding turtles".[207] Although NMFS had made these determinations in December 1996, actual removal of the approval of these TED designs was not scheduled to take effect until December 1997. Specifically, in a Conference Report accompanying the Omnibus Consolidated Appropriations Act, 1997, the NMFS had been directed "not to decertify any turtle excluder devices until every effort has been made, working with industry and others, to improve or modify existing devices to increase turtle escapement".[208] NMFS had also found problems with certain bottom-opening TEDs. Specifically, tests in June 1996 revealed "previously unknown problems with turtle capture in straight-bar, bottom-opening TEDs installed at high angles and fitted with long webbing flaps".[209] Thus, it was not true that TEDs technology was tried, tested and effective as suggested by the United States. This technology was still very much under development.

3.87. The **United States** noted that none of the complainants had questioned the effectiveness of TEDs in allowing sea turtles to escape. Since the United States had begun requiring TEDs, populations of Kemp's ridley and loggerhead sea turtles found in the United States had stopped declining and were well on their way to recovery. Indeed, there was no other effective way known to protect sea turtles from drowning in shrimp trawl nets. As to the alleged "30-40 per cent" losses of shrimp from trawl nets equipped with TEDs, the United States noted the following. A very recent report on *Experiments on the Use of Turtle Excluder Devices in Malaysian Waters*[210] documented a total of 47 trawling experiments done in Malaysian waters to test the suitability of TEDs for Malaysian fishermen. The report concluded that, while a minimal amount (between 0.01 per cent and 7.7 per cent) of fish and "trash fish" might have escaped from the TED-equipped trawl nets, "the result showed that TEDs prevented marine turtles from being trapped in the net but did not affect the catch of fish and shrimp ... Therefore, the

[204] Sea Turtle Conservation; Revisions to Sea Turtle Conservation Requirements; Restrictions to Shrimp Trawling Activities, 61 Fed. Reg. 66, 933 (19 December 1996), p. 66, 935.

[205] *Ibid.*, p. 66, 937.

[206] *Ibid.*, p. 66, 933.

[207] *Ibid.*, p. 66, 938.

[208] *Ibid.*, p. 66, 935.

[209] *Ibid.*, p. 66, 940.

[210] A. Ali, S.S. Sayed Alwi and S. Ananpongsuk, (1994), *Experiments on the Use of Turtle Excluder Devices (TEDs) in Malaysian Waters*, paper presented at the regional workshop on Responsible Fishing, 24-27 June 1997, Bangkok, Thailand.

small and medium size of TEDs were found to be suitable for use by Malaysian fishermen".[211] This report also referred to another 1997 study prepared by C. Bundit et. al., on recent experiments conducted in Thailand on the "Thai Turtle Free Device". The Malaysian report cited the Bundit study as having found average escape rates of shrimp and fish from trawl nets equipped with the Thai Turtle Free Device as "1.8 per cent and 1.04 per cent for day and night time operation, respectively".[212] This finding disproved Thailand's assertions that TEDs caused shrimp losses of 30-40 per cent. The United States also referred to a document produced by Malaysia, which described the results of experiments with the "Super Shooter" TED and the Thai Turtle Free Device in Thai waters and indicated: "[a]fter the second experiment, results showed that by using [the] Super Shooter and [the] TTFD, the escape rate for the total catch [not just shrimp] was acceptable at a percentage range of 1.91 and 1.84, respectively".[213]

3.88. The United States disagreed with India's claim that NMFS gear specialists had found that only the "Georgia Jumper" TED was suitable for Indian waters off the coast of Orissa. In fact, the United States had never stated that any particular TED design was most appropriate. Rather, during training sessions, the United States often demonstrated the Super Shooter TED, and constructed a TED from locally available material. Both types of TEDs were left with the host country. In the particular case of India, the NMFS gear specialist had concluded that any type of TED would work in Indian waters off the coast of Orissa and had informed the Indian participants accordingly. Thailand's assertion that TEDs cost fishermen thousands of dollars did not withstand scrutiny. The cost of a TED to individual Thai fishermen had been zero because their government had supplied them TEDs free of charge. Moreover, Thailand tried to impute to its fishermen the cost to the government of implementing a TED programme. The United States also questioned the governmental costs claimed by Thailand in this respect, and noted that Thailand did not factor in the savings in sea turtles produced. The claims regarding the supposed loss of shrimp conflicted directly with studies of TEDs conducted in the United States, Malaysia, Thailand and elsewhere which showed that TEDs caused virtually no shrimp loss. Moreover, the documents submitted by Thailand purporting to show higher loss rates was based largely on interviews with shrimp fishermen, who had a strong incentive to overstate problems in using TEDs. Thailand had not submitted the same sort of evidence that the United States had provided, i.e. scientific studies and data generated by neutral observers stationed aboard shrimp trawl vessels. Finally, TEDs could save shrimp fishermen money. TEDs excluded from the nets not only sea turtles but large debris, and thus allowed more shrimp to be caught in a given tow. TEDs prevented the shrimp in the nets from being crushed by the debris. TEDs also saved the fishermen time in sorting the catch at the end of the tow.

3.89. The United States disagreed with the assertions made by some of the complainants that it was not effectively enforcing the use of TEDs in US waters. The

[211] A. Ali, S.S. Sayed Alwi and S. Ananpongsuk, (1994), *Experiments on the Use of Turtle Excluder Devices (TEDs) in Malaysian Waters*, paper presented at the regional workshop on Responsible Fishing, 24-27 June 1997, Bangkok, Thailand.p. 1.

[212] *Ibid.*, p. 7. The United States also noted that, during a TEDs workshop held in Songkla, Thailand, officials from the US National Marine Fisheries Service pulled one TED-equipped trawl net along side a trawl net without a TED. The amount of shrimp caught by each was the same.

[213] *TED gained Thai fisherment's acceptance*, SEAFDEC Newsletter, July-September 1996.

requirements with respect to US vessels were enforced vigorously and had achieved a high rate of compliance. The United States only asked that shrimp imported into its market be harvested in accordance with comparable standards. The United States considered that the complainants mischaracterized several elements of the US TEDs programme. The use of soft TEDs was already prohibited in much of US shrimp fishery, particularly in those areas designated as "Shrimp Fishery Sea Turtle Conservation Areas", where sea turtles faced the highest risk if incidental capture. TEDs were required in try nets in these areas as well. Moreover, the use of soft TEDs would be prohibited everywhere in US waters as of 19 December 1997. The United States conceded it experienced elevated levels of sea turtle strandings in 1994. Those sea turtles deaths had been attributed primarily to improperly installed TEDs and improperly floated TEDs. In response, the United States had increased enforcement and implemented an Emergency Response Plan. As a result, strandings had decreased significantly, demonstrating that TEDs, when used properly, were very effective in protecting sea turtles from mortality in shrimp trawls.

3.90. **India** could not agree with the United States that TEDs were simple: the simplicity of TEDs was still a matter of adapting their design to the local conditions. This was yet to be examined in India. Moreover, TEDs were expensive, as explained in paragraph 3.81. India was unable to accept the US estimate that the price of constructing a TED from locally available materials was approximately US$8-12. As noted earlier, TEDs were not in commercial use in India at the moment. From India's experience in fabricating TEDs locally, the cost varied from location to location, and would be higher than the figure given by the United States. The assertion that TEDs virtually eliminated sea turtle mortality in shrimp trawl nets could be true in the case of the United States, but was not applicable to India. This was so because in areas of high turtle congregation (i.e. in concentrated breeding and mating grounds) substantial mortality of adult turtles occurred by the slashing of propellers of all types of mechanized fishing vessels. Promoting trawling activity through the use of TEDs in such high turtle congregation zones might have an adverse impact by disturbing the mating pairs during the peak breeding season, thus in fact affecting the reproductive potential of the population as a whole. Therefore, India believed in giving full protection to this area by restricting fishing rather than allowing trawling with TEDs. Further, in such high turtle congregation areas, there was evidence that, during the peak breeding season, large numbers of adult turtles, including mating pairs and gravid females, very often got simultaneously entangled in fishing nets. In such situations, there was every possibility that the turtles would block the escape route of any TED which might be installed, resulting in the death of turtles as well as loss of fish catch. No study had been done so far regarding the effectiveness of TEDs in such situations.

3.91. Regarding the alleged recovery of the Kemp's ridley and loggerhead populations in the United States, **Malaysia** submitted that a study on Kemp's ridley indicated that the recovery of that population was due to egg protection and to protection of turtles at sea.[214] In the case of loggerheads, not all populations had shown recovery, as stated in a document submitted by the United States.[215]

3.92. **Thailand** noted that the Bundit study[216] referred to by the United States had been conducted under conditions that did not replicate normal operating circumstances in the Thai shrimp fleet. Specifically, the study methodology explained that trawling occurred over a period of only one hour. Trawling over more representative periods increased the amount of debris caught in the TEDs, thereby increasing shrimp loss. The study already referred to by Thailand, representing actual operating experience, showed a much higher shrimp loss.[217] Moreover, reports published in the United States indicated that US shrimpers were routinely disabling their TEDs. It was unlikely that they would take the time and trouble to do this, as well as incurring the risks of detection, if they were not also experiencing losses of catch exceeding the very low rates indicated by the United States.

3.93. The **United States** replied that India offered no evidence to disprove that a TED made from local materials would cost from US$8 to 12. Second, it would be more meaningful to compare the cost of a TED to the total capital costs to an owner of a shrimp vessel of operating that vessel, rather than to the earning of an individual fisherman on the vessel. Even in developing countries, such a comparison would show that TEDs represented a very small fraction of such costs. Shrimp vessels in many developing nations, including Belize, Brazil, Colombia, Costa Rica, Ecuador, El Salvador, Guatemala, Guyana, Honduras, Indonesia, Mexico, Nicaragua, Nigeria, Panama, the People's Republic of China, Trinidad and Tobago, and Venezuela were using TEDs in a cost-effective way. Tests on TEDs conducted in Malaysia and Thailand had proved their effectiveness in those waters.[218] India provided no evidence to show that shrimp trawling conditions in India were different than those in Malaysia and Thailand. The otter trawl gear used in India was the same as that used in most other places of the world, including the United States. Moreover, the United States and other nations had tested TEDs in all marine habitats where shrimp were found, including in the complainants' region during workshops, and had found no meaningful differences of conditions from those elsewhere in the world. As to the argument that pairs of mating turtles could block the escape route of a TED, the United States was not aware of any scientific data on the question and noted that if such sea turtles would definitely not escape from a trawl net without a TED, they might escape from a TED-equipped net.

---

214 *Kemp's Ridley Sea Turtle (Lepidochelys Kempii) Statut Report*, (1996), Report of the Marine Turtle Expert Working Group.

215 *Status of the Loggerhad Sea Turtle Population (Caretta caretta) in the Estern North Atlantic*, (1996), Report of the Marine Turtle Expert Working Group.

216 B. Chokesanguan, et. al., (1997), *The Experiments on Turtle Excluder Devices (TEDs) for Shrimp Trawl Nets in Thailand"*, South Asian Fisheries Department.

217 K. Kwanming, *Impacts of Shrimp Trawl Fishing from TTFD Installation*, Fisheries Economic Division, Department of Fisheries.

218 A. Ali, (1997), *Experiments on the Use of Turtle Excluder Devices (TEDs) in Malaysian Waters*, paper presented at the Regional Workshop on Responsible Fisheries, 24-27 June 1997, Bangkok, Thailand. SEAFDEC, (1996), *TED Gained Thai Fishermen's Acceptance*, SEAFDEC Newsletter, Vol. 19, No. 3, p. 11.

### 5. *International Environmental Agreements and the Use of TEDs*

3.94. The **United States** considered that the use of TEDs had become a recognized multilateral environmental standard, fulfilling twin commitments on the part of the international community to conserve endangered species, such as sea turtles, and to minimize their unintentional mortality in fishing operations. The international community had long recognized the need to protect endangered species such as sea turtles. All species of sea turtles appeared on Appendix I to CITES, having first been placed on that Appendix in 1975. Under the terms of CITES, trade in these species must accordingly be subject to "particularly strict regulation in order not to endanger their survival and must be authorized only in exceptional circumstances".[219] As a consequence of their listing on Appendix I to CITES, international trade in sea turtles, and in their eggs, parts and products, was virtually prohibited. As parties to CITES, the complainants were obligated under international law to impose import prohibitions as a means of conserving these sea turtles. The United States observed that by requiring its parties to prohibit international trade in sea turtles, CITES undoubtedly had advanced the cause of sea turtle conservation. By itself, however, this prohibition did nothing to address the incidental mortality of sea turtles in trawl nets, which for many years has constituted a far more serious threat to sea turtles than international trade. The CITES prohibitions, like the prohibitions on the intentional killing of sea turtles, had not prevented the continuing decline of sea turtles worldwide.

3.95. The international community had also long been aware of the threat to sea turtles and to other living resources as a result of their incidental mortality in marine fishing operations. The 1982 United Nations Convention on the Law of the Sea ("LOS Convention") generally required States, both within areas under their national jurisdiction and on the high seas, to ensure through proper conservation and management measures, that the maintenance of living resources was not endangered by over-exploitation. In taking such measures, States had to "take into consideration the effects on species [such as sea turtles] associated with or dependent upon harvested species with a view to maintaining or restoring populations of such associated or dependent species above levels at which their reproduction may become seriously threatened".[220] Since the adoption of the LOS Convention in 1982, the need for stricter regulation of bycatch had become increasingly critical. That was why Agenda 21 declared that it was necessary to "promote the development and use of selective fishing gear and practices that minimize ... bycatch of non-target species".[221] The United States further argued that this multilateral environmental standard to minimize bycatch had been strengthened further, and made a treaty obligation, in a new global convention regulating marine fisheries, the 1995 Agreement for the Implementation of the Provisions of the United Nations Convention on the Law of the Sea of 10 December 1982 Relating to the Conservation and Management of Straddling Fish Stocks and

---

[219] CITES, Article II(1).

[220] United Nations Convention on the Law of the Sea, UN Doc.A.CONF.62/122, reprinted in 21 I.L.M. 1261 (1982), Article 61(2) & (4) and Article 119(1)(b).

[221] Report of the United Nations Conference on Environment and Development, Rio De Janeiro (3-14 June 1992), UN Doc. A/CONF.151/26, Agenda 21, paragraph 17.46(c).

Highly Migratory Fish Stocks ("UN Fish Stocks Agreement"), whose Article 5(f) required Parties to "minimize ... catch of non-target species (both fish and non-fish species) ... and impacts on associated or dependent species, through measures including, to the extent practicable, the development and use of selective, environmentally safe and cost-effective fishing gear and techniques".

3.96. In 1993, the United States had joined with Mexico in leading negotiations toward a new multilateral agreement for the Western Hemisphere devoted specifically to protecting sea turtles from extinction. This three-year negotiating effort had concluded on 5 September 1996 with the adoption of the Inter-American Convention for the Protection and Conservation of Sea Turtles ("Inter-American Convention"). This new treaty required parties to take a variety of measures to protect and conserve sea turtles and their habitats, and stipulated, in particular that "[e]ach Party shall require shrimp trawl vessels subject to its jurisdiction that operate within the Convention Area[222] to use recommended TEDs that are properly installed and functional"[223] (Annex III, paragraph 3 of the Convention). The countries in the Western Hemisphere understood that, because of the highly migratory nature of sea turtles, a treaty that afforded protection to sea turtles in only one region of the world would not succeed unless countries in other regions adopted comparable measures. For this reason, Article XX of the Inter-American Convention encouraged its parties to negotiate complementary protocols to that treaty with states in other regions in order to promote the protection and conservation of sea turtles outside the Western Hemisphere.

3.97. The United States submitted that, following the conclusion of negotiations on the Inter-American Convention in the latter part of 1996, its Government had proposed to the governments of certain Asian nations, including those of the four complainants, the negotiation of such a protocol or other international agreement for sea turtle protection that would apply to the Asian region. The Governments of India, Malaysia, Pakistan and Thailand had declined to accept the offer of multilateral negotiations. Despite the fact that these governments had not, to date, agreed to negotiate a multilateral agreement for the protection of sea turtles in the Asian region, the required use of TEDs, both in Asia and throughout the Western Hemisphere, had become a multilateral environmental standard. Today, at least the following nations required TEDs on shrimp trawl vessels subject to their jurisdiction: Belize, Brazil, Colombia, Costa Rica, Ecuador, El Salvador, Guatemala, Guyana, Honduras, Indonesia, Mexico, Nicaragua, Nigeria, Panama, the People's Republic of China, Thailand, Trinidad and

[222] Article III of the Inter-American Convention defined the "Convention Area" to comprise "the land territory in the Americas of each of the Parties, as well as the maritime areas of the Atlantic Ocean, the Caribbean Sea and the Pacific Ocean, with respect to which each of the Parties exercises sovereignty, sovereign rights or jurisdiction over living marine resources in accordance with international law, as reflected in the United Nations Convention on the Law of the Sea".

[223] Inter-American Convention, Annex III, paragraph 4. The United States noted that the Inter-American Convention also required parties, *inter alia*, to prohibit the intentional take of sea turtles (except for limited subsistence use by traditional communities), to ban domestic as well as international trade in sea turtles and in their eggs, parts and products, to reduce the incidental capture, injury and mortality of sea turtles associated with all commercial fisheries, and to cooperate in international scientific research for the purpose of protecting sea turtles.

Tobago, the United States and Venezuela. Other nations in Asia and Africa had informed the United States of their intention or desire to establish TEDs programmes.

3.98. With respect to the assertion by the United States that the use of TEDs had become a multilateral environmental standard, **India** referred to the argument made by Thailand in paragraphs 3.101 to 3.104. India further responded that prior to the introduction of the embargo, the United States had not made any effort to initiate negotiations of an international agreement on the protection of sea turtles. Subsequent to the consultations held under the WTO dispute settlement mechanism in Geneva in November 1996, a proposal had been made by the United States to India to enter into a regional agreement on the lines of the Inter-American Convention. However, this proposal was conditional upon India abandoning the proceedings in the WTO. India had been unable to respond positively to the US proposal in view of the fact that India had been subject to trade restrictions which were inconsistent with the GATT and were not in conformity with CITES. In addition, India had declined the US proposal based on the fact that any proposal for a regional agreement on the protection and conservation of endangered species of sea turtles should, in India's view, emanate from the countries of the region in question. Regarding CITES, India added that the only trade restrictions which CITES obliged parties to take concerned the endangered species specified in the relevant Annexes to the Convention. Shrimps were not covered as an endangered species under the provisions of CITES, and therefore could not under those provisions be put under an import prohibition. Since the Unites States was of the view that the CITES prohibitions had not prevented the continuing decline of sea turtles worldwide, it had to address what it perceived as a problem facing endangered species of sea turtles in the forum of the CITES, which was the international agreement competent to deal with such a problem relating to sea turtles, and not to introduce discriminatory trade restrictions on shrimps in disregard of its WTO obligations.

3.99. **Malaysia** refuted the claim that the required use of TEDs had become a multilateral environmental standard or a standard that was acceptable to all countries. Although signatories to the Inter-American Convention for the Protection and Conservation of Sea Turtles recognized TEDs, there were still many countries which did not recognize the use of TEDs.[224] In that regard, Malaysia noted that Indonesia had banned trawling in 1980; this contradicted the US assertion that TEDs use was required in that country. The various treaties and multilateral agreements mentioned by the United States promoted conservation through multilateral mutual agreements and not by the imposition of import prohibitions. They made reference to the use of selective, environmentally safe and cost-effective fishing gear and not to the use of TEDs specifically. Furthermore, Agenda 21 provided for the need to develop agreed criteria and not unilateral measures. Malaysia observed that multilateral environmental treaties like the Convention on Biological Diversity (CBD), the United Nations Convention on Climate Change (UNFCC) and CITES shared the same principles, i.e. the principle of

[224] In commenting on Annex JJ of the United States (see below Section III.D), Malaysia noted that the Inter-American Convention had been cited as an important milestone in the global recognition of TEDs. Nevertheless, very few countries had actually ratified it. As of February 1997, only six countries of the entire region had signed the Convention, i.e. two short of the minimum number required to put this instrument into force.

international cooperation and that of national sovereignty.[225] It was only through this process that a measure would become a multilateral environmental standard. Malaysia declared that no sincere or serious effort had been made by the United States in establishing a arrangement similar to the Inter-American Convention with certain Asian countries. The import prohibition had been imposed on Malaysia on 1 May 1996. The only approach by the US Embassy in Malaysia had been to give a copy of the Inter-American Convention on an informal basis to the Ministry of International Trade and Industry of Malaysia in December 1996, i.e. two months after the consultation procedures between the United States and Malaysia had started in WTO. Since then, there had been no approach or indication, whether on an official or unofficial basis, that the United States intended to negotiate or discuss any arrangement. Malaysia further stated that the United States had not exhausted the bilateral and multilateral channels foreseen in Section 609 (a) (1) to negotiate and cooperate with Malaysia for the purpose of conserving sea turtles. The drastic measures taken by the United States in imposing the import prohibition had made that provision redundant.

3.100. With respect to the assertion by the United States that TEDs had become a multilateral environmental standard, **Pakistan** referred to the arguments made by Thailand in paragraphs 3.101 to 3.104. Pakistan further responded that it was unaware of any efforts made by the United States to initiate negotiations and/or reach bilateral or multilateral agreements on the protection of sea turtles relevant to the issues at stake in this proceeding.

3.101. **Thailand** responded that if the use of TEDs had become a multilateral environmental standard, this was largely due to the effectiveness of US coercion applied through the trade measure in dispute in this case. Certainly this was true of Thailand. Based on the evidence at Thailand's disposal, TEDs were not a cost-efficient means of avoiding sea turtle mortality in Thai waters and would not continue to be required in the absence of Section 609 and the consequences of abandoning TEDs use for Thailand's exports to the United States. The international conventions and conferences cited by the United States evidenced general international agreement that each State had the right to determine its own conservation measures. These conventions further evidenced a consensus that conservation issues relating to shared resources should be resolved through international cooperation, not unilateral action. Under CITES, Thailand and the other signatories had agreed that sea turtles were in need of protection and that "trade in these species must be subject to particularly strict regulation in order not to endanger further their survival".[226] However, parties to CITES had not agreed to trade limitations on species not listed in the Appendices, such as shrimp. Nor did CITES authorize signatories to take action against other signatories which did not limit bycatch by means specified by one signatory to the treaty as being essential or necessary. In fact, the preamble to CITES recognized that "peoples and States are and should be the best protectors of their own wild fauna and flora" and that "international cooperation is essential for the protection of certain species of wild fauna and flora against over-exploitation through international trade". CITES represented an international

[225] Malaysia referred, in particular, to Articles XIII and XIV of CITES, Article 3 and 5 and the Preamble of the CBD, Articles 3 and the Preamble of the UNFCC.
[226] Article II:1 of CITES.

consensus concerning what each State had to do to protect endangered or threatened species. By reverse inference, because the measures adopted by the United States were not authorized by CITES, there was no international consensus on their necessity or desirability. If the United States believed that other nations needed to take specific actions to protect sea turtles within their jurisdiction or on the high seas, the answer was to seek amendment to CITES or to negotiate other consensual international agreements to address the problem.

3.102. Thailand further argued that the 1982 United Nations Convention on the Law of the Sea ("LOS Convention")[227] recognized the sovereignty of States over their territorial waters and exclusive economic zones. Specifically, Article 2 provided that the sovereignty of a coastal State extended, beyond its land territory and internal waters and in the case of an archipelagic State, its archipelagic waters, to an adjacent belt of sea, described as the territorial sea. In addition, Article 56 provided that a coastal State had sovereign rights in its exclusive economic zone for purposes of exploring and exploiting, conserving and managing natural resources, whether living or non-living. The concept of sovereignty and the right to exercise jurisdiction over a State's own nationals was also set forth with respect to shared resources on the high seas. Specifically, Article 117 provided that "all states have the duty to take, or to co-operate with other States in taking, such measures for their respective nationals as may be necessary for the conservation of the living resources of the high seas". Article 62 of the LOS Convention provided that nationals of other States fishing in the exclusive economic zone of a State had to comply with the conservation measures and with the other terms and conditions established in the laws and regulations of the coastal State, including laws relating to the types, sizes and amount of gear used. While, as noted by the United States, this Article also provided that proper conservation and management measures should be taken, the Article provided the coastal State with the authority to make a determination as to which measures were necessary and appropriate.

3.103. Thailand recalled that, with respect to shared resources such as stocks occurring within the exclusive zones of two or more coastal States or highly migratory species, Articles 63 and 64 of the LOS Convention provided that states which fish for such shared resources should seek, directly or through appropriate sub-regional or regional organizations, to agree on measures necessary to ensure conservation and should cooperate directly or through appropriate international organizations with a view to ensuring conservation and promoting the objective optimum utilization of such species. With respect to the conservation of shared living resources on the high seas, Article 118 of the LOS Convention provided that "States shall cooperate with each other in the conservation and management of living resources in the areas of the high seas. States whose nationals exploit identical living resources, or different living resources in the areas, shall enter into negotiations with a view to taking the measures necessary for the conservation of the living resources concerned. They shall, as appropriate, co-operate to establish sub-regional or regional fisheries organizations to this end".

3.104. Thailand further mentioned that Principle 2 of the 1992 Rio Declaration provided that "States have, in accordance with the Charter of the United Nations and the

[227] United Nations Convention on the Law of the Sea, UN Doc. A.CONF.62/122, reprinted in 21 I.L.M. 1261 (1982).

principles of international law, the sovereign right to exploit their own resources pursuant to their own environmental and developmental polices, and the responsibility to ensure that activities within their jurisdiction or control do not cause damage to the environment of other States or of areas beyond the limits of national jurisdiction".[228] Principle 12 of the Rio Declaration provided that "States should cooperate to promote a supportive and open international economic system that would lead to economic growth and sustainable development in all countries, to better address the problems of environmental degradation. ... Unilateral actions to deal with environmental challenges outside the jurisdiction of the importing country should be avoided. Environmental measures addressing transboundary or global environmental problems should, as far as possible, be based on an international consensus". In the preamble to the Inter-American Convention for the Protection and Conservation of Sea Turtles, the drafters recognized that the protection and conservation of sea turtles required cooperation and coordination among States within the range of such species. Thus, the Agreements cited by the United States did not authorize or anticipate the unilateral regulation or determination of conservation policies with respect to shared global resources. To the contrary, the agreements demonstrated that there was an international consensus that such measures should be avoided in favour of international cooperation and regional or multilateral agreement with respect to conservation of shared global resources.

3.105. Thailand argued that the US offer to enter into multilateral negotiations for the protection of sea turtles had taken place after the embargo had been put in place and after the first round of WTO consultations. A copy of the Inter-American Convention had been submitted to the Thai authorities as a proposed model for the negotiations; however, that agreement required the use of TEDs. In addition, Thailand had been asked to abandon the WTO proceeding. In January 1997, the Thai Department of Fisheries responded to the US letter with a series of questions about the model agreement which were never answered. It then did not appear that the offer of negotiations had been seriously put forward by the United States or that the United States was open to any negotiated outcome other than one requiring TEDs to protect sea turtles. As to CITES, which required parties to take action to protect animals in other jurisdictions, Thailand conceded that parties could multilaterally agree to a derogation to GATT rights. Moreover, CITES required that action be taken with respect to the importation, sale, handling or exportation of the endangered species itself once it came within the jurisdiction of the party. The measure at issue in this dispute, in contrast, sought to bar access to the US market for imports of a species that was not endangered - shrimp - and represented a unilateral determination of the appropriate means to conserve resources outside the jurisdiction of the United States.

3.106. As to the argument that CITES represented an international consensus concerning what each State had to do to protect endangered or threatened species and that, by reverse implication, there was no international consensus on the need for TEDs, the **United States** replied that CITES only addressed international trade in endangered species, not other threats to these species. CITES did not purport to limit other measures

[228] Adoption of Agreements on Environment and Development, The Rio Declaration on Environment and Development, A/Conf.151/5/Rev. 1, 13 June 1992, reprinted in 31 I.L.M. 876.

that its Parties might take to protect endangered species. In fact, CITES expressly reserved the rights of its Parties to take such other measures. Moreover, since CITES required countries, including the complainants, to restrict trade in endangered species located in the jurisdiction of other countries, CITES helped to show that there was no general principle of international law prohibiting countries from taking measures to conserve endangered species located in the jurisdiction of other countries. Regarding Principle 12 of the Rio Declaration, the United States noted that the Rio Declaration did not mandate cooperation; rather, it only stated that "unilateral actions ... should be avoided". This was language of exhortation, not obligation. The United States further noted that the United Nations Convention on Climate Change referred to by Malaysia also stated that "[m]easures taken to combat climate change, including unilateral ones, should not constitute a means of arbitrary or unjustifiable discrimination or a disguised restriction on trade". This Convention explicitly acknowledged that countries could take so-called "unilateral" actions in order to prevent harm to the environment. The United States maintained that the US government was quite serious in proposing to the complainants the negotiation of a multilateral agreement to protect sea turtles, and that it remained serious in extending this offer. The United States regarded the Inter-American Convention for the Protection and Conservation of Sea Turtles as a model of international cooperation and hoped that similar agreements could be concluded for other regions, including Asia. Regarding the assertion by Malaysia that Indonesia had banned trawling in 1980 and thus had no TEDs programme, the United States maintained that Indonesia had an operative TEDs programme since 1982. On the invitation of the Indonesian Government, the United States Government had recently conducted a TEDs training seminar in Indonesia to assist them with continued implementation of its TEDs programme for its shrimp trawl fishery, which did exist. Indonesian representative also attended a TEDs workshop held by the United States in Thailand.

### 6. *Transfer of TEDs Technology*

3.107. The **United States** considered that one reason why TEDs use had become so widespread was that the United States Government had undertaken extraordinary efforts to transfer TEDs technology to governments and industries in other countries, particularly in developing countries. Since 1983, when gear specialists from NMFS first began working with foreign government officials, the United States had conducted more than 50 workshops on the design, construction, installation and use of TEDs, both in the United States and in other countries. These workshops usually lasted one week, beginning with classroom lectures and videos and continuing with a hands-on programme on the construction and installation of TEDs. Many workshops also involved fishing vessel demonstrations and evaluations at sea. Through these workshops and related efforts, the United States had transferred TEDs technology to at least the following countries: Australia, Belize, Brazil, Brunei, Colombia, Costa Rica, Ecuador, El Salvador, Eritrea, Guatemala, Guyana, Honduras, India, Indonesia, Japan, Kenya, Mexico, Madagascar, Malaysia, Mozambique, Nicaragua, Panama, the People's Republic of China, the Philippines, Singapore, Suriname, Tanzania, Thailand, Trinidad and Tobago, and Venezuela. In many cases, the United States has provided multiple TEDs workshops in a given country. Recently, the United States had intensified its TEDs technology transfer efforts. In 1996 alone, the United States conducted TEDs training workshops in Mombasa, Kenya; in Songkla, Thailand; in Tegal, Indonesia; in Guayaquil, Ecuador; and in Orissa, India. The workshop in Thailand had been particularly well-attended, including participation by fisheries managers and shrimp fishermen from Australia, Brunei, Japan, Malaysia, the Philippines, Singapore and Thailand. In 1997, to date, the United States had held TEDs workshops in Mombasa, Kenya (for the second time); in several locations in Australia; in Cochin, India; and in Chittagong, Bangladesh. Thus, through the efforts of the United States Government and other governments, in cooperation with industry and environmental groups, TEDs had become a true environmental success story.

3.108. **India** submitted that prior to the introduction of its import restriction, the United States had not made any effort to transfer TED technology to the Government of India or, to India's knowledge, to any industries in India. Since the introduction of the embargo, the US NMFS had organized two workshops in India in collaboration with the authorities of two of India's coastal States, and concerned Indian agencies. While TEDs were demonstrated at the workshops, India did not believe such demonstration constituted a transfer of TED technology. In fact, at the Cochin workshop, officials from the United States had demonstrated TEDs brought by NMFS experts from the United States. Although the US experts participating were shown TEDs fabricated by the Central Institute of Fisheries Nautical and Engineering Training (CIFNET), Cochin, these Indian-fabricated TEDs were not used by the participants in the workshop during demonstration sessions. Consequently, the TEDs demonstrated during this workshop were made in the United States, and were not specifically designed for the use in Indian waters. Recommendations issued after the Paradeep workshop called for further work on the possible use of TEDs in India. No recommendations were issued at the end of the Cochin workshop. During these two workshops, there was no indication given by US experts regarding the sharing of any new TED technology with India.

3.109. **Malaysia** responded that there had been no transfer of TED technology to its Government or to industries in Malaysia. No workshop had been conducted by the United States in Malaysia itself apart from the participation by Malaysia in a 1996 regional workshop organized by the Thai Department of Fisheries in cooperation with the Department of Foreign Trade and NMFS. Two experiments had also been carried out with TEDs, one prior to the workshop, and the other after the workshop. It was to be noted that whilst the cooperation extended by NMFS involved an NMFS official giving a talk on the use of TED, the experiments did not involve any US participation at all. Malaysia noted, furthermore, that the conservation strategies and TEDs workshops mentioned by the United States recommended and endorsed the use of TEDs through bilateral collaboration and friendly technology transfer. Much more could be achieved for sea turtles in this manner as opposed to the imposition of the import prohibition.

3.110. **Pakistan** responded that it was unaware of any efforts made by the United States, either before or after the imposition of the embargo, to transfer TEDs technology to Pakistan. The United States itself had recognized that there were serious costs and implementation issues associated with the manner in which the embargo had been implemented. In addition, a document submitted by the United States indicated that "in most countries there is a shortage of personnel adequately trained and supported to design and carry out research and conservation programmes, liaise with diverse sectors of society ... and enforce laws and regulations related to the conservation of sea turtles and the habitats on which they depend".[229] Nor had the United States conducted any TEDs training workshops in Pakistan.

3.111. **Thailand** noted that the United States met twice with Thai officials for the purpose of transferring technology. In the first instance, one gentleman from the US embassy visited Thai officials in February 1996 and provided a diagram of a TED together with indications where TEDs could be purchased in the United States. In the second instance, a four-person team from the NMFS attended a four day workshop in October 1996, for Thai fishermen. This workshop was financed and organized by the Thai Department of Fisheries and Department of Foreign Trade. The US representatives made some introductory comments concerning TEDs installation and use, and showed a video which described how TEDs were used in the United States. The video also briefly described how to install a TED. The major focus of the workshop was to convey the results of TEDs experiments and experience in Thailand, Australia, Malaysia and the Southeast Asian Fisheries Development Center (SEAFDEC).

3.112. The **United States** replied that Malaysia had attended a TEDs training workshop in Songkla, Thailand, held on 7-10 October 1996. More than 200 hundred participants were present, including 88 Thai fishermen and officials from Malaysia, Singapore, Brunei, The Philippines, Australia and Japan. This workshop included class training, a demonstration on the installation of TEDs and actual use of TEDs in Thai shrimp trawl nets. Moreover, the government of Malaysia had invited the US NMFS to conduct a workshop in Malaysia, but had withdrawn the invitation at the last minute. Pakistan had never asked for a TEDs workshop to be conducted in Pakistan and the Government of that country had recently declined an invitation to attend a TEDs workshop in Chittagong, Bangladesh. If Pakistan or any other country needed further information on TEDs, the United States would be glad to provide it. Two TEDs training sessions had been held in India. The TEDs workshops conducted by the United States provided comprehensive training in the design, construction, installation and use of TEDs. The workshop usually lasted for 3-4 days, starting with classroom lectures and video instruction, and continuing with hands-on demonstrations in which the participants themselves installed a TED in a net. US gear technicians usually constructed at least one TED from local materials and provided training in the construction of TEDs using those materials. During the October 1996 workshop conducted in Songkla, Thailand, US officials had constructed seven TEDs from local materials. The workshops concluded with a full-day demonstration of the proper way to use a shrimp trawl net with a TED installed. The at-sea sessions repeated the instruction on the installation of a TED, and also provided direction on deploying, retrieving and handling a TED. US officials accompanied shrimp fishermen on two or three vessel trips to nearby fishing grounds for the purpose of further teaching them the practical aspects of using TEDs in the local fishing conditions. The United States left the TEDs it constructed, along with instruction manuals, free of charge, once the training was completed. The United States also invited foreign fisheries officials and fishermen to visit the NMFS harvesting systems laboratory in Pascagoula, Mississipi for further training. Representatives from many nations had responded favourably to these

[229] IUCN (World Conservation Union), (1997), *A Marine Turtle Conservation Strategy and Action Plan for the Western Indian Ocean.*

invitations, including a delegation from the Thai Department of Fisheries, who had come to the laboratory in mid-July 1996. On that visit, the Thai delegation had also invited a TEDs manufacturer and had observed trawl operations with TEDs in the Gulf of Mexico. The United States remained ready and willing to provide technical assistance to make TED technology available to any nation that requested it.

### 7. *Scope and Purpose of Section 609*

3.113. **India, Pakistan and Thailand** stated that pursuant to Section 609, nations had been forced to quickly adopt TEDs requirements or lost the right to trade with the United States. The US Government had recognized during the litigation before the CIT that "[e]ven assuming the willingness of affected nations to comply with Section 609, a May 1, 1996 compliance date will achieve no conservation benefit". Specifically, a memorandum filed by the US government during the course of that litigation stated:

> "Even assuming the willingness of affected nations to comply with Section 609, a May 1, 1996, compliance date will achieve no conservation benefit. Significant training and practice in the construction, installation and maintenance of TEDs are required before TEDs can be effective in protecting sea turtles. ... In fact, the National Marine Fisheries Service ("NMFS") still engages in numerous training workshops for domestic fishermen, though the TEDs requirement has been in place for nearly a decade. ... For this reason, it is unlikely that shrimp fishermen will be able to use TEDs effectively in the short term to protect sea turtles. ... Immediate implementation of this Court's order, therefore, will not result in any benefit to sea turtles in those nations newly covered, because fishermen with no experience in TEDs use are not likely to be able to use them effectively in the near term to protect sea turtles. ... Furthermore, there are difficulties inherent in the implementation of a TEDs programme that will be exacerbated by the short time period imposed by the Court's order. These include limitations on funding for the adoption of a TEDs programme, acceptance by the affected industry of newly imposed requirements and loss of shrimp associated with the improper use and installation of TEDs. ... Without the time needed to resolve these problems, and the benefit of a cooperative training programme, these countries may abandon initial attempts at compliance, resulting in a net loss to sea turtle conservation".[230]

While the stated goal of Section 609 may have been to promote the protection and conservation of sea turtles, India, Pakistan and Thailand were of the view that, as recognized by the US Government, Section 609 as applied did not accomplish this goal.

---

[230] United States Court of International Trade, *Earth Island Institute* v. *Warren Christopher and National Fisheries Institute, Inc.*, Memorandum in Support of Defendants' Motion for Modification of 29 December 1995, Order, pp. 11-12.

3.114. India, Pakistan and Thailand further argued that this case was not about preventing imports of "turtle-unsafe" shrimp into the United States. Current US regulations provided that shrimp caught in trawl nets equipped with TEDs might not be imported into the United States unless the exporting nation was certified under Section 609. In order to be certified, a country had to show that all shrimp, whether consumed domestically, exported to the United States, or exported to other Members, was harvested using TEDs.[231] Thus, the purpose of the shrimp embargo was not simply to prevent importation into the United States of shrimp caught with technologies that might or might not pose a threat to sea turtles, it was to dictate the environmental policy that was to be followed by other Members with respect to all shrimp caught within their jurisdiction if they wished to export any shrimp to the United States.

3.115. The **United States** responded that, contrary to what the complainants asserted, the US Administration had never claimed that the applicability of Section 609 to shrimp harvested by nations outside the Wider Caribbean/Western Atlantic region would not promote sea turtle conservation. Section 609 initially applied only to shrimp harvested in the Wider Caribbean/Western Atlantic region. On 29 December 1995, the CIT determined that Section 609 applied on a global basis as of 1 May 1996. The US Administration asked that court to delay the effective date of its ruling by one year. In support of that request, it noted that most of the newly affected countries would be unlikely to adopted comprehensive TEDs programmes by 1 May 1996. However, the United States had never stated that the application of Section 609 to shrimp harvested in nations outside the Wider Caribbean/Western Atlantic region would not promote sea turtle conservation once these nations adopted comprehensive TEDs programmes. Despite the arguments of the US Administration, the Court had denied the request to delay the effective date of its ruling, which prompted the US Administration to redouble its efforts to provide TEDs technology to the newly affected countries, particularly in the South Asia region, so as to maximize their access to TEDs and to decrease the amount of time it would take them to adopt effective TEDs programmes. The United States further argued that the complainants appeared to seriously misapprehend the scope of Section 609; they appeared not to understand the categories of shrimp and products of shrimp to which the statute applied. The complainants accurately recognized that Section 609 did not apply to (and thus did not affect the importation of) shrimp or products of shrimp harvested by aquaculture ("aquaculture shrimp"). Aquaculture shrimp constituted the large majority of shrimp harvested in each of these nations. What the complainants appeared not to understand was that Section 609 also did not apply to (and thus did not affect the importation of) shrimp or shrimp products harvested by other means that were not harmful to sea turtles, which, for ease of discussion, could be referred to as "TED-caught shrimp", "artisanal shrimp", and "cold-water shrimp", respectively.[232]

---

[231] India, Pakistan and Thailand referred here to wild shrimp caught by mechanical means in warm waters.

[232] The United States referred here to "shrimp harvested exclusively by means that do not involve the retrieval of fishing nets by mechanical devices or by vessels using gear that, in accordance with the US programme described above, would not require TEDs" and to "species of shrimp, such as the pandalid species, harvested in areas in which sea turtles do not occur" (1996 Guidelines, 61 F.R. 17343). The United States noted that the term "artisanal shrimp" in this situation actually covered a

3.116. The United States believed that some of the misunderstanding may have its origins in the issuance of two rulings on this point by the CIT in *Earth Island Institute v. Christopher* on 8 October and 25 November 1996. The effect of those two rulings had been to reaffirm that Section 609 did not apply to aquaculture shrimp, artisanal shrimp or cold-water shrimp. These rulings had, however, determined that Section 609 did apply to TED-caught shrimp. The US Administration believed the ruling on TED-caught shrimp to be in error and had appealed it to the US Court of Appeals for the Federal Circuit. The United States noted, however, that the outcome of this appeal would appear to have no bearing on the four complainants since Thailand had adopted a comprehensive requirement for TEDs use in 1996 - and was accordingly certified pursuant to Section 609 - while the other three complainants had not instituted any TEDs requirements at all.

### *C. Trade Impact*

3.117. **India** explained that, as a result of its large size and a coastline extending more than 8,085 kilometres, it had a well-developed but fragmented fishing industry. The number of mechanized vessels in India was estimated to be 47,000. Most of these vessels were rudimentary. In addition to the mechanized vessels, there were approximately 200,000 traditional boats. India submitted that the United States began enforcing the embargo on shrimp consignments in October 1996. Since that time, there had been a variety of adverse effects on India's once-thriving shrimp industry. The discriminatory effects of the embargo imposed by the United States had led to a dramatic decline in India's shrimp exports to the United States. Two major Harmonized Tariff Schedule (HTS) categories of shrimp had been affected by the embargo: HTS 0306.13.00, Shrimps and Prawns, Not Frozen and HTS 1605.20.10, Other Prepared Shrimp and Prawn Products.

3.118. India noted that the data from US imports statistics clearly demonstrated that the rapid decline in India's shrimp exports was proximately caused by the embargo. US import data indicated that the value of imports of fresh shrimp from India classified in HTS category 0306.13.00 fell from US$10.9 million to US$6.8 million, a decline of nearly 60 per cent, from October to November 1996. While shipments had begun to increase slightly in January 1997, they would not reach the levels that would be possible, absent the embargo. The decline in Indian shrimp sales classified under HTS 1605.20.10 had been even more dramatic, falling from approximately US$1.6 million in October 1996 to only US$935,500 in November 1996 and only US$750,500 in December 1996. This rapid decline in shipments had hurt the Indian shrimp industry, which was already suffering on the account of a disease that struck some of India's coastal districts during 1995 and 1996.

3.119. India argued that the US embargo had had a ripple effect on the entire Indian shrimping industry. For example, because shrimp raised in aquaculture was allowed to

---

wide variety of shrimp harvested with gear that did not harm sea turtles, including certain kinds of modern trawl gear in which sea turtles did not get caught. Similarly, the term "cold-water shrimp" in this situation covered shrimp harvested in all environments in which sea turtles did not occur; e.g. in fresh water.

be shipped to the United States, a larger proportion of the total share of farm-raised shrimp was now being exported to the United States, denying local and other export markets the benefits of aquaculture shrimp. This had harmed India's commercial shrimp vessels, as the foreign demand for wild harvested shrimp had fallen. The US action had also had the effect of causing a great deal of uncertainty within the Indian shrimp industry. The socio-economic condition of the coastal community in India was closely linked with fishing and the embargo had adversely affected their livelihood. The embargo had also created great difficulties to many processing units in India. There were a number of collection centres where raw materials from various sources were collected, iced and sent to the processing units for processing. The embargo had forced these centres to maintain separate tubs and storage facilities for material from different sources, which had lead to considerable waste of time and under-utilization of facilities already created. The US actions had also had additional extraterritorial effects on India's shrimping industry. For example, because a certification form had to accompany an export of shrimp, the Government of India had had to implement a system to enable government inspectors to sign the *Shrimp Exporter's Declaration*. In a country the size of India, this had proved to be very difficult. Moreover, many shrimpers had been inconvenienced since it was time-consuming for exporters to prepare the necessary forms and obtain the required authorization from the competent Indian authorities.

3.120. **Malaysia** argued that its exports of shrimps to the US market - its fifth largest importer of that product - constituted about 5.6 per cent of its total export of shrimp in 1995. Malaysia contended that the enforcement by the US of Section 609 had significantly affected the shrimp export industry in Malaysia. In 1995 the total value of exports of shrimp to the US was US$9.1 million. In 1996, it was US$4.86 million. Exports had fallen from US$2.87 million (May-October 1995) to US$1.8 million in the corresponding months of 1996 which amounted to a drop of 38 per cent. The import prohibition had affected most of the exporters who had ceased their exports of shrimp to the United States after the import prohibition came into effect in May 1996. The company Great Ocean Seafood Sdn. Bhd. had their last consignment exported on 8 August 1996. As of September 1996 the company Rex Canning Sdn. Bhd. was the only exporter of shrimp to the United States since 60 per cent of its shrimp came from aquaculture. Several exporters had ceased exporting to the United States and were now exporting to other markets. Most of Malaysia's exports of shrimps to the United States were from the States of Sabah and Sarawak. The export from these two states constituted about 92.6 per cent of the total of Malaysia's shrimp export to the United States for 1995 and 87.8 per cent (January-October) for 1996. About 95 per cent of the shrimp exported to the United States were wild harvested.

3.121. **Pakistan** argued that the shrimp embargo had dramatically decreased shrimp exports to the United States and disrupted Pakistan's domestic shrimp market. There had been an adverse effect on Pakistan's shrimp industry since October 1996, when the United States began enforcing the embargo against Pakistan. Even though shrimp was harvested in Pakistan exclusively by manual means, the United States insisted that Pakistan implement a programme requiring the use of TEDs. Because Pakistan remained uncertified, it had led to a dramatic impact on shrimp sales to the United States. The embargo had decimated Pakistan's exports to the United States. Pakistan noted that, according to US import data, the value of imports of fresh shrimp from Pakistan classified in HTS category 0306.13.00 fell from US$1.8 million in

October 1996 to US$707,000 in November and only US$115,000 in December. Pakistan's export statistics showed a similar trend. Obviously, this steep decline in shipments had had a negative impact on Pakistan's fishermen and shrimp industry. Moreover, the US embargo had had, and continued to have, a negative psychological effect on Pakistan's shrimp industry. It had been quite difficult attempting to disseminate the details concerning the US embargo to the small fishing villages located on Pakistan's coast. Simply put, the US action had caused a great deal of uncertainty in Pakistan's shrimp industry. The US actions had also had additional extraterritorial effects. For example, because a certification form had to accompany an export of shrimp, the Government of Pakistan had had to train government officials and to implement a system to enable government inspectors to sign the *Shrimp Exporter's Declaration*. Moreover, many shrimpers had been greatly inconvenienced since they had to worry about filling out US government forms proving their method of fishing.

3.122. **Thailand** submitted that the US shrimp embargo imposed pursuant to Section 609, effective on 1 May 1996, had resulted in a loss of trade for Thailand. Statistics prepared by the Global Trade Information Service compiled from official US import statistics, showed that between May 1996 and December 1996, the period during which Thailand was not certified, exports of shrimp from Thailand to the United States had declined by approximately 18 per cent from the same period in 1995. On 8 November 1996, the United States had certified Thailand pursuant to Section 609. The State Department had not previously certified Thailand because "the Government of Thailand had not required all commercial shrimp trawl vessels subject to its jurisdiction that operated in waters where there is a likelihood of intercepting sea turtles to use turtle excluder devices at all times". However, Thailand's present and future ability to export wild-harvested shrimp to the United States was conditioned on maintaining its status as a certified country. Certification could be revoked at any time, as illustrated by the cases of Ecuador and Colombia which had been decertified on 1 May 1997 because an on-site investigation conducted by US officials had indicated that there had been wide-spread non-compliance with each country's law requiring the use of TEDs. Certification was therefore dependent on US review of the measures which had been taken by Thailand in order to achieve certification (i.e. requiring TEDs use on its shrimping vessels and maintaining a credible programme of enforcement).

3.123. The **United States** argued that the measures at issue in this dispute had not disrupted the importation of shrimp into the United States. Those measures went into effect with respect to the complainants and other shrimp harvesting nations outside the Wider Caribbean/Western Atlantic region on 1 May 1996.[233] Even though the measures were in effect throughout the last two thirds of 1996, 1996 US shrimp imports in 1996 were within 1 per cent of the average annual level from 1993-1995. Furthermore, were the US measures at issue in this dispute truly disruptive of trade, one would expect that a restriction in supply would have resulted in a corresponding increase in the price of shrimp imports into the United States. The opposite had occurred. The average unit value of US shrimp imports had declined between 1995 and 1996, falling from

[233] The United States noted that the measures did not, however, affect importation of shrimp harvested in these nations and shipped to the United States before 1 May 1996, even if such shrimp did not actually reach the United States until after 1 May 1996.

US$9.52 per kg to US$9.30 per kg. The United States further argued that US shrimp imports from India had increased since 1 May 1996, rising by 7.85 per cent in value terms and 6.9 per cent in volume terms. Comparing the eight month period from May-December 1996 with the same period in 1995 revealed an even more startling increase: US imports of shrimp from India had risen 27.1 per cent in value terms, and its share of total US shrimp imports had also increased by 29.4 per cent. India's exports of shrimp to the United States had also increased since 1 May 1996 relative to the average of the three preceding years. Finally, virtually none of these increases was attributable to an increase in the per unit price of India's shrimp exports, which had gone up less than 1 per cent during this period. Similarly, US imports of shrimps from Pakistan had increased by 8.3 per cent from 1995 to 1996. A comparison of the May-December periods in 1995 and 1996 showed an increase of 19.7 per cent in value terms, 5.7 per cent in volume terms. As with India, virtually none of these increases was attributable to an increase in the per unit price of Pakistani shrimp exports to the United States, which had increased only 4 cents per kg (from US$5.76 to US$5.80).

3.124. **India Pakistan and Thailand** maintained that their exports of shrimp and shrimp products to the United States dropped substantially after the imposition of the embargo. The fact that total imports into the United States had not decreased did not mean that the measure had not disrupted trade, it simply meant that the measure had resulted in preference for countries that had been certified and that other nations had had to alter trading patterns by sending only exempted shrimp to the United States.

3.125. **India** added that the reported increase in the India's exports from May to December 1996 could only have occurred because of an increase in the exportation to the United States of shrimp harvested in India by non-mechanical artisanal means or by aquaculture farming. Thus, even assuming that the Panel chose to overlook the decline in India's exports to the United States, the very fact that India had to shift its exports based on method of harvest and country of destination, and then incur administrative expenses associated with ensuring that only non-mechanical artisanally harvested shrimp and aquaculture shrimp was exported to the US market, while mechanically harvested shrimp was exported to other countries, meant that the embargo affected trade. India noted that figures provided by the United States indicated that imports from India in May-December 1996, totalling US$1.821 million, was in fact lower than imports from India during the same period in 1995, totalling US$1.856 million.[234] India refuted the US assertion that imports in volume terms from India during the calendar year 1996 were higher than in the calendar year 1995. In volume terms, figures from the United States[235] showed clearly that the embargo had affected general shrimp exports from India to the US market, with the worst effect on HTS 0306.13.00, which had declined from a level of 2,165,110 kgs in September 1996 to 1,544,510 kgs in October 1996, and had continued to decline steadily thereafter to register 1,134,930 kgs in November and 1,113,639 kgs in December 1996. This declining trend was significant in comparison to the upward trend in India's export of this product to the United States during the same October-December period both in 1995, when India's overall shrimp

[234] Data derived from official US Department of Commerce statistics in four HTS tariff categories (03061300, 03062300, 16052005 and 16052010).

[235] Bureau of Census (IM-145) # 723948.

exports were adversely affected by a disease that struck India's coastal districts where shrimp was harvested, and in 1994. In 1995, exports in the month of November were 1,282,511 kgs and in December 1,686,536 kgs. In 1994, corresponding figures were for November 1,538,009 kgs and for December 2,039,976 kgs.

3.126. **Malaysia** stated that, although the import prohibition had not disrupted the volume of import of shrimp into the United States, exporting countries affected by the import prohibition suffered a loss of market share. The US market share which was held by exporting countries now affected by the import prohibition (uncertified countries) had been taken over by certified countries. Thus, even if the total imports had not been affected, it did not necessarily mean that exports of countries affected by the action had not been adversely affected by the import prohibition. In the case of Malaysia there had been a decline in the export of shrimp and shrimp products to the US as previously indicated.

3.127. For **Pakistan**, the fact that total US shrimp imports had remained relatively constant since the imposition of the embargo and that US shrimp import prices had dropped slightly, demonstrated only that US shrimp demand was fairly constant, not that the embargo had had no effect on trade. The US analysis failed to consider the impact of the embargo on exporting countries, such as a shift in markets for non-certified countries (as was the case for Pakistan), or an increase in market share for certified countries.

3.128. **Thailand** submitted that, according to information received by the Thai Department of Fisheries, in the spring of 1996, the imminent embargo and unknown form that the US regulations would take created such uncertainties in the marketplace that middlemen told Thai shrimp fishermen they could not continue to pay the market price and take the risk that the shrimp they purchased could not be sold in the United States. The price charged by the Thai shrimpers dropped accordingly. At least part of this decline was then passed on to customers in the United States on shrimp that could still be exported to the US market with a declaration that such shrimp had been caught by a vessel deploying a TED (this particular form of declaration was ruled unlawful by the CIT in October 1996). In short, the embargo had two adverse trade effects: it reduced the total volume and the average unit value of shrimp exported to the United States. The embargo had resulted in a substantial amount of uncertainty in the industry even before its imposition. For example, in March 1996, when exporters of Thai shrimps were aware of the possibility of the embargo, it was unclear whether the embargo would apply to both aquaculture and wild-harvested shrimp. Many exporters did not want to export shrimp due to the perceived risk of absolute loss. There was also a sharp decline in prices associated with this uncertainty: the middlemen claimed they could not pay prevailing prices due to the uncertainty regarding the ability to export to the United States. Finally, the embargo resulted in a loss to Thailand of US market share. For instance, from May-December 1995, imports of shrimp from Thailand under the 0306 HTS heading accounted for 31 per cent of total imports to the United States. However, during May-December 1996, Thai fishermen accounted for only 27 per cent of total imports to the United States, a decrease of 4 per cent.[236] Thailand had therefore

---

[236] Thailand indicated that these percentages were based on US import statistics which showed total value of shrimp imports under the 0306 Harmonized Tariff Schedule heading of approximately

been forced to explore the possibility of increasing exports to other markets, which had resulted in the expenditure of both time and money.

### D. *Communications Received from NGOs*

3.129. The Panel received two *amicus briefs* submitted by non-governmental organizations (NGOs). The first one was submitted on 28 July 1997 jointly by the Center for Marine Conservation (CMC) and the Center for International Environmental Law (CIEL); the second one, submitted by the World Wide Fund for Nature (WWF), was received by the Panel on 16 September 1997. The Panel acknowledged receipt of the two *amicus briefs*. The NGOs concerned had also sent copies of these documents directly to the parties to the dispute. In a letter dated 1 August 1997 and at the second substantive meeting of the Panel, India, Malaysia, Pakistan and Thailand requested the Panel not to consider the content of the *amicus briefs* in its examination of the matter under dispute. At the second substantive meeting of the Panel, the United States, stressing that the Panel could seek information from any relevant source under Article 13 of the DSU, urged the Panel to avail itself of any relevant information in the two *amicus briefs*, as well as in any other similar communications. Taking the view that it had not requested such information under Article 13 of the DSU, the Panel informed the parties to the dispute that it did not intend to take these documents into consideration. The Panel observed, however, that if any of the parties to the dispute wanted to put forwards these documents, or part of them, as part of their own submission to the Panel, they were free to do so; the other parties would then have two weeks to respond to the additional material. The United States availed itself of this opportunity by designating Section III ("Statements of Facts") of the *amicus brief* from CMC and CIEL, as Exhibit JJ to its second submission to the Panel (hereinafter "Exhibit JJ").

3.130. Regarding the procedural aspects, **India** noted that the Panel had acted in an appropriate manner under the provisions of Article 13 of the DSU by refusing to accept the *amicus brief* submitted by the Centre for Marine Conservation, a non-governmental organization. In India's view, by adopting the "factual portions" of the *amicus brief*, as an attachment to its oral statement made at the second substantive meeting of the Panel, the United States had acted against the provisions of paragraph 1 of Article 12 and paragraph 7 of Appendix 3 of the DSU, especially since the latter clearly stipulated that the purpose of the second substantive meeting was for formal rebuttals to be made. The United States had decided to attach the "factual portions" of the *amicus brief* to its oral statement only at the end of the second substantive meeting of the Panel with the parties, after the formal rebuttal statements had been made and the question-and-answer session completed. Therefore, the attachment of this material in this manner could not be considered as an integral part of the United States' formal rebuttal, especially since the United States, as the party complained against, had exercised its right to take the floor first, and in its oral statement formally rebutted the written rebuttals submitted to the Panel by the co-complainants, including India. In this oral statement, the United

US$1,872,708,000 in 1995 and US$1,726,520,000 in 1996; imports under the same heading from Thailand were approximately US$571,717,000 in 1995 and US$469,891,000 in 1996.

States had not indicated that the "factual portion" of the *amicus brief* would be attached to its oral statement. In fact, the United States' oral statement made the following reference to the *amicus brief*: "Under Article 13 of the DSU, the Panel may seek information from any relevant source ... We submit that the Panel should avail itself of any relevant information in the Centre for Marine Conservation communication, as well as in any other similar communications". It was therefore clear that the *amicus brief*, either in its entirety or in its "factual portions", was not an integral part of the formal rebuttal made by the United States under the DSU procedures. Indeed, if any portion of the *amicus brief*, including its "factual portion", were an integral part of the oral statement made by the United States, then the oral statement made at the commencement of the second substantive meeting of the Panel should have referred to such portions in order to provide the necessary linkage between Exhibit JJ and the specific arguments made by the United States in its statement. In the absence of any such reference, this Exhibit could not be considered to be relevant to any specific arguments contained in the US formal rebuttal. India would therefore submit that all the information contained in Exhibit JJ attached to the oral statement of the United States should be rejected on these procedural grounds by the Panel.

3.131. **Malaysia** recalled that, by a letter dated 1 August 1997 addressed to the Chairman of the Panel, Malaysia and the other complainants had objected to the consideration of the *amicus brief*. This objection was based on Article 13 of the DSU which did not permit anyone to make unsolicited submissions. Article 13 merely provided that the Panel itself might seek information and technical advice from any individual or body which it deemed appropriate. It was to be noted that the *amicus brief* comprised not only technical advice but also legal and political arguments. Thus, the brief did not fall within the purview of Article 13. Malaysia wished to seek clarification from the Panel as to the position of the *amicus brief* vis-à-vis the parties. There was no legal premise upon which the Panel could rule that a party was free to adopt the arguments of the *amicus brief* and have it endorsed as part of their submission. Article 13 did not allow for the acceptance of an *amicus brief* from NGOs. The only instance where a non-party to a dispute could appear before the Panel or gain access to it was through Article 10 of the DSU, which provided third parties an opportunity to be heard by the Panel or to make a written submission.

3.132. **Thailand** objected to the participation in this dispute by the Center for Marine Conservation or by any other non-governmental organization through the filing of briefs or oral presentations. The WTO dispute settlement procedures nowhere provided that parties which were not Members could participate in the proceedings. Under Article 13 of the DSU, the panel itself could seek information or technical advice from any individual or body within the jurisdiction of a Member.

3.133. **Pakistan** endorsed the comments made by India, Malaysia and Thailand.

3.134. The Panel noted that the arguments presented in Exhibit JJ are in essence the same as those put forward by the United States and reflected in Section III.B of this Report. In their responses to Exhibit JJ, India, Malaysia, Pakistan and Thailand maintained their arguments as developed in Section III.B.

### E. Legal Arguments

#### 1. Articles I, XI and XIII of GATT

3.135. **India, Pakistan and Thailand** argued that the embargo on shrimp and shrimp products was inconsistent with the most-favoured-nation ("MFN") principle embodied in Article I:1 of GATT 1994 because physically identical shrimp and shrimp products from different nations were treated differently by the United States upon importation based solely on the method of harvest and the policies of the foreign government under whose jurisdiction the shrimp were harvested. Imports of shrimp and shrimp products from some shrimp harvesting nations were denied entry into the United States while imports of like shrimp and shrimp products from other nations were permitted entry into the United States. Further, even assuming, *arguendo*, that the method of harvest did affect the nature of the shrimp, the embargo violated Article I:1 because, pursuant to the embargo, wild shrimp harvested by use of TEDs were forbidden entry into the United States if harvested by a national of a non-certified country, while shrimp harvested by the same method by a national of a certified country would be permitted entry into the United States. The embargo, as applied, was also inconsistent with Article I:1 of the GATT 1994 because initially affected nations had been granted a phase-in period of three years, while newly affected nations had not been given a similar phase-in period. Thus, initially affected nations had been given the opportunity to implement the required use of TEDs without substantially interrupting shrimp trade to the United States. Products from these countries had therefore been given an "advantage, favour, privilege or immunity" over like products originating in the territories of other Members.

3.136. India, Pakistan and Thailand submitted that Article XI:1 of GATT 1994 provided for the general elimination of quantitative restrictions on imports and exports. The scope of Article XI:1 was comprehensive, applying to all measures instituted or maintained by a Member prohibiting or restricting the importation, exportation or sale for export of products other than measures that took the form of duties, taxes or other charges.[237] Measures prohibited by Article XI:1 included outright quotas and quantitative restrictions made effective through import or export licenses.[238] The US embargo on imports of shrimp and shrimp products pursuant to Section 609 violated Article XI:1 of the GATT. The embargo constituted a prohibition or restriction on the importation of shrimp and shrimp products from the complainants. Further, the embargo plainly was not in the nature of "duties, taxes or other charges". The fact that Thailand was now certified and therefore was not presently subject to the embargo did not alter the fact that Section 609 violated Article XI:1. Certification was contingent on the country in question acting in conformity with the certification requirements of US law and, as evidenced by the recent de-certification of Ecuador and Colombia, could be revoked at any time. The *Tuna I*[239] and *Tuna II*[240] Panel Reports involved a measure

---

[237] Panel Report on *Japan - Trade in Semi-conductors*, adopted 4 May 1988, BISD 35S/116, paragraph 104.

[238] See for instance the Panel Report on *Thailand - Restrictions on Importation of and Internal Taxes on Cigarettes*, adopted 7 November 1990, BISD 37S/200.

[239] Panel Report on *United States - Restrictions on Imports of Tuna*, circulated 3 September 1991, not adopted, BISD 39S/155.

virtually identical to the restriction on shrimp imports at issue in this dispute. These two Panels reviewed primary and secondary embargoes maintained by the United States on tuna imported from nations that had not implemented conservation programmes "comparable" to those in effect in the United States to protect dolphins incidentally taken by commercial fishermen harvesting tuna. In both cases, they found that the restriction constituted a violation of Article XI.[241]

3.137. India, Pakistan and Thailand further argued that Section 609 was inconsistent with Article XIII:1 of GATT 1994 because it restricted the importation of shrimp and shrimp products from countries which had not been certified, while "like products" from other countries which had been certified could be imported freely into the United States. The United States permitted or denied entry of shrimp and shrimp products based on the method of harvest. However, the method of harvest did not affect the nature of the product, as noted by the *Tuna II* Panel. Indeed, all foreign shrimp and shrimp products had the same physical characteristics, end-uses, and tariff classifications and were perfectly substitutable.[242] Thus, shrimp products which may be imported into the United States pursuant to Section 609 were "like" shrimp products from non-certified countries which were denied entry. The differential treatment of "like products" from certified and non-certified countries violated Article XIII:1 of the GATT.

3.138. Even assuming, *arguendo,* that the method of harvest did affect the nature of the product, the embargo violated Article XIII:1 because, pursuant to the embargo, wild shrimp harvested by use of TEDs were forbidden entry into the United States if harvested by a national of a non-certified country, while shrimp harvested by use of TEDs by a national of a certified country would be permitted entry into the United States. In other words, the identical product (shrimp caught by use of TEDs) was permitted entry if imported from a certified country and denied entry if imported from a non-certified country.

3.139. India, Pakistan and Thailand further argued that the embargo as applied, was inconsistent with Article XIII:1 because newly affected nations had received only four months notice before shrimp and shrimp products harvested without use of TEDs would be refused entry into the United States, while initially affected nations had been granted a three-year phase-in period. Thus, importation of like products from initially affected nations was not "similarly" prohibited. Finally, the fact that Thailand had been certified and therefore was not presently subject to the embargo did not alter the fact that the embargo violated Article XIII:1. Certification was contingent on the country in

---

[240] Panel Report on *United States - Restrictions on Imports of Tuna*, circulated 16 June 1994, not adopted, DS29/R.

[241] Panel Report on *United States - Restrictions on Imports of Tuna*, circulated 16 June 1994, not adopted, DS29/R; Panel Report on *United States - Restrictions on Imports of Tuna*, circulated 3 September 1991, not adopted, BISD 39S/155. See also Panel Report on *United States - Prohibition of Imports of Tuna and Tuna Products From Canada*, adopted 22 February 1982, BISD 29S/91.

[242] India, Pakistan and Thailand referred to the Panel Report on *United States - Standards for Reformulated and Conventional Gasoline*, adopted 20 May 1996, WT/DS2/9, paragraph 6.9 ("Chemically identical imported and domestic gasoline by definition have exactly the same physical characteristics, end-used, tariff classification, and are perfectly substitutable and are therefore like products").

question acting in conformity with the certification requirements of US law, such as requiring a declaration form to accompany all shipments and, as evidenced by the recent de-certification of Ecuador and Colombia, could be revoked at any time.

3.140. **Malaysia** argued that the import prohibition imposed by the United States under Section 609 on the importation of shrimp and shrimp products was contrary to Article XI of GATT 1994. The United States intended to coerce other nations to follow its regulatory programme and deemed that other nations' conservation efforts were totally inadequate to ensure the survival of sea turtles. The policy requirement was that exporting countries had to ensure that their fishermen use TEDs approved in accordance with US standards while trawling for wild harvested shrimp. It was a policy condition as there were definitely other conservation methods or practices which were equally effective if not better to ensure the survival of sea turtles. As explained in Section B, Malaysia was practising effective turtle conservation policies. Therefore the import prohibition was arbitrary, discriminatory and was nothing else but a disguised restriction on international trade with a view to protecting their domestic shrimp industry with a total disregard to international law. The import prohibition was not in the nature of "duties, taxes, or other charges" and therefore was inconsistent with Article XI:1

3.141. Malaysia submitted that Article XI provision had been previously considered in *Tuna I* and *Tuna II*. In *Tuna I*, the panel had found that the direct import prohibition and the provisions of the Marine Mammal Protection Act ("MMPA") under which it was imposed were inconsistent with Article XI:1. In *Tuna II*, the panel had found that the embargoes imposed by the United States were prohibitions or restrictions in the terms of Article XI as they banned the import of tuna or tuna products from any country not meeting certain policy conditions, and were not duties, taxes or other charges. In the present case Malaysia contended that Section 609 was contrary to the US obligations under the General Agreement. The import prohibition imposed by the United States fell under Article XI as it banned import of shrimp or shrimp products from any country not meeting certain policy conditions under Section 609. Malaysia submitted that the findings of *Tuna I* and *Tuna II* were equally applicable to the facts of this case and therefore urged the Panel to find that the import prohibition was inconsistent with Article XI. Malaysia further argued that the import prohibition imposed by the United States was not justified under paragraph 2 of Article XI since that paragraph referred to situations of "critical shortages of foodstuffs or other essential products" (paragraph 2(a)) or "the application of standards and regulations for the classification, grading or marketing of commodities in international trade", (paragraph 2(b)). Nor is paragraph 2(c) applicable, since it refers solely to "restrictions".

3.142. Malaysia further submitted that nations within the wider Caribbean region had been allowed three years to adopt a programme after the publication of the US requirement, while newly affected nations had received only four months notice (29 December 1995 to 1 May 1996) before being subject to the embargo. Malaysia itself had had only three months to comply before the import prohibition came into effect, as shown by a letter dated 22 January 1996 from the US Embassy in Kuala Lumpur to the Department of Fisheries, Ministry of Agriculture which stated that "the United States Department of State must receive from your government all necessary information for a certification by April 1, 1996". Malaysia argued that this differential treatment was discriminatory and inconsistent with Article XIII:I of GATT 1994.

3.143. With regard to the violation of Articles I, XI and XIII of GATT 1994 alleged by the complainants, the **United States** submitted that the complainants had the burden of proving the violation.[243] Since under Article XX nothing in the GATT 1994 was to be construed to prevent the adoption or enforcement of the measures at issue, there was little practical significance to attempts by the complainants to establish an inconsistency between these measures and other provisions of GATT 1994 and the United States did not need to address GATT Articles I, XI and XIII. The United States noted it did not dispute that, with respect to countries not certified under Section 609, Section 609 amounted to a restriction on the importation of shrimp within the meaning of Article XI:1 of GATT 1994. However, the United States did not agree with complainants' claims under Articles I and XIII (particularly since the US measures applied equally to all harvesting nations), but if the Panel made a finding with respect to Article XI there would be no need to reach Articles I or XIII.

### 2. *Article XX of GATT*

#### (a) Preliminary Observations

3.144. **India, Malaysia, Pakistan and Thailand** submitted that, according to dispute settlement practice, the burden of demonstrating that a measure fell under one of the general exceptions provided for in Article XX was on the party invoking that provision. Noting that the United States invoked in this case paragraphs (b) and (g) of Article XX, the complainants argued that the United States was not able to demonstrate that the measure at issue fell within the scope of either of these two exceptions.

3.145. The **United States** argued that this dispute concerned the measures it took to protect and conserve sea turtles, an endangered natural resource that all parties to this dispute had agreed needed to be protected and conserved. There had never been a clearer or more compelling case presented to the WTO for the conservation of an exhaustible natural resource or the protection of animal life or health than this dispute. The United States required its shrimp fishermen to harvest shrimp in a manner that was safe for sea turtles. In this case, the United States only asked that shrimp imported into the United States should be harvested in a comparable manner. In this way, the US market would not cause a further depletion of endangered sea turtle species and the United States was not forced to be an unwilling partner in the extinction of sea turtles. This dispute dealt with issues that were central to how the rules of the multilateral trading system interacted with the ability of Members, both individually and collectively, to meet critical environmental objectives. The United States considered that, in assessing the facts presented by the parties to this dispute, the Panel was not called on to undertake a study of the most effective methods for sea turtle conservation. Rather, the Panel needed only consider whether the United States had met its burden of showing that the US measures complied with the relevant requirements of Article XX.

---

[243] Appellate Body Report on *United States - Measure Affecting Imports of Woven Wool Shirts and Blouses from India*, adopted 23 May 1997, WT/DS33/AB/R, DSR 1997:I, page 337 ("[A] party claiming a violation of a provision of the *WTO Agreement* by another member must assert and prove its claim").

3.146. The United States noted that the World Trade Organization Agreement ("WTO Agreement"), which was the first multilateral trade agreement concluded after the UN Conference on Environment and Development, provided that the rules of trade must not only promote expansion of trade and production, but must do so in a manner that respects the principle of sustainable development and protects and preserves the environment. Yet, the complainants claimed that in becoming a Member of the World Trade Organization, the United States had agreed to accept imports of shrimp whose harvest and sale in the US market might mean the extinction from the world of sea turtles for all time. This was not true. The WTO promised that nothing in the GATT 1994 might be construed to prevent the adoption and enforcement of measures "necessary to protect human, animal or plant life or health" and of measures "relating to the conservation of exhaustible natural resources if such measures are made effective in conjunction with restrictions on domestic production and consumption", subject to the requirement that "such measures are not applied in a manner which would constitute a means of arbitrary or unjustifiable discrimination between countries where the same conditions prevail, or a disguised restriction on international trade". These provisions of the GATT 1994 promised that Members' measures to conserve natural resources and to protect animal life and health took precedence over any provisions of that instrument to the contrary. The United States noted that the first Appellate Body decision under the WTO also emphasized that the GATT 1994 allowed WTO Members to adopt measures to conserve and protect the environment.[244] As stated by the Appellate Body, Article XX contained requirements designed to safeguard against measures that were intended to serve protectionist ends, rather than the important and legitimate policy objectives within the intended scope of Article XX. The record in this dispute established that the United States measures under Section 609 were *bona fide* measures to protect and conserve an exhaustible natural resource. The measures at issue were clearly within the scope of Article XX paragraphs (g) and (b) of GATT 1994 and thus fully consistent with US obligations.

3.147. The United States concluded that the right of WTO Members to take measures under Article XX of GATT 1994 to conserve and protect natural resources was reaffirmed and reinforced by the Preamble to the WTO Agreement. The first clause of the Preamble recognized that international trade and economic relations under the WTO Agreements should allow for "optimal use of the world's resources in accordance with the objective of sustainable development", and should seek "to protect and preserve the environment". In sum, the WTO Agreement stated affirmatively that protection and

---

[244] The United States referred to the Appellate Body Report on *United States - Standards for Reformulated and Conventional Gasoline*, adopted 20 May 1996, WT/DS2/9, DSR 1996:I, page 17 ("Article XX of the General Agreement contains provisions designed to permit important state interests - including the protection of human health, as well the conservation of exhaustible natural resources - to find expression. The provisions of Article XX were not changed as a result of the Uruguay Round of Multilateral Trade Negotiations ... WTO Members have a large measure of autonomy to determine their own policies on the environment (including its relationship with trade), their environmental objectives and the environmental legislation they enact and implement. So far as concerns the WTO, that autonomy is circumscribed only by the need to respect the requirements of the General Agreement and the other covered agreements.")

conservation of the environment were essential objectives that were to be supported by the WTO regime.

3.148. **India, Pakistan and Thailand** stressed that this case was not about conservation; it was about the imposition of unilateral trade measures designed to coerce other Members to adopt environmental policies that mirrored those in the United States. The US claim that, if not allowed to maintain the measure at issue, the United States would be "forced to be an unwilling partner in the extinction of sea turtles" was a dramatic overstatement. First, because of the conservation measures implemented in India, Pakistan and Thailand respectively, the risk of extinction had abated. Second, the United States had the option to work with other nations on additional measures that could be taken to conserve sea turtles without unilaterally imposing its own solutions to the problem. Third, it was curious that, if universal TEDs usage was the only means of protecting sea turtles from extinction, the United States did not approach the complainants about an agreement on this issue until November 1996, long after the embargo had been put in place, and, indeed, after they had notified the United States and the Members of their intention to bring this dispute to the WTO for resolution.

3.149. India, Pakistan and Thailand noted that the United States referred to, but did not quote in its entirety, the Preamble of the WTO Agreement which recognized the goal of "sustainable development ..., seeking both to protect and preserve the environment". However, the Preamble went on to state that efforts to preserve the environment were to be accomplished by each Member "in a manner consistent with their respective needs and concerns at different levels of economic development", and simply invoking environmental concerns did not guarantee "safe harbour" within the narrow exceptions contained in Article XX. The US measures were therefore inconsistent with the Preamble when that language was considered in its entirety. Specifically, the United States had failed to demonstrate that the environmental policies it was insisting that other countries should adopt as a condition of access to the US market were either necessary to ensure sustainable development or consistent with the respective needs and concerns of Members at different levels of economic development. Moreover, the Preamble did not, by itself, add to or subtract from the obligations of Members under the GATT 1994. As noted by the Appellate Body in the *Gasoline* case, "[t]he provisions of Article XX were not changed as a result of the Uruguay Round of Multilateral Trade Negotiations". Since the language of Articles XI, I, XIII, and XX did not change between the GATT 1947 and the GATT 1994, there was no basis to conclude that Members intended any different interpretation of those provisions than that found by previous panels in their interpretations of the GATT 1947.

3.150. **India** further agreed with the United States that the Panel was not called on to undertake a study of the most effective methods for sea turtle conservation. India requested the Panel to focus on the trade measures introduced by the United States, namely the import prohibition on certain shrimp and shrimp products from India.

3.151. **Malaysia** submitted that the United States gave only a partial citation of the Preamble to the WTO Agreement. The Preamble recognized that the rule of trade was to promote expansion of trade and production in a manner that respected the principle of sustainable development and protected and preserved the environment, but it also specified that such protection and preservation of the environment and the enhancement of the means to do so had to be done in a manner consistent with each Member's respective needs and concerns at different levels of economic development.

3.152. According to the **United States**, the issue was whether the US measures to conserve endangered sea turtles were consistent with WTO rules or, as the complainants claimed, whether those rules required the United States to participate in the extinction of sea turtles. But the complainants' arguments - such as their request that the Panel impose a jurisdictional limitation on Article XX (see sub-section (b)(i)) - had much greater implication. If accepted, GATT 1994 would forbid WTO Members, both individually and collectively, from adopting trade measures needed to conserve the environment. The United States believed that such a severe limitation was not only inconsistent with the text of Article XX, but would be the exact wrong direction for the developing jurisprudence under the WTO, DSU and GATT 1994. The international community was increasingly aware of growing threats to the world environment. Moreover, the Preamble to the WTO explicitly provided that the rule of trade had to be applied in a manner that protected and preserved the environment. The far-reaching limitations to Members' rights suggested by the complainants did not even have support in the language of the Agreement. The GATT 1994, and in particular Article XX, could hardly be more clear in allowing Members to adopt trade measures to promote conservation goals. It was these rules, as written in the Agreement, that had to govern the resolution of this dispute, and not complainants' redrafting of these rules.

3.153. The United States did not agree with India, Pakistan and Thailand that the Preamble to the WTO Agreement should not be considered by the Panel. The United States noted that the complainants' premised their argument on the Appellate Body's statement in the *Gasoline* case that the "provisions of Article XX were not changed as a result of the Uruguay Round". However, the United States had never stated that Article XX had "changed". To the contrary, as shown by the plain text of the Agreement, the circumstances of the drafting of Article XX, and the subsequent practices of the contracting parties, Article XX had never included the jurisdictional limitation claimed by the complainants (see below the arguments made by the United States under sub-section (b)(i)). The United States further argued that India, Pakistan and Thailand misconstrued the statement of the Appellate Body in the *Gasoline* case. The Appellate Body, in its sentence immediately following the statement that Article XX "has not changed" proceeded to look at the Preamble as an aid in interpreting Article XX. The Panel should do the same here. Although Article XX did not "change" between the GATT 1947 and the GATT 1994, a Panel construing the GATT 1994 should look to the Preamble of the WTO Agreement as an aid to interpreting the GATT 1994. Indeed, under the principles of the Vienna Convention, the Preamble of a treaty was part of the "context" to be examined in interpreting the treaty's substantive provisions.

3.154. The United States noted that India, Malaysia, Pakistan and Thailand complained that the United States had not discussed the preambular language regarding sustainable development, nor the language regarding the needs and concerns of Members at different levels of economic development. However, the United States had already addressed both these issues at length. Contrary to what was argued by India, Pakistan and Thailand, the Preamble did not indicate, when referring to sustainable development, that the United States had to demonstrate that the US measures were necessary to ensure sustainable development. Rather, the Preamble stated that international trade relations should "allow[] for the optimal use of the world's resources in accordance with the objective of sustainable development". The US measures were fully consistent with this objective: shrimp fishing practices which led to mass extinction of sea turtles were not consistent with the objective of sustainable development. Conversely, by not allowing its shrimp consumption to contribute to the endangerment of sea turtles, the US measures fostered the objective of sustainable development. Furthermore, the United States had also showed that its measures were consistent with the objective of respecting the "needs and concerns [of countries] at different levels of economic development". In particular, the United States had shown that TEDs were relatively inexpensive, could be fabricated from indigenous materials, and had been successfully adopted by many countries, including developing countries.

3.155. **India, Pakistan and Thailand** replied that in requesting the Panel to find an implied jurisdictional limitation in Article XX(b) and (g), they were not asking the Panel to legislate, but to interpret the language of Article XX in light of the understanding of its original drafters and the structure of the Agreement (see below the arguments made by India, Pakistan and Thailand under sub-section (b)(i)). Important, indeed overriding, objectives of the GATT would be undermined if one party was given the power, under the rubric of natural resource conservation, to dictate the environmental policies that had to be followed by other governments. The interpretation proposed by the complainants would, however, not prevent WTO Members from collectively adopting trade measures necessary to conserve the environment. As found in *Tuna II*, Members could agree among themselves to waive GATT rights and Members as a whole could, of course, amend the agreement. India, Pakistan and Thailand also noted they did not request the Panel to ignore the Preamble to the WTO Agreement, but they asked the Panel to consider that the Preamble did not, by itself, confer any rights or exemptions from GATT obligations and that the language of Article XX remained unchanged from the GATT 1947 to the GATT 1994. The complainants also requested that the Panel consider the Preamble in its entirety.

3.156. **Malaysia** replied that in Malaysia trawling for shrimp did not result in extinction of sea turtles and Malaysia had adequate conservation and protection measures with respect to sea turtles which were consistent with the concept of sustainable development, as recognized in the first preambular provision of the WTO Agreement. Malaysia further did not agree that the US measures were consistent with the objectives of respecting the "needs and concerns [of countries] at different levels of economic development". The principle of sustainable development in the WTO Preamble meant that each country had a right to determine its own level of development commensurate with its needs and concerns.

### (b) Jurisdictional Application of Article XX(b) and (g)

#### (i) Text of Article XX

3.157. **India, Pakistan and Thailand** argued that Article 3.2 of the DSU directed Panels to apply customary rules of interpretation of public international law when interpreting the provisions of the GATT. The rules of interpretation set forth in the Vienna Convention on the Law of Treaties ("Vienna Convention") constituted customary rules of interpretation of public international law within the meaning of Article 3.2 of the DSU. Article XX did not expressly limit its coverage to the humans, animals or plants located within the jurisdiction of the Member taking the measure. Nor did Article XX(b) expressly permit a Member to take measures concerning humans, animals or plants located within the jurisdiction of another Member. The language of Article XX(b), when construed in accordance with its ordinary meaning, was ambiguous on this point. However, the terms of a treaty were not to be interpreted in a vacuum. Rather, pursuant to Article 31(c) of the Vienna Convention, "relevant rules of international law applicable in the relations between the parties" shall be taken into account together with the context of the terms. Rules of international law applicable in relations between the parties included Articles 1.2, 2.1 and 2.7 of the Charter of the United Nations, which recognized the sovereign equality of states and the principle of non-interference in the internal affairs of another state. In light of these general rules of international law, it should be presumed that Article XX(b) did not extend to measures taken by one Member that affected the life or health of the people, animals and plants within the jurisdiction of another Member, absent specific treaty language to the contrary. Regarding Article XX(g), India, Pakistan and Thailand further argued that the language of that provision was silent as to whether the exception covered only exhaustible natural resources located within the jurisdiction of the Member enacting the measure, or whether it extended to all natural resources, wherever located. However, as previously discussed, the terms of a treaty were not to be interpreted in a vacuum and the "relevant rules of international law applicable to the relations between the parties" had to be taken into account together with the context of the terms. In addition, Article 32 of the Vienna Convention stipulated that the drafting history of a provision could be resorted to in order to resolve the ambiguity.

3.158. **Malaysia** argued that Article XX had to be read with due consideration to the general principles of international law governing the issue of jurisdiction, as stipulated by Article 3.2 of the DSU which made it mandatory for the DSB to apply customary rules of interpretation of public international law.

3.159. The **United States** argued that the argument made by India, Pakistan and Thailand that a jurisdictional limit should be imposed on Articles XX(b) and XX(g) was entirely without merit, and should be rejected by the Panel. The United States noted first that the sea turtles protected and conserved by the US measures in fact did not fall exclusively within the complainants' respective jurisdiction. To the contrary, sea turtles were a shared global resource. They had ranges extending thousands of kilometres, and navigated through the coastal waters of many countries. If any one country in the range of a sea turtle population adopted practices resulting in high sea turtle mortality, the population would be endangered throughout its entire range. Thus, even if India, Pakistan and Thailand could support their proposal for a jurisdictional limitation on Article XX (and they could not) such a limitation would not apply to sea turtles, as their ranges extended throughout the high sea and waters under the jurisdiction of many nations, including the United States.

3.160. The United States further argued that Article XX paragraph (b) and (g) were not ambiguous with regard to their jurisdictional scope. Nothing in the language of these two paragraphs raised any question with regard to a possible limitation on the jurisdiction in which the animals or other natural resources were located. Contrary to what was asserted by India, Pakistan and Thailand, the absence of an explicit statement of inclusion did not create an ambiguity. For example, Article XX(b) also did not explicitly state that the animals could be found on the land or in water - but certainly no one would claim that Article XX(b) was "ambiguous" with regard to coverage of both terrestrial and aquatic animals because the language did not explicitly include them. In short, Articles XX(b) and XX(g) were clear on their face: they unambiguously applied to "animals" and "natural resources", without any limitation to the location of the animals or natural resources. In addition, the interpretation proposed by India, Pakistan and Thailand was not supported by past adopted panel reports. Nowhere in the *U.S.-Canada Tuna*, *Herring and Salmon,* or *Gasoline* decisions had the panels first analyzed whether the resource to be protected was outside the jurisdiction of the country taking the measure.[245]

3.161. The complainants' proposed jurisdictional argument was not supported by the Charter of the United Nations and the principles embodied therein concerning "the sovereign equality of States and the principle of non-interference in the internal affairs of another state". General sovereignty principles in the Charter of the United Nations did not address whether endangered species located in one country could be the subject of concern of another country. And, in fact, Malaysia stated in this case that "the concept of permanent sovereignty had not prevented international law from treating conservation issues within a state's territory as a question of common concern in which the international community possesses a legitimate interest" (see below paragraph 3.274). Moreover, CITES, to which each of the four complainants was a party, did explicitly address this issue. As noted above, CITES prohibited the trade in certain endangered species - including endangered species located in the jurisdictions of all other countries - even in countries not parties to CITES. Thus, under CITES, each of the complainants currently was obligated to take trade measures to conserve natural resources located in the jurisdiction of other countries. This showed that, contrary to what was argued by the complainants, there was no general principle of international law prohibiting countries from taking measures to conserve endangered species located in the jurisdiction of other countries. Further, the GATT itself refuted any argument that trade measures generally should not have effects on the internal affairs of exporting countries. For example, Article VI allowed for the imposition of countervailing duties in response to internal subsidies granted by exporting countries, and Article XX(e) provided that measures may be taken with regard to the products of prison labour.[246] Moreover, the *Gasoline* Panel had had no difficulty accepting that the United States, in its desire to conserve clean air pursuant to Article XX(g), was entitled to apply requirements that affected refineries located in Venezuela and owned by the Venezuelan State.[247]

---

[245] Panel Report on *United States - Standards for Reformulated and Conventional Gasoline*, adopted 20 May 1996, WT/DS2/R; Panel Report on *Canada - Measures Affecting Exports of Unprocessed Herring and Salmon*, adopted 22 March 1988, BISD 35S/98; Panel Report on *United States - Prohibition of Imports of Tuna and Tuna Products from Canada*, adopted 22 February 1982, BISD 29S/91.

[246] The United States noted that, as the Panel stated in *Tuna II*, measures "could in principle be taken under other paragraphs of Article XX and other Articles of the General Agreement with respect to things located, or actions occurring, outside the territorial jurisdiction of the party taking the measure. An example was the provision in Article XX(e) relating to the products of prison labour". Panel Report on *United States - Restrictions on Imports of Tuna*, circulated 16 June 1994, not adopted, DS29/R, paragraph 5.16.

[247] Panel Report on *United States - Standards for Reformulated and Conventional Gasoline*, adopted 20 May 1996, WT/DS2/R, paragraph 3.14.

3.162. The United States believed that India, Pakistan and Thailand also confused the extrajurisdictional application of a country's laws with the application by a country of its laws, within its own jurisdiction, in order to protect resources located outside its jurisdiction. In determining that shrimp was produced in a manner that undermined the conservation of sea turtles, the United States did not require any country to follow the US conservation policy nor did the United States undermine the sovereignty of other nations. Countries remained free to use any methods they considered appropriate in harvesting shrimp. However, if those countries chose harvesting methods that threatened sea turtles and that would undermine US conservation measures, those countries could not expect the United States to accept shrimp produced by those methods. This was no different than, for example, permitting WTO Members to refuse to support prison labour by prohibiting imports of products produced by prisoners.

3.163. **India, Pakistan and Thailand** responded that Article XX was silent on whether human, animals and plant or the natural resources could be protected or conserved by means of measures that would otherwise violate provisions of the GATT, included resources outside the jurisdiction of the party imposing the measure. However, this provision had to be interpreted in light of relevant rules of international law. The Charter of the United Nations was relevant to the interpretation of Article XX because it illustrated a fundamental rule of international law that individual nations had the sovereign right to regulate persons, animals or things within their jurisdiction. In light of this rule, it would be illogical to conclude the drafters of the GATT intended to permit contracting parties, under Article XX, to adopt trade measures for the purpose of coercing other contracting parties to modify their policies affecting human, animals, plants or natural resources within their jurisdiction (broadly defined), including within their territorial waters or exclusive economic zones.

3.164. India, Pakistan and Thailand considered that, contrary to what the United States claimed, CITES did not establish a rule of international law allowing states to impose trade measures to conserve natural resources located outside of their jurisdiction. The United States did not - and could not - show that CITES authorized an import embargo on a non-endangered species - shrimp - in order to protect or conserve an endangered species - sea turtles. Nor were the complainants "currently [is] obligated to take trade measures to conserve natural resources located in the jurisdiction of other countries". The only action that was in fact required or authorized under CITES was the prohibition of trade in, or possession of, certain endangered species themselves (Article VIII - Measures to be Taken by the Parties); i.e. CITES required that action be taken with respect to the importation, sale, handling or exportation of the endangered species itself once it came within the jurisdiction of the party. Therefore, CITES did not authorize the US action in this dispute nor did it illustrate why this Panel should find that the US action fell within one of the general exceptions to the GATT. CITES only demonstrated that for exceptions to these general principles of international law to be tolerated by the international community, there had to be international agreement.

3.165. The reference made by the United States to GATT provisions - Article VI and Article XX(e) - to suggest that all other provisions of Article XX should be interpreted to permit Members to take trade measures affecting the internal affairs of an exporting country was without merit. The imposition of countervailing duties under Article VI was a remedial measure expressly permitted in the GATT. The additional duty was intended to offset the effect of a subsidy on products imported into the Member imposing the measure; Article VI did not depend for its effectiveness on changes in the behaviour or policies of the exporting country. Under Article XX(e), a signatory might prohibit or otherwise regulate trade in products of prison labour. In this case, a very specific form of labour exploitation was targeted for special treatment in the GATT. The fact that these provisions were targeted at policies or practices outside of the jurisdiction of the country imposing the measure said nothing about the intended reach of Article XX(g) or (b). In fact, the presence of these very specific measures pointed to the opposite conclusion. When Members intended to allow a country to take actions which involved matters generally considered to be under the control of another country, the actions that could be taken were plainly described and the foreign policies or practices were highlighted. That was not the case here. (Indeed, to the extent that a goal of Article XX(e) was to protect the life and health of prisoners, the exception would be unnecessary if Article XX(b) were applicable to all measures taken to protect the life and health of people, animals and plants, regardless of location.) Article XX(b) was intended to protect sanitary measures from GATT scrutiny and Article XX(g) was intended to permit Members to place limits on exports of finite, physical resources within their jurisdiction so as to reserve them for later domestic use.

3.166. India, Pakistan and Thailand submitted that the location of the resource to be protected had not been raised by the parties in any of the three disputes cited by the United States. In addition, the natural resource at issue in the *Gasoline* dispute was clean air in the United States, not in Venezuela. India, Pakistan and Thailand were of the view that the "policy concerns" raised by the *Tuna I* Panel Report were probative of the issues before this Panel. Contrary to what was suggested by the United States, India, Pakistan and Thailand were not issuing an invitation to the Panel to legislate, but were asking the Panel to interpret the words of the Agreement itself. In doing so, the Panel had to be mindful of the consequences of its interpretation on the core obligations protected by the GATT. If Article XX(g) was interpreted as proposed by the United States, there would be a serious erosion of GATT rights in which the exception swallowed the rule.

3.167. The **United States** replied that the US measures in no way violated the principle, found in the Charter of the United Nations or in other agreements, such as the UN Convention on the Law of the Sea, that nations had the sovereign right to regulate persons, animals, or things within their jurisdiction. The only "regulation" imposed by the US measures was on the importation of shrimp into the jurisdiction of the United States; the United States did not and could not impose its sea turtle conservation measures on persons within the jurisdiction of other countries. In fact, under general principles of sovereignty, nations had the right to regulate imports into their jurisdictions. The question here, which the United Nations Charter did not answer because it did not mention trade at all, was whether WTO Members had agreed to let products into their jurisdiction if to do so would contribute to grave environmental harm. The answer to this question was found in the WTO Agreement itself: Article XX provided that no other provision of the GATT might prevent a Member from adopting measures under Article XX(g).

3.168. The United States further argued the US measures were not taken pursuant to CITES. CITES involved trade in endangered species, their parts and their products. It neither authorized or prohibited the sea turtle conservation measures of the United States which were at issue in this dispute. However, the complainants were wrong when they characterized CITES as not allowing states to impose trade measures to conserve natural resources located outside their jurisdiction. CITES restricted trade not only in live endangered species, but also in dead specimens, as well as in "any readily recognizable part or derivative thereof" (Article I(b)). For example, CITES restricted trade in rhinoceros horn powder, as well as in live rhinoceroses. The exhaustible natural resource to be conserved - the living members of endangered species - did never need to enter the jurisdiction of a CITES member for the CITES trade restrictions to apply. In short, there was no way around the fact that complainants, as parties to CITES, were obligated to take trade measures to protect exhaustible natural resources located outside their jurisdiction. Thus, CITES conclusively rebutted the complainants' claim that "general international law principles" forbade measures having the purpose of conserving resources outside a nation's jurisdiction.

3.169. The United States addressed the policy concerns raised by the complainants in support of their argument on jurisdiction, in particular that without a jurisdictional limitation on Article XX(g), there would be a "serious erosion of GATT rights in which the exception would swallow the rule". The United States noted that it was not the role of Panels under the DSU to conduct a general policy review of the GATT. Nevertheless, the United States stressed three points regarding the complainants' arguments. First, by assuming the conclusion - i.e. that the US measure violated US obligations under the GATT - and then arguing that a ruling in favour of the United States would further "erode" these obligations, the complainants were making a completely circular argument. The central question in this case was whether or not the GATT imposed on the United States the obligations claimed by the complainants. More specifically, the question was whether the United States had the obligation to accept imports of shrimp regardless of the resulting impact on the environment, or whether the United States had retained the right to limit such imports in furtherance of a *bona fide* conservation measure. Since the inception of the GATT, the United States, as well as many other nations, including the complainants under CITES, had continued to hold and to exercise the right, as preserved by Article XX, to regulate trade for the purpose of conserving exhaustible natural resources outside their jurisdiction. Second, the WTO Agreements did not provide for unfettered trade at all costs. Rather, the WTO Agreement, in both the Preamble and GATT Article XX, recognized that the rule of trade had to allow Members to pursue valid conservation goals. Third, the arguments that the Panel needed to impose a jurisdictional limitation on Article XX - despite an absence of textual support - in order to prevent abuses of Article XX exceptions was contrary to the reasoning of the Appellate Body in *Gasoline*. In that case, the Appellate Body explained that the very purpose of the Article XX chapeau was to prevent abuse of the Article XX exceptions by excluding measures applied in a discriminatory manner that would constitute arbitrary or unjustifiable discrimination, or disguised restrictions on trade. Finally, the complainants' argument that Article XX incorporated a jurisdictional limitation was contradicted by the position they had taken in the negotiation of the draft decision on Domestically Prohibited Goods (DPGs).[248] That draft decision, unequivocally supported by all the complainants, expressly provided that a country

[248] Working Group on Exports of Domestically Prohibited Goods and Other Hazardous Substances, Report by the Chairman of the Working Group, L/6872, 2 July 1991.

could ban exports of a product when necessary to protect the health of persons located in another country. Exports restrictions being generally prohibited under GATT Article XI, it would appear that the negotiators had relied implicitly on the applicability of Article XX to export restriction under the draft DPGs decision. In other words, the GATT consistency of the DPGs decision implicitly relied on the protection of persons located outside the country imposing the measure. Yet, neither complainants, nor any other country, ever raised an issue concerning the GATT consistency of the DPGs decision due to some sort of jurisdictional limitation on Article XX.

3.170. **India, Pakistan and Thailand** replied the US response to the complainants' policy concerns was just as circular. Notwithstanding the results reached by *Tuna I* and *Tuna II*, the United States assumed that it had always retained the right to hold its market hostage to changes in other Members' environmental measures and then asserted that there was therefore no erosion in GATT rights threatened by upholding this asserted "right". Second, the WTO Agreement did not permit unfettered resort to Article XX(g) to justify unilateral trade embargoes of non-endangered natural resources. Third, the Appellate Body never considered in *Gasoline* whether a measure of this type exceeded the implied jurisdictional limitation in Article XX(g) because the natural resource to be protected in that case was clean air in the United States, not in Venezuela. The reference made by the complainants to the Charter of the United Nations and the Law of the Sea intended to show that the United States did not have jurisdiction over the method of harvest of shrimp in the complainants' territorial waters or exclusive economic zones, or on the high seas where US nationals and vessels were not involved. The purpose was to demonstrate that, by enacting this measure, the United States was seeking to influence the regulation of persons or things over which it had no internationally recognized jurisdiction. More specifically, the principles embodied in the UN Charter were pertinent because they established that each nation was sovereign within its jurisdiction and that no nation had the right to interfere in the sovereign affairs of another state. This fundamental understanding, adopted in the United Nations Charter contemporaneously with the drafting of the GATT 1947, informed the drafters' conception of the scope of measures that could be taken under Article XX(g) to "conserve natural resources". The drafters would not have presumed to give one contracting party the power to insist that its preferred environmental strategies be adopted by all other contracting parties as a condition of exercising normal GATT rights to free trade in non-endangered species. The drafters' understanding on the scope of the exemption being given to individual contracting parties in 1947 could be given effect by this Panel by finding an implied jurisdictional limitation in Article XX(g).

3.171. While CITES required parties to take action to protect animals in other jurisdictions, the complainants conceded that parties could multilaterally agree to a derogation of GATT rights existing between them. However, in the absence of a multilateral agreement by all affected parties, attempts to regulate persons, things or activities taking place outside the legal jurisdiction of the party seeking to impose such regulation was inconsistent with international law. CITES required that action be taken with respect to the importation, sale, handling or exportation of the endangered species itself, once it came within the jurisdiction of the party. Moreover, CITES was a multilateral agreement evidencing broad consensus regarding appropriate measures that should be taken to protect and conserve endangered species. The measure at issue in this dispute, by contrast, sought to bar access to the US market for imports of a species that was not endangered - shrimp - and represented a unilateral determination of the appropriate means to conserve resources outside the jurisdiction of the United States. Article XX was not available to protect a GATT-inconsistent measure that affected trade in a non-endangered species, nor was it available to insulate from GATT liability measures taken to force other Members to change environmental policies within their sole discretion and control. The decision on Domestically Prohibited Goods, which had not yet been finalized, would have represented an agreement by all parties to the GATT, and therefore would have represented a subsequent modification to Article XI. Members could agree among themselves to derogations of GATT rights and all of the Members could amend the agreement.

3.172. India, Pakistan and Thailand concluded that if the unfettered right to ignore GATT obligations in the pursuit of an environmental objective were secured by Article XX, there would be no limit to the types of goods that could be embargoed in the name of environmental aims. It would not be necessary to limit one's measure to things that were harvested in the same net. Under its understanding of Article XX, the United States could freely choose to embargo computer chips if it thought that such an embargo would be more effective in securing action by the complainants to implement a TEDs programme in shrimp trawl fisheries. In other words, there was no necessary connection, under the US view of Article XX(g), between the article subject to the embargo and the conservation of an endangered species. The United States could even embargo imports of prepared foods in order to secure adoption of a favoured US timber conservation programme. By imposing an embargo on one product in order to achieve the conservation of another, the United States had broken the link between the measure and the thing to be conserved. If that link could be freely broken under Article XX, there was no limit to the types and kinds of GATT-inconsistent measures that could be maintained in the name of conservations. Abuse of the GATT system in the name of conservation could only be prevented by refusing to give "safe harbour" to unilateral trade measures that affected trade in resources whose conservation was not the object of the measure.

3.173. The **United States** stressed the limited purpose for examining general principles of international law in the resolution of this dispute. The Panel's terms of reference were to examine the complainants' claim in light of the obligations of the United States under the "relevant provisions of the covered agreements", in this case the provisions of GATT 1994. The relevant provisions of GATT 1994, in particular Article XX, did not incorporate general rules of international law. Thus, general rules of international law were only relevant in so far as they served as aids to interpreting the text of the GATT, pursuant to Article 31(3)(c) of the Vienna Convention. However, as already explained, Articles XX(g) and (b) were clear on their face. The text did not mention any limitations based on the jurisdiction in which the persons, animals or other natural resources to be conserved or protected were located. In fact, the term "jurisdiction" was not even used in Article XX. In short, the complainants asked the Panel not to use rules of international law to interpret any particular language in Article XX, but rather asked the Panel to redraft Article XX by incorporating an entirely new limitation based on complainants' purported rules of international law.

3.174. Regarding CITES, the United States noted that the complainants acknowledged that CITES required parties to take action to protect animals in other jurisdictions. This aspects of CITES, to which the complainants are parties, disproved their theory that general rules of international law forbade countries from taking such action. Moreover, the complainants' response to this point - i.e. that parties could multilaterally agree to a derogation of GATT rights that existed between them - did not even address the point that the existence of CITES disproved their theory. Rather, the complainants' response regarding mutually agreed derogations was addressed to a different issue - the relationship between multilateral environmental agreements and a GATT Article XX rewritten to include the complainants' proposed jurisdictional limitation. Specifically, the complainants were responding to the point of the United States that under the complainants' proposed jurisdictional limitation, no multilateral environmental agreements calling for trade measures would be allowed under Article XX. The complainants failed to rebut this point. Trade measures under CITES, for instance, applied even to countries that were not parties to CITES, and thus to countries that had not agreed to any "derogations" of their rights under the GATT.

3.175. The complainants' response regarding the draft DPGs decision departed from historical facts. Pursuant to Article XXV:1 of the GATT 1947, the DPGs Working Group was meeting to "give effect to" provisions of the Agreement, with a view to "facilitating the operation and furthering the objectives of the Agreement". The DPG Working Group never proposed or considered any amendment to the GATT 1947, nor any derogations from GATT rights and obligations. The draft instrument prepared by the Working Party would have been a decision of the CONTRACTING PARTIES, not an amendment or waiver, and as such could not change or derogate from the GATT 1947. In short, the draft decision reflected the understanding of all delegations that measures for the protection of persons outside of a party's jurisdiction would be consistent with the GATT.

### (ii) Drafting History of Article XX

3.176. **India, Pakistan and Thailand** argued that the preparatory work of Article XX(b) which, pursuant to Article 32 of the Vienna Convention could be consulted "... in order to confirm the meaning resulting from the application of Article 31 or to determine the meaning when the interpretation according to Article 31:(a) leaves the meaning ambiguous or obscure ...", also supported an interpretation whereby Article XX(b) could not be invoked to justify measures applying to animals outside the jurisdiction of the country enacting the measure. The drafting history of Article XX(b), revealed that the contracting parties' intent was to protect sanitary laws from GATT challenge. The drafting history confirmed therefore that it was the contracting parties' intent to insulate from GATT challenge only those measures designed to protect human, animal or plant life or health within the jurisdiction of the party taking the measure. The conclusion of the *Tuna I* Panel Report was fully supported by the drafting history.[249] Throughout the drafting process, several delegates had provided examples of the measures at issue. All of these examples involved sanitary measures to protect human, animal or plant life or health in an importing country from exposure to infected or

[249] India, Pakistan and Thailand referred the Panel Report on *United States - Restrictions on Imports of Tuna*, circulated 3 September 1991, not adopted, BISD 39S/155 paragraph 5.26.

pest-ridden imports.[250] Recourse to the supplementary means of interpretation therefore demonstrated that Article XX(b) was intended to apply only to measures necessary to protect the life and health of humans, animals or plants located within the jurisdiction of the Member enacting the measure.

3.177. This interpretation was further confirmed by US government publications released concurrently with the conclusion of the General Agreement in 1947 and with the adoption of amendments to the General Agreement in 1955. In *Analysis of General Agreement on Tariffs and Trade*, Department of State Publication 2983, Commercial Policy Series 109 (released November 1947), the following explanation of Article XX of the GATT was provided:

> "Article XX contains a number of exceptions which customarily appear in international commercial agreements, together with certain other exceptions growing out of the economic conditions peculiar to the transitional post-war period. Among the customary exceptions *are those permitting the application of measures to protect human, animal or plant life or health* (*sanitary regulations*); measures to protect public morals; measures relating to international movements of gold or silver; measures to enforce the customs laws and prevent deception or fraud; measures to conserve exhaustible natural resources, if made effective in conjunction with restrictions on domestic production or consumption; and measures applied under approved international governmental commodity agreements".[251]

3.178. Further, the drafting history of other provisions contained in the original text of the General Agreement confirmed that this exception applied only to sanitary regulations. Article XXII of the original text of the General Agreement provided as follows:

> "Each contracting party shall accord sympathetic consideration to, and shall afford adequate opportunity for consultation regarding, such representations as may be made by another contracting party with respect to the operation of customs regulations and formalities, anti-dumping and countervailing duties, quantitative and exchange regulations, subsidies, state-trading operations, *sanitary laws and regulations for the*

---

[250] India, Pakistan and Thailand referred to E/PC/T/A/PV/25, p. 21 (during the Second Session of the Preparatory Committee, the Chairman of the commission drafting the exception discussed the level of proof necessary when "a country refuses to import a product in order to protect domestic animals, ..."); E/PC/T/A/PV/30, p. 8 (Chairman of Commission A of Second Session of the Preparatory Committee discussed level of proof necessary when "a country decides to restrict the importation of goods in order to protect its human, animal or plant life or health"); p. 11 (US delegate to Commission A noted that the safeguard taken at the time of importation to "protect yourself" from a disease such as bubonic plague was exclusion); and p. 13 (French delegate to Commission A discussed misuses which had been made in the past of "sanitary regulations" and the damages caused in this way to "exporting countries").

[251] India, Pakistan and Thailand also referred to *The General Agreement on Tariffs and Trade (GATT), An Explanation of Its Provisions and the Proposed Amendments,* Department of State Publication 5813, Commercial Policy Series 147 (Released April 1955), p. 16 ("Among the customary exceptions listed in Part I of this Article [Article XX] are measures to protect public morals or human, animal, and plant life (sanitary regulations)..."). (emphasis added)

> *protection of human, animal or plant life or health*, and generally all matters affecting the operation of this Agreement".[252]

This language appeared in the original (30 October 1947) GATT Article XXII, as adopted by the CONTRACTING PARTIES. In 1955, Article XXII was amended to exclude the list of subjects to which the right of consultation applied.[253] However, this had been done in order to expand the scope of the provisions pursuant to which consultation could be requested, not to alter the meaning and scope of the particular exception provided by Article XX(b).

3.179. India, Pakistan and Thailand argued that there were compelling systemic considerations which supported this interpretation. As noted in the *Tuna I* Panel Report:

> "Article XX(b) allows each contracting party to set its human, animal or plant life or health standards. .... The Panel recalled the finding of a previous panel that this paragraph of Article XX was intended to allow contracting parties to impose trade restrictive measures inconsistent with the General Agreement to pursue overriding public policy goals to the extent that such inconsistencies were unavoidable. The Panel considered that if the broad interpretation of Article XX(b) suggested by the United States were accepted, each contracting party could unilaterally determine the life or health protection policies from which other contracting parties could not deviate without jeopardizing their rights under the General Agreement. The General Agreement would then no longer constitute a multilateral framework for trade among all contracting parties but would provide legal security only in respect of trade between a limited number of contracting parties with identical internal regulations".[254]

3.180. These same systemic concerns were echoed in a 1992 report on trade and the environment issued by the GATT Secretariat. The report noted that a country had a right, consistent with GATT rules, "to protect its own environment against damage from either domestic production or the consumption of domestically produced or imported products".[255] However, the report further opined that:

> "[w]hen the environmental problem is due to production or consumption activities in another country, the GATT rules are more of a constraint, since they prohibit making market access dependent on changes in the domestic policies or practices of the exporting country. The rationale for this is that to do otherwise would invite a flood of import restrictions as countries (especially those with large markets) either attempted to impose their own environmental, economic and

---

[252] GATT, (1995), *Analytical Index: Guide to GATT Law and Practice*, Vol. 2, p. 621 (emphasis added).

[253] GATT, (1995), *Analytical Index: Guide to GATT Law and Practice*, Vol. 2, p. 621 (emphasis added).

[254] Panel Report on *United States - Restrictions on Imports of Tuna*, circulated 3 September 1991, not adopted, BISD 39S/155, paragraph 5.27 (citing Panel Report on *Thailand - Restrictions on Importation of and Internal Taxes on Cigarettes*, adopted 7 November 1990, BISD 37S/200, 222-223, paragraphs 73-74).

[255] GATT, (1992), International Trade 1990-91, Vol. 1, p. 23.

social policies on other countries, or use such an attempt as a pretext for reducing competition from imports".[256]

After noting that GATT rules could not be used to block the adoption of environmental policies which had broad support in the world community because the GATT contracting parties could either amend the rules or grant a waiver, the report noted that the real danger was the use of unilateral trade measures: "If the door were open to use trade policies unilaterally to offset the competitiveness effects of different environmental standards, or to attempt to force other countries to adopt domestically-favoured practices and policies, the trading system would start down a very slippery slope".[257] To avoid this threat, the exception contained in Article XX(b) should not be read to permit measures taken by one Member which affected the life or health of animals located within the jurisdiction of another Member.

3.181. Regarding Article XX(g), India, Pakistan and Thailand argued that the drafting history also supported that fact that this provision did not apply to natural resources located beyond the jurisdiction of the contracting parties enacting the measures. A review of the drafting history of the ITO Charter demonstrated that the purpose of Article XX(g) was to allow a contracting party to impose limits on the exportation of scarce natural resources located within its jurisdiction. For example, during discussion of the draft Charter provision containing the same exception set forth in Article XX(g), the following discussion occurred:

> "Mr. Johnsen (New Zealand) pointed out in reference to [Article XX(g)] that it would not be advisable to differentiate between natural and manufactured products that were exhaustible. A country might have valid reason for desiring *to curtail the exportation* of manufactured products in short supply ... but he felt that it should be specifically laid down that no Member country should be compelled to export both manufactured and natural products which it wished to conserve for domestic purposes. It was obvious that no country would restrict its export trade except for valid reasons. He therefore proposed to amend the wording of [Article XX(g)] ... to read: "relating to the conservation of exhaustible natural or other resources ..."
>
> "Mr. Ganguli (India) ... He proposed deletion of [Article XX(g)]. He felt that his country might have to conserve for domestic use its exhaustible and scarce resources, even if such a measure was not "pursuant to international agreements", [a phrase originally included within the Charter article which became Article XX(g), but which was subsequently deleted] or was not "made effective in conjunction with restrictions on domestic production or consumption".[258]

During a subsequent discussion, the Brazilian delegation suggested that "export restrictions should be permitted for the preservation of scarce natural resources even if

[256] GATT, (1992), International Trade 1990-91, Vol. 1, p. 22.

[257] *Ibid.*

[258] E/PC/T/C.II/50, p. 4-5 (emphasis added).

there is no restriction on domestic consumption ...".[259] The drafting history therefore supported the interpretation that Article XX(g) applied only to natural resources located within the jurisdiction of the Member applying the measure.

3.182. The decision of the *Tuna II* Panel that Article XX(g) could be applied to measures relating to resources located outside of the jurisdiction taking the measure was not instructive because it failed to take this drafting history into account. Further, in reaching its decision, the *Tuna II* Panel also relied, in part, on the fact that "two previous panels have considered Article XX(g) to be applicable to policies related to migratory species of fish, and made no distinction between fish caught within or outside the territorial jurisdiction of the contracting party that had invoked the provision".[260] However, the *Tuna II* Panel's reliance on the two prior Panel decisions was misplaced because this precise question was never directly addressed by either of the panels referred to.[261]

3.183. Moreover, there were compelling systemic considerations which supported this interpretation. As noted in the *Tuna I* Panel Report:

> "[A]rticle XX(g) allows each contracting party to adopt its own conservation policies. The conditions set out in Article XX(g) which limit resort to this exception, namely that the measures taken must be related to the conservation of exhaustible natural resources, and that they not "constitute a means of arbitrary or unjustifiable discrimination ... or a disguised restriction on international trade" refer to the trade measure requiring justification under Article XX(g), not, however, to the conservation policies adopted by the contracting party. The Panel considered that if the extrajurisdictional interpretation of Article XX(g) suggested by the United States were accepted, each contracting party could unilaterally determine the conservation policies from which other contracting parties could not deviate without jeopardizing their rights under the General Agreement. The consideration that led the panel to reject an extrajurisdictional application of Article XX(b) therefore apply also to Article XX(g)".[262]

These same systemic concerns were echoed in the 1992 report on trade and the environment issued by the GATT Secretariat, referred to above in paragraph 180. In light of these concerns, Article XX(g) should be interpreted to apply only to measures

---

[259] E/PC/T/C.II/QR/PV/5, p. 79 (emphasis added). India, Pakistan and Thailand also referred to E/PC/T/A/PV/25, p. 29 (Indian delegate to the Second Session in Geneva noted that the easiest and most effective way to conserve a mineral for beneficial and planned later use was through limiting exports); E/PC/T/A/PV/30, p. 6 (Australian delegate discussed imposition of export quotas or prohibitions).

[260] Panel Report on *United States - Restrictions on Imports of Tuna*, circulated 16 June 1994, not adopted, DS29/R, paragraph 5.15.

[261] Panel Report on *Canada - Measures Affecting the Exports of Unprocessed Herring and Salmon*, adopted 22 March 1988, BISD 35S/98; Panel Report on *United States - Prohibition of Imports of Tuna and Tuna Products from Canada*, adopted 22 February 1982, BISD 29S/91.

[262] Panel Report on *United States - Restrictions on Imports of Tuna*, circulated 3 September 1991, not adopted, BISD 39S/155, paragraph 5.32.

relating to the conservation of exhaustible natural resources located within the jurisdiction of the party enacting the measure.

3.184. The **United States** argued that, since the language of Article XX(b) and Article XX(g) was not ambiguous with respect to the jurisdictional scope, there was no need to resort to Article 32 of the Vienna Convention as a supplementary means of interpretation to see that there was no mention of, let alone differentiation based upon, the location of the animal whose life or health was protected, or of the natural resource to be conserved. Nonetheless, if the Panel did examine the historical record concerning the language in Article XX(b) and Article XX(g), that record did not support the argument for imposition of a jurisdictional limitation. India, Pakistan and Thailand relied for their claim on, and adopted wholesale, the reasoning of the unadopted *Tuna I* panel report, which found that Article XX(b) and Article XX(g) did not allow measures to protect animal life or health outside the jurisdiction of the country taking the measure. However, that finding of the *Tuna I* panel was without solid support in the text or the drafting history and that panel had not thoroughly analyzed contemporaneous and subsequent practice regarding legitimate exceptions to prohibitions on quantitative restrictions. Moreover, India, Pakistan and Thailand failed to note that the *Tuna II* panel flatly rejected the finding of the *Tuna I* panel that a jurisdictional limit should be read into Articles XX(b) and XX(g).[263]

3.185. With regard to the drafting history of Article XX(b), the United States argued that the arguments made by India, Pakistan and Thailand proceeded from just one small part of the history, reached faulty conclusions even in the context of that one small part, and disregarded the remainder of that history. Contrary to what was asserted by the three complainants, the proposal for Article XX(b) did not date from the Draft Charter of the International Trade Organization (ITO) proposed by the United States, but had a much longer and richer heritage that contradicted the reading of that provision as proposed by India, Pakistan and Thailand. The complainants' reading of the drafting history of Article XX(b) was narrow and fragmentary, and even this narrow treatment of

---

[263] Panel Report on *United States - Restrictions on Imports of Tuna*, circulated 3 September 1991, DS21/R; Panel Report on *United States - Restrictions on Imports of Tuna*, circulated 16 June 1994, not adopted, DS29/R. The United States noted that in *Tuna II*, it was argued that "Article XX(b) could not justify measures taken to protect living things located outside the territorial jurisdiction of the party taking the measure." In rejecting this argument, the Panel explained as follows (paragraphs 5.31 and 5.32).

> "The Panel recalled its reasoning under Article XX(g). It observed that the text of Article XX(b) does not spell out any limitation on the location of the living things to be protected. It noted that the conditions set out in the text of Article XX (b) and the Preamble qualify only the trade measure requiring justification ("necessary to") or the manner in which the trade measure is applied ("arbitrary or unjustifiable discrimination", "disguised restriction on international trade"). The nature and precise scope of the *policy area* named in the Article, the protection of living things, is not specified in the text of the Article, in particular with respect to the location of the living things to be protected.
>
> "The Panel further recalled its observation that elsewhere in the General Agreement measures according different treatment to products of different origins could in principle be taken with respect to things located, or actions occurring, outside the territorial jurisdiction of the party taking the measure. It could not therefore be said that the General Agreement proscribed in an absolute manner such measures".

only one part of the historical record contained a number of leaps of logic. The fact that Article 37(b) of the New York Draft of the ITO Charter referred to "corresponding domestic safeguards under similar conditions exist[ing] in the importing country" did not itself indicate that the measures under that Article were only those to safeguard life or health of humans, animals or plants within the jurisdiction of the importing state. In fact, the opposite inference could be drawn: this language would have required a country to put equivalent domestic safeguards in place when it applied measures to protect resources outside its jurisdiction. The sources referred to by India, Pakistan and Thailand) merely indicated that Article XX included sanitary regulations, but in no way did they indicate any limitation. Further, as discussed below, the history of Article XX(b) covered far more than just sanitary regulations. Similarly, the 1947 version of Article XXII (Consultations) of the GATT, subsequent to its amendment in 1955, did include a reference to sanitary laws and regulations, but, contrary to what was asserted by the three complainants did not even refer to Article XX, and in no way indicated that Article XX(b) was limited to sanitary regulations. The history thus indicated that Article XX(b) was broader in scope than just sanitary measures.[264] In fact, there was little doubt that Article XX(b) covered such measures as those prohibiting the importation of weapons.[265] These were not sanitary measures. Accordingly, it was wrong to conclude that Article XX(b) was limited to sanitary measures, let alone that it was limited to sanitary measures to safeguard life or health of humans, animals or plants within the jurisdiction of the importing state. Furthermore, it did not follow that "focusing" on a particular set of measures was equivalent to concluding that a provision was exclusive of other measures.

3.186. The United States further argued that the historical analysis of India, Pakistan and Thailand was not only illogical, it was also based on an incomplete history of the provision. As one commentator stated:

> "[D]rawing a conclusion from the ITO deliberations alone would neglect the historical background that so clearly shaped Article XX(b). The reason why there was no comprehensive debate on the scope of this exception at the U.N. Conference is that the debate had already taken place — twenty years earlier. Since the exception in the ITO Charter was equivalent to what the 1927 Convention [for the Aboli-

[264] The United States noted that, at Havana, the Third Committee stated concerning the corresponding provision in the Charter: "[t]he Committee agreed that quarantine and other sanitary regulations are a subject to which the Organization should give careful attention with a view to preventing measures "necessary to protect human, animal or plant life or health" from being applied in a manner which would constitute a means of arbitrary or unjustifiable discrimination or a disguised restriction on international trade and to advising Members how they can maintain such measures without causing such prejudice". The fact that quarantine and other sanitary regulations were singled out for careful attention under this provision indicated that the provision was intended to cover more than sanitary measures.

[265] Measures restricting the importation of dangerous weapons were notified to the GATT since at least 1950. (GATT/CP/93/Add.1, "Quantitative Import and Export Restrictions Addendum: Note by the Executive Secretary on the statements submitted by contracting parties in response to GATT/CP/93"). In the negotiations on the draft text regarding sanitary and phytosanitary measures in the Uruguay Round governments recognized that Article XX(b) covered more than just sanitary and phytosanitary measures.

> tion of Import and Export Restrictions] and many bilateral treaties had, there would be little point in rehashing the obvious".[266]

3.187. The language in Article XX(b) had not been newly invented for the ITO Charter, but rather was standard language in trade agreements. The 1927 Convention for the Abolition of Import and Export Prohibitions and Restrictions ("1927 Prohibitions Convention") required that the parties thereto eliminate all quantitative restrictions, but permitted them to retain certain enumerated types of quantitative restrictions taken for non-protectionist purposes. The list of permitted legitimate restrictions, in Article 4 of the 1927 Prohibitions Convention, provided for restrictions to protect animal and plant life or health; the exception in question was phrased in language nearly identical to that later used for Article XX(b). It was clear that this exception permitted the protection of life or health of plants and animals outside the jurisdiction of the contracting party maintaining the measures. The language adopted in the ITO Charter was first debated in the discussions regarding Article 4 of the 1927 Prohibitions Convention.[267] The same language adopted in that Convention was then used in many subsequent bilateral agreements.

3.188. The 1927 Prohibitions Convention was considered to be the first multilateral trade agreement. Article 4 of the 1927 Prohibitions Convention stated, in relevant part:

> "The following classes of prohibitions and restrictions are not prohibited by the present Convention, on condition, however, that they are not applied in such a manner as to constitute a means of arbitrary discrimination between foreign countries where the same conditions prevail, or a disguised restriction on international trade:
>
> (4) Prohibitions or restrictions imposed for the protection of public health or for the protection of animals or plants against disease, insects and harmful parasites".[268]

The scope of Article 4(4) was clarified by the drafters of the Prohibitions Convention in an accompanying Protocol. This Protocol stated that "[t]he protection of animals and plants against disease also refers to measures taken to preserve them from degeneration or extinction and to measures taken against harmful seeds, plants, parasites and animals".[269] All nations that signed the Convention also signed the Protocol. Furthermore, the Draft Convention made separate reference to public health and the protection of plants and animals:

> "The following classes of prohibitions and restrictions are not prohibited ... :
>
> 2. Prohibitions or restrictions on the grounds of public health;
>
> 3. Prohibitions and restrictions having in view the protection of animals and plants against disease, degeneration and extinction".[270]

---

266 S. Charnovitz, (1991), *Exploring the Environmental Exceptions in GATT Article XX*, Journal of World Trade, Vol. 25, No. 5, p. 37, 44.

267 97 L.N.T.S. 393.

268 97 U.N.T.S. p. 405.

269 *Ibid.*, Section III(a).

270 Preliminary Draft Agreement Established by the Economic Committee.

3.189. Thus, the language used in the 1927 Prohibitions Convention (virtually identical in key respects to the language used in the ITO Charter and in GATT Article XX(b)) included protection against extinction, and thus was not limited to purely domestic concerns or to sanitary measures alone. This interpretation of the Prohibitions Convention was bolstered by the drafters' perceptions of the provision and by practice at the time. The United States had numerous environmental statutes in effect at the time of drafting, none of which was challenged during treaty negotiations.[271]

3.190. The United States further submitted that many of the national conservation laws in force at the time of the Prohibitions Convention contained import and export restrictions for solely conservation purposes. For example, the Alaska Fisheries Act, as amended in 1926[272], prohibited domestic salmon fishing in certain waters and during certain times of the year for the preservation of salmon stocks. It also prohibited the importation of "salmon from waters outside the jurisdiction of the United States taken during any closed period provided for by this Act". The Lacey Act of 1900 prohibited the importation of wild animals and birds without a special permit.[273] Other laws included the Underwood Tariff of 1913, prohibiting the importation of certain feathers and plumes of wild birds. In addition to these national laws, there were also several multilateral treaties for purposes of conservation in existence at the time of the Abolition Convention. Two such treaties included a 1911 Convention for Preservation and Protection of Fur Seals and a 1916 Convention for the Protection of Migratory Birds. Both of these treaties contained trade restrictions.

3.191. During the period between the 1927 Prohibitions Convention and the negotiation of the ITO Charter and the GATT, governments used varying formulas in providing for exemptions for conservation and sanitary measures. For example, the 1927 Prohibitions Convention exempted "prohibitions or restrictions imposed for the protection" of plant and animal life or health.[274] Some bilateral trade treaties to which the United States was a party exempted prohibitions or restrictions "imposed for protection of" plant and animal life or health, while others exempted prohibitions or restrictions "designed to protect" plant and animal life and health.[275] Bilateral

---

[271] The United States noted that it was the understanding of the US delegation that these existing statutes were not abrogated by the provisions of the Abolition Convention. Shortly before the United States signed the Convention, a representative of the United States Tariff Commission informed the US negotiator that:

> "The import prohibitions and restrictions now in force in the United States are entirely, as was frequently made clear in the course of the debates, of a non-economic nature. They consist of measures for the protection of public health and public morals, for safeguarding plants and animals against disease and extinction, and of measures which are intended to apply to imports and exports the same control as is applied to corresponding commodities in domestic trade.
>
> "Our right to maintain these prohibitions and restrictions would in no way be affected by our signing the Convention. We have abundant evidence, both in the debates in plenary sessions and in committees, that the right of any country to maintain such measures of control would not be infringed".

[272] Act for the Protection of the Fisheries of Alaska, sec. 1, 69 Cong. 1st sess., ch. 621, p. 752.

[273] 31 Stat. 187-88 (1900)(56th Cong. Sess. 1, ch. 553).

[274] International Convention for the Abolition of Import and Export Prohibitions and Restrictions, 97 L.N.T.S. 393 (signed 8 November 1927).

[275] The United States mentioned, *inter alia*, the Trade Agreement Between the United States and Canada, Article XII(2)(b), 199 L.N.T.S. 92 (1940), ("designed to protect" life and health) (signed on

commercial treaties between other countries contained similar language. A commercial agreement between Australia and the Belgo-Luxemburg Economic Union exempted all prohibitions or restrictions "imposed for the protection of animals and plants".[276] A commercial convention between Estonia and France allowed for "import and export prohibitions to the following cases: war time measures, measures imposed for reasons of health or public security, the protection of animals or plants...".[277] The British government, in an exchange of notes with Brazil constituting a temporary agreement regarding commercial relations, exempted "prohibitions or restrictions upon imports into the United Kingdom for the purpose of protecting animals and plants (that is to say, protection against disease, degeneration or extinction, as well as measures taken against harmful seeds, plants and animals)".[278] The existence of these laws and agreements at the time of the drafting of the Prohibitions Convention demonstrated that Article 4(4) indeed was intended to encompass measures that protected both domestic and non-domestic animal and plant life and health.

3.192. The United States argued that the practice of governments since the entry into force of the GATT 1947 further supported that Articles XX(g) and (b) were not subject to a jurisdictional limit. Treaties that protected plants and animals outside the territory of the parties existed in 1947, and more were agreed afterward. These treaties included both sanitary measures and conservation measures, and provided for trade restrictions and measures which protected the environment beyond the territories of the parties thereto. At no time were these treaties challenged as being inconsistent with the GATT because they protected plants and animals extraterritorially, or because they imposed trade restrictions for non-economic reasons. For example, the Convention Relative to the Preservation of Fauna and Flora in their Natural State provided that "the import of trophies which have been exported from any territory to which the present Convention is applicable in full, whether a territory of another Contracting Government or not, shall be prohibited".[279] Similarly, the Convention on Nature Protection and Wild Life

17 November 1938, ratifications exchanged 19 June 1939); Trade Agreement Between the U.S. and the U.K., 200 L.N.T.S. 294 (1940) ("imposed for protection" of life and health) (signed on 17 November 1938, ratifications exchanged 24 November 1939); Commercial Agreement Between the U.S. and Republic of Nicaragua, Article VI(2)(a)(3), 1936 L.N.T.S. 142 ("designed to protect" life) (signed 11 March 1936, entered into force 1 October 1936); Commercial Agreement Between the United States and Switzerland, 1936 L.N.T.S. 232 ("designed to protect" life or health) (signed 9 January 1936, ratifications exchanged 7 May 1936).

[276] Provisional Commercial Agreement Between the Commonwealth of Australia and the Belgo-Luxemburg Economic Union, Article VII, 1937 L.N.T.S. 272 (signed 3 October 1936, entered into force 1 January 1937).

[277] Commercial Convention Between Estonia and France, Article 6, 1937 L.N.T.S. 43 (signed 16 October 1937, entered into force 1 December 1937).

[278] Exchange of Notes Between the Brazilian Government and His Majesty's Government in the United Kingdom Constituting a Temporary Agreement Regarding Commercial Relations Between the Two Countries, 1936 L.N.T.S. 274, 277 (signed 10 August 1936, entered into force 10 August 1936).

[279] Article 9(3). Article 9(1) of the Convention stated that: "[e]ach Contracting Government shall take the necessary measures to control and regulate in each of its territories the internal, and the export and export, traffic in ... trophies ... with a view to preventing the import or export of, or any dealing in trophies other than [in accordance with the laws of the territory]". Animals protected under the treaty included "all vertebrates and invertebrates ... their nests, eggs, egg-shells, skins and

Preservation in the Western Hemisphere stated that "[e]ach Contracting Government shall take the necessary measures to control and regulate the importation, exportation and transit of protected fauna and flora or any part thereof".[280] The International Convention for the Protection of Birds prohibited "the import, export, transport, sale, offer for sale ... of any live or dead bird or any part of a bird killed or captured in contravention of the provisions of the Convention".[281] The Agreement on Conservation of Polar Bears stated that "[a] Contracting Party shall prohibit the exportation from, the importation and delivery into, and traffic within, its territory of polar bears or any part or product thereof taken in violation of this agreement".[282] The Convention on Conservation of North Pacific Fur Seals required that each party "prohibit the importation and delivery into and the traffic within its territories of skins of fur seals taken in the area of the North Pacific Ocean mentioned in Article III [which includes the high seas] ...".[283] The Convention on the Prohibition of Fishing with Long Drift Nets in the South Pacific, which allowed each party to "prohibit the landing of driftnet catches within its territory ..., prohibit the importation of any fish or fish product, whether processed or not, which was caught using a driftnet".[284]

3.193. The United States added that the practice of governments in this area continued today. In recent years, nations had negotiated a number of multilateral treaties for the purpose of protecting the environment and conserving living and natural resources.[285] Most of these treaties had extraterritorial ramifications for the nations party to the treaties, and many of the treaties included trade measures. In drafting these treaties, governments had been cognizant of the requirements of the GATT and had perceived that Article XX would permit them to implement the trade measures.[286] The Montreal Protocol on Substances that Deplete the Ozone Layer provided one example of nations

plumage". This included highly migratory species. *Ibid.*, Article 2(3). Adopted 8 November 1933, entered into force 14 January 1936. Parties included Belgium, Egypt, India, Italy, Portugal, South Africa, Sudan, United Kingdom and United Republic of Tanzania.

[280] Article IX ("fauna and flora" included migratory species). Adopted 12 October 1940, entered into force 30 April 1942. Parties included: Argentina, Brazil, Chile, Costa Rica, Dominican Republic, Ecuador, El Salvador, Guatemala, Haiti, Mexico, Nicaragua, Panama, Peru, Trinidad and Tobago, the United States, Uruguay, and Venezuela.

[281] Article 3. Adopted 18 October 1950, entered into force 17 January 1963. Parties included Belgium, Iceland, Italy, Luxembourg, Netherlands, Spain, Sweden, Switzerland, Turkey and Yugoslavia.

[282] Article V. Adopted 15 November 1973, entered into force 26 May 1976. Parties, limited to signatories, included Canada, Denmark, Germany, Norway, USSR (current status unknown), USA.

[283] Article VIII. Adopted 7 May 1976, entered into force 10 December 1976. Parties, limited to signatories, include Canada, Japan, USSR (current status unknown), USA.

[284] Article 4(2). Adopted 23 November 1989.

[285] The United States referred in particular to the Vienna Convention for the Protection of the Ozone Layer and the Montreal Protocol on Substances that Deplete the Ozone Layer; the Basel Convention on the Control of Transboundary Movements of Hazardous Wastes and Their Disposal; the London Guidelines for the Exchange of Information on Chemicals in International Trade; Convention on International Trade in Endangered Species of Wild Fauna and Flora; the Framework Convention on Biological Diversity.

[286] The United States referred to the Report of the Fifth Meeting of the Open Ended Working Group of the Parties to the Montreal Protocol, paragraph 14, U.N. Doc. UNEP/OzL.Pro/WG.1/5/3 (1990): "[t]he Working Group concluded that there appeared to be no conflict between GATT rules and Article 4 ... and other articles of the Montreal Protocol. The Working Group further concluded that no specific conflict between GATT rules and Article 4 ... could be identified".

seeking to protect life and health of humans, animals and plants without regard to their location.[287] The Montreal Protocol required, *inter alia*, that countries restrict production and consumption of ozone-depleting substances and implement trade restrictions against countries that did not institute such a restriction. There was no specific reference to, and no distinction within, the Protocol for protection of life or health within a country's jurisdiction and protection of life or health outside the country's jurisdiction. As noted above, CITES imposed trade restrictions for the purpose of conserving endangered species, regardless of where those species were located. The Basel Convention on the Control of Transboundary Movements of Hazardous Wastes and Their Disposal prohibited the import and export of hazardous waste to ensure the environmentally sound disposal of that waste. In 1995, at the third Conference of Parties to the Basel Convention, an amendment to the Convention was adopted, with the support of the complainants, to ban trade in hazardous wastes between developed and developing countries. This ban extended, *inter alia*, to exports of valuable recyclable wastes from developed country parties to developing countries that were not parties to the agreement.

3.194. The United States was therefore of the view that, as could be seen from the actions engaged in by governments, there had been a long-standing practice, continuing through today, of contracting parties maintaining measures to protect and conserve animal and plant life and health outside their jurisdiction. There had never been a historical distinction between the protection of domestic plants and animals and non-domestic plants and animals. Rather, the obligation of a contracting party had been to ensure that the burden imposed by any such measure was placed equitably on domestic and foreign products. The territorial limitation called for by India, Pakistan and Thailand regarding the scope of Article XX would call into question a broad range of agreements entered into by governments. If India, Pakistan and Thailand sought such a limitation, it should negotiate with other governments, not request the Panel to legislate such a limitation and proclaim that it had lain hidden within the GATT for decades. This analysis indicated that, in order to accommodate multilateral treaties relating to the environment, nations had interpreted Article XX to allow for global -territorial and extraterritorial- protection of life and health.

3.195. Regarding the drafting history of Article XX(g), the United States noted that the only examples of drafting history cited by India, Pakistan and Thailand were statements by three delegations indicating that export restrictions should be included within the scope of measures covered by Article XX(g). Nothing in these examples indicated that Article XX(g) measures should be limited to measures involving the export of natural resources within a country's jurisdiction. In fact, the text of Article XX showed that when the drafters intended to limit Article XX exceptions so that only export restrictions would be permitted thereunder, they did so explicitly. Article XX(i) covered measures necessary to ensure adequate supplies of domestic materials during periods when a stabilization plan was in effect, and Article XX(i) was explicitly limited to restrictions "on exports". Article XX(g) contained no similar limitation, and India,

[287] Adopted 16 September 1987, entered into force 1 January 1989. The United States noted that more than 75 countries were party to the Montreal Protocol.

Pakistan and Thailand provided no rationale for reading such a limitation into the text of the GATT.

3.196. The United States submitted that the argument made by India, Pakistan and Thailand to request this Panel to construct a jurisdictional limitation to Articles XX(b) and XX(g)[288] because if there would be no jurisdictional limitation, "... each contracting party could unilaterally determine the international life and health protection policies from which other contracting parties could not deviate without jeopardizing their rights under the General Agreement" amounted to urging the Panel to legislate and to requesting for a policy review of the GATT 1994. Nowhere did the complainants demonstrate that the drafters of the GATT had these particular policy concerns in mind, either in the drafting history or the text of the GATT. As demonstrated above, the GATT was drafted to permit countries to take action to protect animal and plant health both within and outside their borders. The three complainants' arguments amounted to a *post hoc* "bootstrap" for an erroneous proposition. Their concern was that additional conditions were needed on Article XX(b) and XX(g) to protect them from their spectre of "unilateralism". Additional conditions to deal with policy concerns were the province of negotiations, not panel proceedings. The complainants did not explain how these conditions were to suddenly appear in the GATT 1994 as a result of this proceeding.

3.197. The United States further argued that the rationale of India, Pakistan and Thailand was circular in nature. They argued that without a jurisdictional limitation, the "rights" of other Members under the GATT 1994 would be jeopardized. This reasoning, however, assumed that those "rights" of other Members were such as to be infringed in the absence of a jurisdictional limitation, and then deduced that a jurisdictional limitation was needed in order to ensure that the rights were not infringed. This became an interesting exercise in tautology, but hardly shed any light on Article XX. Instead, the interpretation proposed by India, Pakistan and Thailand would attempt to dictate to importing contracting parties that their markets must be available as an incentive for the destruction of exhaustible natural resources. Contracting parties over the years since the inception of the GATT had adopted and enforced a number of measures, both required by their obligations under other international agreements and not so required, to protect the environment. There had been no questioning of the ability of these parties to adopt these measures consistent with their obligations under the GATT, since Article XX provided for them. However, the interpretation of Article XX proposed by the complainants would mean that suddenly a broad range of legitimate environmental protection measures would be thrown into question under the GATT 1994. The practices of the contracting parties before and after the GATT 1947 demonstrated that there was no perceived limitation under the GATT on the ability of contracting parties to take these trade measures for conservation and plant and animal protection purposes. It did not make sense to suggest that the GATT 1994 now should be interpreted to create difficulties for these measures. A Panel should hesitate before accepting an interpretation of the GATT that would have such broad-ranging implications for a large number of important measures maintained by contracting parties - including those

[288] The United States noted that the complainants did not address whether their argument would also apply to all of Article XX, for example Article XX(e) relating to products of prison labour. If not, then it was unclear how other provisions could be distinguished.

pursuant to other international obligations - particularly where that interpretation was unsupported by the plain language of the Agreement.

3.198. **India, Pakistan and Thailand** maintained that the drafting history of Article XX(g) supported the inference of a jurisdictional limitation, and rejected the US assertion that the language of Article XX(g) was ambiguous on its face regarding the presence or absence of a jurisdictional limitation. As an initial matter, the complainants noted that *Tuna I* had concluded there was a jurisdictional limitation inherent in Article XX(g). That panel must have concluded therefore either that the language was ambiguous in this respect or that the language was unambiguous but nevertheless supported a jurisdictional limitation. Moreover, using a primary means of treaty interpretation (i.e., relevant rules of international law applicable in relations between the parties), India, Pakistan and Thailand had demonstrated that the best interpretation of Article XX(g) was that it did not apply to measures taken to coerce other nations to adopt policies to conserve natural resources under their jurisdiction. To the extent that this interpretation was or could be in conflict with other possible interpretations of the language of Article XX(g), resort to the drafting history was appropriate. That history confirmed the interpretation defended by the three complainants.

3.199. The US attempts to minimize the impact of the drafting history by suggesting that India, Pakistan and Thailand quoted selectively from the history was unavailing. The US had not, and could not, point to any drafting history to show that the negotiators intended to include import restrictions within the scope of Article XX(g). Rather, the history clearly showed that the negotiators thought of Article XX(g) as applying to exempt certain export restrictions from normal GATT disciplines. Indeed, even the single statement cited by the United States in support of its interpretation of the term "exhaustible" showed the intent of the drafters that export restrictions aimed at conservation of scarce or valuable domestic resources be exempted from GATT obligations under Article XX(g) (see paragraph 3.243). Moreover, inclusion of the term "export" within Article XX(i) did not mean, as claimed by the United States, that the drafters used the word "export" whenever they intended to limit Article XX exceptions to export restrictions. Article XX(i) covered measures "involving restrictions on exports of domestic materials necessary to ensure essential quantities of such materials to a domestic processing industry during periods when the domestic price of such materials is held below the world price as part of a governmental stabilization plan; ..." Since it would not make sense to impose import restrictions to ensure essential quantities of a domestic material, it was illogical to claim, as did the United States, that the term "export" was included within Article XX(i) for purposes of limiting the scope of the exception.

3.200. India, Pakistan and Thailand argued that the agreements referred to by the United States to suggest that *Tuna I* did not thoroughly analyze or take into account contemporaneous and subsequent practice regarding legitimate exceptions to prohibitions on quantitative restrictions did not represent an appropriate means of interpretation of the GATT. The US criticism therefore was wholly without merit. Prior treaties were not generally relevant to construction of a treaty under the general rules of interpretation set forth in the Vienna Convention.[289] Moreover, because none of these treaties could be construed as establishing the agreement of "all" of the parties to the GATT regarding interpretation of the GATT, such agreements did not constitute an appropriate means of interpretation of the GATT. The US arguments were equally unpersuasive with respect to the agreements which the United States claimed constituted subsequent practice. First, it was not clear why the United States had included the Convention Relative to the Preservation of Fauna and Flora in their Natural State or the Convention on Nature Protection and Wild Life Preservation in the Western Hemisphere as "subsequent practice" since that agreement had entered into force on 14 January 1936 and 30 April 1942, respectively. Moreover, with respect to those agreements that were "subsequent" to the GATT, the United States had provided no evidence that they established the agreement of the parties regarding the interpretation of the GATT 1994. As noted by *Tuna II*, agreements of this kind did not constitute appropriate secondary means of interpretation.[290]

3.201. India, Pakistan and Thailand argued that *Tuna II*, contrary to statements made by the United States in this proceeding, never expressly found that a Member could impose measures respecting persons or things outside of its jurisdiction under Article XX(g). While the panel found in response to an argument made by one of the parties that there was no territorial limitation inherent in Article XX(g), the permissible actions or permissible regulation of persons or things outside of the territory of a Member discussed by the Panel were all premised on some other basis for the exercise of legal jurisdiction by the Member imposing the measure. The *Tuna II* Panel Report stated, in its concluding remarks on the jurisdictional issue, that:

> "... under general international law, states are not in principle barred from regulating the conduct of their nationals with respect to persons, animals, plants and natural resources outside their territory. Nor are states barred, in principle, from regulating the conduct of vessels having their nationality, or any persons on these vessels, with respect to persons, animals, plants and natural resources outside their territory. A state may in particular regulate the conduct of its fishermen, or of vessels having its nationality or any fishermen on these vessels, with respect to fish located in the high seas.
>
> "In view of the above, the Panel could see no valid reason supporting the conclusion that the provisions of Article XX(g) apply only to policies related to the conservation of exhaustible natural resources located within the territory of the contracting party invoking the provision. The Panel consequently found that the policy to conserve dolphins in the eastern tropical Pacific Ocean, which the United States

---

[289] Inasmuch as the United States had failed to provide any evidence that US domestic legislation had any persuasive value in interpreting the GATT 1994, India, Pakistan and Thailand noted they would not address the US domestic legislation cited as evidence of "contemporary" practice.

[290] Panel Report on *United States - Restrictions on Imports of Tuna*, circulated 16 June 1994, not adopted, DS29/R, paragraph 5.20.

pursued *within its jurisdiction over its nationals and vessels*, fell within the range of policies covered by Article XX(g)".[291]

3.202. The Panel never stated or concluded that, under Article XX(g), a contracting party could adopt a measure related to the conservation of natural resources wholly outside its legal jurisdiction, territorial or otherwise. Rather, the panel moved on to other issues and ultimately found that Article XX(g) did not apply because the measure in question did not "relate to" the conservation of dolphins. Thus, *Tuna II* did not reach the issue raised by India, Pakistan and Thailand in this proceeding. The complainants' claim was not that there should be a territorial limitation read into Article XX(g), it was that there should be a jurisdictional limitation such that the Member imposing the measure had some legitimate claim of jurisdiction over the persons or things it was seeking to regulate or conserve and was not impinging upon the regulatory prerogatives of other Members. Nothing in the *Tuna II* Panel Report was inconsistent with the complainants' position that the US measure at issue in this case was beyond the scope of Article XX(g) because it was addressed to the conservation of natural resources exploited in the complainants' territorial waters or exclusive economic zone by their vessels and nationals over which the United States had no legitimate claim of jurisdiction.

3.203. Regarding the drafting history of Article XX(b), India, Pakistan and Thailand declared that the United States had pointed to nothing which demonstrated that the parties intended it to apply to measures to protect the life or health of people, animals, or plants outside of the jurisdiction of the Member applying the measure. The one example cited by the United States, prohibitions against the importation of weapons, was also directed at protecting the life and health of citizens of the Member applying the measure. Contrary to the US assertions, the 1927 Convention for the Abolition of Import and Export Prohibitions and Restrictions was not relevant to this Panel's inquiry. First, inasmuch as it had entered into force prior to the GATT 1947, it constituted neither subsequent agreement nor subsequent practice pursuant to Article 31 of the Vienna Convention. Nor had the United States suggested that the provisions of that Convention rose to the level of relevant rules of international law applicable in the relations between the parties. Moreover, as noted by the *Tuna II* Panel in response to almost identical arguments by the United States, this agreement did not constitute supplementary means of interpreting the GATT 1994.[292] Finally, the language of the 1927 Convention cited by the United States did not even support the proposition that the provision cited was intended to apply outside the jurisdiction of the party enacting the prohibition or restriction.[293] If any conclusions could be drawn from the cited provision, it was that conservation measures relating to animals should be analyzed

[291] Panel Report on *United States - Restrictions on Imports of Tuna*, circulated 16 June 1994, not adopted, DS29/R, paragraphs 5.17, 5.20 and 5.33 (emphasis added).

[292] Panel Report on *United States - Restrictions on Imports of Tuna*, circulated 16 June 1994, not adopted, DS29/R, paragraph 5.20

[293] India, Pakistan and Thailand noted that, while the terms degeneration and extinction, pointed out by the United States, might have served to clarify concerns which could be addressed as relating to life and health", these terms in no way defined the jurisdictional scope of the measures which could be taken.

pursuant to Article XX(b).[294] If the US interpretation were to be accepted, the United States could decide, for instance, that it was in a better position than Thailand to determine how clean the air should be that Thai citizens breathed. It might then undertake to prohibit the importation of products made in factories that did not follow US mandated air emissions standards. Or, the United States might decide that water quality was of importance to the life and health of freshwater fish in China and might then ban the importation of goods that were manufactured by water polluting industries. Who could deny that clean air and clean water were necessary to the health of living things? The issue was who had the right to decide; who had the right to make the trade-off between additional environmental protection and economic growth. The drafters of the GATT clearly never intended to hand to a contracting party the right to make market access contingent upon the adoption of that party's preferred environmental policies in the territory or under the jurisdiction of another contracting party. Only by finding an implied jurisdictional limitation in Articles XX(b) and (g) could the GATT and this Panel definitely avoid reaching this absurd result.

3.204. The **United States** maintained that all the multilateral trade agreements cited above, adopted before and after the GATT 1947, in which the Parties agreed to trade measures for the conservation of natural resources outside of their jurisdiction, were relevant under Article 31(3)(c) of the Vienna Convention. In particular, all these agreements rebutted the complainants' argument that measures to conserve resources outside of a country's jurisdiction were inconsistent with international law. It was quite ironic that the complainants placed such heavy reliance on the UN Charter which never even mentioned trade, and then argued that multilateral trade agreements calling for trade measures were not relevant to the issues in this dispute. In addition, the post-1947 Agreements referred to were subsequent practice in the application of the treaty, pursuant to Article 31(3)(c) of the Vienna Convention, while the Agreements completed prior to the GATT 1947 were valid supplementary means of interpretation under Article 32 of the Vienna Convention. In particular, the pre-1947 Agreements "confirm[ed] the meaning resulting from the application of Article 31" that Article XX had never been intended to have any sort of jurisdictional limitation. As the United States had already explained, these treaties were particularly helpful in that they reflected the understanding of the 1927 Prohibitions Convention, which was a direct precursor of GATT Article XX. The United States agreed with the complainants that the two pre-1947 Conventions[295] should have been referred to not as subsequent practice, but as circumstances of conclusion of the GATT 1947.

3.205. The United States considered that India, Pakistan and Thailand mischaracterized the findings of the *Tuna II* panel when claiming that the *Tuna II* Panel "never expressly found that a Member could impose measures respecting persons or things outside of its jurisdiction under Article XX(g)". The *Tuna II* panel stated as follows:

---

[294] As to the US arguments concerning "contemporaneous" practice and subsequent practice, the arguments made by India, Pakistan and Thailand with respect the Article XX(g) were equally applicable to the US arguments with respect to Article XX(b) (see paragraph 200).

[295] 1936 Convention Relative to the Preservation of Fauna and Flora in their Natural State, and 1942 Convention on Nature Protection and Wild Life Preservation in the Western Hemisphere, see paragraph 200.

> "The Panel noted that two previous panels have considered Article XX(g) to be applicable to polices related to migratory species of fish, and had *made no distinction between fish caught within or outside the territorial jurisdiction* of the contracting party that had invoked this provision. ... The Panel then observed that measures providing different treatment to products of different origins could in principle be taken under other paragraphs of Article XX and other Articles of the General Agreement *with respect to things located, or actions occurring, outside the territorial jurisdiction* of the party taking the measure. An example was the provision in Article XX(e) relating to products of prison labour. It could not therefore be said that the General Agreement proscribed in an absolute manner measures that related to things or actions *outside the territorial jurisdiction* of the party taking the measure".[296]

The distinction the complainants tried to make between a "territorial" and a "jurisdictional" limitation was in fact only terminology. The *Tuna II* Panel explicitly relied on Article XX(e) which acknowledged that Members could take trade measures with respect to persons located solely within another country. Likewise, the *Tuna II* Panel found that Article XX(g) and XX(b) extended to measures intended to conserve resources outside the country imposing the measure. This finding applied equally to both the dolphins involved in the *Tuna* cases, and to the sea turtles involved here. It was simply not the case, as India, Pakistan and Thailand asserted, that the Panel in *Tuna II* had not rejected the argument that Article XX contained a jurisdictional limitation. Furthermore, the EC made this very same point regarding the *Tuna II* Panel Report in its third party submission (see paragraph 4.30). The EC also noted, as did the United States, that "no jurisdictional limitation on use of Article XX was imposed by the Appellate Body in the Reformulated Gasoline case" (Ibid).

3.206. **India, Pakistan and Thailand** replied that the United States misread the Vienna Convention when arguing the pre-1947 international Agreements were "relevant rules of international law". The complainants considered that in interpreting treaties, the Vienna Convention permitted reference to contemporaneous or subsequent agreement by "all of the parties" and contemporaneous or subsequent agreement by fewer than all of the parties which was later accepted by "all of the parties". The Vienna Convention also permitted reference to other "relevant rules of international law". However, this did not mean that reference could be made to agreements that did not involve all of the parties in order to interpret a term or terms in the Agreement, or the scope of the Agreement. "Relevant rules of international law" meant customary international law or rules to which all Members could be said generally to subscribe. Similarly, the post-1947 Agreements cited by the United States were not subsequent practice in application of the treaty because those agreements made no reference to the GATT and were not signed by "all parties to" the GATT 1947.

3.207. With respect of the *Tuna II* Panel Report, India, Pakistan and Thailand explained that by the term "jurisdiction" they referred not only to territorial jurisdiction,

---

[296] *United States - Restrictions on Imports of Tuna*, not adopted, DS29/R, circulated 16 June 1994, paragraphs 5.15 and 5.16 (emphasis added).

but to any form of legal jurisdiction appropriately exercised under recognized principles of international law. The complainants' view that Article XX(g) contained an implied jurisdictional limitation was supported by customary rules of international law which recognized the sovereignty of States to control persons or things within their legal jurisdiction, and by the drafting history of Article XX(g). An implied jurisdictional limitation was also vital to avoid a fundamental redistribution of rights and obligations under the GATT; one that handed nations with large markets the means to coerce other states to conform their environmental laws, conservation and health policies with those of the importing party as a condition of exercising rights that were otherwise guaranteed by the GATT. India, Pakistan and Thailand maintained that the *Tuna II* Panel Report never expressly found that a contracting party could impose measures with respect to persons or things outside its legal jurisdiction under Article XX(g). Rather, the Panel found that "the policy to conserve dolphins in the eastern tropical Pacific Ocean, which the United States pursued within its jurisdiction over its nationals and vessels, fell within the range of policies covered by Article XX(g)". That Panel never found that a contracting party could adopt a measure involving citizens and vessels or related to the conservation of natural resources falling within the exclusive economic zone of another contracting party. Indeed, the fact that some or all of the shrimp harvested in this case was harvested within the complainants' exclusive economic zone gave rise to an important distinction between the *Tuna* case and this case. There was even less justification for the assertion of jurisdiction by the United States in this case than in the *Tuna* case. Rather than reaching the issue of whether the United States could assert its jurisdiction on the high seas to foreign nationals and vessels harvesting tuna, the *Tuna II* Panel moved on to other issues and ultimately found that the measures taken to force other contracting parties to change their environmental policies did not "relate to" the conservation of exhaustible natural resources as set forth in Article XX(g) and were not "necessary" under Article XX(b). Thus, the Panel never specifically ruled on the precise jurisdictional issue raised by the complainants in this case. All of the drafting history reviewed by India, Pakistan and Thailand concerning this provision illustrated that the drafters were concerned to provide contracting parties with the latitude to conserve finite economic resources within their respective jurisdictions from depletion through unrestricted exploitation and exportation. The only drafting history cited by the United States was fully consistent with this interpretation. Thus, the framers had understood Article XX(g) to extend to things within the legal control of the contracting party enacting the measure. There was nothing in the expressed intent of the framers that was inconsistent with the notion of an implied jurisdiction limitation in this provision.

3.208. The **United States** replied that the complainants, not the United States, misread the Vienna Convention in noting the relevance of international agreements. The complainants' paraphrasing was inaccurate, and the words they quoted twice ("all of the parties") were not even found in Article 31. The United States also disagreed with the explanation given by the complainants that the "relevant rules of international law" mentioned in Article 31(3)(c) were "rules to which all contracting parties could be said generally to subscribe". In fact, the sources of customary international law were generally considered to include international conventions; international custom, as evidence of a general practice accepted as law; general principles of law recognized by nations; judicial decisions; and scholarly writings.[297] Nonetheless, the complainants proposed definition of "relevant rules of international law" did not even support their position. Certainly, not all GATT contracting parties could be said to subscribe to the complainants' posited rules of international law when many of those nations, including the complainants themselves, had entered into agreements calling for trade measures for the purpose of conserving resources outside of their jurisdiction. The United States also disagreed with the complainants' claim that the *Tuna II* Panel did not "reach" the issue of jurisdictionality. The Panel did reach this issue and ruled against the *Tuna II* complainants on their theory that Article XX did not apply because the measures sought to conserve dolphins outside of the United States. The United States repeated that the drafting history of Article XX included its precursor, the Prohibitions Convention, and that history was not consistent with the complainants' theory. Moreover, a number of international conservation agreements that called on parties to take actions to deal with matters beyond their jurisdiction existed at the time Article XX was drafted. The complainants showed no evidence that the drafters of GATT were seeking to change or limit this practice.

### (c) Article XX(b)

3.209. The **United States** argued that, since the measures under Section 609 fell within the scope of Article XX(g) and met each requirement of the Article XX chapeau (see section (d) and (e) below), the Panel needed not, in accordance with the principle of "judicial economy" favoured by the Appellate Body[298], decide on the issue of whether the US measures fell within the scope of Article XX(b). However, should the Panel find that the US measure met the requirements of the Article XX chapeau but that for some reason Article XX(g) did not apply, then the Panel should find that the US measures were within thc scope of Article XX(b).

3.210. **India, Pakistan and Thailand** responded that, since the United States did not meet the requirements under Article XX(g) and under the chapeau of Article XX (see section (d) and (e) below), the analysis of Article XX(b) was needed. Moreover, because the measures at issue purported to protect the life and health of sea turtles, a biological resource, the measures should be analyzed under Article XX(b) rather than XX(g).

#### (i) Policy Purpose of the Measure

3.211. **India, Pakistan and Thailand** argued that the policy for which Section 609 was invoked did not fall within the range of policies designed to protect human, animal or plant life or health. By failing to provide newly affected nations with a phase-in period comparable to the period provided to initially affected nations, the United States

---

[297] The United States referred to Shaw, *International Law*, (3d ed. 1991), (quoting Article 38(1) of the Statute of the International Court of Justice).

[298] The United States recalled that the Appellate Body Report on *United States - Measure Affecting Imports of Woven Wool Shirts and Blouses* (adopted 23 May 1997, WT/DS33, DSR 1997:I, page 240) approved of the principle of "judicial economy" in Panel rulings. In particular, the Appellate Body explained that "[a] panel need only address those claims which must be addressed in order to resolve the dispute".

had required foreign shrimp harvesters to use TEDs even though they might not have had time to acquire the TEDs and become trained in their use and might not be able to use them effectively, or forego exports to the United States. However, the United States itself had recognized that requiring use of TEDs with such little notice "will not result in any benefit to sea turtles in those nations newly covered, because fishermen with no experience in TEDs use are not likely to be able to use them effectively in the near term to protect sea turtles".[299] In light of this and similar statements, the United States could not credibly argue that the policy behind the embargo was the protection of sea turtle life and health.

3.212. Moreover, the legislative history of Section 609, pursuant to which the embargo was enacted, indicated that the purpose of the provision was to restrict imports. The bill which ultimately became Section 609 first emerged as a floor amendment to the Foreign Relations Authorization Act, 1990.[300] During debate on this bill, the principals sponsors discussed the need to redress the "competitive disadvantage of US shrimp fishermen *vis-à-vis* foreign fishermen". Further, a concern was expressed that foreign nations would "export a flood of shrimp into our country".[301] Although this bill did not pass, Section 609 was later included in the 1990 appropriations measure for the Departments of State, Justice, and Commerce.[302] In commenting on the provision, one senator explained that the embargo would mean that "... the price of shrimp obviously will go up because the supply will be down, so that Louisiana shrimpers, Texas shrimpers, Florida shrimpers will in effect have some form of compensation in the form of higher prices for their shrimp ...".[303] Further, another senator stated that it was "... patently unfair to say to the US industry that you must abide by these sets of rules and regulations, but other countries do not have to do anything, and, yet we will then give them our market".[304] This language, together with the fact that Section 609 did not provide the same phase-in period that US shrimp harvesters had been granted, indicated that the policy pursuant to which the embargo was enacted was protection of the US shrimp industry, not sea turtles. Further, while Section 609 was later codified as a note to the Endangered Species Act, the US legislative branch did not specifically make it an amendment to the Endangered Species Act. It could be inferred from this that the purpose of the provision was something other than protection of endangered species.

3.213. **Malaysia** noted that in the present case, Section 609 appeared at the very most to be a legislation designed to reduce the mortality rate of turtles and, therefore, might possibly, if at all, fall under the policy to protect animal life.

3.214. The **United States** argued that the measures under Section 609 involved the protection of animal life or health. Sea turtles were obviously animals. As noted, Section 609(a) called for the negotiation of bilateral and multilateral agreements for the protection and conservation of sea turtles, i.e. to protect the life and health of these

---

299 United States Court of International Trade, *Earth Island Institute* v. *Warren Christopher*, Memorandum in Support of Defendants' Motion for Modification of 29 December 1995, Order, p. 11.

300 135 Congressional Record S.1160.

301 135 Congressional Record S. 8373-8376.

302 House Resolution 2991.

303 135 Congressional Record S. 12266.

304 *Ibid.*

animals. Similarly, Section 609(b) was intended to protect and conserve the life and health of sea turtles by requiring that shrimp imported into the United States had not been harvested in a manner that would harm these animals. The United States rejected the argument made by India, Pakistan and Thailand that the United States had enacted Section 609 primarily for protectionist purposes, i.e., to protect its domestic shrimping industry from foreign competition. It considered that such argument was based on isolated excerpts from the legislative history of Section 609 in the US Congress. Given that the United States had negotiated a multilateral agreement with Western Hemisphere nations to require the use of TEDs, and had made extensive efforts to disseminate TEDs technology worldwide, this argument was simply not credible. In fact, Malaysia conceded in this proceeding, albeit grudgingly, that Section 609 was designed to protect sea turtles. Furthermore, an examination of the full legislative history confirmed that the overriding intent of Section 609 was to protect endangered species of sea turtles. Senator Breaux, who introduced Section 609 in the US Senate, described his intentions in doing so as follows:

> "[T]he amendment I am offering today is intended to promote the international conservation of sea turtles, and to provide the groundwork for ensuring that foreign fishermen bear as great a conservation burden as our own industry ... This amendment focuses on the role that other nations must play if we are to fulfil our goal of effective sea turtle conservation. The amendment before the Senate would facilitate international conservation efforts".[305]

Senator Breaux's colleagues echoed his sentiments:

> "I rise today to support the Breaux amendment as it serves to strengthen our Nation's commitment to protect endangered sea turtles from drowning in commercial shrimp nets". (Senator Chafee)[306]

> "I rise in support of the Breaux amendment to strengthen US efforts to conserve threatened and endangered sea turtles". (Senator Shelby)[307]

These comments reflected the prevailing view of the United States Congress in enacting Section 609 that the measures taken within the United States to protect endangered sea turtles would not be effective unless other nations with shrimp trawl fisheries that killed sea turtles took comparable action.

3.215. The United States explained that India, Pakistan and Thailand misunderstood the US legal system when claiming that the fact that Section 609 was placed in the United States Code (U.S.C.) as a note to Section 1537 of Title 16 of the U.S.C., instead of as an amendment, indicated that "the purpose of the provision was something other more than protection of endangered species". This, in fact, did not provide an indication of the intent of Congress in enacting the provision. When, as here, a new law was a stand-alone provision that did not amend an existing law, Congress did not specify where it would be placed on the U.S.C. Instead, that decision was made by the Office of Law Revision Counsel (OLRC), an independant office of the House of Representatives

305 Congressional Record S8373-4 (20 July 1989).
306 Congressional Record S8375 (20 July 1989).
307 Congressional Record S8375 (20 July 1989).

that was responsible for compiling the U.S.C. The OLRC was not involved in the legislative process, and, as held by the Supreme Court of the United States, the OLRC's decisions regarding the organization of the U.S.C. did not provide an indication of Congressional intent in enacting a law.[308] Accordingly, whether Section 609 was placed in Title 16 as a note, or, for example, was assigned to a new section of Title 16, was a choice made at the discretion of the OLRC, and provided no indication of Congressional intent.

(ii) "Necessary ..."

3.216. Assuming, *arguendo*, that the embargo was enacted for the purpose of protecting sea turtle life and health, **India, Pakistan and Thailand** submitted that the embargo was not necessary to accomplish that purpose. As stated in a previous case, "[i]n the ordinary meaning of the term, 'necessary' mean[s] that no alternative exist[s]".[309] Another Panel interpreting the term "necessary" in the context of Article XX(b) had stated that "the import restrictions imposed by Thailand could be considered to be "necessary" in terms of Article XX(b) only if there were no alternative measures consistent with the General Agreement, or less inconsistent with it, which Thailand could reasonably be expected to employ to achieve its health policy objectives".[310] In this case, the United States had not and could not demonstrate that alternative GATT-consistent measures were not available to it at the time that it had promulgated the shrimp embargo. Indeed, Section 609(a) specifically required the US Secretary of State to "initiate negotiations as soon as possible for the development of bilateral or multilateral agreements with other nations for the protection and conservation of such species of sea turtles".[311] This mandate indicated that no such attempts had been made prior to enactment of the legislation which authorized the embargo.

3.217. The embargo was not "necessary" because the complainants already had an adequate programme in place for the protection of sea turtles within their jurisdiction. Inasmuch as the sea turtles in question occurred in waters within the jurisdiction of other nations, the United States could have sought to protect them through international agreements which did not include unilateral import restrictions. Such measures would achieve the US policy goal, while being consistent with the GATT. Pursuant to the CIT's 8 October 1996 Order, the embargo applied to all wild harvested shrimp or shrimp products from non-certified countries, whether or not such shrimp had been harvested in a manner that harmed or could harm sea turtles. In order to become certified, other nations had to adopt conservation policies comparable to US policies.[312]

---

[308] See *United States* v. *Welden*, 377 U.S. 95, 98 n.4.

[309] Panel Report on *United States - Restrictions on Imports of Tuna*, not adopted, circulated 16 June 1994, DS29/R, paragraph 5.35.

[310] Panel Report on *Thailand - Restrictions on Importation of and Internal Taxes on Cigarettes*, adopted 7 November 1990, BISD 37S/200, paragraph 75. See also Appellate Body Report on *United States - Standards for Reformulated and Conventional Gasoline*, adopted 20 May 1996, WT/DS2/R.

[311] 16 USC. § 1537 note (a)(1) (emphasis added).

[312] The complainants noted that Earth Island Institute had challenged the CIT's interpretation of the scope of shrimp subject to the embargo. Earth Island Institute claimed that all shrimp from non-certified countries, including shrimp harvested in aquaculture, was subject to the embargo.

Thus, the embargo could not be considered "necessary" because it was a measure taken to force other countries to change their policies and practices and could be effective only if such changes occurred.[313] Finally, the embargo, as implemented, could not be considered "necessary" when the United States itself had stated that implementing the embargo without providing a sufficient phase-in period for newly affected nations "will not result in any benefit to sea turtles in those nations newly covered, because fishermen with no experience in TEDs use are not likely to be able to use them effectively in the near term to protect sea turtles".[314] Indeed, prior to enforcing the embargo pursuant to the CIT's 29 December 1996 Order, the United States had gone so far as to state that "[e]ven assuming the willingness of affected nations to comply with Section 609, a May 1, 1996, compliance date will achieve no conservation benefit".[315]

3.218. **Malaysia** submitted that in its examination of whether inconsistent measures were necessary to achieve the policy objectives of the United States, the *Gasoline* Panel Report noted that the term "necessary" had been interpreted in the context of Article XX(d) by the Panel in the *Section 337* case which had stated that:

> "a contracting party cannot justify a measure inconsistent with another GATT provision as "necessary" in terms of Article XX(d) if an alternative measure which it could reasonably be expected to employ and which is not inconsistent with other GATT provisions is available to it. By the same token, in cases where a measure consistent with other GATT provisions is not reasonably available, a contracting party is bound to use, among the measures reasonably available to it, that which entails the least degree of inconsistency with other GATT provisions".[316]

The *Gasoline* Panel also relied on the *Cigarettes* case, which had followed the same reasoning under Article XX(b)[317], and found that the aspect of the baseline establishment methods found inconsistent with Article III:4 was not justified under Article XX(b) as "necessary to protect human, animal or plant life or health".[318]

3.219. Applying the principle pronounced by previous panels to the present case, Malaysia submitted that the US import prohibition was not necessary to further the US policy objectives of protecting human, animal or plant life or health for the following reasons. In *Tuna II*, the Panel noted that the text of Article XX was not explicit as to whether under Article XX(b) measures necessary to protect the life or health of animals could include measures taken so as to force other countries to change their policies

[313] Panel Report on *United States - Restrictions on Imports of Tuna*, not adopted, circulated 16 June 1994, DS29/R, paragraph 5.39.

[314] United States Court of International Trade, *Earth Island Institute* v. *Warren Christopher*, Memorandum in Support of Defendants' Motion for Modification of 29 December 1995, Order, p. 11

[315] *Ibid.*

[316] Panel Report on *United States - Section 337 of the Tariff Act of 1930*, adopted 7 November 1989, BISD 36S/345, paragraph 5.26.

[317] Panel Report on *Thailand - Restrictions on Importation of and Internal Taxes on Cigarettes*, adopted 7 November 1990, BISD 37S/200, paragraph 75.

[318] Panel Report on *United States - Standards for Reformulated and Conventional Gasoline*, adopted 20 May 1996, WT/DS2/9, paragraph 6.29.

within their own jurisdictions and requiring such changes in order to be effective. The Panel held the view that Article XX should be interpreted narrowly and in a way that preserved the basic objectives and principles of GATT.[319] The Panel concluded that "measures taken so as to force other countries to change their policies, and that were effective only if such changes occurred, could not be considered 'necessary' for the protection of animal life or health in the sense of Article XX(b)".

3.220. Malaysia regarded the import prohibition as an application of force by a foreign nation to change its turtle conservation policy without the slightest consideration for its serious, effective and continuous efforts to ensure the survival of turtles both domestically and internationally. As such the US import prohibition had the effect of forcing Malaysia to change its policy with regard to the protection of turtles over and above the turtle conservation measures currently in place. As Malaysia had stated, TED was not the only effective conservation method. Moreover, the import prohibition being directed at shrimp and not at turtles would not necessarily result in the adoption of TEDs by legislation or administrative action in the countries concerned. Other willing markets were available. Malaysia, while studying the effectiveness of TEDs, had directed its exports to other markets. Similar action would be taken by other affected countries. Thus, the import prohibition could not be deemed necessary for the conservation of sea turtles. In the *Tuna I* Panel Report Mexico had submitted the import prohibition imposed by the US was not necessary because alternative means consistent with GATT were available to protect dolphin life or health, namely international cooperation between the countries concerned.[320] This alternative means was in fact envisaged in Section 609(a)(1)(2) and (3) which provided that the US Secretary of State may in consultation with the US Secretary of Commerce with respect to the conservation of the five species of sea turtles, *inter alia*, initiate negotiations for the development of bilateral or multilateral agreements with other nations and all foreign governments and encourage such other agreements to promote such purpose. The United States had concluded the Inter-American Convention for the Protection and Conservation of Sea Turtles on 5 September 1996 with only five governments in the Western Hemisphere. Malaysia therefore submitted that the United States had not shown that it has exhausted all options reasonably available to it to pursue its sea turtle protection objectives through measures consistent with GATT, in particular through the negotiation of international cooperative arrangements on a multilateral basis considering especially that turtles were highly migratory. There was nothing to stop the United States from concluding a similar agreement with Malaysia or any other country instead of relying on the unilateral action of imposing an import prohibition.

[319] Panel Report on *United States - Restrictions on Imports of Tuna*, not adopted, DS29/R, circulated 16 June 1994, paragraphs 5.38-39: "[i]f Article XX(b) were to be interpreted to permit contracting parties to deviate from the basic obligations of GATT by taking trade measures to implement policies within their own jurisdiction, including policies to protect living things, the objectives of GATT would be maintained. If however Article XX(b) were interpreted to permit contracting parties to impose trade embargoes so as to force other countries to change their policies within their jurisdiction, including policies to protect living things, and which required such changes to be effective, the objectives of GATT would be seriously impaired".

[320] Panel Report on *United States - Restrictions on Imports of Tuna*, not adopted, circulated 3 September 1991, BIDS 39S/155, paragraph 5.24.

3.221. The United States, like Malaysia, was a party to the CITES. This Convention gave recognition to the sovereignty principle whereby each Party was free to protect its own endangered species of plants or animals. This principle was echoed in the following preambular provision, which recognized that "peoples and States are and should be the best protectors of their own fauna and flora". CITES' Preamble also recognized the principle of international cooperation by stating that "international cooperation is essential for the protection of certain species of wild fauna and flora against over-exploitation through international trade". Appendix I to the CITES was a list including all species of sea turtles which were threatened with extinction and which were or could be affected by trade. Malaysia noted that the United States had not entered a reservation with regard to the species of turtles specified for protection in the application of Section 609 and was therefore governed by CITES. The relevant provisions of CITES allowed both international and domestic measures to be taken by any country based on the principle of mutual understanding and cooperation and with due regard to a nation's sovereignty. No nation which was a party to CITES should resort to any measure such as an import prohibition which was inconsistent with GATT.[321] Malaysia therefore submitted that other alternative means were clearly available to the United States to protect the life and health of sea turtles under Article XX(b), such as multilateral or bilateral agreements for the conservation of sea turtles with other countries; the import prohibition was therefore not necessary to protect the live and health of sea turtles as such.

3.222. The **United States** replied that the US measures under Section 609 were "necessary", in two different senses. First, efforts to reduce sea turtle mortality were "necessary" because, as noted, all species of sea turtles were threatened with extinction. Again, each of the complainants had adopted at least some measures to conserve sea turtles, and each agreed that sea turtle conservation was necessary. Second, the measures under Section 609 relating to the use of TEDs were "necessary" because other measures to protect sea turtles were not sufficient to allow sea turtles to recover from the brink of extinction. Even though each complainant was a party to CITES, which prohibited trade in sea turtles, and each complainant stated that it had adopted certain sea turtle conservation measures - such as beach conservation - sea turtle populations exhibited alarming declines in the Southeast Asian and Indian Ocean regions. This result was not surprising since, as noted, accidental drowning in trawl nets accounted for a greater number of sea turtle deaths than all other human-induced causes combined. Without the use of TEDs, other measures to protect sea turtles were insufficient to produce an increase in sea turtle populations because these measures had not been demonstrated to have any significant effect on the number of sea turtles that survived to adulthood and reproduced. Further, in regions where TEDs were used in conjunction with other sea turtle conservation measures, there were signs of encouraging increases in sea turtle populations.

3.223. The United States further submitted that the grounds asserted by India, Malaysia, Pakistan and Thailand to argue that the US turtle conservation measures under Section 609 were not "necessary" within the meaning of Article XX(b) were without merit. The United States disagreed with statements in earlier panel reports,

---

[321] Article XIII and Article XIV of CITES.

referred to by the complainants, that the word "necessary" should be interpreted to mean that the United States had to demonstrate that "there were no alternative measures consistent with the GATT 1994, or less inconsistent with it, which [the United States] could reasonably be expected to employ to achieve its ... policy objectives". The adoption of this complex, multi-step test, in place of the single word "necessary" actually used in the text of the GATT 1994, was not supported in the text of the GATT 1994 or in its negotiating history. Moreover, the replacement of the actual treaty language in Article XX with a gloss developed by one or more panels was contrary to the teachings of the Appellate Body in the *Gasoline* case. Addressing in that case Article XX(g) and the differing introductory terms (such as "necessary", "essential", and "relating to") used in the various paragraphs of Article XX, the Appellate Body explained that:

> "The relationship between the affirmative commitments set out in, e.g. Articles I, III, and XI, and the policies and interests embodied in the "General Exceptions" listed in Article XX, can be given meaning within the framework of the *General Agreement* and its object and purpose by a treaty interpreter *only on a case-by-base basis, by careful scrutiny of the factual and legal context in a given dispute, without disregarding the words actually used by the WTO Members themselves* to express their intent and purpose".[322]

Further, even though the participants in the *Gasoline* appeal agreed that "relating to" in Article XX(g) could be interpreted as "primarily aimed at", the Appellate Body cautioned that "the phrase 'primarily aimed at' was not itself treaty language and was not designed as a simple litmus test for inclusion or exclusion from Article XX(g)".

3.224. The same principles applied to the complainants' proposed gloss on the meaning of the term "necessary". The proposed "least inconsistent measure" test was not itself treaty language, and could not serve as a "simple litmus test" for measures covered by Article XX(b). Instead, whether a measure was "necessary" under Article XX(b) was to be determined "on a case-by-case basis, by careful scrutiny of the factual and legal context in the given dispute".[323]

3.225. The United States submitted that the test for "necessary" proposed by the complainants was complex. First, a WTO Member maintaining a measure was required to prove a negative by being required to establish that it had no other measure reasonably available to it that was consistent with the GATT 1994: it had to establish the non-existence of other measure. Second, the WTO Member had to demonstrate that, among the measures reasonably available to it, it had employed the measure that entailed the least degree of inconsistency with other provisions of the GATT 1994: the WTO Member had to establish the range of alternatives available and rank them according to "least inconsistency" with the provisions of the GATT 1994. The use of one word, "necessary", was a slender reed indeed on which to hang such an extensive and complex set of obligations. Rather than attempt to impose a reading of the text that

[322] Appellate Body Report on *United States - Standards for Reformulated and Conventional Gasoline*, adopted 20 May 1996, WT/DS2/9, DSR 1996:I, page 17 (emphasis added).
[323] *Ibid.*

no reader could be expected to know, it would be wiser to interpret the language in accordance with its normal meaning.

3.226. This was even more so where there was no discussion of the significance of the term "necessary" in the drafting history of Article XX. No trade agreement prior to the Havana Charter had used the term "necessary" in reference to protecting plant and animal life and health. Article XX itself had not been interpreted by a dispute settlement panel under the GATT until relatively recently, and each panel had modified the interpretation of this provision with each dispute. Where there was no basis in the text of an agreement itself, in the negotiating history, or in the context of the provision for a proposed interpretation of a provision, no panel should attempt to create an interpretation and then assert after the fact that this was the obligation assumed by a WTO Member when it subscribed to the WTO Agreement including GATT 1994. This was particularly true where there was no need for such an interpretation. The complainants' proposed interpretation appeared to be aimed at ensuring that purported health, safety and other measures were not really a form of trade protectionism. That concern was more properly met by addressing the requirement in the chapeau that measures under Article XX were not to be applied in such a manner that they would constitute a disguised restriction on international trade, rather than by reading into a word such as "necessary" a series of complex requirements that were never negotiated or discussed. It was peculiar to propose creating an interpretation with no basis in the text for a term such as "necessary" when in the same article there was explicit language that would serve to guard against the abuse of the measures listed in Article XX by applying them for protectionist purposes. After all, the basic thrust of the GATT was to prevent protectionism, not to intrude on the decision making of the contracting parties when pursuing legitimate policy objectives such as environmental protection.

3.227. The United States argued that, in practice, under the complainants' proposed rule, a WTO Member would not be able to determine whether a measure it was considering would be consistent with its obligations under the GATT 1994 until after the fact. This was because that determination depended on the alternatives that a dispute settlement panel considered to be reasonably available to the WTO Member. This would engage panels in second-guessing domestic legislative or regulatory decision-making based on a factual inquiry beyond the competence of trade panels. For example, a panel would need to decide whether an alternative measure adequately achieved the legitimate policy objectives of the WTO member concerned, which could involve complex technical questions and scientific judgements. The United States noted that, while panels had access to technical experts, the question was not one of having expert advice available, but whether a panel was to substitute its judgement on these issues for that of the government concerned.

3.228. The complainants' proposed interpretation was also too intrusive on the decision-making of each WTO Member. To accept such an interpretation would require dispute settlement panels to dictate the specific measure to be adopted by a WTO Member, since presumably there was only one measure among all the alternatives that was the "least inconsistent" with the GATT 1994. This run counter to the agreed course of practice for dispute settlement panels. Again, it should not be assumed that the contracting parties had agreed to such an intrusive obligation by implication. Such an interpretation should be based on an explicit agreement to these obligations. The complainants not only urged the adoption of a gloss that "necessary" meant the "least

GATT-inconsistent measure", but they further expanded the scope of that gloss beyond that found in any adopted or unadopted panel report. In particular, the complainants argued that the "least GATT-inconsistent measure" had to include the negotiation of bilateral or multilateral agreements. No panel had made such a finding.[324] Rather, panels examined whether the country imposing a requirement on an imported product could have imposed a less burdensome requirement.

3.229. The United States observed that, if adopted, the complainants' position would entirely rewrite Article XX(b). Nothing in the text of the GATT 1994 would limit this new "international cooperation" requirement to environmental measures. Instead, Article XX(b) would no longer apply to any measures necessary for the protection of animal life or health, including sanitary measures, unless the importing country first asked all exporting countries to agree to negotiate a multilateral agreement containing similar requirements. As there was no mention of this in the text of Article XX, it was inconceivable that the drafters intended such a sweeping limitation. The complainants' position was also clearly at odds with the *Agreement on the Application of Sanitary and Phytosanitary Measures*, which in part interpreted Article XX(b). That agreement contained no requirement to seek international negotiation before taking a sanitary or phytosanitary measure. Although the United States strongly disagreed with the complainants' unprecedented proposal to write an "international cooperation" requirement into Article XX(b), in this case the United States did indeed offer to negotiate a multilateral sea turtle conservation agreement with Asian countries, including the four complainants. The complainants, however, exhibited no interest in the United States offer. Thus, the negotiation of a bilateral or multilateral agreement to further sea turtle conservation was not an option reasonably available to the United States.

3.230. The United States rejected the complainants' arguments that their existing turtle conservation measures were sufficient for sea turtle conservation, and thus that a measure such as Section 609, which encouraged the use of TEDs, was not "necessary". The scientific data showed, on the contrary, that sea turtle populations were declining in the Southeast Asian and Indian Ocean, that accidental drowning in shrimp trawl nets was the greatest single cause of human-induced sea turtle mortality, and that the use of TEDs greatly reduced the harm to sea turtles. Moreover, the quotation made by India, Pakistan and Thailand from a brief filed by the United States in domestic litigation concerning the application of Section 609 to nations outside of the Caribbean Basin was out-of-context since the issue in that proceeding was the timing of when Section 609 would be applied to shrimp harvested in nations outside with Wider Caribbean/Western Atlantic region. In this context, the United States had explained to the Court that a delay in the effective date of its ruling to apply Section 609 on a global basis as of 1 May 1996 would allow more time for the governments and shrimp fishermen in foreign nations to become accustomed to TEDs. The United States had not argued, as implied by India, Pakistan and Thailand, that application of Section 609 on a global basis would not promote sea turtle conservation.

---

[324] The United States considered that Malaysia's argument was somewhat misleading by stating that in the *Tuna I* case, Mexico had submitted that international cooperation was a less GATT-inconsistent alternative. However, the *Tuna I* Panel had not adopted Mexico's position on this issue.

3.231. Finally, the four complainants argued that Section 609 was not "necessary" because it would "force" other nations to change their sea turtle conservation policies. Malaysia, and implicitly India, Pakistan and Thailand, based this argument on a finding in the *Tuna II* report. That finding, however, was totally without foundation in the text of the GATT 1994. And, in fact, the GATT 1994 indicated that trade measures could take effect through their influence on countries. For example, Article XX(e) covered measures relating to the products of prison labour. Since the management of prisons was almost universally within the sphere of governments, Article XX(e) unquestionably was intended to allow trade measures to that could serve to influence the policies and practices of governments.

3.232. **India, Pakistan and Thailand** argued that the United States confused the necessity of protecting sea turtles from extinction with the necessity of the specific trade measure purportedly chosen for that purpose, i.e. Section 609. While Thailand agreed with the general goal of protecting sea turtles from extinction, it disagreed with the means chosen to this end by the United States, and in particular that Section 609 was necessary to achieve this goal. Contrary to US assertions, the fact that all species of sea turtles were threatened with extinction did not make the US measures necessary. In fact, the US success in negotiating the Inter-American Convention demonstrated that sea turtles could be, and should be, protected through international cooperation rather than unilateral measures. Further, while the United States put forth scientific evidence to demonstrate that it was important to protect juvenile sea turtles, it did not demonstrate that a TEDs requirement applicable to the shrimp fisheries of all nations was necessary to accomplish that goal. The United States did not demonstrate that the incidental taking of sea turtles in shrimp trawl fisheries was a significant problem in Asia, Australia and Oceania or that there could not be other measures of equal or greater importance that could be taken to protect juvenile sea turtles. As noted previously, sea turtle populations in the complainants' waters was stable and slight declines were not related to shrimping. Even where it could be demonstrated that shrimp trawling was a primary cause of sea turtle mortality, there might be other measures that could reduce that mortality at less cost, such as reduced tow-times or time and area closures. The US claim that this Panel should ignore the interpretation of the term "necessary" adopted by other panels was also without merit. Indeed, the United States made virtually the same arguments to the *Tuna II* Panel, which found that a virtually identical restriction on tuna imports did not meet the necessity test. The only new aspect of the argument related the *Gasoline* Appellate Body Report. However, the *Gasoline* report specifically found that the treaty language "relating to" could be interpreted as meaning "primarily aimed at" and nothing in its decision led to the conclusion that the term "necessary" could not be interpreted to mean that there were no alternative measures consistent with the GATT 1994, or less inconsistent with it, as several previous panels had found.

3.233. **Malaysia** submitted that the United States was not interpreting the term "necessary" in a manner consistent with the *Tuna II* and the *Gasoline* panel reports. First, there were other options "consistent or less inconsistent" with the General Agreement that the United States could reasonably consider. Second, Section 609 could not be considered as "necessary" as it forced other countries to change their policies on the conservation of sea turtles and was ultimately effective only if such changes occurred. The United States should only resort to an import prohibition upon the exhaustion of all other reasonable options open to it, including entering into multilateral, regional or bilateral agreements with other countries. In this respect, it was not up to the Panel to decide what was the best option, but merely to conclude whether the United States had acted within the ambit of Article XX in imposing the import prohibition.

3.234. The **United States** argued that the measures under Section 609 were "necessary" in two different senses. First, efforts to reduce sea turtle mortality were "necessary" because, as noted, sea turtles were threatened with extinction. Second, the US measures under Section 609 relating to the use of TEDs were "necessary" because shrimp trawling without TEDs was the largest source of human-induced sea turtle mortality. Regarding the argument made by India, Pakistan and Thailand that the United States had confused the necessity of protecting sea turtles with the necessity of the specific trade measure chosen for that purpose, the United States responded that, to the contrary, it had addressed both of these matters separately and distinctly (see above paragraph 3.222). The United States noted that the complainants agreed with the general goal of protecting sea turtles from extinction, but disagreed with whether Section 609 was necessary to achieve this goal. Although only the second point was in dispute in this case, there certainly was no "confusion" in the United States discussion. Rather, the United States submitted that it was helpful to the Panel to establish that the complainants agreed with the United States that it was necessary to protect sea turtles from extinction. Indeed, all complainants accepted not only that sea turtles needed to be protected from extinction, but also the principle that import restrictions or prohibitions were needed to protect sea turtles, regardless of whether those sea turtles were outside their "jurisdiction". Under CITES, all complainants had committed to imposing import restrictions on endangered sea turtle and sea turtle products, regardless of where the sea turtles were harvested.

3.235. **India, Pakistan and Thailand** replied that, while it might be true that TEDs installed in shrimp trawl nets were necessary to protect sea turtle population in US coastal waters, the same could not be said of the complainants. In fact, sources cited by the United States specifically cited egg harvest as the cause of recorded declines of the complainants' sea turtle populations. Moreover, the measures were not "necessary" because they were measures taken to change policies and practices of other Members and could be effective only if such changes occurred. As found by the *Tuna II* Panel, measures that could be effective only if they were followed by changes in the policies or practices of other Members were not necessary to protect animal life or health. Finally, the measures were not necessary because there were other, GATT consistent or less inconsistent measures that could be taken to achieve the same objective. The United States did not deny this point, but argued that past panels criteria for determining the necessity of the measure should be disregarded by this Panel. India, Pakistan and Thailand were, however, of the view that these panels had correctly interpreted the term "necessity", and such an interpretation was essential to maintain the balance of rights and obligations in WTO, particularly if the Panel were to find that there was no implied jurisdictional limitation in Article XX(b). This interpretation was also consistent with the generally accepted view that the exceptions contained in Article XX had to be construed narrowly, because they were derogations from normal GATT obligations. As to the US argument that under CITES the complainants had accepted that import restrictions or prohibitions were needed to protect sea turtles, India, Pakistan and Thailand replied that their CITES membership demonstrated in fact that they had the sovereign right to determine which measures should be taken to protect the life and health of animals located within their jurisdiction, as well as the right to agree with other nations after engaging in negotiations what those measures would be. The fact that the complainants had agreed to import restrictions in another context did not make the unilateral action taken by the United States "necessary" in this dispute.

3.236. According to **Malaysia**, the argument that TEDs were necessary because shrimp trawling was the largest source of human-induced sea turtle mortality was not applicable to Malaysia, where the incidental capture of turtles was in fish trawls and not shrimp trawls. Moreover, the United States unduly generalized when stating that the complainants agreed that import restrictions or prohibitions were needed to protect sea turtles, regardless of whether those sea turtles were outside their "jurisdiction". Finally, Section 609 did not apply to flatback and olive ridley turtles. This demonstrated that the United States implicitly recognized the fact that they could not impose restrictions on sea turtles outside their jurisdiction.

### (d) Article XX(g)

#### (i) Policy to Conserve Exhaustible Natural Resources

3.237. **India, Pakistan and Thailand** argued that the language contained in Article XX(g) providing an exception for measures "relating to the conservation of exhaustible natural resources if such measures are made effective in conjunction with restrictions on domestic production or consumption" was to be interpreted "in good faith in accordance with the ordinary meaning to be given to the terms of the treaty in their context and in the light of its object and purpose".[325] A reasonable interpretation of the term "exhaustible" was that it referred to finite resources, such as minerals, rather than biological or renewable resources. Such finite resources were exhaustible because there was a limited supply which could and would be depleted unit for unit as the resources were consumed. If, however, all natural resources were considered to be "exhaustible", the term "exhaustible" would be rendered superfluous. Such a result was inconsistent with general rules of treaty interpretation.[326] In the view of India, Pakistan and Thailand, the conclusion in the *Gasoline* case that Article XX(g) applied to the measure at issue notwithstanding the fact that clean air was "renewable"[327], was based on misplaced reliance on two prior panel reports. In *Salmon/Herring*, the meaning of the term "exhaustible" was not at issue; rather, both parties had agreed that salmon and herring were exhaustible natural resources.[328] Nor had this issue been raised in the *Tuna*

---

[325] Article 31 of the Vienna Convention on the Law of Treaties.

[326] Appellate Body Report on *United States - Standards for Reformulated and Conventional Gasoline*, adopted 20 May 1996, WT/DS2/9, DSR 1996:I, page 21 ("One of the corollaries of the "general rule of interpretation" in the Vienna Convention is that interpretation must give meaning and effect to all the terms of a treaty").

[327] Panel Report on *United States - Standards for Reformulated and Conventional Gasoline*, adopted 20 May 1996, WT/DS2/9, paragraph 6.37.

[328] Panel Report on *Canada - Measures Affecting Exports of Unprocessed Herring and Salmon*, adopted 22 March 1988, BISD 35S/98, paragraph 4.4.

*II* Panel Report; in that dispute, the EC had argued that dolphins were not a "resource" because there was no trade in dolphins.[329]

3.238. The fact that the term "exhaustible" was intended to mean finite physical resources, rather than biological resources, was further confirmed by the drafting history of Article XX(g). The exceptions which appeared in Article XX originated during the drafting of the commercial policy chapter of the draft ITO Charter. Throughout the preparatory meetings held for purposes of drafting the ITO Charter, discussion of the exception reflected in Article XX(g) focused on "raw materials", "products" and "minerals".[330] For example, much debate occurred over the language requiring the measure to be made effective in conjunction with restrictions on domestic product or consumption. After noting that "export restrictions should be permitted for the preservation of scarce natural resources even if there is no restriction on domestic consumption", the delegate from Brazil made the following comment:

> "I gave an example when I first raised this point of our having resources of manganese, for example, which are really ample for our present or prospective uses, but if we continued exporting them without limit, as we have been doing in the past, then they might very soon be exhausted. The main objection, which I recognize [is] a very fundamental objection, raised against this was that such permission might be used in order to prevent the establishment, based on your raw material, in another country of a like industry as we have at home".[331]

During discussions at the Second Session in Geneva, the delegate from India repeated a suggestion that had been made by his delegation in London that the words following "natural resources" be deleted. The Indian delegate then explained his suggestion as follows:

> "I shall give an illustration which will clarify the reason for this suggestion. A mineral of much strategic and industrial importance is being extensively mined, and practically the whole production is being exported. We wish to conserve it for more effective or beneficial and planned use later. The easiest and most effective way to secure this is by limiting exports. We cannot do this with Article XX(g)] as it stands, unless we link it with a somewhat unrealistic restriction on domestic production or consumption. It is to avoid having recourse to such steps that we made this suggestion, and if the Commission sees no objection, I would request that the suggestion be left on the record".[332]

3.239. India, Pakistan and Thailand considered that the drafting history of Article XX(g) supported the interpretation that "exhaustible natural resources" was intended to mean finite resources only. Since sea turtles were a renewable, rather than an

---

[329] Panel Report on *United States - Restrictions on Imports of Tuna*, not adopted, DS29/R, circulated 16 June 1994, paragraph 3.52.

[330] E/PC/T/C.II/50, p. 4-5; E/PC/T/C.II/QR/PV/5, p. 79; E/PC/T/A/PV/25, p. 30.

[331] E/PC/T/C.II/QR/PV/5, p. 79.

[332] E/PC/T/A/PV/25, p. 30.

"exhaustible" natural resource, the United States embargo could not be justified pursuant to Article XX(g).

3.240. **Malaysia** submitted that, for the purpose of interpreting Article XX(g), the Panel should follow the systemic approach adopted by the Appellate Body in the case *Taxes on Alcoholic Beverages* premised on Article 31 of the Vienna Convention of the Law of Treaties (VCT) which provided that "a treaty shall be interpreted in good faith in accordance with the ordinary meaning to be given to the term of the treaty in their context and in the light of its object and purpose".[333] Using this systemic approach, the interpretation to be ascribed to a measure under Article XX(g) could not be ascribed to a measure under Article XX(b) because it would render the systemic approach advocated by the Appellate Body meaningless. Sea turtles being living things, they could only be considered under Article XX(b) whereas Article XX(g) was meant for non living exhaustible natural resources. Malaysia therefore submitted that, given the systemic approach in the interpretation of Articles XX(b) and (g), the United States could not invoke both the exceptions simultaneously, for to do so would be inconsistent with the findings of the Appellate Body.

3.241. The **United States** submitted that sea turtles were important natural resources. They were an ancient and distinctive part of the world's biological diversity, and served key functions in the ecosystems they inhabited. That sea turtles were important natural resources did not appear to be at issue in this dispute; each of the four complainants stressed that it had adopted at least some measures to conserve sea turtles. Furthermore, sea turtles were exhaustible. This was underscored by the fact that all species of sea turtles faced the danger of extinction. CITES - to which all four complainants were parties - included an Appendix I listing species threatened with extinction. All species of sea turtles had been included in CITES Appendix I since 1975. Other international agreements also recognized the endangered status of sea turtles. That sea turtles were threatened with extinction - and thus nearly exhausted - confirmed that they were certainly exhaustible. This, too, did not appear to be at issue in this dispute.

3.242. The United States further argued that the four complainants' argument that Article XX(g) could not apply to "biological or renewable resources" was completely unsupported by the text of the GATT 1994, was contrary to the findings of prior panels, and unsupported by the drafting history of the GATT 1994. In short, the Panel should roundly reject this unsupportable reading. As to the argument made by India, Pakistan and Thailand, the United States considered that, regardless of whether "all natural resources" were exhaustible, there could be no doubt that sea turtles were exhaustible. Indeed, as endangered species, they were nearly exhausted. Once a species was extinct, it was gone forever, just as oil from a well or ore from a mine. India, Pakistan and Thailand were simply wrong in stating that the term "exhaustible" was superfluous unless one somehow read "natural resources" to exclude biological resources. In the view of the United States, India, Pakistan and Thailand completely mischaracterized the *Gasoline* Panel Report by stating that it was "based on misplaced reliance on two prior panel reports" when finding that clean air was an "exhaustible natural resource". In fact, the *Gasoline* panel correctly cited to the *Salmon/Herring* and *Tuna II* Panel Reports.

[333] Appellate Body Report on *Japan - Taxes on Alcoholic Beverages*, adopted 8 November 1996, WT/DS8/11, WT/DS10/11, WT/DS11/8, DSR 1996:I, page 104.

Contrary to the complainants' claims, both panels did find that renewable natural resources could be exhaustible under Article XX(g).[334] Moreover, the *Gasoline* Panel also relied on a plain reading of the text of Article XX(g). With regard to whether clean air was a "natural resource", the Panel explained that "clean air was a resource (it had value) and it was natural". With regard to whether clean air was exhaustible, the Panel explained that "it could be depleted". India, Pakistan and Thailand had no answer to this plain reading of the text of Article XX(g). Finally, India, Pakistan and Thailand's citation to the drafting history of Article XX(g) was completely unpersuasive. As an initial matter, reliance on this supplementary aid to interpretation in order to context the plain meaning of the text was not warranted when, as here, Article XX(g) was not ambiguous.[335]

3.243. Aside from that, India, Pakistan and Thailand merely cited to certain "examples" or "illustrations" from the drafting history of Article XX(g) indicating that measures to be covered under Article XX(g) included those relating to minerals. But India, Pakistan and Thailand simply ignored other drafting history showing that Article XX(g) in fact was also intended to apply to biological resources. In particular, during the negotiation of the ITO Charter, the delegate from Australia questioned whether Article 25 (prohibiting quantitative restrictions) would prevent Australia from limiting exports of merino sheep.[336] The delegate explained that due to dire drought conditions, Australia had lost 20 million merino sheep, and was thus prohibiting exports. The Belgian delegate responded that regardless of the scope of Article 25, Australia's prohibition was allowed by the exception for exhaustible natural resources.[337] In short, the drafting history in fact refuted the complainants' argument that Article XX(g) was intended to be limited so as to exclude biological resources.

3.244. The United States further argued that Malaysia made a similarly flawed argument when contending that Article XX(g) had to be read to exclude animals because animals were explicitly included in Article XX(b), and Article XX(g) or Article XX(b) would thus be rendered superfluous. Just because in certain cases a single measure could fall under two or more paragraphs of Article XX(g), this in no way rendered meaningless a provision of the GATT 1994. Under the natural reading of Article XX(g) (which was to include animals as "exhaustible natural resources"), Articles XX(b) and XX(g) were not coextensive because they contained different requirements. Article XX(b) applied, for example, only to plants and animals, while Article XX(g) applied to all natural resources; Article XX(g) required that the measure be made effective in conjunction with restrictions on domestic production or

[334] The United States referred to the Panel Report on *Canada - Measures Affecting Exports of Unprocessed Herring and Salmon*, adopted 22 March 1988, BISD 35S/98, paragraph 4.4 ("[t]he Panel agreed with the parties to the dispute that salmon and herring stocks are 'exhaustible natural resources' ... within the meaning of Article XX(g)"); Panel Report on *United States - Restrictions on Imports of Tuna*, not adopted, DS29/R, circulated 16 June 1994, paragraph 5.13 ("[t]he Panel noted that the United States maintained that dolphins were an exhaustible natural resource. The EEC disagreed. The Panel, noting that dolphin stocks could potentially be exhausted, ... accepted that a policy to conserve dolphins was a policy to conserve an exhaustible natural resource".)

[335] Vienna Convention, Article 32.

[336] E/PC/T/A/SR/40(1) (15 August 1947) and E/PC/T/A/PV/40(1) (15 August 1947).

[337] The United States noted that Article, 37(j) was the precursor of GATT Article XX(g).

consumption, while Article XX(b) did not; and Article XX(g) required that the natural resource be exhaustible, while Article XX(b) contained no such requirement for the plants and animals within its scope. The United States also noted that two of the third parties (the EC and Japan) expressly noted their disagreement with this unsupportable reading advocated by the complainants (see below paragraphs 4.33 and 4.52).

3.245. **India, Pakistan and Thailand** maintained that the term "exhaustible" should be interpreted as referring to finite, physical resources, such as minerals, which were depleted unit-for-unit as they were consumed. A distinction had to be drawn between resources that were necessarily "exhausted" as they were consumed and resources that were renewable, such as those that were biological. The protection of biological resources was within the scope of Article XX(b). If the term "exhaustible" were extended to include all natural resources, even those that were renewable, then the term "exhaustible" would be rendered superfluous. The United States did not show the Panel how its interpretation of the language of Article XX(g) avoided this result. Moreover, an interpretation of the term exhaustible to include biological resources ignored the structure of Article XX, which provided for a separate exception for measures necessary to protect the life or health of biological organisms (people, animals and plants). Finding that Article XX(g) encompassed biological organisms necessarily meant that the measures had to be scrutinized under two different standards, the "relating to" and the "necessary for" standards, and it was illogical to assume that such a result had been intended by the drafters. It was a fundamental rule of construction that every term or word in a treaty should be given an independent meaning. The US argument that paragraphs (b) and (g) of Article XX were not coextensive and contained different conditions confirmed precisely the point made by the complainants. Indeed, why establishing different legal conditions for the same subject matter? If anything "necessary to" protect the "life" or "health" of sea turtles (or any other biological resource) could be done under Article XX(b), why was it necessary or desirable to create a separate set of conditions for the protection of those organisms under Article XX(g)? The answer could only be that the two provisions were never intended to cover the same subject matter. Therefore, the meaning that ought to be given to the term "exhaustible" was that, as outlined by the complainants, it referred to finite, physical resources, not to renewable resources such as those that were biological. This meaning preserved the separation of the subject matter of Articles XX (b) and (g), while giving concrete, independent meaning to the term that was consistent with the preoccupation of the drafters over the risks of untimely depletion of exhaustible mineral resources through unfettered exploitation and exportation.

3.246. The findings of the *Gasoline* Panel were not on point because the resource at issue in that case was not biological.[338] In addition, the Panel's reliance for its conclusion that renewable resources were within the scope of Article XX(g) on *Herring/Salmon* and the *Tuna II* Panel Reports was misplaced. In *Salmon/Herring*, there had been no dispute between the parties over whether the resource at issue was

[338] India, Pakistan and Thailand noted that the finding of the Panel that clean air was an "exhaustible natural resource" was not appealed and therefore not addressed by the Appellate Body. See Appellate Body Report on *United States - Standards for Reformulated and Conventional Gasoline*, adopted 20 May 1996, WT/DS2/9, DSR 1996:I, page 9.

renewable and therefore not "exhaustible" and thus there was no decision by the Panel on this issue. In the *Tuna II* dispute, the EC disagreed with the United States' position that dolphins were an exhaustible natural resources based on an argument that dolphins were not commodities and therefore were not "resources".[339] Once again, the Panel did not have the opportunity to consider the question of whether a renewable resource qualified as an "exhaustible" resource. Finally, there was no evidence in the text of the *Gasoline* Panel Report that it considered the drafting history cited by India, Pakistan and Thailand. Therefore, there was ample basis for revisiting this issue.

3.247. **Malaysia** did not deny that sea turtles were an exhaustible natural resource, but contended that Article XX(g) was meant only for non living exhaustible natural resources whilst turtles, being living things, could only be considered under Article XX(b). Such an approach logically required that the interpretation to be ascribed to a measure under Article XX(g) could not be ascribed to a measure under Article XX(b) because it would make meaningless the systemic approach advocated by the Appellate Body in the *Gasoline* case.[340] Malaysia noted that previous GATT Panel Reports had held that fish (living) was an exhaustible natural resource.[341] However, these cases had been adjudicated before the entry into force of the WTO. The approach of the Appellate Body in the *Gasoline* case was to be preferred. Malaysia also noted that the United States misread the submissions presented by the EC and Japan on this point. In fact, the EC was merely of the view that sea turtles might be regarded as an exhaustible natural resource, whilst Japan merely did not challenge the US view that sea turtles were an "exhaustible natural resource" within the meaning of Article XX(g).

3.248. The **United States** noted that the complainants did not dispute that sea turtles were "exhaustible natural resources" as that term was normally used. Indeed, this point was beyond argument since sea turtles were listed in Appendix I of CITES as "species threatened with extinction which may be affected by trade." Each complainant was party to CITES. However, despite the plain meaning of the text, the complainants argued that "exhaustible natural resources" under Article XX(g) had to be limited to finite physical resources, such as minerals, which were depleted unit for unit. The United States urged the Panel to reject this interpretation which would violate a fundamental rule of treaty interpretation whereby the terms of a treaty should be interpreted in accordance with the "ordinary meaning to be given to the terms in their context and in light of its object and purpose". Nothing in the text or context limited Article XX(g) to measures involving the conservation of minerals. Contrary to what was

---

339 Panel Report on *United States - Restrictions on Imports of Tuna*, not adopted, DS29/R, circulated 16 June 1994, paragraph 3.52 ("The EEC replied that, although the United States and the EEC both agreed that dolphins were in need of conservation, this did not make them into an exhaustible natural resource. Since CITES ensured that there was no trade in dolphin species, one could question whether dolphins were resources in any economic sense of the term".)

340 Appellate Body Report on *United States - Standards for Reformulated and Conventional Gasoline*, adopted 20 May 1996, WT/DS2/9. Malaysia also referred to the Appellate Body Report on *Japan - Taxes on Alcoholic Beverages*, adopted 8 November 1996, WT/DS8/11, WT/DS10/11, WT/DS11/8.

341 Panel Report on *Canada - Measures Affecting Exports of Unprocessed Herring and Salmon*, adopted 22 March 1988, BISD 35S/98; Panel Report on *United States - Restrictions on Imports of Tuna*, not adopted, circulated 3 September 1991, BISD 39S/155; Panel Report on *United States - Restrictions on Imports of Tuna*, not adopted, circulated 16 June 1994, DS29/R.

claimed by the complainants, the inclusion of non-mineral resources in the scope of Article XX(g) in no way made the term "exhaustible" superfluous. Rather, it instructed the Panel to examine whether the natural resource subject to the conservation measure was "exhaustible" based on the facts of the particular case. Some natural resources, such as solar power, might not be exhaustible, Further, on the facts of this case, it was beyond dispute that sea turtles were exhaustible. Indeed, some species of sea turtles were on the brink of extinction. The analysis suggested by the United States had been followed in the *Gasoline* case, where the Panel had found that clean air was an exhaustible natural resource under Article XX(g). Contrary to the complainants' theory for limiting Article XX(g), clean air was not depleted unit-for-unit like a mineral resource. The new theory proposed by the complainants for limiting Article XX(g) to non-biological resources was, like the prior one, without any basis in the text of the Agreement.

3.249. The United States further argued that the ordinary meaning of the text of Article XX was that both paragraphs (b) and (g) covered biological organisms. This reading did not, as implied by the complainants, make Article XX(b) superfluous. Rather, although there was some overlap, the two provisions had a number of different requirements, and were not coextensive. For example, Article XX(g) required that the measure be made effective in conjunction with restrictions on domestic production or consumption, Article XX(b) did not; Article XX(g) required that the natural resource be exhaustible, Article XX(b) did not; and Article XX(g) applied to "conservation", while Article XX(b) applied to "protection of life and health". The complainants did not and could not point to any reason for departing from the ordinary meaning in order to avoid overlap between two Article XX provisions. Indeed, Article XX included other examples of overlapping provisions. For example, Article XX(c) applied to "gold and silver", and overlapped with Article XX(g), which applied to exhaustible natural resources. Should then gold and silver be excluded from the scope of Article XX(g)?

(ii) "Related to ..."

3.250. Recalling the arguments made in relation with Article XX(b), **India, Pakistan and Thailand** argued that, while the general purpose of Section 609 might have been to benefit sea turtles, the United States could not credibly contend that the objective of the embargo was to protect the lives of sea turtles. By providing only four months notice prior to implementation of the embargo against newly affected nations, the United States had required these newly affected nations to implement regulatory programs requiring 100 per cent TEDs use. This was done even though the foreign shrimp harvesters might not have had time to acquire TEDs and receive instruction on their use, and thus might not have been able to use them effectively. The United States itself had recognized that requiring use of TEDs with such little notice "will not result in any benefit to sea turtles in those nations newly covered, because fishermen with no experience in TEDs use are not likely to be able to use them effectively in the near term to protect sea turtles".[342] Indeed, the United States had gone so far as to state that

[342] United States Court of International Trade, *Earth Island Institute* v. *Warren Christopher*, Memorandum in Support of Defendants' Motion for Modification of 29 December 1995, Order, p. 11.

"[e]ven assuming the willingness of affected nations to comply with Section 609, a May 1, 1996, compliance date will achieve no conservation benefit".[343] In light of these and similar statements, the United States could not credibly argue that the policy behind the embargo was intended to conserve sea turtles. Moreover, as had been argued under Article XX(b), the legislative history of Section 609, pursuant to which the embargo was enacted, indicated that the purpose of the provision was to restrict imports. Furthermore, Section 609 was codified as a note and not as an amendment to the Endangered Species Act; it could be inferred from this that the purpose of the provision was something other than protection of endangered species.

3.251. India, Pakistan and Thailand further argued that the analysis made in the *Tuna II* Panel Report applied to this case. In *Tuna II*, the Panel had noted that the embargo at issue prohibited imports from a country of any tuna, whether or not the particular tuna was harvested in a way that harmed or could harm dolphins, as long as the country's tuna harvesting practices and policies were not comparable to those of the United States. The Panel had noted that the primary and intermediary tuna embargoes at issue were "taken so as to force other countries to change their policies with respect to persons and things within their own jurisdiction" and could achieve the desired effect only if followed by changes in policies and practices in exporting countries.[344] That is, the embargo could not conserve dolphins by itself; a conservation purpose could be achieved only if the foreign governments and foreign fishermen changed their policies and practices. The Panel had concluded that "measures taken so as to force other countries to change their policies, and that were effective only if such changes occurred, could not be primarily aimed at", and therefore did not "relate to", conservation of an exhaustible natural resource.[345] India, Pakistan and Thailand submitted that the shrimp embargo at issue in this case applied to any wild shrimp and shrimp products of nations that had not been certified as having a regulatory programme comparable to that of the United States, whether or not the shrimp was harvested in a way that harmed or could harm sea turtles. Further, the shrimp embargo was not a measure "relating to" the conservation of sea turtles because it was effective only if it forced other nations to change their policies and practices.

3.252. India, Pakistan and Thailand were of the view that, in order to be considered "related to" the conservation of sea turtles, the embargo had to be "primarily aimed at" the conservation of sea turtles.[346] In light of statements made by the United States to the Court of International Trade that the immediate implementation of the embargo against newly affected nations "would not result in any benefit to sea turtles", the embargo could not be said to be primarily aimed at the conservation of sea turtles. Rather, based on the litigation which occurred in the United States and the statements made by the United States Government during its defense, the conservation goal cited as

---

[343] United States Court of International Trade, *Earth Island Institute* v. *Warren Christopher*, Memorandum in Support of Defendants' Motion for Modification of 29 December 1995, Order, p. 11.

[344] Panel Report on *United States - Restrictions on Imports of Tuna*, not adopted, DS29/R, circulated 16 June 1994, paragraphs 5.23 and 5.24.

[345] *Ibid.*, paragraph 5.27.

[346] *Ibid.*, paragraph 5.22 (citing the Panel Report on *Canada - Measures Affecting Exports of Unprocessed Herring and Salmon*, adopted 22 March 1988, BISD 35S/98, paragraph 4.6).

justification for implementation of the embargo appeared to be incidental to the goals of implementing judicial interpretation of United States law, protecting the American shrimp industry, and of placating the demands of US environmental interest groups.

3.253. The **United States** argued that Section 609 as a whole clearly "relate[d] to" the conservation of sea turtles. Section 609(a) called for the negotiation of bilateral and multilateral agreements for the protection and conservation of sea turtles. Section 609(b) was intended to conserve and protect sea turtles by requiring that shrimp imported into the United States had not been harvested in a manner that would harm sea turtles. Shrimp trawl nets caused the greatest number of human-induced sea turtle deaths, accounting for more sea turtle deaths than all other human activities combined, and TEDs were highly effective in preventing such mortality. Thus, by calling for international agreements to protect and conserve sea turtles, and by requiring that shrimp imported into the United States had not been harvested in a manner that endangered sea turtles, Section 609 related to the conservation of sea turtles. The United States submitted that, in applying the "relating to" criterion of Article XX(g), the Appellate Body in the *Gasoline* case noted that the measure met this criterion because it had a "substantial relationship" to the conservation-related requirements of the measure, and was not "merely incidental or inadvertently aimed" at conservation.[347] The Appellate Body also accepted the participants' view that "relating to" could be interpreted as "primarily aimed at", although the Appellate Body also cautioned that "primarily aimed at" was "not itself treaty language" and was "not designed as a simple litmus test".[348] In any event, regardless of whether "relating to" was interpreted as "primarily aimed at" or as having a "substantial relationship", the United States measures met the "relating to" criterion.

3.254. **India, Pakistan and Thailand** maintained that the US measure did not "relate to" the conservation of exhaustible natural resources. Several panels found that the phrase "relate to" meant "primarily aimed at".[349] Further, although Appellate Body had noted in the *Gasoline* case that this language was not treaty language, it applied the same test in its analysis.[350] The United States argued that Section 609 as a whole clearly related to the conservation of sea turtles. However, Section 609 prohibited shrimp imports from non-certified countries whether or not the shrimp was caught with technologies that the United States considered to be "turtle-safe" (i.e. with TEDs). Moreover, while the evidence presented by the United States demonstrated that shrimp trawl nets caused the greatest number of turtle deaths from anthropogenic sources in US waters, the same was not true of sea turtle populations located outside the United States and specifically those located in the complainants' waters, Australia and other parts of Asia. Other forms of fishing and egg harvesting appeared to be the most significant anthropogenic threats to sea turtles in those areas of the world. By requiring the

---

[347] Appellate Body Report on *United States - Standards for Reformulated and Conventional Gasoline*, adopted 20 May 1996, WT/DS2/9, DSR 1996:I, page 18.

[348] *Ibid.*, p. 17.

[349] Panel Report on *Canada - Measures Affecting Exports of Unprocessed Herring and Salmon*, adopted 22 March 1988, BISD 35S/98, paragraph 4.6; Panel Report on *United States - Restrictions on Imports of Tuna*, not adopted, DS29/R, circulated 16 June 1994, paragraph 5.21.

[350] Appellate Body Report on *United States - Standards for Reformulated and Conventional Gasoline*, adopted 20 May 1996, WT/DS2/9, DSR 1996:I, page 18.

Members to expend significant sums on the deployment of TEDs in shrimp fisheries as a condition of access to the US market, the United States was diverting scarce resources from conservation measures that would in fact appear to be more effective in conserving sea turtles. India, Pakistan and Thailand stressed that, for the reasons developed in paragraph 3.251, the analysis made in the *Tuna II* Panel Report applied to this case.

3.255 India, Pakistan and Thailand further noted that the *Tuna II* Panel Report found that a measure which could not achieve its conservation purpose without action being taken by other countries to modify their environmental policies bore no "substantial relationship" to the conservation of the natural resource. In this case, Section 609 did not "relate" to the conservation of sea turtles because no "substantial relationship" had been established between shrimp trawling and sea turtle mortality in the complainants' waters, not had it been shown that the installation of TEDs was, standing alone, an efficient means of increasing sea turtle populations. Moreover, this case was different from the *Gasoline* case where there was a direct connection between the baseline requirements and the conservation of clean air in the United States. In that case, the adherence to the baseline requirements would have the effect to produce clean air; thus, there was a substantial relationship between the measure in question and a policy of conservation. In this case, however, the shrimp embargo could not, by itself, have any direct effect on sea turtle conservation; preventing the importation of shrimp could not, by itself, increase the number of sea turtles in the world. Sea turtle conservation was only achieved if other nations implemented a change in their environmental policies and that change affected sea turtle mortality. An embargo on imports of steel or machinery, or indeed, all goods from affected nations, which was tied to a condition that foreign nations took steps to protect their sea turtle populations, would have the same effect on sea turtle populations that the measure at issue had.

3.256. In addition, **India** recalled that, in the *Gasoline* case, the Appellate Body noted that the baseline establishment rules at issue were designed to permit scrutiny and monitoring of the level of compliance and that without baselines of some kind, such scrutiny would not be possible. Without a baseline, the Gasoline Rule's objective of stabilizing and preventing further deterioration of the level of air pollution would be substantially frustrated.[351] The goals of Section 609, however, would not be substantially frustrated without the embargo. Indeed, as the United States itself noted:

> "[I]mplementation of the Court's order could also irreparably harm the efforts of the US government to protect endangered sea turtles from threats other than shrimping. Defendants have been working for several years toward development of a multilateral agreement for the protection of Sea Turtles (Spero Decl. at paragraphs 16-17). This agreement would require nations to take a wide variety of measures for the benefit of sea turtles, including the protection of sea turtle habitat, strict control over harvest of sea turtles and their eggs, as well as the reduction of sea turtle mortality from fishing operations other than shrimping. (Id.) Nations which had previously cooperated with

[351] Appellate Body Report on *United States - Standards for Reformulated and Conventional Gasoline*, adopted 20 May 1996, WT/DS2/9, DSR 1996:I, page 17.

> the United States in these efforts have reacted negatively to the imposition of the embargo that could result from this Court's order. These nations may have little desire to cooperate when faced with the immediate embargo required by the current court order, thus jeopardizing further negotiations for an international agreement to protect sea turtles from wider threats to the species' survival".[352]

While the United States had negotiated one regional agreement, India understood that this agreement was not yet in force. Moreover, the same effects discussed above could ripple into other US efforts to protect sea turtles. Thus, it could not be said that the US goal would be substantially frustrated without the embargo.

3.257. Recalling the Appellate Body findings in the *Gasoline* case[353], **Malaysia** argued that Section 609 was not "primarily aimed at" the conservation of sea turtles. "Primarily aimed at" implied a substantial relationship between the measures under Section 609(b) and the conservation of sea turtles; it was up to the United States to demonstrate the existence of this substantial relationship, and to prove that the measure was not incidentally or inadvertently aimed at conservation. The United States failed to show such requirements. Malaysia was of the view that there was no such substantial relationship in this case, because, unlike the baseline establishment rules, which represented the benchmark for determining the level of compliance of importers and blenders with the non-degradation requirements, the use of TEDs was not the only method in preventing turtle mortality. This fact was recognized in the 1982 UN Convention on the Law of the Sea (UNCLOS), and the 1995 Agreement for the Implementation of the Provisions of UNCLOS Relating to the Conservation and Management of Straddling Stocks and Highly Migratory Fish Stocks. These agreements made reference to the use of selective, environmentally safe, cost-effective fishing gear but did not make specific mention to the use of TEDs. Furthermore, Malaysia had repeatedly shown that shrimp trawl nets were not the greatest cause of human-induced sea turtle deaths in Malaysia. Hence, there was no substantial relationship between the measures under Section 609 and the conservation of sea turtles. Malaysia recognized that Section 609(b) provided for the imposition of an import prohibition on the importation of shrimp or shrimp products harvested with commercial fishing technology which might adversely affect the conservation and protection of five species of sea turtles. However, the US Congressional Records indicated that the intention behind Section 609 was not primarily aimed at the conservation of sea turtles as the use of TEDs was not the most effective method or the best solution for the conservation of sea turtles. Thus the measures at issue could not come within the ambit of Article XX(g).

3.258. The **United States** maintained that Section 609 as a whole clearly "relate[d] to" the conservation of sea turtles. As the Appellate Body explained in the *Gasoline* case, this criterion was met where there was a "substantial relationship" between the measure and the conservation of an exhaustible natural resource, and where the measure was not

---

[352] United States Court of International Trade, *Earth Island Institute* v. *Warren Christopher*, Memorandum in Support of Defendants' Motion for Modification of 29 December 1995, Order.

[353] Appellate Body Report on *United States - Standards for Reformulated and Conventional Gasoline*, adopted 20 May 1996, WT/DS2/9, DSR 1996:I, pp. 17-18.

"merely incidentally or inadvertently aimed" at conservation.[354] In this case, the United States had shown a substantial relationship between its measures under Section 609(b) and the conservation of sea turtles. Shrimp trawl nets were the greatest cause of human-induced sea turtle deaths, accounting for more sea turtle deaths than all other human activities combined. TEDs were highly effective in preventing such mortality. By requiring that US imports of shrimp found in regions inhabited by sea turtles were harvested with TED-equipped trawl nets, or by other gear that did not harm sea turtles, the United States was ensuring that its importation of shrimp did not further endanger sea turtles. The relationship between the measures and the goal was clear, direct and substantial. By requiring that shrimp imported into the United States be harvested in a manner not harmful to sea turtles, the US measures were an important step in promoting sea turtle conservation.

3.259. The United States further argued that the argument made by the complainants that human activities other than shrimp trawling were a greater cause of sea turtle mortality in their waters missed the point. The US measures "relate[d] to" sea turtle conservation regardless of whether other types of conservation measures would also contribute to the protection of sea turtles. Article XX(g) only required that a measure "related to" conservation of an exhaustible natural resource, but did not require that a measure address each and every threat to such resource. The United States questioned whether the complainants would be any more satisfied if the US measures were extended to apply to fish, as well as shrimp, harvested in a manner harmful to sea turtles. Second, the reference made by India, Pakistan and Thailand to *Tuna II* that a measure could not be "related to" conservation if, to be effective, a foreign government had to change its policies was not supported by the text of the Agreement. Such a restrictive interpretation was moreover inconsistent with the reasoning of the Appellate Body in the *Gasoline* case. Nothing in the text of the GATT indicated that the issue of whether a measure was "related to" conservation depended on whether the measure entailed policy changes by governments, exporters or producers. In essence, the three complainants raised an issue regarding the means by which the measure met the goal of conserving an exhaustible natural resource. However, the GATT addressed such issues in the chapeau, and not in the text of Article XX(g). In particular, the chapeau required that measures should not be applied in a manner which would constitute a means of arbitrary or unjustifiable discrimination.

### (iii) "In Conjunction with ..."

3.260. **India, Pakistan and Thailand** submitted that the United States had not demonstrated that the measure at issue was made effective in connection with restrictions on domestic production or consumption. As noted by the Appellate Body in the *Gasoline* case, this prong referred "to governmental measures being promulgated or brought into effect together with restrictions on domestic production or consumption of natural resources". Specifically, the Appellate Body stated that the language was a "requirement that the measures concerned impose restrictions, not just in respect of [the imported product] but also in respect to [the domestic product]". Thus, the Appellate

[354] Appellate Body Report on *United States - Standards for Reformulated and Conventional Gasoline*, adopted 20 May 1996, WT/DS2/9, DSR 1996:I, p. 20

Body had concluded that the clause was a requirement of even-handedness.[355] However, for India, Pakistan and Thailand, restrictions imposed on domestic and foreign shrimp trawlers had not been imposed even-handedly. While domestic shrimp trawlers had been given a ten-year phase-in period before restrictions were placed on their access to the US market, the embargo had been imposed on the newly affected nations with only four months notice. The manner in which the embargo had been implemented thus provided US shrimp harvesters with a competitive advantage over foreign harvesters. While the United States required both domestic and foreign harvesters to use TEDs, these measures were not "promulgated or brought into effect together".

3.261. The **United States** argued that Section 609 was "made effective in conjunction with restrictions on domestic production or consumption". The Appellate Body interpreted this criterion to mean that the measures concerned imposed restrictions not just on the imported product but also with respect to the comparable domestic product.[356] This test was met here. The United States required its shrimp trawl vessels that operated where there was a likelihood of intercepting sea turtles to use TEDs at all times, and Section 609 applied comparable standards to imported shrimp. The Appellate Body also stated that the "made effective in conjunction with" requirement was a requirement of "even-handedness", although there was no textual basis for identical treatment of domestic and imported products.[357] Again, Section 609 met the test. The statute allowed any nation to be certified - and thus to avoid any restriction on shrimp exports to the United States - if it met criteria for sea turtle safety in the course of shrimp harvesting that were comparable to criteria applicable in the United States. For those nations whose shrimp trawl vessels operated in areas where there was a likelihood of intercepting sea turtles, Section 609 allowed for certification if such nations adopted TEDs requirements comparable to those in effect in the United States.

3.262. The United States considered that the argument made by India, Pakistan and Thailand was based on a misunderstanding of both the relevant facts and of the proper application of Article XX(g). First, United States shrimpers had not been given a "10-year" period in which to comply with TEDs regulations. While it was true that approximately 10 years had elapsed between the time that the United States Government had first begun seeking ways to reduce sea turtle mortality in shrimp trawl nets in 1978 and the time that the first regulations had been promulgated requiring the use of TEDs in 1987, this time could hardly be considered a "grace period" for US shrimpers during which foreign exporters of shrimp to the United States had been somehow disadvantaged. Indeed, to the extent that the US TEDs requirements could be seen as imposing any competitive disadvantage, that disadvantage had been borne by US shrimpers for several years, not those from the complainants. As noted, the 1987 TEDs regulations went into full effect in 1990. Since then, TEDs requirements in the United States had become ever stricter. By contrast, Section 609 was applying to

[355] Appellate Body Report on *United States - Standards for Reformulated and Conventional Gasoline*, adopted 20 May 1996, WT/DS2/9, DSR 1996:I, page 19.

[356] Appellate Body Report on *United States - Standards for Reformulated and Conventional Gasoline*, adopted 20 May 1996, WT/DS2/9, DSR 1996:I, page 19.

[357] *Ibid.*

imports of shrimp from the complainants only since 1 May 1996. By the mid-1990's, moreover, the design of TEDs had become extraordinarily advanced in terms of turtle protection (97 per cent effective) and shrimp retention (virtually no shrimp lost). Due to the considerable efforts of the United States and other governments, TED technology was also inexpensive and readily available at that time. Thus, by the time that Section 609 became applicable to the complainants, they were able to reap the benefits of the research and development that the United States had been undertaking on TED technology for many years.

3.263 Secondly, the United States argued that India, Pakistan and Thailand were correct in citing to the statement in the *Gasoline* Appellate Body report that the "in conjunction with" clause of Article XX(g) generally required "even-handedness" in the imposition of restrictions. But the complainants had left out the Appellate Body's admonition that "[t]here is, of course, no textual basis [in Article XX(g)] for requiring identical treatment of domestic and imported products". In any event, none of the complainants had experienced anything less than even-handed treatment as a consequence of the application of Section 609 to their shrimp imports. Section 609 sought to apply the comparable standards of turtle protection to imported shrimp as to domestic shrimp. To the extent that there was any difference in those standards, US shrimpers were subject to stricter standards than shrimpers from other nations, and had been subject to those standards for much longer. The United States recognized that the period between 29 December 1995 (when the US Court of International Trade ruled that Section 609 applies on a worldwide basis) and 1 May 1996 (when that ruling took effect) was five months. The complainants were correct that the US Administration unsuccessfully sought a one-year delay in the effective date of that ruling. At the same time, the United States undertook considerable efforts to assist the complainants and other nations newly affected by the ruling toward the prompt adoption of TEDs programmes. Thailand, with one of the world's largest shrimp fleets, had been able to adopt a comprehensive TEDs programme quickly.

3.264. **India, Pakistan and Thailand** maintained that the embargo, or for that matter, Section 609, had neither been promulgated with nor brought into effect with restrictions on domestic production or consumption. As discussed above, restrictions had first been placed on domestic production, and then, several years later, on the initially affected-nations, and finally, several years later and with only four months notice, on the newly-affected nations. Thus, while US laws and regulations now required TEDs use by both initially-affected nations and newly-affected nations, they had not been promulgated or brought into effect with regulations on US domestic consumption. Moreover, the US measures did not meet the "even-handedness" requirement established by the Appellate Body for purposes of interpreting the "made effective with" requirement of Article XX(g). One reason for this was the disparity in time provided by the United States for US shrimpers, shrimpers from initially-affected nations and shrimpers from newly-affected nations to comply with the TEDs requirement. US shrimpers had been given ten years (or, at least seven if the time during which the US voluntary TEDs programme was in effect excluded) to implement a TEDs requirement. The initially-affected nations had been permitted several years to establish and implement TEDs requirements. However, India, Pakistan and Thailand and the other newly-affected nations had been required to have TEDs requirements in place within four months, or lost access to the US market.

3.265. India, Pakistan and Thailand explained they were not suggesting that there needed to be identical treatment of domestic and imported products. However, the difference in time allowed to phase-in the TEDs requirement clearly disadvantaged the newly-affected nations in very substantial terms. As the United States itself had recognized in statements before the Court of International Trade, four months was not long enough to change domestic regulations, outfit an entire fleet with TEDs and train shrimpers in TEDs use so that such use would be both effective and minimize loss of catch. Advances in TEDs design were hardly sufficient to make up for the severe disadvantages imposed on the newly affected nations by the very short phase-in of the embargo. The haste with which Thailand had been forced to adopt a universal TEDs requirement led to considerable additional cost, waste, uncertainty and disruption. Thailand's current and continuing problem with loss of catch highlighted the problems caused by implementing a TEDs requirement over such a short period of time. The US claim that such disparate treatment did not violate the even-handedness requirement because of advances in TEDs technology was belied by statements made by the United States in the course of US domestic litigation, and by the actual experience of TEDs use in both the United States and Thailand, which showed considerable difficulty in using TEDs effectively without substantial loss of catch.

3.266. **Malaysia** submitted that the United States had not satisfied the requirement of "even-handedness" spelled out by the Appellate Body Report.[358] The requirement that the measure concerned imposed restrictions on both imported and domestic gasoline was correct because if such restrictions were not equally imposed then the objective of the Clean Air Act could not have been achieved. However, in the case at hand, exports of shrimp to the United States from countries which did not use TEDs would not result in the depletion or even extinction of sea turtle populations in the United States. Section 609 allowed any nation to be certified if it met the criteria for sea turtle safety in the course of shrimp harvesting that were comparable to criteria applicable to the United States. It was Malaysia's view that the criteria for certification was subjective and arbitrary as the United States was ultimately to decide whether a nation's scientific study was credible or not, and would evaluate any information that a nation submitted in support of claims that sea turtles were not present in shrimping grounds or that shrimping operations did not harm sea turtles. Furthermore, countries were subject to yearly review, which created uncertainty and was disruptive to trade.

3.267. The **United States** argued that the Appellate Body interpreted the criterion "made effective in conjunction with restrictions on domestic production or consumption" to mean that the measures concerned imposed restrictions not just on the imported product but also with respect to the comparable domestic product.[359] The Appellate Body also stated that this requirement was one of "even-handedness", and that there was no textual basis for identical treatment of domestic and imported products.[360] Section 609 met these tests. The United States required its shrimp trawl vessels that operated where there was a likelihood of intercepting sea turtles to use

[358] Appellate Body Report on *United States - Standards for Reformulated and Conventional Gasoline*, adopted 20 May 1996, WT/DS2/9.
[359] *Ibid.*, p. 19.
[360] *Ibid.*, p. 19.

TEDs at all times. Section 609 applied comparable standards to imported shrimp. The statute allowed any nation to be certified - and thus to avoid any restriction on shrimp exports to the United States - if it met criteria for sea turtle safety in the course of shrimp harvesting that were comparable to criteria applicable in the United States. In particular, for those nations whose shrimp trawl vessels operated in areas where there was a likelihood of intercepting sea turtles, Section 609 allowed for certification if such nations adopted TEDs requirements comparable to those in effect in the United States. In short, the US measures were even-handed as between domestic shrimp production and the shrimp production of the complainants. Complainants' argument that the measures at issue were not made effective "in conjunction with" US domestic TEDs requirements because the United States had adopted the domestic requirements first would, if adopted, be harmful to environmental goals and the world trading system alike. If this suggestion were to become the rule, any country adopting a domestic environmental measure would have little choice but to simultaneously impose the measure internationally, even if uncertain of the need to do so. Otherwise, the country would be forever barred from adopting a measure falling within the scope of Article XX. Nothing in the GATT led to this absurd result.

### (e) Chapeau of Article XX

3.268. **India, Pakistan and Thailand** submitted that, under the chapeau of Article XX, the United States bore the burden of establishing that the embargo had not been applied in a manner which had resulted in arbitrary and unjustifiable discrimination between Members and was not a disguised restriction on international trade.[361] India, Pakistan and Thailand were of the view that the United States would not be able to establish these requirements. While, as currently written, the embargo applied equally to all Members, a review of the history of the import restrictions established that the newly affected nations, including India, Pakistan and Thailand, had been given substantially less notice than other countries before being forced to comply with TEDs use. While the initially affected nations had been given three years to phase in the requirement of 100 per cent TEDs use, during which period they were permitted to continue exporting shrimp to the United States regardless of the method of harvest, the newly affected nations had been given only four months notice before being subject to the embargo following the CIT's 29 December 1996 Order. Moreover, the relevant US authorities were fully aware that four months was an inadequate period of time in which to outfit the newly affected nations' fleets with TEDs or to train shrimp fishermen to use the equipment properly. Thailand, for instance, which had expended significant time and resources in the installation and implementation of its own Thai Turtle Free Devices, could not be certified by the 1 May 1996 deadline and therefore was subject to the embargo, while many of the initially affected nations were not. Thus, the embargo had been applied in a manner that resulted in arbitrary or unjustified discrimination among nations and was a disguised restriction on trade.

3.269. India, Pakistan and Thailand further argued that, while the United States also required 100 per cent TEDs use by US shrimp trawlers in the Atlantic Area and Gulf

[361] Appellate Body Report on *United States - Standards for Reformulated and Conventional Gasoline*, adopted 20 May 1996, WT/DS2/9, DSR 1996:I, page 21.

Area, this requirement had been gradually implemented over a period of approximately 10 years. The United States thus had not required its own shrimp harvesters to use TEDs within a period of just four months. A similar situation had been explored by the Appellate Body in the *Gasoline* dispute. In finding that the Gasoline Rule at issue did not meet the requirements of the chapeau of Article XX, the Appellate Body stated as follows:

> "Clearly, the United States did not feel it feasible to require its domestic refiners to incur the physical and financial costs and burdens entailed by immediate compliance with a statutory baseline. The United States wished to give domestic refiners time to restructure their operations and adjust to the requirements in the Gasoline Rule. This may very well have constituted sound domestic policy from the viewpoint of the EPA and US refiners. At the same time we are bound to note that, while the United States counted the costs for its domestic refiners of statutory baselines, there is nothing in the record to indicate that it did other than disregard that kind of consideration when it came to foreign refiners".[362]

Consistent with this line of reasoning, a regulatory scheme which had been applied so as to suddenly prohibit importation of shrimp and shrimp products of certain nations unless they met standards that the United States and other nations had been given years to meet constituted arbitrary and unjustifiable discrimination between countries. It further demonstrated that the application of the embargo had resulted in arbitrary or unjustified discrimination between Members and was a disguised restriction on trade. It was clear that while the United States had carefully considered the costs associated with requiring the United States shrimp fleet to use TEDs, such costs had not been taken into account with respect to the newly affected nations. Therefore, the embargo did not meet the requirements of the chapeau of Article XX.

3.270. India, Pakistan and Thailand recalled the legislative history of Section 609 which, in their view, further supported the conclusion that the embargo was a disguised restriction on trade. As previously noted, several United States legislators discussed the embargo in terms of the competitive position of the US shrimp industry. In light of this fact, the United States could not demonstrate that the measure was consistent with the chapeau of Article XX.

3.271. **Malaysia** submitted that the chapeau of Article XX was concerned with the manner in which that measure was applied, and not with the measure itself. In the event that the Panel in this case was of the view that the measures taken by the United States were consistent with any of the exceptions under Article XX (which Malaysia did not admit) Malaysia submitted that the Panel had to examine the chapeau to Article XX. In the *Gasoline* case, the Appellate Body held that "disguised restriction" included disguised discrimination on international trade.[363] In that case, there was more than one alternative course of action available to the United States in promulgating regulations implementing the Clean Air Act; these included the imposition of statutory baselines

[362] Appellate Body Report on *United States - Standards for Reformulated and Conventional Gasoline*, adopted 20 May 1996, WT/DS2/9, DSR 1996:I, page 26.
[363] *Ibid.*, p. 25.

without differentiation as between domestic and imported gasoline. This approach, if properly implemented, could have avoided any discrimination at all. The Appellate Body therefore found that the United States had not pursued the possibility of entering into cooperative arrangements with the governments of Venezuela and Brazil or, if it had, not to the point where it encountered governments that were unwilling to cooperate. With respect to this proceeding, the fact that Malaysia had been allowed only a period of three months to comply with the US requirements as compared to the three years given to the fourteen countries in the wider Caribbean region amounted to an unjustifiable discrimination.

3.272. Malaysia observed that Section 609 had two relevant parts. Section 609(a) provided for the alternative course of action which was the collective effort among countries to conserve sea turtles. Section 609(b) provided for the imposition of the import prohibition. The United States should first exhaust the option under Section 609(a) before resorting to the import prohibition under Section 609(b). In that regard, the United States had not demonstrated that it had exhausted all the options under Section 609(a). Therefore the import prohibition constituted a disguised restriction on international trade. Furthermore, Malaysia submitted that the United States intended to ensure that its domestic shrimp industry would not be unnecessarily disadvantaged. This was evident from the US Congressional Records stating that Section 609 needed to be enacted to complement domestic legislation[364] to level the playing field for the US domestic shrimpers. If Section 609 had not been enacted, it would have resulted in the US domestic shrimpers suffering a competitive disadvantage as compared to foreign shrimpers. This was also a form of disguised restriction on international trade.

3.273. Malaysia noted that the United States had not taken into account the actual situation of Malaysia when it listed Malaysia as falling within Section 609. Malaysia was a nesting ground, but was not known for being a feeding ground for sea turtles. This distinction was of prime importance because sea turtles immediately left to their feeding ground after nesting. The nesting season in Malaysia did not overlap with the shrimp trawling season, whereas the United States was both a feeding and nesting ground for sea turtles. It was therefore appropriate to require trawlers to use TEDs in the United States because there was an interaction between the turtles and the trawlers during the shrimping season. Malaysia therefore submitted that the omission by the United States to establish Malaysia's status as a feeding ground before imposing the import prohibition was an unjustifiable discrimination. The application of the import prohibition was therefore clearly a disguised restriction on trade.

3.274. Malaysia noted that the Declaration on Permanent Sovereignty over Natural Resources of 14 December 1962 (UNGA Resolution 1803 XVII) proclaimed that "the right of peoples and nations to permanent sovereignty over their natural wealth and resources" was protected and the permanent right of every state to dispose of its natural wealth and resources should be respected in accordance with their national interest. The concept of permanent sovereignty had not prevented international law from treating conservation issues within a state's territory as a question of common concern in which the international community possessed a legitimate interest. Treaties such as the 1972 World Heritage Convention, the 1973 CITES Convention, the 1979 Berne Convention

[364] Endangered Species Act, 1973 and the Regulations thereunder.

on the Conservation of the European Wildlife, the 1968 African Convention on the Conservation of Nature and the 1985 ASEAN Convention on the Conservation of Nature and Natural Resources exemplified this point. Migrating species such as sea turtles fell under shared natural resources. A succession of the United Nations General Assembly resolutions had recognized the general principle that states did not have unlimited sovereignty with regard to shared resources. In 1973, UNGA Resolution 3129 XXVIII called for adequate international standards for the conservation and utilization of natural resources common to two or more states to be established, and affirmed that there should be cooperation between states on the basis of information exchange and prior consultation. Article 3 of the 1974 Charter of Economic Rights and Duties of States (UNGA Resolution 3281 (XXIX)) provided that in the exploitation of natural resources shared by two or more countries, each state had to cooperate on the basis of a system of information and prior consultation in order to achieve optimum use of such resources without causing damage to the legitimate interests of others.

3.275. Malaysia was of the view that international law therefore only allowed the conservation of shared natural resources on a cooperative basis and not unilaterally. Malaysia therefore submitted that since Section 609 allowed the United States to unilaterally take actions to conserve a shared natural resource it was therefore in breach of the sovereignty principle under international law. The sovereignty principle was a norm of *jus cogens* for which no derogation was permitted. No nation had a right under international law to impose on a fishing vessel owned by a Malaysian national fishing in Malaysian waters any requirement other than that imposed by Malaysian law. To do otherwise would be contrary to international law, and GATT being a branch of international law was governed by the fundamental norms of international law. Malaysia further submitted that GATT could not subsist on its own and was still subject to principles of public international law. This principle was recognized in Article 3.2 of the DSU which provided that the DSB should "clarify the existing provisions of the [covered agreements] in accordance with customary rules of interpretation of public international law". The application of the import prohibition was therefore a disguised restriction on international trade.

3.276. The **United States** argued that the measures relating to imports of shrimp, as required by Section 609 and implemented on the basis of US Department of State Guidelines, were carefully and justifiably tied to the particular conditions of each country exporting shrimp to the United States and, thus, were not applied in a manner that constituted a means of arbitrary or unjustifiable discrimination between countries where the same conditions prevailed. In particular, the criteria for certification under Section 609 were finely tailored to conditions in the exporting country's shrimp fishery. For example, all nations having shrimp fisheries only in cold waters, where there was essentially no risk of taking sea turtles, were certified under Section 609.[365] All nations whose shrimp vessels only harvested shrimp by the use of small-crewed, manually-retrieved nets - means which were highly unlikely to result in high sea turtle mortality - were certified under Section 609.[366] And all nations which had adopted turtle conservation programmes comparable to the US programme, including requirements for

[365] The United States noted that 16 nations were currently certified under this criterion.
[366] The United States noted that 8 nations were currently certified under this criterion.

the use of TEDs in waters where there was a likelihood of intercepting sea turtles, were certified under Section 609.[367] In sum, the United States had diligently applied Section 609 in a manner that related to exporting countries based on specific and reasonable criteria tightly tied to the goal of conserving sea turtles.

3.277 Nor were the measures of the United States a "disguised restriction on international trade". In fact, the evidence was overwhelming that United States' sea turtle conservation measures under Section 609 were not some artifice intended to protect the US fishing industry. As reflected by the inclusion of sea turtles in CITES Appendix I, the international community had made the commitment to protect and conserve sea turtles. By virtue of the 1982 United Nations Convention on the Law of the Sea and UNCED Agenda 21, the international community had made the commitment to minimize by-catch of non-target species (including endangered sea turtles) in fishing operations. And, as illustrated by Inter-American Convention on the Protection of Sea Turtles, there had recently developed a specific, multilateral standard requiring the use of TEDs by shrimp trawl vessels in waters where there was a risk of intercepting sea turtles. The strong and growing international consensus regarding sea turtle conservation and the mandatory use of TEDs belied any claim that the US measures encouraging the use of TEDs were some sort of disguised restriction on trade. In addition, the United States had made extensive efforts to disseminate TEDs technology worldwide, including to shrimp fishermen of the complainants. The success of these efforts was shown by the fact that 18 nations had adopted TEDs requirements, including Thailand. The successful efforts of the United States to disseminate TEDs technology rebutted any claim that Section 609 was a disguised restriction on trade, since the United States would hardly be spending resources on helping other countries meet US standards relating to the importation of shrimp if the United States' motivation was to protect US domestic production.

3.278 Furthermore, as recognized by the complainants, Section 609 had become applicable to them as a result of a decision by the US Court of International Trade in a case brought by environmental and conservation groups. These groups pursued the application of Section 609 not because it would protect domestic production but because it would conserve and protect sea turtles. Section 609 also was narrowly crafted to affect imports of shrimp harvested in ways that were harmful to sea turtles. Section 609(b) did not apply to all shrimp. Shrimp harvested in ways that did not harm turtles (such as shrimp harvested by aquaculture, shrimp caught with a wide variety of gear that did not kill turtles, and shrimp harvested in cold or fresh water) were completely outside the scope of Section 609(b). The United States noted that the large majority of shrimp harvested by each of the complainants, and by many other nations, was aquaculture shrimp. Had the United States intended to adopt a disguised restriction on trade in shrimp, Section 609 would not be so narrow in its scope. Finally, the US measures at issue in this case had not disrupted the level of imports of shrimp into the United States. Since 1 May 1996, when these measures became applicable to the complainants and to other nations outside the Wider Caribbean/Western Atlantic region, total US imports of shrimp had remained essentially constant and the price of

[367] The United States noted that 19 nations were currently certified under this criterion.

imported shrimp had declined. If Section 609 were in fact a disguised restriction on trade, one would expect substantially reduced imports and higher prices.

3.279. The United States further argued that none of the arguments advanced by India, Malaysia, Pakistan and Thailand supported a finding that US measures under Section 609 somehow failed to meet the requirements of the Article XX chapeau. The four complainants' argument that they were allowed only three to four months to comply with US requirements under Section 609, while the Wider Caribbean/Western Atlantic countries were allowed three years was not factually accurate. Section 609 applied to shrimp harvested in the Wider Caribbean/Western Atlantic region as of 1 May 1991. It was true that the initial State Department Guidelines allowed those countries to phase in the use of TEDs over three years, so long as they met specific progress toward a comprehensive TEDs programme along the way. But the phase-in for these nations was justified in light of the fact that, at that time (1991-1994), TED technology was neither as well-developed nor as readily available, especially for developing countries. By the mid-1990's, i.e. by the time Section 609 had become applicable to shrimp harvested in the complainants' countries, extraordinarily effective TEDs were both inexpensive and easily available, making the adoption of TEDs programs considerably more feasible. Indeed, as noted, Thailand had adopted such a programme with great speed.

3.280. The United States submitted that Malaysia failed to point out how the different periods between notice and compliance for different nations, in practice, had had any effect on Malaysia. Malaysia provided no indication that it ever intended to adopt a TEDs requirement. Thus, with respect to Malaysia, the time allowed for compliance with Section 609 was simply not relevant. Regarding Malaysia's argument that US measures under Section 609 constituted a disguised restriction on international trade because the United States had not exhausted all collective efforts among countries to conserve sea turtles, the United States recalled that Article XX(b) did not include an "international cooperation" requirement, and the same held true for the Article XX chapeau. Furthermore, the United States in fact had approached Malaysia concerning the negotiation of a sea turtle conservation agreement, and had not received a positive response.

3.281. The United States also rejected Malaysia's argument that the legislative history of Section 609 showed that the statute was intended to benefit US shrimp fisherman, and that this intent constituted a disguised restriction on international trade was based on unidentified legislative history. The shortest answer to this argument was that the legislative history of Section 609, as well as the practice of the United States in certifying nations under Section 609 and disseminating TEDs technology, completely rebutted any argument that Section 609 was a pretence intended to benefit US shrimp fishermen. Malaysia failed to provide any support for its proposition that international law only allowed the conservation of shared natural resources on a cooperative basis, and not unilaterally. It merely referred to a UN resolution advocating cooperation in the exploitation of shared natural resources; Malaysia cited to nothing which indicated that a country should not take measures to conserve natural resources outside its jurisdiction. And indeed, as noted above, Malaysia was a party to CITES, and was obligated for conservation purposes to take trade measures against all countries, even those not a party to CITES. Thus, CITES rebutted Malaysia's contention that conservation measures under international law must be taken on a "cooperative basis". Other multilateral agreements cited in paragraphs 3.192 and 3.193 similarly served to rebut

Malaysia's contention regarding principles of international law. Finally, the United States noted that Malaysia could not cite a single source of international law that directly stated its supposed general principles regarding sovereignty. Therefore, the implied limitations advocated by Malaysia, based on purported general principles of international law, should be disregarded, and the Panel should not depart from the text of the GATT. Similarly, Malaysia cited no international agreement providing that countries had to cooperate in taking trade measures aimed at the conservation of shared natural resources. Multilateral environmental agreements exhorted countries to cooperate, but exhortations did not reflect a shared international consensus that cooperation was a required precondition for the adoption of trade measures. In fact, the very instruments cited by the four complainants showed that cooperation was not a requirement.

3.282. **India, Pakistan and Thailand** maintained that the US measures had been applied in a manner which constituted arbitrary and unjustifiable discrimination because the US provided longer phase-in periods for domestic shrimpers and for initially affected nations *vis-à-vis* the newly-affected nations. While allowing longer phase-in periods for domestic shrimpers could have constituted wise domestic policy, the United States had not provided equal consideration to the costs associated with immediate application of the TEDs requirement to newly-affected nations. Such discrimination was in fact specifically recognized by the US government during the litigation before the Court of International Trade. In light of these facts, this Panel should conclude that the US measures constituted unjustifiable discrimination and a disguised restriction on trade. The US attempted to suggest that its discriminatory application of the TEDs requirement was somehow justified because of the difference in available TEDs technology. First, as the complainants had demonstrated, TEDs were not "inexpensive" for their respective fishermen. Moreover, the claim that TEDs approved by the United States were "extraordinarily effective" was belied by recent tests and the high levels of stranding which had occurred in the United States in recent years. Finally, India, Pakistan and Thailand noted that in arguments made before the US Court of International Trade, the United States had cited many reasons why newly-affected nations would have difficulty meeting the four month deadline, including the lack of time to provide significant training and practice in the construction, installation and maintenance of TEDs and the limited funding for the adoption of a TEDs programme. India, Pakistan and Thailand noted that the United States attempted to dismiss the importance of the statements made during the domestic litigation by stating that the issue before the US Court of International Trade was timing. However, there was no factual basis for this differentiation which had resulted in the measures being applied so as to constitute a means of arbitrary and unjustifiable discrimination and a disguised restriction on trade.

3.283. Regarding the interpretation of the phrase "where the same conditions prevail", India, Pakistan and Thailand noted that the Appellate Body in the *Gasoline* case accepted the views of the parties that the phrase referred to comparative conditions in the exporting country and in the importing country maintaining the measure in dispute and as between exporting countries.[368] India, Pakistan and Thailand believed that this was the correct interpretation of the phrase and had demonstrated that the measures at issue unjustly and arbitrarily discriminated between the newly-affected countries and the initially affected countries and between the newly-affected countries and the shrimp industry in the United States. Further, India, Pakistan and Thailand believed that the phrase meant that similarly-situated countries had to be treated equally. For example, while the complainants did not concede that it was legitimate to distinguish between nations based on whether or not they had adopted a production method forced upon them by another Member, this clause made clear that if the United States were to permit entry of shrimp from one certified nation, but to deny entry of shrimp from other certified nations, such action would constitute discrimination between countries in which the same conditions prevailed. In short, to the extent that the fact of certification was legitimate and constituted "the same conditions", certified countries were to be treated equally. In the dispute before the Panel, all certified nations had not been treated equally. Specifically, Thailand had been arbitrarily and unjustifiably discriminated *vis-à-vis* other certified nations because, without any basis, Thailand had not been given the same opportunity as the initially-affected nations to become certified without disruption of trade.

3.284. India, Pakistan and Thailand did not agree that Section 609 was narrowly crafted to affect imports of shrimp harvested in ways that were harmful to sea turtles. First, as applied, Section 609 prohibited the entry of shrimp caught using TEDs from non-certified countries. Further, Section 609 currently allowed for the importation of shrimp caught using soft-TEDs, even though soft-TEDs had been found to be ineffective at excluding sea turtles. How such shrimp was captured in manner which was any less harmful to sea turtles than simply not using a TED was not clear.[369]

3.285. **Pakistan** added that, by refusing to certify Pakistan even though 8 other countries harvesting wild shrimp by manual means had been certified, the US measures had been applied in a manner which constituted a means of arbitrary or unjustifiable discrimination between countries where the same conditions prevailed and a disguised restriction on international trade. In addition, the distinction made by the United States between so-called "cold-water" shrimp fisheries and "warm-water" shrimp fisheries constituted arbitrary and unjustified discrimination where the same conditions prevailed and a disguised restriction on trade. For example, one of the species of sea turtle which did occur in US waters ranged as far north as Canada, yet Canada had been certified as one of the 16 nations that had "shrimp fisheries in only cold waters whether there was essentially no risk of taking sea turtles". Even if the United States had some evidence that its shrimpers along the northern Atlantic coast did not encounter sea turtles often, it was not clear that the same evidence existed with respect to the cold-water shrimp fisheries of other nations. At the very least, such nations should be required to provide

[368] Appellate Body Report on *United States - Standards for Reformulated and Conventional Gasoline*, adopted 20 May 1996, WT/DS2/9, DSR 1996:I, page 22.

[369] India, Pakistan and Thailand noted that the United States also argued that the fact that the US litigation involved environmental groups demonstrated that Section 609 was not a disguised restriction on trade. While the complainants would not quibble with the relevance of this point, they would note that one of the parties to the legal action in question was the Georgia Fishermen's Association, Inc.

the same type of evidence as the nations with warm-water shrimp fisheries that claimed that their shrimp trawl fisheries did not take place in areas where sea turtles occurred.

3.286. **Malaysia** argued that the agreements referred to by the United States in paragraph 3.277 made reference to the fact that States had to ensure through proper conservation and management measures that the maintenance of living resources was not endangered by over-exploitation and by the use of selective, environmentally safe and cost-effective fishing gear, but did not mention the use of TEDs specifically. These agreements did not in any way fortify the US claim that Section 609 was a measure intended to conserve sea turtles and was not a disguised restriction on international trade. The Inter-American Convention on the Protection of Sea Turtles provided that parties to the regional agreement had to take appropriate and necessary measures in accordance with international law and on the basis of the best available scientific evidence. This included, *inter alia*, the reduction of the incidental taking of sea turtles in the course of fishing activities through, for instance, the development and use of appropriate gear, including TEDs. However there were still countries which had not recognized the use of TEDs. This factor also did not further the US contention that Section 609 was not a disguised restriction on international trade. Malaysia refuted the US contention that the dissemination of TEDs technology rebutted any claim that Section 609 was a disguised restriction on trade. Malaysia had not gained from the United States in this regard, save for a regional workshop organized by the Thai Department of Fisheries, in cooperation with the Department of Foreign Trade and NMFS, US Department of Commerce. As to the US contention that "Malaysia provided no indication that it ever intended to adopt a TEDs requirement", Malaysia recalled that (i) it had participated in the regional workshop titled "[t]he Utilization of Shrimp Trawls Equipped with TED" organized by the Department of Fisheries, Thailand, in cooperation with the US Department of Foreign Trade and NMFS, and (ii) Malaysia had undertaken, with SEAFDEC, work to localize where the SEAFDEC developed TED should be used in Malaysia, which had led to the introduction of TEDs at Sigari, Perak. With regard to the US contention that Section 609 had been narrowly crafted so as to exclude any element of a "disguised restriction", Malaysia submitted that the different time period provided by the United States to Malaysia and to the newly affected countries to comply with Section 609 requirements, as compared to the 3 years given to the 14 countries of the wider Caribbean region and a period of about 10 years to the US domestic shrimpers, constituted an unjustifiable discrimination. Even if Malaysia had been given 3 years to phase-in TED use, it would still be unacceptable from a legal and practical point of view. Legally, the same 3 years would still cause the import prohibition inconsistent with GATT Article XIII because a 3 year phase-in would not change the fact that there is a different treatment between the complainants and the initially affected countries, inconsistent with Article XIII. Practically, even after certification, Malaysia would still be subject to a yearly assessment and review by the US State Department, as required under Section 609; such an assessment was subjective and created an element of uncertainty which was disruptive to trade. Moreover, that fact that Malaysia and other uncertified countries had suffered a loss of market share refuted the US contention that Section 609 was not a disguised restriction on trade.

3.287. According to Malaysia, "where the same conditions prevail" applied to both the position of the United States vis-à-vis Malaysia and the position of Malaysia *vis-à-vis* other countries affected by Section 609. The same conditions had to apply to the United

States and Malaysia in order to fulfil the requirements of the chapeau and the treatment had to be the same for other affected countries. Regarding the concept "the same conditions prevail", Malaysia stressed the following facts. The major sea turtle species which were of concern in the United States were the loggerhead and the Kemp's ridley. These two species had been more extensively studied than the other species, in particular in publications addressing mortalities in shrimp trawls. On the other hand, loggerheads rarely nested on Malaysian beaches, and Kemp's ridleys did not occur in Malaysian waters. In Malaysia, the major sea turtle species was the green turtle, followed by the hawksbill, the leatherback and the olive ridley. The high mortality of sea turtles reported in shrimp trawls in the United States actually referred to loggerheads and Kemp's ridleys. These two species lived in nearshore waters where they fed on bottom invertebrates such as crabs, shrimp and mollusc. These habitats were heavily trawled by shrimpers in the United States. The residence of loggerheads and Kemp's ridleys in trawling grounds in the United States naturally accounted for the facts that large numbers of these turtles were caught in shrimp trawl nets, and explained why in the United States it was essential that TEDs be applied to shrimp trawlers to save these two species from extinction. Since neither loggerheads nor Kemp's ridleys lived in nearshore waters in Malaysia, the same conditions did not prevail in Malaysia. Malaysia further argued that green turtles were residents in seagrass beds, which were found in shallow coastal waters, and hawksbill were found in coral reef; trawling was prohibited in these areas. During the nesting season, green turtles remained close to shore, in areas where, again, trawling was prohibited. During long-distance migrations between feeding and nesting grounds, turtles were actively swimming close to the surface of the water, which made them more vulnerable to driftnets and longlines rather than trawlnets. In Malaysia, trawling targeted fish for the most part of the year and, thus, the incidental capture of sea turtles was due to fish trawls and not shrimp trawls. Again, this demonstrated that the same conditions did not prevail in Malaysia.

3.288. With regard to the relevance of public international law in interpreting the chapeau, Malaysia agreed with the United States that the Panel should not depart form the text of the GATT. However, this did not preclude the Panel from following customary rules of interpretation of public international law in deciding this case, as required by Article 3.2 of the DSU. Malaysia stressed that the multilateral agreements cited by the United States in paragraphs 3.192 and 3.193 were primarily used to show that countries had jurisdiction over a matter regardless of where the matter was located. Malaysia questioned which provisions of these multilateral agreements cited by the United States required countries to take conservation measures against a country not party to the agreement and recalled its arguments in this regard, contained in paragraphs 3.274 and 3.275. Malaysia further noted that multilateral environmental treaties generally resorted to the soft law approach and their provisions were written in a persuasive language, as could be seen from the provisions requiring parties to undertake obligations under the agreement. This contrasted with the mandatory language of treaties based on hard law, such as the 1949 Geneva Convention I for the Amelioration of the Condition of the Wounded and Sick in Armed Forces in the Field, and the 1949 Geneva Convention II Relative to the Treatment of Prisoners of War.

3.289. The **United States** considered that the term "where the same conditions prevail" had to be interpreted "in accordance with its ordinary meaning", in its "context and in the light of its object and purpose".[370] As the Appellate Body explained in the *Gasoline* case, the object and purpose of the Article XX chapeau was generally to prevent the abuse of the Article XX exceptions.[371] Accordingly, the term "where the same conditions prevail" should include the "conditions" in a country that related to the policy goal of the applicable Article XX exception. In other words, if a measure discriminated among countries based on conditions that were legitimately connected with the policy of an Article XX exception, the measure did not amount to an abuse of the applicable Article XX exception. Here, the United States was invoking Article XX(g), which had the goal of conserving exhaustible natural resources. In particular, the United States submitted that its restrictions on shrimp importation related to its goal of conserving endangered species of sea turtles. Thus the relevant "conditions" in this case were those conditions of shrimp harvesting that related to the conservation of sea turtles. In fact, the United States measures were tailored to the conditions of the exporting country's shrimp fishery, as those conditions related to sea turtle conservation, as explained in paragraph 3.276.[372]

3.290. The United States noted that the only discrimination alleged by the complainants related to the timing of the application of the US measures. However, as already noted, the difference in timing, at most, benefitted the complainants. They had not been subject to measures under Section 609 for a full three years after those measures had been first applied to nations in the wider Caribbean Western Atlantic region. And, by the time Section 609 had been applied to countries outside the wider Caribbean/Western Atlantic region, TEDs had developed to the point where they were extraordinarily effective, easily available, and inexpensive. Nor were the US measures a disguised restriction on international trade.

3.291. **India, Pakistan and Thailand** replied that, since the United States had failed to show that shrimp trawling was the primary cause of sea turtle mortality in the complainants' waters, it could not demonstrate that it had discriminated between the complainants and other nations based on conditions legitimately connected to the Article XX exceptions. The Preamble to the WTO Agreement, which the United States considered pertinent to interpreting Article XX, required, *inter alia*, that measures to protect the environment be undertaken "in accordance with the objective of sustainable development" and "in a manner consistent with [Members'] respective needs and concerns at different levels of economic development". India, Pakistan and Thailand were of the view, however, that the United States had failed to demonstrate, in enacting the measure at issue, that it had considered whether it was more appropriate under the concept of sustainable development to address other, more significant, local causes of sea turtle mortality than shrimp trawling. The United States had also failed to

370 Vienna Convention on the Law of Treaties, Article 31.1.

371 Appellate Body Report on *United States - Standards for Reformulated and Conventional Gasoline*, adopted 20 May 1996, WT/DS2/9, DSR 1996:I, page 20.

372 The United States noted that, even if the Panel were to find discrimination with respect to countries where the same conditions prevailed, such discrimination would be neither "arbitrary" nor "unjustifiable". Section 609 was applied in a manner based on specific and reasonable criteria tied to the goal of conserving sea turtles.

demonstrate that it had considered the complainants' needs and concerns based on their level of economic development. Even accepting the US argument that "the condition in this case were those conditions of shrimp harvesting that related to the conservation of sea turtles", there was no justification for allowing the initially affected nations nearly three years in which to attain the required "conditions", while providing the complainants with less than five months to comply. India, Pakistan and Thailand also considered that TEDs had not been "extraordinarily effective" in the United States and the TEDs programme had been very expensive to implement in Thailand.

3.292. India, Pakistan and Thailand stressed they did not contend that the US TED programme had been implemented as a disguised restriction on international trade; the US programme was a response to clear scientific evidence regarding the principal threat to sea turtles swimming along the coastline of the United States. However, India, Pakistan and Thailand contended that extending the same programme outside the United States was a disguised restriction on international trade, because scientific evidence did not demonstrate that shrimp trawling was the principal threat or even an immediate threat to sea turtles elsewhere in the world. India, Pakistan and Thailand were of the view that TEDs were not an "international environmental standard" and believed that TEDs use by many countries did not indicate a recognition of their necessity to protect sea turtles but rather the necessity to adhere to this standard if they desired to sell shrimp in the United States. Thus, the US argument that TED requirement was not a disguised restriction on trade because it was an international environmental standard was unpersuasive. The complainants' contention that the measure acted as a disguised restriction on international trade flowed from the fact that several in Congress who had supported this measure were apparently more concerned with equalizing the costs of environmental regulation imposed on the domestic industry with that imposed on its foreign competitors, regardless of the relative merits of regulating shrimp trawl fisheries, as opposed to taking other measures to protect and increase sea turtle populations in other parts of the world. Furthermore, the dissemination of information on TEDs by the United States had been rather limited in India, Pakistan and Thailand and did not reduce the costs of implementing a universal TEDs programme, or the costs imposed on individual shrimp trawlers. Finally, the fact that the total level of shrimp imports into the United States had not been disrupted did not compel the conclusion that the US measures were not a disguised restriction on trade. The nature of the trade restriction was the imposition of an additional cost on the foreign industry making that industry less cost-competitive in the United States and the risk that the right to export to the United States might be revoked if a country lost certification. The fact that the foreign industry was still able to collectively ship the same amount of shrimp to the United States did not mean that there had been no restriction on international trade. It might mean that overall consumption was increasing or that foreign profitability had been squeezed, discouraging future investment in the exporting countries. This was precisely the intent of those in the Unites States Congress who had sought to impose on foreign shrimp fisheries the additional regulatory costs of protecting sea turtles through the mandatory use of TEDs. These facts contradicted the US assertions that its measures were not a disguised restriction on trade.

3.293. **Malaysia** responded that the United States had failed to prove that the same conditions had to apply to the United States and Malaysia. The reasons given by the United States in paragraph 276 attempted to show that the same conditions existed between countries which were affected by Section 609. However, Malaysia had proved that the same conditions did not prevail between the United States and Malaysia.

3.294. The **United States** first noted that, contrary to what was claimed by India, Pakistan and Thailand, nothing in the text of the Article XX chapeau required that a measure address the "primary cause" of an environmental problem. The United States further argued that the US measures under Section 609 were not abuses of the Article XX exceptions, but rather *bona fide* measures for the conservation of sea turtles. First, the complainants seemed to agree in substance with the United States that the relevant conditions to consider when interpreting the phrase "where the same conditions prevail" were those conditions of shrimp harvesting that related to the conservation of sea turtles. In that regard, the United States reiterated that all exporting nations with the same shrimp-harvesting conditions were treated equally, without discrimination. The complainants had actually benefited from the difference in timing they pointed out. As to the argument that the United States currently did not permit imports of shrimp caught with TEDs from nations that were not certified under Section 609, the United States recalled that none of the complainants were uncertified nations that were attempting to export TED-caught shrimp to the US market. Indeed, the United States was unaware of any uncertified nation that would like to export TED-caught shrimp to the United States. Moreover, the question of the application of Section 609 to TED-caught shrimp from uncertified nations was currently under consideration by a US Appellate Court. Finally, the US measures under Section 609 were not a "disguised restriction on international trade" because they did not represent an "abuse or illegitimate use" of the individual paragraphs of Article XX. To the contrary, the record showed that sea turtles were endangered by shrimp trawling practices, that TEDs prevented such harm, and that, by restricting the importation of shrimp caught without TEDs, Section 609 sought to ensure that the US shrimp market did not contribute to the endangerment of sea turtles.

3.295. The United States further noted that the aggregate US import data provided to the Panel showed that the US measures under Section 609 had not affected aggregate shrimp import quantity or price, and thus had not provided any protection to the domestic industry. These data further supported the point that Section 609 was not a disguised restriction on trade. Finally, the fact that shrimp caught with so-called soft TEDs could be imported into the United States, while hard TEDs had been found more effective missed the point. Once again, the India, Pakistan and Thailand tried to turn the issue from the application of Article XX to questions of sea turtle conservation policy. The United States measures did not amount to a "disguised restriction" regardless of whether the United States allowed the importation of shrimp caught with soft TEDs.

3.296. **India, Pakistan and Thailand** responded that the United States misapprehended their point when claiming that nothing in the Article XX chapeau required that a measure address the "primary cause" of an environmental problem. The chapeau forbade unjustified discrimination between countries "where the same conditions prevail". The United States claimed that it did not discriminate unfairly against the complainants because it based its discrimination on whether or not a country had a TED programme in place and whether or not a TEDs programme was necessary in the circumstances to protect sea turtles. (In cases in which the United States considered TEDs of limited or no effectiveness in protecting sea turtles, including certain regions in the United States itself that sea turtles were known to inhabit, shrimp trawl industries were exempted from the TEDs requirements.) However, India, Pakistan and Thailand maintained that there was unjustified discrimination between them and countries with no TEDs requirements (including portions of the United States) because the United States had failed to demonstrate in such case that the "same conditions" did not prevail in India, Pakistan and Thailand on one hand, and in those other nations on the other hand. Specifically, the United States had failed to demonstrate that the imposition of a TEDs requirement was any more necessary to protect sea turtles in India, Pakistan and Thailand than it was for those other countries and US regions for which no TEDs were required.

### *3. Article XXIII:1(a)*

3.297. **India, Pakistan and Thailand** recalled that Section 609 and the resulting embargo and certification process represented a clear infringement of GATT Articles I, XI and XIII. It was well-established that "in cases where there is a clear infringement of the provisions of the General Agreement, or in other words, where measures are applied in conflict with the provisions of the GATT ..., the action would, *prima facie*, constitute a nullification or impairment" within the meaning of Article XXIII of GATT.[373] In particular, import restrictions had been found to constitute a *prima facie* case of nullification of impairment and the party imposing the restriction had the burden to rebut the presumption.[374]

3.298. **India and Pakistan** further submitted that this case presented a clear-cut example of a measure imposed by one Member nullifying and impairing the rights and benefits of another Member. As noted, the volume and value of Indian and Pakistani shrimp exported to the United States had declined dramatically since the embargo had been imposed. Moreover, the embargo had led to an increase in transaction costs associated with exporting shrimp to the United States since all exporters had to obtain the signature of an authorized government agent before the merchandise was shipped. Furthermore, the US embargo had created a great deal of uncertainty and confusion in the Indian and Pakistani shrimp industry. This was conclusory evidence that the two complainants' rights had been nullified or impaired by the shrimp embargo. In similar circumstances, prior dispute settlement panels had found "the existence of a quantitative restriction should be presumed to cause nullification or impairment not only because of any effect it had on the volume of trade but also for other reasons, e.g. it would lead to increased transaction costs and would create uncertainties which could affect investment plans".[375]

3.299. **Thailand** further submitted that, in addition to the fact that Section 609 and the embargo represented a *prima facie* nullification or impairment of the benefits accruing to Thailand under the General Agreement, the embargo proximately had caused a decline in exports of shrimp and shrimp products to the United States. As noted, from the date of application of the embargo to Thailand to the date on which Thailand had

[373] Panel Report on *Uruguayan Recourse to Article XXIII*, adopted 16 November 1962, BISD 11S/95, paragraph 15.
[374] Panel Report on *Japanese Measures on Imports of Leather*, adopted 15/16 May 1984, BISD 31S/94, paragraphs 47-48, 53, 55-56.
[375] *Ibid.*

been certified, exports of shrimp from Thailand to the United States had declined by approximately 18 per cent from the same period in 1995. Moreover, since the United States could decertify Thailand without notice or recourse, Thailand's shrimp trade could face similar declines in the future, and, because of this threat, was subject to uncertainties which might limit investment in the shrimp industry in Thailand. In addition, application of the embargo and certification procedures had created uncertainties in the marketplace and had increased transaction costs associated with shrimp trade with the United States.[376] Among the increased transaction costs were the cost of installing TEDs on Thailand's commercial shrimp trawl fleet, the cost of creating education programmes to teach Thai shrimp trawlers how to use TEDs, and the cost to the Royal Thai Government of implementing and enforcing the regulation regarding the use of TEDs.

## IV. ARGUMENTS PRESENTED BY THIRD PARTIES

### *1. Australia*

4.1. Australia submitted that its exports of shrimp to the United States had been subject to the requirements laid down under Section 609 since May 1996. The unilateral, and selectively abrupt, imposition by the United States of an import embargo under Section 609 raised important trade and environmental policy concerns, including the fact that it was pursuing the objective of turtle protection through the unilateral imposition of an import embargo rather than working cooperatively at the bilateral level and through multilateral fora to address any transboundary or global issues involved. Australia's concerns were not about the validity of the US environmental objectives to protect and conserve turtles, but the particular measures it had chosen to use in pursuit of these objectives and their consistency with its WTO obligations.

4.2. In spite of having submitted a request for certification in April 1996, Australia had not been certified on 1 May 1996. In support of its request for certification, Australia had presented a detailed submission on its marine turtle conservation regime which extended well beyond protecting turtles from shrimping nets.[377] That conservation regime included cooperative programmes with the shrimp industry to limit turtle/trawler interaction. Six of the world's seven species of marine turtles were found in northern Australian waters. They were migratory animals whose populations were shared between Australia and its regional neighbours in the Indo-Pacific. There was international concern over the impact of human activities on turtle populations which included commercial and subsistence hunting, egg harvesting, damage to nesting beaches and feeding areas, fisheries bycatch, marine debris, and boat-strike. The Australian fishing industry was committed to continuous improvement in its understanding and amelioration of the effects of shrimp trawling on the environment generally and specifically on animals which were of conservation significance.

[376] Panel Report on *Japanese Measures on Imports of Leather*, adopted 15/16 May 1984, BISD 31S/94, paragraphs 47-48, 53, 55-56.

[377] *US Embargo on the Import of Wild-Caught Shrimp*, Submission by Australia to the US Secretary of State in support of its request for certification under Section 609(b), April 1996.

Research efforts to minimize bycatch was also well advanced in the Northern Prawn Fishery (NPF).

4.3. Australia submitted that total Australian exports of shrimp were valued at A$ 223 million in 1995/96. Annual exports accounted for 60 to 70 per cent of the total Australian shrimp harvest. Therefore, Australia had a substantial trade interest in this dispute, although direct exports to the US market had not been significant in recent years. Australia had a particular concern with the medium to long term implications of disruption to global markets, increased competition from embargoed shrimp, potential for existing markets to lever down prices, and consequent changes to other countries' import requirements.

4.4. Australia argued that the US measures were inconsistent with Articles I and XI and were not covered by Article III of GATT 1994. Moreover, the United States did not demonstrate that its measures were in conformity with the requirements of Article XX.

4.5. The differential treatment of shrimps from certified and non-certified countries was inconsistent with the requirements of Article I:1 of GATT 1994. The US import restrictions were based solely on country of origin of shrimps, including between WTO Members. The United States had granted certification to some forty countries on the basis that they were cold water shrimping nations, or that they did not use mechanical means to harvest shrimp or that they required the use of TEDs. However, the United States had refused certification to Australia and certain other shrimp exporters, and exports of certain shrimp from these countries were prevented entry into the United States except for specific categories such as aquaculture shrimp. Shrimp from certified countries were not subject to such limitations. Certification was granted not on the basis of any differences in the products exported by certified and non-certified countries but on the basis of differences in their domestic conservation policies. There was nothing in the US certification requirements that provided a basis for considering that shrimp and shrimp products from certified and non-certified countries were not "like" products, and the US measures did not require any differences in products in granting certification. Consequently, the US measures granted an advantage to imports of shrimp and shrimp products from certified countries which was not available to the imports of like products from non-certified countries. This constituted discriminatory treatment of products on the basis of country of origin as the US measures distinguished between imports on the basis of the domestic conservation policies of the exporting countries and not on the basis of differences in the nature or character of the products. The measures were therefore inconsistent with US obligations under Article I:1.

4.6. Australia further argued that the US measures did not come within the scope of Article III as they were not measures relating to internal taxation and regulation of imported goods, but were conditions attached to the importation of a product. The measures constituted an import embargo on shrimps which were not harvested using TEDs and, as such, came within the scope of Article XI. Even if the United States was to claim that the measures were internal regulations enforced at the border, and within the scope of the Note *Ad* Article III, the measures would still not meet the requirements of Article III. Under the US measures, certification and therefore import approval was contingent upon the exporting nation instituting and enforcing a "comparable" regulatory regime which modified prawn harvesting practices to reduce turtle mortality. Such measures were clearly not intended to be covered by Article III. The *Tuna II* Panel

Report, for instance noted that "Article III calls for a comparison between the treatment accorded to domestic and imported like products, not for a comparison of the policies or practices of the country of origin with those of the country of importation". The Panel also found that Note *Ad* Article III could, therefore, only apply to "those laws, regulations and requirements that affected or were applied to the imported and domestic products considered as products".[378] The US measures distinguished between shrimp and shrimp products on the basis of the domestic conservation policies of the country in which they were harvested. Other than specified exceptions, imports were prevented of products from countries judged not to have a programme to reduce the incidental capture of sea turtles in shrimp fisheries comparable to that in the United States, specifically through the mandatory use of TEDs. This distinction did not relate to shrimp as products and therefore could not be covered by the provisions of Article III.

4.7. With respect to Article XI, Australia submitted that the US measures banned the import of shrimp and shrimp products from non-certified countries except for some specified categories including aquaculture shrimp or shrimp harvested in areas where there was no risk of capturing sea turtles. As certification was granted on the basis of differences in countries' domestic conservation policies, the US measures essentially banned imports of shrimp from countries not meeting certain policy conditions. In *Tuna II*, the panel found that a ban on the import of tuna or tuna products from any country not meeting certain policy conditions were "prohibitions or restrictions" in the terms of Article XI of GATT.[379] The US measures were therefore inconsistent with the requirements of Article XI:1. As they represented import prohibitions and not restrictions, and as the United States had not claimed that the measures related to the application of standards or regulations for the classification, grading or marketing of commodities, the measures did not come within the scope of paragraph 2 of Article XI.

4.8. Australia considered that, by not contesting the inconsistency of the import embargo under other GATT provisions and by invoking the provisions of Article XX, the United States had the burden of demonstrating that it had the exceptional right to maintain measures which were not in conformity with other GATT provisions. Australia did not contest that measures having the claimed objective of protecting animal life and of conserving exhaustible natural resources came within the scope of Article XX(b) and (g). The fundamental issue in the present case was whether the import embargo on certain shrimp caught in other locations, which had been imposed on the basis of unilaterally determined US standards for the protection of turtle life and for the conservation of turtles in the United States, constituted measures which were necessary for the protection of turtles or were related to the conservation of turtles as an exhaustible natural resource.

4.9. In Australia's view, the dispute did not concern the relationship between the GATT and obligations under another international treaty or international legal norms in regard to the use of TEDs in shrimp harvesting in all locations. For instance, the provisions of the Inter-American Convention could only involve a regional standard agreed between parties to that Convention. No party was contesting the GATT

[378] Panel Report on *United States - Restrictions on Imports of Tuna*, not adopted, DS29/R, circulated on 16 June 1994, paragraph 5.8.
[379] *Ibid.*, paragraph 5.10.

consistency of restrictions on trade in sea turtles under other international treaties. As the United States was not required by any other international treaty to impose an import embargo on shrimps from countries such as Australia which did not have regulatory programmes requiring the use of TEDs, conflict between obligations under the GATT and other international treaties was not at issue. The panel had, therefore, to consider whether the United States had demonstrated that import embargoes on certain shrimp, that were imposed on the basis of the regulatory programmes of other countries governing shrimp harvesting in their jurisdiction, met the conditions of Article XX(b) and (g), including the chapeau to Article XX.

4.10. Australia considered that the WTO Agreement on Sanitary and Phytosanitary Measures was not relevant to the present issue because the approach of that Agreement in regard to unilaterally determined measures had no application to circumstances involving measures which did not involve pest or disease control and which applied to animal life and conservation outside the territory of a Member.

4.11. Australia did not contest that measures having the stated purpose of protecting and conserving sea turtles came within the scope of Article XX(b) and (g). However, Australia did not consider that the United States had demonstrated that its discriminatory trade measures on shrimp were either necessary for the protection of sea turtles in all locations or satisfied the conditions attached to the use of discriminatory trade measures for the purpose of sea turtle conservation.

4.12. The only way in which another WTO Member, including Australia, could gain access to the US import market for certain shrimp was to meet the US certification requirements. Except in regard to cold water, artisanal and aquaculture shrimping, the only way in which a Member could be certified was by adopting the same mandatory TED requirement as the United States, and irrespective of the turtle conservation policies of that Member. The United States was not obligated to impose the specific certification requirements on other Members in accordance with either US or Australian obligations under another international treaty. Rather, the United States was imposing a trade measure on other Members with the effect of "burden sharing" in terms of the economic consequences of harvest loss associated with the use of TEDs. US mandatory requirements for the use of TEDs effectively hindered international cooperation in commercial bycatch issues.

4.13. It was difficult to see how the US measures could have any direct effect on the conservation or protection of turtles. For example, shrimp caught with TEDs in non-certified countries were still subject to the embargo. Furthermore, shrimp subject to the embargo could come from countries which had effective policies and programmes for turtle conservation, or were developing such programmes, but which were not certified simply because their policies differed from that of the United States in not mandating the use of TEDs. There could be environmental, commercial and regulatory reasons why a different approach to addressing bycatch issues was appropriate in other countries. The US import embargo therefore prohibited imports from non-certified countries, whether or not the particular shrimp was harvested in a manner that harmed or could harm turtles, and whether or not these countries had shrimp harvesting practices and policies that harmed or could harm turtles. The embargo could not, by itself, further the US conservation objectives. The only way in which the embargo could possibly contribute to these objectives would be if it was followed by changes in the policies and practices of the exporting countries. As pointed out in the *Tuna II* Panel

Report, measures which could only have a conservation or wildlife protection effect if they resulted in changes in the policies pursued by other countries, could not be primarily aimed at the conservation of an exhaustible natural resource, or at rendering effective restrictions on domestic production or consumption, in the meaning of Article XX(g), nor could they be considered "necessary" for the protection of animal life or health in the sense of Article XX(b).[380]

4.14. By claiming that discriminatory import restrictions had been imposed for the purposes of ensuring that US conservation measures were not "undermined", while considering that countries remained "free to use any methods they consider appropriate in harvesting shrimp", the United States appeared to be confusing "measures" and "policies". The "measures" in this instance were discriminatory trade measures. The United States had not claimed that access for shrimp from non-certified countries would prevent it from attaching and enforcing bycatch harvesting conditions to shrimp of US origin, or to shrimp from countries with which it had reached agreement on bycatch harvesting conditions, for the purposes of achieving domestically or internationally agreed conservation policies. Nor had the United States claimed that non-certification would prevent it from enforcing any of its bilateral, regional or multilateral obligations under another treaty. As such, the purposes of the trade restrictions would appear to relate to US domestic consensus about trade related domestic conservation policies. The "necessity" to maintain trade measures for the stated purpose of ensuring that domestic non-trade practices were not "undermined" did not translate into a demonstration that the trade measures were "necessary" for the protection of animal life, or that they "related" to conservation of an exhaustible natural resource. Australia further argued that the United States did not demonstrate that its domestic sea turtle conservation measures, or that sea turtle conservation measures involving trade restrictions and agreed upon with other countries, could only be maintained by recourse to discriminatory trade measures against products of third country origin. It did not demonstrate that other GATT consistent measures were not reasonably available to it in order to maintain its own measures, or measures agreed in common with other countries, for the purposes of implementing unilateral or internationally agreed policies in regard to international sea turtle conservation. Indeed, alternatives were specifically identified in Section 609(a)(1) to (4).

4.15. Australia further argued that, in addition to failing to meet the requirements of Article XX(b) and (g), the application of the US measures constituted an "unjustifiable discrimination" and a "disguised restriction on international trade" inconsistent with the requirements of the chapeau of Article XX. The United States had failed to demonstrate the contrary. In particular, it did not supply evidence that it had adequately explored means of addressing its concerns about shrimp harvesting practices and turtle conservation in other countries - the concerns it had used to justify its discriminatory import embargo - through cooperation with the governments concerned. The United States had offered to certain countries to negotiate a multilateral sea turtle conservation agreement but this offer was conditioned on acceptance of the mandatory use of TEDs and therefore could not be regarded as an adequate exploration of the scope for

[380] Panel Report on *United States - Restrictions on Imports of Tuna*, not adopted, DS29/R, circulated on 16 June 1994, paragraphs 5.27 and 5.39.

international cooperation on the issues involved. Furthermore, the offer had been made after the imposition of the import ban and the initiation of WTO consultations. The United States sought to defend its measures as consistent with the chapeau of Article XX by stating that the chapeau did not include an international cooperation requirement. However, the United States failed to address the fact that it was difficult to see how a discriminatory trade ban that addressed transboundary and global conservation concerns could meet the requirements of the chapeau of Article XX when the United States had not adequately explored the scope for international cooperation. Accordingly, there must be a presumption that the US measures were being applied in a manner that involved "unjustifiable discrimination" and constituted a "disguised restriction on international trade", in line with the Appellate Body's findings in the *Gasoline* case. Also relevant to the current dispute was the observation by the *Tuna I* Panel over the failure to explore the scope for international cooperative arrangements to address conservation objectives "which would seem to be desirable in view of the fact that dolphins roam the waters of many states and the high seas".[381] In its own submission the United States clearly recognized and identified the transboundary and global aspects of turtle conservation but failed to demonstrate that it had sought to address these aspects in order to avoid discriminatory trade measures through properly exploring the scope for international cooperation.

4.16. Australia noted that this dispute did not concern the validity of the environmental objectives of the US to protect and conserve turtles, but the particular trade measures chosen in pursuit of these objectives and their consistency with its WTO obligations. As observed by the Appellate Body in the *Gasoline* case, the fact that the US measures were inconsistent with its WTO obligations did not mean that the ability of any WTO Member to take measures to protect the environment was at issue, as "that would be to ignore the fact that Article XX of the General Agreement contains provisions designed to permit important state interests - including the protection of human health, as well as the conservation of exhaustible natural resources - to find expression".[382] Furthermore, the preamble to the Marrakesh Agreement Establishing the World Trade Organization stated the desire of WTO Members to conduct their relations in the field of trade and economic endeavour in a way which allowed for the optimal use of the world's resources in accordance with the objective of sustainable development. WTO Members were giving practical effect to this desire through the Committee on Trade and Environment (CTE) in considering the issues raised by the relationship between trade and the environment and with the aim of making international trade and environmental policies mutually supportive.

4.17. In its November 1996 Report, the CTE recalled Principle 12 of the Rio Declaration that "[u]nilateral actions to deal with environmental challenges outside the jurisdiction of the importing country should be avoided. Environmental measures addressing transboundary or global problems should, as far as possible, be based on an international consensus," and noted "there is a clear complementary between this

[381] Panel Report on *United States - Restrictions on Imports of Tuna*, not adopted, BISD 39S/155, circulated on 3 September 1991, paragraph 5.28.

[382] Appellate Body Report on *United States - Standards for Reformulated and Conventional Gasoline*, adopted on 20 May 1996, WT/DS2/9, DSR 1996:I, page 28.

approach and the work of the WTO in seeking cooperative multilateral solutions to trade concerns".[383]

4.18. Australia added that both the CTE's Report and the Singapore Ministerial Declaration had underlined the importance of policy coordination at the national level in the area of trade and environment, and the Declaration had welcomed the participation of environmental as well as trade experts in the CTE's work. These provided appropriate avenues for Members to seek to ensure that trade and environment policies were mutually supportive in promoting the objective of sustainable development.

### 2. *Ecuador*

4.19. Ecuador submitted that the international marketing of shrimp and shrimp products was extremely important for its economy, which was one of the world's foremost exporters of farmed shrimp. In 1996, Ecuador exported a total of 85,649 metric tonnes, for an amount of US$ 624,330,000. Shrimps accounted for 20 per cent of Ecuador's total exports and their share of Ecuador's GDP was currently 4 per cent.

4.20. For a number of years, countries on the Atlantic coast and in the Caribbean Basin had had to adapt their fishing practices to meet the requirements of Section 609 in order to be able to export shrimp to the United States. Countries that did not use TEDs were put on an embargo list and could not export to the United States. Ecuador was not included in the first list of countries that violated US standards because it submitted sufficient proof that its fishing practices protected sea turtles on the basis of legislation enacted in April 1996, which made it mandatory to use TEDs when taking shrimp in Ecuadorian waters. In November 1996, the first US mission visited Ecuador and found that every effort was being made to use TEDs. Certification being an annual procedure, a second official inspection visit to Ecuador was made in March 1997. On 2 April, Ecuador learned that the report by the NMFS inspectors was negative and that the Department of State had decided to include Ecuador in the list of countries whose shrimp could not be imported to the United States as from 1 May 1997. Finally, after the Ecuadorian Government had made several efforts and following its request for re-certification, on receipt of a technical report on the inspection mission by the NMFS, on 30 May 1997, the Department of State announced the decision to lift the ban on imports of sea shrimp from Ecuador. In any event, this situation created a great deal of insecurity for shrimp exporters, who were subject to arbitrary measures that did not allow them the necessary predictability to pursue their commercial operations properly. Ecuador also noted that the "Galápagos" species of turtle was found only in Ecuador; this species was not aquatic and was protected since 1970. Three species of turtles nested in Ecuador, but only in the extreme north of the country, an area protected since 1979. The other turtles were pelagic and lived 30 to 40 miles off the coast, whereas shrimp were fished between 8 to 10 miles offshore. Thus, the United States imposed on Ecuador standards and procedures to protect turtles that were not found off its coasts.

---

[383] Report (1996) of the Committee on Trade and Environment, WT/CTE/1, 12 November 1996, paragraph 171.

4.21. The shrimp industry started up in Ecuador in 1968. In 1997, as a result of the efforts made by Ecuadorian enterprises, the utilization of existing natural resources and the training of Ecuadorian technicians, the production performance achieved by this sector made it one of the mainstays of Ecuador's economy, occupying the third place for foreign currency earnings after bananas and petroleum. Ecuador was currently the biggest producer in the western hemisphere and occupied second place at the global level. Shrimp production was mainly based on two activities:

(a) Shrimp farming, which production accounting for 95 per cent of the volume exported. In 1995 a total of 178,000 hectares of seashore and beach were used to farm shrimps in captivity, 82 per cent of this area was farmed by 1,974 farmers produced shrimp.

(b) wild caught shrimp, which was carried out by fishermen on a small scale and by a trawling fleet composed of 179 legally registered fishing boats, of which 150 were operational. The share of wild caught shrimp in the total volume of shrimp exports was barely 5 per cent, although it corresponded to 8 per cent of the value because these shrimps were larger.

4.22. The trend in exports of farmed shrimp in recent years was mainly due to improvements in technology. In 1991, for example, Ecuador had exported 79,029 metric tonnes for an amount of US$491.4 million, corresponding to an increase of 49.7 per cent in volume and 44.39 per cent in foreign currency in comparison with 1990. In 1992, it had exported a peak volume of 86,796 metric tonnes for an amount of US$525.7 million. In 1995 and 1996, production conditions had improved: 86,567 metric tonnes and 85,650 metric tonnes respectively had been exported, with high foreign exchange earnings of US$673.4 and US$624.3 million respectively for these two years. Between January and April 1997, the volume of exports had been 30,559 metric tonnes, equivalent to US$ 249.6 million, an increase of 25.12 per cent over the value for the period January-April 1996. In 1996, the major importers of Ecuadorian shrimp had been the United States with 51 per cent, Europe, 36.5 per cent, Far East with 10.1 per cent, and others with 2.4 per cent. In addition to contributing towards the development of Ecuador's economy, the shrimp industry also created skilled and unskilled jobs. The number of persons directly employed in this sector was estimated at about 150,000, and indirectly around 250,000.

4.23. Ecuador noted that the desirability of implementing a particular conservationist policy was not under discussion in this case since all countries agreed on the need to protect the planet's resources; the problem was how to implement this policy in practice. Obviously, relations between States had to be set within the framework of international law, and it could not be acceptable that one country's domestic policy objectives should be applied to other sovereign States. This principle of mutual respect among States was one of the keystones that had enabled mankind to achieve a relative degree of peace and prosperity in the second half of this century: this was a benefit that had to be carefully safeguarded. Nor was this case about establishing the degree of injury caused to the exports of countries that did not obtain certification. The problem was that this situation created serious insecurity for shrimp exporters, who were subject to arbitrary measures that did not allow them to have the proper predictability as to the future development of their trade operations.

4.24. Endorsing the legal arguments put forward by Thailand, Ecuador argued that the US legislation was inconsistent with its obligations under GATT 1994, specifically Articles I:1, III:4 and XI:1. Moreover, the embargo was not justified under the exceptions provided for in Article XX(b) and (g). Regarding Article I.1, Ecuador considered that a single product, shrimp, was treated differently according to the method used to take it. Shrimp taken without TEDs could not be imported into the United States. Furthermore, some countries had had several years to adapt their fishing practices to the provisions of US legislation, whereas others, including Ecuador, had had to do so in a few months, with the ensuing financial burden and training problems for fishermen. With respect to Article III:4, Ecuador submitted US shrimp fishing boats operating in Pacific Ocean waters did not appear to be obliged to use TEDs and their catch was marketed in the United States without any restrictions. This difference in treatment would constitute discrimination according to the principle of "national treatment". All shrimp producers should receive the same treatment as was accorded to US producers in the Pacific area, particularly if the species of turtles it was sought to protect did not exist in their countries. Ecuador considered that the United States was not complying with Article XI:1 because it was restricting imports of a product on the basis of domestic conservation policies and not duties, taxes or other charges. Previous panels had found that such prohibitions established by the United States in the past, for example in the *Tuna* cases, were contrary to GATT, and more specifically to Article XI:1. Lastly, the rules laid down by the United States could not be justified under Article XX(b) and (g). The scope of these provisions was explained in greater detail in the *Tuna I* Panel Report.

### *3. El Salvador*

4.25. El Salvador stated that its interest in participating as a third party in this Panel stemmed from the fact that shrimps and shrimp products were an important part of its exportable supply of non-traditional products. The line of conduct pursued by El Salvador had been one of faithful respect and support for the multilateral principles and disciplines governing trade. El Salvador therefore considered that the application of unilateral and extraterritorial measures having a restrictive effect on trade were unacceptable and incompatible with the multilateral system. The reputation and credibility of the WTO, resulting from long years of negotiation which established a delicate balance of rights and obligations among Member countries, could be threatened by the application and maintenance of such measures. El Salvador trusted that the work of the Panel would uphold the fundamental principles and rules which made the multilateral system a bulwark for the liberalization of trade in goods and services and for the protection of its Members' trade interests.

### *4. European Communities*

4.26. The European Communities ("EC") considered that this dispute did not relate to the desirability of protecting and conserving sea turtles, a species listed in Appendix I of the CITES and therefore generally recognized to be a species threatened by extinction. Rather, it concerned the methods employed to achieve conservation of sea turtles and in particular measures taken to ensure that other countries employed the same means as, or at least means comparable to, those employed by the United States. In this respect certain of the issues before this Panel were similar to those in issue before earlier panels, such as *Tuna II*. However, the issues raised were not identical in view, *inter alia*, of the particular status of sea turtles. The Panel was called upon once again to consider the scope of application of the exceptions contained in Article XX of GATT 1994. The case raised a number of important questions of general principle relating to international law and WTO law, and the circumstances in which Members could take measures to conserve what could be considered to be "shared global resources". The EC noted in this respect the first preambular paragraph of the Agreement establishing the World Trade Organization.

4.27. The EC shared the concerns about the imperiled status of sea turtles. However, it considered that, in general, the attainment of shared objectives relating to the conservation of global resources, including endangered species, should follow the process of international negotiation. The EC remained of the view that, as a general principle, it was not acceptable for a state to impose restrictions on trade in order to force other states to adopt certain measures or face economic sanctions which included the withdrawal of rights enjoyed under the WTO Agreements. This view was consistent with Principle 12 of the Rio Declaration on Environment and Development. The EC considered that there was a broad degree of consensus among the parties to the dispute as to the precarious status of sea turtles and the need to take steps for their preservation. Since sea turtles were listed on Appendix I of CITES the parties agreed to restrict trade accordingly. Moreover, as the United States pointed out, sea turtles were protected under the CMS. The EC did not intend to make detailed observations on the factual data submitted by the United States to the panel but would simply note that the factual evidence it had presented showed that the use of TEDs was, at least in some cases, a reasonable and effective solution to minimize the incidental killing of marine turtles resulting from certain fishing activities.

4.28. Turning to the legal aspects, the EC submitted that the United States apparently did not dispute there was a *prima facie* infringement of the GATT and, hence, that it had the burden of proving that the measures at issue could be justified under Article XX. With respect to the infringements to GATT 1994 alleged by the complainants, the EC observed that, whilst there were certain differences between the US legislation at issue in this case and that at issue in the *Tuna II* case, the basic features were similar. In particular, a country could not export certain wild-harvested shrimp to the US market unless it had been certified. This legislation was mandatory and the EC was of the view that it amounted to a quantitative restriction contrary to Article XI:1.

4.29. Regarding the US argument that the measure at issue was justified by Article XX paragraphs (b) and (g), the EC considered that, as ruled by the Appellate Body in the *Gasoline* case, the provisions of Article XX were "not changed as a result of the Uruguay Round of Multilateral Trade Negotiations".[384] Article XX was an exceptional provision and the long standing practice of panels had been to interpret it narrowly, in a manner which preserved the basic objectives of the General Agreement. The EC supported the exhortations of the complainants to the effect that the General Agreement should be interpreted in the light of fundamental rules of treaty interpretation as

[384] Appellate Body Report on *United States - Standards for Reformulated and Conventional Gasoline*, adopted on 20 May 1996, WT/DS2/9, DSR 1996:I, page 28.

codified in the Vienna Convention on the Law of Treaties and recalled the recent ruling of the Appellate Body in the *Gasoline* case that "the General Agreement is not to be read in clinical isolation from public international law".[385]

4.30. Regarding the jurisdictional scope of Article XX, the EC recalled that in *Tuna II*, the Panel had concluded there was no valid reason for supporting the conclusion that either Article XX (b) or (g) applied only to policies in respect of things located or actions occurring within the territorial jurisdiction of the party taking the measure.[386] Moreover, no jurisdictional restriction on use of Article XX was imposed by the Appellate Body in the *Gasoline* case. In the light of these rulings, the EC considered that Article XX could, in certain circumstances, be relied upon to justify measures taken to protect global commons (globally shared environmental resources) or resources located outside the territory of a Member, provided, of course, that the other conditions of application of the relevant exception in Article XX, and the introductory clause thereof, were complied with. However, such circumstances should indeed be exceptional. This followed from the fact that Article XX, as an exception to the rules of the General Agreement, should be construed restrictively, and from the fact that, in general international law, states could normally not apply their legislation so as to coerce other states into taking certain actions, including modifying their own domestic standards.[387]

4.31. The EC considered that current international law and practice showed that environment was one area where such exceptional circumstances could exist. In this field, the application of agreed rules beyond the normal jurisdictional limits of Members might indeed be necessary to ensure effective application of such rules. Hence, as noted by the United States, CITES prohibited trade in certain endangered species, including endangered species located within the jurisdiction of other countries and of countries which were not Parties to CITES. The EC did not deny that certain species, in particular migratory species, might require application of measures beyond usual jurisdictional boundaries. The EC noted in this respect that WTO rules should not hinder the pursuit of commonly shared environmental goals, including where such goals might justify the taking of measures against third parties. However, for the criterion that exceptional circumstances existed to be fulfilled, the EC submitted that a state had to be able to demonstrate it had made genuine and sustained efforts to seek a multilateral solution before taking the measures in question, as underlined by the Appellate Body in the *Gasoline* case. The EC noted that, in the absence of such a requirement, countries would be permitted to enforce their conservation policies on other countries by unilateral action. In this case, the United States asserted that it had proposed the

---

[385] Panel Report on *Japanese Measures on Imports of Leather*, adopted 15/16 May 1984, BISD 31S/94, paragraphs 47-48, 53, 55-56, p. 17.

[386] With regard to the use to be made of unadopted panel reports, the EC referred to the statement of the Appellate Body Report on *Japan-Taxes on Alcoholic Beverages*, adopted on 8 November 1996, WT/DS8/AB/R, WT/DS10/AB/R, WT/DS11/AB/R, DSR 1996:I, page 108 to the effect that whilst unadopted panel reports had no legal status in the GATT or WTO systems since they had not been endorsed through decisions of the Contracting Parties to GATT or WTO members, "a panel could nevertheless find useful guidance in the reasoning of an unadopted panel report that it considered to be relevant".

[387] See Oppenheim's International Law, Ninth Edition, pp. 456-498.

negotiation of a multilateral agreement for Asia comparable to the Inter-American Convention, but that this proposal had not been accepted so far. No details were, however, given as to what steps had been taken, or the content of the Agreement the United States proposed should be negotiated. The EC observed that the short time period which elapsed between the rulings of the CIT and the imposition of the ban implied that there was little possibility to engage in genuine efforts to find a negotiated solution.

4.32. The EC noted, that whilst the United States relied on CITES and the provisions of other relevant international conventions, it did not demonstrate that the method which it imposed for shrimp fishing was required by CITES or by any other multilaterally agreed standard. The US submission was based solely on the assertion that, because the United States considered the use of TEDs to be the most effective method of protecting sea turtles during shrimp fishing, and because a regional agreement advocating the use of TEDs had been concluded, the required use of TEDs had become a "multilateral environmental standard", a concept whose precise meaning was unclear to the EC. To conclude, the EC considered that in order to justify unilateral measures outside the jurisdiction of a Member in pursuit of commonly shared environmental concerns, a Member had to demonstrate that it had made genuine efforts to reach an agreed multilateral solution. Such efforts were to go beyond the mere imposition of its own domestic standards on other Members. Moreover, the Member invoking Article XX had to demonstrate that it had no objective alternative to the unilateral measure taken.

4.33. With respect to Article XX(g), the EC agreed with the United States that sea turtles might be regarded as an "exhaustible natural resource". This followed from the definition of that term adopted in the *Salmon/Herring*[388] and *Tuna II* cases, as well as the ruling of the Appellate Body in *Gasoline*. It followed also from the fact that sea turtles were included in Appendix I of CITES and protected under the CMS, which the EC considered to be relevant in interpreting the definition to be given to that term in Article XX(g). In the light of the Appellate Body's ruling in the *Gasoline* case, which confirmed on that point the *Salmon/Herring* Panel Report, it seemed clear that "related to" in this context meant "primarily aimed at". The United States asserted that Section 609 related to the preservation of sea turtles since it was intended to require that shrimp imported into the United States had not been harvested in a manner harmful to sea turtles. However, it seemed to the EC that the measure at issue was the import ban on shrimps. As was the case for the measures at issue in *Tuna II*, the desired effect of that measure would only be achieved if the ban on importation of shrimps was followed by changes in practices and policies of the exporting countries with respect to the manner in which shrimp was harvested. Hence, the manner the legislation was framed and the fact that, should exporting countries not change their practices and policies they were no longer allowed to export shrimps to the United States, showed that the purpose of the legislation was to require third countries to conform to the same standards as the United States. The EC noted in this regard that an interpretation of Article XX allowing the United States to impose unilateral trade restrictions in order to enforce its environmental

388 Panel Report on *Canada - Measures Affecting Exports of Unprocessed Herring and Salmon*, adopted 22 March 1988, BISD 35S/98.

standards would seriously undermine the General Agreement, in particular its vocation to serve as a multilateral framework for trade among Members. The EC argued that "in conjunction with" meant rendering "effective equivalent restrictions on domestic production". The EC noted that the burden of proving that this criteria was satisfied and that the purpose of the US measures was not merely the creation of equivalent conditions of competition for the domestic fishing industry, rested with the United States.

4.34. Turning to Article XX(b), the EC agreed, in the light the *Tuna II* case, that the protection of sea turtles was a policy which could come within Article XX (b). As to the term "necessary", the EC noted that previous panels had interpreted it as meaning that the measures taken were "indispensable" or "unavoidable".[389] Furthermore, these panels emphasized that a Member was bound to use, among the measures reasonably available to it, that which entailed the least degree of inconsistency with other provisions of the General Agreement. The EC submitted that the United States had not demonstrated that, in view of their purpose, the measures taken could be considered to be "necessary" for the protection of animal life. More particularly, the United States had not demonstrated that the import ban was the only possible means of attaining its objectives with respect to sea turtle conservation; it was not clear that unilateral measures were indispensable and that a negotiated solution in respect of measures to protect sea turtles could not be found.

4.35. The EC considered that the question of compatibility with the chapeau of Article XX needed not be addressed since the United States had not demonstrated that the measures taken fell within one of the exceptions laid down in Article XX. To conclude, the EC considered that the United States measures under Section 609 constituted a quantitative restriction inconsistent with Article XI:1 of GATT 1994 and which were not justified by any of the exceptions in Article XX.

### 5. *Guatemala*

4.36. Guatemala submitted it shared the belief in preserving the environment and ensuring ecological sustainability. It therefore supported measures aimed in that direction, including those designed to preserve threatened species, as in the case of certain species of sea turtles. Guatemala recognized that it was desirable to achieve multilateral understandings in this regard. The WTO was the most appropriate forum for discussing and seeking trade agreements. Guatemala was concerned that the practice of adopting unilateral trade restrictive measures, as a form of disguised and legalized protectionism, could become widespread, especially when the countries applying such measures were those with developed economies which had greatest relative weight in the trade regulatory framework. The fundamental interest of Guatemala in this dispute was to ensure that the measures adopted by the United States to ban imports of shrimp and certain shrimp products did not serve as a precedent for other importing countries in future to apply measures aimed at indirectly and unilaterally restricting access to their

[389] Panel Report on *United States - Restrictions on Imports of Tuna*, not adopted, DS29/R, circulated on 10 June 1994; Panel Report on *United States - Section 337 of the Tariff Act of 1930*, adopted 7 November 1989, BISD 36S/345; Panel Report on *Thailand - Restrictions on Importation of and Internal Taxes on Cigarettes*, adopted 7 November 1990, BISD/37S/200.

market in a manner inconsistent with the provisions of the WTO, and particularly of GATT 1994.

### 6. *Hong Kong*

4.37. Hong Kong submitted that both the US legislation and its implementing measures violated Article XI:1 and could not be justified by Article XX of GATT 1994. According to constant GATT case-law, a Member could attack the legislation of another Member (independent of its eventual application) if the legislation as such did not leave any room for discretion to the implementing domestic authorities. Hong Kong did not intend to address the issue of whether the approach preferred by GATT panels so far should be also followed in the future as well. In Hong Kong's view, even if such legislation left discretion to the implementing authorities it could still run counter to that Member's international obligations to the extent that it permitted GATT-inconsistent action: this was the obligation of Members to implement *bona fide* their international obligations. But even if the most conservative, currently followed, approach were to guide the Panel's considerations in this respect, Hong Kong submitted that Section 609 left no room for discretion to the competent implementing authorities. The wording of Section 609 was unambiguous in this respect. Section 609 left some discretion to the competent US authority to exceptionally allow importation of shrimp and shrimp products from third countries following a certification to this effect: this meant that until the moment when certification was granted, the implementing US authority did not enjoy any discretion. Taking into account the fact that so far, except for the field of anti-dumping duties, GATT case-law knew of no remedies with an *ex tunc* effect, exporters found themselves in an awkward situation whereby they had to prove their innocence after having been convicted. This was why Section 609 as such should be condemned by the Panel as GATT-inconsistent. There was no doubt that the measures in application of such legislation should be condemned as well. Were, however, the Panel to follow a different route (by accepting, e.g., that the legislation at hand was purely discretionary), it should still find fault with the US measures in application of Section 609 for the reasons elaborated below.

4.38. Hong Kong submitted that the US arguments did not address specifically the issue whether the measures in question should be recognized as a border or as internal measures. The implication of this approach could be that Article XX of GATT 1994 be recognized as a stand-alone provision. This was, however, clearly not the case. As made plain by its title, Article XX provided the list of permissible exceptions to GATT's obligations laid down in the various provisions of the General Agreement. Moreover, previous GATT panels had consistently approached Article XX as an exception to GATT's obligations. Consequently, recourse to that provision should be made only if inconsistency with a GATT obligation had been previously established.

4.39. By requiring that "the importation of shrimp or products from shrimp which have been harvested with commercial fishing technology which may affect adversely such species of sea turtles shall be prohibited ...", Section 609 clearly violated Article XI of GATT 1994, since it established a quantitative restriction prohibited by the letter of that provision. Such actions could be eventually justified by recourse to the exceptions mentioned in the GATT and not to any other provisions. In such a case, the Member wanting to avail itself of such a possibility carried the burden of proof to demonstrate that an otherwise GATT-inconsistent measure could be justified by recourse to a GATT provision justifying such departures. In this context, it seemed that the only provision that could help justify the measure at hand was Article XX. Hong Kong submitted that the United States could not justify its action under Article XX in this case and urged the Panel to conclude accordingly. In Hong Kong's view, the US measures violated the chapeau of Article XX, did not meet the requirements of Article XX(b) as they were not necessary to protect animal life, and did not fall under Article XX(g).

4.40. Hong Kong recalled that, in its first interpretation of the chapeau of Article XX, the Appellate Body had noted that panels would first have to examine whether an allegedly GATT-inconsistent measure passed the test mentioned in the chapeau and then establish whether the other conditions (e.g., the "necessity" test in Article XX(b) of GATT) were met as well, in order to pronounce on the consistency (or inconsistency) of the measure under examination. Hong Kong agreed that this approach was in conformity with the wording of the chapeau: "Subject to ...". Hong Kong considered that the two requirements contained in the chapeau of Article XX meant that a WTO Member which wanted to avail itself of such a possibility would have to ensure that, for example in the context of environmental protection, it set standards which would be observed by domestic and foreign products alike: in other words, the chapeau of Article XX of GATT contained an Articles I and III-type obligation addressed to Members.[390] This in turn meant that Members wanting to avail themselves of the possibility offered in Article XX would have to establish certainty concerning the competitive conditions in their market.

4.41. In stating that the chapeau of Article XX included an Articles I and III-type obligation, Hong Kong meant that once standards had been set by a Member in pursuance of an objective mentioned in Article XX, such standards would have to be observed in respect of both domestic and foreign products. In other words, while such standards of themselves constituted exceptions to the Member's obligations elsewhere under the GATT, their application to all Members had to be on equal footing (Article I), and to apply to domestic and foreign products alike (Article III). The GATT reflected at this point the lack of harmonization of the various policies mentioned in the body of Article XX among Members. Moreover, the GATT was neither an instrument for harmonization (i.e. all Members should pursue identical health/environmental policies), nor an instrument for deregulation (i.e. no Member could pursue any such policy). To the contrary, each Member pursuing its own health or environmental policy could justifiably depart from GATT obligations provided that it respected the conditions laid down in Article XX. In this sense, Article XX gave the "green light" to regulatory diversity among Members with respect to policies mentioned in its body. Consequently, Members wanting to avail themselves of such a possibility could reveal their "preferences". Such revealed preferences, though, would have to be enforced *erga omnes*, i.e. they would have to be respected for both domestic and foreign products.

4.42. Hong Kong argued that the US legislation failed to meet this requirement. Foreign producers, even after they had provided documentary evidence according to which they demonstrated that their regulatory program was comparable to that adopted

[390] Hong Kong noted these were the views of John H. Jackson, in *The World Trading System* (1989).

by the United States, would still have to show that their average rate of incidental taking of sea turtles was comparable to that of US vessels. The word "and" which figured between the first two conditions mentioned in the supplementary information contained in the 1996 Guidelines for determining comparability of national programmes with the US programme made this point clear. Sub-section II of the Guidelines stipulated that incidental taking would be deemed comparable provided exporting governments required their fishing vessels to use TEDs in a manner comparable in effectiveness to those used in the United States. In Hong Kong's view, the United States was clearly not applying the same standards to foreign and domestic products, in that domestic producers did not have to meet any specific standard. Furthermore, the information on incidental taking would reach exporters to the US market only *ex post* and never *ex ante*. This meant foreign producers would continuously be in a state of uncertainty as far as their export possibilities to the US market were concerned. As mentioned above, it was precisely this form of uncertainty that the chapeau of Article XX aimed to outlaw.

4.43. Furthermore, under the US legislation, importation of shrimps harvested by individual shrimp trawl vessels in uncertified countries was prohibited even if *de facto* the vessels were fitted with the required TEDs. This meant individual foreign producers, even after having fully met the US requirements, would not be allowed to export shrimps to the United States. Hong Kong considered that the US measures were applied in a manner that constituted an arbitrary and unjustifiable discrimination between countries where the same conditions prevailed, thus violating the chapeau of Article XX. Were the Panel to agree with Hong Kong on the interpretation of the chapeau of Article XX and, consequently, find that the US measures at hand were inconsistent with the requirements of the chapeau, it needed not examine whether the US measures were justifiable under Article XX(b) or (g). However, were the Panel to adopt a different approach, Hong Kong would still urge it to find a case of inconsistency in that the US measures did not meet the requirements of Article XX(b), and Article XX(g) was not applicable to the measures.

4.44. Hong Kong noted that, for a measure to be justified under Article XX(b), it must be deemed necessary to achieve the stated objective (revealed preference). According to constant GATT case-law in this field, the "necessity" requirement was interpreted as obliging Members to take the least restrictive option in order to achieve the stated objective. The US action at hand was at the other end of the spectrum, since it amounted to an embargo. It should be pointed out that the panel reports on *Tuna I* and *Tuna II*, which concerned actions strikingly similar to the one at hand, had found the US measures to be GATT-inconsistent. Moreover, it was questionable whether TEDs were a necessary option in order to achieve the stated objective. Article XX imposed on Members an obligation of result: they could use any measure they deemed necessary in order to achieve the stated objective. This essential characteristic of Article XX should be preserved when Members adopting measures were about to establish equivalence of foreign standards to their own ones. This approach was in full conformity with the fact that the WTO did not impose on its Members harmonized approach to the policies mentioned in Article XX. Consequently, to impose TEDs on foreign producers who could, by means of other methods, reach an incidental rate of taking comparable to that reached by US vessels, would clearly be inconsistent with the spirit of Article XX. In other words, to the extent that alternative measures could be used without prejudging the desired level of the attainment of the objective, they should be accepted. This point was in line with previous GATT panel reports.[391]

4.45. Hong Kong submitted that Article XX(g) was not applicable to the case at hand. Article XX(b) and Article XX(g) established two different legal standards; while the first one established the "necessity" requirement, the second merely requested that a measure be related to (i.e. without it being necessary) a stated objective. If there was an overlap in the coverage of the two paragraphs, then obviously Article XX(b) would have fallen into *desuetudo*, since Members wanting to avail themselves of the possibility of Article XX would always prefer the framework of XX(g) which established a much less stringent standard. Moreover, the wording of Article XX(g) "exhaustible natural resources" seemed to support their systemic conclusion: "exhaustible" meant "non reproducible". This interpretation was in full conformity with the Vienna Convention, whose principle of effective treaty interpretation required that by interpreting an agreement one should ensure that no term become redundant. An interpretation condoning an overlap between the coverage of Article XX(b) and XX(g) run counter to this principle.

4.46. Hong Kong argued that the US view on the absence of any jurisdictional limitation in the body of Article XX(b) and (g) relied on an erroneous application of public international law. The GATT was an international agreement and should be interpreted in accordance with customary principles of interpretation (Article 3.2 DSU). The GATT/WTO system had no jurisdictional clause. It did not, however, operate in a vacuum. There was no *a priori* division of jurisdiction at the international plane. Jurisdiction was defined at the domestic level. Public international law could only impose limits to such definitions. This principle was reflected in a myriad of instruments which dealt with this issue. Multilateral environmental agreements (MEAs) belonged to this category. For some externalities to be effectively addressed (and this was predominantly the case in the field of environmental protection), states should have recourse either to extraterritorial application of domestic laws, or to international treaties. The former could violate the relevant rules of public international law; the latter constituted a voluntary transfer of sovereignty. Hence, MEAs also defined the jurisdictional reach. It could be said that MEAs in effect served to address such externalities in a way consistent with public international law. This was also a clear recognition of the territorial limitations in Article XX, as GATT was an international treaty and operated within the realm of public international law. To conclude, there was no room for extraterritorial application of domestic laws in the context of Article XX.

4.47. As to the relevance of CITES to the present case, Hong Kong submitted that examination of any obligations under that Convention was outside the remit of the Panel because the US had not cited any such obligations as justifications for their measures. In any case, it should be noted that CITES concerned the regulation of trade in endangered species, and that the case before the Panel did not concern trade in endangered species but rather trade in shrimp. Also under no circumstances should incidental taking of sea turtles be equated to trade.

[391] Panel Report on *United States - Section 337 of the Tariff Act of 1930*, adopted on 7 November 1989, BISD 36S/345, paragraph 5.26.

### 7. *Japan*

4.48. Japan noted there had been a rising global awareness of the importance of conservation of endangered species and exhaustible natural resources. When addressing transboundary or global environmental problems, Japan believed the solution should be sought in a multilateral framework and attached great importance to Principle 12 of the Rio Declaration that called for actions based on international consensus and stipulated the avoidance of unilateral actions to deal with environmental challenges outside the jurisdiction of the importing country. Based on this conviction, Japan had been implementing appropriate domestic policy and measures and participating actively in international cooperative actions to tackle transboundary or global environmental problems. Japan shared the recognition that sea turtles were endangered species included in Appendix I of CITES and were in serious need for international conservation actions. Numerous measures had been taken by Japan to protect them, including the restriction on capture of sea turtles, the conservation of nesting grounds and a programme for the enhancement of reproduction. Japan also expected that other countries would take appropriate actions to ensure the international effort for conservation of sea turtles.

4.49. Japan noted that it had no commercial shrimp trawl vessels or any other type of trawl vessels to catch shrimps, and a very small amount of shrimps were taken incidentally by vessels operating for other fish. Consequently, any occurrence of incidental killing or serious injury of sea turtles had not been recognized in Japanese fishing activities. Given this situation, the Government of Japan had requested on several occasions that its shrimp export to the United States should be categorized separately from those subject to the US legislation. Nonetheless, the United States had gone ahead and imposed a ban covering fishing activities of Japanese vessels. Japan argued that the import ban on shrimp and shrimp products - the species not subject to protection - pursuant to Section 609 had been imposed as trade sanctions for countries whose vessels did not use TEDs, and was inconsistent with the basic principles of the WTO and obligations of the United States under Articles I:1, XI:1 and XIII:1 of GATT 1994, and could not be justified under Article XX of GATT 1994. The US measures in dispute were also unacceptable extraterritorial applications of domestic conservation policies.

4.50. Japan submitted that the US import prohibition on shrimp and shrimp products pursuant to Section 609 violated Article XI:1, which stipulated a general elimination of quantitative restrictions. The measure was also inconsistent with Articles I:1 and XIII:1. The United States imposed the import ban on shrimp and shrimp products only from the countries whose vessels did not use TEDs. However, based on the finding of the *Tuna II*, the difference in practices, policies and methods of harvesting shrimp did not have any impact on the inherent character of shrimp and shrimp products as products. Thus, the import ban on shrimp and shrimp products under Section 609 accorded a different treatment to "like products". However, in view of the increased awareness of the importance of policy objectives of environmental protection and resource conservation, it should be noted that certain cases required differential treatment according to process and production methods (PPMs) to tackle global and transboundary environmental problems. Japan believed that the international community should further address the issue of PPM in order to avoid conflict between WTO rules and multilateral efforts to tackle global and transboundary environmental issues.

4.51. Noting that Article XX had to be interpreted on a case-by-case basis, as stated by the Appellate Body in the *Gasoline* case, Japan was not convinced that the US import ban under Section 609 was "necessary" within the meaning of Article XX(b). Japan did not contest the US argument that the installation of TEDs might be an effective method for conservation of sea turtles and that the US intention to implement the measure pursuant to Section 609 was to achieve that goal. However, Japan doubted that it was necessary to impose an import ban on shrimp or shrimp products from countries whose vessels did not use TEDs. As in the *Tuna* cases, the import ban could not possibly, by itself, further the United States objective of protecting the life of sea turtles. This point was vividly illustrated when the ban applied to non-certified countries regardless of whether the shrimps were caught in waters inhabited by sea turtles or of whether or not TEDs were actually installed and used. Secondly, Japan did not believe that there was no other alternatives which could contribute to the same objective but were consistent or less inconsistent with WTO provisions. Considering that the United States itself acknowledged that the US efforts to promote technology transfer had successfully facilitated the international situation where the use of TEDs had become a multilateral standard, the United States claim that there was no alternative available other than the import ban was difficult to accept. While accepting that Article XX(b) might not oblige Members to take specific measures such as negotiations of international cooperation arrangements with the countries concerned, this did not mean that the US import ban was the only alternative and justified as such under that provision.

4.52. As to the US argument that the measures under Section 609 met the requirements of Article XX(g), Japan did not challenge the US view that sea turtles were "exhaustible natural resources" within the meaning of that provision, but considered that the extraterritorial application of the US measure in the form of an import ban seriously impaired the right of Members under GATT 1994. In Japan's view, the control over the fishing activities of foreign vessels in the exclusive economic zones of a country did not constitute extraterritorial application of domestic measures; this was supported by the general principle that an individual nation should bear responsibility for conservation and management of fisheries resources in its exclusive economic zone pursuant to the United Nations Convention on the Law of the Sea. However, imposing an import ban designed to force other countries to change their policies concerning the conservation of sea turtles under the jurisdiction of those countries was clearly beyond the scope envisaged by Article XX(g), for the reasons explained in the two *Tuna* cases. In this regard, Japan supported the remark of Appellate Body in the *Gasoline* case that WTO Members' autonomy to determine their own policies on the environment, including its relationship with trade, was circumscribed by the need to respect the requirements of the General Agreement and the other covered agreements. Moreover, though not clearly stated, the United States appeared to rely its claim on CITES. In this regard, Japan argued that CITES prohibited the international trade of sea turtles, but did not regulate their capture. Therefore, the United States could not rely on CITES for justifying the requirement that other countries used TEDs.

### 8. *Nigeria*

4.53. Nigeria stated that it shared the unanimous concern for the conservation and protection of sea turtles. However this dispute did not relate to the desirability of protecting and conserving sea turtles but rather to the methods and measures for doing so. In this regard, Nigeria's position was defined by and would remain committed to paragraphs 169 and 171 of the 1996 Report of the Committee on Trade and Environment to the Singapore Ministerial Conference.[392]

### 9. *Philippines*

4.54. The Philippines submitted that it exported shrimp and shrimp products in quantities and values which it deemed substantial. Undue interference with market forces resulted in distortion and adversely affected the Philippines. This dispute likewise had systemic implications. Therefore, as exporter and as a WTO Member, the Philippines had a substantial interest in the matter before the Panel. In line with "judicial economy", an approach ratified by the Appellate Body, the Philippines' arguments focused on specific issues the resolution of which was sufficient, in the Philippines' view, to resolve this dispute without the necessity of delving into other issues.

4.55. The Philippines argued that proper resolution of this dispute would be expedited by prior inquiry into the legal characterization of Section 609, as enacted, interpreted,

---

[392] Report (1996) of the Committee on Trade and Environment, WT/CTE/1, 12 November 1996. Paragraph 169 of the Report states: "WTO Member governments are committed not to introduce WTO-inconsistent or protectionist trade restrictions or countervailing measures in an attempt to offset any real or perceived adverse domestic economic or competitiveness effects of applying environmental policies; not only would this undermine the open, equitable and non-discriminatory nature of the multilateral trading system, it would also prove counterproductive to meeting environmental objectives and promoting sustainable development. Equally, and bearing in mind the fact that governments have the right to establish their national environmental standards in accordance with their respective environmental and developmental conditions, needs and priorities, WTO Members note that it would be inappropriate for them to relax their existing national environmental standards or their enforcement in order to promote their trade. The CTE notes the statement in the 1995 Report on Trade and Environment to the OECD Council at Ministerial Level that there has been no evidence of a systematic relationship between existing environmental policies and competitiveness impacts, nor of countries deliberately resorting to low environmental standards to gain competitive advantages. The CTE welcomes similar policy statements made in other inter-governmental fora."

Paragraph 171 of the Report states: "The CTE notes that governments have endorsed in the results of the 1992 U.N. Conference on Environment and Development their commitment to Principle 12 of the *Rio Declaration* that "Unilateral actions to deal with environmental challenges outside the jurisdiction of the importing country should be avoided. Environmental measures addressing transboundary or global problems should, as far as possible, be based on an international consensus." There is a clear complementarity between this approach and the work of the WTO in seeking cooperative multilateral solutions to trade concerns. The CTE endorses and supports multilateral solutions based on international cooperation and consensus as the best and most effective way for governments to tackle environmental problems of a transboundary or global nature. WTO Agreements and multilateral environmental agreements (MEAs) are representative of efforts of the international community to pursue shared goals, and in the development of a mutually supportive relationship between them due respect must be afforded to both."

and implemented. If it was a "point of importation" measure (see Note *Ad* Article III of GATT 1994), its consistency with GATT 1994 was appropriately assessed basically in light of the national treatment obligation specified in Article III. Otherwise, such consistency was appropriately assessed primarily in light of other provisions of GATT 1994, including, but not limited to, the obligations specified under the provisions of Article XI and Article I.

4.56. The products subject to regulation under Section 609 were "shrimp or products from shrimp which have been harvested with commercial fishing technology which may affect adversely" the species of sea turtles "the conservation of which is the subject of regulations promulgated by the Secretary of Commerce on June 29, 1987". The Philippines noted that, for purposes of this dispute, the United States had no relevant internal "law, regulation or requirement of any kind" affecting shrimp or products from shrimp as products. There was no relevant US law, regulation or requirement affecting the "internal sale, offering for sale, purchase, transportation, distribution or use of products, and internal quantitative regulations requiring the mixture, processing or use of products in specified amounts or proportions" (Article III:1). As products, there was no distinction whatsoever between shrimp and shrimp products harvested or processed elsewhere and the "like domestic product" (shrimp and shrimp products harvested and processed in the United States by vessels or nationals subject to the jurisdiction of the United States). Thus, Section 609 was not a "point of importation" measure within the context of Note *Ad* Article III of GATT 1994. In determining whether certain regulations would qualify as "point of importation measures" under Article III, two as yet unadopted GATT panel decisions (*Tuna I & II*) ruled that measures must in some way have an effect on the regulated product. Based on this distinction, these panels found that an attempt at the point of importation to regulate a product based on the manner in which it was produced, a so-called process and production method, would not have a sufficient effect on the product to be considered an internal measure enforced at the point of importation. The Philippines further argued that the relevant US internal "law, regulation or requirement" was a regulatory programme governing the incidental taking of sea turtles by US vessels in the course of such harvesting. While there could be a difference in the incidental taking rate of sea turtles in the course of harvesting shrimp based on the technology used, there was no distinction, as such, between shrimp harvested using a particular technology and shrimp harvested using another technology. For purposes of the resolution of this dispute, Section 609 was not a "point of importation" measure.

4.57. The Philippines submitted that Section 609, by subjecting the importation of shrimp and shrimp products into the United States to a certification requirement, was a restriction "on the importation of any product of the territory of any other contracting party" in violation of Article XI:1 of GATT 1994. At the same time, Section 609 discriminated in favour of Members which had been so certified by allowing the importation of "like product". If at all discrimination was permissible under an otherwise authorized quantitative restriction regime, the basis of such discrimination had to have in some way an effect on the regulated product as product. The Philippines further argued that, since there was no distinction between the meaning of "like product" in Article XIII, and "like product" in Article III, Section 609 was likewise administered in a discriminatory manner, in a manner contrary to Article XIII:1.

4.58. The Philippines further argued that Section 609 accorded in favour of Members which had been certified the opportunity to export shrimp and shrimp products to the United States, while at the same time withholding the same opportunity from Members not so certified, in violation of the basic obligation of WTO Members to "immediately and unconditionally" accord the same "advantage, favour, privilege" to the "like product originating in or destined for the territories" of all other Members (Article I). Again, if at all discrimination was permissible, the basis of such discrimination had to have in some way have an effect on the regulated product as products. Since there was no distinction between products of Members which had not been certified and the like products of Members so certified, Section 609 was in violation of the MFN treatment obligations contained in Article I.

4.59. The Philippines submitted that the SPS Agreement was the authoritative and definitive interpretation by WTO Members for the coverage of Article XX(b) of GATT 1994. The SPS Agreement provided, in particular, that "the provisions of GATT 1994 which relate to the use of sanitary or phytosanitary measures, in particular the provisions of Article XX (b)" (Preamble) and that "sanitary or phytosanitary measures which conform to the relevant provisions of this Agreement shall be presumed to be in accordance with the obligations of the Members under the provisions of GATT 1994 which relate to the use of sanitary or phytosanitary measures, in particular the provisions of Article XX (b)" (Article 2.4). In clear and unequivocal terms therefore, the SPS Agreement categorically declared that Article XX(b) of GATT should be interpreted in light of the "use of sanitary or phytosanitary measures". The Philippines argued that it needed no elaboration to establish that Section 609, which sought to regulate the entry into the United States of shrimp and shrimp products based on the incidental taking of sea turtles in the course shrimp trawl operations, was not a sanitary or phytosanitary measure, as defined in Annex A of the SPS Agreement. Therefore, Article XX(b) of GATT 1994 was not applicable to this dispute and could not be invoked as a defense by the United States.

4.60. Referring to arguments made by India, Pakistan and Thailand, the Philippines argued that Article XX(g) of GATT 1994 was not applicable. In the Philippines' view, all animals were "renewable" natural resources in that they were capable of reproduction. At the same time, all animals were subject to extinction. Animals were thus "renewable" natural resources subject to extinction. Inanimate natural resources, which were not capable of reproduction, were "non-renewable" and were "exhaustible". For purposes of interpreting Article XX(g), a distinction had to be made between (a) the state of being renewable and subject to extinction, and (b) the state of being non-renewable and therefore "exhaustible". Otherwise, if no such distinction were made, and both renewable and non-renewable natural resources were intended to be covered by Article XX(g), the word "exhaustible" qualifying "natural resources" would be unnecessary. The word "exhaustible" could then very well be deleted without changing the meaning of Article XX(g). It was a basic rule of legal interpretation that every word had to be accorded its reasonable meaning, and to assume that no word was unnecessary. The Philippines further observed that, while some species of sea turtles were indeed endangered species, this was not relevant for purposes of interpreting and applying Article XX(g). The state of being an endangered specie was not an inherent state; rather, it was a circumstance brought about by several factors, and was therefore a dynamic factual concept. On the other hand, being "exhaustible" was an inherent state, a static legal concept. While a legal text might seek to cover a potentially infinite number of circumstances, its meaning did not change depending on the circumstances. Therefore, animals were not "exhaustible natural resources" within the context of Article XX(g). Even assuming that animals were "exhaustible" natural resources (which would mean that Article XX(g) was interpreted so as to include both renewable and non-renewable natural resources), Article XX(g) could not be invoked in this dispute because there was a specific rule applicable to animals, i.e. Article XX(b). Under the principle of *lex specialis*, rules applicable to a specific category forming part of a general category prevailed over the rules applicable to the general category as far as the specific category was concerned. And as earlier stated, Article XX(b) was applicable only in the context of sanitary and phytosanitary measures. Therefore, Article XX(g) was likewise not applicable to this dispute and could not be used by the United States as a defense.

### *10. Singapore*

4.61. Being equally concerned with the continued survivability of endangered sea turtles and as a party to CITES, Singapore was sympathetic to the US efforts to conserve sea turtles. As part of its overall conservation efforts, Singapore prohibited the operation of trawl-nets in its territorial waters, as well as the taking, netting, keeping or killing of local wildlife, which included sea turtles. Whilst applauding the US policy to conserve sea turtles, Singapore was of the view that the imposition of the embargo under Section 609 was over-reaching. It was a barrier to legitimate trade and disregarded the expectations of WTO Members under the General Agreement as to the competitive relationship between their products and those of other Members. Singapore, therefore, requested the Panel to find that the US embargo on the importation of certain shrimp and shrimp products pursuant to Section 609 was inconsistent with the US obligations under GATT Articles XI:1, XIII:1 and I:1 and was not justified under GATT Article XX(b) and (g). Singapore urged the US to bring it to conformity with their obligations under the GATT. Besides having substantial trade interest, Singapore was also concerned with the systemic implications of the US extra-territorial application of domestic conservation policy on the multilateral trading system.

4.62. Although Singapore was not a shrimp harvesting nation, it had substantial trade interests in this dispute. In 1996, exports of shrimp and shrimp products to the United States amounted to S$13.5 million. The United States was Singapore's single largest market for shrimp and shrimp products accounting for almost 10 per cent of its world-wide exports of shrimp and shrimp products of S$161 million. Most of these exports were re-exports. Singapore observed that its exports of shrimp and shrimp products had been adversely affected by the embargo. From the effective date of the embargo on 1 May 1996 to 30 April 1997, exports had fallen by 66 per cent to S$8.2 million from an export value of S$24.2 million during the comparable preceding twelve months from May 1995 to April 1996.

4.63. Singapore argued that, since Section 609 banned the importation of shrimp and shrimp products from countries that harvested shrimp with commercial fishing technology which could affect sea turtles, the embargo, which was not a duty, tax nor charge, was inconsistent with Article XI:1. There was no difference between shrimp harvested in aquaculture facilities and those that were harvested in the open seas: they were like products. There was also no difference between shrimp harvested using TED technology and shrimp harvested in the open seas by other means: they, too, were like products. By imposing a ban on the importation of shrimp and shrimp products from certain Members but allowing the importation of like products from other Members, Section 609 discriminated between like products, in a manner contrary to the requirements of Article XIII:1. Finally, Section 609 contravened Article I:1 because it allowed the importation of shrimp and shrimp products from certain Members but prohibited such importation from other Members. It did not grant the same advantage, favour, privilege or immunity to like products originating from different Members.

4.64. Turning to Article XX of GATT 1994, Singapore observed that the long-standing practice of panels had been to interpret this provision in a manner that preserved the basic objectives and principles of the GATT. If Article XX were interpreted to permit Members to deviate from obligations under the GATT by taking trade measures so as to force other Members to change their policies within their jurisdiction, including their conservation policies, the balance of rights and obligations among Members, in particular the right of market access, would be seriously impaired. Under such an interpretation, the GATT could no longer serve as a multilateral framework for trade (see *Tuna II*). Singapore asked the Panel to bear this in mind when considering whether the embargo under Section 609 fell within the permitted exceptions of Article XX(b) and (g). Singapore could not agree with the United States that the embargo was justified under GATT Article XX(b) and (g).

4.65. As to Article XX(b), Singapore submitted that the measure for which the exception was being invoked was not necessary and did not conform to the requirements of the introductory clause of Article XX. Singapore noted that previous panels had concluded that a Member could not justify a measure inconsistent with another GATT provision as "necessary" if an alternative measure which it could reasonably be expected to employ and which was not inconsistent with other GATT provisions was available to it. In cases where a measure consistent with other GATT provisions was not readily available, a Member was bound to use, among the measures reasonably available to it, that which entailed the least degree of inconsistency with other GATT provisions.[393] Singapore observed that the United States applied the Appellate Body's reasoning in the *Gasoline* case to argue that whether a measure was "necessary" under Article XX(b) must be determined "on a case-by-case basis, by careful scrutiny of the factual and legal context in the given dispute". According to the United States, Article XX(b) was not a "least inconsistent measure" test. Singapore was of the view that the rationale behind the Appellate Body's reasoning was to avoid any subversion of affirmative GATT obligations through an overly expansive reading of Article XX exceptions or conversely, emasculation of Article XX exceptions through an overly broad reach of GATT obligations. Bearing this in mind, the decision of earlier panels on the necessity test was consistent with the Appellate Body's reasoning. Otherwise, Members could easily circumvent their GATT obligations even if there were

[393] Panel Report on *United States - Section 337 of the Tariff Act of 1930*, adopted 7 November 1989, BISD 36S/345, paragraph 5.26; Panel Report on *Thailand - Restrictions on Importation of and Internal Taxes on Cigarettes*, adopted 7 November 1990, BISD 37S/200; Panel Report on *United States - Restrictions on Imports of Tuna*, not adopted, DS29/R, circulated 16 June 1994; Panel Report on *United States - Standards for Reformulated and Conventional Gasoline*, adopted 20 May 1996, WT/DS2/R.

measures that were less inconsistent with their GATT obligations. Under such circumstances, the GATT could not effectively serve as a multilateral framework for trade among contracting parties. The United States had not discharged its burden of proving that the embargo under Section 609 was necessary. It had not demonstrated that it had exhausted all other options available to it to pursue its turtle protection objectives through measures consistent with the GATT. In any event, the panel in the *Tuna II* case had concluded that measures taken so as to force other countries to change their policies, and that were effective only if such changes occurred, could not be considered necessary for the protection of animal life of health in the sense of Article XX(b). The embargo under Section 609 clearly fell within this category of measures.

4.66. Singapore observed that the introductory clause of Article XX set out further restrictions on the use of GATT-inconsistent measures. The fundamental theme was to be found in the purpose and object of avoiding abuse or illegitimate use of the exceptions to substantive rules.[394] Measures should not be a means of arbitrary or unjustifiable discrimination, nor a disguised restriction on international trade. For Singapore, the measure contained in Section 609 was an arbitrary or unjustifiable discrimination. There was arbitrary or unjustifiable discrimination in respect of the period of notice given to different countries to employ TED technology. In the case of the wider Caribbean region, a three-year phase-in period had been given. However, other countries had been allowed only a four-month period to institute comparable programmes. The United States contended that the difference in notice period was directly related to improvements in TED technology, lowering of costs and greater availability of TEDs. However, this assumed that all countries were able to implement comparable turtle conservation programmes within four months. This also assumed that all governments were able to inform and train their shrimp harvesters within four months. For these reasons, the embargo did not meet the requirements of Article XX(b).

4.67. Regarding Article XX(g), Singapore submitted that the measure for which the exception was being invoked did not relate to the conservation of exhaustible natural resources and/or was not made effective in conjunction with restrictions on domestic production or consumption. Furthermore, the measure did not conform to the requirements of the introductory clause of Article XX. Previous panels had concluded that the term "relating to" should be taken to mean "primarily aimed at".[395] This interpretation was also accepted by the United States in the *Gasoline* case. Though not treaty language nor a simple litmus test, as clarified by the Appellate Body in that case, the terms nonetheless provided valuable guidance when considering the balance of rights under the GATT. In the context of this dispute, it meant that the embargo was to be primarily aimed at the conservation of natural resources. Section 609 was clearly an attempt by the United States to force other countries to change their policies. Therefore, it could not be said to be primarily aimed at the conservation of exhaustible natural resources. A similar conclusion had been reached by the *Tuna II* Panel.

[394] Appellate Body Report on *United States - Standards for Reformulated and Conventional Gasoline*, adopted 20 May 1996, WT/DS2/9.

[395] Panel Report on *Canada - Measures Affecting the Exports of Unprocessed Herring and Salmon*, adopted 22 March 1988, BISD 35S/98, paragraph 4.6; Panel Report on *United States - Restrictions on Imports of Tuna*, not adopted, DS29/R, circulated 16 June 1994.

4.68. Applying the reasoning of the *Tuna II* Panel Report to this case, Singapore considered that the embargo could not be regarded as primarily aimed at rendering effective restrictions on domestic production or consumption since it was clearly directed at the conservation policies of other countries and could not be effective unless such policy changes occurred. Singapore observed that a US official had submitted that the current imposition of the embargo under Section 609 could jeopardize efforts for the world-wide protection of sea turtles. It had also been pointed out by other US officials that proficiency in the use of TEDs would generally take time because of the need for significant training and practice. This was the case in the United States during the mid-1980s, and it was the case in the Wider Caribbean Area in the early 1990s, and would likely be the case in the other countries now. In other words, the embargo as it was now being enforced world-wide would not be effective. Singapore noted that in the *Gasoline* case, the Appellate Body had felt that the phrase "if made effective in conjunction with restrictions on domestic production or consumption" was not intended to establish an empirical "effects test". However, it also clarified that it was not suggesting that consideration of the predictable effects of a measure could never be relevant. It concluded that the phrase was a requirement of even-handedness in the imposition of restrictions, in the name of conservation upon the production or consumption of exhaustible natural resources. Applying this reasoning, the embargo at issue also failed to meet the requirements of the exception. It was not implemented even-handedly. The embargo was targeted at the entire shrimp imports from a foreign country rather than at particular shipments. Domestically, the United States only imposed the prohibition on the harvests of individual vessels that did not employ TEDs during harvesting. This strongly suggested that the interests of foreign harvesters were given lesser consideration than those of domestic harvesters. In Singapore's opinion, this was clearly not even-handed.

4.69. With respect to the chapeau of Article XX, Singapore submitted that, for the same reasons highlighted under in paragraph 4.66, the embargo was an arbitrary or unjustifiable discrimination. Therefore, it did not meet the requirements of Article XX(g).

4.70. Singapore observed that the US government had admitted before the CIT that Section 609 might be inconsistent with the GATT. It had acknowledged that there were very serious questions relating to the consistency of Section 609 with United States' GATT obligations and that a GATT challenge would likely lead to the conclusion that the embargo provisions were violating GATT principles. Indeed, by objecting to the US court decision requiring the application of Section 609 to TED-caught shrimp, the United States appeared to recognize that the embargo did not comply with Article XX provisions. Singapore submitted that the issues raised in the present controversy were identical in all material respects to the *Tuna II* dispute. The United States did not attempt to distinguish such proceedings or contend that its shrimp embargo complied with Article XX(b) and (g) exceptions as interpreted by that Panel. Instead, the United States urged this panel to reject the interpretation, analysis and findings of the prior Panel. However, the United States did not contest the validity of the prior panel's central finding that Article XX requirements were violated by measures that embargoed imports without regard to whether particular products had been harvested in a manner that could harm the species intended to be protected.

4.71. Singapore subscribed to Principle 12 of the Rio Declaration and Section B of Agenda 21, which clearly stated that unilateral action should be avoided and that environmental measures addressing transboundary or global environmental problems should, as far as possible, be based on international consensus. This principle found consensus in the WTO Committee on Trade and Environment.

*11. Venezuela*

4.72. Venezuela submitted that Section 609 was inconsistent with GATT 1994 and not covered by its general exceptions. Venezuela considered this case to be particularly important because the United States argued that the provisions of Article XX, paragraphs (g) and (b), did not impose jurisdictional limitations on the measures covered by these paragraphs. Venezuela disagreed with that interpretation and had already expressed it on previous occasions (in particular as a third party in the two *Tuna* disputes). In Venezuela's opinion, the fact that the text of the provisions of Article XX did not refer expressly to the territorial jurisdiction of the measures covered by these exceptions did not imply that they could be invoked without any limitations. Furthermore, although a Member could adopt measures affecting common natural resources, such as migratory species, or measures affecting the activities of its nationals outside its own territory, this was not to be interpreted as entitling them to legislate on the activities of nationals of other Members. To claim otherwise would be to accept that a Member could apply trade restrictions to other Members simply because they maintained different domestic policies. This needed not be confined to environmental policies but could also extend to other policies in which states exercised their sovereign right to legislate in accordance with their own specific circumstances, as happened in the fields of health, education and other social policies. Moreover, the measure under consideration by this Panel was based on the way in which shrimp were fished and not on shrimp as a product. In Venezuela's view, the WTO provisions did not cover measures based on production processes and methods when these were not incorporated in the product itself. Venezuela believed that the Panel should maintain this approach, because otherwise there would be a risk that Members could discriminate in their treatment of similar products that were basically distinguished by the production processes used in manufacturing or obtaining them. Venezuela considered, therefore, that the Panel should weigh very carefully the implications of this case for the multilateral trading system.

4.73. Venezuela was not directly affected by the challenged measure. Venezuela required the use of TEDs by its shrimp fishing fleet as a part of a national and regional policy for protecting sea turtles. It was also the depository country of the Inter-American Convention for the Protection of Sea Turtles. However, in this respect it was worth pointing out that the Convention had a provision stipulating that parties should act in accordance with the WTO Agreement, particularly the TBT Agreement and Article XI of the GATT 1994. Venezuela's interest in this case was thus a systemic one, because it considered the unilateral, extra-jurisdictional application of measures based on production processes and methods not incorporated in products, aimed at imposing a country's own domestic policies on other Members, to be unacceptable and incompatible with WTO rules. There were better, compatible alternatives that should be used to attain the objectives of environmental protection: fundamentally, multilateral cooperation among states and technical assistance.

# V. PANEL'S CONSULTATION WITH SCIENTIFIC EXPERTS

## A. *Introduction*

5.1. The Panel noted that none of the parties to the dispute had requested the Panel to consult experts. However, the Panel noted that parties had submitted a number of studies by experts and often quoted the same scientific documents to support opposite views. Under those circumstances, the Panel informed the parties that it had decided, acting on its own initiative, to seek scientific and technical advice pursuant to paragraph 1 and paragraph 2, first sentence, of Article 13 of the DSU. The Panel focussed its questions on two main areas: (i) approaches to sea turtle conservation in light of local conditions, and (ii) habitat and migratory patterns of sea turtles.

5.2. Regarding the criteria for selecting the experts, **India, Malaysia, Pakistan and Thailand** noted that the experts should be neutral, diverse in areas of expertise and geographically distributed as much as possible. The emphasis should be placed on experts who had knowledge and first-hand experience with respect to sea turtle populations in the areas of contention, namely Asia and South-East Asia. They should not come from the same university or the same team of research. Moreover, the experts should be asked to provide citations to all sources that they consulted for the purpose of providing information to the Panel and to attach copies of cited sources to any submissions to the Panel. India, Malaysia, Pakistan and Thailand further noted that the Panel had decided to seek expert opinion under the provisions of paragraph 1 and paragraph 2, first sentence, of Article 13 of the DSU, and had decided, therefore, not to establish an expert review group as foreseen in paragraph 2, second and third sentences, of Article 13 and Appendix 4 of the DSU. India, Malaysia, Pakistan and Thailand requested the Panel to conform as far as possible with the provisions of Appendix 4 of the DSU, and in particular with paragraph 3 of Appendix 4 which stated that, unless there was joint agreement of the parties to the dispute, citizens of parties to the dispute should not be called upon to render expert advice.

5.3. The **United States** fully supported the Panel having access to expert advice that it considered useful for the resolution of this dispute. The advice of qualified and impartial experts would support the scientific and technical information that the United States had presented to the Panel and would thus assist the Panel in resolving this dispute on the basis of the best available scientific data. According to the United States, the Panel's enquiry should be limited to resolving those factual issues necessary to determining whether the US measures met the criteria of Article XX(g) and (b); the Panel was not asked to address and decide general policy issues relating to shrimp trawling and sea turtles conservation. In order to determine whether the US measures related to the conservation of an exhaustible natural resource, or were necessary for the protection of animal life or health, the core scientific and technical issues were the following: (i) are sea turtles threatened or endangered worldwide?, (ii) does shrimp trawling without TEDs result in the death of large numbers of sea turtles?, (iii) do TEDs, when properly installed and used, significantly reduce the mortality of sea turtles caused by shrimp trawl nets?

5.4. According to the United States, the Panel should use two basic criteria in selecting the experts: (i) the persons selected should be "experts" with respect to those aspects of the dispute for which their opinions were sought; (ii) as stipulated in the Rules of Conduct for the Understanding on Rules and Procedures Governing the

Settlement of Disputes they must be "independent and impartial, and shall avoid direct or indirect conflict of interest".[396] In particular, no expert consulted by the Panel should be associated with the government of a party to the dispute. The disclosure requirements regarding the existence of any interest, and in particular employment interests, that could affect or raise doubts concerning a person's independence or impartiality also applied to the experts.[397] Given the broad field covered by the questions, it was unlikely that many persons would have expertise with respect to each and every one of these questions. Each expert should therefore be instructed to answer only those questions in which they had expertise.

### Panel Procedures with Regard to Scientific Expertise

5.5. The Panel asked the parties to the dispute to provide it with names of possible experts. The Secretariat, then sollicited brief *curricula vitae* from all proposed experts who were ready to assist the Panel. The parties were provided the opportunity to comment on these potential experts on the basis of the *curricula vitae*, and in particular to state any compelling objections they might have with regard to any individual.

5.6. After careful consideration of the *curricula vitae* and of the comments made by the parties, the Panel selected the following five experts:

> Dr. Scott A. Eckert, Ph. D., Hubbs Sea World Research Institute, San Diego, United States;
>
> Dr. John G. Frazier, Ph. D., Centro de Investigación y de Estudios Avanzados, Mérida, Mexico;
>
> Mr. Michael Guinea, Northern Territory University, Darwin, Australia;
>
> Mr. Hock-Chark Liew, University Putra Malaysia Terengganu, Malaysia;
>
> Dr. Ian Poiner, Commonwealth Scientific and Industrial Research Organization, Queensland, Australia.

5.7. These experts were requested to serve, in their own personal capacities, as individual advisers under the authority of the Panel. The Panel noted that, in their disclosure forms, three of the proposed experts disclosed what might be considered to be potential conflicts of interest. However, the Panel decided to confirm their appointments being of the view that the disclosed information was not of such a nature as to prevent the individuals concerned from being impartial in providing the scientific information expected of them. The Panel has also taken into account the disclosed information when evaluating the answers provided. The Panel underlined that, in making its choice, it had been guided primarily by the need to gather expertise of the best quality and covering as wide a field as possible. In the small community of sea turtle specialists, it was difficult - if not impossible - to reconcile this need with an agreement by all the parties to the dispute on each and every individual concerned.

5.8. The Panel, in consultation with the parties, prepared specific questions which it submitted to each expert individually. The experts were requested to answer only those questions which fell within their field(s) of expertise. The parties agreed that their

[396] See WT/DSB/RC/1, Article II.1 (hereinafter the "Rules of Conduct").
[397] Article III.1 and VI.2 of the Rules of Conduct.

written submissions to the Panel, including the written versions of their oral statements, be provided to the selected experts. The written responses of the experts, as well as copies of the sources cited in support of their responses, were provided to the parties, which were afforded the opportunity to comment on them. The questions asked by the Panel and the answers provided by the experts are presented in Section V.B. The comments by the parties are reflected in Section V.C. The United States raised the fact that, in their comments, some parties had submitted new material, i.e. material which had not been submitted by the time of the second meeting of the Panel. The Panel specified that it did not intend to take this new material into account in evaluating the comments made by the parties; the Panel would take into account only those comments which were strictly related to the scientific issues under discussion with the experts.

5.9. On 21-22 January 1998, the experts were invited with the Panel and the parties to discuss their written responses to the questions and to provide further information. A transcript of this meeting is contained in Annex IV.

### *B. Questions by the Panel and Views of the Scientific Experts*

5.10. The Panel requested the experts to focus their answers on the situation prevailing in India, Malaysia, Pakistan, Thailand and the United States, and on the following species of sea turtles: loggerhead (*Caretta caretta*), Kemp's ridley (*Lepidochelys kempi*), olive ridley (*Lepidochelys olivacea*), green turtle (*Chelonia mydas*), leatherback (*Dermochelys coriacea*), and hawksbill (*Eretmochelys imbricata*). The experts were also asked to cite references where appropriate.

#### General Comments by the Experts

**Dr. J. Frazier:**

5.11. The questions cover a wide range of topics, and many of them are broadly phrased, so to provide complete answers requires considering a large number of variables. In general, differences between species, time and place all bear on different biological interpretations. Several of the questions are phrased in such a way that it would appear that what was expected was not only a concise, simple answer, but also the reduction of a series of options to one single alternative. If biology and biological conservation were as simple as rocket science, it might have been possible to provide brief, clear-cut answers. But biology is the study of life, of variation and change. It would be both arrogant and deceitful to pretend that biology, and even worse, that I myself, could consistently produce simple answers to simple questions. Furthermore, biological conservation is an interactive, iterative process, during which there are endless events of learning and experimenting. Since biological conservation is an attempt to use the information that we have in order to steward the resources on which we depend, the challenge becomes all the greater, for the needs and desires of many people and societies become paramount.

5.12. Hence, in many cases it seemed that as much as an answer, what was warranted was an explanation, at least from my point of view; and my intention has been to not only respond to the questions presenting my point of view, but also to provide citations to information which bears on my opinion. There are several general principles which I espouse: (i) do not assume that a lack of information is negative information, nor a justification for denying or asserting a case; (ii) to paraphrase from the United

Convention on the Law of the Sea: be more cautious when information is uncertain, unreliable or inadequate, the absence of adequate scientific information shall not be used as a reason for postponing or failing to take conservation and management measures; (iii) develop and implement integrated approaches - not "either-or" alternatives - for conservation biology and resource management; (iv) thus, in concerns of resource management and conservation, especially when they confront various threats, the Precautionary Approach, as explained in the FAO Code of Conduct for Responsible Fisheries is essential.

5.13. While it is fully understood that the case at hand deals with a dispute before the WTO in which five countries are directly involved, there are several aspects of this initial orienting statement that warrant comment, concerning the issue of endangered species of sea turtles and their conservation.

(a) All of the six listed species of marine turtles disperse and migrate over vast distances, with no respect to national boundaries. This has been amply proven in the scientific literature, with contributions by nationals of many of the five countries that are involved; the research includes tag and recapture, satellite telemetry, genetic analyses (notably of the D-loop of mitochondrial DNA), and geographic distribution/life history information. A few of the better known examples, and review papers that synthesize many citations are discussed below. Because of the biological realities, it would be artificial, incomplete, inadequate and deceptive to limit the responses to what is known for just the five nations involved in a dispute. The issue at hand involves many other nations neighbouring those five: the conservation and management of migratory marine animals - marine turtles in this case - can only be accomplished through full international cooperation. Furthermore, many basic aspects in the biology of marine turtles are poorly known, and information available for some of the countries involved is very limited. Hence, it is frequently necessary to draw from studies done elsewhere in order to provide a response.

(b) The issue at hand is far greater than sea turtle conservation. Human activities - in this case fishing, and in particular, bottom trawling - have major effects on marine organisms and environments, some of which are critical to sea turtle survival, and many of which are utilized for human consumption. The subject in dispute is a small, though highly visible part of a gargantuan dilemma before modern society: the destruction of bycatch as a major contributor to the declining status of the world's fisheries. The focus on marine turtle conservation is justified in and of itself. At the same time marine turtles are "flagship species", charismatic, highly visible, and easily identified; and they are employed as ambassadors of the seas in a strategy to facilitate the resolution of other resource conservation dilemmas, less visible and attractive to the general public. A brief description of this conservation strategy, in relation to a new regional convention, is presented in Frazier (1997a).

(c) Finally, no resource conservation or management can be effective without including humans and their societies in the equation. Limiting the discussion of sea turtle conservation to biological and technical questions, risks ignoring the basic social problems, on which the conservation problems rest. Problems of biological conservation and the human situation are tightly inter-linked, and can only be solved in concert. A discussion of this argument, as part of a critique of the magic of "sustainable development", is developed in Frazier (1997b).

**Mr. M. Guinea:**

5.14. The base unit for sea turtle conservation and management is the demographic unit (Chaloupka and Musick, 1997)[398] or breeding unit (gene pool). A country may have a single, or several, breeding units within its territorial waters. Sea turtles feeding in the waters of that country may not belong to the breeding unit. This has been demonstrated by mixed populations of hawksbill turtles on a feeding ground in Northern Australia (Broderick et. al., 1994). The paradigm of breeding units is essential to assess the threats and status of the sea turtle resources of a geographic area (Limpus, 1997). The concept of sea turtles being a global resource is philosophically laudable, but cumbersome in terms of conservation strategies.

5.15. Generalizations regarding sea turtles "... [being] found in the same general habitats and [feeding] on the same types of food throughout the world. Their feeding habits and habitat put them in the direct path of shrimp trawls where they were captured"[399] are incorrect and hamper management options of individual countries in managing their breeding units of sea turtles. Some species e.g., loggerhead, olive ridley, Kemp's ridley and flatback are generally at risk from shrimp trawling. But because of their preferred habitats most greens, and usually hawksbills and leatherbacks, are relatively unaffected by trawling. Sea turtles are very long lived with several decades required before hatchlings grow to sexual maturity. Any management strategy employed to increase the number of hatchlings will not be obvious on the nesting beaches, the accepted reference for the condition of the breeding unit, for some decades.

5.16. The embargo imposed by the United States on the affected countries has been ineffective in reducing any sea turtle mortality because the trawling effort remained unchanged in the affected countries, and alternative markets were found for shrimp banned from the US market. In Australian waters, the incidental catch of sea turtles is directly related to the fishing effort (Poiner et al., 1990). A similar relationship exists in the United States (US National Research Council, 1990). There is no indication that fishing effort decreased in any of the affected countries. The figures given relating to trade pre and post 1 May 1996 relate to exports of shrimp to the United States. India has indicated that other markets for their non-TED shrimp were found.[400] This indicates that shrimp previously destined for the US market before 1 May 1996 could flood existing markets that do not require the use of TEDs for their imported shrimp. This was anticipated by Australia which exports considerable amounts of shrimp of which only a small proportion has been exported to the US market (Stanley, 1996). The embargo imposed by the United States has readjusted trade in shrimp without reducing the alleged mortality of sea turtles in the affected countries.

5.17. Affected countries may still export shrimp to a third country(s) for either processing or transshipment to the US market.[401] A number of countries in their third

---

[398] The complete references of the literature and other sources cited by the experts can be found in Annex III.

[399] See above paragraph 3.61.

[400] See above paragraph 3.125.

[401] Verbal presentation by India at FAO Responsible Fishing Workshop Darwin, NT, Australia, 24-26 July 1997.

party submissions indicated that they did not have trawl fleets and did not allow trawling in their waters, but were involved with trade in shrimp.[402]

5.18. The report "Decline of Sea Turtles" (US National Research Council, 1990) was a fine body of work by a highly respected group of scientists, but it focused on mainland Unites States of America with some references to its Caribbean Territories but scarcely mentioned the Pacific Ocean States and the Pacific Ocean Territories. Its outlook is therefore ethnocentric and relates to the decline of sea turtles in the Gulf of Mexico, Western Atlantic Ocean and Caribbean Sea by essentially the US shrimp trawling fleet. I have difficulty extrapolating its conclusions to the global scale. The Australian Endangered Species Scientific Subcommittee has been evaluating a nomination for otter trawls as a key threatening process. After nearly two years of deliberation, it is unprepared to so make such a recommendation because of the equivocal reports of the relative effects of trawling on Australian sea turtles and other causes of decline e.g., egg predation. It will seek further advice before making another statement in approximately one year's time.[403]

**Question 1: Status of sea turtle populations - Past and current threats**

**1(a) Biologists consider that sea turtle populations around the world are affected by various factors, mainly anthropogenic. Are sea turtles threatened or endangered worldwide? Have the causes of any decline of sea turtle populations been the same for all species of sea turtles? Have these causes been similar in different parts of the world? Have these causes been similar over time?**

**Dr. S. Eckert:**

5.19. There can be no question that global sea turtle populations have declined significantly to the point where all species are in danger of extinction. Leatherbacks, green turtles, hawksbills, olive ridleys, and the Kemp's ridley are classified as Endangered in International Union for Conservation of Nature and Natural Resources (IUCN) Red Data Book and the loggerhead is classified as Vulnerable. Such listing reflects on the global status for each species. Further, all of these species are included on Appendix I of the Convention on International Trade In Endangered Species of Wild Flora and Fauna (CITES). While such listing is designed to regulate cross border trade in listed species and not control within country utilization, listing by CITES does reflect on the global status of the species.

5.20. Relative to commenting on the status of the species within the regions of the disputing parties, some discussion of how population status is determined is necessary. It is possible to evaluate the status of stocks within different regions, but these values cannot be applied as though regional populations were independent management units. The reason for such limitation is that we do not know the full geographic distribution of each stock, and that stock status is assessed by nesting beach census. Our current rudimentary understanding of sea turtle life history and cohort movements or migrations does not yet allow us to define individual stock boundaries or home ranges (Musick and

402 See above paragraphs 4.49 and 4.61-62.

403 Interim Advice to the Minister of the Environment from the Endangered Species Scientific Subcommittee of a Public Nomination to Schedule 3 of the Endangered Species Protection Act 1992.

Limpus, 1996). For example, all sea turtle species except one (Australian Flatback) have a pelagic phase in their development, whose duration is not yet well defined but is apparently in excess of 5 years (Musick and Limpus, 1996). Loggerhead sea turtle hatchlings dispersing from Japanese nesting beaches move across the North Pacific Ocean and reside off the US west coast and the Baja Peninsula of Mexico, before returning to Japan to continue development to maturity (Bowen et. al., 1995). A similar developmental migration occurs in the Atlantic with loggerheads hatched on the US east coast, migrating to Eastern Atlantic developmental habitats. Unfortunately, these are the only sea turtle stocks that we understand where the pelagic developmental phase of theirs lives is spent. All other species are unknown, but similar cycles are likely. Without a clear understanding of the distribution of individual stocks, it is not feasible to determine their population status. Thus, consideration of population status must still be based on the global species status.

5.21. Research into individual stock boundaries is still in its infancy. Improvements in stock identification techniques using mitochondrial and nuclear DNA, as well as improved satellite telemetry are rapidly changing what we know about stock ranges of turtle populations. Unfortunately, both are relatively new methods and sample sizes are still very small. Often information gathered using these new methods cause us to extend what we previously considered the home range of an individual stock. In 1996 I discovered that leatherback turtles distribute across ocean basins covering far greater ranges than had been expected from tag return data (S. Eckert, 1997). By satellite tracking 3 leatherbacks from the nesting beaches on the Caribbean island of Trinidad it is apparent that leatherback females circumnavigate the north Atlantic ocean annually. In the Pacific my ongoing satellite tracking studies of leatherbacks indicate that these turtles migrate from Mexican and Central American nesting beaches to Chile and Peru and probably also circumnavigate the entire Pacific Ocean. DNA analysis of leatherback caught in the north Pacific and stranded on the west coast of the US indicate that leatherback nesting stocks from Malaysia (and probably Thailand as well), Indonesia, the Solomon Islands, Mexico, and Costa Rica distribute throughout the ocean basin (Peter Dutton, NMFS pers. com.).

5.22. Disagreements on population status often revolve around confusion on what constitutes a population. To compound this confusion, what is usually referred to as a population by the scientific community actually refers to a nesting population or nesting stock. A nesting population describes only the mature females utilizing a particular beach or area for nesting. Traditional monitoring methods for a sea turtle "nesting population" is to count the number of females annually nesting at particular beach, and utilize these counts to calculate nesting population status. The primary reason for this approach is that nesting activities are obvious and can last for many days or weeks after nesting. However, it should be realized that such methods have limitations that must be accounted for when conducting trend analysis.

5.23. There are often stochastic fluctuations in the annual numbers of females nesting in any given year that may be brought about by environmental conditions such as the southern oscillation or El Niño events (Limpus and Nicholls, 1988). Such fluctuations can be quite large. There are also regional differences in what is known as the remigration interval, or the time between nesting seasons for an individual turtle. Generally for most species and most regions this interval is 2-3 years, but in some areas may extend to 5-7 years (Van Buskirk and Crowder, 1994, Limpus et. al., 1992, Dodd,

1988, Witzell, 1983, Hughes, 1974). The reasons for this difference is yet unclear, but may be reflective of local foraging habitat quality. Thus it is recommended that when defining a population trend, census coverage be maintained for 3 times the average remigration cycle, which for most species and most populations requires a nesting beach be monitored for a 6-9 years. One exception to this monitoring duration is for the ridley species which tend to nest annually. Confusion as to population status is often due to trend analysis being carried out on census durations that are too short and thus overly influenced by stochastic fluctuations.

5.24. Determining population or stock status based on the numbers of nesting females can also sometimes mask population status because female sea turtles generally require between 20 and 35 years to reach maturity. Thus, conservation actions or perturbations to the nesting beach population can take many years to be reflected on the number of females nesting annually. This is likely why the leatherback nesting population at Terengannu, Malaysia took so long to collapse. It took at least 40 years of almost 100 per cent egg harvest for this population to be reduced to an effectively extinct nesting population (Chua, 1988a, 1988b, Chan and Liew, 1996). When examining population status, it is critical to remember that these long lag times can confound trend analysis.

5.25. Some analysis of each species current status can be summarized as follows:

5.26. Global population outlook for the *leatherback* sea turtle is extremely poor. Since 1980 most data indicates that the global population has declined substantially. Of the 28 nesting areas reviewed by Spotila et. al., 1996, 10 may be in decline, 5 may be increasing and 13 may be stable. Even more importantly the largest nesting populations (Mexico, French Guiana/Suriname, Irian Jaya, Gabon, Malaysia), only one may be stable (French Guiana/Suriname). Most of the decline has been in the Pacific Ocean with the nesting populations of Malaysia virtually gone, the nesting populations of Irian Jaya in doubt (Bhaskar 1985, Stark, 1993 ), but likely reduced, and the once largest nesting population in the world in Mexico almost gone (Spotila et. al., 1996, Sarti et. al., 1996).

5.27. Of all the species, leatherbacks have the most regular long distance migration through the waters of a large number of countries. In the Atlantic, leatherbacks tracked by satellite travelled to the North Atlantic and then south to Africa in a single year (Eckert, 1997). During this single year migration, the turtles passed through the jurisdiction of as many as 7 countries. In the Pacific it appears that females nesting in Mexico and Central America reside for some time in the coastal waters of Chile, but based on DNA data, will also migrate to the northeast Pacific and then down the coast of the Western United States to Mexico. Thus, it can be predicted that the home range for all nesting populations of the leatherback in the Pacific extends to virtually every government region of the Pacific.

5.28. *Green turtle* populations for the region(s) are also in decline. According to Groombridge and Luxmoore (1989 ) "around half of the extant nesting populations are either known or suspected to be depleted or in decline, ...". The draft Recovery Plan for US Pacific Populations of the green turtle (NMFS and USFWS, 1996b), which describes all US Pacific ocean populations as well as those of the Republic of Palau, the Federated States of Micronesia and the Republic of the Marshall Islands, states that "green turtle throughout the insular Pacific region has likely continued to decline due to directed harvest (both illegal and legal) and negative impacts to essential habitats".

5.29. Green turtles nesting populations throughout Malaysia are also in decline (de Silva, 1982, 1987, Eckert, 1993, Chan and Liew, 1996). On peninsular Malaysia, green turtle nesting populations declined 43 per cent between 1956 and 1982 (Eckert, 1993). Given the large and continuing (illegal) egg take in Sabah and Sarawak these nesting populations will continue to decline. Between 1965 and 1973 more than 6 million eggs were harvested from the Turtle Islands (de Silva, 1982 in Eckert, 1993) and turtle egg poaching continues (Francis Liew, in Eckert, 1993) despite the areas classification as a marine turtle refuge. In neighbouring Sarawak 1-3 million eggs were collected per year between 1927 - 1960, 500,000 per year in the 1960's and <300,000 eggs collected until 1986 (Banks, 1986 in Eckert, 1993). In 1989 and 1990, 185,461 and 117,701 eggs respectively were collected (Eckert, 1993). Further, recent information suggest that development pressures from Malaysian business interests at the Turtle Islands may also threaten nesting populations there (Romeo Trono, pers. com.).

5.30. As tropical coral reef residents, *hawksbill* sea turtles are faced with very much the same suite of threats faced by green turtles. However, the global populations are generally considered to be in far worse condition than green turtles. The Recovery Plan for the US Pacific Populations of the hawksbill turtle (NMFS and USFWS, 1996e) describes that status of the species very well:

> "Anecdotal observations throughout Micronesia, from across the Pacific, and from other tropical oceans of the world are in near total agreement that current stock sizes are significantly below historical numbers. Although quantitative historical records are few, dramatic reductions in numbers of nesting and foraging hawksbills have apparently occurred in Micronesia (Johannes 1986; Pritchard 1981a) and Pacific Mexico just South of California (Cliffton et. al., 1982) since World War II, largely because of increased access to remote nesting beaches by indigenous fisherman equipped with spear guns, outboard motors, SCUBA, and other high-tech fishing gear (Johannes 1986; Pritchard 1981a and 1981b). Market pressures from Asia, sustained by a vast fleet of Taiwanese and other fishing vessels of various national origins, are overwhelming the existing stocks. Most important of all, hawksbills are threatened by a pervasive tortoise shell trade, which continues particularly in southeast Asia and Indonesia even though the once lucrative Japanese markets were closed in 1994."

This latter issue is the primary reason that hawksbill population are in so much worse shape than the green turtle.

5.31. While the *olive ridley* is considered the most numerous species of sea turtle, its populations have also been reduced. In Pacific Mexico, overexploitation of the nesting females and their eggs caused the collapse of 3 of the 4 arribada beaches (Eckert, 1993). Harvest of nesting females was so extensive (for the leather trade) that between 75,000 and 100,000 females were killed each year (despite a legal limit of 20,000). In May of 1990, the harvest of turtles was banned in Mexico. Population status for stocks nesting in India are far less clear. Based on my review of data presented by Dash and Kar (1990) there is no clear trend in nesting population status at Gahirmatha.

5.32. Globally *loggerhead* populations are considered in less danger of immediate extinction than most other sea turtle species. However regionally there have been serious population declines, particularly in the south-east United States (NRC, 1990).

The primary cause for these local population collapses have been shrimp fishing (NRC, 1990). However, some re-consideration of the global status of loggerhead may be warranted in light of the rapid growth of longline fishing methods. Beside shrimp trawling loggerheads are the most frequently caught sea turtle species in longline type fisheries. (Aguilar et. al., 1992, 1993, Balazs and Pooley, 1994).

5.33. It is extremely difficult to credit any one particular cause with decline for all sea turtle species. In the Draft Recovery Plans for US Pacific populations of sea turtles (NMFS and USFWS, 1996 drafts a-f) we identified 29 different general categories of threats to marine turtles, 26 of those were anthropogenic. Those anthropogenic sources fall under 3 headings: (a) direct intentional take of turtles for food or commercial product; (b) incidental take by fisheries; and (c) destruction of habitat. Historically the most significant threats fall within headings (a) and (b).

5.34. The tremendous decline in *leatherback* sea turtle populations can probably be attributed to over-harvest of eggs, and incidental take in fisheries. The best example of the destruction of any nesting population of sea turtles by over-harvest of eggs was the leatherback nesting population at Terengannu, Malaysia. Mortality of adult turtles was limited at this nesting colony due to religious constraints but commercial egg take was in excess of 90 per cent for over 50 years and caused a slow decline to less that 100 females (Chua, 1988a, 1988b). Some mortality to this population can likely be attributed to the high-seas driftnet fishery which operated through the 1980's and early 1990's, and to trawl fisheries operating off the coast in the early 1980's (Wetherall et. al., 1993, Chan and Liew, 1996). The once large Mexican/Costa Rican populations of nesting leatherback is likely a good example of the impact gillnet and longline fisheries can have to a sea turtle population. Throughout the 1980's the high seas driftnet fleet caught approximately 1000 leatherbacks per year (Wetherall et. al., 1993, Eckert and Sarti, 1997). While this take was likely from all of the nesting stocks in the Pacific, the exceptionally large numbers of leatherbacks nesting in Mexico and Central America, has probably meant that the majority of those killed in the north Pacific were from those stocks. In the mid-1980's, Chile and Peru initiated large scale gillnet and longline fisheries for swordfish and it is estimated that they kill in excess of 2000 leatherbacks per year in this fishery (Eckert and Sarti, 1997). In only 10 years, the population of leatherbacks nesting in Mexico alone has declined over 95 per cent (Sarti et. al., 1996). This decline occurred despite extensive efforts by Mexico to protect their nesting stocks of sea turtles on the beaches.

5.35. *Green turtle* population declines can generally be attributed to intense harvest for meat, eggs and turtle products, and secondarily to incidental take in fisheries. This species has been highly sought as a source of food, both commercially and by indigenous peoples (Groombridge and Luxmoore, 1989). While most countries have laws to limit such take, those laws have generally been ineffective, such that large scale harvest still continues (Eckert, 1993). However in some areas such as the Pacific coast of Mexico and NE South America and Thailand shrimp trawling has also been a significant source of mortality for these species Hill, 1991, Eckert, 1993, Chantrapornsyl, 1997).

5.36. There are 2 primary causes of population decline for the *loggerhead* sea turtle. In the southeastern United States, it was estimated that shrimp trawling accounted for the mortality of 50,000 loggerheads per year (NRC, 1990). However, this threat in the United States has been largely eliminated with the application of TEDs in shrimping trawls (Henwood and Stuntz, 1987). In the Pacific Ocean, the high seas driftnet fleets also caught large numbers of loggerheads during the 1980's and early 1990's, but this threat has been largely removed by the outlawing of that fishery (Wetherall et. al., 1993). A particularly serious and growing source of mortality for this species is pelagic longline fisheries in the Pacific and the Mediterranean. Loggerhead turtles will feed on bait used in longline fisheries and become hooked. Large numbers of mostly juvenile loggerheads are killed or injured by these fisheries (Aguilar, 1992, Aguilar, 1993, Argano, 1983, Balazs and Pooley, 1994).

5.37. *Olive ridleys* have long been harvested in Central America for eggs, meat and skin. This harvest was so intense in Mexico that 3 of the 4 arribada beaches were extirpated by the 1980's (Eckert, 1993). Such harvest was banned in Mexico by 1990 and there is some evidence that the remaining arribada population may be recovering (Marquez, 1996b). Olive ridleys are also heavily impacted by shrimp fishing in Central America, India, Suriname (Hoekert and Schouten, 1996) and to a lesser extent in Mexico. The incidental take of olive ridleys in India is exceptionally severe which supports the largest nesting aggregation of this species in the world. Annually 5,000 - 8,000 dead turtles wash up on the beaches of Orissa which are attributed to incidental take in shrimp trawls. Despite laws banning such fishing, large scale shrimp fishing is occurring within the Bhitara Kinika Sanctuary (the primary nesting area for olive ridleys in India) and more than 4,000 olive ridleys stranded dead on the nesting beach during 1996/97 (Das, 1998). Finally there is evidence that the incidental mortality of olive ridleys due to shrimp fisheries is not limited to reproductive adults, but also to what are likely resident juveniles (Pandav and Choudhury, 1995). Two things are clear relative to the incidental take of olive ridleys in India. The first is that there are severe problems with enforcement of regulations protecting these important olive ridley nesting beaches and, secondly, there seems to be conflicts between the State and Federal government as well as the fisheries resource management agencies in India over the need to protect sea turtles. This latter problem is well defined by incidents in which the State of Orissa attempted to build fishing harbours within and alongside the sanctuary to support increased shrimp fishing, despite the protected status of the area (Andrews, 1993, Mohanty-Hejmadi, 1994, Das, 1998 in press).

**Dr. J. Frazier:**

5.38. It is certainly true that "biologists consider that sea turtle populations around the world are affected by various factors". The life cycles of all species of sea turtles are very complex: the animals depend on terrestrial areas of sandy beaches to make their nests and deposit their eggs (Miller, 1997; Ackerman, 1997); hatchlings (newly-hatched turtles) of all species, except the Australian flatback, disperse into open ocean, and live as part of the epipelagic (open ocean) assemblage on the high seas (Musick and Limpus, 1997); immatures of many species take up residence in coastal areas, and may pass through a series of "developmental habitats" before reaching maturity; adults migrate between feeding areas and nesting areas (Musick and Limpus, 1997). Depending on the species and "population", these migrations may occur every one, two, three or more years, and can involve displacements of thousands of kilometers, in some cases crossing ocean basins (Meylan, 1982a; Bowen and Karl, 1997). In the wild, sea turtles require more than a decade (several decades in some species) to reach maturity (see references in Bjorndal and Zug, 1995; Chaloupka and Musick, 1997), and they have the capability to live for many decades, during which time they continue to reproduce.

5.39. Hence, during its long life, an individual sea turtle will pass through many different environments, traversing a substantial - often vast - surface of the planet; in any one of these environments, and at any time during its long life, it may meet a large variety of predators and other threats. For turtle eggs laid on beaches, these threats include ants, flies, beetles, crabs, snakes, and lizards, as well as birds and mammals of many varieties; the hatchling turtles are liable to many of the same terrestrial predators, as well as a diversity of marine fishes. Even immature and adult sea turtles are not free from predation, and can be attacked by large fishes and carnivorous mammals, both in the sea and on land (Stancyk, 1982). The list of human-caused (anthropogenic) threats to sea turtles is also long and includes fishing activities, coastal development, marine and coastal pollution, and even upland pollution and deforestation (Eckert, 1995; Lutcavage et. al., 1997).

5.40. For this reason, depending on the time, place and circumstances, the factors affecting a particular sea turtle, or stock of sea turtles, will vary. Anthropogenic factors add to an already enormous list of threats that sea turtles face during the course of their normal life cycle. People can prey on and impact those stages of the life cycle when turtles would otherwise be least vulnerable to predation. Anthropogenic risks can also include large scale perturbations of habitat, thereby increasing mortality, both in time and in space, e.g., the chronic effects of marine pollution or the total devastation of a nesting beach.

5.41. Because sea turtles live for long periods of time and they require decades to reach maturity, it may take years to perceive the effects of loss from the "population". Hence "current" threats may in effect be the results of past actions and damage, which only now are being detected. It is also worth clarifying that the concept of "population" is not easily defined for sea turtles, due to their complex migratory patterns and life cycles; recent information on genetic composition is resolving this problem (Bowen, 1995; Bowen and Karl, 1997; Chaloupka and Musick, 1997: 235). However, in the absence of such information, many specialists prefer to employ the terms "reproductive unit", "breeding stock" (Chaloupka and Musick, 1997) or "management unit" (Bowen and Karl, 1997). In the present review, the term "population" is used simply because it is in common use.

5.42. The terms "threatened" and "endangered" have specific significance to organizations such as the IUCN (World Conservation Union) and CITES. A recent evaluation of these categories, by specialists of the IUCN (Bailley and Groombridge, 1996), concluded that the appropriate categories for sea turtles are as follows:

| | |
|---|---|
| *Caretta caretta* | endangered |
| *Chelonia mydas* | endangered |
| *Dermochelys coriacea* | endangered |
| *Eretmochelys imbricata* | critically endangered |
| *Lepidochelys kempii* | critically endangered |
| *Lepidochelys olivacea* | endangered |
| *Natator depressus* | threatened |

5.43. At a general level, the decline of any animal population can be attributed to the same causes: that recruitment of new animals into the population cannot keep up with loss of animals from the population. On a more detailed level, the causes of decreased recruitment and/or increased mortality (or emigration) vary according to time, place and a variety of conditions. Unfortunately, there are several basic factors in sea turtle biology which are not well known, these include: age at maturity, reproductive lifetime, reproductive output, rate of mortality in different life stages, and sex ratio in the wild. Hence, in many cases our lack of fundamental information makes it difficult to dogmatically assign simple "causes" to any decline (or recovery) of a population.

5.44. What is known and widely accepted, is that - with few exceptions - the numbers of marine turtles that are found nesting around the world are far less today than they were historically or within living memory (e.g., Frazier, 1980; King, 1982; Ross, 1982; National Research Council, 1990; Chan, 1991; Limpus, 1994; 1995; Limpus and Reimer, 1994; Witzell, 1994; Chan and Liew, 1996b; Liew, in press). In many instances, although systematic or quantitative data are not available, general historic accounts or comments of long-time residents of coastal areas reveal clear declines in numbers of turtles (e.g., Clifton et. al., 1982; Cornelius, 1982; Frazier, 1982; Kar and Bhaskar, 1982; King, 1982; Polunin and Nuitja, 1982; Ross, 1982; Spring, 1982; Jackson, 1997). Indeed, systematic, quantitative information on status is available for very few sea turtle populations.

5.45. With few exceptions, the status of sea turtle populations is evaluated on the basis of the numbers of females, or more commonly, the numbers of nests (or even numbers of eggs) recorded on a nesting beach during a nesting season. The reason for this is simply because it is far easier, and much less expensive, to observe and count what happens on a beach than what happens in the sea.

5.46. Attempts to estimate the number of turtles in a population (immatures, adult males and adult females) are foiled by a lack of basic information on demography of sea turtles (Crouse et. al., 1987; Van Buskirk and Crowder, 1994; Crouse and Frazer, 1995). In fact, even estimating the numbers of reproductive females in a population presents a major challenge. With the exception of ridley turtles, female sea turtles typically nest several times during a season, and then not again for two or three years, or more. Individual females may nest at two-year intervals and then change to three-year intervals, or vice versa (Carr et. al., 1978) so even though they return periodically to lay their eggs on the same beach, there is not even a simple - reliable - way to estimate the number of adult females in a sea turtle population (Crouse and Frazer, 1995).

5.47. In the case of ridley sea turtles, which in addition to nesting annually, nest in great concentrations, arribadas, the challenge of estimating the numbers of nesting females is complicated for additional reasons. During arribadas, the density and commotion of females on the beach makes it physically impossible to accurately count every female that nests. At different arribada beaches different methods have been used to estimate the numbers of females, but these methods tend to be rather rough, without clear consistency between years, and rarely statistically sound (viz. they rarely are based on defensible statistical procedures, and do not include confidence limits, making statistical comparisons between numbers impossible). Two different methods, designed to derive confidence limits, are used at Nancite, Costa Rica, and they produce results which can be very different (Clausella, pers. com.). The most thorough attempt to develop a statistically defensible counting procedure for concentrated nesters has recently been presented by Gates et. al. (1996), but it is not yet in common use.

5.48. Whatever the species, numbers from nesting beaches must be interpreted with great care. In the first place, the methods and effort involved in counting must be comparable. It is not uncommon for effort and efficiency in patrolling a beach, or collecting eggs, to increase as personnel in a programme acquire more experience, and perhaps more support. For example, over the past five years increasing numbers of hawksbill nests have been recorded on the Yucatan Peninsula, in southern Mexico. In part, this is because more turtle camps have been established, some of the camps are better equipped, and there is more attention and concern on part of the local populace to protect sea turtles. However, there are also indications that at some individual beaches, the numbers of nests per season has increased.

5.49. Even when methodology and effort are comparable from year to year, data from nesting beaches must be interpreted with caution. Nesting populations, thought to be free from large scale predation, can show tremendous changes in numbers from one year to the next. For example, on Heron Island, Great Barrier Reef, about 1,100 green turtles nested in 1974-75, and the following year only about 50 nested. During peak nesting season on remote Raine Island, also in Australia, it was estimated that 11,000 females came ashore in one night during the 1974-75 season, but there were only about 100 on the beach in any one night the following year (Limpus, 1982). Similar large variations have been recorded on other green turtle nesting beaches (Meylan, 1982b; Hirth, 1997: 73). In the case of Australian beaches, these fluctuations in numbers of nesting green turtles can be predicted by an index of the Southern Oscillation ("El Niño"), but in other cases it is unknown what causes the fluctuations (Limpus and Nicholls, 1988).

5.50. Yearly variations in nesting are reported to be greatest with green turtles, but annual fluctuations in nesting activity (numbers of nesting females, numbers of nests and/or numbers of eggs) occur in all species of sea turtles; some loggerhead beaches have had tremendous variation from year to year, for which there are no simple nor clear explanations (Meylan, 1982b; National Research Council, 1990; Chaloupka and Musick, 1997). Thus, to fully understand the dynamics of a population requires long-term data, for apparent trends over a few years may not reflect true changes in the total numbers of animals in the population but rather the physiological condition of those animals that migrate to breed, the condition of their feeding areas, etc. (Limpus and Nicholls, 1988; National Research Council, 1990; Crouse and Frazer, 1995; Chaloupka and Musick, 1997).

5.51. A further complication is that individual females generally nest more than once in a single nesting season. But, the number of nests per female varies, even for the turtles sharing the same beach, during the same nesting season. Hence, there is no precise conversion from number of nests to number of nesting females. Using numbers of eggs to derive numbers of females in a season is even more tenuous, because of the added variation in clutch size, both between females and between subsequent clutches of the same female.

5.52. This having been said, there are some cases in which it is possible to relate certain documented changes in a population indicator to a major perturbation in the environment which clearly has had a significant impact on a sea turtle population. For example, direct, unrelenting exploitation of reproductive green turtles in the Seychelles, directed for an export market, was quickly followed by dramatic declines in "annual production" (i.e., numbers of animals captured per year), and in the general abundance of the animals (Frazier, 1980). Similar examples of direct exploitation of both breeding and non-breeding green turtles accompanied by decimation of their numbers are known for the Caribbean (Jackson, 1997), the southern United States (Witzell, 1994), Pacific Mexico (Clifton et. al., 1982), and many other parts of the world (King, 1982; Ross, 1982). Breeding olive ridleys in Pacific Mexico were also heavily exploited, with consequent decimation in their numbers (Clifton et. al., 1982). Throughout the Caribbean, hawksbills have declined drastically, in conjunction with heavy exploitation in both nesting and non-nesting animals (Meylan et. al., in prep.).

5.53. Where no direct exploitation on breeding turtles is recorded, declines in populations have been attributed to intense direct exploitation of eggs, for example in Sarawak, East Malaysia (Limpus, 1994; 1995; Chan and Liew, 1996a). But at least in the case of the Terengganu leatherbacks in Western Malaysia, the decline is thought to have also been influenced by incidental capture and mortality, first in a local fishery, and then in a high seas fishery (Chan and Liew, 1996a).

5.54. In addition to direct exploitation, indirect factors are also known to cause major impacts on sea turtles. For example, declines in loggerheads in Georgia and South Carolina are clearly linked to incidental mortality in shrimp trawls (National Research Council, 1990). Dramatic declines in Pacific leatherbacks have been related to an increase in fisheries activities in South America, and incidental mortality in fisheries using drift- and gillnets (Eckert and Sarti, 1997).

5.55. It is important to realize that multiple, sequential causes can be attributed to the decline of a population, as was explained by Chan and Liew (1996a) in the case of the Terengganu leatherbacks. This case illustrates the danger of attributing simple causes to what appear to be simple phenomena relating to sea turtles. Because of their complex life history, the researcher must be ever vigilant of effects which may take place in some area or time, out of view, and distant to one's area or period of operation; important sources of mortality may take place on the other side of an ocean basin, or a decade before a study is carried out. This is even further complicated because the same beach may be used by turtles that feed in very different places, or turtles that feed in the same areas may nest in very different places (Carr et. al., 1978). Hence, a significant source of mortality may occur at some point during the long generation time of a cohort of sea turtles, but if that factor is not observed during a study, it will be easy to ignore it and attribute the decline to other causes. The challenge in explaining the demography of sea turtles is one of identifying major factors over large periods of time, and over large expanses of the sea.

5.56. In regards to the five countries specifically involved in this report, reasons attributed to declines can be summarized as follows:

*India*: Green turtles in the Gulf of Mannar appear to have declined, following heavy exploitation of animals at sea for local consumption and occasionally for export (Frazier, 1980). In general, however, systematic data are wanting for the majority of sea turtle populations in India, and it is only possible to compare what little is known of the present-day situation with general accounts of naturalists or long-term coastal residents. For example, intensive development and human immigration on the coast of Tamil Nadu has resulted in extensive habitat perturbation as well as intense exploitation of olive ridley turtle nests. Thus, it is thought that the numbers of olive ridleys here are much lower than years ago. There is a similar supposition that green turtles in Gujarat have declined, but clear trends are not possible to determine in the absence of systematic information. There are conflicting opinions about the current trends of the massed nesting beach for olive ridleys at Gahirmatha (Mohanty-Hemadi and Sahoo, 1994; Pandav et. al., 1997).

*Malaysia*: Declines in egg production has been attributed to heavy harvest of eggs of green turtles at Sarawak (de Silva, 1982; Limpus, 1994; 1995), and in Sabah heavy pressure from hunting at sea and on nesting beaches as well as intensive egg harvests occurred prior to declines in egg production (de Silva, 1982; Eckert, 1993; Limpus, 1994; 1995; Chan and Liew, 1996b). In both Sabah and Sarawak, habitat degradation (marine and terrestrial), and fishing activities - notably trawls - have been identified (Leh, 1989; Suliansa et al., 1996). Egg production of green turtles in Terengganu (as well as Kelantan and Pahang) declined following heavy egg harvest, coastal development and intensification of coastal fisheries activities (Siow and Moll, 1982). Numbers of eggs of leatherback turtles at Terengganu show a well documented precipitous decline (Siow and Moll, 1982; Chan, 1991; Limpus, 1994, 1995) which has been related to nearly complete egg harvest for decades, as well as incidental mortality first in coastal fisheries, and then in high-seas fisheries (Chan and Liew, 1996a). Nesting by green and hawksbill turtles on the west coast of Malaysia has declined following intensive coastal development and fisheries activities, especially prawn trawling (Siow and Moll, 1982). Limpus (1995) states that from possible thousands of olive ridleys nesting annually in Terengganu, there may now be 20 per year nesting. Chan (1991) explained that in Malaysia, all five species of sea turtles are considered to be critically endangered.

*Pakistan*: Data on the numbers of nests at Hawksbay, Sind, indicate declines in both green turtles and olive ridleys from 1979 to 1995 (Firdous, in press). However, there has been no detailed analysis of these data. Very little is known from Baluchistan, but sizable populations of green turtles are thought to occur (or to once have occurred) there. Groombridge et al., (1988) reported commercial exploitation (thought to be green turtles) from remote beaches in Baluchistan. The levels of harvesting were claimed to have been many thousands of turtles in a year; a short-term exportation to Japan was involved, but there was also evidence that much of the exploitation was for local consumption. Later, Groombridge (1989), in reporting on Baluchistan, stated "Incidental catch appears to be a problem in surrounding waters...". He suggested that the nesting colony in the Sonmiani region of Las Bela may have been extirpated by heavy direct exploitation. As the area is remote, and much of the exploitation is for locally consumed products not recorded in normal statistics, it is next to impossible to know what happened historically or even what has happened in recent years.

*Thailand*: Polunin and Nuitja (1982) explained that little systematic information has been available, but data on egg yields from Phangnga and Ko Khram (probably mainly green turtles) indicated clear declines. Intensive coastal development and reef blasting were reported to have eliminated much nesting habitat. All evidence pointed to serious depletion in the Gulf of Thailand (Polunin and Nuitja, 1982). Phasuk (1982) identified uncontrolled harvest of eggs and turtles, as well as incidental drowning in trawls; to these causes were added habitat modification (Lekagul and Damman, 1977; Ginsberg, 1981). Direct and heavy ("near total, long term") harvest of eggs has been described as the principal cause of declines of green turtles and leatherbacks (Limpus, 1995). Limpus (1995) stated that overharvest of eggs has been responsible for the dramatic declines of olive ridleys that once nested on the Andaman Sea coast of Thailand, which have been decimated to only tens of females per year. This focus on egg harvest is because there is some systematic information available on this activity, unlike incidental kill and harvest of turtles (Eckert, 1993). The most recent review of the situation at Khram Island and other main nesting areas, including the Andaman sea coast, has concluded that there have been significant declines in green and hawksbill turtles. In Khram this was reported to have been caused by heavy fishing activities, while at other areas coastal development, egg poaching and incidental capture in gill nets, long lines, and trawls have been implicated (Supot, in press).

*United States*: Historic declines of green turtles, due to intensive exploitation at sea for commercial purposes, has been documented for coastal waters from Texas to Florida (Witzell, 1994). Loggerhead nesting has declined in Georgia and South Carolina, due especially to incidental capture in shrimp trawls (National Research Council, 1990). Population declines of loggerheads in these two states are thought to continue, but to a lesser extent, because of reduced mortality from the use of TEDs (Crowder et al., 1995). There have been dramatic declines of sea turtles - notably green turtles - in Hawaii (Balazs, 1980). Declines of both green and hawksbill turtles have been documented for most other US island territories in the Pacific, related to hunting (legal and illegal) eggs and meat, habitat degradation and incidental catch (Eckert, 1993).

5.57. In general terms, the causes have been similar in different parts of the world: an inability of recruitment to match mortality. (Little is known of the processes of immigration and emigration in sea turtle populations, so for simplicity, these terms will not be used here.) However, specific conditions vary, depending on different circumstances (see comments above), so recruitment and mortality may vary from beach to beach and from year to year.

5.58. Nonetheless, there are some aspects that are known to be relatively constant on a global level. When reproductive animals are removed from a population, the decline tends to be relatively rapid (e.g., the case of green turtles in Texas, Florida (Witzell, 1994) and Seychelles (Frazier, 1980); when eggs are removed, it takes longer for the decline to manifest itself (e.g., the case of Sarawak (Limpus, 1994)). In some cases, a complex of factors is thought to be related to the decline, but lack of fundamental information, including good baseline data, makes it a challenge to explain many declines in simple, precise terms. This is not to mention that marine and coastal environments are extremely dynamic, and many non-human effects may interact with anthropogenic threats.

5.59. A constant cause for decline, independent of time, is when mortality is greater than recruitment. Mortality and recruitment vary, depending on predation, food availability and quality, habitat quality, and many other factors. Because the life cycle of a sea turtle is complex, and includes large periods of time and large expanses of the planet, mortality can occur at many places and many times during an individual turtle's life. If mortality occurs anytime before reproductive maturity, the individual will not have the opportunity to contribute to the maintenance of the population. In the case of sea turtles, this means that mortality anytime during the first decade or more of pre-reproductive life will eliminate that individual's potential for reproducing, and contributing to recruitment and maintenance of the population. During the period of maturation a sea turtle will have lived in diverse environments, including spending the first two months of its life in a nest on a beach, years in the open ocean, and more years in coastal waters; in each of these environments it will have to evade diverse sources of mortality.

**Mr. M. Guinea:**

5.60. The conservation status of the world's sea turtles are presented in the IUCN Red data book of threatened animals (IUCN 1996). The hawksbill is critically endangered. Green, loggerhead and olive ridley, Kemp's ridley and leatherback are listed as endangered. The endemic Australian flatback is listed as vulnerable. The status of each species is achieved by nomination of the decline of the nesting population and the nomination of regional threatening processes. Pritchard (1997) states "[t]he IUCN in close cooperation with the Secretariat and Parties to CITES, has now adopted a set of complex numerical and ostensibly objective criteria by which the status category of a species should be deduced… The criteria incorporate considerations of actual global population numbers, fragmentation of habitat and populations and demonstrable population trends. For the great majority of species, the necessary data are unlikely to be currently available." All marine turtles are included in Appendix I of CITES..." (IUCN, 1995).

5.61. The causes of decline have been the same for all species. Limpus (1997) reviewed the causes of decline in sea turtle numbers in Southeast Asia. Human activities have been nominated as the causative agents in every decline. However, the breeding unit has to be examined to identify what activity or process is responsible for the decline. Trawling may affect some species while egg harvesting and habitat destruction may be more significant for other breeding units. Sea turtles are threatened at all periods of their life. Their critical habitats are also threatened. The nature and level of threat varies for each breeding unit. Threats may be natural and impact on the breeding unit during the nesting season, e.g. Hurricane Pauline destroyed 40 million olive ridley eggs in Mexico (Marine Turtle Newsletter), or affect the morphology of the nesting beach, e.g., storm surges drastically altered the nesting beach at Gahirmatha, India (Satapathy Rajaram, 1997). At least one breeding unit was affected by Cyclone Kathy, which stranded sea turtles on their feeding ground at 1057 km from their rookery (Limpus and Reed, 1985). These unpredictable natural events are less damaging than continuous human utilization.

5.62. Great attention has been given to the decline of modern day sea turtles (Poiner et. al., 1990). Anthropogenic causes are attributable to negative impacts of human activities at any and all stages of the life history of sea turtles and their critical habitats. Direct alteration to the nesting environment by beach modification, through armouring, replenishment, nourishment and their environs by light and waste pollution as well as from recreational pursuits of beach driving and intensive human beach visitation, all have the potential to harm sea turtles, their eggs and/or hatchlings. Introduced and native predators of sea turtles eggs and hatchlings can have significant negative impacts on sea turtle rookeries. Almost every omnivorous vertebrate and many invertebrates within the vicinity of a sea turtle rookery has the potential to be a predator of sea turtle eggs and hatchlings (Carr, 1973). Yet, predation pressures are greatest as the hatchlings cross the shallow coastal waters on their dispersal into the open ocean (Limpus, 1997a).

5.63. Little is known about survivorship of sea turtles in the open sea and through their intermediate years (US National Academy of Sciences, 1990). Most of the interactions between sea turtles and humans are usually to the detriment of the former. Threats include subsistence, artisanal and direct commercial hunting in the vicinity of the nesting beaches and feeding grounds (Frazier, 1980), succumbing to pollution (e.g., petroleum products (Lutcavage et. al., 1997), discarded plastics and fishing gear (Chatto et. al., 1995)), and accidental capture in fishing activities, including bottom set gill nets (Guinea and Chatto, 1992), protective shark meshing (Paterson, 1979), long lines, drift gill nets (Eckert and Sarti, 1997) and shrimp trawls (US National Academy of Sciences, 1990).

5.64. When the above natural and anthropogenic causes of the decline in sea turtle populations are examined few target a single species, although each has the potential to negatively impact on any group of sea turtle species within an area. Natural threats are indiscriminate and may affect any species. Natural predation on eggs and hatchlings is thought to be kept in check by natural balances of predator prey relationships. Predation is so high that it is obvious that a number of terrestrial, marine and avian species depend on sea turtles as a source of protein. Anthropogenic threats to nesting habitats are again indiscriminate and driven more by coastal development, industrialization and the recreational opportunities provided by coastal environments. Direct human exploitation of sea turtle eggs and adults, if unchecked by legislation, will markedly reduce sea turtle numbers even in the absence of trawling activities e.g., Fiji (Guinea, 1993). The eggs of all species are targeted but major industries have been established in the past for green (meat, cartilage and oil), hawksbill (tortoise shell), olive ridley (leather, oil) and leatherback (oil) sea turtles. Incidental capture in fishing gear has the potential to reduce the population levels of some species. Shallow water fisheries in turtle habitats, using large meshed bottom set nets to capture sharks and rays will inevitably capture sea turtles. These nets are traditionally used to capture green (Travis, 1967) and olive ridley (Marquez, 1990) sea turtles.

5.65. Modern shrimp trawling is a relatively new technology. It should be used in conjunction with a number of management tools e.g., exclusion zones, time of trawl activity, vessel size, number of nets, net mesh size and the duration of individual trawls. The trawl fishery is sustained by this reduction of effort while improving the catch of the target species. Bycatch reduction or sorting devices remove unwanted species and objects or alternatively sort fish from prawn species giving a cleaner catch. Trawls of long duration over areas inhabited by benthic feeding sea turtles i.e., loggerhead, olive ridley, Kemp's ridley, flatback and some adult greens or in waters adjacent to their rookeries will capture a proportion of the sea turtles present. TEDs will allow the majority of adult turtles to escape.

5.66. Natural destruction and replacement of nesting beaches occur throughout the tropical region. Native and introduced predators of eggs and hatchlings occur on most rookeries. Coastal development, recreational pursuits and industrialization of the shore are common throughout the nesting range of sea turtles. Shallow water net and trawl fisheries are present throughout the tropical seas. Essentially all of the threats are present in the majority of tropical countries that have sea turtle populations. It is the intensity of those threatening activities, their duration and the subsequent abatement measures, that determine the viability of the sea turtle populations. Abatement measures vary with the socio-economic structure within various countries. The high technology approach to conservation of so-called developed countries appears at odds when dealing with artisanal fishers and trawl fleets of countries that are still developing. The decline of sea turtles has been driven by development of markets for turtles, their eggs, their habitats and other marketable marine species e.g., shrimp.

5.67. Natural threats to the habitat and native predation pressures have been present throughout time. Subsistence utilization of sea turtles has been in operation for some thousands of years by indigenous peoples. Non-indigenous exploitation of sea turtles and their products i.e., eggs, meat, oil, leather and tortoise shell have been operating for some centuries in areas which were close to centres of trade. With a global increase in commercialism, transport and trade, sea turtle breeding units have come under increasing pressures as a commodity. Their habitats are sought for coastal development. Modern fishing techniques place some species that coexist with shrimp at risk. The increase in human demand for tropical marine products and coastal facilities places increasing pressure on the more vulnerable species, such as sea turtles.

**Mr. H.-C. Liew:**

5.68. On a global scale, IUCN (International Union for the Conservation of Nature) recognizes that all sea turtle species are threatened and endangered as all species of sea turtles are listed in CITES Appendix I.[404] However, different populations are in different states of health. Some populations have disappeared, some near extinction, some threatened but a few have shown some apparent recovery.

5.69. The factors that are known to cause decline in sea turtle populations are generally similar but differences do exist in terms of importance for different populations i.e. in different parts of the world, and with changing laws and technologies through time. For example, before the widespread use of trawlers and high seas gill-nets, turtle mortality caused by fishing was minimal but laws were not in force then to protect turtles and their products. Hence, there was widespread hunting of turtles for meat, shell and leather. Eggs were also collected extensively for food. Seas were not as polluted then, hence mortality caused by plastics, tar balls, pollutant induced diseases were not as extensive. Similarly, the degree of importance of factors threatening turtles in different parts of the world does differ. Presently in the United States, shrimp trawlers may be the most important threat as the United States has managed with various laws, education and conservation programmes through the years to reduce mortalities caused by killing of turtles and egg harvesting. In Hawaii, the main threats to their green turtle population is not shrimp trawling but the widespread occurrence of the fibriopapilloma disease. In Indonesia, turtle mortalities caused by commercial

[404] Under the new IUCN criteria, sea turtles are designated as follows: Lepidochelys kempii critically endangered; *Eretmochelys imbricata* critically endangered; *Caretta caretta* endangered; *Chelonia mydas* endangered; *Lepidochelys olivacea* endangered; *Dermochelys coriacea* endangered; *Natator depresus* vulnerable. From CTURTLE List (Internet Source). Marydele Donnelly, 10:47 am 02-10-96, IUCN status of sea turtles.

exploitation of eggs and large scale hunting for the turtle meat markets are significant to be primary causes of population decline.

**Dr. I. Poiner:**

5.70. Sea turtles are very long lived animals that mature at a relatively late age (ca. 30 to 50 years). The interval between breeding events is also extended (ca. 5 to 15 years, depending on the species). While many eggs are produced, and egg predation is high, natural mortality of sub-adults and adults is probably relatively low. Because recruitment to the adult population is low, population modeling studies suggest even small increased mortality rates in adults and sub-adults could impact substantially on population numbers and viability (Crouse et. al., 1987; Crowder, et. al., 1994 Heppell et. al., 1995; Chaloupka and Musick 1997).

5.71. Most sea turtle populations in the world are severely depleted. All seven species are included in CITES Appendixes and the World Conservation Union's (IUCN) Red Data Book lists. Most species have been listed as endangered or threatened under various national legislation. For example, all five species found in the United States waters are listed under the Endangered Species Act of 1973 and the five species found in Australian waters are listed under the Commonwealth Endangered Species Protection Act 1992. Recovery from low population number (if non-natural sources of mortality have been removed) will be slow, and there are no clear documented cases of recovery in the world.

**Table 1:** Sea turtle species that have declined and current anthropogenic threat to sea turtle populations in Thailand (Monanunsap 1997; Limpus 1997; Settle 1995), Malaysia (Chark 1997; Limpus 1997; Liew 1995; Chan et. al., 1998) and United States (Lutcavage et. al., 1997).

| Turtle Species and Threat | Thailand | Malaysia | United States |
|---|---|---|---|
| *Turtle species* | *Documented* | *Population* | *Declines* |
| Loggerhead (Caretta caretta) | | | * |
| Kemp's ridley (Lepidochelys kempi) | | | * |
| Olive ridley (Lepidochelys olivacea) | * | * | |
| Green turtle (Chelonia mydas) | * | * | * |
| Leatherback (Dermochelys coriacea) | * | * | * |
| Hawksbill (Eretmochelys imbricata) | * | * | * |
| *Threat* | | | |
| Habitat alteration and loss | Yes | Yes | |
| Beach armouring (e.g., concrete sea walls) | | | Yes |
| Beach nourishment/sand mining | | | Yes |
| Beach cleaning and beach driving | | | Yes |
| Human presence on beach | | | Yes |
| Artificial light | | | Yes |

| Turtle Species and Threat | Thailand | Malaysia | United States |
|---|---|---|---|
| *Turtle species* | *Documented* | *Population* | *Declines* |
| Boat strikes | | | Yes |
| Dredging and explosive platform removal | | | Yes |
| Feral and domestic animal predation at rookeries | | Yes | Yes |
| Oil pollution | ? | ? | Yes |
| Other pollution sources and entanglement | | | |
| Debris ingestion | Yes | ? | Yes |
| Entanglement | Yes | Yes | Yes |
| Fishing and incidental capture | | | |
| Shrimp trawling | Yes | Yes | Yes |
| Pelagic fishing gear | Yes | Yes | Yes |
| Gill nets | Yes | Yes | Yes |
| Traditional and commercial fishing | | | |
| Egg harvests (legal and illegal) | Yes | Yes | Yes |
| Adult harvests (legal and illegal) | Yes | No | No |

5.72. There is data documenting declines in sea turtle populations and the causes of declines have included: habitat alteration and loss of nesting and foraging habitats, pollution and entanglement, and fishing and incidental capture (Table 1). However, apart from estimates of the incidental capture and mortality of sea-turtles in some shrimp trawl fisheries (United States and Australia) (Henwood and Stuntz, 1987; Poiner and Harris 1996; Robins 1992), estimates of mortalities from boat strike, oil pollution and explosive platform removal mortalities in the United States (Lutcavage et. al., 1997), most mortality factors are not well quantified and it is difficult to rank mortality sources either currently or over time. Furthermore, there is a paucity of information about total population size, age structure, age-specific growth and mortality rates of the turtle populations and turtle distributions (patch dynamics) (Chaloupka and Musick, 1996). Without this, and information on the size and age structure of the segment of the population impacted by the anthropogenic activity, it is difficult to rank the relative impact of the different sources of mortality on sea turtle species and populations.

**1(b) Is it possible to rank the various sources of mortality according to their impact on sea turtle populations? In particular, is it possible to determine the relative role played by past practice of egg harvesting and direct catch as compared to more recent threats at sea (such as those related to modern fishing practices) on the depletion of sea turtle populations? If these determinations are possible, please explain the basis for them, in particular if the studies cited cover sea turtle populations in the countries parties to the dispute.**

**Dr. Scott Eckert:**

5.73. Our perspective on the impacts of various types of mortality to sea turtle populations has evolved as sea turtle population models have become better refined. This process will likely continue; however, based on work by Frazer, Crouse, Crowder, and Heppell, the current perspective is quite different than that of 20 years ago (see review by Chaloupka and Musick, 1996). What has been determined is that it simply is not adequate to concentrate all efforts on protecting reproducing females and eggs as has been the traditional approach to restoring sea turtle populations. While it is obviously necessary to preserve the reproductive capacity of any sea turtle population, no population can be preserved by such methods alone. What both Frazer (1983) and Crouse et. al., (1987) pointed out in their population models is that it is vital to protect large juvenile and sub-adult turtles (so called "stage 3" turtles). Based on the reproductive value curves of Frazer (1983) for loggerheads, these larger turtles represent the highest reproductive value to the population, because significant reproductive investment has gone into their survival. There has not been any data presented to date to suggest that these value curves are not applicable to all species of sea turtle.

5.74. What is particularly critical to understand is that for many species (in particular those that have a neritic existence), stage 3 turtles are often the most subject to trawl fisheries (Crouse et. al., 1987). This is likely because this size class seems to pick foraging habitats that are most strongly correlated with shrimp fisheries. A number of possibilities have been proposed for this overlap. One is that this size class is more subject to chumming, i.e. the large quantity of bycatch discarded by the fishing boats attracts the turtle to scavenge. The other possibility is that this habitat is simply the developmental habitat for this size class of turtles. It is likely that these smaller size classes cannot dive as deeply nor as long as larger mature animals, and their ability to handle large prey is reduced. Thus, they forage in shallower waters with soft bottoms that characterize shrimp habitat.

5.75. It is my belief that nothing is as destructive to any turtle population as incidental mortality caused by fishing operations. Beside the issue of how some fisheries focus mortality on critically important size classes, fishery impacts can cause population declines far more rapidly than mortality associated with beaches. Good examples of this are the loggerhead populations in North Carolina, South Carolina and Georgia. All have declined approximately 80 per cent in 26 years, due primarily to shrimp fishing (NRC, 1990). The crises of the Pacific leatherback, has undoubtedly been due to high mortality in the high seas driftnet fishery and the South American swordfish driftnet and longline fisheries. In this latter case we have seen the world's largest leatherback nesting population (estimated by Pritchard, 1982, to support 75,000 females in 1980) decline more than 95 per cent to less than

1,000 females by 1997 (Sarti et. al., 1996). The rate of decline caused by these impacts are often too fast for us to respond until it is too late. This latter situation is near to my own experience, as I have been working with colleagues from Mexico on one of the primary nesting beaches for the leatherback in Mexico since 1986. We should have seen this terrible decline, but I have described how long a nesting beach must be monitored before a trend will become apparent. We were not concerned that this decline was real until about 5 years ago, and it took 3 more years to confirm our suspicions. Finally it took until this year to determine that the problem lay with gillnetting in South America, and it may be too late to reverse this trend. The rate of decline caused by incidental fisheries mortalities is simply too rapid to respond with mitigation actions.

5.76. With declines associated with egg mortality such problems take substantially longer and they tend to be far more gradual, as was the case in Terengannu, Malaysia. Thus, our ability to detect these declines is enhanced, and while such perturbations to the population may require many years to turn around, there are many techniques available to mitigate (beach protection programmes, *in situ* beach hatcheries, enforcement of egg harvest regulation etc.). In the case of Terengannu, the problem was that when the population decline was identified, too little was understood about population dynamics of turtles to realize that preserving approximately 10 per cent of the harvested eggs was not enough.

**Dr. J. Frazier:**

5.77. Turtles that reproduce contribute to the maintenance of the population; hence, those animals are critical to sustaining the population: without reproduction, there will be extinction, sooner or later. Individuals that are not yet reproducing are not yet contributing to the maintenance of the population. Therefore, turtles that have survived the many and diverse risks over a period of decades, growing to reproductive maturity, are essential to the maintenance of the population, because they are capable of reproducing for many more years (decades, apparently). These adult animals are the immediate key to the future of the population. Animals that are not yet mature, still have to survive more years before they can contribute to the maintenance of the population. The younger a sea turtle is, the more time will have to pass before it will begin breeding; during this time, it will be liable to different sources of mortality, and in the end it may not survive to reproduce.

5.78. Therefore, removing a reproductive female from a population will have an immediate impact on the population, by reducing the amount of reproduction in the population. As there is a high probability that a breeding female will nest for many seasons, removing her will eliminate her reproductive contribution, not only in the short term but also in the long term. In comparison, removing a recently hatched turtle ("hatchling") from a population will have no immediate impact on reproduction. This animal would need to evade different sources of mortality for decades, before it began to reproduce. If we assume - for the sake of argument - that the chances of a hatchling surviving to maturity are 1 in 1,000, then on average the removal of 1,000 hatchlings would have an impact comparable to removing one animal that has just reached maturity, but the reproductive contribution of the hatchling that survived to maturity would not be manifested for more than a decade after it had hatched. Clearly, a healthy population needs individuals in all stages of development and maturity; there must be constant recruitment of young animals into the population to gradually replace the older animals as they die or cease reproducing. Thus, even although removing a hatchling may have no immediate effect on the reproduction of a population, continual removal of hatchlings will produce a situation in which the population would "die of old age", that is, there would be no new animals to replace the old ones.

5.79. The purpose of the above simplified example is to clarify the immediate impacts of different sources of mortality. A very clear explanation of the issues of mortality, survivorship and life stages is given in National Research Council (1990: Chapter 5). In more precise, scientific terms population models provide quantitative ways to evaluate how different sources of recruitment or mortality are likely to impact a population. The studies of Crouse et. al. (1987), Crowder et. al. (1994; 1995), and Heppell (1996a; 1996b) have used population models to predict the relative effects of increasing recruitment or increasing mortality on different phases of the life cycle, and how these relate to conservation priorities. Because basic information is lacking, and only two populations of loggerheads have sufficient data to even begin constructing population models, the work has been limited to loggerheads. While some details of life history parameters will be different with other species and other populations, these models are the best predictive tools that we have at the moment. Furthermore, it is not likely that general conclusions will change, given the general similarity in life history parameters between the different species of marine turtles.

5.80. A concept that is used to integrate the above ideas is that of "reproductive value". According to the work of Crouse et. al. (1987), if the reproductive value of an egg is 1, then the reproductive value of a subadult would be 116 and that of a breeding animal would be 584. These numbers are indices of the relative "value" of an individual, at different stages during its life cycle, for reproduction and maintenance of the population.

5.81. Given the above paradigm, a population would be resistant to mortality concentrated on early life stages (e.g., egg harvesting), but mortality of animals that are reproducing, or just about to reproduce, would have an immediate effect on the level of reproduction in the population, and these deficits would continue for many years. The closer to maturity the turtles get, the more they are worth to the population, and the less it can afford to lose them. On the other hand, continual egg harvesting will in the end result in the collapse of a population, but a few years of total loss of eggs, or moderate levels of egg loss over a period of years would have less impact on the status of a population than would several years of removing breeders - this would be true both in the short term and in the long term.

5.82. Hence, sources of mortality that affect animals that are mature, or nearly mature, have far greater instantaneous impact on the status of the population than taking the same number of eggs or young animals, for they reduce levels of reproduction very quickly. Harvesting of breeding animals, or incidental capture in fishing gear, are examples of these very "costly" sources of mortality. Modern fishing practices have been repeatedly documented to cause mortality; and more specifically, large-sized, especially adult, turtles are known to be caught and drown in shrimp trawls in Australia (Poiner and Harris, 1994; Robins, 1995); Pacific Costa Rica (Arauz, 1990; 1996b); and the United States (National Research Council, 1990).

5.83. Systematic data on present population size, trends in population size, rates and sources of mortality, population structure, and indeed geographic distribution are incomplete for many areas. Hence, many decisions related to conservation and management of sea turtles are made with imperfect knowledge, "splicing" together the best information available, from wherever it can be obtained. While this clearly has drawbacks and limitations, the logic is to adopt a conservative approach so that mistakes in decision making will be "conservative", i.e., least likely to be detrimental to the population. In terms of the present discussion, this means paying special attention to those animals that are of greatest value to the maintenance of the population: in other words, making sure that the animals that are breeding, or close to breeding, are protected. Clearly, all stages of a population are important for its long-term continuity, but where risks are focused on individuals with the greatest reproductive value, an immediate priority is to reduce these risks. This is particularly true of populations that are under risk, because they have been decimated.

5.84. A study was carried out using a population model to evaluate the effect of mortality on different stages of the life cycle of loggerheads from eastern Australia. They found that even if hatchling emergence success could be elevated to 90 per cent (well above the natural average), with the present rate of mortality of adult and subadult females, the population may be headed for extinction in what are the equivalent of 3 turtle generations (Heppell et. al., 1996b). Since a major source of mortality for these turtles is incidental capture in prawn trawls (Poiner and Harris, 1994; Robins, 1995), a priority for the survival of these populations is significantly reducing this risk; Heppell et. al. concluded that the use of TEDs, together with other conservation measures, would be instrumental in the survival of these populations. Similar analyses, giving comparable results, have been carried out for the east coast of the United States, where once again it was concluded that eliminating, or significantly reducing, mortality of breeders and large juveniles in shrimp trawls was critical to the long term survival of these populations (Crouse et. al., 1987; Crowder et. al., 1994; 1995).

5.85. Along the Pacific coast of Central America it is estimated that some 60,000 turtles are caught annually in shrimp trawls; and in Costa Rica, which contributes a third of the total, there may be 24 to 60 per cent mortality (Arauz, 1996a). Systematic data are not available for other populations (neither for the countries involved in this dispute, nor for any others). Thus, these sorts of determinations can only be carried out for other populations by analogies based on existing knowledge of the basic similarities in life history parameters. Until systematic information is available to refute these assumptions, it is generally considered that the most conservative approach is to use the results of the population models as indicators for conservation priorities.

**Mr. M. Guinea:**

5.86. It is difficult to rank the various threats to sea turtles on a global scale. Hence the paradigm of breeding units becomes an essential tool to assess, for that unit, the relative impacts of human pressures. The major threats to each breeding unit must be independently assessed and managed. Sea turtle populations have declined in some countries which have had a long period of intensive egg harvest. As have the populations in countries that have focused on the exploitation of tortoise shell or meat. This has happened regardless of modern fishing practices such as trawling. Other countries with intensive trawling activities have also experienced a decline in their sea turtle numbers. It is the breeding unit of each species that has to be examined. If nesting beaches have been destroyed by commercial or industrial development, then abatement measures should be directed to halt, modify or remove that development. If introduced predators have reduced the productivity of rookeries, then their reduction becomes the target of abatement measures. If adults are being killed while nesting and by set nets off shore, then legislation to protect rookeries and their off shore refuges needs to be enacted or enforced. Should trawling be responsible for the deaths of sea turtles of any age, then management regulations involving reduction of fishing effort, by exclusion areas, closed seasons, vessel and gear size restrictions, limits to tow duration, adoption and enforcement of bycatch reduction devices such as TEDs, should be adopted.

5.87. As indicated, the sources of mortality should be examined in relation to the breeding units. Malaysia and Thailand because of their proximity may share breeding units of some species. Malaysia may share breeding units with the Philippines and Indonesia. India and Pakistan could share breeding units of some species. The United States and Mexico may share breeding units as well. It is speculative to suggest that southeastern United States shares a breeding unit with any of the other countries in the dispute.

**Mr. H.-C. Liew:**

5.88. The truth and accuracy of whatever ranks produced are only as good as the information that is available. There will always be shortcomings of such reports and their reliability will vary from country to country depending on how accurate and extensive the information is made available. Scientific studies are still being conducted to improve on the information but gaps still exist especially on mortalities at sea of hatchlings, juveniles and adults. For example, we still do not know what degree of mortalities is affecting our hatchlings at sea. How many are killed by natural predation or by consuming floating debris like tar balls and styrofoam beads, etc. Attempts have been made to estimate these unknowns by modeling, but these estimates are hinged on assumptions made of what is unknown. Turtle landings, egg production, or turtle catch statistics produced by governments or NGOs are sometimes extrapolated figures, misreported, biased or even falsified. With the absence of any other data, they are often assumed to represent the true situation. The degree of error does vary from country to country depending on expertise available to collect the data and various other limitations. Bearing these limitations in mind, attempts can still be made to rank them when such requests are made.

5.89. In developed countries like the United States where the human population is generally rich, educated, with cheap protein available, they could afford to have strict conservation management policies and effective enforcement. Hence turtle mortalities caused by egg harvesting or killing for meat is negligible (ranked low). With mortalities by these causes removed, mortalities caused by their high technologies like shrimp trawling becomes more prominent and overshadows the other causes (ranked high). In developing countries like India, Pakistan, Malaysia, Thailand, Indonesia, etc., conservation management policies and their enforcement are at a different level. Egg harvesting for consumption is still legal or poorly enforced in many of these countries. Turtles are still being slaughtered for meat in some of them. Fishing technologies like shrimp trawling may not be as developed or still artisanal to be of prime impact on turtle populations. They may even be using other fishing methods which may have a greater impact on sea turtles than shrimp trawling, like the sunken set-net or "pukat pari" in Malaysia.

**Dr. I. Poiner:**

5.90. It is not possible to rank the various sources of mortality according to their impact on sea turtle populations especially with respect to relative role of past practices.

**1(c) A survey of current anthropogenic threats to sea turtle populations in the five countries involved in this dispute would be appreciated. In particular, are anthropogenic threats currently more important at sea or on the nesting grounds? What is the relative impact on sea turtle populations of egg harvests and direct harvesting of sea turtles vs. incidental capture of sea turtles in fishing operations, in particular shrimp trawling? Is this situation similar in different parts of the world? Are different species of sea turtles affected differently?**

**Dr. Scott Eckert:**

5.91. Identifying primary sources of mortality within these countries is quite challenging, primarily because most of these countries (with the exception of the United States) are simply not putting much effort into studying the problem. This seems particularly true for measures of fishery bycatch. The purpose of most government fisheries agencies is to support fisheries with research and technology advances. Generally, measuring bycatch is not a high priority. Hence, bycatch data is rarely gathered. Furthermore with fisheries such as shrimp fishing, the boats are relatively small and numerous, making the application of an observer programme difficult and very expensive. However, without an independent observer programme any data (such as logbook data or even port sampled data) must be suspect. In my experience captains uniformly under-report bycatch data, sometimes unintentionally but often out of concern for what reporting turtle mortalities will mean to their livelihood. It is not surprising to me, therefore, to find a great paucity of rigorous study on incidental take in shrimp fishing in Malaysia, Thailand, Pakistan or India. In the United States there is a large body of information (see NRC, 1990, Crouse et. al., 1992, Murphy and Murphy, 1989), driven primarily by the requirements of the Endangered Species Act. All that is generally reported in these other 4 countries are anecdotal or very limited reports, most gathered during interviews with fishermen.

5.92. In the United States threats to sea turtles are somewhat species and regionally dependent; however, a few generalizations can be made. For green, loggerhead and Kemp's ridley turtles in the Atlantic, the most serious threat was shrimp trawling (NMFS and USFWS 1992, 1991a, 1991b, NRC, 1990). This threat has been well documented and is probably indisputable (Maley et. al., 1994, NRC, 1990). The requirement that TEDs be utilized in all waters at all times has reduced this threat. At this time the most significant threat has to be enforcement of existing regulations, and the scope of this problem is minor when compared to the previous unlimited incidental take. Also, of significant importance to green turtles and hawksbills occurring within the US insular Pacific Ocean (except in Hawaii) and Caribbean is the direct killing of turtles. (NMFS and USFWS 1996a, 1996e). However, the scale of this problem is substantially less than in other countries of the region. The primary threats to olive ridleys in the United States is the due to incidental take of turtles in the Hawaiian-based longline fishery (NMFS and USFWS, 1996f). Threats to the leatherback in US waters include the shrimp fishery on the Atlantic seaboard, the Hawaii longline fishery and gillnet fishing in Northern California.

5.93. In Malaysia, it is apparent that egg harvest is still a serious problem for green, hawksbill and possibly leatherback turtles, despite regulations designed to limit such harvest (Eckert, 1993, and paragraphs 5.34 and 5.75). During research I conducted in 1989 in Terengannu, Malaysia, leatherback and green turtle eggs were openly sold in the local markets despite their protected status. Trawling has also been described as a threat to turtles residing off Terengannu, though this report may be out-of-date to the current situation (Chan, et. al., 1988). However, in 1991, Chan reported that incidental capture in fishing gear "is now recognized at one of the most serious threats to the survival of the remaining sea turtles in Malaysia." (Chan, 1991). I have no other information on the situation in Malaysia, but based on my general experience with trawl fisheries and sea turtles, I would not be surprised that any area in southeast Asia which support trawl fishing also has incidental catch of sea turtles.

5.94. In Thailand there appear to be a number of threats to sea turtle populations, the most serious appear to be shrimp trawling, killing of turtles and taking of eggs on nesting beaches (Eckert, 1993, Hill, 1991, Hill, 1992, Chantrapornsyl 1997). There also seems be problems with enforcement of trawling regulations (Hill, 1991, Hill, 1992). Both green and hawksbill populations in Thailand are severely depleted (Eckert, 1993, Chantrapornsyl, 1997).

5.95. As described earlier, there are a host of anthropogenic threats to sea turtles in India, including the killing of nesting females, harvest of eggs and incidental mortality associated with shrimp fishing. However, the large numbers of olive ridley killed by legal and illegal trawling operations is extraordinary and must represent the single largest threat to sea turtle populations in India.

**Dr. J. Frazier:**

5.96. Recent reviews of the topic of anthropogenic threats are provided by Eckert (1995) and Lutcavage et. al., (1997). For several of the countries involved, there simply are no (or very little) systematic data.

*India*: Kar and Bhaskar (1982) reported the consumption of turtles and eggs in most coastal states and Union Territories. In the south of Tamil Nadu and West Bengal there is a long history of direct exploitation of turtles (Frazier, 1980; Kar and Bhaskar, 1982; Silas et al., 1983b; 1983c; 1985; Pandav et. al., 1997); although illegal, these activities persist in the Bay of Bengal (Pandav et. al., 1997). For over a decade incidental capture and drowning in fishing gear has been known to be an important source of mortality of adult turtles, particularly in the Bay of Bengal; and trawlers, specifically shrimp trawlers, in Tamil Nadu, Andhra Praesh, Orissa and West Bengal have consistently been singled out for impacts that they cause (e.g., Kar and Bhaskar, 1982: 367, 368; Silas et. al., 1983a; 1983b; 1983c; 1985; James et. al., 1989; 1991; Dash and Kar, 1990; Mohanty-Hejmadi and Sahoo, 1994; Department of Fisheries et.

al., 1996). Sand mining from beaches and coastal development have also been identified as threats for over a decade (Kar and Bhaskar, 1982).

Recent reviews identify development along the beach front (roads, buildings, tourist resorts), development of capital-intensive fishing operations (jetties and fish processing centers) and military installations, casuarina (Australian pine) plantations (which often make nesting impossible because of the dense cover of trunks and needles), incidental capture in fishing gear (notably trawl nets) and artificial lighting (Behera, 1997a; Pandav et. al., 1997; Choudhury, in press). With a long tradition of an active civilian population and free speech, there have been countless articles in the popular press, as well as initiatives from NGOs, focused on these various anthropogenic threats to sea turtles - particularly the problems of incidental capture in mechanized fishing boats, viz. trawlers and gill netters (e.g., Anon, 1982; Wright, 1984; Anon; 1985; Anon, 1986; Anon, 1992; West, 1995; Anon, 1996; Anon, 1997a; 1997b; 1997c; 1997d; 1997e; 1997f; 1997g; 1997h; 1997i; 1997j; Behera, 1997b; 1997c; Mishra, 1997; Panda, 1997, Rai, 1997; Sridhar, 1997a; 1997b).

*Malaysia*: Intensive, long-term egg harvest has occurred up until recently at most nesting beaches on both East and West Malaysia, and has been clearly identified as having been a major threat (de Silva, 1982; Siow and Moll, 1982; Mortimer, 1990; Chan, 1991; Eckert, 1993; Limpus, 1994; 1995; Chan and Liew, 1996a; 1996b). Hunting of turtles, namely in Sabah, has also been identified (de Silva, 1982; Eckert, 1993). Coastal development and habitat loss have been pointed out for some time (Siow and Moll, 1982; Leh, 1989; Mortimer, 1990; Chan, 1991; Chan and Liew, 1996a); this involves both terrestrial and marine environments, for example light and oil contamination at sea (Eckert, 1993; Chan and Liew, 1996a). Incidental capture in fishing gear, including drift/gill nets, long lines, traps, trawls (especially prawn trawls) and other gear (as well as dynamiting in Sabah) has also been identified for years (de Silva, 1982; Siow and Moll, 1982; Chan et al., 1988; Leh, 1989; Mortimer, 1990; Chan, 1991; Eckert, 1993; Chan and Liew, 1996a; 1996b; Suliansa et. al., 1996). Improper hatchery practices have also been singled out (Chan, 1991; Chan and Liew, 1996a).

The most recent review of Malaysian sea turtles (Liew, in press) lists several threats including: direct harvesting for tortoise-shell and leather, over-harvesting eggs, poaching, inadequate hatchery techniques, incidental captures in fishing gear and coastal and offshore development for tourism and industrialization.

*Pakistan*: At Hawksbay, Karachi, there have long been problems with development of weekend houses, which usurp nesting habitat along the beach. In addition, adult turtles have been washing up dead for decades. Kabraji and Firdous (1984) reported stranded turtles, especially during the monsoon. They had no direct evidence of cause of death, but proposed shark attack, as well as "Drowning in fishermen's nets as part of incidental catch, Poisoning by pollutants such as oil, Disease". Firdous (1989) reported that 69 dead turtles were counted on the beach between June 1983 and June 1989. Most of the strandings were documented in the month of June, when tides and waves were the highest; 65 of the specimens were green turtles. There have been no systematic studies of this problem, but the evidence matches trawl-related strandings in other parts of the world. More recently, commercial trade, poaching of eggs, accidental capture in fishing nets, extensive shore-line development, disturbance and pollution have all been identified as threats (Asrar, 1995?).

The little information available from Baluchistan indicates that direct exploitation has been a serious source of mortality, but there seems to be no recent information. Groombridge et. al., (1988) reported commercial exploitation (thought to be green turtles) from remote beaches in Baluchistan. The levels of harvesting were claimed to be many thousands of turtles (mainly breeders) in a year; a short-term exportation to Japan was evidently involved, but there was also evidence that much of the exploitation was for local consumption. This all occurred in contravention of provincial legislation. As the area is remote, and much of the exploitation yield products is not recorded in normal statistics, it is next to impossible to know what happened historically or even what has happened in recent years. Groombridge (1989), later reported that "incidental catch appears to be a problem in surrounding waters." He suggested that the nesting colony in the Sonmiani region of Las Bela may have been extirpated by heavy exploitation.

*Thailand*: Harvest of eggs of most (all) species is known to be have been intensive for many years (Lekagul and Damman, 1977; Gilbert, 1981; Phasuk, 1982; Polunin and Nuitja, 1982; Hill, 1992; Eckert, 1993; Stuart and Cartin, 1994; Limpus, 1995; Settle, 1995). The same is true with the harvest of turtles of most (all) species (Lekagul and Damman, 1977; Gilbert, 1981; Phasuk, 1982; Eckert, 1993; Limpus, 1995; Settle, 1995). Coastal development and loss of nesting and feeding habitat is another widespread threat (Lekagul and Damman, 1977; Gilbert, 1981; Polunin and Nuitja, 1982; Settle, 1995). Incidental capture in fishing gear, including drift nets, purse seines, push seines, and notably trawlers, as well as cyanide and bombing, has been identified as a major threat (Lekagul and Damman, 1977; Gilbert, 1981; Phasuk, 1982; Polunin and Nuitja, 1982; Hill, 1992; Eckert, 1993; Stuart and Cartin, 1994; Settle, 1995). Inadequate management, notably headstarting and hatcheries, is also a problem (Stuart and Cartin, 1994; Settle, 1995 (see Donnelly, 1994; Mortimer, 1995; Crouse, 1996; Heppell et al., 1996a)). There have been notices in the popular press about turtles being caught and killed by trawlers (Matchima, 1996; Walakkamon, 1996). The most recent review of the status of marine turtles in Thailand identifies commercial exploitation of sea turtles and their eggs, coastal development, heavy fishing activities (trawling, gill nets, and long lines) (Supot, in press).

*United States*: Intense, direct exploitation of turtles, especially greens, in the continental United States ended in the mid 1970's, after decimation of these populations (Witzell, 1994), but evidently continues in many of the island territories of the Pacific (Eckert, 1993). A recent detailed analysis of anthropogenic threats for the Gulf of Mexico and Atlantic concluded that by far the most important source of mortality was incidental capture in shrimp trawls (National Research Council, 1990). Other threats include beach erosion, beach armouring, beach nourishment, beach cleaning and utilization, artificial lighting, gill nets, pound nets, fish trawls, traps, long lines, and a variety of other fishing gear, dredging actives, boat collisions, use of explosives underwater, ingestion of plastics and other contaminants (Lutcavage et. al., 1997). Oceanic drift nets and debris are of major concern, notably in the Pacific

(Balazs, 1982; 1985; Balazs and Wetherall, 1991; Laist, 1995). The high incidence of fibropapilloma tumors - notably in Florida and Hawaii, and the devastating impacts on sea turtles has become a major concern, and there are suspicions that marine contamination is involved (George, 1997).

5.97. Without a doubt, reproductive and near-reproductive animals are most critical to the maintenance of a population. As sea turtles spend the vast majority of their lives in the sea, they are more subject to threats at sea in terms of the time spent at sea; these threats can be direct harvest (e.g., in nets), incidental capture (e.g., in fishing gear) or effects of contamination and marine pollution. However, while sea turtles are at their nesting grounds, they are concentrated in time and space, and generally this attracts concentrations of predators and exploiters. Hence, in general, they are more liable to predation while at their nesting grounds. However, the importance of a threat depends not on where mortality occurs, but how that mortality affects the population. As explained above, a few hundred eggs and hatchlings are less important to a population than is one breeding adult.

5.98. Different sources of mortality produce the same effects on the same stages of the life cycle: killing a reproductively mature turtle at sea for its meat, killing it as it comes to a nesting beach to lay eggs, or drowning it in a shrimp trawl means the same thing to the population - the removal of a breeding animal. In terms of the dynamics of the population, it really does not matter what killed the turtle, but rather how many were killed.

5.99. What is important is the life stage where the mortality occurs. One female may lay several clutches, each more than 100 eggs, and this she may do several times during one nesting season; and she can potentially nest for a period of decades. Thus, taking every single egg that she lays over a period of two nesting seasons, say, 1,000 eggs, means stopping her reproduction for two nesting seasons, but not completely. She has the potential (if she is not killed by any one of a variety of threats, both human and non-human) to return to the nesting beach on subsequent seasons and lay more eggs. If she can avoid mortality, she might successfully nest during 10 to 20 nesting seasons, each time laying perhaps 500 eggs. In this case, a female that lost 1,000 eggs in her first two nesting seasons, could successfully lay 5,000 to 10,000 eggs. What is critical, is that the turtle be able to survive to continue reproducing.

5.100. Fishing operations cause mortality - albeit incidental - which impacts large turtles, including those that are breeders and close to breeding. Shrimp trawling is one such fishing operation, which causes incidental mortality on large sized turtles (those that live in coastal waters). The special concern with shrimp trawling stems from several points. Because shrimp are generally most concentrated in coastal waters, trawling tends to concentrate in coastal waters (this occurs routinely, despite regulations and bans on trawling in these waters). Around the world, shrimp trawl fleets have grown faster than the shrimp stocks can sustain levels of exploitation, so the activity is regularly overcapitalized, and investments find decreasing returns. Shrimp trawling is targeted as a valuable export product, for which there is generally intense competition. Hence, shrimp trawling generally is carried out with considerable intensity, resulting in large areas of the benthos having the trawl pulled across them repeatedly. (One clear exception to the above paradigm is Australia, where shrimp fishery is closed entry (Tucker et. al., 1997), so the intensity of fishing effort has not spiraled out of control, as is the case for nearly every other fishing ground in the world.)

5.101. Where shrimp trawling is intense, and concentrated in coastal waters, there is a high probability that sea turtles will be caught and accidentally drowned. If these fishing activities occur near to breeding grounds (nesting beaches or mating areas) or in the migratory routes used by turtles to get to and from the breeding areas, or in feeding grounds, there is an extremely high probability that large numbers of turtles will be caught and drown. Where this happens, the numbers of turtles that are breeders and near-breeders killed incidentally can be relatively large. If this sort of operation continues, it can decimate a healthy population, make it impossible for a recovering population to recover, or even finally exterminate a population.

5.102. In terms of the general demographic phenomena, described above, the situation is similar in different parts of the world. However, each sea turtle population may have specific sources and intensities of mortality, at different times in the life cycle, which may occur at different places in the geographic distribution of the individuals, as they pass through different stages of the life cycle. Put another way, a dead turtle in Louisiana is just as dead as a dead turtle in Sabah.

5.103. Different stocks are under different situations, and different species have variations in the details of their life history. As such, each one may be affected somewhat differently by different types of mortality. For example, species that mature faster than others (ridleys for example) should be able to sustain relatively more mortality in the breeding adults, than species that require more time to mature. Nonetheless, there will be certain constants: increased mortality of reproductive, or near reproductive animals, will have more affect on the population than the same level of mortality on eggs or newly hatched turtles.

**Mr. M. Guinea:**

5.104. Threats to sea turtles have been compiled for the various countries. Few have ranked the order of the perceived threats. The ranking is as indicated in the references listed. It is unclear if the authors would give their consent to such ranking given the nature of the question.

5.105. The United States lists (Lutcavage et al., 1997): (i) beach modification by armouring etc.; (ii) Boat strikes; (iii) dredging and explosive platform removal; (iv) depredation of nests by animals; (v) pollution: oil, plastics and debris; (vi) incidental capture in fishing gear particularly shrimp trawls.

5.106. Thailand lists (Monanunsap, 1997): (i) the overuse of marine turtles and their eggs as sea food in the past; (ii) the sale of marine turtle products to tourists and for international trade; (iii) the deterioration of nesting habitats and marine pollution (light and plastics); (iv) the incidental capture of marine turtles in commercial fishing operations offshore.

5.107. Pakistan Lists (WWF, Marine Turtles of Pakistan): (i) Commercial trade for turtle skin, shell medicines and cosmetics; (ii) destruction of eggs by predators and poachers; (iii) accidental capture of turtles in fishing nets; (iv) extensive shore-line development, human disturbance and pollution.

5.108. Malaysia lists (*Threats to Sea Turtles*, http://www.opmt.edu.my/seatru/cons2.htm): (i) beach front development; (ii) heavy egg exploitation; (iii) incidental capture in set nets, drift nets, trawls and longlines; (iv) pollution (both light and industrial).

5.109. India lists (IUCN, 1995): (i) direct mortality: intentional catch by local and artisanal fisheries and on commercial long-lines; (ii) indirect mortality: unintentional catch causing drowning in trawls and gill nets; (iii) habitat degradation: beach destruction due to human activities, sand mining. Walking and driving litter and surface obstructions, disturbance by residential and commercial lights. Coastline modification due to construction etc. Beach destruction due to coastal erosion. Feeding, resting and developmental habitat destruction due to pollution and development; (iv) pollution: plastics and debris in the sea cause entanglement and drowning and death following ingestion; (v) boat collision; (vi) hatcheries: poor management of egg hatcheries; (vii) lack of information on sea turtle population sizes, migrations and natural and anthropogenic mortality levels hampers effective planning.

5.110. Human threats to sea turtles depend on the intensity and duration of the impacting activity. It is difficult to generalize between ocean and shore based threats. However, once the nesting beach has been lost the breeding unit has lost a critical habitat. As long as the nesting beach is intact there is a chance for seriously depleted populations to recover, should they be given enough protection.

5.111. Once eggs and adults are targeted as a commercial commodity, the breeding unit can suffer serious and rapid decline. Essentially, sea turtles are easy to capture and their eggs are easy to locate. Incidental capture is a relative modern term. Before the 1960's sea turtles were actively harvested in most countries in which they occurred. Modern fishing practices through effective management, should have little impact on sea turtles. This is embedded into the ethos of responsible fishing.

5.112. The species most at risk from shrimp trawling in the United States are the benthic feeding loggerhead, Kemp's ridley and to some extent the green (Robins, 1995). In Australia, flatback, olive ridley and loggerhead are the species most commonly caught in shrimp trawls of the Northern Prawn Fishery (Poiner et. al., 1995). However in the Queensland Trawl fishery, the order changes to loggerheads, greens, and flatbacks, olive ridley and hawksbills (Robins, 1995). The differences may be attributable to the species present in the different trawl fields and composition of habitats and depths on each of the trawl fields. Green turtles will be caught if the trawl field contains seagrass or abundant growths of algae. Hawksbills will be more commonly encountered amongst soft corals and algae. Leatherbacks are seldom caught in shrimp trawls.

**Mr. H.-C. Liew:**

5.113. The major anthropogenic threats to sea turtles are:

(a) Sea turtles are hunted for their meat and other products. Even though sea turtles are endangered and various countries have regulations to protect them, the hunting of adults and juveniles is still rampant. Some countries still permit such activities by imposing quotas but the quota numbers are in the thousands per year, often far exceeding what is sustainable considering the other threats facing sea turtles today. Very often, the numbers hunted illegally are estimated to be 2 to 5 times higher than the legal quota. Enforcement is generally very poor and difficult. All countries party to the dispute have banned such activities but their neighbouring countries like Costa

Rica and Indonesia still condone hunting which invariably affect their population of sea turtles also.

(b) Incidental catch in fishing gears, e.g. shrimp trawlers, high seas gill-nets and other fishing gears. The impact of shrimp trawling on sea turtles appears to be the most important factor today threatening sea turtles in the United States. Thousands of olive-ridleys are also killed in Orissa, India, each year which conservationists attributed largely to shrimp trawlers. Incidental captures of sea turtles in shrimp and fish trawlers are also known to occur in Malaysia and Thailand; however, there is insufficient studies conducted to survey the extent of such impacts. Numerous other fishing gears are also known to kill turtles in Malaysia (Suliansa et al., in press), which, in some locations, appear more important than shrimp trawlers.

(c) A fair amount of turtles are killed or drowned in man-made structures (e.g., oil-rigs) or by speedboats and other powered watercrafts. Many of these go unreported except for stranding of dead turtles with lacerations on them. However, the number of turtles that do get stranded and reported is only a small portion of the true situation. Such problems occur in all countries with turtles.

(d) No estimates are available on the mortality caused by marine pollution to hatchlings, juveniles and adults. There are numerous reports of plastic debris in the stomach of autopsied stranded sea turtles, especially leatherbacks. Large numbers of hatchlings are probably killed or weakened due to the accidental feeding on marine debris like tar balls, styrofoam beads, plastics, etc. This is because hatchlings aggregate at oceanic drift lines where floating seaweed and other food items are found. Unfortunately, these are the same locations marine debris accumulate. Due to the scarcity of food items in the ocean surface, hatchlings would often attempt to feed on any small items that drift by.

(e) Mortality caused by diseases that may be anthropogenically induced, e.g., fibriopapillomas, is recent but spreading fast. It has affected several populations in the world from the Caribbean to the Indo-Pacific. Among the severe cases are the turtle populations in Hawaii.

(f) Trawlers, fish bombing, pollution, land reclamation and development are continuously destroying the feeding grounds of sea turtles. Large areas of sea-grass beds and coral reefs have been damaged or lost by these activities. All the countries concerned face these problems.

(g) Similarly, nesting beaches of sea turtles also face severe threats from beach front development, coastal protection structures like seawalls, land reclamation, sand mining, etc.

(h) Losses due to unsuitable or poorly managed hatchery practices also occur. Some of these losses can be very significant especially if hatcheries are the primary conservation effort practiced in those countries. Some Asian countries still practice the wrong conservation strategy of withholding newly emerged hatchlings for many days, or months to "harden" them before release, often termed as "headstarting".

(i) Commercial exploitation of eggs both legal and illegal is also still rampant especially in the poorer and developing nations like in some parts of Malaysia, Indonesia, Thailand, India, Maldives, Australia, Latin American nations and many others (Limpus, 1997).

5.114. The relative impact on sea turtle populations through egg harvests and direct harvesting of sea turtles vs. incidental capture of sea turtles in fishing operations, in particular shrimp trawling varies in different parts of the world. As mentioned earlier, egg harvesting and turtle hunting are well controlled in the United States, hence do not pose a major problem. Incidental capture in fishing operations, therefore, stands out as a major threat due to the large number of modern and efficient shrimping fleets, supported by the high demand for shrimps in the United States. The same cannot be said for developing countries in Asia. Even though these countries do have turtle conservation programmes, are signatories to CITES, and have laws to protect turtles, the level of enforcement can be quite different. Some of these countries even allow varied levels of commercial egg harvest or even killing of turtles for meat. Moreover, these countries do not have good statistics on turtle mortalities caused by fishing or shrimp trawling but records are available for commercial egg and turtle harvests where legal. Yet, many may go unreported. Thus, their reports would show egg harvest or turtle harvest as major causes.

5.115. The relative importance of threats does vary from species to species. For example, hawksbill turtles are hunted for their shell, hence largely decimated because of this activity. Leatherback turtles are largely pelagic, not known to rest on the seabed and feed primarily on jellyfish. Hence, threats caused by high seas drift nets and discarded plastic bags may be more important compared to shrimp trawling. Loggerhead turtles, Kemps ridleys and olive ridleys feed on crustaceans and shellfish found on the seabed, often in the same areas where shrimps are found, hence are most susceptible to being caught in shrimp trawlers. Green turtles forage primarily over seagrass and algal beds. Fishing and boating activities, and pollution in these shallow areas become more of a threat. However, for all these species of turtles, they are also vulnerable in the waters off their nesting grounds during the nesting season where they aggregate in numbers depending on the size of the nesting population. If some form of protection is accorded to these coastal areas during the nesting season, they may help reduce the threat caused by fishing.

**Dr. I. Poiner:**

5.116. I am only qualified to comment on current threat to sea turtle populations in the United States, Malaysia and Thailand. It appears that all sea turtle populations of all species in the three countries are severely depleted, and/or subject to over-harvesting and/or excessive incidental mortality. Anthropogenic threats in the three countries are similar (see Table 1, paragraph 5.71) but their relative importance is different. Most notably the indigenous harvests of eggs and adults in South East Asia is an important source of mortality not present in the United States, especially since the same stock will be fished in several countries in South East Asia. For example, the Malaysian green turtle population in Sarawak which has declined >90 per cent in egg production since the 1930s and is still under threat despite Malaysian conservation measures. One reason for the lack of recovery is egg harvests and adult fishing in neighbouring Indonesia since they are likely to be the same stock (Limpus, 1997).

5.117. As stated above, apart from estimates of the incidental capture and mortality of sea turtles in shrimp trawl fisheries (United States and Australia), and estimates of mortalities from boat strike, oil pollution and explosive platform removal mortalities in the United States, many mortality factors are not well quantified. It is not possible to estimate the full range of impacts on a stock and this is needed to assess population stability and the relative importance of different anthropogenic threats at sea or on the nesting grounds. None of the mortality factors are well quantified for south east Asia sea turtle populations.

5.118. In the United States the incidental capture of sea turtles in shrimp nets was identified as the major source of anthropogenic mortality for loggerhead, Kemp's ridley and green turtles when compared to other known sources of mortality (Henwood and Stuntz, 1987). However, there is no quantitative data on the various mortality factors in Malaysia and Thailand to make this assessment. In Australia, shrimp trawling has been identified as an important but not a key source of mortality for the six species of turtles that occur in Australian waters (loggerhead, olive ridley, green turtle, leatherback and hawksbill). The assessment is based on robust estimates of the incidental capture of sea turtles in shrimp nets (Poiner and Harris, 1996; Robins, 1995; Anon, 1997) and a variety of numerical population models (dynamic stage-structured and stochastic simulation models) for green and loggerhead turtles developed to help design and evaluate conservation policy and management (Chaloupka and Musick, 1997). Furthermore, there is significant variation in the relative catch and mortality rates for the different sea turtle species both within and between Australian prawn trawl fisheries (Poiner and Harris, 1996; Robins, 1995).

**1(d) Is it possible to differentiate between shrimp trawl and other fishing gear in terms of the threat they represent to marine turtles? Are there regional differences in this respect?**

**Dr. S. Eckert:**

5.119. By far the most serious threat to sea turtle stocks living in coastal environments are trawl fisheries. Trawling is particularly serious in that there seems to be a cumulative effect of capture stress. As a trawl net approaches a turtle's response is to flee directly away from the net (Ogren et. al., 1977). Observers suggest that the "doors" which hold the nets open act as "blinders" and they keep the turtle from veering away. Thus, the turtles swim directly in advance of the net until they are exhausted and are overtaken (Ogren et. al., 1977). While most species of turtles are capable of long term submergence in excess of 1 hour (the notable exception to this is the leatherback who routinely only makes 12-15 minutes dives (Eckert et. al., 1996), the exhaustion and depletion of oxygen stores during "the chase" renders them highly susceptible to asphyxiation. Even if the turtle escapes it may be physiologically stressed and subsequent captures may kill the animal (Stabenau, 1991). Another problem for turtles in areas that are bottom trawled is that such fishing methods degrade the habitats many species of turtle rely on as foraging areas (Dayton et. al., 1995). If seagrases are present, such fisheries uproot the sea grass and destroy the area for green turtle foraging or habitat for mollusca and crustaceans relied upon by loggerhead or the ridley species. Further, the constant perturbation may reduce the quantity of prey species that neritic carnivores, such as loggerhead and ridley turtles, rely on for food.

5.120. A close second to trawl fisheries in terms of potential to harm sea turtle populations are gillnet fisheries. Gillnets are very effective at drowning turtles in large numbers. While high-seas driftnets are banned by international agreement (primarily due to the massive bycatch problems caused by this fishery), coastal gillnets are still in use in many places. This type of fishery has probably been the primary cause of the recent decline in the Pacific leatherback population (Eckert and Sarti, 1997). Unlike trawling, there is no known solution to the incidental turtle bycatch problem with gillnets.

5.121. Longline fisheries are not entirely as destructive to turtles as the previous fishery style; however, they do have a large bycatch of turtles, and it is the largest growing fishing method in the world. The reason it may not be quite as destructive is that the drowning rate (=acute mortality) is lower for this type of fishery. However, there is data suggesting that post release mortality is substantial. (Balazs and Pooley, 1994, Aguilar et. al., 1992, 1993, Dayton et. al., 1995). Purse seine fishing does catch turtles, but the mortality rate of such fisheries is negligible for turtles (S. Eckert, unpub data).

**Dr. J. Frazier:**

5.122. The characteristics of the gear - where, when and how it is used - will determine the organisms that are likely to be impacted by it. For example, gear that is used in coastal waters will affect the turtles when they are in coastal waters; gear that is used on the high seas will affect the turtles when they are in the open sea. Many types of modern fishing activities are known to have deleterious effects on a wide variety of marine organisms, including sea turtles. Modern fishing techniques, such as, drift nets, long lines and trawls are responsible for incidental catch and mortality. Because of its nature, bottom trawling is known to cause major impacts on non-target species because it is an unselective method of fishing (Norse, 1997a). Shrimp trawls are notoriously unselective, and on a world level it has been estimated that they are responsible for more than a third of all bycatch (Alverson et. al., 1994). Hence, shrimp trawls not only catch and drown turtles, but they are responsible for an extraordinary amount of bycatch and discards in world fisheries: it is estimated that approximately 10 million tons of bycatch result from shrimp trawling. This level of environmental perturbation carries with it many other risks, both ecologically and socially. In the end, any of these gear used where there is a likelihood of incidentally capturing turtles poses a threat to the animals, and when a population is at risk all of these sources of mortality must be drastically reduced.

5.123. Since individual marine turtles migrate and disperse over vast distances, they are vulnerable to incidental capture in many different regions. The environmental and social impacts of shrimp trawls are most acute in the tropics (Alverson et. al., 1994) where the intensity of trawling is high, bycatch ratios are high, human populations are high, human food needs are high, dependency on fish is high, proportion of trawled catch which is exported is high, and local availability to traditional fisheries resources is declining. For this reason, there have been calls, nationally and internationally, to ban this form of exploitation of common marine resources (O'Riordan, 1994; SAMUDRA, 1994).

**Mr. M. Guinea:**

5.124. Few quantitative data are available on the numbers of sea turtles caught in fish trawls, set nets (Chan et. al., 1987), long lines and driftnets (Eckert and Sarti,

1997). Sea turtle mortality in shrimp trawls increases with trawl duration (Poiner et. al., 1990). Short tows of less than 60 minutes pose little threat to sea turtles. Trawls lasting longer than 60 minutes have a proportionally greater influence on sea turtle mortality. Set nets may be set for any length of time. This depends on the target species. Nets set for shark products may be checked only once a day. Others may be set for several hours to coincide with a tidal stream. A single bottom-set, large-mesh, gill-net killed in excess of three hundred turtles in four days of netting in Northern Australia (Guinea and Chatto, 1992). This was approximately equal to the expected annual mortality of sea turtles in the entire Australian Northern Prawn (Shrimp) Fleet which trawls along more than 10,000 km of coastline each season (Poiner et. al., 1990).

5.125. There will be regional differences between shrimp trawl and other fishing gear in terms of the threat they represent to sea turtles depending on the species of sea turtle present and the nature of the nets being used (see paragraph 5.124).

**Mr. H.-C. Liew:**

5.126. Sea turtles are threatened by numerous fishing methods ranging from hook and lines, drift or gill nets, purse seines, trawlers, fish traps, fish bombing, etc. How much of a threat are they depends on whether the fishing activity occurs during the period and in regions where significant numbers of turtles occur, e.g. feeding and nesting grounds, migration routes. It also depends on whether the gear or methods cause severe injury or entangle the turtle, resulting in drowning. The differing habits of the different species during feeding, resting, swimming, etc, can also influence the threats by different gears. For example, leatherback turtles are known to feed primarily on jellyfish in the pelagic zone of deep oceans. They would be less likely to be caught by shrimp trawling but are more susceptible to high seas gill-nets and longlines.

**Dr. I. Poiner:**

5.127. Since there is no quantitative data on the mortality from other fishing gear on sea turtles, it is not possible to make this assessment. However, given the variation in the type and size of the different bottom trawl and other fisheries around the globe there is likely to be significant regional differences in this respect.

**Question 2: Conservation measures**

**2(a) Since most countries regulate the direct exploitation of sea turtles and sea turtle products (quotas and/or prohibitions on egg harvests and sea turtle catch, for instance), can one consider that such direct exploitation no longer represents a threat to sea turtle populations? What is the impact of these regulatory measures on sea turtle conservation efforts? Are you aware of any country where such regulatory measures are in place, but where sea turtles and their products are nevertheless still excessively exploited?**

**Dr. S. Eckert:**

5.128. Direct exploitation is still a serious problem for turtles in the countries involved in this dispute. In the United States the problem is highly reduced, but the taking of eggs, killing of nesting females and in a few cases netting of foraging turtles still take place. Most of such illegal take is limited to US territories in the Western Pacific (American Samoa, Guam, the Northern Marianas Islands) and the Caribbean (Puerto Rico, US Virgin Islands) (NMFS and USFWS, 1996a-f, pers. obs.). Sometimes such illegal take is by foreign fishing vessels that stop at uninhabited islands and atolls within US jurisdiction (NMFS and USFWS, 1996a-f). Generally, however, direct harvest is a minor problem in the US when compared to other countries.

5.129. In Malaysia, it is clear that illegal egg harvest continues at a level which threatens sea turtle populations (Eckert, 1993). In Thailand, both the illegal taking of eggs and the killing of nesting females and foraging turtles continues (Hill, 1991, 1992; Chantrapornsyl, 1997). In India, the direct harvest of eggs and meat is apparently still a problem. I have no information on sea turtle threats in Pakistan. Thailand, Malaysia, India, and the United States (and likely Pakistan) have regulations in place to protect sea turtles and their habitats, yet these stock are still stressed by anthropogenic sources; thus it is clear that lack of wildlife law enforcement is a problem. It is generally clear that more resources need to be applied to protecting turtles than is currently being done in all countries.

**Dr. J. Frazier:**

5.130. To put this question in context, it is useful to reflect on the contemporary situation regarding hallucinogenic drugs, such as cocaine, crack, hashish, marijuana, and opium, to name just a few. In theory, most modern states have strict controls on the import, export, sale and consumption of some, if not all of these drugs. Nonetheless, illegal commerce in these items is probably higher now than it has ever been in the history of the planet. Man-made laws do not necessarily result in a significant modification of the human activities that they are meant to regulate. If drug trafficking cannot be controlled - despite the fact that it is an international priority, there is little chance that the illegal use of sea turtles and their products will be controlled.

5.131. Depending on the place and situation, direct exploitation of sea turtles (legal or illegal) may or may not represent a major risk to the survival of the populations. Little systematic information seems to be available from Thailand, but what is known indicates that direct exploitation on eggs and turtles has resulted in major declines, and that the practice continues. Since these populations are evidently badly decimated, any source of mortality - especially concentrated on animals that are breeding or near breeding - will reduce the chances of population recovery.

5.132. Up until recently, there has been sustained direct exploitation on most nesting populations in both East and West Malaysia. However, recently enacted, strict regulations for fuller protection are reported to have stopped, or greatly reduced direct exploitation. Depending on how effectively the regulations are observed and enforced, specific populations may or may not be under continued risk from direct exploitation. In Pakistan, there is very little information from the remote Province of Baluchistan, but what is available indicates that direct exploitation - especially on breeders - has been, and continues to be, a major risk to these populations. There is apparently no significant direct exploitation in Sind. Strict laws and regulations may be observed in some parts of India, but there are continuing accounts of heavy predation on turtles at sea, off the coast of Gahirmatha, Orissa (Pandav et. al., 1997).

Egg harvesting surely also continues, along vast stretches of remote beach. However, there are no quantitative data. Illegal exploitation of turtle eggs may occur occasionally in the southeast of the continental United States, but it is thought to be minimal (National Research Council, 1990). Persistent exploitation (illegal) on turtles and eggs apparently continues in some Pacific islands, and the populations may be so small in some cases that this mortality may be a major risk (Eckert, 1993).

5.133. Since conservation involves the integration of biological information with social and political actions, impacts important to conservation can (and must) be evaluated in the organisms involved (in the present case, sea turtles) as well as in the societies that interact with these organisms and/or the environments in which they live. Hence, impacts of regulatory measures must be evaluated in different ways. Public awareness of the plight of marine turtles often increases because of regulatory measures; from personal experience, I know that this is the case in India, Malaysia, Pakistan and the United States (I have never been to Thailand). Clearly, actual protection of turtles or their habitats has also been achieved by regulatory measures. Protection of nesting beaches and nesting turtles has been facilitated by these means in each of these countries. In the United States, stiff fines for poaching sea turtles have been published in the newspapers, and are likely to have dissuaded would-be poachers. Reglementation for the use of TEDs on the Atlantic coast of the United States, where forward looking state governments took the initiative before the federal government, have resulted in reducing mortality of turtles in shrimp trawls (Crowder et. al., 1995).

5.134. There is probably not a country in the world where despite the existence of national (or indeed regional and/or international) regulatory measures, there is not an active trade in some parts or products of sea turtles. What is open to debate is the phrase "still excessively exploited"; by definition illegal activities are difficult to trace and document. Bearing this limitation in mind, according to the best information available, it is thought that excessive exploitation may be occurring with ridley turtles off Gahirmatha and West Bengal (Silas et. al., 1983b; Pandav et. al., 1997); green turtles in Baluchistan (Groombridge, 1989); green and ridley turtles in Thailand (Supot, in press); and green and hawksbill turtles in South Pacific Islands under US jurisdiction (Eckert, 1993).

**Mr. M. Guinea:**

5.135. Direct exploitation of sea turtles, their eggs and their products continues to be a threat to sea turtle populations. In spite of excellent legislation some countries have problems with the enforcement of their laws in relation to wildlife. Wildlife law infringements may be perceived as less important when compared with crimes against persons or property. Laws that cannot be enforced are an impediment to genuine progress in wildlife conservation.

5.136. Legislation prohibiting the direct exploitation of sea turtles are essential for establishing a base from which prosecutions can proceed.

5.137. Enforcement of legislation is a problem in all countries. There will be cases of non-compliance with every conservation measure. I am unaware of any first hand knowledge of where sea turtle quotas have been flouted.

**Mr. H.-C. Liew:**

5.138. In some countries, especially the developing countries, direct exploitation are still very much a threat to sea turtle populations. For example, egg harvest is still significant in Southeast Asia due to insufficient quotas, poaching, poor enforcement and management problems. There may be hatcheries that practice very good conservation but neighbouring islands or countries that share the same population of turtles may not. In a recent paper, Limpus (1997) showed that excessive egg harvests are still serious threats while the total green turtle kills in Bali approached 30,000 annually in recent years. The impact of such large kills would overshadow the impact caused by shrimp trawling.

5.139. Table 1 below summarizes Limpus's findings. In this table, there was no indication of fisheries bycatch mortality for green turtles, hawksbill turtles, olive ridleys and leatherbacks. It may be insignificant compared to the other causes or no information is available. However, shrimp or prawn trawling in Australia was indicated as a major threat to the loggerhead and flatback turtle populations. All the countries listed in Table 1 have turtle conservation programmes and regulatory measures but most are still experiencing declining trends in their turtle populations. Similar situations exist in many other countries in Latin America, Africa and Asia.

**Table 1**: Critical regional problems that must be addressed if conservation of Indo-Pacific marine turtles in Southeast Asia and the Western Pacific is to be achieved. (Taken from Limpus, 1997).

| Species | Excessive egg harvests | Excessive turtle harvests (all continuing) | Predation of eggs | Fisheries bycatch mortality |
|---|---|---|---|---|
| Chelonia mydas | Malaysia<br>Terengganu<br>Sarawak<br>Sabah (past)<br>Philippines<br>Indonesia<br>Continuing at multiple sites | Indonesia<br>Bali + other Market<br>Papua New Guinea<br>Daru + other coastal<br>Solomon Islands<br>Coastal villages<br>Fiji<br>Coastal villages<br>Australia<br>Indigenous, Torres | Indonesia<br>Irian Jaya<br>(pigs) | |
| Caretta caretta | | | Australia<br>SE Queensland<br>(foxes) | Australia<br>(trawling & crabbing) |

| Species | Excessive egg harvests | Excessive turtle harvests (all continuing) | Predation of eggs | Fisheries bycatch mortality |
|---|---|---|---|---|
| Eretmochelys imbricata | Malaysia Terengganu Malacca (cont'd) Johor (cont'd) Thailand West coast Indonesia (cont'd) Solomon islands (cont'd) Australia (indigenous, cont'd) | Fiji | | |
| Lepidochelys olivacea | Malaysia Terengganu | | | |
| Dermochelys coriacea | Malaysia Terengganu (past) Thailand West coast Indonesia Irian Jaya Papua New Guinea Northern (cont'd) | Indonesia Kei | Indonesia Irian Jaya (pigs) | |
| Natator depressus | Australia (indigenous, cont'd) | Australia (indigenous) | Australia Cape York Peninsula (pigs) | Australia Northern Eastern Indonesia Irian Jaya |

**Dr. I. Poiner:**

5.140. All sea turtle populations in the Indo Pacific region including southeast Asia, are severely depleted and/or are subjected to over-harvest (legal and illegal) and/or excessive incidental mortality. Some countries (e.g., Malaysia and Thailand) have instigated management measures to prohibit or control egg and sea turtle harvests but there is no evidence of recovery of these populations (Limpus, 1997). The current Indonesian meat and egg harvest (legal and illegal) is likely to be unsustainable despite a variety of conservation management measures introduced by the Indonesian government (Monanunsap, 1997; Limpus, 1997).

5.141. Local/regional approaches to management are unlikely to be successful since sea turtle breeding stocks usually comprise multiple rookeries within a region while foraging areas and developmental habitats comprise a mix of turtles from several genetically distinct stocks (Bowen et. al., 1995; Broderick et. al., 1994). The breeding adults usually migrate relatively long distances from the foraging areas to the traditional breeding rookeries. For example, the Australian nesting populations of loggerhead sea turtles are genetically distinct from those in other countries and within Australia there are two genetically independent breeding populations. Breeding females migrate up to 2,600 km from feeding areas to aggregate at traditional nesting beaches (breeding males have not been studied). In Eastern Australia, females migrate from northern and eastern Australia, Indonesia, Papua New Guinea, Solomon Islands and New Caledonia. In Western Australia, recorded migrants come from Northern and Western Australia and Indonesia. Mean remigration period is 3.8yr. At the completion of the breeding season the female returns to the same feeding site as she occupied before the breeding migration.

**2(b) Could you comment on how the socio-economic factors prevailing in the five countries involved in this dispute (e.g. history of direct exploitation of sea turtles and sea turtles products, practices and techniques of the fishing industry) interact with sea turtle conservation requirements? Do these factors influence the choice and enforcement of conservation programmes?**

**Dr. S. Eckert:**

5.142. Probably the greatest effect of socio-economic that I am aware of is on enforcement of environmental regulations and on amount of information gathered on the fisheries themselves. Countries with less financial resources seem unable or unwilling to expend these limited resources on wildlife law enforcement. A similar situation exists for the monitoring of fishery efficiency. There are seldom the financial resources or personnel to monitor fisheries, or fish resources. Thus, resource managers seldom understand the resource they are assigned to manage or what factors may be impacting this resource.

5.143. Socio-economic can also play a role in how various shrimp fisheries treat bycatch. It has been my experience that in the US bycatch is regularly discarded in favour of keeping only the target species (shrimp) as the market for bycatch product is limited. The only bycatch utilized is taken home by the fisherman for their own use. In other countries, bycatch seems to be utilized more often for both personal and commercial use. I do not have quantified data for this impression as it is just based on personal experience after having worked in a number of third world countries. One note about this bycatch. In studies of bycatch by shrimp trawling it has been found that such bycatch is often made up of undersized commercially viable species. If these species were left to grow to commercial size, the resulting economic gain can be significant (Amelang, 1994, Dayton et. al., 1995). Limiting (or eliminating) bycatch by shrimp fisheries, whether that bycatch has immediate commercial value or not, is probably a better strategy for long term resource management.

5.144. Relative to how socio-economic might affect the application of TEDs as a conservation tool, I see very little reason to suspect that there would be an effect. Except for the possible impact of reducing commercially utilized bycatch, TEDs should not change the economics of a shrimp fishery. TEDs are incredibly simple devices to construct from local materials, require little special skills above what is already in use by shrimp fisherman and plans for their construction are available (e.g. Mitchell et. al., 1995). Considering the costs of fuel, nets and other required equipment for such a fishery, it is doubtful that TEDs would add significantly to the cost of fishing and may actually be advantageous (Easley, 1982). Further, my limited experience working on shrimp boats suggests that deploying and operating these devices take very little special skills or handling. It must be remembered that the first TEDs were developed and used by shrimp fisherman as a way to reduce fouling and bycatch problems, long before sea turtles were of concern.

**Dr. J. Frazier:**

5.145. Conservation activities, for sea turtles or any other biological resource, must be seen within a matrix of social and political interactions. Biological conservation is not exclusively a sub-discipline of biology, but rather an activity with clear political dimensions (as clearly illustrated by the present dispute). In this respect, it must be understood that issues of biological conservation and human rights are intricately intertwined, and that without resolving one, meaningful advancements with the other are not possible (Frazier, 1997b). Clearly, nutritional rights, or food security, is a fundamental component of human rights, and as long as large sectors of modern nation states persist in a state of malnutrition and hunger, human rights abuses will continue. In this circumstance, true conservation of biological resources will be an illusive dream. Hence, with or without TEDs, with or without integrated sea turtle conservation plans, there will be no lasting conservation of sea turtles on this planet while the majority of humanity slides ever deeper into poverty and finds ever fewer alternatives for survival. While this problem is worldwide, and present in all modern nation states, it is most intense in the "Third World". It is therefore fundamental to understand how modern fisheries practices have developed and how they relate to the question of food security and human rights.

5.146. Mathew (1990) provided a brief evaluation of the fishing industry in five different Asian countries, making comparisons between historic, social and legal aspects. In his description of the situation in Malaysia, he drew from various in-country studies (e.g., Gibbons, 1976). He described how the introduction of trawling resulted very quickly in violent conflicts, including physical attacks, the burning of trawlers, and murder of fishermen. The small-scale fishers charged that trawlers destroyed their gear and would deplete their fishing grounds. This was unlike the situation in most other countries in the region, where it took several years for conflicts to manifest themselves. After a study, the Government of Malaysia established zoning regulations to keep the trawlers out of the coastal areas; ahead of many other countries, the government introduced legislation to eliminate conflict. Yet, it was reported that enforcement was inadequate, and social conflict - fueled by ethnic divisions - became very violent and bloody. In the end, countless full-time, traditional fishermen lost control of, and access to, their traditional fisheries resources. The fishing sector was restructured from autonomous full-time fishers to capital-intensive enterprises. Although these organizations were called "co-operatives", the authors observed that "they are 'cartels' of local political and economic elites". with little if any active participation of fishermen in management. Evidently, the people who depended directly on the resources being exploited were excluded from the major decision-making process.

5.147. The authors explain that although (as is the case everywhere) scientific information necessary to plan or manage properly is inadequate: "Malaysia is the first developing country to attempt seriously to limit fishing effort in response to indications of overfishing". Yet, while in theory the zoning regulations drawn up by Government make good sense, diverse sources cited in Mathew (1990) - including the Head of the Legislation Department - have highlighted the inadequacies of enforcement and the lack of trawler's respect for the zones (e.g., only 9 per cent of respondents answered that the ban of trawlers within 5 miles of shore is effective). The authors indicate that, like in most other countries in the world where fisheries have been "modernized" and markets "liberalized", the activity is controlled by the elite hegemony, resulting in a socio-political situation in which the full-time, traditional fishers would be the last to benefit from "modernization" and the liberalization of market forces.

5.148. For Thailand, Mathew (1990) describes how the well-intentioned, and generally well-conceived fisheries management plans of the government were foiled by political clout from an industry that is export oriented (and provides a major share of the country's foreign exchange earnings). He explains that Government has been unable to implement critical management measures: "the state has a tendency to swap foreign exchange for long-term sustenance of the fishery". In the end, the trawler owners basically do as they like, even scuttling plans to close entry to the fishery, a measure which is widely recognized as being urgently needed. The fleet provides a classic example of an overcapitalized venture, and because of the degree of overfishing, the Gulf of Thailand is often characterized as an "underwater desert", even by local establishments.

5.149. While there were no immediate, violent conflicts with the introduction of trawling in Thailand, as occurred in neighbouring nations where small-scale fishers depend strongly on fisheries resources, violent clashes with trawlers did eventually occur. Mathew (1990) suggests that the relatively few social problems related to impacts of trawling was largely due to two major factors. Firstly, he suggests that Thais may be "more tolerant of injustice", than are some other people. Secondly, there was no well established, or well organized, sector of society that had traditionally depended on marine fisheries. Hence, according to Mathew (1990), the affected groups were not sufficiently organized and animated to resist incursions of the trawlers.

5.150. Yamamoto (1994) provided a later synthesis of the fisheries situation in Thailand, giving a much more critical view of the social and environmental effects of trawling. He reported that nearly 90 per cent of the "fishery establishments", were "households" which worked in the coastal fishery, as compared to the remainder which were enterprises, focused on offshore and distant water fisheries. He observed that "since its inception, the Thai trawl fishery has come into conflict with coastal fishery, as it tends to operate in the coastal waters". With the rapid growth of the trawler fleet, some of which operated without permits, demersal resources were overexploited. The coastal fishers experienced declining resources, conflicts and lowered standard of living. In order to resolve this, he proposed a new law that would, inter alia assign clear access to resources, and "discourage the continued operation of trawl fishery...".

5.151. In the case of India, Debnath (1994) has described the situation regarding the fishworkers, some 7,000,000 people who live by artisanal fisheries. He clearly describes how the "development" and mechanization of fisheries has left the vast majority of these people actually worse off than they were before "development". Social conditions related to equity, gender, job stability and security, are worse than before, while many basic fisheries resources are over-exploited, making traditional food sources inaccessible and insufficient for this enormous number of people. The ever-present problems between industrialized/mechanized fisheries and artisanal fisheries were explained: the artisanal fishers have not just lost access to their resource base, but through a process of "modernization" have been subjected to violence. Of the imported technologies which are responsible for these dire social and environmental problems, bottom trawling was singled out as one of the most prominent causes (see also Norse, 1997a).

5.152. This process of modernization and consequent loss of access to resources by a large segment of the fishing community has been abundantly documented in the studies of social scientists. What is remarkable is that although these scientists are trained to evaluate the functioning of human social systems and human interactions, their opinions and participation are routinely absent from discussions about fisheries development and resource management. The writings of Professor Conner Bailey (e.g., 1985: 1986; 1988a; 1988b; 1988c; 1988d; 1989; Bailey and Zerner, 1988; Bailey and Jentoft, 1990; Bailey et al., 1986) provide in-depth analyses, drawing mainly from South East Asia, with central relevance to the shrimp/prawn and trawling industries. He has shown, in case after case, how fisheries development activities that focus on gross productivity and income generation have resulted in increasing social and economic polarization, which produce grievous social degradation, stress and disorder, exacerbating problems of poverty. This is to say nothing of the gross depletion of marine resources on which millions of people have depended for generations, resources no longer available or adequate for feeding their families or for sustaining their participation in local, national or regional markets. These people are not just passive bystanders to change and development. Since at least the 1940's, coastal fishing communities have participated in material modernization processes in Southeast Asia. The sale of fresh and preserved fish, shellfish and other marine products has provided cash incomes for other consumer goods, including investments in modernization of boats and equipment (Frith, 1946; Fraser, 1960).

5.153. Bailey's analyses have shown that development initiatives, fueled by foreign aid from diverse sources, are commonly linked also to foreign investments and interests. Of those technologies introduced into the Third World in an effort to increase fisheries productivity, the bottom (or otter board) trawl is a prime example, and because of the extraordinarily export value of shrimp\prawn products, shrimp trawling provides some of the clearest examples of these unpredicted (and often unspoken) environmental and social consequences to development. Taken together, the usual result of these events is that the traditional resource base of a powerless majority is expropriated by a powerful minority, routinely with extra-national interests. In Bailey's words: "Emerson (1980:20) noted that, in the context of fisheries development, 'free-market forces may only reinforce absolute poverty and structural inequality in the name of economic efficiency...' ". "But it became obvious that producing evidence of resource depletion was not the same thing as mobilizing political will to restrict the operations of wealthy and politically well connected entrepreneurs." (Bailey, 1988d:41). As Bailey et. al. (1986:1270) explain: "In the context of an open access resource, the result of this process is a de facto reallocation of access favoring the minority which limits the ability of the majority to earn adequate incomes from traditional pursuits". "By promoting the use of highly productive technologies without simultaneously strengthening institutional capacities to manage and allocate finite resources among competing users, international development assistance agencies are contributing to structural problems and policy distortions which pose serious threats to the majority of those employed in the fisheries sector".

5.154. The studies of Professor George Kent (e.g., Kent, 1980; 1983; 1984; 1985; 1986; 1987; 1989; 1994) provide an additional lens for evaluating the socio-economic underpinnings of fisheries development, characterized by export-oriented shrimp fisheries. For years, and in diverse fora, he has shown that pledge of feeding the Third World, equity and social justice has not been met by increased fisheries production. There are several reasons for this. Much of what is caught is wasted: Alverson et. al. (1994) estimated that more than 27 million metric tons of bycatch are dumped back into the sea, most of it dead or mauled. Furthermore, more than a third of what is caught and landed is not for direct human use, but processed for fertilizer, livestock feeds, etc. (i.e., a third of the landed catch, instead of being used for feeding people, is destined for more round-about routes to producing food, directed by processes of income generation). In summary, this is an industry that is characterized for being grossly overcapitalized, with a distribution of resources heavily biased toward the industrialized countries: fish is caught in the Third World, where there are intense problems of malnutrition and protein need, and exported to the richer nations, where there is an excess of food. Kent (1994) shows that there is a clear inverse relationship between dependence on fish as a basic food and income level. At the same time, there are clear cases of countries, for example Bangladesh, where despite a traditional dependency on fish for food, and burgeoning human populations, annual exports of fish increase, while available fish for national consumption decreases (Kent, 1994). Recent affairs in Thailand serve as another clear example: in 1996 it was the world's largest exporter of both rice and farmed shrimp, yet the cost of food increased more than that of housing or clothing (from a 1990 base of 100, food had risen to 132 by 1995) (Europa, 1997:3191-3195), this is for a 1995 population with a GNP of US$2,800 *per capita* (World Bank, 1997:9).

5.155. As Kent states: "Fish, like other food products entering the market system, tends to flow toward the rich simply because the rich can outbid the poor." (Kent, 1980:7); "Thus, fish continue to migrate after they are caught. They tend to move from the more needy to the less needy." (Kent, 1983:13). "The fish and other food which moves in international trade is only a small share of the total amount of food produced and consumed. But the pattern of the poor feeding the rich is found within as well as among nations. The thesis that the poor feed the rich is not only about international relations; it is about social structures based on the market system wherever they occur. This regular flow of food toward the top, within countries as well as among countries, helps to account for the chronic undernutrition at the bottom." (Kent, 1985:288). "Often there is some compensation for increasing exports by the increasing imports of food. Typically, however, the foreign exchange earned from the export of food is not devoted to purchasing low cost nutritive foods for the needy, but is diverted to the purchase of luxury foods and other products in demand by local elites." (Kent, 1985:289). In addition to negative effects on that part of society that is most at risk, there are also deleterious effects on the fishery: "When people fish for their own food there is such a thing as sufficiency. In the commercial orientation, however, when people fish for profit, there is no such thing as enough. As one observer put it, 'technology makes overfishing possible, but profits provide the incentive'". (Kent, 1986:138).

5.156. Kent (1987) provides an evaluation of fish and nutrition in India, and the statistics that he presents are remarkable. Although India is one of the top fish producing nations in the world, it is has one of the lowest rates of per capita consumption. Religious and food preferences do not provide a simple explanation for this anomaly, because many people in coastal states have the habit of consuming fish. Over the last few decades, there have been outstanding increases in fisheries production as well as exports. At the same time, the cost of fish for Indians has skyrocketed, especially in comparison to other food articles, and other commodities. Hence, major increases in fisheries production are not helping to feed nationals.

5.157. Explaining fisheries production in Thailand, Kent (1984:7) described the same phenomenon. He wrote: "High export levels, low import levels, declining overall production, increasing trashfish production and increasing [human] population have combined to reduce available per caput fish supplies". "The Philippines and Thailand have well developed fisheries. At the same time there is widespread protein-energy malnutrition, vitamin A deficiency, iron deficiency, and iodine deficiency in these countries. Fisheries products can be used to respond to these problems." (Kent, 1984:25). Yet, there is overwhelming evidence that shows that increased fishing effort - notably for shrimp - is to fuel "increasing needs for exports" (Tuoc, 1995), not to feed local populations.

5.158. A number of writers have explained that fishing is a way of life and resource base for millions of small scale fishers; the fate of these people is germane to any discussion of fisheries, and marine conservation for many reasons. To start with, small scale fishers comprise about 90 per cent of all those employed in the fishing sector; furthermore, they produce a third of the world's food fish, and the bulk of all fisheries products consumed in the Third World derive from small-scale fishers (Ben-Yami in: Bailey et al., 1986). Yet, these millions of people have little if any political clout and few economic resources; they are at the mercy of development activities, run by national and international elites.

5.159. These evaluations of the social impacts of modern fisheries are not new, nor are they ensconced in hard-to-find academic literature. Social scientists have been writing about this serious problem for decades. Recent publications in the non-academic press also have described these issues in great detail. Two excellent sources of recent information on the contemporary state of fisheries, highly readable and thoroughly documented are Professor James R. McGoodwin's book *Crisis in World's Fisheries: People, Problems, and Politics* (1990) and a special issue of the *Ecologist*, edited by Simon Fairly (1995) and containing a dozen major and minor articles describing the intricacies of modern fisheries. In addition, O'Riordan (1994) reviewed the crux of modern fisheries in the widely read weekly, *New Scientist*. Finally, Dr. Daniel Pauly - dean of southeast Asian fisheries biology - has been elucidating these points for more than a decade (e.g., Pauly, 1988; 1995; Pauly and Neal, 1985; Pauly and Chua, 1988).

5.160. What is more, the same general conclusions were arrived at recently at a regional meeting on Coastal and Marine Biological Diversity, held at Subic Bay, Philippines from 24-25 October, 1996; at least three of the countries involved in the present dispute were represented: Malaysia, Thailand and US (DENR and WRI, 1997). The first Key Issue identified as needing to be regulated was: "Excessive levels of fishing effort - both commercial and artisanal - and the use of destructive fishing gears and methods. One of the key points which was detailed in this synthesis was: "Protection of CBCRM (Community-Based Coastal Resources Management) areas from external predators that local communities are unable to fend off on their own - such as *commercial trawlers*, cyanide fishing operators, and coastal developers." (p. 5, emphasis added). It is noteworthy that in this regional report, commercial trawlers were identified alongside cyanide fishers. The report goes on to state that: "Artisan fishermen constitute one of the poorest social sectors in the region and are highly dependent on fish for protein and cash income, but are exploited by middlemen and squeezed by commercial vessels operating in nearshore waters." (pp. 6-7). "Livelihoods of artisan fishermen throughout the region are increasingly threatened by competition with commercial vessels fishing in nearshore waters - despite the many laws reserving these waters for local fishermen." (p. 7). "Subsidies for development of commercial fisheries have in many cases led to over-capacity - and thus to overfishing." (p. 7).

5.161. It is also important to point out that the United Nations Research Institute for Social Development has clearly described the social and political risks involved in globalization, and the form of development characterized by modern fisheries (e.g., Utting, 1995). *See also Annex I: The Issue of Bycatch in Modern Fisheries, with Special Reference to Shrimp Trawls.*

5.162. In summary, the good intentions of development programmes for the modernization (= mechanization and technification) of Third World fisheries, as a rule have not taken into account fundamental social factors, especially the distribution and availability of food for those sectors of the population that are at risk. The people who are in a position to benefit from development initiatives are those who have access to capital and political power. For example, it is normal for those people who already have substantial financial resources to influence the creation of, and then gain access to (if not monopolize), government subsidies, while those who lack such financial resources are unable to obtain the subsidies, which purportedly were created for them. Those who do not enjoy economic and political advantages, are by definition the majority - in developing countries, they are the vast majority of citizens and producers. Yet, under these sorts of development schemes, this majority is unable to compete for limited fisheries resources, even though they may have a longer term dependence and interrelationship with them than do those who take advantage of the new technology. The end result is typically an increase in productivity with concomitant decreases in equity of income and wealth, as well as increasing social polarization: greater excesses in wealth for the elite and deeper depression of poverty for the masses. Analysis of civil conflicts in South East Asia have repeatedly referred to this process of social polarization as a primary contributing factor to unrest (Phillips, 1965; Nakahara and Witton, 1971; Milne and Mauzy, 1986; Europa, 1997). Thus, an ever-widening gap between an elite minority and an impoverished majority can lead to intense civil disorder and strife - even open warfare. This is hardly an environment in which effective conservation and resource management can be implemented.

5.163. As pointed out earlier in this section, resource conservation (for sea turtles in this case) will not be effective without considering - and resolving - basic social problems. If traditional sources of livelihood are taken away, people are likely to resort to the simplest alternatives available, despite laws and conservation plans. When the less powerful sectors of society perceive growing social inequity, it only exacerbates the lack of compliance with state regulations, and the greater the social polarization, the greater the chances of conflict and anarchy. Civil strife and lawlessness are by no means absent from industrialized societies (Kaplan, 1994). Indeed, there is a long and bellicose history of conflict in the specific case of the US shrimp fishery, notably in the Gulf of Mexico (Weber et. al., 1995; Tucker et. al., 1997). At one level, the reasons for conflict may appear distinct from those of the "Third World", simply because degrees of socio-economic development are so different. However, in the end, the root causes are comparable, for they have to do with struggles for access to and control of both resources and political power.

5.164. Hence, socio-economic factors do influence the choice and enforcement of conservation programmes.

**Mr. M. Guinea:**

5.165. In countries such a India, Pakistan, Thailand and Malaysia, the so-called bycatch, in US terms, is a commodity with either a subsistence or retail value. The entire catch has a value. Sea turtles do not have a commodity value in the shrimp trawls and are released according to cultural or religious beliefs. India, Pakistan and Malaysia have indicated that because of these religious beliefs, sea turtles are not killed, but only their eggs are eaten. As these countries are multiracial, "outsiders" are implicated in the direct mortality of sea turtles. The sea turtle research unit in Malaysia is educating people about the presence of a living embryo in each sea turtle egg. This may prove effective in reducing the consumption of sea turtle eggs in that country. Other countries may follow this example, as few convincing arguments had been provided to dissuade people from eating turtle eggs.

5.166. Conservation programmes should emanate from within a country so that implications on cultural, economic and social issues can be addressed at the same time. Reasons for such general conservation measures may have their origins elsewhere but the conservation programmes should have a national focus and flavour.

**Mr. H.-C- Liew:**

5.167. In a developed country like the United States, the level of education is higher, there is extensive mass media communication, cheap protein available, and people are more aware of their environment and the need for conservation. They could also afford to have strict conservation management policies and effective enforcement. Turtle meat producing farms that used to operate in the Cayman Islands have stopped operations and all turtle eggs are saved and protected for hatching. Hence, turtle mortalities caused by egg harvesting or killing for meat is well under control and no longer an issue in turtle conservation. These causes of mortality being removed, turtle conservationists in the United States could concentrate their efforts on other more apparent causes of mortalities, like incidental capture in shrimp trawls.

5.168. In developing countries like India, Pakistan, Malaysia, and Thailand, conservation management practices and their enforcement may not share the same effectiveness. Turtle eggs are still eaten, either through legalized harvesting or poached due to poor enforcement or poverty. Their turtles are still being slaughtered for meat in some of these countries or by neighbouring countries. Thousands of green turtles are still being slaughtered in Bali each year to sustain a cultural practice there. Fishing technologies like shrimp trawling may not be as developed or still artisanal to be of prime impact on turtle populations. They may even be using other fishing methods which may have a greater impact on sea turtles than shrimp trawling, like the ray-net or "pukat pari" in Malaysia. Some Asian cultures believe that the act of releasing turtles into the sea will bring good luck and longevity. As such, thousands of hatchlings are not released immediately to the sea on hatching but kept in enclosures for days or even months for release by the public. All these factors do influence the way conservation programmes are run and can differ from country to country.

**Dr. I. Poiner:**

5.169. I am not qualified to comment.

**2(c) What are the sea turtle conservation measures that should be implemented on a priority basis? Are those the same for all sea turtle populations and all countries concerned, or do they differ among countries and regions, and species or populations of sea turtles?**

**Dr. S. Eckert:**

5.170. While it is difficult to speak to socio-economic aspects of the fishing industry in the countries involved in the dispute, there are some ideas I can put forward relative to sea turtles and sea turtle conservation and economics. By far the best and most economical approach to conserving sea turtle populations is to eliminate the problems that caused sea turtle populations to decline in the first place (Frazer, 1992). Sea turtle populations have incredible resilience and ability to restore themselves once the anthropogenic perturbations have been removed. With the generally plastic reproductive capacities (faster growth in times of good food abundance = shorter maturity times and possibly higher reproductive output) of reptiles, turtle populations probably have the capacity for rapid growth and for sustaining very large population sizes, once they are left alone.

5.171. The most commonly utilized conservation method to restore sea turtle populations is to enhance reproductive output. Generally this means protecting reproductive females on the beach and during interesting intervals in the water (which Malaysia is doing very effectively for leatherbacks nesting at Rantau Abang by combining on-shore nest protection with an offshore sanctuary) and by protecting nests on the beach. Such an approach can be done quite economically, and often local peoples can be employed to assist in the conservation activities, thus benefiting the local economy as well as investing local people in the process. Every country involved in this dispute has such programmes. However, given the structure of sea turtle populations, nesting beach protection alone is not enough to restore sea turtle populations (Crouse et. al., 1987).

5.172. With the exception of passing laws to limit (or prohibit) the intentional harvest of turtles, very little is being done by most of the countries in this dispute to protect juvenile or resident adult sea turtles. The United States with the regulatory strength of the Endangered Species Act its TED regulations and for the US mainland, its lack of cultural desire to harvest sea turtles is the one exception. The reasons for this are probably both economical as well as social. Local peoples in many of the countries have harvested turtles for generations and unenforced regulations are not going to limit the opportunistic efforts to harvest turtles (Johannes, 1986). Economically, sea turtles can provide income, either for meat or shell, and despite its illegality, turtle products are often available in many of these countries. Even in the United States, there are problems where historically turtles were harvested (e.g. territories in the Western Pacific). Thus conservation efforts which include regulatory enforcement and environmental education are still needed.

5.173. A frequently touted method proposed to enhance survival of sea turtle offspring is known as headstarting. The basic strategy is to rear sea turtle hatchlings for between a few months and 1 year and release them to the wild when it has been assumed that they should have a higher survival rate. This is a labour and cost intensive procedure, and it is not yet proven to be successful for enhancing sea turtle populations. Two problems with the technique have challenged its application as a conservation measure. The first is that it has not been demonstrated that such turtles will reproduce on their natal beach. To date, and despite the release of over 20,000 yearly turtles, only 2 head started turtles have been known to nest in the Kemp's ridley head start project in the United States (Shaver, 1996). While these nestings provide some hope that head started turtles might reproduce, such nestings may have also been anomalous. There is a very valid concern that interrupting the typical life cycle of hatchling turtles, which requires a crawl to the sea and a pelagic life stage will yield turtles unable to return to nest. The second problem is that such efforts are very expensive and no cost benefit analysis has been undertaken. The United States spent millions of dollars to rear and release approximately 1,000 Kemp's ridley hatchlings per year. Further, there has not been any determination of whether head started turtles have a survival advantage over *in situ* produced hatchlings. The questions that must be answered before undertaking such an exercise are: (i) will head started turtles become reproductive members of the population; (ii) will they reproduce on beaches suitable for their species/population; (iii) are their survival rates significantly higher than *in situ* hatched turtles; and (iv) is this approach more cost effective than simply fixing the problem that reduced the population in the first place (e.g. TED's) and/or is there a more cost efficient means to mitigate for the problem (e.g., enhancing beach production). At this time headstarting is not considered a valid conservation tool.

5.174. Priority actions that must be taken by all countries irrespective of species or region are (i) identify turtle stock boundaries; (ii) assess threats in all stages of the life history for each stock; (iii) eliminate all incidental take in fisheries; (iv) eliminate all on-the-beach sources of mortality; and (v) enhance production of offspring. As noted earlier, we are finding it more difficult to restore sea turtle populations than previously anticipated precisely because we are unable to account for the entire ranges of each stock and what problems they face. Clearly, eliminating all sources of anthropogenic mortality is critical to restoration of declining populations. However, it is very easy to miss major sources of mortality until we understand where to look for those sources. This is particularly true in international waters, where jurisdiction of stocks is unclear.

**Dr. J. Frazier:**

5.175. Biological priorities for sea turtle conservation programmes, independent of where they are carried out, focus on providing adequate protection of the habitat which is critical for the animals, during the different stages of their life cycle; this means protecting nesting beaches, feeding grounds, areas of refuge and migratory routes. In addition, the populations must be protected from levels of mortality, independent of what those sources of mortality are, which are greater than the population's capacity of regeneration. Since most sea turtle populations have declined - some dramatically - and since mortality on animals that are breeding or near breeding is most costly to the population, a general priority is to reduce mortality on those animals that have a high reproductive value.

5.176. Because of the complex nature of the sea turtle life cycle, and long period to maturity, individuals are vulnerable to multiple sources of mortality. Hence, to increase the chances of recovery of the population, each of these sources of mortality must be reduced, for simply reducing one of many sources of mortality is unlikely to provide adequate protection, if significant numbers are being removed for other causes. This involves an integrated approach to reducing diverse threats, as has been described in various global and regional strategies for sea turtle conservation (e.g., World Conference on Sea Turtle Conservation, 1982; IUCN, 1995; 1996; in press).

5.177. Each conservation programme must take into account the environmental, social and political conditions where it is to be carried out, hence the assigning of priorities involves social, political and economic considerations. One consideration - especially in these times of privatization - is for conservation activities to be carried out in such a way that they do not cost the State, but are self-supporting, or are born by a segment of society. When a segment of society is involved in an activity which has direct repercussions on the environment and resources used by the rest of society, it is normal to require this sector to contribute to conservation actions. Where an industry makes a profit, carrying out actions that present a risks to the rest of society, it is just that this industry bear the costs of eliminating, or in the very least reducing, the risks.

5.178. Take for example an enterprise which carries out activities, exploiting resources that are public property or property of the nation; consider that this extraction for private gain is done without investing in the nurturing or maintenance of these resources. Further, the actions involved in extracting these resources have direct repercussions on the environment; they reduce other immediately harvestable resources, as well as resources potentially useful to society at a later date. In addition, the undertaking is subsidized by public funds, on both a national and international level. Should this enterprise be completely free to profit, causing multiple costs to society?

5.179. The case of modern fishing industry fits the above example (McGoodwin, 1990; Fairley, 1995): it is highly profit oriented; it exploits common property marine resources, regularly with great intensity; it does not routinely invest in the maintenance of these resources; its patterns of exploitation have direct effects on resources that other enterprises and society could benefit from; there are usually substantial subsidies from public funds to develop and run these modern fisheries. Of the different types of modern fishery, shrimp trawling fits the above description easily. What is more, on a global level although shrimp constitutes less than 2.3 per cent of annual landings of marine catches, shrimp trawling is responsible for more than a third of annual bycatch discards - some 9.5 million tons (Teutscher, 1995b:11; Clucas, 1997a:7); this problem is especially critical in tropical waters (Alverson et. al., 1994). Clearly, the relative benefits of shrimp trawling must be evaluated in the context of the environmental and social problems that it causes.

5.180. On an international level, fisheries scientists have identified that a major priority is to reduce bycatch destruction from fishing activities, notably from shrimp trawling. Thus, eliminating, or at least substantially reducing, mortality of large turtles from shrimp trawling activities conforms with both biological and socio-political priorities. One way to accomplish this is to completely ban trawling, as has been done in much of Indonesia, and as has been called for by fishers from many nations of the Third World (O'Riordan, 1994; SAMUDRA, 1994). A less drastic measure is to use bycatch exclusion devices (BEDs) in shrimp trawling; the TED is a BED developed to exclude turtles (see Appendix 1 "The Issue of Bycatch in Modern Fisheries, with Special Reference to Shrimp Trawls", contained in Annex II of this Report).

**Mr. M. Guinea:**

5.181. The nesting habitats should be preserved as should the offshore refuge habitats for nesting females. Only those fishing activities that do not harm adult sea turtles or hatchlings should be permitted within the offshore sanctuary. Mitochondrial DNA techniques should be used to determine the genetic make up of the breeding unit. This will assist in determining the relative impact of anthropogenic activities on members of that unit. The survivorship of each stage of the life cycle should be maximized (Limpus, 1997). This should involve either leaving the nests *in situ* on the nesting beach or relocating the eggs to a hatchery within 2 hours, or using ice to cool the eggs during long periods of transport. Hatchery techniques should aim for an 80 per cent hatching success with a bias of about 70 per cent females. Hatcheries should not hold hatchlings, but ensure that hatchlings enter the water at night in a manner as close as possible to a normal hatching event. Responsible fishing techniques should be employed. Bottom set gill nets and tangle nets should be set at seasons and at times when sea turtles are neither abundant nor active. Mesh size, hanging ratio, gauge and material should be such that non-target species are not in danger of being caught. Nets should be checked regularly for entangled sea turtles. Trawls over areas where sea turtles occur should be of short duration (60 minutes) and employ TEDs.

5.182. The procedures should be similar in many countries. There will be some behavioural differences displayed by the sea turtles and cultural differences present in the human custodians. The procedure of securing the nesting beach and increasing survivorship at each stage in the life cycle should ensure the breeding unit will increase to a stable level.

**Mr. H.-C. Liew:**

5.183. All measures that prevent sea turtles from being killed would be of priority. These are:

- Conservation measures or techniques that reduce the incidental catch of adult and juvenile turtles in fishing gears e.g.: (i) use of TEDs in trawlers (shrimp and fishing); (ii) regulate or ban the use of high seas gill-nets; (iii) regulations to protect turtles or restrict the use of fishing methods harmful to turtles off their nesting grounds during the nesting season.
- Conservation measures to curb the hunting and trade of live turtles, adults and juveniles, for meat and other turtle products.
- Conservation measures to curb commercial exploitation of eggs, both legal and illegal.
- Conservation measures to curb the destruction of nesting grounds by beachfront development, seawalls, land reclamation, etc.
- Conservation measures to curb the destruction of feeding grounds by trawlers, pollution, land reclamation, etc.
- Conservation measures to prevent the killing or drowning of turtles in man-made structures (e.g. oil rigs) or by powered watercrafts.
- Conservation measures to curb marine pollution to reduce the mortality of hatchlings, juveniles and adults caused by marine debris like plastic bags, tar balls, styrofoam, etc.
- Conservation measures to prevent the inducement and spread of diseases that may be anthropogenically related, e.g. fibriopapillomas.
- Measures to reduce losses due to unsuitable or poorly managed hatchery practices

5.184. In general, ranked high in the list would be measures that protect the adults and juveniles but in places where exploitation of eggs is still substantial, they would still be ranked high. Differences in priority would exist for different populations, regions and species as explained in earlier answers given.

**Dr. I. Poiner:**

5.185. Priority conservation measures for sea turtle conservation will not be the same for all sea turtle populations and all countries concerned. It would be inappropriate to implement uniform measures. For example, in the United States the incidental capture of sea turtles in shrimp nets was/is identified as the major source of anthropogenic mortality for loggerhead, Kemp's ridley and green turtles when compared to other known sources of mortality. Management measures e.g., use of TEDs to reduce this mortality was/is a high priority. In the Indo-Pacific the major sources of anthropogenic mortality on loggerhead turtles are egg predation, incidental capture of sub-adult and adult sea turtles in shrimp nets and the incidental capture of the pelagic phase in high-seas long-line fishing. For green turtles it is egg predation and the harvest of sub-adult and adults for meat; for olive ridley turtles it is egg predation and the incidental capture of sub-adult and adults in trawl and gill net fisheries. In developing and evaluating conservation measures it is important to assess the impact of the full range of mortalities on a stock using both robust population models complemented by empirical studies of the sources of mortalities (Chaloupka and Musick, 1996).

**2(d) Have some sea turtle populations found in the waters of the countries involved in this dispute stabilized or recovered so that there is not or will soon not be a risk of extinction of the populations concerned? If so, where has the stabilization or recovery occurred, what measures permitted it, and would the same measures also be effective with respect to other sea turtle populations found in the waters of the countries involved in this dispute?**

**Dr. S. Eckert:**

5.186. To the best of my knowledge, no nesting population of sea turtles has shown any recovery in any of the countries of dispute. There are encouraging signs that the Kemp's ridley nesting population may be growing (Marquez et. al., 1996a); however, this opinion has been challenged (Ross, 1996). If there is a recovery it is likely due to the required use of TED's in the United States and Mexico and to the protection afforded nesting females. However, it is far too early to state conclusively that this population is recovering and it will take quite a few years of continued population growth before this population can be considered "recovered". As I noted earlier, it takes many years of monitoring before a population trend can be determined when using nesting females or egg production as an indicator. In that regard, it is erroneous to assume that a trend in green turtle populations can be determined after only a few years.[405] This is simply not the case, and particularly so for green turtles in the western Pacific which seem to have exceptionally long remigration intervals (Limpus, 1995). The "trend" described by Malaysia will not be valid for at least another 15 or more years, depending on the maturity time of the turtles within this population. To conclude that this stock is recovering is optimistic but not defendable based on the data presented Malaysia.

**Dr. J. Frazier:**

5.187. Examples of recovery of sea turtle populations are few and far between. Limpus (1995) felt that green turtles in Florida, Hawaii and Sabah, hawksbills in Sabah, and Kemp's ridley in Tamaulipas (and the Gulf of Mexico) showed signs of recovering. The case of Kemp's ridley has been evaluated in detail by the Turtle Expert Working Group (TEWG, 1996:18), and it was concluded that "the Kemp's ridley population appears to be in the early stage of exponential expansion".

5.188. This not withstanding, I am unaware of conclusive evidence for the recovery of any sea turtle population in any of the five countries involved in this dispute so that there is not or will soon not be a risk of extinction. TEWG (1996:18) made it clear that, despite the exponential increase in numbers of nests of Kemp's ridley, an "intermediate recovery goal" could not be expected before the year 2020.

[405] See above paragraph 3.9 (a) and (b).

Furthermore, it is unclear if the "stabilization" of a population after a decline removes it from risk, or is desirable in terms of biological conservation.

**Mr. M. Guinea:**

5.189. Few data are available about the size and stability of the breeding units of the species that nest in Pakistan. India has one of the largest populations of olive ridleys. Data are scant about the size and regularity of the arribadas at Gahirmatha. Estimates of the size of the nesting population are 150,000 in 1976 but none in 1977 (Davis and Bendi, 1978), 200,000 in 1978, 130,000 in 1979 (Kar and Bhaskar, 1992), 286,00 in 1985 and 600,000 in 1991.[406] This indicates that the population is increasing or at least stable. Malaysia's leatherback population has been in decline for some years.[407] However, the green turtle population at Terengganu has declined to about 2,945 nests per year which is 38 per cent of 1956 figures. Because of a history of egg harvesting the population is expected to decline further. The green turtle nesting on the Turtle Islands of Sabah have staged a remarkable recovery, as have the hawksbills.

5.190. In the above areas, the stability has been obtained by conservation measures aimed at protecting the nesting beaches and offshore refuges by a system of reserves and sanctuaries. Legislation to protect nesting turtles and their eggs was passed and enforced. In Malaysia, great effort has gone into hatcheries which have had varied, but improving, success in their hatch rates. As eggs were purchased from collectors, the coastal communities were involved to some extent with the conservation of the sea turtles.

**Mr. H.-C. Liew:**

5.191. As quoted by Limpus (1997), .."[t]he Sabah (Malaysia)/Philippines stock (of green and hawksbill turtles) may be showing recovery after 25 years of intensive conservation management in Sabah and 12 years in the Philippines". The conservation efforts accorded here were to protect the islands where turtles nest and to operate hatcheries in these islands for the eggs. Though shrimp trawlers do operate around these islands and do catch sea turtles, no TED use is enforced. Apart from some turtle stranding records and boat inspections by park rangers of trawlers that infringe the park boundary (Suliansa et. al., in press), there is no comprehensive study on the impact of shrimp trawlers on sea turtles in these waters. The impact, if found to be significant, may negate other conservation efforts and would need urgent attention.

5.192. The same measures can be effective for other sea turtle populations but they must work in tandem with other conservation strategies to be successful. Saving the eggs and protecting nesting turtles on the beach only while allowing them to be killed in the sea will not work. Neither would the use of TEDs on shrimp trawlers, while allowing turtles to be hunted or killed by other gears, or eggs collected for consumption, or destroying feeding and nesting grounds be effective. It is important

[406] See above paragraph 3.51.

[407] The Status of Major Sea Turtle Populations in Malaysia, (http://www.upmt.edu.my/seatru/mals3.htm).

for each region, country or state to assess their own sea turtle populations, examine the threats affecting them, and prioritize the conservation strategies accordingly.

**Dr. I. Poiner:**

5.193. Sea turtles are very long lived animals that mature at a relatively late age (ca 30 to 50 years). The interval between breeding events is also very extended (ca 5 to 15 years, depending on the species). While many eggs are produced, and egg predation is high, natural mortality of sub-adults and adults is probably relatively low. Because recruitment to the adult population is low, recovery from low population number (if non-natural sources of mortality have been removed) will be slow, and there is no clear documented cases of recovery in the world. Modeling studies of loggerhead turtles in the United States following the introduction of TEDs which should have reduced mortalities suggest recovery will be slow e.g., 70 years or more was required for the simulated population to increase by an order of magnitude (Crowder et. al., 1994).

**2(e) What are the different reproductive values of sea turtles at different life stages? Given those differences, if any, how do programmes to protect eggs and hatchlings compare to programmes that protect large juvenile and adult sea turtles in terms of their likely benefit to the populations and species as a whole?**

**Dr. S. Eckert:**

5.194. The life tables and reproductive value curves of Frazer (1983) and Crouse et. al., (1987) for the loggerhead turtle have clearly demonstrated that large juvenile and adult size classes have the highest reproductive value to the population. These conclusions have recently been supported by Chaloupka and Musick (1996). Crouse utilized these tables and curves to demonstrate in her model that populations of sea turtles will not recover without minimizing the mortality of these size classes, despite rigorous protection of nesting females and their nests. While these models were for loggerheads, there is little reason to suspect that they will be different for other species. In practical conservation terms it must be realized what it means to replace a juvenile turtle. Each juvenile represents 500 or more eggs (based on the survivorship values determined by Frazer (1983) for loggerheads). For most species this represents between 5 and 6 clutches of eggs. Economically, this means that resources equal to the cost of preserving 500 eggs could be invested in the conservation of 1 juvenile turtle.

**Dr. J. Frazier:**

5.195. "Reproductive value" is an abstraction, not a component of a sea turtle that can be measured directly. It is calculated by taking into account basic characteristics of the life history of the animal, notably rates of mortality, time to maturity, and reproductive contribution. Reproductive value serves as a simple index, which is easier to visualize than a complex of other interacting measures. To calculate the reproductive value, basic information on the life history is needed, and long-term, systematic studies are fundamental for obtaining this kind of information. Up until now only two populations have been adequately studied: loggerhead turtles in the southeast of the United States and loggerhead turtles in Eastern Australia.

5.196. Crouse et. al. (1987) were the first to calculate reproductive values, using detailed, long-term information from loggerheads in the southeast of the United States. They reported:

| *Life History Stage* | *carapace length (cm)* | *estimated age (years)* | *reproductive value* |
|---|---|---|---|
| eggs or hatchlings | < 10 | < 1 | 1.0 |
| small juveniles | 10 to 57 | 1 to 7 | 1.4 |
| large juveniles | 55 to 79 | 8 to 15 | 6.0 |
| subadults | 80 to 86 | 16 to 21 | 116.0 |
| breeders | > 87 | 22 to 54 | 584.0 |

5.197. Although the details of sea turtle life history differ between species and from population to population, all sea turtles share a relatively common life cycle. Hence, although precise values for the reproductive value will vary, the large difference between reproductive value for eggs and reproductive value for breeders will be a standard feature for all populations. Given this situation, the protection of those life stages which represent the greatest investment for the population takes precedence over those life stages in which rates of mortality are normally rather high, and the reproductive value to the population is low. Nonetheless, every live stage needs to be protected, for the complete removal of any life stage from a population will sooner or later result in its collapse.

**Mr. M. Guinea:**

5.198. The figures most often quoted indicate that the reproductive value of a nesting female loggerhead is 584 times that of a single loggerhead egg in a Southeastern United States breeding unit (Crouse et. al., 1987). This was the first stage based population dynamics model for any sea turtle species, but other models had been tried for different populations and all have their limitations (Chaloupka and Musick, 1997). Other models are sure to follow. However the general perception is that between 1,000 and 10,000 eggs are required to produce a single nesting female.[408] There are some assumptions inherent in these models: male to female ratios are 1:1, survivorship is assumed between stages, reproductive longevity is assumed. However, studies of Australian loggerheads place the reproductive values of adult females at between 200 and 400, depending on the population (Heppell et. al., 1996). Reproductive values of each stage of the life cycle appear to differ for each breeding unit.

5.199. All stages of the life cycle require protection. Eggs may have lower reproductive value to larger turtles but all require protection. It depends on the threats to which the breeding unit is exposed. For example, yearly 50 million eggs are deposited on the beaches at Gahirmatha. Using Crouse's figure of 584, this is equal to a recruitment to the nesting population of over 85,000 adult females annually at one generations duration in the future. In view of this figure, an annual mortality of

[408] See above paragraph 3.19.

5,000 from fish trawls and set nets[409] from a nesting population of 600,000 with a recruitment of 85,000, appears relatively minor.

**Mr. H.-C. Liew:**

5.200. It is generally believed that out of between 1,000 to 10,000 eggs, only one will survive to adulthood. These figures are, however, estimates as they are not based on scientific evidence but on some models with numerous assumptions. Using such figures, one would be inclined to conclude that the reproductive values of adults are much higher than the young. Similarly in humans, each female can produce 5 - 10 or more children. If one were asked to choose, would it be natural for us to sacrifice all the children leaving only one and save the mother? Knowing also that the child has many more years to go, with many threats before he/she reached adulthood? One should also realize that the probability of survival of humans are much higher as mothers take care of their young. For turtles, there is absolutely no parental care. Many will die, and in fact in nature many do die of natural mortality. Turtles, like may other animals, compensate for this by producing many young. It is thus as important to protect the babies, as much as the mother. Protect the children, they are our future, but we also need mothers and fathers to produce them.

**Dr. I. Poiner:**

5.201. Crouse et. al., (1987) and Crowder et. al., (1994) used a stage-based-model for United States loggerhead sea turtles to conclude from sensitivity analysis that reducing annual mortality of large juveniles, sub-adults and adults was most important to ensure long-term viability of the stock. This was because of the high relative reproductive value individuals at these stages/ages in the model. Somers (1994) developed a similar stage structured model for an Australian loggerhead stock but concluded that protection of eggs/hatchlings would also have a major impact on long-term stock viability. The reason for the difference was a higher egg/hatchling stage mortality rates used by Somers (Chaloupka and Musick (1997). Chaloupka and Limpus (MS) have developed stochastic simulation model for an Australian loggerhead stock which also suggested that predation on eggs makes a significant contribution to increased mortalities. These different results either reflect the different conditions the United States and Australian sea turtle stocks are exposed to or the limited data on size - and age - specific growth and mortality rates and the lack of data on distribution of stage transition rates.

[409] See above paragraphs 3.49, 3.51, 3.59 and 3.77.

## Question 3: Conservation measures at sea

**3(a) Do TEDs, when properly installed and used, significantly reduce the mortality of sea turtles caused by shrimp trawl nets? Do different socio-economic conditions and level of education among fishermen, in particular in developing countries, influence the proper installation and use of TEDs?**

### Dr. S. Eckert:

5.202. Based on the extensive testing so-called hard TEDs have received in the United States (in contrast to the soft TEDs which have been recently decertified in the United States due to poor performance), there can be no question that TEDs reduce sea turtle mortality when installed and operated properly. (Crouse et. al., 1992., Renaud et. al., 1991, Renaud et. al., 1990, Henwood and Stuntz, 1987, Henwood et. al., 1992, Crowder et. al., 1995). While it is certainly possible to deploy a TED incorrectly, my experience with shrimp fisherman in Georgia indicates that most experienced fisherman understand net deployment methodology very well irrespective of formal education, and thus I would expect that deploying a TED equipped net would pose no particular challenges. While I do not have any direct experience working with trawler fisherman from other countries involved in this dispute, I would not expect them to necessarily be less skilled at operating their own equipment than US fisherman.

### Dr. J. Frazier:

5.203. Studies carried out in Australia (Robins-Troeger et. al., 1995), Costa Rica (Arauz, 1997; Arauz et. al., 1997b) and the United States (e.g., Watson and Seidel, 1980; Easley, 1982; Seidel and McVae, 1982; National Research Council, 1990) show that when properly installed and used, different kinds of TEDs can significantly reduce the incidental capture and mortality of sea turtles in shrimp trawl nets. In a recent study, Crowder et. al. (1995) analyzed long-term data from South Carolina and concluded that TEDs "reduce strandings by about 44 per cent relative to the estimated effects of shrimp trawls without TEDs". Furthermore, depending on the design of the TED and conditions of its use, it may successfully exclude more than half the bycatch (e.g., National Research Council, 1990; Robins-Troeger et. al., 1995; Olguin, 1996; Olguin et. al., 1996).

5.204. Under the aegis of the Southeast Asian Fisheries Development Center, trials with the Thai Turtle Free Device (TTFD) (a Thai version of the TED) have been carried out in Malaysia (Ali et. al., 1997), Philippines (Dickson, 1997) and Thailand (Bundit et. al., 1997). The trials in Malaysia showed that a mature hawksbill was successfully excluded (Ali et. al., 1997; SEAFDEC, 1997b). In all three cases the findings indicated that the gear was suitable for use by local fishermen. These results were also reported on by the Southeast Asian Fisheries Development Center, in their newsletter (SEAFDEC, 1996; 1997a; 1997b; 1997c), and results of further tests are awaited. Dr. E. G. Silas, former Director of the Central Marine Fisheries Institute, Cochin, India, proposed the testing of TEDs in Orissa (Silas et. al., 1983a; 1983b), and apparently trials were carried out (Rajagopalan, pers. com.), but further information is not available. A preliminary trial recently carried out in Orissa showed that TEDs installed in local trawls successfully excluded turtles (Department of Fisheries et. al., 1996).

5.205. Fishermen who can successfully use the equipment required to trawl for shrimp will have all the skills needed to properly install and use a TED. As with any new gear, they will require some training and some experience (e.g., Renaud et. al., 1993). Socio-economic distinctions between fishermen are not likely to be relevant to this question. Although in the United States many shrimpers are also boat owners, in developing countries fishermen are routinely employees, working on trawlers owned by investors, for whom fishing is just a business, not a way of life (Mathew, 1990). Level of formal education is not likely to be relevant either, for the skills needed are learned by experience; and certainly in the United States the average level of education for shrimpers is primary school, and a large proportion is illiterate.

**Mr. M. Guinea:**

5.206. When properly installed and used, a TED will significantly reduce, but not eliminate, the mortality of sea turtles in some shrimp trawls. It would be condescending and culturally insensitive to suggest that any fisherman could not operate a net fitted with a TED. For TEDs to be accepted the technology has to become adapted for the local area. This gives a sense of ownership of the technology and removes the imposition exerted by other countries. Thailand developed two TEDs of which one (Thai Turtle Free Device) is now used on each shrimp trawl net. Australia developed a TED, the AusTED, for use with Australian species of sea turtles on Australian trawl fields (Robins and Campbell, 1997).

**Dr. H.-C. Liew:**

5.207. Studies conducted by the United States have shown that proper use of TEDs can significantly reduce the mortality of sea turtles caused by shrimp trawl nets. However, even though TED use is mandatory in the United States and in their neighbouring countries, large numbers of turtle stranding still occur there. All shrimp trawlers operating in areas where the likelihood of incidental turtle capture is high should be encouraged to use TEDs or other similar devices. However, proper studies need to be conducted to determine where these areas occur and the seasons involved. Fishermen would not respond positively to the use of TEDs if they hardly catch turtles in their operations. Neither would they use TEDs if they have intentions of eating or selling the turtle.

5.208. After many years of experiments, publicity campaign and TED trials, the United States mandated their use in 1989. Yet, as recent as in 1994, NMFS concluded that poor compliance and enforcement of TED requirements contributed to record numbers of dead sea turtles washed ashore (Crouse, 1996). Considering the socio-economic conditions, educational level, language differences and history of turtle exploitation, it would take at least as long to introduce the use of TEDs, train all the shrimp fishermen, convince them to comply and have effective enforcement. It is important to introduce TED use properly to these fishermen, show how they can benefit from them and getting their full cooperation. To suddenly force them to use TEDs would only be met with blind resistance. Even in the United States where there is mandated use of TEDs, studies are still being conducted to determine if they are needed. NMFS is funding a U$500,000 study conducted by Gary Graham, Texas

A&M, Galveston, to determine if TEDs are needed in the offshore waters of the Gulf of Mexico where the "year-long" will place observers on six vessels to see if turtles are caught (Steiner, 1997a).

**Dr. I. Poiner:**

5.209. Studies of TEDs and other bycatch reduction devices (BRDs) in the United States (Henwood et. al., 1992) and Australia (Brewer et. al., 1995, 1997; Robins-Troeger et. al., 1994) demonstrate that properly installed TEDs are very effective at virtually eliminating the trawl catch of sea-turtles. I am not qualified to comment on the effect of different socio-economic conditions on TED installation and use.

**3(b) During the course of this proceeding, it has been stated that TEDs can reduce the number of turtles killed in shrimping activities by 97 per cent or more. This statistic is apparently based on data collected during TEDs testing. Is there any data on TEDs efficiency during commercial shrimping? If so, what does it indicate? Are your aware of data on the rate of turtle stranding in areas where TEDs are currently required or on the relationship between turtle stranding and shrimping activities in areas where TEDs are required?**

**Dr. S. Eckert:**

5.210. Probably the most thorough review of the efficacy of TEDs in the United States is Crouse et. al., (1992) in which they summarize a number of studies on TED use and shrimp catch rates and debunk a large number of anecdotal reports on TED performance. Controlled tests described in Renaud et. al., 1990, 1991 seem to confirm data described in the Crouse et. al., report. (1992). Crowder et. al., (1995) published the most recent and thorough model of the effects TEDs will have on turtle stranding rates and benefits to loggerhead sea turtle populations in South Carolina. Conclusions were that stranding rates should decrease significantly (44 per cent) and that the probability of recovery of this stock (which is currently declining at 5.3 per cent annually) is good.

5.211. Generally three conclusions are put forth in studies on TED effects on commercial fisheries: (i) commercial shrimp catch rates were higher in years after TED's were required (though it is probably not valid to suggest that TED use necessarily resulted in increased catch rates); (ii) shrimp loss ranged from 0.7 - 10 per cent per boat and 0 - 2 per cent for the fleet; however, this value was statistically not significantly different from 0.0 per cent given the sample size and variability in the data; and (iii) performance of TED equipped nets improved with operator experience.

5.212. For other countries, there is one study of TEDs (in this case called Thai Turtle Free Devices (TTFDs)) and shrimping (Senalak and Sujittosakul, 1997); however, the study is probably invalid due to poor data gathering methodology and data analysis. In particular, the data collection seems to rely on dock-side interviews with shrimp boat captains as the sole means of obtaining catch statistics. Such technique is not valid without a means of independent validation of the reported data. Logbook and interview data can often provide important qualitative information, but is usually quantitatively inaccurate. Even more significantly is that the experimental and control groups were fishing in two different years (e.g., non TTFD data was from 1991 and TTFD equipped trawl boat data was from 1992). No attempt was made to correct for between year variation in the data sets. For example, 1991 and 1992 should have been compared to average catch rates over the previous 5 or 10 years to determine if the reported values fall within expected annual variation in catch rates. Without such an analysis it is impossible to know whether the reported differences in catch rates are simply due to annual variation in CPUE or to the use of TTFDs.

5.213. In Malaysia a recent experiment on the use of TEDs in shrimp fisheries concluded that "this study showed that TEDs will prevent marine turtle[s] from being trapped in the net without effecting [sic] the catch of shrimp and fish" (Ali, A. et. al., 1997). Although this study cannot be considered conclusive due to the very small sample size, it does seem to be a well executed and analyzed preliminary experiment.

**Dr. J. Frazier:**

5.214. The figure of 97 per cent is an arbitrary value which was established by gear specialists from the Pascagoula laboratory of the National Marine Fisheries Service (NMFS), United States. In early tests of TEDs they established a standard for evaluating different designs of TEDs. Because the NMFS design successfully excluded 97 per cent of the turtles that entered the trawl net it was decided that a TED, irrespective of its design, should exclude at least 97 per cent of the turtles in order to be approved by NMFS. This standard was set to provide as much protection as possible for sea turtles, but at the same time allow for a small - and realistic - margin of error. Some of the first experiments on keeping turtles out of shrimp trawls, carried out 20 years, were carried out aboard commercial vessels in Florida, Georgia and South Carolina. Two gear modifications were used, the "reverse barrier trawl" and the "turtle excluder device"; and in both cases they caught significantly less turtles than normal nets ($p< 0.001$) (Watson and Seidel, 1980; Seidel and McVea, 1982).

5.215. During the last few years there have been clear indications from the commercial shrimp fishery in the United States, that TEDs have significantly reduced turtle mortality. Stranding data from South Carolina for the period 1980 to 1993 show remarkable declines, particularly when TED regulations were in place. Crowder et. al. (1995) concluded that the decline in strandings was because of reduced mortality from TED use. Preliminary analyses of results of a study of "naked net" trawling (i.e., shrimp trawling without TEDs) along the coast of South Carolina in 1997, indicates that the rate of capture of loggerheads (CPUE) is now considerably more than it was when these waters were studied a decade ago by Henwood and Stuntz (1987) (Bransdetter, pers. com.). This increase in turtles, together with the decrease in strandings documented by Crowder et. al. (1995) clearly points to the effect of TEDs in reducing mortality.

5.216. TEDs designed in the United States, and TEDs modified locally have been tested on commercial shrimp trawlers in Australia, Costa Rica, Mexico and Venezuela. Robins et. al. (1997) reported on results of 151 test trawls ("tows") using eight commercial trawlers in north-eastern Australia. They found that the catch of large animals (including turtles) was significantly less in nets with the AusTED both in the subtropical estuarine fishery ($p = 0.041$) and in the tropical gulf fishery ($p<0.01$). Arauz et. al. (1997b) reported on the results of 165 test trawls ("drags") using 11 commercial trawlers in Pacific Costa Rica. They found that Super Shooter and Seymour TEDs successfully excluded turtles (as long as bar spacing was not greater than 8 inches): 14 caught in control nets and 2 caught in 1 net with a TED that had been jammed with logs.

5.217. The only country where I know that there is systematic information on turtle strandings is the United States. Increased strandings of Kemp's ridleys, notably in Texas and Louisiana, in 1994 and 1995 (Shaver, 1994; 1995; Steiner, 1994), are thought to be related to improper use of TEDs, use of inadequate TEDs and "intense pulse fishing" (TEWG, 1996:18). As a rule, strandings increase when shrimping activity increases, notably immediately before and immediately after the closure of a shrimping area. This "pulse fishing", very intense trawling in certain coastal areas, results in repeated sweeps of an area over a short period of time which increases the chances that an individual turtle will be captured repeated during a day, undergo successive physiological stress (Lutcavage and Lutz, 1991; Stabenau et. al., 1991), and finally succumb from exhaustion. Pandav et. al., (1997) compiled information on strandings from the Gahirmatha area of Orissa, but the area covered and effort from year to year have varied. TEDs are not used in India. Recently, Guinea and Whiting (1997) have provided evidence of trawl related strandings of four species from the remote coast of Northern Australia, indicating that prawn trawling is a significant source of mortality in these waters. It must be emphasized that the turtles that are found stranded represent only a part - and in certain conditions, only a small part - of all the turtles that have died. Current; tide; tow time; turtle species and size; water depth; water temperature; wind; predator and scavenger densities and behavior; and other factors will affect the way in which turtle carcasses are deposited on the shore. There is no scientifically substantiated conversion factor to convert number of strandings to total number of drown turtles.

5.218. Murphy and Hopkins-Murphy (1989:15) reviewed the results of two experiments that examined the question of what proportion of carcasses are documented as strandings. They reported:

| *Experiment* | *Marked* | *Stranded* | *Per cent Stranded* |
|---|---|---|---|
| A | 13 | 4 | 31 |
| B | 9 | 2 | 22 |
| Total | 22 | 6 | 27 |

Under the conditions of these two experiments, less than a third of the free-floating carcasses were recovered; hence, mortality will be considerably greater than indicated by just stranding data.

**Mr. M. Guinea:**

5.219. Data from the Northern Prawn Fishery in Australia indicate: a reduction in small fish bycatch by about 30 per cent, a reduction in large fish, no sea turtles were captured during the trials. Other studies reported a slight increase in prawn catch (4 per cent and 7 per cent) (Mounsey, 1995) which may have been a result of the otter boards spreading wider in response to the reduction in bycatch and therefore in drag at the cod end. The catch was of better quality with fewer broken or damaged shrimp. The better catch of unbroken shrimp could command a higher price.

5.220. Data on turtle stranding are only available from the United States where sea turtles continue to wash ashore even where TEDs are compulsory. Compliance appears to be a problem.[410]

**Mr. H.-C. Liew:**

5.221. Mandatory use of TEDs by commercial shrimpers has been enforced in the United States for the most number of years. Hence, they would provide the best statistics. However, even as recent as in 1997, large numbers of turtle stranding still occur (Coyne, 1997). It even reports that while the 96.9 per cent of the vessels were using TEDs, biologists still see a big decline in dead turtles washing ashore when the Gulf of Mexico is temporarily closed each year to shrimping. In a message by Todd Steiner (1997), he stated that "18 turtles washed up dead in Texas last week, nine had straight-edge cuts at Padre Island National Seashore. Shrimpers were observed by Seashore rangers fishing so close to the beach that it looked like they would run aground. When the shrimper left the area, the strandings ceased." All these examples indicate that problems still exist in the use of TEDs and mandating fishermen to use them does not guarantee that sea turtles will be safe from shrimp trawlers.

**Dr. I. Poiner:**

5.222. For certification purposes TEDs in the United States need to be at least 97 per cent effective in reducing turtle catches. I am not familiar how this is measured in the certification process. Monitoring of TEDs and other bycatch reduction devices (BRDs) in the United States (Henwood et. al., 1992) and Australia (Brewer et. al., 1995, 1997; Robins-Troeger et. al., 1994) under commercial conditions demonstrate that properly installed TEDs are very effective at virtually eliminating the trawl catch of sea-turtles. Caillouet et. al., (1995) compared the relationship between sea turtle stranding rates and shrimp fishing intensities in the northwestern Gulf of Mexico in 1986-1989 (pre-compulsory compulsory introduction of TEDs) versus 1990-1993 (post introduction of TEDs). They found no difference in stranding rates whereas the expectation was that the introduction of TEDs would reduce the incidental capture of sea turtles and hence diminish or eliminate the statistical relationship between sea turtle stranding rates and shrimp fishing intensities. A variety of hypotheses were suggested to explain the continuation of the statistical relationship, including violation of TED regulations in the fisheries.

[410] See above paragraphs 3.51, 3.83 and 3.84.

**3(c) In your view, is the obligatory use of TEDs for shrimp trawling an essential conservation measure in all areas where sea turtles occur? Or can alternative measures such as seasonal and time closures, areas closures or tow-time limitations achieve equivalent or better results?**

**Dr. S. Eckert:**

5.223. It is my belief that TEDs provide the best opportunity to reduce turtle bycatch with the greatest efficiency and lowest cost to the fishing industry. Further, as I noted above, I believe it is the most easily enforced conservation measure available. The problem with seasonal and time closures are that: (i) enforcement requires extensive and continual law enforcement presence on the water in the closed area. With the costs of operating enforcement vessels and the extensive areas fished, this is generally beyond the capacity of most countries (including the United States) to support; (ii) such closures do not facilitate rapid adjustment for stochastic fluctuations in the migratory patterns of turtles; and (iii) tow time limitations are almost impossible to enforce and actually do not provide much protection to turtles subject to multiple captures (Stabenau, 1991).

**Dr. J. Frazier:**

5.224. Nationals from three of the countries involved have expressed the need to employ, or at least test and seriously consider TEDs in their fisheries: India (e.g., Silas et. al., 1983a; 1983b; James et. al., 1989; Department of Fisheries et. al., 1996; Mohanty-Hejmadi, 1996; Sarkar et. al., 1996; Behera, 1997c; Pandav et. al., 1997); Malaysia (e.g., Suliansa et. al., 1996); and United States (e.g., National Research Council, 1990; Weber et. al., 1995). In addition, tests carried out in four of these countries have indicated that TEDs are suitable for local use: India (e.g., Department of Fisheries et. al., 1996); Malaysia (Ali et. al., 1997); Thailand (Bundit et. al., 1997); and United States (e.g., National Research Council, 1990; Weber et. al., 1995).

5.225. As a stop-gap measure, the use of TEDs in all shrimp trawlers should slow the rate of destruction of marine resources, including sea turtles. The real problem, however, is much, much deeper and involves the environmental and social effects of bottom trawling and bycatch destruction as carried out by modern fisheries. In my view, there is ample evidence for banning trawling from countries with dense human populations, high dependency on fish for food, and where modern fisheries (e.g., the tropical shrimp fishery) are focused on exporting food to industrialized nations while local citizens of these exporting countries find it more and more difficult to find adequate food for themselves and their families. Certainly, people from many different fishing communities around the world have called for a ban on trawling (O'Riordan, 1994; SAMUDRA, 1994), and ample evidence in the fisheries literature shows without a doubt that modern fisheries are overcapitalized, grossly destructive of the environment, and supporting greater social polarization and degradation on national, regional and international levels.

5.226. Area closures do not work because of a lack of enforcement. This has been widely documented in many countries, including those involved in this dispute (e.g., Mathew, 1990; Yamamoto, 1994; Pauly, 1995; Behera, 1997a; Pandav et. al., 1997). Area closures, designed to minimize bycatch of protected species, may actually create problems, for the effect may be simply to displace fishing effort to other areas.

To accomplish the goals of the closure, it may be necessary to close a much larger area than originally contemplated, or even to stop fishing (Murawski, 1995:8). The logic behind seasonal and time closures is to remove fishing effort from a particular species, during a critical period. However, the shrimp trawl industry is heavily overcapitalized, and shrimp stocks are generally in decline, so there is intense competition to fish and catch shrimps. Hence, even if enforcement were possible, the usual result of temporal closures is to concentrate fishing effort just before and just after the closure ("pulse fishing"). In general, seasonal and time closures simply offset mortality around the time of the closure.

5.227. Tow-time (the period of time that the trawl net is in the water) limitations are least enforceable of all measures. Furthermore, recent information indicates that forced submergences of more than 30 minutes may be fatal to many sea turtles (Lutcavage and Lutz, 1991; Stabenau et. al., 1991), so to be effective, maximum tow-times would have to be 30 minutes, not 60 as has been frequently claimed. Even 60 minute two times are inconvenient and uneconomical for most trawlers, so there is little chance that they would abide by 30 minute tow-times.

5.228. It must be pointed out that in a well managed fishery, with controlled fleet size and closed entry, such as found in Australia, it has been possible to work with the fishermen and enlist their collaboration (Kennelly and Broadhurst, 1995; Tucker et. al., 1997). However, this is very much the exception, and not anything like the case for any of the countries involved in this dispute where the fishery is open entry and basically a free-for-all.

**Mr. M. Guinea:**

5.229. "TEDs are not an ultimate solution, they should only be seen as part of an integrated approach to sea turtle conservation and restoration." (Steiner, 1993, p. 180). I agree with the above quote by Todd Steiner in that TEDs are just one option in the array of management options open to the managers of shrimp fisheries. Any of the options mentioned previously in my submission could be employed with or without TEDs. The management options should be tailored to the Fishery. Recent population models have shown that when TEDs are used in conjunction with egg protection, the population has a greater chance of survival than if either egg protection or TEDs were used individually (Grand and Beissinger, 1997).

**Mr. H.-C. Liew:**

5.230. In certain areas, TED use is essential, but scientific studies must be conducted with unbiased data to show its necessity and to convince the fishermen in those areas why they should used them. TED use should not be mandated blindly without proper studies. When the Gulf of Mexico is temporarily closed each year to shrimping, biologists in the United States found a significant decline in dead turtle strandings compared to shrimpers using TEDs even with a 96.9 per cent compliance by the fishing vessels.

**Dr. I. Poiner:**

5.231. The obligatory use of TEDs to reduce the incidental mortality of sea turtles in shrimp trawls is one management tool that can be used but there are others, including area, seasonal and time closures and tow-time limitations that either individually or together may achieve the same reductions in catch. Which suite of management tools to be used will depend on management objectives, the nature of the fishery and ease of surveillance and enforcement. Tucker et. al., (1997) compared the Australian and United States approaches to the introduction of TEDs to reduce turtle mortalities. They suggest a participatory (non legislative) solution to trawl bycatch issues via negotiation and mediation between stakeholders has substantial advantages in the Australian situation (nature of the fisheries, nature of the people, political system, etc.) over a litigation and legislation approach as was/is use in the United States.

**3(d) Does variety in geographical and environmental conditions (e.g. different sea bottom topography, vegetation, current) affect significantly the efficiency of TEDs, both in term of loss of catch and protection of the various species of sea turtles? More particularly, do the geographical and environmental conditions prevailing in the Indo-Pacific waters require a different approach to that chosen in the Gulf of Mexico and Caribbean Sea?**

**Dr. S. Eckert:**

5.232. Renaud et. al., (1991) noted that there were differences in catch rates between TED equipped nets and non-TED nets when comparing tests in the Atlantic Ocean and the Gulf of Mexico. However, he also noted that there were no statistical differences in catch rates between different areas within the Gulf of Mexico. Because no data was given to characterize the habitats used in this test, it is difficult to draw any conclusions from this data. Poiner et. al., (1990) compared catch rates between the North Australian prawn fishery and the US shrimp fishery and found comparable catch rates (between the US Gulf of Mexico and Northern Australia). To the best of my knowledge, there is no study that attempts to compare geographic differences in TED performance based on habitat or geographical area.

**Dr. J. Frazier:**

5.233. To work properly, TEDs must be adapted for the local conditions where they are to be used, taking into account: fishing gear, fishing technique, substrate type, bottom cover, and water depth, among other things. These sorts of adaptations are not unlike the modifications that fishermen have made to gear to be able to fish in different conditions. Sr. Randall Arauz, who has been working on TEDs in Costa Rica for the last four years, stated: "with proper modifications of the TED technology and fishing practices, together with scientific documentation, research to make TEDs work efficiently under virtually any fishing conditions, as we have proven in Costa Rica". (Arauz, 1997).

5.234. There is great variation in the fishing grounds of the Gulf of Mexico, Caribbean and East Pacific, where TEDs are being used. Fishing grounds of the Indo-Pacific are likely to be both similar and divergent from fishing grounds in the Americas. However, the principle of TED modification for local requirements is the same. Indeed, Thai gear specialists have carried out tests and devised two unique designs, the Thai Turtle Free Device (TTFD) and the Thai-Ku (Bundit et. al., 1997). Under the aegis of SEAFDEC, Thai fisheries officers have been disseminating this gear in other countries of the region (SEAFDEC, 1996; 1997a; 1997b; 1997c).

5.235. It must also be pointed out that the gear specialists of the Pascagoula Laboratory of the National Marine Fisheries Service have decades of experience in devising, modifying and testing TEDs. They have been actively training people as well as distributing gear and information in many different countries, in workshops both in the United States and abroad, since 1983 (see Appendix 2 "Transfer of TED Technology" contained in Annex II of the Report).

**Mr. M. Guinea:**

5.236. For TEDs to be effective in reducing the mortality of sea turtles, they have to be functional in the fishery. Part of their functionality is the willingness with which they are accepted by the fishery. This involves considerable modification and experimentation not only to provide the previously mentioned sense of ownership, but also to convince operators of the usefulness of new technology. Australian trawl fields are considerably different to the trawl fields of the Gulf of Mexico and the Caribbean Sea.[411] Options such as bottom or top opening for the removal of sponge or sea turtles respectively, have to be explored. The set angle of the TED and the position in the net have to be modified for the nature of the benthic habitat and the species of sea turtles and their size as well as the nature of any other bycatch. There needs to be considerable modification and trials before TEDs or any other bycatch reduction device, e.g., fish eye etc., is accepted by the fishery.

5.237. From trials in Australia (Robins, 1995; Mounsey, 1995) and Thailand (Chokesanguan et. al., 1996), it is possible that the environmental conditions vary greatly between the localities. This is reflected in the performance and unacceptability of the unmodified TEDs.

**Mr. H.-C. Liew:**

5.238. Not able to comment.

**Dr. I. Poiner:**

5.239. Monitoring of TEDs and other bycatch reduction devices (BRDs) in tropical northern Australia (Brewer et. al., 1995, 1997; Robins-Troeger et. al., 1994) under commercial conditions demonstrate that TEDs performance depends on the nature of the sea bottom. Different areas require different types of TEDs. These results should be transferable to other parts of the Indo-Pacific waters. What these results show is that if TEDs are to be used they need to be selected and adapted to local fishing conditions and approaches to fishing. TEDs that are effective in the Gulf of Mexico and Caribbean Sea may not be appropriate for Indo-Pacific fisheries.

**Question 4: Conservation measures on nesting grounds**

**4(a) What is your assessment of conservation programmes focusing on protection of eggs and hatchlings? Are there examples where these programmes**

---

[411] *US Embargo on the Import of Wild-Caught Shrimp*, Submission by Australia to the US Secretary of State in support of its request for certification under Section 609(b), April 1996. See above paragraph 4.2.

**have been proved effective in restoring a population of sea turtles, or in maintaining it at a sustainable level? Are their regional differences in this regard?**

**Dr. S. Eckert:**

5.240. In my response to question 2(b), I have provided some assessment of sea turtle conservation methods. Of greatest importance to any sea turtle conservation programme is to address the problem that led to the "endangered" status of the stock or population as a first priority in conservation (Frazer, 1992). To the best of my knowledge, there has never been a case where enhancing reproductive output has been able to mitigate for juvenile and adult turtle mortality. Thus, while nesting beach programmes are important and useful in mitigating for historical over-harvest of eggs, I cannot advocate this technique as a mitigation for incidental mortality associated with fishing. The reason for this stance in sea turtle conservation is obvious when you consider what it means in terms of sea turtle population dynamics. Due to the low survival rate of sea turtle hatchlings and juveniles, one large juvenile or sub-adult turtle represents many hundreds (or thousands of eggs). Thus, for each turtle killed incidentally many eggs must be hatched and released over and above those that would survive naturally. With the highly depleted status of most nesting populations it is simply not feasible to increase hatch production at the levels required to mitigate for even small levels of incidental mortality.

5.241. An example of where protecting only nesting stocks as a conservation strategy has failed is for the loggerhead nesting stocks of North Carolina, South Carolina, and Georgia. This stock constitutes a unique nesting assemblage and is separated genetically from the larger Florida nesting population (Bowen et. al., 1993). The index nesting beach for this stock is on Little Cumberland Island. This is the best studied loggerhead nesting population in the world and thus much of our information on sea turtle population dynamics is based on this data from this beach (Frazer, 1983; Frazer, 1985; Richardson, 1978; Taylor, 1993, Bell and Richardson, 1978, Bowen et. al., 1993, Frazer and Richardson, 1985, Frazer and Richardson, 1986, Hillestad et. al., 1978, Frazer and Richardson, 1985b, Hillestad et. al., 1979, Kraemer and Richardson, 1979, Mrosovsky et. al., 1984. Stoneburner et. al., 1982, Richardson et. al., 1976a, Richardson et. al., 1979b, Richardson et. al., 1976, Richardson, 1978, Stoneburner and Richardson, 1981, Richardson, 1982, Richardson, 1992). Little Cumberland Island has provided an interesting test of nesting beach conservation, because prior to the initiation of nest protection in 1964, virtually 100 per cent of the nests were consumed by raccoons. After the initiation of protection by beach patrol and maintenance of an on-beach hatchery, almost 100 per cent of the eggs have been protected. Yet, between 1964 and 1991 the population declined approximately 65 per cent (NRC, 1990, Richardson, 1992). Accounting for a 20 -25 year delay in nesting population response due to maturity time in loggerhead (Frazer, 1983), nesting population numbers should have begun to rebound if egg protection was an appropriate conservation tool, and they have not. Similar trends in nesting have been seen in North and South Carolina. Such lack of recovery has been due to the mortality associated with shrimp fishing on the Atlantic coast (NRC, 1990).

**Dr. J. Frazier:**

5.242. As stated in earlier responses, the protection of eggs and hatchlings of sea turtles is essential for the long-term health of the population; without recruitment into the population from eggs and hatchlings, it will gradually "die of old age". However, "focusing" on protection of just eggs and hatchlings, and not reducing mortality in older animals will be doomed to failure (see my answers to questions 1(b), 1(c), 2(c) and 2(d)). It makes little sense to invest time, money, materials and effort protecting just eggs, only some of which will hatch, and fewer of which will grown into young turtles, if those turtles are under high risk, and their chances of survival are very low. Because egg protection produces rapid, tangible results (i.e., hundreds of scrambling baby turtles, just two months after eggs are laid) it provides quick and attractive rewards for conservation activities; furthermore, it is much simpler and less expensive than protection of animals in the sea or marine environments. Hence, as a rule egg protection attracts more attention than the more difficult, complex and time-consuming tasks of protecting turtles at sea. For decades, egg protection and head-starting (captive rearing) programmes have been carried out with the best of intentions, and the rapid, tangible results have consistently been activities that have been reported as evidences of success - routinely taken advantage of by politicians. However, over the last decade sea turtle conservationists have come to realize that concentrating on nesting beaches has routinely taken attention away from other, more needy activities (e.g., Mortimer, 1990; 1995; Suliansa et. al., 1996). As explained in several sea turtle conservation strategies (World Conference on Sea Turtle Conservation, 1982; IUCN, 1995; 1996; in press), the priority is integrated management and conservation.

**Mr. M. Guinea:**

5.243. Conservation measures devoted to eggs and hatchlings have been successful for some breeding units of some species e.g., olive ridleys in Orissa. Mortimer (1995) elegantly distils the evidence for protecting eggs and adults. Each strategy has its individual strengths and possible scenarios for delaying such conservation measures. Conservation involving coastal communities will gain popular support and have a greater chance of being maintained, than a piece of legislation which affects only a small proportion of the population i.e., fishers, or companies and which is out of sight of the community. Like fishing, conservation can become an industry, if properly structured.

5.244. The conservation measures employed by Malaysia (Liew, 1997) and Thailand (Monansunsap, 1997) appear to be successful. The measures have community support and sponsorship from a number or organizations.

5.245. There will be regional differences regarding the effectiveness of conservation programmes focussing on protection of eggs and hatchlings. These will be based on the culture of the area and the socio-economic climate that prevails as well as depending on the breeding unit to which the sea turtles belong. The sea turtles may display plasticity in life history strategies which may be confounded by differing pivotal temperatures, sex ratios and stable age structure. Each breeding unit will respond in a similar manner but at a differing rate to identical conservation measures. Conservation measures that protect nests or eggs will make a significant contribution to the continued survival of the breeding unit.

**Mr. H.-C. Liew:**

5.246. Protection of eggs and hatchlings are important to ensure the continued sustainability of sea turtle populations. However, they must be conducted properly and in tandem with other conservation strategies determined for each locality. Where possible, eggs should be incubated in natural nests *in situ* and hatchlings immediately released on hatching and not retained for long periods as still practised in some countries. There are a few examples where turtle populations have shown apparent recovery or sustained where conservation efforts focus on protection given to turtle nesting beaches, their eggs and hatchlings. However, such recoveries were only apparent after many years of strict conservation measures due to the long periods turtles need before they mature after emergence as hatchlings. Some of these include the green and hawksbill populations in the Turtle Islands of Sabah, Malaysia; the leatherback populations of South Africa, the leatherback population in St. Croix and Surinam and the green turtles of the French Frigate Shoals, Hawaii.

**Dr. I. Poiner:**

5.247. All sea turtles populations in the Indo-Pacific region including southeast Asia are severely depleted and/or are subjected to over-harvest (legal and illegal) and/or excessive incidental mortality. Some countries (e.g., Malaysia and Thailand) have instigated management measures to prohibit or control egg harvests as a conservation measure but there is no evidence of recovery of any of these populations (Limpus, 1997).

**4(b) Considering the long timeframe some species of sea turtles need to reach reproductive age, is it still difficult for biologists to anticipate the effects of the more recent programmes on the populations concerned or is it now possible to assess whether egg protection methods are capable of ultimately preventing marine turtle extinction and, if properly implemented, will in fact do so?**

**Dr. S. Eckert:**

5.248. In previous answers I have touched on the disadvantages of using nesting counts for determining population trends. The same is pretty much true for understanding the effect of conservation actions or nesting beach perturbations. Due to the long time it takes for turtles to reach reproductive maturity, it will often take a generation time (25-50 years) to see the fruits of such efforts revealed on the beaches. However, as noted in the example provided by the Little Cumberland Island loggerhead study, we are reaching a point in some projects that enough time has elapsed for the effects of nesting beach conservation actions to be determined. This, combined with improvements in our sea turtle population models (for a review see Chaloupka and Musick, 1996) is indicating the need for a balanced conservation approach and illustrating the fallacy of focusing only on nest beach conservation as a means to restore depleted turtle populations. Finally, consider this illustration. If it takes 1000 eggs to produce 2 adult turtles (Frazer, 1983) (this is probably a minimum estimate) and only slightly less for 2 sub-adult (stage 3) turtles, then for every turtle we want to replace we must hatch just under 500 eggs. If there is a relatively minor incidental shrimping mortality of stage 3 turtles, 100 as an example, then just under 50,000 eggs will need to be protected to mitigate for the fishery mortality. Further, this 50,000 has to be in excess of what is already being produced on the beach, since the current beach production is likely not enough to maintain the population (based on the assumption that most population are already in decline). From this example it can be seen why it is so difficult to use nesting beach conservation as a mitigation for fishery mortality, and why such an approach simply will not work, as was demonstrated at Little Cumberland Island.

**Dr. J. Frazier:**

5.249. As yet, no species of sea turtle is known to reach reproductive age in less than 10 years. Green and loggerhead turtles, for which the best information on growth rates is available, are generally thought to require about 30 years to reach maturity. The long time needed to reach maturity means that only long-term data will permit a true understanding of trends in the population. As was explained earlier, turtle populations are evaluated by counting nesting females, nests, or eggs. These counts represent only a small segment of the total population and there is tremendous variation in clutch size, number of clutches per female, inter-nesting intervals, and nesting activity from year to year. Hence, estimating population size from what is seen during a nesting season on a beach has clear limitations.

5.250. It does not matter whether the conservation measure is egg protection or use of TEDs; it takes years of systematic information to be able to decipher the trends in size of a sea turtle population. Because the animals have complex life cycles and need a long time to maturity, they are subjected to many different sources of mortality over long periods of time. It is most prudent to carry out integrated conservation, providing a variety of measures for habitat protection and reducing mortality. This strategy of integrated conservation for sea turtles has been adopted in numerous international fora, for well over a decade (e.g., World Conference on Sea Turtle Conservation, 1982; IUCN, 1995; 1996; in press).

**Mr. M. Guinea:**

5.251. Egg protection strategies have been employed for less than one sea turtle generation. The nesting beaches are the only points of reference to measure the success of such conservation measures. Ideally if the developmental habitats were known, then an increase in relative abundance of sea turtles may be demonstrated, but developmental habitats may, in fact, be defined more by carrying capacity than the absolute abundance of sub-adult sea turtles. Egg protection measures for olive ridleys in India and green turtles in Malaysia appear to be successful. The relative significance of egg protection is difficult to determine without knowing the other threatening processes impacting on the breeding unit.

**Mr. H.-C. Liew:**

5.252. Egg protection methods alone is not sufficient especially if other threats are still present and have significant impacts on the population. For populations, if any, where egg exploitation is high while the threats from the other factors are negligible, then egg protection methods would suffice.

**Dr. I. Poiner:**

5.253. Sea turtles are very long lived animals that mature at a relatively late age (ca 30 to 50 years). The interval between breeding events is also very extended (ca 5 to 15 years, depending on the species). While many eggs are produced, and egg predation is high, natural mortality of sub-adults and adults is probably relatively low. Because recruitment to the adult population is low, recovery from low population number (if non-natural sources of mortality have been removed) will be slow, and there is no clear documented cases of recovery in the world. Our only estimates of recovery times come from modeling studies.

5.254. Crouse et. al., (1987) and Crowder et. al., (1994) used a stage-based model for United States loggerhead sea turtles to conclude from sensitivity analysis that reducing annual mortality of large juveniles, sub-adults and adults was most important to ensure long-term viability of the stock and suggested egg protection programmes are ineffective. Modeling studies of loggerhead turtles in the United States following the introduction of TEDs which should have reduced mortalities suggest recovery will be slow e.g., 70 years or more would be required for the simulated population to increase by an order of magnitude (Crowder et. al., 1994). This was because of the high relative reproductive value individuals at these stages/ages in the model. However, other models by Somers (1994), and Chaloupka and Limpus (MS) concluded that protection of eggs/hatchlings would also have a major impact on long-term stock viability but give no estimation of recovery times.

**Question 5: Migratory patterns**

**5(a) What are the migratory patterns of the various species of sea turtles mentioned above? Are the migratory patterns similar in different regions of the world? In particular, do sea turtles migrate seasonally -and if so, are those seasons clearly defined- or do they migrate all year round?**

**Dr. S. Eckert:**

5.255. Despite many years of sea turtle flipper tagging, and an increasing number of satellite telemetry studies, our understanding of the migratory movements for sea turtle populations are still very limited. In particular, we know almost nothing of the migratory movements of juvenile turtles during early development or even after they have settled in coastal habitats. As noted earlier, we have only one clear pattern of migration resolved for the loggerhead during this part of its life phase, yet even for that species our sample sizes are small and we know nothing of the timing of the migration. Further, virtually all other migration information is associated with mature female turtles.

5.256. However, some hints at what sea turtles are capable of can be gleaned from recent studies. Early in this document, I described something of what my own satellite telemetry studies are telling us of the migratory capabilities of the leatherback. They have demonstrated a capacity to travel in excess of 11,000 km in a single year, and all indications are that they make north/south migrations annually. In the Pacific it is likely that mature female leatherbacks circumnavigate the Pacific Ocean during the 2 or 3 years between nesting seasons. My current hypothesis for the movement of leatherbacks in the Pacific is that females from the 2 major colonies (Mexico/ Central America and Irian Jaya/Solomon Islands) as well as the minor colonies (e.g. Malaysia) distribute into a clockwise migration of the Pacific Ocean with turtles stopping to feed in areas of high productivity. What I have shown for the Atlantic Ocean is that leatherbacks are very adept at knowing where to anticipate areas of high food availability and will readily migrate great distances to access those resources. Supporting data for the theory of the migration cycle of Pacific leatherbacks is currently being gathered by satellite telemetry and DNA stock assessment, and thus far the hypothesis is supported. Significantly, this make the leatherback a species that shares many government jurisdictions. It is highly probable that Malaysia, Thailand and the United States all share responsibility Pacific leatherbacks during a single nesting migration.

5.257. Green turtle females have well-documented long distance post-nesting migrations. Most of the data is from tag returns, which are somewhat problematic when trying to understand migratory cycles. Such data usually only represents a one-way trip or a stop along a possibly longer journey, because invariably the turtle is killed and thus the tag is recovered. Most green turtle post-nesting migrations are between 1,500 and 3,000 km (Kolinski, 1991, 1992, Meylan, 1982, Mortimer and Carr, 1987, Pritchard, 1973, Balazs, 1976). Even more valuable has been a recent plethora of satellite tracking studies of female green turtle post-nesting migrations, though in most cases the duration of tracking has been too short for the determination of annual movement patterns (Balazs, G.H. 1994, Balazs et. al., 1994, Liew et. al., 1995, Luschi et. al., 1996).

5.258. Migrations or movements of juvenile or foraging green turtles are not as well investigated. It is likely that the species exhibits the same planktonic existence of other species for the first years after hatching. Balazs (1976) proposed for the Hawaiian green turtle nesting population at the French Frigate Shoals that hatchling probably disperse to the west, though how far and how long is unknown. Generally loggerhead females also make long post nesting migrations in excess of 1000 km; they are generally shorter than what is documented from green turtles (Bell and Richardson, 1978, Hughes 1974, Meylan, 1982, Margaritoulis, 1988). Developmental migrations of juvenile loggerheads is probably better understood than any other species. In both the Pacific and Atlantic, hatchling loggerheads circle their respective ocean basins during their first years of life (Carr, 1987, Bowen et. al., 1995) and return to the coast they were hatched on to settle. From those foraging area they will make migrations to their natal beaches to nest. Early literature on the migration behaviour of hawksbill suggested that they were relatively sedentary and did not make long migrations (Bustard, 1979). Meylan et. al., (1997) summarizes hawksbill migrations and concludes that they migrate comparable distances to green or loggerhead turtles. The longest migration was 2,925 km, with a large number in excess of 1,000 km. Meylan et. al., (1997) also summarizes studies on hawksbill juveniles both in the Caribbean and Pacific that suggests that juveniles probably remain in the same habitat or area for many years and may only move to other developmental habitats as they grow.

5.259. Annual migrations for most species are only poorly documented or understood. I have noted where it appears that Atlantic leatherbacks make annual north-south migrations. There is also a seasonal presence of leatherbacks at various areas along the US East and West Coasts (Shoop and Kenney, 1992, Stinson, 1984). Stinson (1984) also documented the seasonal abundance of loggerheads, olive ridley and East-Pacific green turtles on the US West coast, and concluded that these species follow the 18°C isotherm. Morreale (1990) has also indicated that there is a strong correlation between temperature and presence of Kemp's ridleys and loggerhead sea turtles in Long Island sound and the coastal waters of New York. With the exception of reproductive migrations and leatherback, migratory movement of most species seem to be temperature driven. Given the relatively warm waters of Malaysia, Thailand, India and Pakistan it would not be expected that resident turtle population would exhibit annual or seasonal migrations in those countries.

**Dr. J. Frazier:**

5.260. The individuals of a population of sea turtles, that nests on a nesting beach, are likely to have migrated to a variety of feeding grounds. Leatherbacks make the largest movements, while in general hawksbills migrate the shortest distances. Olive ridleys take up a pelagic existence, at least in the Eastern Tropical Pacific (Plotkin et al., 1995; 1997). In any event, information on "migratory patterns" is very incomplete, and we are only beginning fully to appreciate the degree to which sea turtles move around the oceans. It has been known for decades - even centuries - that sea turtles migrate over vast distances; Brongersma (1972) compiled hundreds of records from the Atlantic coast of Europe (where sea turtles do not breed), the first of which was from the 1300s. Today, with the exception of the Australian Flatback, there are records of every species of sea turtle crossing ocean basins: viz loggerhead (e.g., Brongersma, 1972; Dodd, 1988; Bowen, 1995; Bowen and Karl, 1997); green (e.g., Brongersma, 1972; Bowen, 1995; Hirth, 1997); leatherback (e.g., Brongersma, 1972; Pritchard and Trebbau, 1984; Eckert and Sarti, 1997); hawksbill (e.g., Marcovaldi and Filippini, 1991; Meylan et. al., in press); Kemp's ridley (e.g., Brongersma, 1972; Pritchard and Marquèz, 1973); and olive ridley (e.g., Pitman, 1990; Plotkin et. al., 1995). The absence of information simply is not evidence with which to conclude that turtles do not migrate. New scientific tools such as genetic analyses (Bowen, 1995; Bowen and Karl, 1997) and satellite transmitters, are providing valuable new insights into the question of sea turtle migrations.

5.261. Generally nesting is seasonal, although in some populations nesting may occur through the year, or much of the year, with a peak in activity at a certain time of year. The migrations for which sea turtles are famous occur between nesting grounds and feeding grounds, and between feeding grounds and nesting grounds. When nesting is seasonal, these migrations will also be seasonal However, some turtles may move over large areas between nesting seasons, as seems to be the case with the leatherback. In addition to the migrations of breeding adults to and from nesting grounds, the immature turtles disperse over vast areas of the oceans, apparently taking up temporary, sequential residence in various "developmental habitats" as they mature. These movements are often referred to as migrations also, although they generally are thought not to involve return trips. Little is known about these "immature migrations".

**Mr. M. Guinea:**

5.262. All sea turtle species except the Australian flatback undergo extensive ocean migrations during their life. Hatchlings, after they leave the nesting beach, spend a long period, possibly a decade, at sea. In response to an unknown trigger they take up residence in an inshore feeding area. Several of these inshore feeding areas may be used as the turtle grows to maturity. Adult sea turtles are thought to migrate to nesting beaches and back to their feeding areas using the magnetic field of the earth (Lohman et. al., 1997). They are capable of crossing deep water (>2,000 m) on these migrations. The migration may be independent of the coastline of alternatively may be along the coast. The return path appears to be essentially the same route. This is done individually without any social facilitation of others or herding within the breeding unit.

5.263. The migrations are similar but at the same time they are uncoordinated. Reproductive migrations are in response to conducive nesting conditions developing in the coming months at a rookery, possibly over 1,000 km from the feeding area. In mixed feeding grounds, turtles from one breeding unit may leave at a different time and in a different direction to those of another breeding units. Some turtles may not breed that year and will remain resident on the feeding area.

5.264. The migration of a breeding unit will be seasonally to the rookery at the beginning of the breeding season and away from the rookery at the end of the nesting season. This largely goes unnoticed, except where the sea turtles pass through straits, cross shallow water or around geographic projections. This seasonality of green sea turtle migration through the waters of the Torres Straits, north of Australia, have been exploited for centuries by the indigenous islanders (Johannes and MacFarlane, 1991).

5.265. The timing and intensity of the migrations through the straits varies with the number of sea turtles nesting that season and the number of males that migrate to the breeding areas. Males leave the breeding area early in the nesting season and return to their feeding ground. Within the nesting area, movements by the female will be relatively short, 2-20 km, and coincide with movements to the nesting beach to lay the clutch and return to the offshore refuge while awaiting the maturation of the next clutch. After her final clutch the female returns to her distant feeding grounds.

**Mr. H.-C. Liew:**

5.266. Much has yet to be learned about sea turtle migration. From various evidences gathered, sea turtle hatchlings do not seem to migrate but head offshore on entering the sea to drift and be carried by oceanic currents for about 5-7 years. The oceanic currents may carry some of these hatchlings thousands of kilometres along oceanic gyres and may be transported across the Pacific or Atlantic Ocean. On becoming juveniles, only the leatherback will continue this ocean-pelagic existence while the other species would begin to work their way towards shallower waters. When they find suitable feeding areas, they would establish these areas as their foraging or feeding grounds, where they may remain for many years. The range of these feeding grounds may vary between species and between turtles. As to whether they have multiple distant feeding grounds and migrate amongst them is not known. The most significant migration that sea turtles perform is their migration between feeding grounds and nesting grounds (see answer below).

**Dr. I. Poiner:**

5.267. Sea turtle breeding stocks usually comprise multiple rookeries within a region while foraging areas and developmental habitats comprise a mix of turtles from several genetically distinct stocks (Bowen et. al., 1995; Broderick et al., 1994). The breeding adults usually migrate relatively long distances from the foraging areas to the traditional breeding rookeries. I will illustrate this life history pattern using Australian loggerhead (Caretta caretta) and green (Chelonia mydas) turtle populations (Limpus 1997).

5.268. The Australian nesting populations of loggerhead sea turtles are genetically distinct from those in other countries and within Australia there are two genetically independent breeding populations. Breeding occurs in the summer months for both populations. Breeding females migrate up to 2,600 km from feeding areas to aggregate at traditional nesting beaches (breeding males have not been studied). In eastern Australia, females migrate from northern and eastern Australia, Indonesia, Papua New Guinea, Solomon Islands and New Caledonia. In Western Australia, recorded migrants come from Northern and Western Australia and Indonesia. Mean remigration period is 3.8yr. At the completion of the breeding season the female returns to the same feeding site as she occupied before the breeding migration.

5.269. The green turtle has a global distribution in all oceans with nesting occurring mostly in tropical areas. The Australian nesting populations are genetically distinct from those in neighbouring countries. Within Australia there are at least 5 genetically independent stocks. In addition, there are green turtles that feed in Australia that are part of stocks that breed in other countries: Indonesia (Java), northeastern PNG, New Caledonia and Pacific Mexico. Breeding occurs in the summer months for the east coast and west coast populations and during the winter for the northern populations. Breeding females and males migrate up to 3000 km from feeding areas to aggregate at traditional nesting beaches. In Eastern Australia, females migrate from Northern and Eastern Australia, Indonesia, Papua New Guinea, Vanuatu, Fiji and New Caledonia. In Western Australia, recorded migrants come from Northern and Western Australia and Indonesia. Mean remigration period = 5.8 years for females and 2.1 years for males. At the completion of the breeding season the adult returns to the same feeding sites it occupied before the breeding migration.

**5(b) What is the typical range of migration of the various species of sea turtles, in particular in relation to the territories (including overseas territories) of the countries concerned? What is the maximum range?**

**Dr. S. Eckert:**

5.270. See my response to question 5(a).

**Dr. J. Frazier:**

5.271. It would be difficult to derive a value for a "typical range of migration" for a population of sea turtles, much less for a species. Firstly, precise information on migrations of sea turtles from the Indo-Pacific region is only recently becoming available. Secondly, much information is from tag returns, and this only reveals where the turtle was caught - not the route it traveled, nor where it was actually headed. Third, there is often tremendous variety in the final destinations and distances where turtles are recaptured, after being tagged and released.

5.272. A very brief review of some of the more remarkable data on migrations from the Indo-Pacific follows, all it is from nesting females. As more studies are carried out, especially using satellite telemetry, a much better information will come to light on the intricate relationships between nesting beaches, feeding ground, and migratory routes.

- Although at least 2,351 green turtles and 42 olive ridleys have been tagged at Hawksbay, Pakistan (Firdous, in press), there seems only one tag recovery from outside Pakistan. One green turtle tagged in Hawksbay was recaptured in the Gulf of Kutch, India (Firdous, 1991). The distance involved is relatively short, considering the distances that green turtles are known to have moved in other populations.
- Tens of thousands of olive turtles have been tagged at Gahirmatha, Orissa, India, but few if any have been reported recaptured away from India. There are observations that flotillas of these turtles may migrate from offshore Sri Lanka to Gahirmatha (Silas, 1984; Silas et. al., 1984).
- Long-range migration data are available for three species of sea turtle in Malaysia. Leatherbacks tagged at Terengganu have been captured at tremendous distances from their home beach, as far away as Taiwan, Japan and Hawai'i (Leong and Siow, 1980). Green turtles tagged in Sarawak have been recovered as far off as Philippines and California (Leh, 1989). During recent years, a wealth of information on migrations has been coming out of Malaysia. Green turtles nesting on Redang Island, off the coast of Terengganu, Peninsular Malaysia, have been tracked with satellite transmitters more than 1,600 km east to Sabah and Philippines, as well as some 1,000 km southeast into Indonesian waters (Liew et. al., 1995a; 1995b; Papi et. al., 1995). Once they have finished nesting in the Sabah turtle islands, green turtles disperse north and east to the Philippines and even to Palau Islands, as well as south into Indonesian waters; some of the distances between sites of marking and recapture are close to 2,000 km (Chan and Liew, 1996b). Hawksbills from the Sabah turtle islands also disperse east to Philippines (Chan and Liew, 1996b).
- There seems to be no information on tagging or tag returns or sea turtle migration from Thailand.
- From the United States there is a considerable amount of information on long-range tag returns, and more recently satellite telemetry. Eckert (1993) has reviewed findings from the North Pacific. Since then several studies of satellite telemetry have documented movements of green turtles from French Frigate Shoals to Hawaii and Johnson Atoll (Balazs, 1994; Balazs and Ellis, in press), as well as from Rose Island to Samoa (Balazs et. al., 1994). Hawksbill turtles have made shorter movements, within the Hawaiian Islands (Balazs et. al., 1997; in

press). Pultz et. al. (in press) found that one of six green turtles tagged while nesting on Tinian Island, Commonwealth of Northern Mariana Islands, was recaptured in Philippines a year later. Dutton et. al. (in press) have found that one of two leatherbacks caught in Hawaii had a haplotype that has been found in Indonesia.

5.273. It is important to understand that in those regions with more active research activities, more scientific information is available. The absence of information is no proof of the absence of a phenomenon; until a systematic study has been carried out to objectively show that a specific phenomenon does not occur, one cannot draw defensible conclusions on the basis of the lack of information.

**Mr. M. Guinea:**

5.274. The years that juvenile sea turtles spend in their pelagic existence after leaving the rookery enable them to drift around an ocean gyre. At any one time they may be thousands of kilometres away from their natal beach. (The Australian flatback is exceptional in not having a pelagic phase to its life cycle.) The coastal developmental habitats through which they pass as they mature, do not necessarily bring the sub-adult closer to its natal beach. The movement from the adult feeding ground to the nesting beach and return is considered a true migration. Tagging studies in Australia have indicated that loggerheads travel hundreds and even several thousand kilometres to nesting beaches and return during a reproductive migration. Green turtles have been recorded travelling up to 2600 km from rookery to feeding area, but most travel less than 1000 km. Hawksbills travel up to 2369 km in one instance but most travel a shorter distance. In Malaysia, green turtles travel over 1700 km after nesting (Liew, 1997). In India, olive ridleys travel within the country from Orissa to the Gulf of Mannar, over 1,000 km. Leatherbacks appear to retain their pelagic existence in adulthood and may, in their non reproductive state, be several thousand kilometres from their natal beach.

5.275. The concept of maximum range is attributable to sea turtles that migrate from a feeding area to a nesting area and return to the feeding area. The maximum ranges as reported above are in the order of 2,000 km. Breeding units from nesting beaches may be detected on feeding grounds. Comparisons between the genetic profiles of a sample of sea turtles at a nesting beach and a sample of adult mature females turtles on the feeding ground may indicate if they are of the same breeding unit. This may be supported further by tagging programmes. If a turtle has been tagged either at the feeding ground or the nesting beach, then its life history may be pieced together from subsequent recaptures on either feeding grounds and the nesting beach. It is the successful completion of the migration that separates a normal sea turtle from a "waif" which has been carried or drifted out of its "normal" range.

**Mr. H.-C. Liew:**

5.276. Turtles migrate from their feeding or "home" grounds to the nesting grounds when they are physiologically ready and are in the reproductive phase. This does not occur every year for the individual female but happens in cycles of between 2 to 7 or more years. This is because the females need to build up sufficient fat (or food) reserves to sustain them throughout the breeding season which may last up to 3-4 months before they are able to return back to their feeding grounds. What is known of the green turtles throughout this period, i.e. during migration and at the nesting grounds, they hardly feed. Hence migration ranges would be somewhat restricted. The migration ranges of most green turtles would be in the region of 500 to 2,500 km. Anything beyond that would put severe restrictions on their survival. Leatherbacks, however, being and ocean-pelagic species are capable of migrating over much longer distances.

**Dr. I. Poiner:**

5.277. See my response to 5 (a).

**Question 6: Relation between sea turtles and shrimping grounds**

**6(a) Does sea turtle biology and in particular the spatial and temporal relation between sea turtles and shrimp differ between the Atlantic and the Indo-Pacific waters? To what extent do habitats and/or nesting grounds of the different species of sea turtles coincide with shrimp fishing grounds?**

**Dr. S. Eckert:**

5.278. Due to the limited information available on the distribution of foraging turtles in Thailand, Malaysia, India and Pakistan I am not able to address the question of where shrimping and turtles might interact. Except for the few reports of where turtles have been killed by shrimping (Orissa, India, Terengannu, Malaysia, United States Atlantic coast and Gulf of Mexico), predicting where such interaction could occur is difficult.

**Dr. J. Frazier:**

5.279. It is important to understand that "sea turtle" refers to any one of five species of sea turtles, and "shrimp" refers to scores of species; in some countries, a dozen species of shrimp and prawn may be harvested. Each species will have its own life history, with different spatial and temporal characteristics. I am not versed in these details. The spatial and temporal relationship between sea turtles and shrimp trawling has been abundantly and systematically documented. The first global review on the subject was presented by Hillestad et. al. (1982), and since then much more information has become available. There have been specific studies in both northern and eastern Australia (Poiner and Harris, 1994; Robins, 1995 Guinea and Whiting, 1997); on the Pacific coasts of Guatemala, El Salvador, Nicaragua and Costa Rica (Arauz, 1990; 1996a; 1996b; Arauz et. al., 1997a; 1997b); Mexico (Olguin, 1996); along the southern Atlantic and Gulf of Mexico coasts of the United States (National Research Council, 1990; Crowder et. al., 1994; 1995; Weber et. al., 1995); and on the Caribbean coast of Venezuela (Marcano and Alio, 1994). There is also information in the scientific literature from many other countries, such as: Eritrea (Hillman and Gebremariam, 1996), India (e.g., Silas et. al., 1983a; 1983b; 1985; Pandav et. al., 1997), Kenya (Wamukoya et. al., 1996), Malaysia (Suliansa et. al., 1996; Ali et. al., 1997), Mauritius (Mangar and Chapman, 1996), Tanzania (Howell and Mbindo, 1996) and Turkey (Oruç et. al., 1997).

**Mr. M. Guinea:**

5.280. Just as there are a number of species of sea turtle there are even more species of shrimp. Generalizations about sea turtles and shrimp interactions should be avoided as different shrimp species of different market value have different preferred habitats. Particular shrimp species are targeted by the operators. In Australian trawl fields, some species e.g., the banana prawn (*Penaeus merguiensis*) form dense aggregations which discolour the shallow water and the schools of prawns form an image on depth sounders. Beam or otter trawls are used to target such aggregations. Tow durations rarely exceed 30 minutes. In such short tows on a targeted school, sea turtles are rarely captured. Other prawn species inhabit deep water (90m). Trawls may be longer, but turtles are seldom found at those depths and any negative impact is unlikely. Trawling for some tiger prawn species is conducted in shallower water, with 3 hours per tow being relatively common. They have the potential, if unchecked by restrictions, to interact with loggerhead, olive ridley and flatback sea turtles. Operators may target different shrimp species at times of the year. Or alternatively they may target different species within a single cruise.

5.281. Regions offshore from sea turtle rookeries, by the soft nature of the sea bed, may support a shrimp ground. These areas offshore from rookeries should have seasonal closures to fishing activities that have the potential to harm sea turtles. The extent of the closed area will depend on the species of sea turtles nesting. Some species may be protected by a 3 km wide refuge, but others e.g., leatherback, may require a width of 20 km for a successful refuge. This is a situation best left to the legislators of the respective countries. All the countries in the dispute have indicated that sanctuaries or seasonal refuges have been established offshore from nesting beaches.

**Mr. H.-C. Liew:**

5.282. In a broad general sense, they are similar but there will also be localized differences. In Asia, we have the wet and dry season brought about by the monsoon, which may be somewhat different in the Atlantic. Even within the same region, some sea turtle populations nest in the dry season, but others may nest in the wet season. There are also some locations, like in the Sabah turtle islands where nestings occur throughout the year. The season for shrimp trawling may also differ. Feeding habitats of different sea turtles would differ depending on their diet but these habitats may overlap. An area of seabed may have green turtles, hawksbills, loggerheads and ridleys occurring together as the area may have pockets of seagrass, sponges, crabs, shrimps, molluscs and fish there. On the other hand, over a seagrass area in an estuary, you may find only green turtles feeding there. Since loggerheads and ridleys feed on crustaceans and molluscs while green turtles and leatherbacks feed on seagrass/algae and jellyfish respectively, shrimping grounds would have a stronger association with loggerheads and ridleys than the other species. Not all sea turtle nesting grounds have good shrimping grounds in the vicinity. Sipadan Island, off Sabah, Malaysia, is a world renown nesting beach for green turtles but no shrimp trawlers can operate there as the waters off the island is 2,000 ft deep. Many such islands and atolls do occur throughout the Indo-Pacific.

**Dr. I. Poiner:**

5.283. Globally, tropical and sub-tropical shrimp fisheries are generally concentrated in relatively shallow coastal waters (< 80m). Sea-turtle nesting and foraging habitats also tend to occur in the shallow coastal waters. Hence there is and will continue to be significant interaction between shrimp fisheries and sea-turtles.

**6(b) Are statistical comparisons of the interaction between shrimp trawling and sea turtle populations in the Atlantic and in the Indo-Pacific waters available? If so, what do they indicate?**

**Dr. S. Eckert:**

5.284. To the best of my knowledge there are no statistical comparisons on shrimp fishery / sea turtle interaction between the waters around Thailand and Malaysia and the United States. However, there are some studies on the Australian prawn fishery (Dredge, and Trainor, 1994, Harris and Poiner, 1990, Poiner et. al., 1990), the latter comparing Northern Australian catch rates directly to Henwood and Stuntz (1987) report of US catch rates. While this study showed comparable catch rates between the US Gulf of Mexico and Northern Australia, the mortality rate for Australia was much lower. Unfortunately, for comparative purposes the Australian study was hampered in that the primary species caught (43 per cent) was the endemic Australian Flatback. This species has a very unique life history as compared to all other marine turtle species and it is not known if it has a higher resistance to drowning than other species. Thus, it is difficult to know if the different mortality rates are due to geographical or species composition differences between Australia and the United States.

**Dr. J. Frazier:**

5.285. Systematic studies of the interactions between shrimp trawling and sea turtles have been carried out in both Northern and Eastern Australia (Poiner and Harris, 1994; Robins, 1995); on the Pacific coasts of Guatemala, El Salvador, Nicaragua and Costa Rica (Arauz, 1996a; 1996b; Arauz et. al., 1997a; 1997b); along the southern Atlantic and Gulf of Mexico coasts of the US (National Research Council, 1990; Crowder et. al., 1994; 1995; Weber et. al., 1995); and on the Caribbean coast of Venezuela (Marcano and Alio, 1994).

**Mr. M. Guinea:**

5.286. Available data indicate that sea turtle mortality rates are higher in the Gulf of Mexico (29 per cent) and Atlantic Ocean Shrimp Fishery (21 per cent) than has been found in the Northern Prawn Fishery (6-10 per cent) and the East Coast Trawl Fishery (1-6 per cent) of Australia (Robins, 1995). The catch rates of sea turtles per unit of effort was greater in the American shrimp fisheries (0.0031-0.0487 per net h) than in the above mentioned Australian fisheries (0.0057-0.01 per net h). The species of turtles impacted also differed, with loggerheads, Kemp's ridleys and greens being present in the US fisheries and loggerheads, flatbacks, olive ridleys, greens and hawksbills present in the Australian fishery.

**Mr. H.-C. Liew:**

5.287. Unable to source such information.

**Dr. I. Poiner:**

5.288. Poiner and Harris (1996) compared the incidental catch of sea turtles in Northern Australia with the Gulf of Mexico and southern North Atlantic. The catch rate of turtles in the Australian Northern Prawn Fishery (mean 0= 0.0113, 95 per cent CI 0.0012 turtles) is higher than the rate Henwood and Stuntz (1987) reported for the Gulf of Mexico (mean = 0.0031, 95 per cent CI 0.0008 turtles) but lower than the rate they reported for the southern North Atlantic (mean = 0.0487, 95 per cent CI 0.0041 turtles). Most prawn trawling in the southern North Atlantic fishery occurs in water depths less than 18 m and, as in the Northern Prawn Fishery, catch rates vary with water depth, with the highest catch rates in water around 14 m deep. In the Gulf of Mexico, prawn trawling occurs in water depths up to 80 m, but unlike the other two fisheries, the turtle catch rate appears to be fairly constant over all depths up to 30 m.

5.289. The turtle mortality rates for the Gulf of Mexico and southern North Atlantic prawn fisheries were estimated as 29 per cent and 21 per cent of captures (Henwood and Stuntz 1987), which is higher than the 14.1 per cent estimated for the Northern Prawn Fishery. The difference may be due to different species having different mortality rates. The loggerhead dominates the American catches: 94 per cent of the southern North Atlantic and 86 per cent of the Gulf of Mexico catches. Its mortality rates were estimated as 29 per cent and 30 per cent respectively (Henwood and Stuntz 1987). The same species is a small component of the Northern Australian catch (10 per cent), but its estimated mortality rate is similar to the American rates (22 per cent). The loggerhead therefore appears to be particularly susceptible to drowning. In contrast, the dominant turtle in the Northern Prawn Fishery catch, the flatback (59 per cent), has a low mortality rate: 11 per cent. This species is endemic to Northern Australia and tends to be found inshore in relatively shallow (<40 m) muddy waters and possibly has a higher resistance to drowning in trawls (11 per cent mortality) compared to the other species. The difference in the overall mortality rates of turtles in the American and Australian fisheries may, therefore, be due to the dominant species being more or less susceptible to drowning.

**6(c) Are all species of sea turtles significantly affected by shrimp trawling in different regions of the world? Or are some species likely to be more or less affected due to their nesting/feeding habits and migratory patterns and such divergences as might occur in those habits and patterns in different parts of the world ?**

**Dr. J. Frazier:**

5.290. Any population of sea turtles that suffers mortality of breeders or near breeders in shrimp trawls will be significantly affected, independent of the species or locality. Some sea turtle populations may be more vulnerable to shrimp trawling than others because of spatial and temporal differences in occurrence of turtles and shrimp. By the same token, some human populations may be more vulnerable to cocaine addiction than others, but in all human populations this drug represents a risk to society.

**Mr. M. Guinea:**

5.291. All species of sea turtles are not adversely affected by shrimp trawls. Some species have preferred habitats which do not always coincide with shrimp trawl fields. These habitats can be identified and, if need be, seasonal closures to turtle threatening activities may be imposed. Even on relatively uniform substrates sea turtle distribution is clumped rather than random. This gives rise to "hot spots" where sea turtles abound while in seemingly similar areas nearby, they are scarce. After almost one year of trials in the Northern Prawn Fishery, the Australian Fisheries Management Authority (Sachse and Wallner, in press) are looking towards a log-book programme of all sea turtle captures, resuscitation procedures for comatose sea turtles, and closure of some areas such as seagrass beds to protect juvenile tiger prawns and green sea turtles as well as the implementation of TEDs on a voluntary basis. This example from Australia demonstrates the complexity of introducing new technology into a fishery as well as adopting an ethos of responsible fishing. Any legislation requiring the use of TEDs on shrimp trawls would require the allocation of additional resources for enforcement of any such legislation. Australia is encouraging voluntary compliance by stressing the advantages of using Trawl Efficiency Devices (TEDs) in the fishery. This will take considerable time.

**Mr. H.-C Liew:**

5.292. All species of sea turtles have the potential of being caught in a shrimp trawl as much as any other sea creature large enough to be retained by the cod-end of the trawl net. The only difference is the probability of encounters. Some of the factors that dictate this probability are:

- Number of trawlers operating in the area, their size, power, efficiency, size of nets, trawl time, etc.
- How much the trawling grounds overlap with turtle feeding grounds.
- Species of turtles which will dictate their feeding habits, resting habits, migration routes, how long they remain on the seabed as opposed to midwater or surface, do they feed in the same area as the operating trawlers.
- Offshore internesting habitats, depth, frequency of shrimp trawlers operating there.
- Whether shrimp trawling seasons coincide with nesting seasons.
- Laws and regulations protecting the turtles.
- Enforcement of regulations.
- Awareness and education of the fishermen to turtle conservation.

All these factors do vary from region to region, hence the probability of encounters cannot be the same. There is no doubt that in some regions of the world, sea turtles are significantly affected by shrimp trawling where the probability of encounters is high but the same cannot apply for all regions. Moreover, threats due to other causes may impact the turtles more significantly than shrimp trawling for some regions.

**Dr. I. Poiner:**

5.293. See my answer to 6(b).

### *C. Comments by the Parties*

#### *1. Comments by India*

5.294. A review of experts' opinions shows that causes of decline of sea turtles should not be broadly categorized as being due to anthropogenic and natural causes. In the *Draft Recovery plans for US Pacific populations of Sea Turtles*[412], Eckert et al. have identified 26 different types of anthropogenic threats. The degree and magnitude of these different types of threats are not the same for all species of sea turtles. Even for the same species differences exist in different geographical regions of the world. All experts have indicated that the causes of decline of sea turtle populations have changed over time for each region and for each species. Again all the experts have emphasized the lack of information in this regard, which makes it difficult for categorization of different threats. For sea turtle populations in different parts of the world, the general consensus is that in the past populations have vanished due to exploitation of eggs, habitats and adults for commercial purposes. There was a great demand for eggs and byproducts all over the world which led to the flourishing trade. Now such large scale exploitation for commercial purposes has completely stopped in many countries including in India. Although eggs have a special value for certain other qualities in addition to nutrition in some countries, in India, there is no such tradition. Again, from the experts' opinions, it emerges that the concept of sea turtles being a global resource, while being philosophically laudable, is cumbersome in terms of conservation strategies.

5.295. The 1997 Limpus study[413] has given an overview of the status of marine turtles of South East Asia and the Western Pacific region. His report does not include the status of turtles in Indian waters. Mr. Guinea has given most extensive answer to the question quoting data from several sources. We generally endorse his views.

5.296. Dr. Eckert's statements regarding "regional populations were independent management units"[414] and that "consideration of population status must still be based on the global species status"[415] are contradictory. Even the DNA analysis and satellite telemetry data by Dr. Eckert show that the Atlantic leatherback turtles migrate within the Atlantic Ocean. Similarly, the Pacific population remains restricted to the Pacific Ocean. The sweeping generalization regarding leatherback nesting stocks from Malaysia/Thailand/Indonesia being distributed throughout the Ocean basin is based on personal communication (Peter Dutton, NMFS)[416] and needs to be reinforced by more objective data. Though the methods of monitoring nesting population status

---

[412] NMFS and USFWS, (1996) drafts a-f, p. 5.

[413] Limpus, C. (1997, *Marine Turtle Population of South East Asia and the Western Pacific Region: Distribution and Status*, Proceedings of the Workshop on Marine Turtle Research and Management in Indonesia, Jember, East Java, Indonesia, November 1996.

[414] Eckert para. 5.20.

[415] *Ibid.*

[416] Eckert para. 5.21.

have limitations, methods remaining the same over years can be used for conducting trend analysis. Dr. Eckert further lists a few causes for population decline for different species. The following are our comments on Dr. Eckert's views.

5.297. Dr. Eckert's views do not include the recent data (MTN, 1996) regarding the recovery of Mexican population of olive ridleys. For population status of ridleys in India he has incorporated old data and not the recent publications which shows recovery in populations (Mohanty-Hejmadi, 1994).[417] Further, Dr. Eckert has quoted several sources regarding the death of some five thousand turtles attributed to incidental catch in trawlers. As pointed out in the presentation by Indian experts to the WTO panel, the paper mostly lists the number and type of fishing vessels in Orissa in which the number of the shrimp trawlers is much less than the other fishing vessels. The conclusion that all the dead turtles are due to shrimp trawler activities is not true. Although 5,000 may seem a large number from other population point of view, India would like to draw attention to Mr. Guinea's comment that "the annual mortality of 5000 from fishing trawls and set nets from the nesting population of 600,000 with a recruitment of 85,000 appears relatively minor".[418] Further, Eckert has mentioned the attempts of State of Orissa to build fishing harbours besides the sanctuary.[419] On this point India repeats that the jetty, specially the Tachua jetty which would have affected the Gahirmatha population, was never commissioned by the Government. Further the whole area has now been declared as a marine sanctuary with the zone up to 20 km from the coast line having been declared as a "No fishing zone". At present the coast guards and the Indian Navy are patrolling the area to enforce the Government's conservation programmes. Regarding loggerhead sea turtles, Dr. Eckert has not provided data on Indo-Pacific populations.

5.298. Dr. Eckert has shown that causes of mortality for sea turtles are different in different parts of the world. For example, decline in the loggerhead populations in North Carolina is due to driftnet fishery in the high seas. The South American swordfish driftnet and longline fisheries are the causes of mortality of Pacific leatherbacks. Dr. Eckert has also shown that gill netting in South America is a major problem. The facts presented by Dr. Eckert show that no generalization can be made about ranking sources of mortality in different geographic areas of the world. Dr. Eckert has given data only about leatherback sea turtles and no data about India to rank sources of mortality. Regarding anthropogenic threats, Dr. Eckert has not included the recent developments in sea turtle protection in India. He has given the status of harvest of eggs and adults prior to 1985. Indian experts have already provided factual data to the Panel to demonstrate the highly successful steps taken by India to conserve and protect its sea turtle populations.

5.299. Dr. Eckert, Mr. Guinea and Mr. Liew have given only qualitative information to differentiate between shrimp trawl and other fishing gear in terms of the mortality they represent to marine turtles. No qualitative information has been provided on the effect on sea turtle mortality due to trawl fisheries, gillnet fisheries, longline fisheries, purse seine fisheries, fish traps, fish bombing. No information has been

417 Eckert para. 5.31.
418 Guinea para. 5.199.
419 Eckert para. 5.37.

provided about the degree of coincidence of the above type of fishing activities in different regions of the world where significant number of turtles occur e.g. feeding, breeding, migrating etc.

5.300. Scott Eckert's view that in India, the direct harvest of eggs and meat is apparently still a problem[420] is not factually correct, as Indian experts have provided the Panel already with factual data to demonstrate that direct harvest of endangered sea turtle eggs and meat is not a problem in India. Regarding the influence of socio-economic factors on the choice and enforcement of conservation programmes, Dr. Eckert has mainly covered the conditions in America relating to application of TEDs. He has not given any answer relating to socio-economic factors in the five countries involved in this dispute. We agree with Mr. Guinea's assessment that the so-called by-catch in US terms is a commodity with either a subsistence or retail value. Mr. Guinea has given a more realistic account on the subject. However, his comment that sea turtle eggs are also eaten is not applicable to India. Large scale exploitation of eggs has been effectively banned since mid 1970s. Mr. Liew's views that turtles are slaughtered in Asia is not true for India.[421] The same applies for eggs.

5.301. In general we agree with the views of Mr. Liew that all measures that prevent sea turtles from being killed are important.[422] We further endorse the views of Mr. Guinea that nesting habitats should be preserved as should the offshore refuge habitats for nesting females.[423] Dr. Eckert's views that very little is being done by most of the countries in this dispute to protect juvenile or resident adult sea turtles[424] is not true. For most of the populations of Southeast Asia, the feeding areas remain unknown. Therefore, more emphasis has been placed on protection to adults and eggs. The offshore turtle sensitive areas declared as Marine Wildlife Sanctuaries have given adequate protection to mating/breeding/feeding/developmental habitats of sea turtles in India. India does not have "headstarting" programme for any species of sea turtle populations at present. We endorse Mr. Guinea's opinion that the Gahirmatha population of sea turtles is increasing or at least stable through protection of the nesting area.[425]

5.302. Dr. Eckert's view is that TEDs reduce sea turtle mortality only when installed and operated properly.[426] Even in the United States, with years of education and conservation programmes, improper use of TED has resulted in continuing mortality of turtles. Dr. Eckert has admitted that he does not have any direct experience working with trawler fisherman from other countries involved in this dispute. In reality, improper use of TEDS, inefficiency in implementation and an ineffective monitoring mechanism can significantly affect the efficiency of TEDS, both in terms of loss of catch and protection of various species of sea turtles. The socio-economic conditions prevailing in the South Asian region require a different approach to that chosen in the United States in so far as the proper use, successful implementation

[420] Eckert para. 5.129.
[421] Liew para. 5.89.
[422] Liew para. 5.183.
[423] Guinea para. 5.181.
[424] Eckert para. 5.172.
[425] Guinea, para. 5.189.
[426] Eckert para. 5.202.

and foolproof monitoring mechanism is concerned. No answer has been given by Dr. Eckert to the question "can alternative measures such as seasonal and time closures, area closures or low-time limitations achieved equivalent or better results". In areas of low congregation TEDs will reduce, but not eliminate deaths of sea turtles caused by shrimp trawl net. So far, there is no study on the efficiency of TEDs in areas of high turtle congregation zones and whether in such areas TEDs can significantly reduce the mortality of sea turtles has to be studied.

5.303. India agrees with the interpretation of Mr. Liew on the points that after many years of experiments, publicity campaigns, TED trials, the United States mandated use of TEDs in 1980. As recently as 1994, NMFS reported poor compliance with US requirements. resulting in a record number of dead sea turtles. India also agrees with his views that considering the socio-economic conditions, educational level, language and cultural differences, it will take some time to convince and introduce the use of TEDs in different countries. These are all time consuming processes. Mr. Guinea has also mentioned that for TEDs to be accepted, the technology has to be adopted for the local area. There is no data on TED efficiency in Indian coastal waters except for demonstration of a few hours. No data has been collected on the efficiency of TEDs or their effect on bycatch. In so far as the "data on rate of turtle stranding in areas where TEDs are currently required or on the relationship between turtle stranding and shrimping activities in areas where TEDs are required", India endorses the views of Mr. Guinea. Data on TEDs efficiency during commercial shrimping seems to be most extensive for the United States and data from other countries and geographical locations would be necessary for comments. On this last question, India further endorses the views of Mr. Liew.

5.304. On question 3(c), India endorses the views of Mr. Guinea and Mr. Liew. On question 3(d) India endorses the views of Mr. Guinea.

5.305. In his answer to question 4(a), Dr. Eckert's data is based on specific populations. It is not clear why he has not quoted some of the recent data. However, India endorses the views of Mr. Guinea and Mr. Liew on the subject. Even Mr. Guinea has specifically cited the conservation measures devoted to eggs and hatchlings of olive ridleys in Orissa, India. Dr. Eckert has restricted his answer to question 4(b) to loggerheads in Little Cumberland Island and has not paid any attention to the data that is available for other areas. In this regard, India endorses the views of Mr. Guinea. It may be noted that he has made a special note on egg protection measures for olive ridleys in India and green turtles in Malaysia.

5.306. When examining the migratory patterns of sea turtles, Dr. Eckert has mainly used data on leatherbacks which, as pointed out by Mr. Liew, are ocean pelagic species, capable of migrating over long distances. In India, the major population is olive ridleys. Mr. Guinea has already indicated that in India olive ridleys travel within the country from Orissa to Gulf of Mannar, i.e. a distance of about 1,000 kms. On question 5(b), India endorses the views of Mr. Guinea.

5.307. On question 6(a), India agrees with Dr. Eckert's view that information is limited on the distribution of foraging turtles in Thailand, Malaysia, India and Pakistan. Dr. Eckert has cited few reports where turtles have been killed by shrimping but he has also said that predicting interactions between sea turtles and shrimp between Atlantic and Indo-Pacific waters is difficult. India would like to mention that the report often cited about turtles being killed by shrimping in Orissa,

India is not true. As Indian experts have demonstrated to the Panel, the death of a relatively minimal number of sea turtles in this area is due to all types of fishing activities, and not to shrimp trawl fishing by itself. On question 6(a), India further endorses the views of Mr. Liew and Mr. Guinea.

5.308. On question 6(c), India agrees with the views of Mr. Liew and would further like to say that the turtle sensitive areas in Orissa, India, have been declared as a Marine Wildlife Sanctuary with a no fishing zone extending up to 20 km from high tide line. Indian Navy and Indian Coast Guard have been deployed for protecting the area and enforcing the Government's sea turtle conservation programmes.

5.309. On the issue of bycatch addressed in Dr. Frazier's Appendix 1 (see Annex II), India would like to recall the point made by its experts to the Panel that in India, shrimps are harvested along with other fish. There is no specific shrimp trawling activity in Indian waters. The concept of bycatch therefore has to be applied in the Indian context with due care, since the catch involves all kinds of fish, and not exclusively shrimp. Endangered species of sea turtles are not the target of fish harvesting activities in India. Indeed, India would note that Dr. Frazier has not mentioned that endangered species of sea turtles do in fact form part of the bycatch in Indian fishing operations in his description of bycatch as contained in paragraphs 1-53 of his Appendix 1 (see Annex II). India would endorse the point made by Dr. Frazier regarding the non-exclusionary approach of India towards TEDs as one of the many ways for conserving and protecting sea turtles. The reference to ban on trawling in Indian waters off the coast of Kerala (paragraph 60 of Appendix 1), the reference to the interest in experiments on the use of TEDs in India (paragraph 77 of Appendix 1) illustrate this point.

5.310. India would like to highlight the fact brought out by Dr. Frazier's account that "the issue of endangered sea turtles, the use of TEDs and the questions of the present dispute" has been focused on in 1997 (paragraph 98 of Appendix 1). This helps to emphasize our point made to the Panel that the embargo imposed on our shrimp exports by the United States was not introduced on the basis of any factual or scientific evidence derived from Indian data known to the United States before 1997. Even data relevant to India in 1997 cannot, on a scientific basis, support the embargo imposed by the United States.

5.311. India is unable to see relevance for Indian sea turtle conservation programmes of the linkage between bycatch as a danger to the marine environment and the conservation and protection of endangered species of sea turtles (paragraphs 103-108of Appendix 1) since the argument appears to be developed on the basis of hypothetical situations, without supporting scientific data derived from Indian waters.

5.312. India would note that Dr. Frazier's views on the transfer of TED technology contained in Appendix 2 (see Annex II) of his report do not contradict the Indian expert opinion provided to the Panel, namely, that the workshops conducted under the auspices of the US NMFS in India were of too short a duration, and used only a limited type of TED made in the United States, to come to any definitive conclusion that TEDs are indeed the only way to protect and conserve endangered species of sea turtles in India. The correspondence provided by Dr. Frazier (p. 28 of Annex II) also demonstrates that India has always been interested in TEDs as one of the many ways to conserve and protect endangered species of sea turtles. Finally, India would like the Panel to disregard the objectivity of the views on the *Amicus Brief* submitted by the Centre for Marine Conservation dated 17 September 1997, as well as the WWF Amicus Brief and the Statement of Scientists attached to Dr. Frazier's opinion (see above section III.D).

### 2. *Comments by Malaysia*

5.313. In general, the views of Mr. Guinea, Mr. Liew, Dr. Pointer and Dr. Frazier (except Appendixes 1 and 2 contained in Annex II) are in conformity with the views of Malaysia. However, Malaysia does not agree with a number of points raised by Dr. Eckert and Dr. Frazier in his Appendixes 1 and 2.

5.314. Malaysia would like to reiterate that all trawling activities in Malaysia are subjected to zoning under the Fisheries (Maritime) Regulations, 1967. Under these Regulations, four zones have been established, as follows:

| | |
|---|---|
| Zone A | The zone within 5 nautical miles for traditional fishing fears owned and operated by Malaysian fishermen. Any form of trawling is prohibited within this zone. |
| Zone B | The zone between 5 to 12 nautical miles is reserved for trawlers and purse seiners less than 40 GRT (Gross Registered Tonnes) owned and operated by Malaysian fishermen. |
| Zone C | The zone between 12 to 30 nautical miles is reserved for trawlers and purse seiners greater than 40 GRT, and other fishing gears owned by Malaysian fishermen. |
| Zone C2 | The zone beyond 30 nautical miles is reserved for foreign or partially - Malaysian owned fishing vessels greater than 70 GRT. |

5.315. Zone A which covers shallow waters within 5 nautical miles (or 9.41 km.) from the shoreline would include all shallow water habitats utilized by sea turtles as feeding or internesting habitats. This zone therefore coincides with the areas where turtles concentrate. The exclusion of trawling in this zone would effectively protect the turtles from trawl nets as well as their habitats from destruction. In a sense, these zoning Regulations can be seen to be superior to TEDs requirements since it serves not only to protect the turtles, but also the habitats of the turtles from destruction by trawling activities. Enforcement as a general rule has its problems in any country. This is due mainly to the extensiveness of coastal waters and constraints imposed by limitations in financial and manpower resources. Enforcing zoning Regulations would be less cumbersome than enforcement of TEDs regulations because in Malaysia, the fishing vessels are required to paint their wheel houses with colours ascribed for each zone, besides having to mark prominently whether their vessels are of the A, B, or C2 classes. Therefore enforcement officers can easily sight cases of encroachment.

5.316. It is recognized that sea turtles do occur in waters beyond Zone A, i.e. when they perform breeding migrations between feeding and nesting grounds. However, during migration, the turtles do not stay at the bottom, but are engaged in constant swimming activities in the pelagic zone. During this time they are more susceptible to being caught in drift nets and longlines, not trawls. Internesting habitats of leatherback turtles may also extend into waters beyond Zone A. However, leatherback turtles do not normally sit on bottom habitats during the internesting period, making them less vulnerable to incidental captures in trawl nets.

5.317. To further protect turtles, Malaysia is amenable to introducing TEDs to trawl fishermen, including both fish (since most trawlers are fish trawlers) and shrimp trawlers. However, its use should be on a voluntary basis, as is in the case of Australia. Further, TEDs should be recommended only in those places where interactions with sea turtles occur and trials must be carried out to test their suitability in fish and shrimp trawls. It is important that fishermen be convinced of the beneficial effects of TEDs for them to voluntarily use them. More educational campaigns and workshops just as the one which had been held in Perak, Malaysia, can be conducted to popularize the use of TEDs. It is clear that in order to execute a sea turtle conservation programme which is comprehensive and addresses all threats faced by sea turtles, financial resources are urgently required. It is hoped that concerned rich nations like the United States can provide funding assistance in this respect.

5.318. There seems to be some disagreement among the experts regarding the status of the green and hawksbill populations of the Sabah Turtles Islands. Limpus[427] gives the recognition of recovering status, with Mr. Guinea, Mr. Liew and Dr. Frazier agreeing, although the latter has expressed some reservations. Dr. Eckert does not acknowledge that the Sabah Turtle Islands population has recovered. His contention is that the population has been monitored only a few years and this is not sufficient to ascertain its status. Malaysia would like to reiterate that the nesting population of the Sabah Turtle Islands has been monitored since the mid-1960s[428]. A declining trend was evident in the first 20 years, from 1966 to 1987. A reversal in trend started from 1988, with the upward trend maintained since then. Chan and Liew[429] provided data up to the year 1994 (i.e. for seven years). We now have additional data for 1995 and 1996, as shown in the table below. Lately, the Sabah Turtle Islands have been subjected to erosion. Notwithstanding, the nestings did not show any appreciable decline:

[427] C.J. Limpus, (1995), *Global Overview of the Status of Marine Turtles*, in D.A. Bjorndal (ed.), Biology and Conservation of Sea Turtles, Smithsonian Institution Press; C.J. Limpus, (1997), *Marine Turtle Populations of Southeast Asia and the Western Pacific Region: Distribution and Status*, Proceedings of the Workshop on Marine Turtle Research and Management in Indonesia, Jember, East Java, November 1996.

[428] C.H. Chan and H.C. Liew, (1996), *A Management Plan for the Green and Howksbill Turtle Populations of the Sabah Turtle Islands: a Report to the Sabah Park*, SEATRU, Universiti Kolej, Universiti Putra Malaysia, Terengganu.

[429] *Ibid.*

*Turtle nestings and egg incubation in the Sabah Turtle Islands for 1995 to 1997*

| Year | 1995 | 1996 | 1997 |
|---|---|---|---|
| No. of green turtle nestings (egg clutches) deposited | 9,120 | 8,359 | Not available* yet |
| No. of green turtle eggs incubated | 910,274 | 833,078 | 1,032,580 |
| No. of hawksbill nestings (egg clutches) deposited | 420 | 615 | Not available yet |
| No. of hawksbill eggs incubated | 40,835 | 60,657 | 55,360 |

* Although this data is not available yet, the number of green turtle nestings have reached the ten thousand mark, based on the total number of eggs which have been incubated (on average, green turtles lay about 100 eggs per nesting).

*Source*: Paul Bisintal, Assistant Director, Sabah Parks.

5.319. With the additional data for the three years 95-97, we now have data which shows an increasing trend for the last nine years (1988-1997). This already fulfils the time series requirement of "6-9" years stipulated by Dr. Eckert.[430] Therefore, we do not understand why he requires "another 15 years" of monitoring before he would accord the status of "recovered" to the Sabah Turtle Islands. Dr. Eckert has criticized Malaysia for being wrong assuming that a trend in the green turtle populations can be determined only after a few years.[431] We would like to point out that the recovering trend in the Sabah Turtle Islands has been observed since 1988, more than a matter of a few years. We now have additional data for years 1995, 1996 and 1997, as shown above.

5.320. Mr. Liew, in his response to question 2(d), says that for the Sabah Turtle Islands population, "the impact (shrimp trawling), if found to be significant, may negate other conservation efforts and would need urgent action". The fact that the nesting population of the Sabah Turtle Islands has shown a recovery, with the current levels fluctuating at a level about 2-3 times the levels of post-recovery years indicates that incidental captures, including trawling mortality have not negatively impacted the current population. Current levels have not been short-lived, but instead, have been sustained since recovery in 1988. If fishing mortality is serious, there would have been a persistent continuing declining trend.

5.321. The argument put forth by Dr. Eckert for the case of the loggerheads of Little Cumberland Island, Georgia,[432] supports our contention. In this case, population recovery has not occurred even though the eggs have been accorded 100 per cent protection since 1964. Dr. Eckert attributes this to mortality associated with shrimp fishing on the Atlantic coast, which has negated the effects of 100 per cent egg protection. By the same token, there must have been an absence of significant mortality attributed to shrimp trawling and other fishing activities around the Sabah Turtle Islands to have made possible the population recovery there.

5.322. It is generally agreed that each stock or population or breeding unit of sea turtle should be identified and managed as an independent unit. These units are genetically

[430] Eckert para. 5.23.
[431] Eckert para. 5.186.
[432] Eckert, para. 5.241.

defined.[433] Limpus (1997)[434] recognizes this when he says that "population genetics studies are clearly showing that each of the geographically separate clusters of rookeries represents an independent management unit". Mr. Guinea similarly recognizes this in his introductory comments.[435] However, Dr. Eckert does not seem to subscribe to this. He maintains that regional populations cannot be viewed as independent management units. However, he subsequently stresses that top priority should be given to the identification of turtle stock boundaries,[436] which appears contradictory to his non-recognition of independent management units.

5.323. In his response on the analysis of population status of the individual species, Dr. Eckert argues against the determinant for population size which is based on nesting density.[437] It is agreed that there are shortcomings since any population or unit stock of sea turtle comprises hatchlings, post-hatchlings, juveniles, sub-adults and adults of both male and female turtles. However, due to current limitations in assessing the status of all life stages of the turtles, nesting density is still universally used as a measure of population size for breeding units of sea turtles. Dr. Eckert's own analysis of the population status of the various species is also based on assessments of the size of nesting populations. Limpus (1997)[438] identifies a population "by the focus of its nesting population, irrespective of where it migrates to feed".

5.324. It is observed that Dr. Eckert regards sea turtles as a global resource. Malaysia refutes this as sea turtles are a shared regional resource as elaborated in Malaysia's arguments to the Panel. The recognition of different breeding stocks of sea turtles as independent management units (see paragraph 5.322) reinforces the fact that sea turtles are a regional resource, and not a global resource. Mr. Guinea essentially captures the essence of the regional status of unit stocks of sea turtles when he says "Malaysia and Thailand because of their proximity may share breeding units of some species".[439] Malaysia may share breeding units with the Philippines and Indonesia. India and Pakistan could share breeding units of some species. The United States and Mexico may share breeding units as well. It is speculative to suggest that southeastern United States shares a breeding unit with any of the other countries in the dispute. Dr. Eckert attempts to justify the status of sea turtles as a global resource by projecting a picture of extensive migrations. He hypothesizes that leatherback turtles "circumnavigate the entire Pacific Ocean" and that "females from the two major colonies (Mexico/Central America and Iran Jaya/Solomon Islands) as well as the minor colonies (e.g. Malaysia)

---

433 M.Y Chaloupka and J.A. Musick, (1997), *Age, growth and population dynamics,*in: P.L. Lutz and J.A. Musick (eds.), The Biology of Sea Turtles, CRC Press, pp .234-276.

434 C.J. Limpus, (1997), *Marine Turtle Populations of Southeast Asia and the Western Pacific Region: Distribution and Status*, Proceedings of the Workshop on Marine Turtle Research and Management in Indonesia, Jember, East Java, November 1996.

435 Guinea para. 5.14.

436 Eckert para. 5.174.

437 Eckert para. 5.20.

438 C.J. Limpus, (1997), *Marine Turtle Populations of Southeast Asia and the Western Pacific Region: Distribution and Status*, Proceedings of the Workshop on Marine Turtle Research and Management in Indonesia, Jember, East Java, November 1996.

439 Guinea para. 5.87.

distribute into a clockwise migration of the Pacific Ocean ...".[440] Malaysia argues against this as follows:

- The work that Dr. Eckert has cited to support his view shows impressive migrations across latitudes (i.e. in a north-south direction, extending from Chile to the Northeast Pacific), but is limited in range with respect to longitudes (i.e. east-west direction). More information on the migration ranges of leatherbacks in the Eastern Pacific is provided in Eckert and Sarti (1997).[441] Here again, migration is limited with respect to longitude. The single individual which migrated westwards, beyond the longitudinal range of all other individuals studied was considered by Eckert and Sarti to be an anomaly, rather than the norm. The claim that leatherback turtles "circumnavigate the entire Pacific Ocean" is highly speculative and cannot be validated by available scientific information.
- Peter Dutton's work through a personal communication to Dr. Eckert cannot be accepted as scientific evidence, unless a written statement is issued from Dutton, outlining his method of study and how samples were procured.

Dr. Eckert's hypothesis that leatherback turtles circumnavigate the entire Pacific is an argument put forward to provide justification for the United States that they have jurisdiction over Malaysian and Thai sea turtles. What hypothesis would be offered to justify the claims of the United States for jurisdiction over the sea turtles of the Indian Ocean?

5.325. All the experts subscribe to the status listings of IUCN and CITES. Mr. Liew specifies that different populations are in different states of health, with some populations having disappeared, some near extinction, some threatened, and a few having shown some apparent recovery.[442] Mr. Guinea recognizes that "the green turtle nesting on the Turtle Islands of Sabah have staged a remarkable recovery, as have the hawksbills".[443] Elsewhere, in South Africa, leatherback turtles have also staged a recovery from 5 nesting females per year in 1963 to over 100 per year in 1995.[444] This demonstrates that although general status listings are recognized, certain populations are in fact doing quite well.

5.326. Regarding the leatherback sea turtles, it is true that, as mentioned by Dr. Eckert[445], some previously large populations, including the Malaysian population, are almost extinct. However, Spotila et. al.[446] had identified the population of 18 out of 28

---

[440] Eckert para. 5.256.

[441] Eckert, S.A. and L.M. Sarti, (1997), *Distant Fisheries Implicated in the Loss of the World's Largest Leatherback Nesting Population*, Marine Turtle Newsletter 78:2-7.

[442] Liew para. 5.68.

[443] Guinea para. 5.189.

[444] G.R. Hughes., (1996), *Nesting of the Leatherback Turtle (Dermochelys coriacea) in Tongaland*, Kwa Zulu-Natal, South Africa, Chelonian Conservation and Biology 282):153-158.

[445] Eckert para. 5.26.

[446] J.R. Spotila, A.E. Dunham, A.J. Leslie, A.C. Steyermark, P.t. Plotkin and F.V. Paladino, (1996), *Worldwide Population Decline of Dermochelys coriacea: Are Leatherback Turtles Going Extinct*? Chelonian Conservation and Biology 2(2):209-222, (cited in Eckert's response).

important leatherback nesting areas reviewed as either increasing or stabilized. The case of the decimated leatherback population in Malaysia is recognized both locally and internationally. The local authorities have put in much effort to save the leatherback (even Dr. Eckert recognizes this).[447] Malaysia would welcome international effort to bring about a recovery of the decimated population.

5.327. Most of the references used by Dr. Eckert to conclude that green turtles in Malaysia are in decline are outdated reports, except for Chan and Liew (1996).[448] Malaysia requests Eckert to review Chan and Liew (1996) again because this report demonstrated population recovery since 1988, and the recovery has now been sustained for almost ten years. The reference used by Dr. Eckert to allege Malaysian business interests at the Turtle Islands is not valid since Romeo Trono is a Filipino and does not have reliable information on Malaysian business interests. The allegation can only be accepted if Dr. Eckert provided a primary source. As a representative of the Malaysian government, we assure this Panel that there is currently no business developments being considered in the Turtle Islands which may destroy the natural habitats or in any way pose any threat whatsoever to the continued recovery and survival of the turtle population there.

5.328. In Malaysia, hawksbill sea turtle are not hunted any more. The outlook for Malaysian hawksbills is not as dismal as Dr. Eckert has made it out to be. The hawksbill population in the Sabah Turtle Island has recovered in the same manner as the green turtles (Chan and Liew, 1996). According to Limpus (1997)[449], "[t]he largest hawksbill nesting population in Southeast Asia appears to be in the Sulu Sea Turtle Islands of Sabah (Malaysia) with a nesting population of several hundred females annually. This .... may currently be increasing significantly". Elsewhere in Malaysia, hawksbill nesting appears stabilized, except in Terengganu where it has declined. Efforts are being made in Terengganu to maximize egg protection.

5.329. It is recognized that the causes of decline of sea turtle populations are generally similar for all species of sea turtles. However, the degree of threat of each of the causes may vary according to time, place, and a variety of conditions. These views are held by Mr. Guinea, Mr. Liew and Dr. Frazier. Dr. Poiner says that it is difficult to rank mortality factors either currently or over time. The views of Mr. Guinea, Mr. Liew, Dr. Frazier and Dr. Poiner are upheld because the same conditions do not prevail uniformly in the United States, India, Malaysia, Pakistan and Thailand. Notwithstanding, Dr. Eckert argues the "...by far the most serious threat to sea turtle stocks living in coastal environments are trawl fisheries".[450]

5.330. Dr. Poiner and Mr. Guinea are of the view that it is not possible to rank the sources of mortality. Mr. Liew believes that in the United States mortality caused by shrimping is high, while in India, Pakistan, Malaysia and Thailand, other fishing methods such as sunken set nets or "pukat pari" may have a greater impact than shrimp

447 Eckert para. 5.171.

448 Eckert para. 5.29.

449 C.J. Limpus, (1997), *Marine Turtle Populations of Southeast Asia and the Western Pacific Region: Distribution and Status*, Proceedings of the Workshop on Marine Turtle Research and Management in Indonesia, Jember, East Java, November 1996.

450 Eckert para. 5.119.

trawling. The information provided by Dr. Eckert and Dr. Poiner that shrimp trawling presents the most serious threat to green turtles[451] is inconsistent with the findings of NRC (1990) which has not even listed shrimp trawling to be among any of the factors responsible for green turtle mortality. The major threats identified in the reference were direct exploitation of eggs and meat, and the degradation of nesting and feeding habitats.

5.331. There is currently no large and continuing illegal egg take in Sabah and Sarawak. Some poaching may occur, but most of the eggs are being conserved. Eckert (1993)[452] mentioned that data supplied by the Sarawak Museum showed that in 1989 and 1990, 185,461 and 117,701 eggs were collected respectively. The implication is that the eggs were still collected and completely marketed. Dr. Eckert failed to provide the rest of the information where, out of these eggs, 107, 237 (57.8 per cent) and 88,869 (75.5 per cent) were respectively replanted in hatcheries (Leh, 1997).[453] In subsequent years, over 90 per cent of the eggs collected have been conserved (Leh, 1997). Leh has also provided turtle landing statistics in Sarawak from 1970 to 1996, which showed population stabilization, rather than decline. In the Sabah Turtle Islands, close to 100 per cent of the eggs collected are conserved (Suliansa, 1997).[454] It is true that legalized egg harvest is still a problem in Peninsular Malaysia. However, numerous hatcheries have been established where increasing percentages of eggs are being purchased from the egg collectors for conservation. Local governments provide funds for the purchase of eggs for incubation and this is supplemented by conservation projects conducted by universities[455], resort and chalet operators and other conservation groups.

5.332. Malaysia agrees that incidental mortality caused by fishing gear does occur, but in Malaysia, shrimp trawling is not the major gear impacting sea turtles. The more serious gear are the fish trawls and bottom gill nets which are used for catching rays. The latter nets have been banned. Dr. Eckert cites Crouse (1987) whose study was based on loggerhead turtles and tries to extrapolate the conclusions to all species of sea turtles. The conclusion that loggerheads "... pick foraging habitats that are most strongly correlated to shrimp fisheries" is true for loggerheads and this is the very reason why loggerheads suffer the most serious impact of shrimp trawls. However, it has not been shown anywhere that leatherbacks, green or hawksbill turtles "...forage in shallow waters with soft bottoms that characterize shrimp habitat".[456] Dr. Eckert is of the opinion that "stage 3" sea turtles of all species, meaning large juveniles and sub-adults, forage in shallower water with soft bottoms which characterize shrimp habitat. He

---

[451] Eckert para. 5.92 and Poiner para. 5.118.

[452] K.L. Eckert, (1993), *The Biology and Status of Marine Turtles in the North Pacific Ocean*, NOAA Tech. Memo, NOAA-TM-NMFS-SWFSX-186, 156 pp. (cited in Eckert's response).

[453] C.M.U. Leh, (1997), *Country Status Report: Status of Marine Turtles Conservation in Sarawak*, Proceedings of the First SEAFDEC Workshop on Marine Turtle Research and Conservation, SEAFDEC MFRDMD RM/3:13-20.

[454] M.S. Suliansa, (1997), *Country Status Report 2: Status Report of Sea Turtle Management at the Turtle Islands Park, Sabah Parks*, Proceedings of the First SEAFDEC Workshop on Marine Turtle Research and Conservation SEAFDEC MFRDMD RM/3:21-34.

[455] See the SEATRU website at http://www.upmt.edu.my/seatru.

[456] Eckert para. 5.74.

thinks that these habitats are the developmental habitats since the turtles at this stage cannot dive as deeply nor as long as larger mature animals. Malaysia would like to point out that this is a generalization, and not a proven scientific fact. This generalization has been extrapolated from studies conducted on loggerhead turtles. However, if this is possible, zoning Regulations in Malaysia prohibit any form of trawling activity in these shallower waters.

5.333. There is some confusion with regards to the word "trawl"; as it is used in Malaysia, trawling means fish trawling, not prawn or shrimp trawling. However, in the United States, trawling is synonymous with shrimp trawling. The Malaysian publications which prescribe turtle mortality to trawls actually refer to mortalities in fish trawls and not shrimp trawls. Dr. Frazier[457] cites Siow and Moll (1982) when he attributes declines in turtle population is Malaysia to prawn trawling. The exact words of Siow and Moll were "... increases in fishing activities, especially trawling and drift-netting were blamed for the ... dead turtles on the beach ...". There was no mention of prawn trawling in the reference. The type of trawling referred to be Siow and Moll (1982) was fish trawling.

5.334. Malaysia recognizes the trans-Pacific and trans-Atlantic movements (not migrations) of hatchlings and post hatchlings sea turtles described by the experts. Malaysia wishes to point out to the Panel that the extensive ranges of the hatchlings and post hatchlings occur only during the first few years of the life cycle of turtles and that at this phase, turtles are found only in the pelagic zones. In terms of vulnerability to shrimp trawls, this phase of the life cycle is of no relevance. It is true that leatherback turtles show extensive migration. However, the circumnavigation of the Pacific Ocean by all leatherback populations which nest in the Pacific area, as alleged by Dr. Eckert is highly speculative and is as yet unsupported by published scientific data. Data available so far indicate that movements of leatherback turtles which nest along the Eastern Pacific range from the north-eastern Pacific to the south-eastern Pacific, but do not extend to the Western Pacific. The satellite tracking work conducted by Dr. Eckert illustrates this point as explained in paragraph 5.324 above. The recent satellite tracking data on green turtles show regional migrations which do not exceed 3,000 km in range, with most within the 2,500 km range. The studies involved were carried out over a few months, and in most cases, were continued well after the turtles had reached their destinations at the feeding grounds. Studies in Australia have shown that adult green turtles do not change feeding grounds, but remain within particular feeding grounds until the next reproductive migration. They also return to the same feeding site they occupied before the breeding migration.[458] Therefore, green turtles do not perform annual movements, their migrations are strictly between feeding and nesting grounds at 2-7 year intervals.

5.335. Dr. Eckert has attempted to discredit the recent satellite tracking studies of post-nesting green turtles by saying that the studies have been carried over too short a duration to determine annual movement patterns. Malaysia would like to point out that adult green turtles, unlike the loggerheads, do not undertake annual migrations. Dr. Eckert himself admits that "given the relatively warm waters of Malaysia, Thailand,

---

457 Frazier para. 5.56.
458 See Poiner para. 5.269.

India and Pakistan, it would not be expected that resident turtle populations would exhibit annual or seasonal migrations in those countries".[459]

5.336. Malaysia notes that the experts are quite divided about the status of breeding populations which have recovered based on protection of nesting beaches, nesting females and 100 per cent protection of eggs. There are examples where conservation programmes focused on protection of eggs and hatchlings have proved effective in population restoration or maintaining it at a sustainable level. Malaysia would like to cite the following examples: Tongaland, South Africa where beach patrols and 100 per cent protection of eggs and nesting leatherbacks on the beach, and in the absence of TEDs application, have resulted in a recovery of the population from 5 to over 100 nesting females per season (Hughes, 1996).[460] This recovery was gradual and occurred over a period of more than 30 years, from 1963 to 1995. In this proceedings, Malaysia also gave the example of the Sabah Turtle Islands. Examples are also provided in the responses of Mr. Guinea and Mr. Liew to question 4(a). In that regard, Malaysia wonders where would the sub-adult and adult turtles come from if the eggs were not protected in the first place? Dr. Poiner has cited several studies conducted in Australia which indicate that protection of eggs and hatchlings also have a major impact on long-term stock viability, and that predation on eggs makes a significant contribution to increased mortalities.[461]

5.337. The priority action for sea turtle conservation would vary, as stipulated by Dr. Poiner.[462] Mr. Guinea mentions protection of nesting habitats and offshore refuges for nesting females as priority.[463] However, Dr. Eckert advocates one set of uniform priority actions for all species and all countries.[464] We hope that Dr. Eckert can appreciate the level of capability and financial resources in poor developing countries. The priority actions given by Dr. Eckert are indeed idealistic and the dream of every sea turtle conservationist. However, each country is able to act only within the limitations of its financial and manpower resources. To the question posed by the Panel "Do these [socio-economic] factors influence the choice and enforcement of conservation programmes", Dr. Frazier puts it in a nutshell by responding very succinctly "Yes, they do". The time when reproductive females are most vulnerable to exploitation and capture are the times when they arrive predictably and concentrate on specific nesting beaches to nest. Therefore, in sea turtle conservation, a top priority should be to eliminate direct capture and harvest of sea turtles on nesting beaches. Malaysia has been practising this for many decades now, in addition to protecting nesting beaches as well as eggs.

5.338. Malaysia would like to draw the attention of the Panel and experts to the fact that TEDs were developed for shrimp trawlers where the targeted species are shrimp and all other catch, including fish are considered to be bycatch. In Malaysia and other developing countries, most of the trawlers in operation are fish trawls which target fish,

---

[459] Eckert paras. 5.257 and 5.259.

[460] G.R. Hughes, (1996), *Nesting of the Leatherback Turtle (Dermochelys coricea) in Tongaland, KwaZulu-Natal, South Africa*, Chelonian Conservation and Biology 2(2):153-158.

[461] Poiner para. 5.201.

[462] Poiner para. 5.185.

[463] Guinea para. 5.181.

[464] Eckert para. 5.174.

both small and large-sized fish. TEDs developed in the United States will not be appropriate under such conditions as they will cause the escape of large fish which are targeted in the trawl fisheries of the region. Dr. Eckert believes that TEDs are extremely simple to use and that the socio-economic conditions in complainant countries would not pose a constraint. Theoretically, this may seem to be the case. However, in the practice of TEDs deployment, an array of situations and problems may arise. This is apparent as seen in the strong resistance of US shrimpers to the mandatory use of TEDs (Weber et. al., 1995).[465] Further, even after TEDs became mandatory in the United States, large numbers of turtles continued to strand.

5.339. Malaysia notes that Dr. Eckert has not answered question 3(b) in context. The question is "Is there any data on TEDs efficiency during commercial shrimping?" The studies of Renaud et. al., (1990, 1991) cited by Eckert were "controlled" tests. Further, Crowder et. al., (1995) cited by Dr. Eckert used a model to predict the effects of TEDs. Dr. Eckert did not attempt to cite the references from which he drew his three conclusions. The examples cited by Dr. Eckert for other countries were results from trials conducted by gear specialists and not from actual commercial shrimping carried out by the fishermen themselves.[466] Dr. Eckert has avoided answering questions concerning rate of turtle stranding in areas where TEDs are currently required. Malaysia has already provided data to the Panel (see Section III.B); in addition, Mr. Liew in his response to question 3(b) refers to Coyne (1997), who states that "while Kemp's ridley are nesting, others are dying in large numbers along the Texas coast ... so far this year (1997), 275 dead turtles have washed ashore up along the Texas coast ... biologists still see a big decline in dead turtles washing ashore when the Gulf of Mexico is temporarily closed each year to shrimping". The last part of the quote shows that closed seasons appear more effective in reducing turtle mortality.

5.340. Dr. Eckert talks about problems in enforcement relative to seasonal and time closures, area closures and tow-time limitations.[467] Similar problems would apply to TEDs enforcement as well. There is information which reveals that US fishermen disengage their TEDs once they are out at sea (Seber et. al., 1995).[468] There is information which shows that TEDs may be exempted after storms. Apparently, debris in the nets prevent TEDs from closing, allowing shrimp to escape, thus reducing shrimp catch efficiency.[469] Malaysia would like to stress again that prohibition of trawling within 5 nautical miles of the coastline eliminates turtle mortalities attributed to both fish and shrimp trawling in these shallow waters. Enforcement of the regulations is facilitated, as explained in paragraph 5.315. What is needed in Malaysia is not an additional regulation but rather more financial resources and personnel to enhance existing enforcement of regulations which are already in place for the protection of sea turtles against trawling activities.

---

[465] M. Weber, D. Crouse, R. Irvin and S. Iudicello, (1995), *Delay and Denial: A Political History of Sea Turtles and Shrimp Fishing*, Center for Marine Conservation, p. 12.

[466] Eckert para. 5.210-213.

[467] Eckert para. 5.223.

[468] M. Weber, D. Crouse, R. Irvin and S. Iudicello, (1995), *Delay and Denial: A Political History of Sea Turtles and Shrimp Fishing*, Center for Marine Conservation, p. 12.

[469] CURTLE List (Internet Source), T. Steiner, 14:30 pm 29-07-97, *Are TEDs Coming Off?*, referred to by Mr. Liew.

5.341. Malaysia notes that some experts have cited several studies conducted on loggerheads and attempted to superimpose or extrapolate the findings uniformly on all species of sea turtles in all geographical regions. This is not acceptable for the following reasons:

- The reproductive values of sea turtles: population modeling of loggerheads in the United States (Crouse et al. 1987)[470] give a reproductive value of 584 for breeders, as opposed to the value of 1 for eggs or hatchlings. Studies on Australian loggerheads put a reproductive value of 200-400 on adult females, depending on the population.[471] These two examples show that even for the same species, the values will vary according to geographical location. This is obviously the case since the same conditions do not prevail.
- Similarly, survivorship values must necessarily differ among species and geographical locations. The extent of threats confronting sea turtles would differ from location to location.
- Dr. Eckert cites the case for loggerheads which "pick foraging habitats that are most strongly correlated to shrimp fisheries".[472] This is true for loggerheads, and accounts for the fact that loggerheads suffer the most serious impacts of shrimp trawls. However, it has not been shown anywhere that leatherbacks, green or hawksbill turtles similarly pick such habitat (see paragraph 5.332).

5.342. Evidence is provided in the experts' responses that green turtles are directly harvested in the thousands annually in some countries (approaching 30,000 annually)[473], but yet, these same countries are given exemption to the import prohibition. Does this not amount to arbitrary or unjustifiable discrimination between countries?

5.343. Malaysia recognizes the effort and time Dr. Frazier has dedicated towards preparing his lengthy discourse on the issue of bycatch in modern fisheries (Annex II, Appendix 1). The international community, Malaysia included, is well aware of all the issues associated with bycatch. In recognizing this, FAO adopted the Code of Conduct for Responsible Fisheries in 1995. Malaysia fully supports the Code, and is especially appreciative of the way in which it has been mediated - through international consensus. Malaysia would like to state that nations should not impose trade prohibition on every fisheries product found to have a relationship with an endangered species. Such actions cannot bring about conservation, and is certainly not the way to bring about cooperation in saving an endangered species. Malaysia believes on a proper balance between the urgent and recognized need for conservation and impact on people and livelihood. Any form of conservation requires the dedicated cooperation of the various groups of people directly dealing with and affected with conservation matters. FAO and fisheries bodies and organizations are working out ways to mitigate the problems recognized in modern fisheries, and they are the ones most competent to do so.

---

[470] Referred to by Frazier, para. 5.196.

[471] Guinea para. 5.198.

[472] Eckert para. 5.74.

[473] Liew paras. 5.138-139 and Poiner para. 5.140.

5.344. With reference to the example mentioned in paragraph 72 of Appendix 1, Malaysia would like to repeat that the TEDs trial referred to in Ali (1997) was conducted in a zone which is off limits to trawling. Therefore, Dr. Frazier should not use the CPUE derived from this study to calculate the potential number of turtles caught per year. For extrapolation, the CPUE should be derived from trawling activities, which are conducted in those zones where trawling is permitted.

5.345. With regard to Appendix 2 provided by Dr. Frazier, Malaysia notes that the Panel did not request the experts to provide information on the issue of transfer of TED technology. However, in Appendix 2, Dr. Frazier has obtained a long list of documents relating to TED technology transfer. Malaysia would only point out that the correspondence appended to Appendix 2 merely lists down individuals who have written to NMFS. There does not demonstrate any actual transfer of TED technology. Malaysia therefore requests the Panel to disregard Appendix 2 as any form of proof that there was technology transfer. Malaysia does not contend that the United States has been incompetent or made inadequate attempts at TED technology transfer. Malaysia, however, wishes to reiterate that the United States has not made any official offer or attempt at a government-to-government level to negotiate an agreement for the protection of sea turtles in Malaysia. Malaysia further reiterates that there has been no workshop conducted by the United States in Malaysia itself, apart from the participation by Malaysia in a regional workshop organized by the Department of Fisheries, Thailand, in cooperation with the Department of Foreign Trade and NMFS, US Department of Commerce. Malaysia similarly reiterates that this workshop was held way after the imposition of the import prohibition which commenced on 1 May 1996.

5.346. To conclude, Malaysia notes that the United States is merely addressing shrimp trawling in its effort to conserve turtles. Malaysia contends that merely introducing TEDs for shrimp trawling only may save certain breeding units in certain places, for example the Gulf of Mexico, where shrimp fishing grounds coincide with habitats of turtles there. In other parts of the world where interactions do not occur, fish trawling, gill nets etc. would cause more turtle mortality rather than shrimp trawling alone. Therefore, there is a need to address the conservation of turtles in a broader spectrum rather than confining one's effort to the effect of shrimp trawling on turtles. Dr. Frazier's report contained in Appendix 1 aptly highlights the issues and concerns for selective fishing and the conservation of turtles and the need for international cooperation rather than a unilateral initiative on the part of the United States in this case. It simply demonstrates the magnitude of the problem which we believe the United States alone, as one of the 132 WTO Members, could never hope to address adequately in a unilateral manner. In conclusion, Malaysia would like to request the Panel to consider the introductory comments of Mr. Guinea[474] which have captured the essence of the present dispute.

### 3. *Comments by Pakistan*

5.347. Pakistan is located along the rich and bountiful Arabian sea which is very rich in species diversity. A large number of marine animals and plants are found along the

[474] Guinea paras. 5.14-18.

coast of Pakistan. Among the reptiles, sea snake and sea turtles are commonly found along the coast of Pakistan sea. Sea turtles, as in other parts of the world, inhabit shallow coastal waters especially along sandy, sandy *cum* rock and rocky shores. Females come to lay their eggs at high water marks on sandy shores. Along the coast of Pakistan turtles are found on a number of sandy beaches; important among them are Sandspits, Hawks Bay, Paradise Point, Cape Monz, Goth Mubarak, Gaddani, Malan, Had Ormara (West Bay), Tay, Sakoni, Astola Island, Shumal Bundar and Jiwani. Five species of marine turtles are known from Pakistan including loggerhead, green turtle, olive ridley, hawksbill, and leatherback, though only the green turtle and the olive ridley seem to be common.[475] Other species are known to have very rare occurrence. Very little work has been done on the population of turtle in coastal waters of Pakistan except Kabrahi and Firdous (1984)[476] who calculated the population of green turtles to be about 24,000 to 36,000 and that of olive ridley turtle to be 800 and 1,200. The figures for green turtles are seemingly overestimated because even visual and casual observations of the coastal area do not verify such high concentrations of green turtle in waters of Sindh. Along the coast of Balochistan, major turtle populations are observed in Taq (Ormara), Sakoni, Astola Island and Jiwani.

5.348. Turtles are very slow growing animals and achieve maturity at about 30 to 50 years. Recruitment is considered to be very low because of high mortality at early ages due to natural predation and human interference. Most turtle species world over are considered to be severely depleted due to human and natural factors. All turtle species are considered to be threatened along the coast of Pakistan. Their populations

---

[475] Butler, E.A., (1877), *Astola, a summer cruise in the Gulf of Oman*, Stray Feathers, Calcutta, 5:293-304; Firdous, F., (1986), *Marine turtle*, Proceedings of International Conference on Marine Science of the Arabian sea, Institute of Marine Sciences, University of Karachi; Ghalib, S.A., and S.S.H. Zaidi, (1976), *Observations on the survey and breeding of marine turtles of Karachi coast*, Agric. Pak 27(1):87-96; Groombridge, B., (1982), *The IUCN Amphibia-Reputilia Red Data Book*, Part I, Testudines, Crocodylia, Rhynchocephalia, IUCN, Gland, Switzerland; Groombridge, B., (1983), *A preliminary environmental profile of the India-Pakistan Bodelands in the Sind-Kutch region*, IUCN Conservation Monitoring Centre, Report for the World Bank; Groombridge, B., (1987a), *A preliminary marine turtle survey on the Makran coast, Baluchistan, Pakistan with notes on birds and mammals*, Unpublished report, IUCN Conservation Monitoring Centre, Cambridge; Groombridge, B., (1987b), *Makran coast: a newly explored habitat for marine turtle*, WWF-Pakistan Newsletter 6(2):1-5; Groombridge, B., (1989), *Marine turtles in Baluchistan: report of an aerial survey*, 9-11 September 1988, World Conservation Monitoring Centre, Cambridge, U.K; Groombridge, B., A.M. Kabraji and A.K. Rao, (1988), *Marine turtle in Baluchistan (Pakistan)*, Marine Turtle Newsletter 42:1-3; Kabraji, A.M., and F. Firdous, (1984), *Conservation of turtle, Hawkesbay and Sandspits, Pakistan*, World Wildlife Fund Project 1451, Unpublished report, WWF International ad Sind Wildlife management board, 52 p.; Khan, M.S. and M.R. Mirza, (1976), *An annotated chcklist and key to the reptiles of Pakistan*, Part I, Chelonia and Crocodilia, Biologia, Lahore, 22(2):211-219; Minton, S.A., (1962), *An annotated key to the amphibians and reptiles of Sind and Las Bela, West Pakistan*, Bull. Am. Mus. Nat. hist. 134; Minton, S.A., (1966), *A contribution to the herpetology of West Pakistan*, Bull. Am. Mus. Nat. hist. 142(2); Pernetta, J.C., (ed.), (1993), *Marine Protected Area Needs in the South Asian Seas Region*, Volume 4, Pakistan, A marine conservation and Development Report, IUCN, Grland, Switzerland, 42 p.; Shockley, C.H., (1949), *Herpetological notes from Ras Jiunri*, Baluchistan Herpetologogica 5:121.

[476] Kabraji, A.M., and F. Firdous, (1984), *Conservation of turtle, Hawkesbay and Sandspits, Pakistan*, World Wildlife Fund Project 1451, Unpublished report, WWF International ad Sind Wildlife management board, 52 p.

are considered to be thin along the entire coastline. Steps have been taken by the Government to enhance population of sea turtles by banning their commercial exploitation through Wildlife acts and through a programme of enhanced recruitment by protection of eggs and juveniles of hatchling. As with most recovery programmes of sea turtles, recruitment is very slow and considerable changes will be seen only after a very long period. In Pakistan the major threats to sea turtles are anthropogenic (Table I).

**Table I**: Anthropogenic threat to sea turtle species along the coast of Pakistan

| Threat | Status |
|---|---|
| Habitat alteration and loss | |
| Beach armouring (e.g. concrete sea wall) | No sea wall is constructed along nesting beaches. |
| Beach nourishment/ sand mining | No sand mining or beach nourishment is done along the coast of Pakistan especially no beach alteration on sea turtle nesting areas. |
| Beach cleaning and beach driving | No beach cleaning is done in Pakistan except for some environmental beach cleaning done by school children on rare occasion to remove debris and solid wastes. But such cleaning do not affect turtles. Beach driving is not done on nesting areas because most of them are not accessible. |
| Human presence on beach | Population in general do not go to beaches frequently. Only on holidays the number of persons visiting various beaches reaches a few thousands otherwise in a normal working day only a few hundred people visit the beaches for recreation purposes. Along the coast of Sandspits, Hawks Bay and Paradise Point, private huts were constructed mainly in 1960's and 1970's. A number of these huts have collapsed except those which are renovated regularly. These beach huts are used by picnickers on holidays. These, however, do not seem to be a threat to turtle population and nesting areas because they are located only on a few beaches, also not inhabited except on holidays and mostly located above high water mark in sand berm areas. |
| Artificial lights | Not used along sea coast. |
| Dredging and explosive platform | No such activities in Pakistan, especially along turtle nesting beaches. |
| Boat strikes | No report of boat strikes with turtles from Pakistan. Only a few speed boats in Pakistan which are not operated in turtle areas. |
| Feral and domestic animal predation at rookeries | Feral dogs are reported to dig out recently laid eggs of turtles on some beaches along Karachi coast. Sindh Wildlife Department with help of municipal agencies regularly carry out elimination of pye dogs from important turtle beaches. However, it is not a serious threat to turtle nesting. |

| Threat | Status |
|---|---|
| Oil pollution | Most of the turtle nesting beaches are located West of Karachi, therefore, not affected from oil pollution generated from Karachi and other ports (because circulation in most parts of the years remain clockwise). Tar balls are found on sandy beaches. But since no major oil spill has occurred in the area, therefore, oil pollution seemingly a threat to turtle nesting beaches. Those turtle found in sea are also not affected because oil pollution is not a major problem in the area. |
| Other pollution sources and entanglement | |
| Debris ingestion | A few reports of debris ingestion report. This problem seems not to be serious at present. |
| Entanglement | No record on any turtle entanglement in debris and solid waste materials. May however, occur if level of such pollutants increase in sea. |
| Fishing and incidental capture | |
| Shrimp trawling | Not a threat because of small mouth opening of shrimping net, short duration of operation, location of shrimping ground in muddy cum sandy areas (not a turtle habitat) and use of manual retrieval system (vs. mechanical retrieval system in other parts of world such as in United States). |
| Pelagic fishing gears | No record of mortality from any other pelagic fishing gears. Encircling nets are used for catching sardinellas and anchovies but because of the their mode of operation these do not pose any threat to turtle population. |
| Gill nets | Major fisheries along the coast of Pakistan. However, seldom any record of turtle in the nets. If a turtle is found in the net, it is released immediately. |
| Traditional and commercial fishing | |
| Egg harvests (legal or illegal | No harvesting of eggs in Pakistan. |
| Adult harvest (legal or illegal) | No legal or illegal harvesting of adult turtle. Considered to religiously forbidden. |

5.349. Decline in sea turtle population is attributed to a number of factors in other parts of the world, including habitat alteration, loss of nesting and foraging areas, pollution and commercial harvesting. In Pakistan, probably pollution may be the only factor which to some extent started affecting turtle populations; however, it is not a serious threat owing to circulation pattern and restriction of pollution to city of Karachi. Fishing operations not targeting sea turtles, shrimp trawling, can lead to incidental catches of sea turtles, especially in the United States. However, this is not a problem in Pakistan because trawl nets have smaller mouth, the operation is done manually, the duration of fishing operation is short and shrimping grounds are located in areas not inhabited by turtles. On very small scale commercial harvest of sea turtles was done along Karachi coast in early 1970's but since then this commercial harvesting was totally stopped. Along Balochistan coast in 1982, turtle commercial harvesting was done for a few months but the Fisheries Department took immediate action and since then no commercial harvesting of turtle is done. Groombridge[477] had reported mortality of turtles in Balochistan owing to commercial harvesting. These statements were based on a rapid assessment trip made to Balochistan coast during late 1980's. The harvesting referred to in these studies occurred in 1982, after which commercial harvesting was altogether stopped. Authentic information cannot be collected during snap visits to one particular area, especially if one is not familiar with the major turtle beaches and because of language barriers. Similar sweeping statements are made in these articles about utilization of sea turtles by local population. These area all based on speculations. Local population do not consume or utilize sea turtle for any specific purposes. Sonmiani has not been visited but nevertheless turtle utilization has been presumed in these areas. It can be categorically stated that turtles are not utilized nor consumed in Pakistan for any specific purpose.

5.350. The major cause of mortality amongst various factors in Pakistan seems to be natural factors. Along the Sindh coast in 1970's and along Balochistan in 1982, the major cause for the mortality was due to commercial harvesting. At that time, eggs on small scale were also harvested for utilization in some bakeries. But these practices were altogether stopped since then. About 3 to 4 turtles die each year entangled in gillnets. However, no mortality is reported from shrimp trawling operations. Habitat alteration and other human activities do not cause any mortality of turtles.

5.351. Disposal of solid waste seems to be the important anthropogenic factor which may interact with turtle populations; in particular, disposal of polyethylene bags may result in accidental ingestion by turtles. Anthropogenic factors seem to be more important at sea, especially around the city of Karachi. The pollution is restricted to Karachi area. Most of the nesting grounds are located in areas not affected by sea pollution. Egg harvesting is not done in Pakistan and no harvesting of sea turtles is practised. With the exception of gillnetting, which may lead to a few turtle mortality, other fishing operations do not affect turtle population in Pakistan. Shrimp trawling, in particular, does not lead to sea turtle mortality. It is worth mentioning shrimp trawling is not practised along the major part of the coastline. There is a total ban on the shrimp trawling along Balochistan coast which covers about 800 km (out of a total of about 1050 km coastline). It is also interesting that along the Sindh coast (about 250 km) the turtle population is restricted to about 50 km along the Western coastline. Turtles are rarely seen along the remaining 200 km of the coastline facing mouth of River Indus, which is mostly muddy. Mortality of turtles in gillnet fisheries is mostly confined to green turtles and olive ridleys are seldom reported entangled in gillnets. Other species, though reported from Pakistani waters, are of very rare occurrence.

---

[477] Groombridge, B., (1987a), *A preliminary marine turtle survey on the Makran coast, Baluchistan, Pakistan with notes on birds and mammals*, Unpublished report, IUCN Conservation Monitoring Centre, Cambridge; Groombridge, B., (1987b), *Makran coast: a newly explored habitat for marine turtle*, WWF-Pakistan Newsletter 6(2):1-5; Groombridge, B., A.M. Kabraji and A.K. Rao, (1988), *Marine turtle in Baluchistan (Pakistan)*, Marine Turtle Newsletter 42:1-3.

5.352. Shrimp trawling in Pakistan does not lead to any sea turtle mortality. A few turtles, however, do die every year in gillnet fishery. Along Balochistan coast, gillnet mortality is comparatively higher (about 4 to 5 each year) as compared to Sindh where about 2 to 3 turtles die entangled in gillnets.

5.353. Direct exploitation of sea turtles is not done in Pakistan. As already pointed out, in the 1970's along Sindh coast and in 1982, commercial harvesting of sea turtle was practised but since then commercial harvesting of sea turtle is effectively banned in Pakistan. Under Sindh and Balochistan Wildlife regulations turtle are declared protected animals and thus no commercial harvesting is allowed. Since turtles are not consumed locally, no illegal fishing is in practice in Pakistan. Conservation measures taken by the Government have led to the protection of the turtle populations in Pakistan.

5.354. Turtle harvesting is not done on a commercial scale in Pakistan; therefore, there is no relation of dispute with socio-economic condition of Pakistan. Turtle harvesting done in 1970's along the Sindh coast was not a regular fishery of the area. It was started by a group of exporters to meet the demand in South East Asian countries. Fishermen and the local population resented this harvesting; in particular, the local population was very much annoyed with commercial harvesting done in Ormara, Balochistan, in 1982. The Fisheries Department had to take action and stopped this operation effectively.

5.355. There is a need to start protection of the nursing ground, especially that of hatchlings and to ensure their safe release in the sea, as has been done by Sindh Wildlife Department in Sanspits area. This programme may be started in Balochistan, as well as in other areas of the Sindh coast. There is also a need to start mass scale tagging programmes to understand migration and population biology of sea turtles. There is also a need to study other aspects of sea turtle biology, such as stock assessment, natality and mortality parameters.

5.356. Turtle population in area of Taq (Ormara), which was exploited at a commercial level in 1982, has started showing signs of recovery for a period of about 3 years. In 1982 commercial harvesting was done on a small scale but because the local population protested, the Fisheries Department stopped this harvesting. Taq now receives a large number of females which lay their eggs on these beaches. Along the Sandy beaches of Sandspits, where the Government of Sindh has started egg protection in fences, more females are reported visiting these beaches for laying eggs. There seems to a stable population of turtles in the Sandspits area. Protection of sea turtles through Wildlife Acts has helped population stabilization. Though not adequately managed, the wildlife acts were instrumental in controlling commercial harvesting. This was supported by the fact that there is no commercial utilization of sea turtles by local population in Pakistan.

5.357. There is not enough long term data from Pakistan on the various life stages (eggs, hatchlings, large juveniles, sub-adults and adults) which may indicate the importance of any particular stage in population recovery or stabilization. However, results from various parts of the world showed the importance of all these stages in population recovery, depending on the areas.[478] The programme of protection of eggs

---

[478] Chaloupka, M.Y. and Musick, J.A., (1997), *Age, growth and population dynamics*, p. 233-276, in: The Biology of Sea Turtle, Eds. P.K. Lutz and J.A. Musick, CRC Press, Boca raton, USA; Crouse, D.T., L.B. Crowder and N. Casewell, (1987), *A stage based population model for loggerhead sea turtles and implications for conservation*, Ecology 68:1412-1423; Crowder, L.B., D.T.

and hatchlings by the Government of Sind may have a bearing on the population of adults after a decade because this programme was started in 1980 and hatchlings released will mature by 2010 or later (because sea turtle mature in about 30 years or so). Since the species of sea turtles are protected by law and mortality due to gillnet fisheries or pollution is negligible, there seems to be no potential threat to turtle stocks in Pakistan. However, this does not mean that further protective measures are not needed. There seems to be a need to start work on various aspects of population biology of turtles, as well as to take steps for protection of eggs and hatchling, so that natural mortality due to predation and other factors may be reduced.

5.358. TEDs are not installed in shrimp trawlers in Pakistan because of following reasons:

- Pakistan has a substantially large shrimping fleet, consisting of about 2,000 medium sized trawlers. The net used on these trawlers is comparatively much smaller. Its opening during operation is about 2m x 15 m. In addition, the net is towed at a very slow speed, usually less that 2 knots. Because of the small size of the opening and the slow speed of the trawler, turtles can easily avoid these nets. The entrapment of turtles is seldom noticed in shrimp trawlers.
- Major shrimping grounds are located along the Sindh coast, in the areas east of Karachi.[479] Indus estuarine creek and adjoining areas of the mouth of the creeks are the main areas of concentration for shrimp catching activity. The bottom of these areas is muddy *cum* sandy, therefore, not suitable for sea turtles. No turtle nesting is reported from the Indus estuary, associated creeks and adjoining areas.
- Major turtle nesting, feeding and breeding areas are located between Sanspits, Hawks Bay up to Cape Monz. These areas have sandy and sandy *cum* rocky bottom, which is ideal for turtles. Shrimp trawling is not carried out in these areas because of the bottom is not suitable. Shrimp are also not reported in these areas.
- Turtle are regarded as sacred animals and killing them is considered to be a bad omen. Fishermen, therefore, do not kill any turtle if accidentally entrapped in the net but release it immediately. In addition, there is no turtle fisheries in the country. Similarly turtles are not eaten and there is also a ban on the export of any products derived from turtles. Turtle mortality because of shrimp trawling is therefore insignificant.
- By-catch studies carried out by research organizations in Pakistan have not reported a single case of turtle entrapment, even juvenile or hatchling, in shrimp by-catch.
- Studies carried out by the Sindh Wildlife indicate that turtle population is static. There is no increase in turtle nesting due to breeding programmes.

---

Crouse, S.S. Heppell and T.H. Martin, (1994), *Predicting the impact of turtle excluder devices on loggerhead sea turtle populations*, Ecological Implications 4:437-445.

[479] Zupanovic, S., (1973), The Pakistan Shrimp resources, FAO TA-3218, FAO, Rome, 76 p.

5.359. Shrimp trawl net used in Pakistan was designed in 1958 when shrimping was introduced for the first time in Pakistan.[480] No change in the design of the shrimp trawl net has been made since then. A typical shrimp trawl has a circumference of 860 meshes by 50 mm stretched mesh and a cod end of 25 mm stretched mesh, lined with a second layer of 10 mm stretched mesh.[481] Wooden trawlers of about 15 m are used for shrimp purposes. There is no mechanical device used on the shrimp trawler and every operation of deployment and retrieval is done manually. The crew consists of about 8 to 16 fishermen. Duration of trawl operation is about 30 minutes to one hour, depending upon the catch rate. In addition to target species, i.e. shrimp, a variety of fish and invertebrates are caught as bycatch. The Marine Fisheries Department started a programme of analysis of shrimp bycatch which indicated a preponderance of juveniles of food fishes, small fishes, invertebrates and flotsam. The study revealed that adult and juvenile turtles are not represented in the bycatch. A creel survey was conducted by Marine Fisheries Department in June and July 1997 and about 146 fishermen were interviewed to find out the frequency of turtle entrapment in shrimp trawl nets. The results revealed that turtles are very rarely entrapped in shrimp trawl nets. In almost all cases where a turtle was accidentally entrapped, it was released immediately. Fishermen have not reported any case of mortality due to drowning in net. It is worth mentioning that along the coast of Balochistan (which covers about 800 km out of 1050 km of the entire coastline of Pakistan) shrimp trawling is not allowed.

5.360. TED's are known to reduce bycatch in various parts of the world. Since no turtle dies in shrimp trawl nets in Pakistan, there seems to be no justification to press upon installation of these gears. However, under a phased programme, TED's or other bycatch reduction devices may be installed in shrimp trawl nets in Pakistan so that catch of non target species may be reduced. There is no data on TEDs efficiency in Pakistan because these gears are not installed in shrimp trawl nets. Turtle stranding has been reported by Firdous recently, especially in June; however, the mortality cannot be attributed to shrimping because June and July are closed season for shrimping. The mortality during this period may be attributed to intensive monsoonic wave action, which may result in colliding of sea turtles with man-made structures or vessels operating in the area or to any other cause but not to shrimping.

5.361. There seems to be not adequate justification for installation of TEDs in all shrimp fisheries. Pakistan shrimp fishery is an excellent example where the size of nets, tow duration and area exclusion result in no mortality of turtles. Similar practices in other parts of the world can lead to protection of sea turtle population. Advocating the installation of TEDs in all shrimping activities is, therefore, not justified. Other

---

[480] FAO, (1995), *Report to the Government of Pakistan on mechanisation of West Pakistan fishing boats*, UNDP/FAO, TA; Jaleel, S.A., (1978), *Fish resources of Pakistan*, UNESCO/IOC Advanced Regional Traning Course in Biological Oceanography, karachi, Pakistan (4-30 November 1978), 21p.; Qureshi, M.R., (1961), *Pakistan's Fisheries*, Central Fisheries Department, Karachi, Pakistan, Government of Pakistan Press, Karachi.

[481] Khan, M.Y., (1994), *Fishing techniques in coastal waters of Pakistan*, in: Proceedings of national Seminar of Fisheries Policy and Planning, Marine Fisheries Department, Government of Pakistan, Karachi 345-364; Van Zalinge, M. Khaliluddin and W. Khan, *Pakistan's Shrimp Fishery*, in: Proceedings of national Seminar on Fisheries Policy and Planning, Marine Fisheries Department, Government of Pakistan, Karachi 130-177.

management tools, if properly used, can result in similar reduction of incidental mortality of sea turtles. Since TEDs are not used in Pakistan, comments on efficiency of TEDs in Pakistan cannot be made. However, there is a need for TEDs to be selected and adapted to individual local fishing conditions, in particular to the design of shrimp trawl net used in a particular area, including Indo-Pacific waters.

5.362. An effective programme of protection of sea turtle eggs and hatchlings was started under the auspices of the Wildlife Department, Government of Sindh in 1980. This work is confined to Sandspits area. It is believed that this programme has helped to at least maintain the population of sea turtles to a static level, if not to restore the population. Stop and control on commercial onslaught of sea turtles and harvesting of their eggs, general public awareness are other benefits of this programme. Long terms effects of these conservation measures will be known only after a few decades because turtles take a very long time to mature. Similar programmes started in other countries, especially to control or prohibit control of egg harvests as a conservation measure, but no evidence of recovery of any of these populations.[482] Although egg protection and hatchling release started in Pakistan in early 1980's, it seems difficult to assess the effects of such a programme on the recovery of the adult population after a period of about two decades. It will take another ten to fifteen years before any substantive evidence on the population recovery is available. However, studies in other parts of the world based on modeling indicate that protection of eggs/hatchlings may have a major impact on long term stock viability.[483]

5.363. Sea turtle migration is not well understood in all parts of the world. However, it is known that breeding adults usually migrate over very long distances from breeding areas to foraging grounds. Such information is especially lacking about sea turtle populations inhabiting the Arabian Sea. One specimen of sea turtle tagged in Pakistan (Sindh coast) was captured in Kutch, India, which indicates that there is a long distance migration involved in populations inhabiting Arabian Sea; however, to understand the actual migration pattern and their seasonality, etc., it is necessary to have regional cooperation amongst the countries of the area, as well as to increase tagging programme. Information on the typical range of migration of sea turtles is not available for sea turtle populations living along the coast of Pakistan. However, sea turtles are known to have extensive migration.

5.364. Shrimp are known to inhabit shallow coastal waters predominantly in areas with muddy *cum* sandy bottom. This is the reason why most shrimping grounds along the coast of Pakistan are located in front of River Indus delta. Other shrimping grounds are Gaddani (in Sonmiani Bay) and Pasni, etc. All these areas have muddy *cum* sandy bottom. Major turtle populations of sea turtles which spend a part of their life cycle in shallow coastal waters inhabit areas with sandy or rocky *cum* sandy bottoms. However, there may be marginal overlapping of shrimping and turtle foraging and breeding areas.

---

[482] Limpus, C., (1997), *Marine turtle population of South east Asia and Western Pacific Region: Distribution and Status*, p. 37-72, Proceedings of Workshop on Marine Turtle Research and Management in Indonesia.

[483] Somers, I., (1994), *Modelling loggerhead turtle populations*, in: Proceedings of the Marine Turtle Conservation Workshop, p. 142-153, (Comp. R. James), Australian National Park and Wildlife Service, Canberra, Australia.

However, because of short tow duration and small mouth opening of the trawl net, turtle entrapments in shrimp trawl operations are very rare. Even if some turtles get entrapped, they do not die because of short tow duration. Since turtles are considered sacred animals in Pakistan, they are released immediately. No nesting ground is located in shrimping areas along Pakistan's coast. Statistically there is significant difference in incidental catches of sea turtle in shrimping nets in various parts of the world.[484] However, since no incidental mortality of sea turtles is reported from Pakistan, a comparison with other fisheries cannot be made.

5.365. Sea turtle populations of all species are not affected by shrimp trawling in Pakistan. Even if it is presumed that mortality of turtles occurs due to shrimp trawl operations, then there should be stranded carcasses of sea turtles on the beaches, especially during peak shrimping period, i.e., August and October. In such instances, strandings should occur on the beaches east of Karachi, especially Clifton, Bundal Island and islands on Indus creeks, since shrimp trawling operations during this period are carried out in the nearshore areas off Karachi and Indus delta. However, no stranding of dead turtles was observed in the area.

### 4. *Comments by Thailand*

5.366. Review of the experts' responses to the Panel's questions reveals that the factual issues before the Panel are highly complex and that much of the available data is subject to varying interpretations. However, in general the responses contradict many of the "facts" that the United States has asserted to support its position that the measures are justified under Article XX of the GATT 1994. Based on the responses, the Panel should determine that the US shrimp embargo is inconsistent with the GATT 1994 and should recommend that the United States dismantle the embargo in conformity with its obligations under the GATT 1994.[485]

5.367. In support of its claim that the conservation measures at issue are "necessary" and therefore justified by Article XX(b), the United States has asserted that: (i) accidental drowning in shrimp trawl nets is the greatest single cause of human-induced sea turtle mortality and (ii) other measures to protect sea turtles are not sufficient to allow sea turtles to recover from the brink of extinction. To support its contention that the measures "relate to" the conservation of an exhaustible natural resources as required by Article XX(g), the United States has asserted that shrimp trawl nets have caused the greatest number of human-induced sea turtle deaths, accounting for more sea turtle deaths than all other human activities combined, and (ii) TEDs are highly effective in preventing such mortality.

5.368. In addition, in response to arguments raised by Thailand, the United States asserted that the measures were "made effective in conjunction with" domestic legislation as required by Article XX(g) because TEDs technology was readily available by the mid-1990's so that, by the time that Section 609 became applicable to the

[484] Pointer, I.R. and A.N.M. Harris, (1996), *Incidental capture, direct mortality and delayed mortality of sea turtles in Australia's Northern Prawn Fishery*, Mar. Biol. 125:813-825.

[485] In presenting these arguments, Thailand does not concede any of its legal arguments concerning whether the Article XX exceptions invoked are applicable to the measures at issue.

complainants, they were able to reap the benefits of the research and development that the United States had been undertaking on TEDs technology for many years and therefore received even-handed treatment irrespective of the fact that they were not give the same phase-in period provided to US shrimpers. Finally, and again in response to arguments raised by Thailand, the United States argued that the measures complied with the Preamble of Article XX since at the time the TEDs requirement applied to initially affected nations, TEDs technology was neither as well-developed nor as readily available, especially for developing countries; by the time Section 609 became applicable to shrimp harvested in the complainants' countries, extraordinarily effective TEDs were both inexpensive and easily available, making the adoption of TEDs programmes considerably more feasible.

5.369. A review of the responses provided by the experts demonstrates that the above assertions are incorrect. In general, the information provided indicates that a majority of the experts disagree with these factual assertions. On the whole, the experts' responses demonstrate that the United States has not, and cannot, meet its burden of establishing that the measures at issue are justified by Article XX.

5.370. The United States has alleged that "the greatest human-related cause of sea turtle mortality is drowning in shrimp trawl nets" and has relied upon this assertion to demonstrate that its conservation measures are "necessary" within the meaning of Article XX(b). However, a majority of the experts consulted by the Panel recognize that different sea turtle species and even different populations or stocks of the same species are subject to different threats in different locations. Additionally, the responses demonstrate that even when the same threat is present in multiple locations, the significance of that threat may vary in each location. Consistent with these general observations, the experts have identified multiple sources of mortality for sea turtles in Thailand; while it is generally stated that the overall impact of each source cannot be quantified, it is clear from the responses that within Thailand, the significance varies by species and location. Thus, while shrimp trawling is the greatest human-induced threat to sea turtles in US waters, the responses demonstrate that this is not categorically true elsewhere, and it is not true in Thailand.

5.371. While several of the experts disagreed as to what constitutes a particular "population" or "stock" of turtles, the experts stated that threats to sea turtles vary in different locations throughout the world.[486] Specifically, it was stated that the causes of

[486] Frazier para. 5.40 ("depending on the time, place and circumstances, the factors affecting a particular sea turtle, or stock of sea turtles, will vary."); Eckert paras. 5.25-5.37 (noting various threats that affect different species in different locations); Poiner para. 5.71 (showing that egg harvest and adult harvests are threats in Thailand and Malaysia, but not in the United States); Liew para. 5.69 (indicating that shrimp trawling is the most significant threat for the US mainland; fibropapilloma disease is a significant threat to green turtles in Hawaii, and egg exploitation and large scale hunting turtle meat is significant in Indonesia); Liew para. 5.89 (noting that in developed countries, mortalities caused by high technologies such as shrimp trawling are prominent, while in developing countries egg harvest and turtle harvest still occur and, other fishing techniques may have a greater impact than shrimp trawling); Liew para. 5.115 (noting that the relative importance of threats varies by species); Liew para. 292 (noting that in some regions threats due to other causes may impact sea turtles more significantly than shrimp trawling); Guinea para. 5.61 (noting that the nature and level of threat varies for each breeding unit). Interestingly, with respect to the impact of shrimp trawling on loggerheads in the United States, Dr. Eckert cites a 1987 source (two years be-

decreased recruitment and/or increased mortality vary according to time, place and a variety of conditions.[487] Further, even when the same threat is present in several locations, its significance or intensity will vary from location to location.[488] Indeed, as Thailand has argued throughout this proceeding, the United States has erroneously extrapolated from conditions in the United States in forcing its conservation measures on other nations. In this respect, Mr. Guinea specifically noted that he has difficulty extrapolating conclusions described in the report *Decline Of The Sea Turtle* to the global scale.[489] In fact, Mr. Guinea cited specific evidence demonstrating that in Northern Australia incidental take from gill nets is far greater than incidental take in shrimp trawls.[490] If, however, resources are diverted from meeting this threat because they are being expended to implement the conservation measures imposed by the United States, there may be a negative net effect on turtle mortality.

5.372. Consistent with the fact that threats and their significance vary between regions and species, the evidence presented by the experts demonstrates that threats and their significance vary throughout Thailand. All of the experts indicate that direct exploitation of both adults and eggs has been a serious threat to sea turtles in Thailand in the past, and continues to be so today. Additionally, threats to sea turtles in Thailand include destruction of habitat through development and incidental mortality in a variety of fishing gear. Quantitative information on the relative significance of the threats is generally not available; however, the responses and cited sources indicate that the significance of the threats varies from region to region in Thailand and from species to species. Further, to the extent that shrimp trawling is identified as a threat in Thailand, it is identified as a threat in certain locations and/or in conjunction with other threats. Moreover, the threat appears to be associated with trawlers operating too close to shore - a situation that is addressed by Thai legislation banning commercial fishing within 3 km.

---

fore the imposition of the US Federal TEDs requirement) for the assertion that "this threat in the United States has largely been eliminated with the application of TEDs in shrimp trawls." (Eckert para. 5.36). Thailand believes this assertion has been largely discredited by information presented by several of the other experts concerning the high strandings of turtles in the United States since imposition of the TEDs requirement.

[487] Frazier para. 5.43.

[488] See Poiner para. 5.116 ("Anthropogenic threats in the three countries [the United States, Malaysia and Thailand] are similar ... but their relative importance is different."); Poiner para. 5.118, (shrimp trawling is the most significant factor in the United States but is not a key factor in Australia); Liew para. 5.69 ("the factors that are known to cause decline in sea turtle populations are generally similar but differences do exist in terms of importance for different populations... The degree of importance of factors threatening turtles in different parts of the world does differ."); Liew para. 5.292 (noting the multiple factors that may impact the interaction between sea turtles and shrimp trawling and that the factors vary from region to region.); Guinea para. 5.15 (generalizations concerning sea turtle and shrimp trawl interaction "are incorrect and hamper management options of the individual countries in managing their breeding units of sea turtles."); Guinea para. 5.15 ("Because of their preferred habitats most greens and usually hawksbills and leatherbacks are relatively unaffected by trawling."); Frazier para. 5.102 ("each sea turtle population may have specific sources and intensities of mortality").

[489] Guinea para. 5.18.

[490] Guinea para. 5.124 (noting a single gill net killed more sea turtles in four days in Northern Australia than are killed annually in the same location in shrimp trawls).

5.373. Mr. Liew presented a table summarizing the findings presented by C. Limpus in a 1997 paper. The table indicates that excessive egg harvest is an issue that must be addressed for all species of sea turtle found in Thailand; however, fisheries bycatch mortality is not listed as a threat to any species in Thailand.[491] Mr. Guinea listed four anthropogenic threats to sea turtle populations in Thailand: (i) the over-use of marine turtles and their eggs as food in the past; (ii) the sale of marine turtle products to tourists and for international trade; (iii) the deterioration of nesting habitats and marine pollution; and (iv) the incidental capture of marine turtles in commercial fishing operations.[492] Shrimp trawling is not singled out in this list as a threat in Thailand, as it is in Mr. Guinea's list of US anthropogenic threats, suggesting that the reference to "commercial fishing operations" is not specifically targeted to shrimp trawling.

5.374. Dr. Poiner also identified several human-induced threats to sea turtles in Thailand: egg harvests, adult harvests, shrimp trawling, pelagic fishing gear, gill nets, debris ingestion, entanglement, and habitat alteration and loss.[493] With respect to Thailand, the chart presented by Dr. Poiner is based on three sources. The Limpus article (Limpus, 1997) has previously been discussed and does not identify shrimp trawling as a threat that must be addressed in Thailand. The Settle article[494] states that the study upon which the article is based did not address threats at sea, that the dominant threat to sea turtle survival includes egg collection and turtle hunting, that indirect take in numerous types of fishing gear, such as trawls, drift nets, and purse seines, plays a significant role, and that loss of nesting habitat to beach from development is another serious threat. Further, the Monanunsap article[495] identifies shrimp trawling as an issue only in some locations in Thailand and states that the ban on in-shore fishing and regulations controlling the number of trawls and pushnets have reduced incidental sea turtle capture in trawls. In general, Dr. Poiner stated that it is difficult to rank the various sources of mortality.[496]

5.375. Dr. Frazier similarly identified a variety of threats to various species and in various locations in Thailand.[497] He noted that "the most recent review of the status of marine turtles in Thailand identifies [the threats as] commercial exploitation of sea turtles and their eggs, coastal development, heavy fishing activities (trawling, gill nets,

[491] Liew para. 5.139. In the source material provided by Mr. Liew, Dr. Limpus notes that the small nesting population of hawksbills at Ko Khram appears to have stabilized in the last 20 years. While, as discussed below, the majority of experts agree that TEDs are not a required conservation measure, this evidence further demonstrates that alternatives such as area closures can be used to achieve conservation purposes.

[492] Guinea para. 5.106. It should also be noted that while Mr. Guinea states that any ranking given is indicated in the references listed, no such references appear to have been listed and therefore further comment is not possible.

[493] Poiner para. 5.71.

[494] Settle S., (1995), *Status of Nesting Populations of Sea Turtles in Thailand and their Conservation*, Marine Turtle Newsletter 68:8-13.

[495] Monanunsap, S., (1997), *Country Paper - Thailand*, Proceedings of the Workshop on Marine Turtle Research and Management in Indonesia, Jember, East Java, Indonesia, November 1996, pp. 139-149.

[496] Poiner para. 5.90.

[497] Frazier paras. 5.56 and 5.96.

and long lines)".[498] Dr. Frazier also cites a 1996 press report by Matchima as indicating that sea turtles have been caught and killed by trawlers. In this respect, we note the 1996 article by Matchima indicates that small trawlers, not deep-sea large trawlers, are responsible for netting and killing most sea turtles and that the small boats are using longline hooks and gill nets.[499] Further, Dr. Frazier indicates that excessive exploitation may be occurring with respect to green and ridley turtles in Thailand.[500]

5.376. Dr. Eckert stated that there are a number of threats to sea turtle populations in Thailand, and that the most serious appear to be "shrimp trawling and killing of turtles and taking of eggs".[501] However, there is substantial evidence calling into question Dr. Eckert's identification of shrimp trawling, as opposed to other forms of incidental take, as one of the three most serious threats in Thailand. In this respect, the sources cited by Dr. Eckert do not rank trawling *vis-à-vis* other human-induced threats, and cite trawling as a factor only in certain areas of Thailand and generally in conjunction with other threats. Further, the sources identify the threat as trawling too close to shore - a threat addressed by Thai legislation. In Hill (1991), the complaint voiced by one villager on the Andaman Sea coast is that "large trawling boats ... illegally lay their seines too close to shore, within the legal three kilometres limit".[502] The K. Eckert (1993) source[503] cited by Dr. Eckert is a compilation of available sources concerning threats to sea turtles undertaken for purposes of analyzing threats posed by high sea drift nets. As an initial matter, we note that this compilation of available data occurred prior to the report on the *Night Trawl Study*[504] or the study by Sujittosakul and Senaluk[505], that demonstrated a lack of interaction between shrimp and trawlers around Kram Island and therefore could not include these sources in the discussion on Thailand. Further, this source similarly identifies the problem as interaction between shrimp and trawlers in shallow waters. With respect to quantification threats, the source identifies the impact of both trawling and longlining as "unknown" but possibly large. The full quote from that article is that

> "[t]he magnitude of the take incidental to other forms of fishing, notably trawling and long-lining in modern times, has not been quantified. Catch rates for single trawlers in the Java Sea ... and southern China Sea ... appear low, but the effect of the entire fishing effort could be large".[506]

---

498 Frazier para. 5.96.

499 Matchima Chanswangpuwana, Thailand: *Small Trawlers Blamed for Sea Turtle Losses*, Bangkok Post, 11 March 1996.

500 Frazier para. 5.134.

501 Eckert para. 5.94.

502 Hill, G., (1991), *Villagers in Thailand Protect Turtle Eggs, Bring Conservation Home*, Marine Turtle Newsletter, 53:8-9.

503 Eckert, K., (1993), *The Biology And Status Of Marine Turtles In The North Pacific Ocean*, NOAA Tech Memo, NOAA-TM-NMFS-SWFSC-186. 156p.

504 *The Night-Trawled Monitoring Survey During 1967-1996,* Marine Fisheries Division, Department of Fisheries, Thailand, January 1997.

505 Sujittosakul, T. and Senaluk, S., (1997), *Relationship Between Sea Turtle Nesting and Number of Shrimp Trawlers Around Kram Island*, Technical Paper No. 6, Marine Fisheries Division, Department of Fisheries, Thailand.

506 N.V.C. Polunin and N.S. Nuitja, (1995 rev. ed.), *Sea Turtle Populations of Indonesia and Thailand*, K.A. Bjorndal, Biology and Conservation of Sea Turtles, p. 359.

Notably, the K. Eckert compilation of sources omits reference to the fact that catch rates from single trawlers appear low. Moreover, it is not even clear that the statement made in the Polunin and Nuitjy article is referring to the effect of individual Thai trawlers in Thai waters; one of the sources referred to in that article relates to single trawlers in the south China Sea and is entitled *Variations in size and composition of demersal trawler catches from the North coast of Java with estimated growth parameters for three import and food-fish species.*[507] Similarly, in another source entitled *Report on the Java Sea Southeast Monsoon trawl survey June-December 1976*, the authors explained in the introduction that because Indonesia "is far richer in sea turtles than is Thailand; most of this account therefore deals with Indonesia".[508] Finally, it is important to note that in the section of the article on conservation methods, the authors do not even mention TEDs or any regulation of the fishing industry. Instead, they focus on measures to address direct exploitation.

5.377. Dr. Eckert also cites *Status of Marine Turtles in Thailand*, by Chantrapornsyl.[509] Thailand already has discussed this source in detail. With respect to green and hawksbill turtles located in the Gulf of Thailand at Khram Island, the article states that a reduction in the number of sea turtles is due to "heavy fishing activities" including trawling, drift gill nets and long-lines. No statement is made as to which particular activity has the greatest impact. With respect to the Andaman Sea Coast, trawling is cited as a problem only near Phrathong island and in conjunction with egg collection, gill nets, and housing and hotel development. The article notes that the prohibition against commercial fishing within 3 km of the coastline was enacted because of a finding that most sea turtles in Thailand are caught from shallow water trawling boats. Finally, Dr. Eckert cites Hill (1992), which is another story about the same Andaman sea village involved in the 1991 Hill story. As is the case with the other sources, the article states that "the main problem remaining is that of the large trawling boats seining within 3 km of shore".[510]

5.378. Based on the responses of the experts, it is clear that the threats and their intensities vary both throughout the world and throughout Thailand. The responses therefore establish that the US assertion that shrimp trawls cause the greatest human-induced mortality to sea turtles is simply not correct with respect to either the world at large, or Thailand.

5.379. The other factual assertion relied upon by the United States to demonstrate that its conservation measures are "necessary" within the meaning of Article XX(b) is that other measures are not sufficient to protect sea turtles. However, since threats and the intensity of threats vary from region-to-region, priority responses also vary. In fact, a majority of the experts concluded that an obligatory TEDs requirement is not an essential conservation measure in all areas where sea turtles occur. Further, some

[507] Sudrajat, A. and U. Beck, (1978), *Variations in Size and Composition of Demersal Trawlers Catches from the North Coast of Java with Estimated Growth Parameters for Three Important Foodfish Species*, Laporan Penelitian Perikanan Laut, 4:1-80.

[508] Losse, G. F. and A. Dwiponggo, (1977), *Report on the Java Sea Southeast Monsoon Trawl Survey, June-December 1976*, Laporan Penelitian Perikanan Laut (Special Report), 3:1-119.

[509] Phuket Marine Biological Center, (1997).

[510] Hill, G., (1992), *The Sustainable Sea Turtle*, Marine Turtle Newsletter, 58:2-5.

experts provided evidence of conservation programmes that do not include TEDs and nonetheless have produced positive results.

5.380. The majority of the experts' responses indicate that priority responses that should be enacted in any particular jurisdiction depend on the threats present - the most serious threats should be addressed first. For example, Dr. Poiner stated that "priority conservation measures for sea turtle conservation will not be the same for all sea turtle populations and all countries concerned. It would be inappropriate to implement uniform measures".[511] Mr. Guinea stated that the conservation measure that should be implemented on a priority basis is the preservation of nesting habitats and the offshore refuge habitats for nesting females[512] - steps that Thailand has already taken in several areas. He further stated that only fishing activities that do not harm adult sea turtles or hatchlings should be permitted within the offshore sanctuary[513] - in effect, advocating an area closure alternative similar to Thailand's ban on fishing within 3 km of the coast.

5.381. Mr. Liew suggested that every measure that prevents sea turtles from being killed is a priority. He noted however, that "in places where exploitation of eggs is still substantial, they would still be ranked high. Differences in priority would exist for different populations, regions and species...".[514] He also noted that if coastal areas are protected during nesting season, the threat caused by fishing may be reduced.[515] Dr. Eckert noted that "of greatest importance to any sea turtle conservation programme is to address the problem that led to the 'endangered' status of the stock or population as a first priority in conservation".[516] Since the experts seem to agree that the factor that has lead to the endangered status of all species in Thailand is historic and continued direct exploitation of turtles and eggs, measures addressing the direct exploitation of turtles and eggs should be Thailand's highest priority. As this review of comments demonstrates, priority responses to sea turtle mortality can vary by location. A conservation programme designed to address the most significant threat in one area is not likely to address the most significant threat in other areas. Therefore, uniform conservation measures are not advisable.

5.382. In addition to noting that priority responses to sea turtle mortality will vary, the majority of experts stated that obligatory use of TEDs is not an essential conservation measure in all areas. In fact, some experts provided examples of successful conservation management programmes that did not include TEDs. Finally, although one expert indicated that TEDs were a necessary conservation measure, the rationale provided is unpersuasive.

5.383. Even in areas where shrimp trawling poses a threat to the sea turtle population, a majority of the experts agree that there are many alternatives to the use of TEDs. Specifically, in response to the Panel's question on whether obligatory use of TEDs for shrimp trawling is an essential conservation measure in all areas where sea turtles occur, both Dr. Poiner and Mr. Guinea referred to TEDs as one of several available

511 Poiner para. 5.185.
512 Guinea para. 5.181.
513 Guinea, *Ibid.*
514 Liew para. 5.183-184.
515 Liew para. 5.115.
516 Eckert para. 5.240.

management tools.[517] Other options include "exclusion zones, time of trawl activity, vessel size, number of nets, net mesh size and duration of individual trawls".[518] The conservation measures chosen depend on a number of factors, including "management objectives, the nature of the fishery and ease of surveillance and enforcement".[519]

5.384. Mr. Liew stated that TEDs, or other similar devices, should only be required on shrimp trawls operating in areas where the likelihood of incidental turtle capture is high[520], and cautioned as follows:

> "Proper studies need to be conducted to determine where these areas occur and the seasons involved. Fishermen would not respond positively to the use of TEDs if they hardly catch turtles in their operations. Neither would they use TEDs if they have intentions of eating or selling the turtle".[521]

In conclusion, he noted that "TEDs use should not be mandated blindly without proper studies".[522] As is clear from his comments, TEDs are not necessary on every shrimp trawl.

5.385. Several of the experts also provided specific examples of management programmes that did not require TEDs but nonetheless produced positive results.[523] For example, Mr. Liew noted that stocks of green turtles and hawksbill turtles from Malaysia/Philippines may be showing recovery after many years of intensive conservation management that involved beach protection and hatcheries.[524] This recovery has occurred without a TEDs requirement even though shrimping occurs in the area.[525] In addition, studies were cited that indicated that in areas where the impact of egg harvest is great, conservation measures that focus on preventing egg harvest may have a significant impact.[526] In materials submitted by Mr. Liew, Dr. Limpus identified

---

517 Poiner para. 5.231 and Guinea para. 5.229.

518 Guinea para. 5.65. Mr. Guinea also noted that "high technology approach to conservation of so called developed countries appears at odds when dealing with artisanal fishers and trawl fleets of countries that are still developing." Guinea para. 5.66 See also, Guinea para. 5.124 (noting that "short [shrimp trawl] tows of less than 60 minutes pose little threat to sea turtles").

519 Poiner para. 5.231.

520 Liew para. 5.207.

521 *Ibid.* See also Liew para. 5.230 ("In certain areas, TEDs use is essential, but scientific studies must be conducted with unbiased data to show its necessity and to convince the fishermen in those areas why the should use them").

522 Liew, *Ibid.*

523 Guinea para. 5.189 (noting the recovery of green turtles and hawksbills on the Turtle Islands of Sabah based on protection of nesting beaches and offshore refuges); Liew para. 5.246 (noting that protection of turtle nesting beaches, eggs and hatchlings has lead to recoveries for greens and hawksbills in the Turtle Islands, leatherbacks in South Africa, leatherbacks in St. Croix and Surinam and greens in the French Frigate Scholes, Hawaii.).

524 Liew para. 5.191.

525 Although Mr. Liew cautioned that urgent attention would be needed if it were determined that the impact of the trawling was significant, mandatory TED use was not required in order to produce these conservation gains.

526 Poiner para. 5.201. Specifically Dr. Poiner discussed two separate studies indicating that protection of eggs/hatchlings could have a major impact on long-term stock viability. The conclusion was based on the fact that the study adopted a higher egg/hatchling stage mortality rate than used in

the Ko Khram rookery (which is a protected nesting beach and offshore refuge due to its location inside a Thai naval base security zone in the Northern Gulf of Thailand) as "the only long-term, stable nesting green turtle population in Southeast Asia".[527] The experience at Ko Khram indicates that Thailand's chosen conservation measures of beach protection, egg and turtle protection, and the ban on commercial fishing within 3 km off shore should effectively protect sea turtles in Thai waters assuming resources do not have to be diverted from enforcing these measures. The majority of the experts, therefore, specifically refuted the US claim that, without TEDs, other measures to protect sea turtles are not sufficient.

5.386. Only one of the experts, Dr. Eckert, considered use of TEDs and essential conservation measure.[528] However, as the following discussion indicates, the rationale Dr. Eckert provides a support for this opinion is unpersuasive. Dr. Eckert indicated that TEDs use should be obligatory because TEDs "provide the best opportunity to reduce turtle bycatch with the greatest efficiency and lowest cost to the fishing industry".[529] Dr. Eckert then indicated that obligatory TEDs requirements should be pursued before other alternatives because of ease of enforcement. He further noted that

> "the problem with seasonal and time closures are that [a)] enforcement requires extensive and continual law enforcement presence on the water in the closed area. With the costs of operating enforcement vessels and the extensive areas fished, this is generally beyond the capacity of most countries (including the US to support)...".[530]

5.387. With respect to efficiency, in actual use TEDs have not been shown to be efficient at excluding sea turtles. Furthermore, no support has been offered for the assertion that TEDs enforcement is more easily accomplished, or less expensive, than enforcement of other measures such as area closures. Due to the ease with which TEDs can be disengaged, the only way to enforce use is for enforcement officers to visit operating trawls individually and inspect the net - even then an inspector may not be able to detect that the TED has been tampered with.[531] In fact, the United States' own

---

a study on a US loggerhead population, an assumption that coincides with the fact that the threat of egg harvest is much greater in countries other than in the United States.

[527] Limpus, C.J., (1997), *Marine Turtle Populations o f Southeast Asia and the Western Pacific Region: Distribution and Status*, Proceedings of the Workshop on Marine Turtle Research and Management in Indonesia, Jember, East Java, Nov. 1996, pp. 37-73.

[528] Dr. Frazier considered TEDs to be only a "stop-gap" measure and instead called for a ban on trawling in all developing countries. Frazier para. 5.225. Further, he stated that "[W]ith or without TEDs, with or without integrated sea turtle conservation plans, there will be no lasting conservation of sea turtles on this planet while the majority of humanity slides even deeper into poverty and finds even fewer alternatives for survival." Frazier para. 5.145. Therefore, apparently Dr. Frazier believes that TEDs are not sufficient to protect sea turtles.

[529] Eckert para. 5.223.

[530] *Ibid.* Dr. Frazier also stated that area closures do not work because of lack of enforcement. Frazier para. 5.226.

[531] See *Decline Of The Sea Turtles Causes and Prevention,* National Research Council, National Academy of Sciences, (1990), p. 134 ("Enforcing proper use of TEDs is also a major concern, because TEDs can be readily disabled by altering the tension of spring cords or tying them in a fashion virtually undetectable by inspectors."). Further, as indicated in an article of the Bangkok Post (*Troubled Waters*, 17 April 1997), inspection in the United States involves visits by the US Coast Guard,

experience calls into doubt the assertion that enforcing TEDs usage is easy or inexpensive.[532] Thus, the rationale for Dr. Eckert's preference for TEDs is unpersuasive. On whole, the experts' responses refute the United States' claim that without TEDs other conservation measures are insufficient.

5.388. In its presentations to the Panel, the United States has argued that the measures at issue "relate to" the conservation of sea turtles within the meaning of Article XX(g) because shrimp trawl nets are the greatest cause of human-induced sea turtle deaths and because TEDs are highly effective in preventing such mortality. Specifically, the United States cited these "facts" to demonstrate a "substantial relationship" between the measures at issue and the conservation of sea turtles. The information presented by the experts contradicts the factual assertions offered by the United States. As previously discussed, the experts' reports conclude that threats to sea turtles vary by region and species. Therefore, the responses do not support the US contention that shrimp trawling is the greatest human-induced cause of sea turtle mortality, one basis for the US claim that there is a substantial relationship between its measures and sea turtle conservation. In fact, the responses indicate that a uniformly imposed measure not targeted to the most significant threats in an area or region may have a negative conservation effect, since, given scarce resources, more serious threats may then go unaddressed.

5.389. Further, evidence presented indicates that while TEDs may be highly effective in theory, they have not been highly effective in practice. Specifically, the evidence presented indicates that, for a variety of reasons, TEDs have not been effective throughout the United States, even though US efforts to develop and implement a TEDs requirement have been underway for at least a decade. Therefore, the responses do not support the second factual premise for the US claim that a substantial relationship exists between the US measures and conservation of sea turtles. The United States has argued that TEDs effectively prevent the drowning of sea turtles in shrimp trawl nets - noting that properly installed TEDs approach 97 per cent efficiency in allowing sea turtles to escape from shrimp trawl nets. Evidence presented by the experts indicates that while TEDs may be effective in tests, in actual use, trawling with TEDs may not lead to a reduction in strandings. For example, Dr. Poiner noted a 1995 study that compared the relationship between sea turtle standing rates and shrimp fishing intensities in the Gulf of Mexico for pre-TEDs and post-TEDs periods and found no difference in stranding rates.[533] Mr. Guinea also noted that sea turtles continue to wash ashore in the United States even though TEDs are compulsory.[534]

---

and since the shrimpers know when an inspection will take place, the US Coast Guard is not likely to catch violators.

532 See Poiner para. 5.222 (after discussing a study that revealed no difference in stranding rates in pre-TEDs and post-TEDs time periods in the Gulf of Mexico, Dr. Poiner stated that "[a] variety of hypotheses were suggested to explain the continuation of the statistical relationship including violation of TED regulations in the fisheries."); Guinea para. 5.220 (noting that in the United States compliance appears to be a problem).

533 Poiner para. 5.222.

534 Guinea para. 5.220 (also noting that in the United States, compliance appears to be a problem). Mr. Guinea further suggested that TEDs will not be effective in all shrimp trawls, stating that "when properly installed and used, a TED will significantly reduce, but not eliminate, the mortality of sea turtles in some shrimp trawls." Guinea para. 5.206.

5.390. Mr. Liew noted that use of TEDs by commercial fishermen has been in force in the United States for the longest time, but that as recently as 1997 there were still large numbers of sea turtle strandings - even though compliance was stated to be 96.9 per cent.[535] Further, he noted that there was a big decline in turtle strandings when the Gulf of Mexico was temporarily closed to shrimping. He concluded that "[a]ll of these examples indicate that problems still exist in the use of TEDs and mandating fishermen to use them does not guarantee that sea turtles will be safe from shrimp trawls".[536] Dr. Frazier's comments evidence a mixed record on TEDs efficiency in the United States. He indicated that studies in South Carolina indicate that TEDs have significantly reduced turtle mortality. However, he also noted that there where high levels of strandings in Louisiana and Texas and stated that they are attributed to "improper use of TEDs, use of inadequate TEDs and intense pulse fishing".[537] This information demonstrates that, even with TEDs, high levels of strandings still occur in the United States. Therefore, in actual use, TEDs have not been nearly as effective at reducing sea turtle mortality as claimed by the United States. Based on this information, the United States cannot support its second factual basis for asserting that there is a substantial relationship between the measures at issue and the conservation of sea turtles.

5.391. A common thread throughout the majority of responses is that to have a positive conservation effect, the development of particular conservation practices must involve the communities that will engage in such practices. On an international level, the issues at hand call for cooperation, not coercion.[538] A conservation measure unilaterally imposed by a foreign country will not have a positive effect because if will not enjoy the support of the community. As the experts make clear, conservation measures must be "owned" by the involved community in order to have a positive effect. Specifically, "[c]onservation programmes should emanate from within a country so that implications on cultural, economic and social issues can be addressed at the same time".[539] Further, "it is important for each region, country or state to assess their own sea turtle population, examine the threats affecting them and prioritize conservation strategies accordingly".[540] Moreover, a participatory solution to trawl bycatch that includes negotiation and mediation with the industry can have substantial advantages over a litigation and legislation approach.[541] The US measures, however, are based on coercion and, therefore, are not "owned" by the affected communities. Based on these comments, and because the US measures are unilateral and externally imposed, it does not appear

[535] Liew 5.221; see also, Liew para. 5.207 ("even though TED use is mandatory in the United States and in their neighbouring countries, large numbers of turtle strandings still occur there").

[536] Liew para. 5.221. Further, he noted that in the United States studies are underway to determine if TEDs should be required in all US waters where shrimping occurs. Liew para. 5.208.

[537] Frazier para. 5.203, referring to Crowder et al. (1995) and para. 5.217. Thailand noted that the same study, which concludes that TEDs reduce strandings by about 44 per cent, is cited by Dr. Eckert (para. 5.210).

[538] Frazier para. 5.13 ("The issue at hand involves many other nations neighbouring those five [United States, Thailand, Malaysia, Pakistan and India]; the conservation and management of migratory animals - marine turtles in this case - can only be accomplished through full international cooperation").

[539] Guinea para. 5.166.

[540] Liew para. 5.192.

[541] Poiner para. 5.231.

that the measures will have the intended effect on the conservation of sea turtles. The United States has usurped each State's ability to address cultural and societal factors, to prioritize conservation measures, and to engage in a dialogue with the affected industry aimed at resolving any incidental sea turtle capture that may occur.

5.392. The information presented by the experts also refutes the contention that Thailand and the other newly affected nations received even-handed treatment as a result of the application of Section 609. Specifically, the responses of several of the experts indicate that there are significant differences between the US shrimp fishery and the geographical area within which it operates and other shrimp fisheries and their area of operations. The technology developed in the United States must be adapted before it can be used in other locations.[542] In addition, development of a "local" TED is tied to acceptance by the local fishery and "[t]here needs to be considerable modification and trial before TEDs or any bycatch reduction device, e.g. fish eye, etc., is accepted by the fishery".[543] Thus, implementation of a TEDs programme takes a substantial amount of time, as noted by Mr. Liew.[544] Dr. Poiner also noted that a requirement imposed through involvement of the stakeholders and negotiation and mediation has worked better in some situations than the litigation/legislation model adopted by the United States.[545] Based on these statements, the United States was not justified in providing Thailand with only four months (a phase-in period that Thailand could not meet) in which to implement a TEDs requirement simply because the United States has developed a TED for use in US waters by US fishermen.

5.393. In defending its contention that the measures at issue are in accordance with the Preamble of Article XX, the United States argued that the shorter phase-in period provided Thailand and the other newly-affected nations *vis-à-vis* the originally affected nations was justified. The basis for this argument was that TEDs technology was not well developed or easily available, especially for developing countries, when the requirement was applied to the originally affected nations, but that extraordinarily effective TEDs were available by the time the requirement was applicable to newly-affective nations.

5.394. As previously noted, TEDs developed in the United States are not extraordinarily effective in practice. Even putting aside this question, as Thailand has just described, the evidence presented by the experts indicates that TEDs designed for US shrimpers in US waters must be modified before they can be used in other waters. This process, which is closely tied to acceptance of the technology, takes time. Therefore, the United States cannot prove that it was justified in providing US shrimpers and shrimpers from originally-affected nations a substantial period of time to implement the TEDs requirement, while provided the newly-affected nations with only four months. Application of the US measures, thus, resulted in arbitrary or unjustified discrimination between Members where the same conditions prevail (in this case, implementation of a conservation measure not previously required) and is a disguised restriction on international trade.

[542] Poiner para. 5.239; Frazier para. 5.233.
[543] Guinea para. 5.236.
[544] Liew para. 5.208.
[545] Poiner para. 5.231.

### 5. *Comments by the United States*

5.395. The United States appreciates this opportunity to provide comments on the responses received from the five experts selected by the Panel. The United States greatly appreciates the time and attention that the experts have devoted to the preparation of their responses. As discussed below, the responses of the experts can make a valuable contribution toward the resolution of this dispute.

5.396. Experts may provide a panel information, advice, and their opinions on certain aspects of the matter that is the subject of the dispute.[546] Experts can provide a panel with vital perspectives, information and advice on technical issues. At the same time, a panel cannot ask experts to advise it on issues or measures which are beyond the panel's own terms of reference, including issues which are outside the scope of any agreement to be interpreted by the panel. Furthermore, it is clear that a panel cannot delegate to experts the panel's central task of interpreting the agreement(s) at issue in a dispute. Experts may advise only on factual issues, not on questions of law nor on the application of the legal standards in the agreement(s) to the facts at hand. The Panel has recognized this principle by selecting persons with expertise in scientific and technical matters, rather than in the *Marrakesh Agreement Establishing the World Trade Organization* ("WTO Agreement").

5.397. Resolution of this dispute depends primarily on a determination of whether the US measures in question relate to the conservation of an exhaustible natural resource which are made effective in conjunction with restrictions on domestic production, or whether the measures are necessary to protect animal life or health. To aid the Panel in making this determination, the parties have presented a substantial amount of factual information that is scientific or technical in nature. The United States believes that, consistent with the WTO Agreement and the Understanding on Rules and Procedures Governing the Settlement of Disputes, the Panel can use the responses received from the experts to better inform their judgment concerning the key scientific or technical questions which lie at the heart of this dispute:

- Are sea turtles threatened or endangered worldwide, including in Complainants' waters?
- Does shrimp trawl fishing without TEDs result in the death of large numbers of sea turtles?
- Do TEDs, when properly installed and used, significantly reduce the mortality of sea turtles caused by shrimp trawl nets?

5.398. The following discussion reviews relevant aspects of the experts' responses as they pertain to these core questions. Subsequently, the United States comments on certain specific responses of the experts (see paragraphs 5.420 to 5.431).

5.399. The experts agree with virtual unanimity that sea turtles are endangered worldwide, including in complainants' waters. Dr. Frazier and Mr. Guinea note that the International Union for the Conservation of Nature lists all species of sea turtles, except the Australian flatback, as either "endangered" or "critically endangered".[547] Dr. Eckert

[546] See Article 13 of the *Understanding on Rules and Procedures Governing the Settlement of Disputes*.

[547] Frazier para. 5.42 and Guinea para. 5.60.

concurs: "[G]lobal sea turtle populations have declined significantly to the point where all species are in danger of extinction".[548] Dr. Poiner adds "most sea turtle populations in the world are severely depleted."[549] Finally, Mr. Liew reports that "some populations have disappeared, some [are] near extinction, some [are] threatened but a few have shown some apparent recovery".[550] As discussed below in more detail, most of the experts believe that there is insufficient evidence for a determination that any sea turtle species or population has recovered.

5.400. Data provided by the experts also underscores that, because of the long-range migrations of sea turtles, efforts by one nation to protect endangered or threatened sea turtles can only succeed if other nations cooperate. Dr. Frazier explains that "all of the six listed species of marine turtles disperse and migrate over vast distances, with no respect to national boundaries ... during its long life, an individual sea turtle will pass through many different environments, traversing a substantial - often vast - surface of the planet".[551] Mr. Guinea agrees: "All sea turtle species except the Australian flatback undergo extensive ocean migrations during their life".[552] Dr. Poiner reports that breeding adults usually migrate relatively long distances from the foraging areas to the traditional breeding rookeries".[553]

5.401. Dr. Eckert provides valuable insight on the migratory habits of leatherback sea turtles:

> Based on very recent data, "leatherback nesting stocks from Malaysia (and probably Thailand as well) ... distribute throughout the [Pacific] ocean basin.... It is likely that mature female leatherbacks circumnavigate the Pacific Ocean during the 2 or 3 years between nesting seasons. ... It is highly probable that Malaysia, Thailand and the United States all share responsibility for Pacific leatherbacks during a single nesting migration".[554]

5.402. In this respect, the experts directly call into question the premise of the complainants that the sea turtles which nest on their beaches are somehow "their" sea turtles, and that the efforts of each of the complainants to protect sea turtles can succeed without regard to the circumstances affecting the same turtles in areas under the jurisdiction of other nations. Instead, as the United States has argued throughout these proceedings, endangered sea turtles are a shared global resource in the sense that they can be effectively protected only through the combined actions of many nations. We therefore concur with the conclusion of Dr. Frazier that "the conservation and management of migratory marine animals - marine turtles in this case - can only be accomplished through full international cooperation".[555]

---

548 Eckert para. 5.19.
549 Poiner para. 5.71.
550 Liew para. 5.68.
551 Frazier paras. 5.13 and 5.39.
552 Guinea, para. 5.262.
553 Poiner para. 5.141.
554 Eckert paras. 5.21 and 5.256.
555 Frazier para. 5.13.

5.403. The experts also agree that shrimp trawl nets used without TEDs in areas and at times where sea turtles occur will capture and drown large numbers of sea turtles, including in complainants' waters. As the United States has previously explained, shrimp trawl nets are dragged along the sea floor for long periods and will capture virtually anything in their path, including endangered sea turtles. Unless the trawl nets are equipped with TEDs, captured animals and debris will remain in the nets until they are emptied on deck. In the words of Dr. Frazier, "bottom trawling is known to cause major impacts on non-target species because it is an unselective method of fishing. Shrimp trawls are notoriously unselective".[556] Mr. Guinea adds that, "trawls of long duration over areas inhabited by benthic feeding sea turtles; i.e., loggerhead, olive ridley, Kemp's ridley, flatback and some adult greens or in waters adjacent to their rookeries will capture a proportion of the sea turtles present".[557]

5.404. Dr. Eckert reports that the incidental mortality of sea turtles in fishing operations is one of the two most significant anthropogenic threats to sea turtle species, the other being direct harvest of sea turtles (which all parties to this dispute have outlawed). He further notes that, while other kinds of fishing gear, including coastal gillnets and longlines, result in some incidental mortality of sea turtles, "by far the most serious threat to sea turtle stocks living in coastal environments are trawl fisheries".[558] On this point, Dr. Frazier discusses the reasons why shrimp trawling (without TEDs) is a particularly dangerous fishing method for sea turtles:

> "The special concern from shrimp trawling stems from several points. Because shrimp are generally most concentrated in coastal waters, trawling tends to concentrate in coastal waters (this occurs routinely, despite regulations and bans on trawling in these waters) ... shrimp trawling is generally carried out with considerable intensity, resulting in large areas of the benthos having the trawl pulled across them repeatedly ... Where shrimp trawling is intense, and concentrated in coastal waters, there is a high probability that sea turtles will be caught and incidentally drowned. If these fishing activities occur near to breeding grounds (nesting beaches or mating areas) or in the migratory routes used by turtles to get to and from the breeding areas, or in feeding grounds, there is an extremely high probability that large numbers of turtles will be caught and drown. Where this happens, the numbers of turtle that are breeders or near-breeders killed incidentally can be relatively large. If this sort of operation continues, it can decimate a healthy population, make it impossible for a recovering population to recover, or even finally exterminate a population".[559]

5.405. Material provided by the experts further supports the contention of the United States that the mortality of sea turtles in shrimp trawl nets is not a phenomenon restricted to US waters or to the Western Hemisphere, but in fact occurs wherever sea turtles and shrimp trawling occur together, including in the complainants' region.

---

556 Frazier para. 5.122.
557 Guinea para. 5.65.
558 Eckert paras. 5.33 and 5.119.
559 Frazier paras. 5.100-101.

5.406. Dr. Poiner identifies the incidental capture of sub-adult and adult sea turtles in shrimp nets as one of the "major sources" of loggerhead and green sea turtle mortality in the Indo-Pacific region, particularly Malaysia and Thailand.[560] Dr. Eckert finds that, in Thailand, shrimp trawling is one of the most serious threats to sea turtle populations and is a significant cause of sea turtle mortality, particularly for green sea turtles.[561] Many of the experts describe the large-scale killings of sea turtles caused by the shrimp trawl industry in India. Dr. Frazier notes that, "for over a decade, incidental capture and drowning in fishing gear has been known to be an important source of mortality of adult turtles, particularly in the Bay of Bengal; and trawlers, especially shrimp trawlers in Tamil Nadu, Andhra Pradesh, Orissa and West Bengal have consistently been singled out for impacts that they cause".[562]

5.407. According to Dr. Eckert, olive ridleys, in particular, are "heavily impacted" by shrimp trawl fishing in India. "The incidental take of olive ridleys in India is exceptionally severe ... Annually 5,000 - 8,000 dead turtles wash up on the beaches of Orissa which are attributable to incidental take in shrimp trawls. Despite laws banning such fishing, large scale shrimp fishing is occurring within the Bhitara Kinika Sanctuary (the primary nesting area for olive ridleys in India) and more than 4,000 olive ridleys stranded dead on the beach during 1996/7 ... The large numbers of olive ridleys killed by legal and illegal trawling operations is extraordinary and must represent the single largest threat to sea turtle populations in India".[563] Mr. Liew states that, "thousands of olive ridleys are also killed in Orissa, India each year which conservationists attributed largely to shrimp trawlers".[564] Citing a study by E.C. Chan, Dr. Eckert also reports that incidental capture in fishing gear, including shrimp trawl gear, "is now recognized as one of the most serious threats to the survival of the remaining sea turtles in Malaysia".[565]

5.408. The responses of the experts also reflect widespread agreement that TEDs, when properly installed and used, substantially reduce the mortality of sea turtles caused by shrimp trawls. "Studies of TEDs ... demonstrate that properly installed TEDs are very effective at virtually eliminating the trawl catch of sea turtles".[566] "[T]here can be no question that TEDs reduce sea turtle mortality when installed and operated properly".[567] "[W]hen properly installed and used, different kinds of TEDs can significantly reduce the incidental capture and mortality of sea turtles in shrimp trawl nets".[568] "TEDs will allow the majority of adult turtles to escape [from shrimp trawl nets]".[569]

5.409. Beyond this general conclusion, the experts elaborate a number of specific points that the United States has advanced throughout these proceedings:

- TEDs help to protect sea turtle populations.

560 Poiner para. 5.185.
561 Eckert paras. 5.94 and 5.35.
562 Frazier para. 5.96.
563 Eckert paras. 5.37 and 5.95.
564 Liew para. 5.113.
565 Eckert para. 5.93.
566 Poiner para. 5.209.
567 Eckert para. 5.202.
568 Frazier para. 5.203.
569 Guinea para. 5.65.

- TEDs are inexpensive and easy to use.
- TEDs cause minimal shrimp loss and produce other benefits.
- TEDs are adaptable to different shrimp fishing environments.
- Other methods to protect sea turtles are insufficient, unless coupled with the use of TEDs.

5.410. The experts describe how the required use of TEDs by shrimp trawlers in the United States has produced significant benefits for sea turtle populations. Dr. Eckert reports that, "for green, loggerhead and Kemp's ridley sea turtles in the Atlantic, the most serious threat was shrimp trawling. ... The requirement that TEDs be utilized in all waters at all times has reduced this threat".[570] Dr. Frazier also states that, "during the last few years there have been clear indications from the commercial shrimp fishery in the United States that TEDs have significantly reduced turtle mortality. Stranding data from South Carolina for the period 1980 to 1993 show remarkable declines, particularly when TED regulations were in place. Crowder et. al. (1995) concluded that the decline in strandings was because of reduced mortality from TED use".[571]

5.411. Similarly, many of the experts attest to the fact that TEDs are inexpensive and easy to use. Dr. Eckert, for example, explains that:

> "TEDs are incredibly simple devices to construct from local materials, require little special skills above what is already in use by shrimp fishermen and plans for their construction are available. Considering the costs of fuel, nets and other required equipment for such a fishery, it is doubtful that TEDs would add significantly to the cost of fishing and may actually be advantageous ... [D]eploying and operating these devices take very little special skills and handling ... The first TEDs were developed and used by shrimp fishermen as a way to reduce fouling and bycatch problems, long before sea turtles were of concern ... Most experienced fishermen understand net deployment methodology very well irrespective of formal education and thus I would expect that deploying a TED equipped net would pose no particular challenges".[572]

5.412. Mr. Guinea adds that, "it would be condescending and culturally insensitive to suggest that any fisherman could not operate a net fitted with a TED". Dr. Frazier concurs that neither socio-economic distinctions nor level of formal education is likely to be relevant to the ability of a shrimp fishermen to use a TED successfully.[573]

5.413. A number of the complainants have alleged that TEDs cause significant losses of shrimp. The experts disagree. Dr. Eckert, for example, reviews studies from the United States which show that "commercial catch rates were higher in years after TEDs were required (though it is probably not valid to suggest that TED use necessarily resulted in increased catch rates)". According to Dr. Eckert, the study submitted by Thailand which purports to show otherwise "is probably invalid due to poor data gathering methodology and data analysis". By contrast, Dr. Eckert found that a recent

[570] Eckert para. 5.92.
[571] Frazier para. 5.215.
[572] Eckert paras. 5.144 and 5.202.
[573] Guinea para. 5.296 and Frazier para. 5.205.

study in Malaysia on TEDs and the Thai Turtle Free Device, which "showed that TEDs will prevent marine turtles from being trapped in the net without effecting [sic] the catch of shrimp and fish", cannot be considered conclusive due to the very small sample size; however, it does seem to be a very well executed and analyzed preliminary experiment".[574]

5.414. Mr. Guinea, summarizing the results of TEDs trials in the Northern Prawn Fishery in Australia, reports: "a reduction in small fish bycatch by about 30 per cent, a reduction in large fish, no sea turtles were captured during trials. Other studies reported a slight increase in prawn catch (4 per cent and 7 per cent) ... The catch was of better quality with fewer broken or damaged shrimp. The better catch of unbroken shrimp could command a higher price".[575] The comments of Mr. Guinea in this regard also demonstrate, as the United States has argued, that TEDs are adaptable to different shrimp fishing environments. Dr. Frazier further mentions studies in Malaysia which "indicated that the gear was suitable for use by local fishermen... [and] a preliminary trial recently carried out in Orissa showed that TEDs installed in local trawls successfully excluded turtles". Dr. Frazier goes on to cite another expert in the use of TEDS: "According to Randall Arauz, who has been working on TEDs in Costa Rica for the last four years: 'with proper modifications of the TED technology and fishing practices, together with scientific documentation, research [can] make TEDs work efficiently under virtually any fishing conditions, as we have proven in Costa Rica'".[576] In light of these findings, it should not be surprising that the experts also generally agree that TEDs should be used wherever there is a likelihood that sea turtles will be incidentally caught in commercial shrimp trawl nets.

5.415. Mr. Guinea argues that the use of TEDs should be one of the management regulations adopted where trawling is responsible for the deaths of sea turtles. "Trawls over areas where sea turtles occur should be of short duration (60 minutes) and employ TEDs".[577] Dr. Eckert simply says that, "TEDs provide the best opportunity to reduce turtle bycatch with the greatest efficiency and lowest cost to the fishing industry ... It is the most easily enforced conservation measure available".[578] Dr. Frazier, summarizing reports of other researchers (including Dr. Poiner), concludes that the use of TEDs, together with other conservation measures, would be instrumental in the survival of marine species, including sea turtles.[579] Mr. Liew concurs that the use of TEDs in trawl nets should be implemented as a matter of "priority" to reduce the incidental catch of adult and juvenile turtles. "All shrimp trawlers operating in areas where the likelihood of incidental turtle capture is high should be encouraged to use TEDs or other similar devices".[580]

5.416. Most of the experts also concur that, while other methods to protect sea turtles may have value, they will not succeed in producing the recovery of decimated sea turtle populations unless they are coupled with the use of TEDs in areas where sea turtles are

574 Eckert paras. 5.211-213.
575 Guinea para. 5.219.
576 Frazier paras. 5.204 and 5.233.
577 Guinea paras. 5.86 and 5.181.
578 Eckert para. 5.223.
579 Frazier paras. 5.84 and 5.225.
580 Liew paras. 5.183 and 5.207.

subject to capture in shrimp trawl nets. For example, Mr. Liew states emphatically that, "saving the eggs and protecting nesting turtles on the beach alone while allowing them to be killed in the sea will not work ... Egg protection methods alone are not sufficient especially if other threats are still present and have significant impact on the population".[581] Dr. Frazier is equally pessimistic about the likelihood of success of these approaches: "focusing on protection of just eggs and hatchlings, and not reducing mortality in older animals, will be doomed to failure."[582] Dr. Eckert also agrees: "It is simply not adequate to concentrate all efforts on protecting reproducing females and eggs ... no population can be preserved by such methods alone. ... Nesting beach protection alone is not enough to restore sea turtle populations". As evidence of the failure of such methods, Dr. Eckert notes that extensive efforts by Mexico to protect nesting stocks of leatherbacks did not prevent a 95 per cent decline in the population over 10 years caused by incidental mortality in fishing operations.[583]

5.417. The experts similarly disfavour the practice of "headstarting", which involves the keeping of hatchlings in protected captivity for some period of time before releasing them into the wild. Mr. Liew describes headstarting as "the wrong conservation strategy".[584] Dr. Eckert adds that headstarting "has not yet proven successful ... at this time, headstarting is not considered a valid conservation tool". According to Dr. Eckert, one primary reason why such other methods cannot work by themselves is that, unlike TEDs, they do not adequately protect adult, subadult and large juvenile sea turtles, which have much higher reproductive values than eggs and hatchlings. These latter classes of sea turtles are most vulnerable to incidental mortality in trawl fisheries.[585] Dr. Frazier further explains that:

> "[A]dult animals are the immediate key to the future of the population.... The closer to maturity the turtles get, the more they are worth to the population, and the less it can afford to lose them.... Hence, sources of mortality that affect animals that are mature, or nearly mature, have far greater instantaneous impact on the status of the population than taking the same number of eggs or young animals, for they reduce levels of reproduction very quickly. Harvesting or breeding animals, or incidental capture in fishing gear, are examples of these very 'costly' sources of mortality. Modern fishing practices have been repeatedly documented to cause mortality.... [S]ince mortality of animals that are breeding or near breeding is most costly to the population, a general priority is to reduce mortality on those animals that have a high reproductive value".[586]

5.418. Furthermore, the experts cast serious doubts on the efficacy of methods, asserted by some Complainants to be effective, consisting of prohibitions on trawling in certain areas or at certain times ("area and time closures") or of requirements that trawling

581 Liew paras. 5.192 and 5.252.
582 Frazier paras. 5.242.
583 Eckert paras. 5.73, 5.171 and 5.34.
584 Liew para. 5.113.
585 Eckert paras. 5.173, 5.73-74.
586 Frazier paras. 5.77, 5.82 and 5.171.

times not exceed a certain duration ("tow-time limitations"). "Area closures do not work because of a lack of enforcement. This has been widely documented in many countries, including those involved in this dispute". Seasonal and time closures are ineffective for similar reasons. "Tow-time limitations are least enforceable of all measures".[587] Similarly, "tow-time limitations are almost impossible to enforce and actually do not provide much protection to turtles subject to multiple captures".[588]

5.419. There is some disagreement among the experts as to the validity of claims by some of the Complainants that they have produced population recoveries through methods not involving the use of TEDs. Mr. Guinea believes that "conservation measures devoted to eggs and hatchlings have been successful for some breeding units of some species e.g., olive ridleys in Orissa", that green and hawksbill turtles nesting on the Turtle Islands of Sabah have recovered and that, in general, the conservation measures of Malaysia and Thailand "appear to be successful".[589] Most of the other experts flatly reject these assessments. Dr. Poiner states that "there is no clear documented case of recovery in the world. ... Some countries (e.g., Malaysia and Thailand) have instigated management measures to prohibit or control egg harvests as a conservation measure but there is no evidence of recovery of any of these populations".[590] Dr. Frazier concurs: "I am unaware of conclusive evidence for the recovery of any sea turtle population in any of the five countries involved in this dispute so that there is not or will soon not be a risk of extinction".[591] Dr. Eckert, for his part, states that, "to the best of my knowledge, no nesting population of sea turtles has shown any recovery in any of the countries of dispute. There are encouraging signs that the Kemp's ridley nesting population may be growing ... If there is a recovery [of Kemp's ridleys], it is likely due to the required use of TEDs in the United States and Mexico and the protection afforded nesting females". Referring to arguments presented by Malaysia in this dispute, he adds that it is erroneous to assume that a trend in green turtle populations can be determined after only a few years. This is simply not the case.... The trend described in this study will not be valid for at least another 15 or more years depending on the maturity time of the turtles within this population".[592]

5.420. To conclude, the United States notes that it is natural that in five sets of separate responses for the experts there would be some differences of view expressed. What is remarkable about these particular responses is the high degree of consensus among the experts on the core factual issues in question. In the view of the United States, the responses of the experts emphatically support our contentions that the measures at issue in this dispute relate to the conservation of an exhaustible natural resource and that they are necessary to protect animal life and health.

5.421. The United States also wishes to comment on certain specific responses of the experts. The responses of Mr. Guinea call for the following comments.

---

587 Frazier paras. 5.226-27.
588 Eckert para. 5.223.
589 Guinea paras. 5.189, 5.243-44.
590 Poiner paras. 5.71 and 5.247.
591 Frazier para. 5.188.
592 Eckert para.186.

5.422. The concept of sea turtles as a shared global resource may be "cumbersome", as Mr. Guinea puts it, but global efforts are necessary for sea turtle conservation to succeed. In fact, Mr. Guinea's very first observation (Introductory Comment #1) is that sea turtle conservation must be based on the "breeding unit", and he notes that "breeding units" may be found in the waters of other countries.[593] As noted in a Limpus study (widely quoted by the experts in this case), "Marine turtles are internationally migratory species that cannot be managed at single localities. Indeed they cannot be successfully managed even at the level of a single country. They are internationally shared resources that need to be managed at the level of individual stocks".[594] Further, in response to Question 5(a), all of the experts, including Mr. Guinea, note that sea turtles commonly feed over 1000 km from their nesting grounds.

5.423. Mr. Guinea also notes that "most greens and usually hawksbills and leatherbacks are relatively unaffected by trawling". While it is true that loggerheads, olive ridleys, Kemp's ridleys and flatbacks may be more susceptible to incidental capture in shrimp trawls, greens, hawksbills and leatherbacks have been documented as bycatch in shrimp trawls. In fact, the paper he refers to in his answer to question 6(c) (Sachse and Wallner, in press) notes that in one study, green sea turtles were the second most captured species of sea turtles. There was also a significant catch of hawksbill sea turtles (368 green and 62 hawksbill sea turtles captured - p. 3). Further, in his response to question 1(c), Mr. Guinea identifies the flatback, olive ridley, loggerhead, green and hawksbill turtles as bycatch in Australian prawn fisheries. He lists greens as the second most prominent sea turtle species found in the bycatch in the Queensland Trawl fishery.[595] Other experts in this case also address the mortality of all sea turtle species in shrimp trawl nets. Dr. Eckert identifies trawl fisheries as a contributing source of decline of leatherbacks[596] and shrimp trawling as a significant source of mortality for greens and hawksbills on the Pacific coast of Mexico, in North Eastern South America and Thailand. Mr. Liew writes, "[f]eeding habitats of different sea turtles would differ depending on their diet but these habitats may overlap. An area of seabed may have green turtles, hawksbills, loggerheads and ridleys occurring together as the area may have pockets of seagrass, sponges, crabs, shrimps, mollusc and fish there".[597] Furthermore, Guinea's statement only takes into account the feeding habitats of sea turtles, it does not consider threats to sea turtles when they migrate from their feeding grounds to the nesting beach or when they are in coastal waters during the internesting period. In discussing the various feeding habitats of different species and the risks they face from incidental capture in fisheries in those habitats, Dr. Liew writes, "[h]owever, for all these species of turtles, they are also vulnerable in the waters off their nesting grounds during the nesting season where they aggregate in numbers depending on the size of the nesting population".[598]

---

593 Guinea para. 5.14.

594 C.J. Limpus, (1997), *Marine Turtle Populations of Southeast Asia and the Western Pacific Region: Distribution and Status*, Proceedings of the Workshop on Marine Turtle Research and Management in Indonesia, Jember, East Java, November 1996.

595 Guinea, paras. 5.15, 5.291 and 5.112.

596 Eckert para. 5.34.

597 Liew para. 5.282.

598 Liew para. 5.115.

5.424. In his introductory, Mr. Guinea further argues that the US measure is ineffective because affected countries may circumvent the US measures by various means, such as by transshipping their shrimp through certified countries. To support this argument, he cites a statement purportedly made by a delegate of India at an FAO Workshop.[599] The United States responds that this issue is outside the purview of the Panel's questions, and, moreover, each one of the Complainants - including India - claims that they have been substantially affected by the US measure. Finally, Section 609 applies to shrimp based on the country of harvest, regardless of whether the shrimp is processed in or shipped through a third country. Thus, it should not be possible for a nation to avoid the requirements of Section 609 simply by transshipping its shrimp through another country.

5.425. In his answer to question 1(c), Mr. Guinea states that he relies on certain cited sources for his ranking of threats to sea turtles. However, Mr. Guinea's ranking of threats to sea turtles in the United States is incorrect. The source he cites, Lutceavage, M.E. et. al. (1997), simply delineates the threats to sea turtles without ranking them. In fact, the authors note that the National Academy of Science study ("Decline of Sea Turtles") found incidental capture in shrimp trawls to be the leading cause of sea turtle mortalities due to human activities. Moreover, his ranking of threats to sea turtles in the other countries that are parties to this dispute supports the United States contention that shrimp trawling is a significant source of mortality for sea turtles. For each of the complainant countries, incidental capture of marine turtles in fishing operations is ranked within the top four threats to sea turtles.

5.426. In answering question 2(d), Mr. Guinea does not provide a citation for his contention that the green and hawksbill turtles on the Sabah Turtle Islands have staged a "remarkable recovery". He seems to be contradicted by other experts. Limpus writes, "[i]t appears that all marine turtle populations in the Indo-Pacific region outside Australia are severely depleted and/or subject to overharvest and/or to excessive incidental mortality".[600] Drs. Eckert and Frazier in their response conclude that there are no sea turtle populations in the countries involved in this dispute that have recovered. Dr. Poiner states, "there is no clear documented cases of recovery in the world." Poiner specifically mentions the sea turtle conservation efforts in Malaysia and Thailand and the fact that there is no evidence of recovery of these populations.[601]

5.427. Answering question 2(e), Mr. Guinea reasons that 5000 deaths in shrimp-trawl nets per year is a sustainable level of mortality for Indian olive ridley turtles. This reasoning is without foundation. Mr. Guinea transfers Dr. Crouse's conclusions on loggerhead sea turtles to olive ridleys which is biologically unsound. The major flaws with this approach are age to maturity differences, reproductive strategy differences (i.e. arribada or mass nesting vs. solitary nesting) and stage-based mortality differences. Under question 3(c), Mr. Guinea's response is misleading. The quoted source, Todd Steiner of Earth Island Institute, said that TEDs are part of an integrated approach

---

599 Guinea para. 5.16-17.

600 C.J. Limpus, (1997), *Marine Turtle Populations of Southeast Asia and the Western Pacific Region: Distribution and Status*, Proceedings of the Workshop on Marine Turtle Research and Management in Indonesia, Jember, East Java, November 1996.

601 Poiner paras. 5.71 and 5.140.

to sea turtle conservation and restoration, not that TEDs were simply one option available to managers, as Mr. Guinea asserts. In his answer to question 3(d), Mr. Guinea states that TEDs, without modification to local conditions, have unacceptably poor performance. The sources cited by Mr. Guinea do not support his contention.

5.428. In answering question 4(a), Mr. Guinea makes a very broad and generalized statement that is not supported by any further facts when he states that the egg/hatchling conservation measures employed by Malaysia and Thailand appear to be successful. Drs. Eckert, Frazier and Poiner contradict his response in their statements. They conclude that there are no sea turtle populations in the countries involved in this dispute that have recovered. Dr. Poiner writes, "[s]ome countries (e.g., Malaysia and Thailand) have instigated management measures to prohibit or control egg and sea turtle harvests but there is no evidence of recovery of these populations.[602] In particular regard to Thailand, it has been noted that "there is no clear link between the high numbers of turtles at Khram island and the headstart programme there. The effects, positive or negative, of headstarting will only be seen after two or four decades if and when the raised creatures return to breed and nest. In the interim, Thailand will lose its sea turtles for sure if 'conservation' is limited to headstarting. ... Simply raising more turtles and introducing them into habitat ill-suited to support them is a waste".[603] Limpus writes, "[i]t appears that all marine turtle populations in the Indo-Pacific region outside Australia are severely depleted and/or subject to overharvest and/or to excessive incidental mortality".[604] Mr. Guinea himself equivocates on this issue later in his statement when he writes, "the relative significance of egg protection is difficult to determine without knowing the other threatening processes impacting on the breeding unit".[605]

5.429. Under question 6(a), Mr. Guinea implies that time and area closures near turtle rookeries may be sufficient measures to protect sea turtles, but he never addresses the serious difficulties with this approach. Time and area closures only protect large juvenile or adult turtles while they are in the closed area near the rookery, or during the time when shrimping is banned and not at other times or places, such as when turtles are feeding in shrimp grounds. In fact, time/area specific closures and sanctuaries are not sufficient to protect sea turtles from incidental mortality in shrimp fisheries.[606] Two other experts in this case, Drs. Eckert and Frazier, disagree that time/area closures are viable management tools in and of themselves. Eckert points out the various problems with seasonal and time closures: (a) they are difficult and expensive to enforce, (b) they do not facilitate rapid adjustment for stochastic fluctuations in the migratory patterns of turtles, and (c) tow time limitations are almost impossible to enforce and actually do not

---

602 Poiner para. 5.140.

603 Settle, (1995), *Status of Nesting Populations of Sea Turtles in Thailand and their Conservation*, Marine Turtle Newsletter, No. 68, p. 11.

604 C.J. Limpus, (1997), *Marine Turtle Populations of Southeast Asia and the Western Pacific Region: Distribution and Status*, Proceedings of the Workshop on Marine Turtle Research and Management in Indonesia, Jember, East Java, November 1996.

605 Guinea para. 5.251.

606 Crowder et al., (1994), *Predicting the Impact of Turtle Excluder Devices on Loggerhead sea Turtle Populations*, 4(3) Ecological Applications, p. 437; Statement of Deborah Crouse, Ph.D. 23 July 1997 (document submitted to the Panel by the United States).

provide much protection to turtles subject to multiple captures.[607] Dr. Frazier also points out the problems with these approaches. Both area closures and tow times are difficult to enforce. Additionally, seasonal and time closures tend to "concentrate fishing effort just before and just after the closure ('pulse fishing'). In general, seasonal and time closures simply offset mortality around the time of the closure".[608]

5.430. The United States also wishes to comment on some aspects of Dr. Poiner's answers.

5.431. In his answer to question 3(c), Dr. Poiner states that although the "obligatory" use of TEDs is one management tool that can be used, he cites with approval a source noting that voluntary TEDs use may be a better alternative, at least for Australia. However, the factual matter at issue in this case is whether TEDs reduce sea turtle mortality, not whether TEDs should be adopted voluntarily, or by regulation. None of the four Complainants claims that their shrimp trawlers voluntarily use TEDs. Furthermore, the Sachse and Wallner study, cited by Mr. Guinea[609], notes,

> "we accept that after the current research, development and voluntary use phases, it may be appropriate to formally include TED use in management arrangements for the fishery. To this end, AFMA [Australian Fisheries Management Authority] and NORMAC (the management advisory committee established to provide management advise to AFMA for the NPF [Northern Prawn Fishery]) are in the process of developing bycatch action plans. These plans are likely to include an implementation timetable for TEDs".

Thus, the study itself seems to call into question the effectiveness of the voluntary approach.

5.432. Dr. Poiner also states that there are other measures such as area, seasonal and time closures and tow-time limitations that can be used to prevent sea turtle mortality. But, like Mr. Guinea's response, his response does not address the sea turtle mortality due to shrimp trawling in areas outside the banned area, or due to trawling at times when the ban is not in effect (see paragraph 5.429).

## VI. INTERIM REVIEW

6.1. On 16 March 1998, Malaysia submitted comments regarding the interim report in accordance with Article 15.2 of the Understanding on Rules and Procedures Governing the Settlement of Disputes (hereafter "DSU"). Malaysia added that, in the event the United States would provide any comments on the interim report, Malaysia, together with the other co-complainants, reserved their rights to respond to such comments and to request a further meeting with the parties to discuss those comments. India, Pakistan and Thailand did not request a review. On 16 March 1998, the United States requested the Panel to review, in accordance with Article 15.2 of the DSU, the interim report that had been issued to the parties on 2 March 1998. The

[607] Eckert para. 5.223.
[608] Frazier para. 5.226.
[609] Guinea paragraph 5.291.

United States also requested the Panel to hold a meeting with the parties to discuss the issues raised in its comments. We met with the parties on 31 March 1998, reviewed the entire range of arguments presented by the parties, and finalized our report, taking into account the specific aspects of these arguments we considered to be relevant.

6.2. With respect to the comments made by Malaysia on the descriptive part, we have taken a number of them into account and accordingly modified paragraph 2.2, paragraph 3.9(f), footnote 80 to paragraph 3.38, and paragraphs 3.84, 3.131, 3.221 and 3.286.

6.3. With respect to the findings, Malaysia and the United States make several specific comments. We have accepted most of them and accordingly have made the appropriate changes in paragraphs 7.2, 7.5, 7.6, 7.19 and 7.48. However, we have not modified paragraph 7.46, as requested by the United States. We agree with the United States that none of the parties cited or discussed the 1952 *Belgian Family Allowances* case[610], but in our view a reference to that case is relevant to our findings because, even though it did not relate to Article XX, it addressed a situation similar to this case, where a country had imposed conditions on access to its market based on the existence in the exporting countries of a family allowance system meeting specific requirements. Finally, we cannot agree with the comment of the United States on paragraph 7.52 that we should review the statement that the 1992 Rio Declaration "stresses the diversity of environmental situations and responsibilities". When we refer to diversity of responsibilities, we do not base ourselves on Principle 2 only, to which the United States seems to refer exclusively, but also to Principle 11 as well. Both Principles are quoted in footnote 661 and our purpose is to illustrate the right of States to design their own environmental policies on the basis of their particular environmental and developmental situations and responsibilities. We have clarified the relevant part of paragraph 7.52 accordingly.

6.4. The United States also makes comments of a more general nature. We address them successively hereafter. First, the United States considers that the findings of the Panel never identified or analyzed the particular terms of the chapeau of Article XX and disregarded the relevant language of the GATT 1994. In response, we have expanded the discussion of the terms of the chapeau in paragraphs 7.33 and 7.34.

6.5. The United States also claims that the Panel adopted a new test based on the Panel's view of the object and purpose of the Article XX chapeau. However, this mischaracterizes our findings, which do not rely solely on the object and purpose of Article XX. They are based on an analysis, pursuant to Article 31(1) of the Vienna Convention on the Law of Treaties (1969), of the ordinary meaning of the terms of the chapeau of Article XX, *taken in their context and in the light of the object and purpose of the WTO Agreement*. Moreover, in our reasoning, we rely also on general principles of public international law such as *pacta sunt servanda*. Consequently, our findings are the result of the application of interpretative methods required by Article 3.2 of the DSU. In our view, our process of interpretation of Article XX in this case does not add to Members' obligations in contravention of Article 3.2 of the DSU.

[610] Adopted on 7 November 1952, BISD 1S/59.

6.6. The United States further claims that the Panel has adopted a so-called "threat to the multilateral trading system" test that is tautological and undermines Article XX. In our view, the concept of "threat to the multilateral trading system" is an application in this case of the principle according to which Members should not deprive the WTO Agreement of its object and purpose. This concept is elaborated in paragraphs 7.44 and 7.45. We have not imposed a new test, but merely found that the type of measure at issue in this case deprives the WTO Agreement of its object and purpose and, thus, is beyond the scope of Article XX. The analysis is not tautological, since it elaborates on the function of Article XX in the WTO framework. As the United States put it in its request for interim review: "A measure meeting the provisions of Article XX, by definition, cannot be a 'threat to the multilateral trading system'." Thus, where a panel believes that a measure does constitute such a threat, it is appropriate to interpret Article XX so as not to permit it. We do not believe that the notion of "threat to the multilateral trading system" entrusts panels with unfettered discretion as to what measure would satisfy the conditions of Article XX. On the contrary, it preserves the right of Members to implement the environmental policies of their choice through trade measures, as long as those trade measures do not affect the multilateral system to the point where the WTO Agreement is deprived of its object and purpose.

6.7. The United States argues in addition that "the interim report contains troubling language indicating that under the object and purpose of the WTO, trade concerns outweigh environmental concerns" and that the Panel's categorical language according to which measures are only allowed if they do not undermine the WTO system is much broader than necessary for the resolution of this dispute. We do not believe that our findings reflect such a view. Our examination of the object and purpose of the WTO Agreement led us to conclude that the central focus of that agreement is the promotion of economic development through trade. That means that there is room for other concerns, and, in particular, environmental concerns, as underlined by the wording of the preamble and the existence of exceptions. Moreover, we have not in any way passed judgement on the relative importance of trade and environmental policies.

6.8. Finally, we reject the US assertion that we have used unnecessarily broad language in our findings. Indeed, our findings have been written narrowly to address certain specific attributes of the US measure at issue, attributes which we do not believe would typically be found in environmental regulations. Indeed, as the United States concedes in its request for interim review, we stated that "there should not be nor need be any policy contradiction between upholding and safeguarding an open, equitable and non-discriminatory multilateral trading system on the one hand and acting for the protection of the environment on the other". In light of such statements, we see no scope for a future panel to misconstrue our narrowly drafted findings in this case.

# VII. FINDINGS

## A. *Introduction*

7.1. We note that the dispute arose from the following facts.[611] Most sea turtles are distributed around the world, in sub-tropical or tropical areas. Sea turtles are affected by human activity. They have been exploited for their meat, shell and eggs but they are also affected by the pollution of the oceans and the destruction of their habitats. In addition, they are subject to incidental capture in fisheries. Presently, most populations of sea turtles are considered to be endangered or threatened. In this respect, all marine turtles are included in Appendix I to the 1973 Convention on International Trade in Endangered Species (hereafter "CITES")[612] as species threatened with extinction.

7.2. Pursuant to the US Endangered Species Act of 1973 (hereafter "ESA"), all sea turtles that occur in US waters are listed as endangered or threatened species. Research programmes carried out by the United States have led to the conclusion that incidental capture and drowning of sea turtles by shrimp trawlers is a significant source of mortality for sea turtles. The United States National Marine Fisheries Service (hereafter "NMFS") has developed, within a programme aimed at reducing the mortality of sea turtles in shrimp trawls, turtle excluder devices (hereafter "TEDs").[613] In 1987, the United States issued regulations under the ESA whereby shrimp fishermen are required to use TEDs or tow time restrictions in specified areas where there is a significant mortality of sea turtles in shrimp trawls. Since December 1994, these regulations have eliminated the option for small trawl vessels to restrict tow times in lieu of using TEDs.

7.3. In 1989, the United States enacted Section 609 of Public Law 101-162 (hereafter "Section 609"). Section 609 calls upon the US Secretary of State, in consultation with the US Secretary of Commerce, *inter alia* to initiate negotiations for the development of bilateral or multilateral agreements for the protection and conservation of sea turtles, in particular with governments of countries engaged in commercial fishing operations likely to have a negative impact on sea turtles. Section 609 further provides that shrimp harvested with technology that may adversely affect certain sea turtles protected under US law may not be imported into the United States, unless the President annually certifies to the Congress that the harvesting country concerned has a regulatory programme governing the incidental taking of such sea turtles in the course of such harvesting that is comparable to that of the United States, that the average rate of that incidental taking by the vessels of the harvesting country is comparable to the average rate of incidental taking of sea turtles by United States vessels in the course of such harvesting, or that the fishing environment of the harvesting country does not pose a threat of incidental taking to sea turtles in the course of such harvesting.

---

[611] For a more detailed presentation of the factual aspects of this case, see Section II of this Report.

[612] Done at Washington, on 3 March 1973, 993 UNTS 243, 12 ILM 1085 (1973), entered into force on 1 July 1975.

[613] A TED is a grid trapdoor installed inside a trawling net that is designed to allow shrimp to pass to the back of the net while directing sea turtles and other unintentionally caught large objects out of the net.

7.4. The United States issued guidelines in 1991 and 1993 for the implementation of Section 609. Pursuant to these guidelines, Section 609 was applied only to countries of the Caribbean/Western Atlantic. In September 1996, the United States concluded the Inter-American Convention for the Protection and Conservation of Sea Turtles with a number of countries of that region. In December 1995, the US Court of International Trade (hereafter "CIT") found the 1991 and 1993 guidelines illegal insofar as they limited the geographical scope of Section 609 to shrimp harvested in the wider Caribbean/Western Atlantic area. The CIT directed the US Department of State to prohibit, no later than 1 May 1996, the importation of shrimp or products of shrimp wherever harvested in the wild with commercial fishing technology which may affect adversely those species of sea turtles the conservation of which is the subject of regulations of the Secretary of Commerce.

7.5. In April 1996, the Department of State published revised guidelines to comply with the CIT order of December 1995. The new guidelines extended the scope of Section 609 to shrimp harvested in all countries. The Department of State further determined that, as of 1 May 1996, all shipments of shrimp and shrimp products into the United States must be accompanied by a declaration attesting that the shrimp or shrimp product in question has been harvested "either under conditions that do not adversely affect sea turtles ... or in waters subject to the jurisdiction of a nation currently certified pursuant to Section 609." The 1996 guidelines define "shrimp or shrimp products harvested in conditions that do not affect sea turtles" to include: "(a) Shrimp harvested in an aquaculture facility ...; (b) Shrimp harvested by commercial shrimp trawl vessels using TEDs comparable in effectiveness to those required in the United States; (c) Shrimp harvested exclusively by means that do not involve the retrieval of fishing nets by mechanical devices or by vessels using gear that, in accordance with the US programme, would not require TEDs; (d) Species of shrimp, such as the pandalid species, harvested in areas in which sea turtles do not occur". The 1996 guidelines provided that certification could be granted by 1 May 1996, and annually thereafter to harvesting countries other than those where turtles do not occur or that exclusively use means that do not pose a threat to sea turtles "only if the government of [each of those countries] has provided documentary evidence of the adoption of a regulatory program governing the incidental taking of sea turtles in the course of commercial shrimp trawl harvesting that is comparable to that of the United States and if the average take rate of that incidental taking by vessels of the harvesting nation is comparable to the average rate of incidental taking of sea turtles by United States vessels in the course of such harvesting." For the purpose of these certifications, a regulatory programme must include, *inter alia*, a requirement that all commercial shrimp trawl vessels operating in waters in which there is a likelihood of intercepting sea turtles use TEDs at all time. TEDs must be comparable in effectiveness to those used by the United States. Moreover, the average incidental take rate will be deemed comparable to that of the United States if the harvesting country requires the use of TEDs in a manner comparable to that of the US programme.

7.6. In October 1996, the CIT ruled that the embargo on shrimp and shrimp products enacted by Section 609 applies to "all shrimp and shrimp products harvested in the wild by citizens or vessels of nations which have not been certified." The CIT found that the 1996 guidelines are contrary to Section 609 when allowing, with a shrimp exporter declaration form, imports of shrimp from non-certified countries, if the shrimp was harvested with commercial fishing technology that did not adversely affect sea turtles. The CIT later clarified its decision in ruling that shrimp harvested by manual methods which do not harm sea turtles, by aquaculture and in cold water, could continue to be imported even from countries which have not been certified under Section 609.

### *B. Rulings Made by the Panel in the Course of the Proceedings*

7.7. In the course of the proceedings, we received two documents called *amicus briefs* and submitted by non-governmental organizations. These documents were also communicated by their authors to the parties to the dispute. In a letter dated 1 August 1997 and at the second substantive meeting of the Panel, India, Malaysia, Pakistan and Thailand requested us not to consider the content of these documents in our examination of the matter under dispute. At the second substantive meeting of the Panel, the United States, stressing that the Panel could seek information from any relevant source under Article 13 of the Understanding on Rules and Procedures Governing the Settlement of Disputes (hereafter "DSU"), urged us to avail ourselves of any relevant information in the two documents, as well as in any other similar communications.

7.8. We had not requested such information as was contained in the above-mentioned documents. We note that, pursuant to Article 13 of the DSU, the initiative to seek information and to select the source of information rests with the Panel. In any other situations, only parties and third parties are allowed to submit information directly to the Panel. Accepting non-requested information from non-governmental sources would be, in our opinion, incompatible with the provisions of the DSU as currently applied. We therefore informed the parties that we did not intend to take these documents into consideration. We observed, moreover, that it was usual practice for parties to put forward whatever documents they considered relevant to support their case and that, if any party in the present dispute wanted to put forward these documents, or parts of them, as part of their own submissions to the Panel, they were free to do so. If this were the case, the other parties would have two weeks to respond to the additional material. We noted that the United States availed themselves of this opportunity by designating Section III of the document submitted by the Center for Marine Conservation and the Center for International Environmental Law as an annex to its second submission to the Panel.

7.9. None of the parties to the dispute requested the Panel to consult experts. However, we noted that parties had submitted a number of studies by experts and often quoted the same scientific documents to support opposite views. Under those circumstances, we decided, acting on our own initiative, to seek scientific and technical advice pursuant to paragraph 1 and paragraph 2, first sentence of Article 13 of the DSU.[614]

7.10. Parties to the dispute were given time to comment in writing on the replies of the experts to the questions of the Panel. However, before and during the hearing of the experts, we recalled that parties should limit their intervention to questions and

[614] For a detailed account of the Panel's consultation with scientific experts, see Section V of this Report.

comments strictly related to the issues raised by the experts. Accordingly, we decided not to take into account in our findings any comment or question raised in relation with the consultation of the experts which would not be strictly related to the scientific issues under discussion with the experts.

## *C. Violation of Article XI:1 of GATT 1994*[615]

7.11. We note that all four complainants[616] raise claims regarding the violation of Article XI GATT 1994. India, Pakistan and Thailand submit that the scope of Article XI:1, which provides for general elimination of quantitative restrictions, is comprehensive and applies to all measures instituted or maintained by a Member prohibiting or restricting the importation, exportation or sale for export of products other than measures that take the form of duties, taxes or other charges. Measures prohibited by Article XI:1 include outright quotas and quantitative restrictions made effective through import or export licences. The embargo applied by the United States on the basis of Article 609 constitutes a prohibition or restriction on the importation of shrimp or shrimp products from the complainants and is not in the nature of a "duty, tax, or other charges" within the meaning of Article XI:1. India, Pakistan and Thailand consider that the 1991 and 1994 reports on *United States - Restrictions on Imports of Tuna*[617] involve a measure virtually identical to the restriction on imports of shrimp and shrimp products at issue in this case. In those cases, the embargo was applied by the United States to imports of tuna from countries that had not implemented conservation programmes comparable to those of the United States to protect dolphins incidentally taken by commercial fishermen harvesting tuna. In both cases, the panels found that the restriction constituted a violation of Article XI.

7.12. Malaysia argues that the import prohibition imposed by the United States under Section 609 falls under Article XI as it bans import of shrimp or shrimp products from any country not meeting certain policy conditions, and are not duties, taxes or other charges. The findings of the *Tuna I* and *Tuna II* cases are equally applicable to the facts of this case. The US prohibition on imports of shrimp and shrimp products is therefore contrary to Article XI:1 and cannot be justified under Article XI:2, as this provision does not address the situation at issue.

7.13. The United States argues that since under Article XX nothing in GATT 1994 is to be construed to prevent the adoption or enforcement of the measures at issue, it need not address Article XI. The United States also considers that the complainants have the burden of establishing any alleged violation of GATT 1994. However, the United States does not dispute that, with respect to countries not certified under Section 609, Section 609 amounts to a restriction on the importation of shrimp within the meaning of Article XI:1 of GATT 1994.

---

[615] For a more detailed presentation of the main arguments of the parties, see Section III of this Report.

[616] India, Pakistan, Malaysia and Thailand are hereafter referred to as the "complainants".

[617] Panel Report on *United States - Restrictions on Imports of Tuna*, 3 September 1991, DS21/R, not adopted (hereafter *"Tuna I"*), and Panel Report on *United States - Restrictions on Imports of Tuna*, 16 June 1994, DS29/R, not adopted (hereafter *"Tuna II"*).

7.14. The arguments put forward by the parties raise the general question of the burden of proof, in terms of who bears this burden and in terms of how much has to be proved in the circumstances of this case. Regarding who bears the burden of proof, we recall the well established general principle of law referred to by the Appellate Body in its report on *United States - Measure Affecting Imports of Woven Wool Shirts and Blouses from India*[618]: "the burden of proof rests upon the party, whether complaining or defending, who asserts the affirmative of a particular claim or defence". We consequently consider that it is up to the complainants to demonstrate that the US measure at issue violates Article XI:1 of GATT 1994. The arguments of the parties also raise the question of when a panel should consider that a party has provided sufficient evidence in support of a particular claim or defence. We recall that the Appellate Body in the *Wool Shirts* case found that "precisely how much and precisely what kind of evidence will be required to establish [a presumption that a claim is valid] will necessarily vary ... from case to case".[619] We therefore have to assess the evidence before us in the light of the particular circumstances of this case. This implies that we may consider any type of evidence, and also that we may reach our conclusions regarding a particular claim on the basis of the level of evidence that we consider sufficient.

7.15. In this respect, we note that the United States, in reply to one of our questions, "does not dispute that with respect to countries not certified under Section 609, Section 609 amounts to a restriction on the importation of shrimp within the meaning of Article XI:1 of GATT 1994".[620] This statement of the United States creates a particular situation where the defendant basically admits that a given measure amounts to a restriction prohibited by GATT 1994. It is usual legal practice for domestic and international tribunals, including GATT panels[621], to consider that, if a party admits a particular fact, the judge may be entitled to consider such fact as accurate.

7.16. Even if the above-mentioned US declaration does not amount to an admission of a violation of Article XI:1, we consider that the evidence made available to the Panel is sufficient to determine that the United States prohibition of imports of shrimp from non-certified Members violates Article XI:1. Article XI:1 reads in part as follows:

> "No prohibitions or restrictions other that duties, taxes or other charges, whether made effective through quotas, import or export licences or other measures, shall be instituted or maintained by any

---

618 Adopted on 23 May 1997, WT/DS33/AB/R (hereafter "*Wool Shirts*"), p. 14.

619 Op. Cit., p. 14.

620 See para. 3.143 of this Report.

621 See Panel Report on *EEC - Programme of Minimum Import Prices, Licences and Surety Deposits for Certain Processed Fruits and Vegetables*, adopted on 18 October 1978, BISD 25S/68, where the panel, at para. 4.9, *inter alia* "noted the assertion by the representative of the Community that this system was a system which fell within the purview of Article XI and XI alone ... Having noted the foregoing, the Panel considered that the minimum import price system, as enforced by the additional security, was a restriction 'other than duties, taxes or other charges' within the meaning of Article XI:1". In *EEC - Quantitative Restrictions against Imports of Certain Products from Hong Kong*, adopted on 12 July 1983, BISD 30S/129, the panel noted, in para. 31, that the EC itself referred to the products concerned as subject to quantitative restrictions. The panel further noted that "no GATT justification had been advanced for the quantitative restrictions referred to in paragraph 31 above" and concluded that "the relevant provisions of Article XI were not complied with".

> contracting party on the importation of any product of the territory of any other contracting party ...".

We note that Section 609(b)(1) provides that:

> "The importation of shrimp or products from shrimp which have been harvested with commercial fishing technology which may affect adversely such species of sea turtles shall be prohibited no later than May 1, 1991, except as provided in paragraph (2) [i.e. the exporting country is certified]".

Thus, Section 609 expressly requires the imposition of an import ban on imports from non-certified countries. We further note that in its judgement of December 1995, the CIT directed the US Department of State to prohibit, no later that 1 May 1996, the importation of shrimp or products of shrimp wherever harvested in the wild with commercial fishing technology which may affect adversely those species of sea turtles the conservation of which is the subject of regulations of the Secretary of Commerce.[622] Furthermore, the CIT ruled that the US Administration has to apply the import ban, *including to TED-caught shrimp*, as long as the country concerned has not been certified. In other words, the United States bans imports of shrimp or shrimp products from any country not meeting certain policy conditions. We finally note that previous panels have considered similar measures restricting imports to be "prohibitions or restrictions" within the meaning of Article XI.[623]

7.17. Therefore, we find that the United States admits that, with respect to countries not certified under Section 609, the measures imposed in application of Section 609 amount to "prohibitions or restrictions" on the importation of shrimp within the meaning of Article XI:1 of GATT 1994. Even if one were to consider that the United States has not admitted that it imposes an import prohibition or restriction within the meaning of Article XI:1, we find that the wording of Section 609 and the interpretation made of it by the CIT are sufficient evidence that the United States imposes a "prohibition or restriction" within the meaning of Article XI:1. We therefore find that Section 609 violates Article XI:1 of GATT 1994.

---

[622] United States Court of International Trade: *Earth Island Institute v. Christopher*, ruling of 29 December 1995 (913 F. Supp. 559).

[623] See Panel Report in the *Tuna I* case, Op. Cit., para. 5.17-5.18, and Panel Report in the *Tuna II* case, Op. Cit., para. 5.10. Speaking of the relevance for panels of previous reports, the Appellate Body has stated, with respect to adopted panel reports:

> "Adopted panel reports are an important part of the GATT *acquis*. They are often considered by subsequent panels. They create legitimate expectations among WTO Members, and, therefore, should be taken into account where they are relevant to any dispute". (Appellate Body Report on *Japan - Taxes on Alcoholic Beverages*, adopted on 1 November 1996, WT/DS8, DS10, DS11/AB/R, p. 14)

Regarding unadopted panel reports, the Appellate Body agreed with the panel in the same case that:

> "a panel could nevertheless find useful guidance in the reasoning of an unadopted panel report that it considered to be relevant". (Appellate Body Report on *Japan - Taxes on Alcoholic Beverages*, Op. Cit., p. 15)

### D. *Violation of Article XIII:1 and of Article I:1 of GATT 1994*[624]

7.18. India, Pakistan and Thailand claim that the import prohibition on shrimp and shrimp products from non-certified countries is inconsistent with the most-favoured-nation principle embodied in Article I:1 GATT 1994 because physically identical shrimp and shrimp products from different Members are treated differently by the United States upon importation. This differentiated treatment is based solely on the method of harvest and the conservation policies of the government under whose jurisdiction the shrimp is harvested. Further, even if one were to assume *arguendo* that the method of harvest does affect the nature of the shrimp, the embargo violates Article I:1 because, pursuant to the embargo, wild shrimp harvested by use of TEDs are forbidden entry into the United States if harvested by a national of a non-certified country, while shrimp harvested by the same method by a national of a certified country is permitted entry into the United States.

7.19. India, Pakistan and Thailand also claim that the embargo as applied is also inconsistent with Articles I:1 and XIII:1 of the GATT 1994 because initially affected countries were given a phase-in period of three years, while newly affected nations were not given a similar period of time. Malaysia further argues that, while newly affected nations generally received only a four month notice, Malaysia actually was given three months (i.e., until 1 April 1996) to adopt a programme complying with the US requirements. For Malaysia, this differential treatment is also discriminatory and inconsistent with Article XIII:1. According to India, Pakistan and Thailand, initially affected countries were given the opportunity to implement the required use of TEDs without substantially interrupting shrimp trade to the United States. Products from these countries have therefore been given an "advantage, favour, privilege or immunity" over like products originating in the territories of other Members, in violation of Article I:1. Likewise, importation of like products from initially affected countries was not similarly prohibited, in violation of Article XIII:1.

7.20. India, Pakistan and Thailand also argue that Section 609 is inconsistent with Article XIII:1 of GATT 1994 because it restricts the importation of shrimp and shrimp products from countries which have not been certified, while like products from other countries which have been certified can be imported freely into the United States. The United States denies entry of shrimp and shrimp products based on the method of harvest, even though it does not affect the nature of the product. Indeed, all foreign shrimp and shrimp products have the same physical characteristics, end-uses and tariff classifications and are perfectly substitutable. Thus, shrimp products which may be imported into the United States pursuant to Section 609 are like shrimp products from non-certified countries which are denied entry. The differential treatment of like products from certified and non-certified countries violates Article XIII:1. Even assuming that the method of harvest does affect the nature of the product, the embargo violates Article XIII because wild shrimp harvested by use of TEDs are forbidden entry into the United States if harvested by a national of a non-certified country, while shrimp harvested by use of TEDs by a national of a certified country are permitted entry into the United States.

---

[624] For a more detailed presentation of the main arguments of the parties, see Section III of this Report.

7.21. The United States does not agree with the complainants' claims under Articles I and XIII, particularly since, in the US view, the US measure applies equally to all harvesting Members. The United States further argues that, if the Panel makes a finding with respect to Article XI, there will be no need to reach the claims under Articles I and XIII.

7.22. Given our conclusion in paragraph 7.17 above that Section 609 violates Article XI:1, we consider that it is not necessary for us to review the other claims of the complainants with respect to Articles I:1 and XIII:1. This is consistent with GATT[625] and WTO[626] panel practice and has been confirmed by the Appellate Body in its report in the *Wool Shirts* case, where the Appellate Body mentioned that "A panel need only address those claims which must be addressed in order to resolve the matter in issue in the dispute."[627]

7.23. Therefore we do not find it necessary to review the allegations of the complainants with respect to Articles I:1 and XIII:1. On the basis of our finding of violation of Article XI:1, we move to address the defence of the United States under Article XX.

### *E. Article XX of GATT 1994*[628]

#### *1. Preliminary Remarks*

7.24. The United States claims that the measures at issue adopted pursuant to Section 609, which were found to be inconsistent with Articles XI:1 GATT 1994, are justified under Article XX(b) and (g) of GATT 1994. India, Pakistan and Thailand argue that Article XX(b) and (g) cannot be invoked to justify a measure which applies to animals not within the jurisdiction of the Member enacting the measure. Malaysia contends that, since Section 609 allows the United States to take actions unilaterally to conserve a shared natural resource, it is therefore in breach of the sovereignty principle under international law. The United States responds that Article XX(b) and (g) contain no jurisdictional limitations, nor limitations on the location of the animals or natural resources to be protected and conserved and that, under general principles of international law relating to sovereignty, States have the right to regulate imports within their jurisdiction.

7.25. The relevant parts of Article XX provide as follows:

> Article XX
>
> *General exceptions*
>
> Subject to the requirement that such measures are not applied in a manner that would constitute a means of arbitrary or unjustifiable dis-

[625] See, e.g., Panel report on *Canada - Administration of the Foreign Investment Review Act*, adopted on 7 February 1984, BISD 30S/140, para. 5.16.

[626] See, e.g., Panel Report on *Brazil - Measures Affecting Desiccated Coconut*, adopted on 20 March 1997, WT/DS22/R, para. 293.

[627] Op. Cit., p. 19.

[628] For a more detailed presentation of the main arguments of the parties, see Section III of this Report.

> crimination between countries where the same conditions prevail, or a disguised restriction on international trade, nothing in this Agreement shall be construed to prevent the adoption or enforcement by any contracting party of measures:
>
> ...
>
> (b) necessary to protect human, animal or plant life or health;
>
> ...
>
> (g) relating to the conservation of exhaustible natural resources if such measures are made effective in conjunction with restrictions on domestic production or consumption;
>
> ...

7.26. The arguments of the parties raise the general question of whether Article XX(b) and (g) apply at all when a Member has taken a measure conditioning access to its market for a given product on the adoption of certain conservation policies by the exporting Member(s). We note that Article XX can accommodate a broad range of measures aiming at the conservation and preservation of the environment.[629] At the same time, by accepting the WTO Agreement, Members commit themselves to certain obligations which limit their right to adopt certain measures. We therefore consider it important to determine first whether the *scope* of Article XX encompasses measures whereby a Member conditions access to its market for a given product on the adoption of certain conservation policies by the exporting Member(s).

7.27. Pursuant to Article 3.2 of the DSU and in accordance with Appellate Body decisions[630], we should, when trying to clarify the scope of Article XX, have recourse to customary rules of interpretation of public international law. We note that Article 31(1) of the Vienna Convention on the Law of Treaties (1969) (hereafter the "Vienna Convention") provides that:

> "A treaty shall be interpreted in good faith in accordance with the ordinary meaning to be given to the terms of the treaty in their context and in the light of its object and purpose".

Therefore, in order to determine the scope of Article XX, it is necessary to consider not only the terms in their ordinary meaning, but also their context and the object and purpose of GATT 1994 and the WTO Agreement itself.[631]

---

[629] See, e.g., Appellate Body report on *United States - Standards for Reformulated and Conventional Gasoline* (hereafter "*Gasoline*"), WT/DS2/AB/R, adopted on 20 May 1996, which provides, at p. 30:

> "WTO Members have a large measure of autonomy to determine their own policies on the environment (including its relationship with trade), their environmental objectives and the environmental legislation they enact and implement. So far as concerns the WTO, that autonomy is circumscribed only by the need to respect the requirements of the *General Agreement* and the other covered agreements".

[630] See, e.g., Appellate Body Report in the *Gasoline* case, Op. Cit., p. 17-18.

[631] See Appellate Body report on *Brazil - Measures Affecting Desiccated Coconut*, adopted on 20 March 1997, WT/DS22/AB/R, p. 15. Where appropriate, we must also consider GATT and WTO panel and Appellate Body reports. See footnote 623 above.

7.28. Article XX contains an introductory provision, or *chapeau*, and a number of specific requirements contained in successive paragraphs. As mentioned by the Appellate Body in its report in the *Gasoline* case[632], in order for the justification of Article XX to be extended to a given measure, it must not only come under one or another of the particular exceptions - paragraphs (a) to (j) - listed under Article XX; it must also satisfy the requirements imposed by the opening clause of Article XX. We note that panels have in the past considered the specific paragraphs of Article XX before reviewing the applicability of the conditions contained in the chapeau. However, as the conditions contained in the introductory provision apply to any of the paragraphs of Article XX, it seems equally appropriate to analyze first the introductory provision of Article XX.

7.29. We also recall that the Appellate Body considered, in the *Gasoline* case[633], that the chapeau by its express terms addresses, not so much the questioned measure or its specific contents, but rather the manner in which that measure is applied.[634] The Appellate Body further underscored that "the purpose and object of the introductory clause of Article XX is generally the prevention of 'abuse of the exceptions of [what was later to become] Article [XX]'". Hence, the chapeau determines to a large extent the context of the specific exceptions contained in the paragraphs of Article XX. Therefore, we shall first determine whether the measure at issue satisfies the conditions contained in the chapeau. If we find this to be the case, we shall then examine whether the US measure is covered by the terms of Article XX(b) or (g).

7.30. Finally, we keep in mind the well-established practice according to which when an affirmative defence, such as Article XX, is invoked, the burden of proof should rest on the party asserting it.[635] We therefore consider that the burden of proving that the measure at issue is justified under Article XX rests on the United States, as the party asserting this affirmative defence.

### 2. *Chapeau of Article XX*

7.31. India, Pakistan and Thailand argue that the embargo applied by the United States is implemented in a manner that constitutes a means of arbitrary or unjustifiable discrimination between countries where the same conditions prevail insofar as the newly affected nations, including India, Pakistan and Thailand, have been given substantially less notice than the other countries, whether the United States or initially

632 Op. Cit., p. 22.

633 *Ibid.*, p. 22.

634 See also the panel report on *United States - Imports of Certain Automotive Spring Assemblies*, adopted on 26 May 1983, BISD 30S/107, which specified, at para. 56, that "the preamble of Article XX made it clear that it was the application of the measure and not the measure itself that needed to be examined."

635 See Appellate Body Report in the *Wool Shirts* case, Op. Cit., p. 16, and the GATT cases cited in footnote 23 to that report. In that case, the Appellate Body mentioned that "Articles XX and XI:2(c)(i) are limited exceptions from obligations under certain other provisions of the GATT 1994, not positive rules establishing obligations in themselves. They are in the nature of affirmative defences. It is only reasonable that the burden of establishing such a defence should rest on the party asserting it". Therefore, we shall apply this principle when we review the US arguments under Article XX.

affected countries, before being forced to comply with TEDs requirements. They maintain that there is not only a discrimination between exporting countries, but also between exporting countries and the United States. Furthermore, India, Pakistan and Thailand consider that, before requiring TEDs application from them, the United States should have demonstrated that the same conditions do not prevail between India, Pakistan or Thailand and the countries with no TEDs requirement. Moreover, for these complainants, the legislative history of Section 609, which includes discussions of this section in terms of the competitive position of the US shrimp industry, further supports the conclusion that the embargo is a disguised restriction on international trade. The effect of the restriction was not so much reduced importation as the additional cost on the foreign industry, making it less competitive, and the risk that the right to export might be revoked. Malaysia claims that disguised restrictions include disguised discrimination in international trade, and that it has been subject to such discrimination because it was given only a few months to comply with the US requirements as opposed to three years in the case of the initially affected countries.

7.32. The United States argues that the measures related to import of shrimp were carefully and justifiably tied to the particular conditions of each country exporting shrimp to the United States. All exporting nations with the same shrimp harvesting conditions are treated equally, with no discrimination. For the United States, the evidence is overwhelming that the conservation measures under Section 609 are not some artifice intended to protect the US fishing industry. The United States argued that the strong and growing international consensus regarding sea turtle conservation and the mandatory use of TEDs belies any claim that the US measures are some sort of disguised restriction on trade. In addition, the United States maintains that the extension of the application of Section 609 to other countries than the United States and the wider Caribbean/Western Atlantic area has not led to a decrease in the quantities imported nor to an increase in prices.

7.33. In order to apply Article XX in this case, we must, as mentioned in paragraph 7.27 above, interpret it in line with Article 31(1) of the Vienna Convention. More particularly, the chapeau of Article XX must be interpreted on the basis of the ordinary meaning of its terms, in their context and in the light of the object and purpose of GATT 1994 and the WTO Agreement. We consider first if the terms of the chapeau of Article XX explicitly address the issue of whether Article XX contains any limitation on a Member's use of measures conditioning market access to the adoption of certain conservation policies by the exporting Member. In this connection, we note that the chapeau prohibits such application of the measure at issue as would constitute "arbitrary or unjustifiable discrimination" between countries where the same conditions prevail. We note that the US measure at issue applies to all Members seeking to export to the United States wild shrimp retrieved mechanically from waters where sea turtles and shrimp occur concurrently. We consider those Members to be "countries where the same conditions prevail", within the meaning of Article XX. We further note that some of those countries have been "certified" and can export shrimp to the United States whereas some have not and are subject to an import ban. Consequently, discriminatory treatment is applied to shrimp from non-certified countries. Pursuant to the chapeau of Article XX, a measure may discriminate, but not in an "arbitrary" or unjustifiable" manner.

7.34. We therefore move to consider whether the US measure conditioning market access on the adoption of certain conservation policies by the exporting Member could be considered as "unjustifiable" discrimination. As was recalled by the Appellate Body in the *Gasoline* case, "the text of the chapeau of Article XX is not without ambiguity". The word "unjustifiable" has never actually been subject to any precise interpretation.[636] The ordinary meaning of this term is susceptible to both narrow and broad interpretations. While the ordinary meaning of "unjustifiable" confirms that Article XX is to be applied within certain boundaries, it does not explicitly address the issue of whether Article XX should be interpreted to contain any limitation on a Member's use of measures conditioning market access on the adoption of certain conservation policies by the exporting Member. For that reason, it is essential that we interpret the term "unjustifiable" within its context and in the light of the object and purpose of the agreement to which it belongs.

7.35. Turning to an examination of the context of the terms and the object and purpose of the WTO Agreement, we note that the notion of "context", on the one hand, and of "object and purpose", on the other hand, are intimately linked. Indeed, Article 31(2) of the Vienna Convention provides that the context for the purpose of treaty interpretation comprises the text of the agreement, including its preamble and annexes. By the same token, determining the object and purpose of an agreement implies an examination of the text of the agreement and of its preamble. Consequently, we consider that the context of the chapeau of Article XX cannot be distinguished from that of Article XX as a whole. Furthermore, as the WTO Agreement is an integrated system including GATT 1994[637], we shall consider as the context of the chapeau and of Article XX as a whole not only the other relevant provisions of GATT 1994 together with its preamble and annexes, but also the WTO Agreement, including its preamble and its other annexes. For the same reasons, the object and purpose to be considered is not only that of GATT 1994, but that of the WTO Agreement as a whole.

7.36. GATT panels had the occasion to address the context and the object and purpose of Article XX. The 1989 panel on *United States - Section 337 of the Tariff Act of 1930* considered that:

> " ... Article XX is entitled 'General Exceptions' ... Article XX(d) thus provides for a *limited and conditional exception* from obligations under other provisions".[638]

Referring, *inter alia*, to the above-mentioned report, the panel in the *Tuna I* case found that:

> " ... previous panels had established that Article XX is a limited and conditional exception from obligations under other provisions of the

---

[636] Previous panels considered situations of discrimination related to import prohibitions. The Panel Report on *United States - Prohibition on Imports of Tuna and Tuna Products from Canada*, adopted on 22 February 1982, BISD 29S/91, considered, at para. 4.8, that the measure had been taken exclusively against imports from Canada, but that *similar actions* had been taken against imports from other countries, and then for similar reasons. The panel concluded that if Canada had been discriminated against, it might not necessarily have been in an arbitrary or unjustifiable manner.

[637] See Appellate Body Report on *Brazil - Measures Affecting Desiccated Coconut*, Op. Cit., pp. 11-12.

[638] Adopted on 7 November 1989, BISD 36S/345, para. 5.9 (emphasis added).

General Agreement, and *not a positive rule establishing obligations in itself*. Therefore, the practice of panels has been to interpret Article XX narrowly ... ."[639]

7.37. The Appellate Body also described Article XX in very similar language. In the *Wool Shirts* case, it found that:

"Articles XX and XI:2(c)(i) are limited exceptions from obligations under certain other provisions of the GATT 1994, not positive rules establishing obligations in themselves".[640]

7.38. The Appellate Body has also discussed the relationship of Article XX(g) to GATT as a whole, in terms that would apply to the relationship to GATT of Article XX taken in its entirety:

"... Article XX(g) and its phrase, 'relating to the conservation of exhaustible natural resources,' need to be read in context and in such a manner *as to give effect to the purposes and objects of the General Agreement*. The context of Article XX(g) includes the provisions of the rest of the General Agreement, including in particular Articles I, III and XI; conversely, the context of Articles I and III and XI includes Article XX. Accordingly, the phrase 'relating to the conservation of exhaustible natural resources' may not be read so expansively as seriously to subvert the purpose and object of Article III:4. Nor may Article III:4 be given so broad a reach as effectively to emasculate Article XX(g) and the policies and interests it embodies. The relationship between the affirmative commitments set out in, *e.g.*, Articles I, III and XI, and the policies and interests embodied in the "General Exceptions" listed in Article XX, can be given meaning *within the framework of the General Agreement and its object and purpose by a treaty interpreter only on a case-to-case basis*, by careful scrutiny of the factual and legal context in a given dispute, without disregarding the words actually used by the WTO Members themselves to express their intent and purpose."[641]

7.39. While the Appellate Body has noted that the rights that Members do have under Article XX must, of course, be respected, it has also noted the existence of limits and conditions on the scope of Article XX. It has expressed those limits and conditions as follows in respect of its analysis of the object and purpose of the chapeau of Article XX:

"... while the exceptions of Article XX may be invoked as a matter of legal right, they should not be so applied as to frustrate or defeat the legal obligations of the holder of the right under the substantive rules of the *General Agreement*. If those exceptions [contained in Article XX] are not to be abused or misused, in other words, the measures falling within the particular exceptions must be applied reasonably,

---

[639] Op. Cit., para. 5.22 (emphasis added, footnote omitted). See, also, Panel Report on *Canada - Administration of the Foreign Investment Review Act*, Op. Cit., para. 5.20.

[640] Op. Cit., p. 16.

[641] Appellate Body Report in the *Gasoline* case, Op. Cit., p. 18 (emphasis added).

with due regard both to the legal duties of the party claiming the exception and the legal rights of the other parties concerned."[642]

7.40. We note that the chapeau to Article XX provides that "nothing in [GATT 1994] shall be construed to prevent the adoption or enforcement ... of measures" otherwise in conformity with Article XX conditions. However, we consider that this wording is not affected by the findings quoted above. As the Appellate Body also put it, Article XX "needs to be read in its context and in such a manner as to give effect to the purposes and objects of the General Agreement" and "the purpose and object of the introductory clauses of Article XX is generally the prevention of 'abuse of the exceptions of ... [Article XX]'."[643] We deduce from this that, when invoking Article XX, a Member invokes the right to derogate to certain specific substantive provisions of GATT 1994 but that, in doing so, it must not frustrate or defeat the purposes and objects of the General Agreement and the WTO Agreement or its legal obligations under the substantive rules of GATT by abusing the exception contained in Article XX.

7.41. We consider this finding of the Appellate Body to be an application of the international law principle according to which international agreements must be applied in good faith, in light of the *pacta sunt servanda* principle.[644] The concept of good faith is explained in Article 18 of the Vienna Convention which states that "A State is obliged to refrain from acts which would defeat the object and purpose of a treaty".[645]

7.42. We consequently turn to the consideration of the object and purpose of the WTO Agreement, of which GATT 1994 and Article XX thereof are an integral part. We note that the preamble of an agreement may assist in determining its object and purpose.[646] On the one hand, the first paragraph of the Preamble of the WTO Agreement acknowledges that the optimal use of the world's resources must be pursued "in accordance with the objective of sustainable development, seeking both to protect and preserve the environment and to enhance the means of doing so in a manner consistent with [Members'] respective needs and concerns at different levels of economic development". On the other hand, the second paragraph of the Preamble of GATT and the third paragraph of the WTO Preamble refer to "entering into reciprocal and mutually advantageous arrangements directed to the substantial reduction of tariffs and other barriers to trade and to the elimination of discriminatory treatment" in

---

642 Appellate Body Report in the *Gasoline* case, Op. Cit., p. 22 (emphasis added).

643 *Ibid.*, referring to EPTC/C.11/50, p. 7; quoted in *GATT, Analytical Index: Guide to GATT Law and Practice, Updated 6th Edition* (1995), Volume I, p. 564.

644 Good faith in the application of treaties is generally considered as a fundamental principle of treaty law. See Article 26 (*Pacta Sunt Servanda*) of the Vienna Convention, which provides that "Every treaty in force is binding upon the parties to it and must be performed by them in good faith." See judgement of the International Court of Justice of 27 August 1952 in the *Case Concerning Rights of Nationals of the United States of America in Morocco (France v. United States)*, ICJ Report 1952, p. 176, at p. 212, where the Court stated that "The power of making the valuation [a power granted by the 1906 Act of Algesiras] rests with the customs authorities, but it is a power *which must be exercised reasonably and in good faith*" (emphasis added).

645 This rule, which applies to the period between the moment when a State has expressed its consent to be bound by a treaty and its entry into force, nevertheless seems to express a generally applicable principle. See Patrick Daillier & Alain Pellet, *Droit International Public* (1994), p. 216.

646 See, e.g., Ian Sinclair, *The Vienna Convention on the Law of Treaties*, 2nd edition (1984), p. 130.

international trade relations. While the WTO Preamble confirms that environmental considerations are important for the interpretation of the WTO Agreement, the central focus of that agreement remains the promotion of economic development through trade; and the provisions of GATT are essentially turned toward liberalization of access to markets on a nondiscriminatory basis.

7.43. We also note that, by its very nature, the WTO Agreement favours a multilateral approach to trade issues. The Preamble to the WTO Agreement provides that Members are "resolved ... to develop an integrated, more viable and durable *multilateral trading system* [and] ... determined to preserve the basic principles and to further the objectives underlying this *multilateral trading system*" (emphasis added). Article III:2 of the WTO Agreement also mentions that:

> "The WTO shall provide the forum for negotiations among its Members concerning their multilateral trade relations in matters dealt with under the agreements in the Annexes to this Agreement. The WTO may also provide for a forum for further negotiations among its Members concerning their multilateral trade relations ...".[647]

This approach is also expressed in Article 23.1 of the DSU which stresses the primacy of the *multilateral* system and rejects unilateralism as a substitute for the procedures foreseen in that agreement.

7.44. Therefore, we are of the opinion that the chapeau Article XX, interpreted within its context and in the light of the object and purpose of GATT and of the WTO Agreement, only allows Members to derogate from GATT provisions so long as, in doing so, they do not undermine the WTO multilateral trading system, thus also abusing the exceptions contained in Article XX. Such undermining and abuse would occur when a Member jeopardizes the operation of the WTO Agreement in such a way that guaranteed market access and nondiscriminatory treatment within a multilateral framework would no longer be possible. As was recalled by previous panels, GATT rules "are not only to protect current trade but also to create the predictability needed to plan future trade".[648] The protection of expectations of Members as to the competitive relationship between their products and the products of other Members is therefore an important principle to be taken into account by panels when reviewing a particular measure. We are of the view that a type of measure adopted by a Member which, on its own, may appear to have a relatively minor impact on the multilateral trading system, may nonetheless raise a serious threat to that system if similar measures are adopted by the same or other Members. Thus, by allowing such type of measures even though their individual impact may not appear to be such as to threaten the multilateral trading system, one would affect the security and predictability of the multilateral trading system. We consequently find that when considering a measure under Article XX, we

[647] The emphasis on multilateralism is also found in the General Agreement on Trade in Services, where the second paragraph of its Preamble states that Members wish to "establish a *multilateral* framework of principles and rules for trade in services ... " (emphasis added). Similarly, the Preamble to the Agreement on Trade-Related Aspects of Intellectual Property Rights stresses the need for a multilateral approach (TRIPS Agreement, Preamble, paras. 3 and 7). See also Marrakesh Declaration, 15 April 1994, para. 2.

[648] Panel Report on *United States - Taxes on Petroleum and Certain Imported Substances*, adopted on 17 June 1987, BISD 34S/136, para. 5.2.2.

must determine not only whether the measure *on its own* undermines the WTO multilateral trading system, but also whether such type of measure, if it were to be adopted by other Members, would threaten the security and predictability of the multilateral trading system.

7.45. In our view, if an interpretation of the chapeau of Article XX were to be followed which would allow a Member to adopt measures conditioning access to its market for a given product upon the adoption by the exporting Members of certain policies, including conservation policies, GATT 1994 and the WTO Agreement could no longer serve as a multilateral framework for trade among Members as security and predictability of trade relations under those agreements would be threatened. This follows because, if one WTO Member were allowed to adopt such measures, then other Members would also have the right to adopt similar measures on the same subject but with differing, or even conflicting, requirements. If that happened, it would be impossible for exporting Members to comply at the same time with multiple conflicting policy requirements. Indeed, as each of these requirements would necessitate the adoption of a policy applicable not only to export production (such as specific standards applicable only to goods exported to the country requiring them) but also to domestic production, it would be impossible for a country to adopt one of those policies without running the risk of breaching other Members' conflicting policy requirements for the same product and being refused access to these other markets. We note that, in the present case, there would not even be the possibility of adapting one's export production to the respective requirements of the different Members. Market access for goods could become subject to an increasing number of conflicting policy requirements for the same product and this would rapidly lead to the end of the WTO multilateral trading system.[649]

7.46. We find support for our reasoning in the *Tuna II* case[650] where the panel considered a similar issue and found as follows:

> "5.26 The Panel observed that Article XX provides for an exception to obligations under the General Agreement. The long-standing practice of panels has accordingly been to interpret this provision narrowly, in a manner that preserves the basic objectives and principles of the General Agreement.[651] If Article XX were interpreted to permit contracting parties to deviate from the obligations of the General Agreement by taking trade measures to implement policies, including conservation policies, within their own jurisdiction, the basic objectives of the General Agreement would be maintained. If however Article XX were interpreted to permit contracting parties to take trade

649 We note that the United States referred to Article XX(e) as evidence that GATT refutes any argument that trade measures generally should not have effects on the internal affairs of exporting countries. We note however that this provision does not permit a Member to make entry of imported goods into its territory conditional upon the exporting Member's policy on prison labour. This paragraph only refers to the products of prison labour.

650 Op. Cit.

651 The footnote in the report referred to the Panel Report on *Canada - Administration of the Foreign Investment Review Act*, Op. Cit., para. 5.20 and to the Panel Report on *United States - Section 337 of the Tariff Act of 1930*, Op. Cit., para. 5.27.

> measures so as to force other contracting parties to change their policies within their jurisdiction, including their conservation policies, the balance of rights and obligations among contracting parties, in particular the right of access to markets, would be seriously impaired. Under such an interpretation the General Agreement could no longer serve as a multilateral framework for trade among contracting parties."[652]

The principle underlying our interpretation of Article XX of GATT 1994 was apparently also at the origin of the findings of the 1952 panel on *Belgian Family Allowances*. This panel addressed a charge imposed by Belgium on imported products purchased by public bodies when these goods originated in a country whose system of family allowances did not meet specific requirements. In that context, the panel considered that "the Belgian legislation on family allowance was not only inconsistent with the provisions of Article I ... , but was based on a concept which was difficult to reconcile with the spirit of the General Agreement".[653]

7.47. In light of this analysis of the terms and context of the chapeau of Article XX in the light of the object and purpose of the WTO Agreement, we turn to a consideration of whether the US measure challenged in this case falls within the scope of Article XX.

7.48. The United States argues that the intent of Section 609 is to protect and conserve the life and health of sea turtles by requiring that shrimp imported into the United States has not been harvested in a manner that will harm sea turtles. As a result of judgements of the US Court of International Trade, the US Administration currently has to apply the import ban, including on TED-caught shrimp, as long as the country concerned has not been certified.[654] In addition, certification is only granted if comprehensive requirements regarding use of TEDs by fishing vessels are applied by the exporting country concerned, or if the shrimp trawling operations of the exporting country take place exclusively in waters in which sea turtles do not occur. Consequently, Section 609, as applied, is a measure[655] conditioning access to the US market for a given product on the adoption by exporting Members of conservation policies that the United States considers to be comparable to its own in terms of regulatory programmes and incidental taking.

7.49. Accordingly, it appears to us that, in light of the context of the term "unjustifiable" and the object and purpose of the WTO Agreement,[656] the US measure at issue constitutes unjustifiable discrimination between countries where the same

---

652 The report of the panel in the *Tuna II* case was not adopted. We nonetheless recall the findings of the Appellate Body in its report on *Japan - Taxes on Alcoholic Beverages*, Op. Cit., that unadopted panel reports have no legal status in the GATT or WTO system but that a panel can nevertheless *find useful guidance in the reasoning of an unadopted panel report that it considers to be relevant.* We consider that the reasoning of the panel in the *Tuna II* case, in the light of the similarities between the issues addressed by that panel and the present Panel, is relevant in the present case and provides useful guidance.

653 Adopted on 7 November 1952, BISD 1S/59, para. 8.

654 United States Court of International Trade: *Earth Island Institute v. Christopher*, rulings of 8 October (942 F. Supp. 597) and 25 November 1996 (948 F. Supp. 1062).

655 As described in para. 7.45.

656 See paragraph 7.34.

conditions prevail and thus is not within the scope of measures permitted under Article XX. However, before making a definitive finding on this issue, we must consider several arguments put forward by the United States that relate generally to our analysis of Article XX.

7.50. The United States argues that the Panel should consider the many examples of import bans under various international agreements that show that Members may take actions to protect animals, whether they are located *within or outside their jurisdiction*. We are of the view that these treaties show that environmental protection through international agreement - as opposed to unilateral measures -have for a long time been a recognized course of action for environmental protection.[657] We note that this US argument addresses the issue of a potential jurisdictional scope of Article XX. However, we consider that this argument bears no direct relation to our finding, which rather addresses the inclusion of certain unilateral measures within the scope *ratione materiae* of Article XX. In addition, in the present case, we are not dealing with measures taken by the United States in application of an agreement to which it is party, as the United States does not claim that it is allowed or required by any international agreement (other than GATT 1994) to impose an import ban on shrimp in order to protect sea turtles. Rather, we are limiting our finding to measures - taken independently of any such international obligation - conditioning access to the US market for a given product on the adoption by the exporting Member of certain conservation policies. In this regard, we note that banning the importation of a particular product does not *per se* imply that a change in policy is required from the *country* whose exports are subject to the import prohibition. For instance, a Member may ban a product on the ground that it is dangerous, and accept a similar product that is safe. This is clearly different from adopting a policy pursuant to which only countries that adopt measures restricting all of their production to products considered safe by a particular Member may export to the market of that Member. We note that a judgement of the CIT interpreting Section 609[658] ruled that the US Administration has to apply the import ban, including on TED-caught shrimp, as long as the country concerned has not been certified. Currently, certification is only granted if *comprehensive requirements* regarding use of TEDs by fishing vessels are applied by the exporting country concerned.

7.51. The United States further argues that the complainants confuse the difference between extrajurisdictional application of a country's law and the application by a country of its law, within its jurisdiction, in order to protect resources located outside its jurisdiction. However, we note that we are not basing our finding on an extra-jurisdictional application of US law. Many domestic governmental measures can have an effect outside the jurisdiction of the government which takes them. What we found

---

[657] We note in this respect that the WTO Committee on Trade and Environment endorsed and supported "multilateral solutions based on international cooperation and consensus as the best and most effective way for governments to tackle environmental problems of a transboundary or global nature. WTO Agreements and multilateral environmental agreements (MEAs) are representative of efforts of the international community to pursue shared goals, and in the development of a mutually supportive relationship between them due respect must be afforded to both". (Report (1996) of the Committee on Trade and Environment, WT/CTE/1, 12 November 1996, para. 171).

[658] United States Court of International Trade: *Earth Island Institute v. Christopher*, rulings of 8 October and 25 November 1996, Op. Cit.

above was that a measure cannot be considered as falling within the scope of Article XX if it operates so as to affect other governments' policies in a way that threatens the multilateral trading system, as described in paragraph 7.45 above. For instance, a US requirement, that US norms regarding the characteristics of a given product be met for that product to be allowed on the US market, would not constitute such a threat. Such types of measures are contemplated by the WTO Agreement on Technical Barriers to Trade and the Agreement on Sanitary and Phytosanitary Measures. However, requiring that other Members adopt policies comparable to the US policy for their domestic markets and all other markets represents a threat to the WTO multilateral trading system. As affirmed by the Appellate Body in its report in the *Gasoline* case, "Members have a large measure of autonomy to determine their own policies on the environment ..., their environmental objectives and the environmental legislation they enact and implement"[659], circumscribed only, so far as concerns the WTO, by the need to respect the requirements of the General Agreement and the other covered agreements. Therefore, a Member's measure which conditions access to its market on the adoption by the exporting Member of certain conservation policies is a denial of such autonomy.

7.52. The United States argues that the right of WTO Members to take measures under Article XX to conserve and protect natural resources is reaffirmed and reinforced by the Preamble to the WTO Agreement. Although we do not disagree in general with this statement, we are not persuaded that this argument is a reason to change our finding. Whilst the central focus of that Agreement is to promote economic development through trade, we note that the Preamble acknowledges that the optimal use of the world's resources must be pursued "in accordance with the objective of sustainable development, seeking both to protect and preserve the environment and to enhance the means of doing so in a manner consistent with [Members'] respective needs and concerns at different levels of economic development". Thus the Preamble endorses the fact that environmental policies must be designed taking into account the situation of each Member, both in terms of its actual needs and in terms of its economic means. Moreover, the record before us and, in particular, the answers of the experts to the questions of the Panel, strongly suggest that the environmental issues at stake in this case should be evaluated to a large degree in light of local and regional conditions. They also suggest that conservation measures should be adapted, *inter alia*, to the environmental, social and economic conditions prevailing where they are to be applied. We further note that the 1992 Rio Declaration on Environment and Development[660] recognizes the right of States to design their own environmental policies on the basis of their particular environmental and developmental situations and responsibilities.[661] It

---

[659] Op. Cit., p. 30.

[660] See Rio Declaration on Environment and Development, The Final Text of Agreements Negotiated by Governments at the United Nations Conference on Environment and Development (UNCED), 3-14 June 1992, Rio de Janeiro, Brazil.

[661] Rio Declaration on Environment and Development, Op. Cit., Principle 2:

> "States have, in accordance with the Charter of the United Nations and the principles of international law, the sovereign right to exploit their own resources pursuant to their *own* environmental and developmental policies, and the responsibility to ensure that activities within their jurisdiction or control do not cause damage to the environment

also stresses the need for international cooperation[662] and for avoiding unilateral measures. In this light, we consider that the Preamble does not justify interpreting Article XX to allow a Member to condition access to its market for a given product on the adoption of certain conservation policies by exporting Members in order to bring them into line with those of the importing Member. On the contrary, the diversity of the environmental and development situations underlined by the Preamble can best be taken into account through international cooperation. The Preamble also implies that attempts to generalize standards of environmental protection would require multilateral discussion, especially when, as here, developing countries are involved. Therefore, we do not consider that the wording of the Preamble referred to by the United States should lead us to a different conclusion than the one reached above.

7.53. The United States further claims that sea turtles are a shared global resource and that, therefore, it has an interest and a right to impose the measures at issue. Firstly, the United States argues that sea turtles are a shared global resource because they are highly migratory creatures which travel through large expanses of sea, within the range of thousands of kilometres, from the jurisdiction of one Member to those of other Members. Secondly, the United States also argues that, even if sea turtles were not migratory at all, they may still represent a shared global resource in terms of biological diversity in the protection of which the United States may have a legitimate interest. Information brought to the attention of the Panel, including documented statements from the experts, tends to confirm the fact that sea turtles, in certain circumstances of their lives, migrate through the waters of several countries and the high sea. This said, even assuming that sea turtles were a shared global resource, we consider that the notion of "shared" resource implies a common interest in the resource concerned. If such a common interest exists, it would be better addressed through the negotiation of international agreements than by measures taken by one Member conditioning access to its market to the adoption by other Members of certain conservation policies. We note in this respect that Article 5 of the 1992 Convention on Biological Diversity provides that:

> "each contracting party shall, as far as possible and as appropriate, co-operate with other contracting parties directly or, where appropriate, through competent international organizations, in respect of areas be-

---

> of other States or of areas beyond the limits of national jurisdiction." (Emphasis added)

Principle 11 states that:

> "States shall enact effective environmental legislation. Environmental standards, management objectives and priorities should reflect the environmental and development context to which they apply. Standards applied by some countries may be inappropriate and of unwarranted economic and social cost to other countries, in particular developing countries."

In this respect, we note that whilst incidental drowning in shrimp nets may be the single most important source of turtle mortality along the East coast of the United States, in other countries egg harvesting and direct sea turtle harvest are factors affecting significantly the survival of sea turtles.

[662] Rio Declaration on Environment and Development, Op. Cit., Principle 12: "Environmental measures addressing transboundary or global environmental problems should, as far as possible, be based on an international consensus".

yond national jurisdiction and on other matters of mutual interest, for the conservation and sustainable use of biological diversity." [663]

We consider that this provision is evidence that "matters of mutual interest" have normally to be addressed primarily through international cooperation.[664] Therefore, we find that if, as alleged by the United States, sea turtles are shared global resources, that would not call for a change in our finding. Instead, it suggests that the United States should have entered into international cooperation with the aim of developing internationally accepted conservation methods, including with the complainants.

7.54. In addition, the United States argues that nothing in Article XX requires a Member to seek negotiation of an international agreement instead of, or before adopting unilateral measures. In any event, the United States claims it offered to negotiate but the complainants did not reply.

7.55. Regarding whether there is an obligation for a Member to negotiate, we recall our finding in paragraph 7.45 above that the WTO multilateral trading system would be undermined if Members were allowed to adopt measures making access of other Members to their market conditional upon the adoption by the exporting Members of certain conservation policies because it would not be possible for Members to meet conflicting requirements of such a nature. This is clearly a situation where elaboration of international standards would be desirable. We note in that respect that the WTO Agreements on Technical Barriers to Trade and on Sanitary and Phytosanitary Measures promote the use of international standards.[665] We also recall our consideration in paragraph 7.52. The nature of the measures that the United States was seeking to obtain from the exporting countries concerned and the principles recalled in several international environmental agreements[666] imply that a country seeking to promote environmental concerns of such a nature should engage into international negotiations. The negotiation of a multilateral agreement or action under multilaterally defined criteria is clearly a possible way to avoid threatening the multilateral trading system.

7.56. We note that Section 609 contains provisions calling upon the US Secretary of State to initiate negotiations as soon as possible for the development of bilateral or multilateral agreements for the protection and conservation of the species of sea turtles covered by that Section.[667] The judgement of the CIT which was handed over on 29 December 1995 required the US Administration to apply Section 609 on a world-wide

---

[663] We also note that the 1979 Bonn Convention on the Conservation of Migratory Species of Wild Animals (to which some parties to this dispute are not parties) lists the relevant species of sea turtles in Annex I as "Endangered Migratory Species" and provides in its preamble as follows:

> "The contracting parties [are] convinced that conservation and effective management of migratory species of wild animals requires the concerted action of all States within the national boundaries of which such species spend any part of their life cycle;"

[664] It appears that WTO bodies support this multilateral approach. See footnote 657 to para. 7.50 above.

[665] See, e.g., Agreements on Technical Barriers to Trade, fourth preambular paragraph and Articles 2 and 9, Agreement on Sanitary and Phytosanitary Measures, Article 3.

[666] See, e.g., the 1992 Convention on Biological Diversity, the 1979 Bonn Convention on the Conservation of Migratory Species of Wild Animals. See, also, the 1992 Rio Declaration on Environment and Development.

[667] Section 609(a)(1) to (4).

basis (and no longer only to the Wider Caribbean/Western Atlantic region) by no later than 1 May 1996. This implied that, unless the exporting countries decided to use TEDs in their shrimp trawling activities - either of their own initiative or through negotiations - the import ban on wild shrimp would be applied to them as of that date. The United States told us of its efforts to have the deadline set in the CIT judgement postponed. However, we have no evidence that the United States actually undertook negotiations on an agreement on sea turtle conservation techniques which would have included the complainants *before* the imposition of the import ban as a result of the CIT judgement. From the replies of the parties to our question on this subject, in particular that of the United States, we understand that the United States did not propose the negotiation of an agreement to any of the complainants until after the conclusion of negotiations on the Inter-American Convention for the Protection and Conservation of Sea Turtles, in September 1996, i.e. well after the deadline for the imposition of the import ban of 1 May 1996. Even then, it seems that the efforts made merely consisted of an exchange of documents. We therefore conclude that, in spite of the possibility offered by its legislation, the United States did not enter into negotiations before it imposed the import ban.[668] As we consider that the measures sought by the United States were of the type that would normally require international cooperation, we do not find it necessary to examine whether parties entered into negotiations in good faith and whether the United States, absent any result, would have been entitled to adopt unilateral measures.

7.57. Finally, we note that the United States argues that the use of TEDs has become a recognized multilateral environmental standard. In support of this, the United States firstly contends that the international community has long recognized the need to protect endangered species such as sea turtles. Secondly, several international conventions require parties to adopt conservation policies and urge them to ensure, through proper conservation measures, the maintenance of living resources, including non-target species caught in fishing operations. In support of these statements, the United States refers to the 1982 United Nations Convention on the Law of the Seas[669] and to paragraph 17.46(c) of the 1992 Agenda 21.[670] Thirdly, the United States claims that, either as a result of the Inter-American Convention on the Protection and Conservation of Sea Turtles or of their own initiative, 19 countries currently require TEDs on shrimp trawl vessels subject to their jurisdiction.

7.58. Moving to examine whether international obligations exist with regard to the protection of sea turtles, we first note that both the United States and the complainants have elaborated at length on the policies they have developed to protect sea turtles. Both the United States and the complainants have referred to the Convention on International Trade in Endangered Species of Wild Fauna and Flora (CITES). Parties to the dispute

---

[668] We note in this respect that, in the *Gasoline* case, the Appellate Body considered that a strong implication arose from the fact that the United States had not pursued the possibility of entering into cooperative arrangements, which would have been a means of alleviating the discrimination suffered by foreign refiners *vis-à-vis* US refiners. In that case, the Appellate Body concluded that the discrimination was not "inadvertent or unavoidable" and that the measure at issue constituted "unjustifiable discrimination" and a "disguised restriction on international trade".

[669] UN Doc.A.CONF.62/122, Articles 61(2), 61(4) and 119(1)(b).

[670] Agenda 21: Programme of Action for Sustainable Development, United Nation Conference on Environment and Development (UNCED), 3-14 June 1992, Rio de Janeiro, Brazil.

are all parties to CITES and the turtles species covered by the US measures at issue are all listed in Appendix I (Species threatened with extinction). The endangered nature of the species of sea turtles mentioned in Appendix I as well as the need to protect them are consequently not contested by the parties to the dispute. However, CITES is about *trade in endangered species* and the subject of the US import prohibition (shrimp) is not the endangered species whose protection is sought through the import ban. We also note that the United States has mentioned that CITES neither authorizes nor prohibits the sea turtles conservation measures which are at issue in this dispute.[671] Therefore, we consider that CITES, even though its object is to contribute to the protection of certain species, does not impose on its members specific methods of conservation such as TEDs.

7.59. We also note that the development of the use of TEDs is the result of regional agreements or voluntary individual practices of States. In our opinion, the existence of regional agreements and individual practices may not as such suffice to reach the conclusion that the use of TEDs has become a recognized multilateral environmental standard applicable to the complainants. We derive from the submissions of the United States that the application of TEDs based on a convention is only regional. Moreover, if the provisions of the multilateral agreements referred to by the United States (the 1982 United Nations Convention on the Law of the Seas and the 1992 Agenda 21) effectively address the objective of limiting by-catches of non-target species in trawling operations, they do not require the application of specific methods nor, *a fortiori*, the use of TEDs.[672] Finally, even if a number of countries individually require TEDs on their shrimp trawlers, the fact that the complainants and third parties have objected to their

---

[671] See para. 3.168 of this Report.

[672] One of the experts referred to the FAO *Code of Conduct for Responsible Fisheries*, unanimously adopted on 31 October 1995 by the FAO Conference. This non-binding text provides for a broad range of guidelines for governments and those involved in fisheries activities with the aim of promoting responsible, sustainable fisheries. We note that the provisions of this document promote, *inter alia*, the further development and application of selective and environmentally safe fishing gear and practices in order to maintain biodiversity and to conserve the population structure and aquatic ecosystems. Existing proper selective and environmentally safe fishing gear and practices should be recognized and accorded a priority in establishing conservation and management measures. Catches of non-target species, both fish and non fish species, should be minimized (Article 6.6). The Code also provides that its provisions should be interpreted and applied in accordance with the principles, rights and obligations established in the WTO Agreement (Article 11.2.1) and mentions that States should cooperate to develop internationally acceptable rules or standards for trade in fish and fishery products in accordance with the principles, rights and obligations established in the WTO Agreement (Article 11.2.13). Finally, the Code also provides that when a State introduces changes to its legal requirements affecting trade in fish and fishery products with other States, sufficient information and time should be given to allow the States and producers affected to introduce, as appropriate, the changes needed in their processes and procedures. In this connection, consultations with affected States on the time frame for implementation of the changes would be desirable (Article 11.3.4). This Code, even though it is not binding, is evidence of the methods currently favoured for the promotion and development of conservation methods (see, *inter alia*, the 1992 Convention on Biodiversity or the 1982 Convention on the Law of the Seas).

use makes it difficult to conclude that the mandatory use of TEDs has been customarily accepted as a multilateral environmental standard applicable to the complainants.[673]

7.60. In conclusion, we do not consider that any of the arguments raised by the United States would justify a finding different from that reached in paragraph 7.49 above. We consider that our findings do not question the legitimacy of environmental policies, including those promoted through multilateral conventions.[674] We consider our findings to be in line with the principles embodied in many international agreements pursuant to which international cooperation is to be sought before having recourse to unilateral measures. Furthermore, the risk of a multiplicity of conflicting requirements clearly is reduced when requirements are decided in multilateral fora. Moreover, we do not suggest that import markets must exist as an incentive for the destruction of natural resources. Rather, we address a particular situation where a Member has taken unilateral measures which, by their nature, could put the multilateral trading system at risk.

7.61. In reaching our conclusions, we based ourselves on the current status of the WTO rules and of international law. As far as the WTO Agreement is concerned, we considered that certain unilateral measures, insofar as they could jeopardize the multilateral trading system, could not be covered by Article XX. Our findings with respect to international norms confirm our reasoning regarding the WTO Agreement and GATT. General international law and international environmental law clearly favour the use of negotiated instruments rather than unilateral measures when addressing transboundary or global environmental problems, particularly when developing countries are concerned. Hence a negotiated solution is clearly to be preferred, both from a WTO and an international environmental law perspective. However, our findings regarding Article XX do not imply that recourse to unilateral measures is always excluded, particularly after serious attempts have been made to negotiate; nor do they imply that, in any given case, they would be permitted. Nevertheless, in the present case, even though the situation of turtles is a serious one, we consider that the United States adopted measures which, irrespective of their environmental purpose, were clearly a threat to the multilateral trading system and were applied without any serious attempt to reach, beforehand, a negotiated solution.

7.62. We therefore find that the US measure at issue is not within the scope of measures permitted under the chapeau of Article XX.

### 3. *Article XX(b) and (g)*

7.63. In line with our approach described in para. 7.29 above, we do not find it necessary to examine whether the US measure is covered by the terms of Article XX(b) or (g).

---

[673] See Article 38.1(b) of the Statute of the International Court of Justice and Brownlie, *Principles of Public International Law*, 4th edition (1990), pp. 4-5, quoting Brierly: "what is sought for [a custom to be considered as a general practice accepted as law] is a general recognition among States of a certain practice as obligatory".

[674] We do not question either the fact generally acknowledged by the experts that TEDs, when properly installed and used and adapted to the local area, would be an effective tool for the preservation of sea turtles.

### F. *Article XXIII:1(a) of GATT 1994*

7.64. We note that India, Pakistan and Thailand claim that the measure at issue represents a clear infringement of Articles I, XI and XIII of GATT 1994 and that it is well established that "in cases where there is a clear infringement of the provisions of the General Agreement, or in other words, where measures are applied in conflict with the provisions of GATT ... the action would, *prima facie*, constitute a nullification or impairment ..." within the meaning of Article XXIII of GATT.[675]

7.65. We have found that the US measure at issue violates Article XI and is not justified under Article XX. We therefore conclude that there is a presumption of nullification or impairment within the meaning of Article 3.8 of the DSU, and that it is for the United States to rebut it. We do not consider that the United States has succeeded in rebutting the presumption that its breach of GATT has nullified or impaired benefits accruing to the complainants under GATT 1994.

## VIII. CONCLUSIONS

8.1. In the light of the findings above, we conclude that the import ban on shrimp and shrimp products as applied by the United States on the basis of Section 609 of Public Law 101-162 is not consistent with Article XI:1 of GATT 1994, and cannot be justified under Article XX of GATT 1994.

8.2. The Panel *recommends* that the Dispute Settlement Body request the United States to bring this measure into conformity with its obligations under the WTO Agreement.

## IX. CONCLUDING REMARKS

9.1. We note that the issue in dispute was not the urgency of protection of sea turtles. The matter we have been asked to review is Section 609 as interpreted by the CIT and as applied by the United States on the date this Panel was established. It was not our task to review generally the desirability or necessity of the environmental objectives of the US policy on sea turtle conservation. In our opinion, Members are free to set their own environmental objectives. However, they are bound to implement these objectives in such a way that is consistent with their WTO obligations, not depriving the WTO Agreement of its object and purpose. We recall the statement contained in the 1996 report of the Committee on Trade and Environment for the Singapore Ministerial Conference to the effect that there should not be nor need be any policy contradiction between upholding and safeguarding an open, equitable and non-discriminatory multilateral trading system on the one hand and acting for the protection of the environment on the other.[676] We also note that we are bound to make findings on the basis of the existing norms, without prejudice to any potential developments in the relevant fora. In our view, and based on the information provided by the experts, the

---

[675] The complainants referred to the Panel Report on the *Uruguayan Recourse to Article XXIII*, adopted on 16 November 1962, BISD 11S/95, para. 15.

[676] See Report (1996) of the Committee on Trade and Environment, Op. Cit., para. 167.

protection of sea turtles throughout their life stages is important and TEDs are one of the recommended means of protection within an integrated conservation strategy. We consider that the best way for the parties to this dispute to contribute effectively to the protection of sea turtles in a manner consistent with WTO objectives, including sustainable development[677], would be to reach cooperative agreements on integrated conservation strategies, covering, *inter alia*, the design, implementation and use of TEDs while taking into account the specific conditions in the different geographical areas concerned.

[677] See para. 7.42.

## ANNEX I

*SEA TURTLES CONSERVATION: International Agreements*
*Fish and Fishing, Maritime affairs, 16USC 1537 note*

SEC. 609. (a) The Secretary of State, in consultation with the Secretary of Commerce, shall, with respect to those species of sea turtles the conservation of which is the subject of regulations promulgated by the Secretary of Commerce on June 29, 1987:

(1) initiate negotiations as soon as possible for the development of bilateral or multilateral agreements with other nations for the protection and conservation of such species of sea turtles;

(2) initiate negotiations as soon as possible with all foreign governments which are engaged in, or which have persons or companies engaged in, commercial fishing operations which, as determined by the Secretary of Commerce, may affect adversely such species of sea turtles, for the purpose of entering into bilateral and multilateral treaties with such countries to protect such species of sea turtles;

(3) encourage such other agreements to promote the purposes of this section with other nations for the protection of specific ocean and land regions which are of special significance to the health and stability of such species of sea turtles;

(4) initiate the amendment of any existing international treaty for the protection and conservation of such species of sea turtles to which the United States is a party in order to make such treaty consistent with the purposes and policies of this section; and

(5) provide to the Congress by not later than one year after the date of enactment of this section:

(A) a list of each nation which conducts commercial shrimp fishing operations within the geographic range of distribution of such sea turtles;

(B) a list of each nation which conducts commercial shrimp fishing operations which may affect adversely such species of sea turtles; and

(C) a full report on:

(i) the results of his efforts under this section; and

(ii) the status of measures taken by each nation listed pursuant to paragraph (A) or (B) to protect and conserve such sea turtles.

SEC. 609. (b)(1) IN GENERAL. The importation of shrimp or products from shrimp which have been harvested with commercial fishing technology which may affect adversely such species of sea turtles shall be prohibited not later than May 1, 1991, except as provided in paragraph (2).

SEC. 609. (b)(2) CERTIFICATION PROCEDURE. The ban on importation of shrimp or products from shrimp pursuant to paragraph (1) shall not apply if the

President shall determine and certify to the Congress not later than May 1, 1991, and annually thereafter that:

(A) the government of the harvesting nation has provided documentary evidence of the adoption of a regulatory program governing the incidental taking of such sea turtles in the course of such harvesting that is comparable to that of the United States; and

(B) the average rate of that incidental taking by the vessels of the harvesting nation is comparable to the average rate of incidental taking of sea turtles by United States vessels in the course of such harvesting; or

(C) the particular fishing environment of the harvesting nation does not pose a threat of the incidental taking of such sea turtles in the course of such harvesting.

# ANNEX II

## Appendix 1

## *THE ISSUE OF BYCATCH IN MODERN FISHERIES, WITH SPECIAL REFERENCE TO SHRIMP TRAWLS*

By Dr. J. Frazier

*Definition of "Bycatch":*

1. The term "bycatch" has been used in different ways, and there may be some confusion over its meaning. When applied to contemporary fisheries, the word refers to animals (and plants to a much lesser extent) which are caught incidental to attempts to catch a "target species".

2. A prime example of bycatch comes from the shrimp/prawn trawl, a type of gear which is dragged along the sea bottom to catch shrimps and prawns; on retrieving the trawl nets, the catch typically includes not just shrimp and prawns, but other organisms which were in the way of the nets as they were trawled. Dividing the catch into target species (shrimp and prawns) and bycatch (animals other than shrimp and prawns), there is sometimes a ratio of 1 to 10 or even 1 to 20, indicating that for every kilogram of shrimp, 10 or 20 kilograms of other animals were extracted from the sea. Sea turtles, when caught in shrimp trawls, form part of the bycatch.

3. The present dispute before the Panel is a bycatch issue: marine turtles caught in shrimp trawls constitute an important component of the bycatch of shrimp trawling. Indeed, the problem of sea turtles drowning in shrimp trawls is the classical "tip of the bycatch iceberg".

*Fate of Bycatch:*

4. Once they have been caught and landed, the animals in the bycatch can be utilized, thus, becoming a "byproduct" of the fishing operation. Alternatively, organisms in the bycatch can be discarded, and thrown back into the sea as "discards".

*Global Relevance of Bycatch:*

5. A recent report by the United Nations Food and Agriculture Organization (FAO) estimates that the annual bycatch in world fisheries totals 29 million metric tons; of this, an estimated 27 million metric tons are discarded. Shrimp trawling - notably shrimp trawling in the tropics - accounts for some 35 per cent of the total world bycatch (Alverson et. al., 1994). To put these numbers in perspective, according to the FAO, the annual total for marine fisheries landings during recent years has been between 80 and 90 million metric tons. In other words, annual discards are equivalent to about a third of the total annual catch that is brought to port.

*Status of Knowledge on Bycatch:*

6. Despite the obvious importance - economic, environmental and social - of bycatch in contemporary fisheries, it is a subject which is little understood and poorly documented. Various recent publications, especially by fisheries experts at the FAO, make it clear that there is a general lack of systematic - and reliable - information on the problem of bycatch, or bycatch utilization (e.g., Andrew and Pepperell, 1992; Everett, 1995:280; Teutscher, 1995a:4; 1995b:16; Eyabi-Eyabi, 1995:19; FAO, 1997a:3-7; Clucas, 1997a:8; Everett, 1997:46; 55; Prado, 1997:42). Likewise, there is a general lack of awareness of the magnitude and gravity of the problem (Everett, 1997:55), and this involves policy makers in various regions, including Southeast and South Asia (Prado and Rahman, 1995:24-25). Although there are very few systematic studies on the levels of mortality due to bycatch, it is widely accepted that this is a major source of fisheries mortality. Hence, experts in the evaluation of global bycatch have summarized the dilemma: "[Fisheries] Management for the better part of this century has operated largely in ignorance of many of the mortality coefficients". (Alverson and Hughes, 1995:17).

*Reactions by Fishers and the Fishing Industry to Bycatch:*

7. When confronted with bycatch, there are several ways in which fishers can respond. The issue may be ignored, and the unwanted animals and plants may simply be discarded and thrown back into the sea. Shrimp fisheries target one of the most commercially lucrative of all fisheries products - shrimp, so the operation is focused on catching, handling, sorting, conserving, storing, transporting, and marketing shrimp. "Typically, if the bycatch from shrimp trawling has any value at all, it can be twenty or thirty times less valuable than the shrimp" (Clucas, 1997c:6); hence, there is often no, or insufficient, economic incentive to deal bycatch, and it is simply discarded. "Various studies on fishery bycatch have made it clear that discarding is pervasive in world fisheries ..." (Alverson and Hughes, 1995:26).

8. Alternately, the fishers may look for a way of using the bycatch, or a part of it. Thus, the bycatch is separated into "other food fish" and "trash fish". The ways in which these components are dealt with is then determined by market prices and/or regulations.

9. Finally, attempts can be made to avoid the bycatch. This may involve modifying the gear so that it does not capture the "non-target" species (for example, by altering the dimensions or other characteristics of nets, using excluder devices, etc.). It is also possible to change the way, place and time that fishing is carried out; for example, fishing can be banned from an area, either on a long term or a seasonal basis.

10. If endangered species are part of the bycatch, other factors come to bear. "The incidental capture of prohibited or endangered species as bycatch is potentially a very serious problem for the future of the fisheries." (Prado, 1997:25). "Avoidance of by-catch through selective trawl designs is considered a high priority in many fisheries, particularly where the incidental capture of turtles is controversial". (Andrew and Pepperell, 1992:527). Hence, when endangered species are involved, solutions to bycatch problems normally involve reglementation by governing authorities, as dictated by society (see Hall, 1995).

*Implications of Discarding, or "Wastage":*

11. Despite its pervasive nature, there are few detailed scientific studies of the effects of discarding, or wastage of bycatch; and although little is known about the proportion of discards that die, bycatch mortality is regarded to be high (except in certain resistant species, such as crabs). At an ecological level, even less is known about what happens when large numbers of dead and mauled marine animals are thrown, *en masse*, back into the sea. It has been argued that the biotic composition of the area changes, not only from the mortality caused by fishing but from the introduction of large quantities of dead animals. Physical and chemical characteristics of the sea floor may also be affected, particularly if discarding is done in shallow waters (Harris and Poiner, 1990).

12. Because of a lack of basic information, there are no simple scientific pronouncements about the impacts of discarding. However, in terms of social and economic considerations, many societies do not accept the present degree of wastage in modern fisheries, and have called upon their governments to find solutions to this practice (e.g., Alverson and Hughes, 1995:13; Dilday, 1995; Everett, 1995; Olsen, 1995; Clucas, 1997c:47-49). The number of international accords, as well as statements from concerned citizens, which focus on this issue is large and growing (see sections below on International Accords Regarding Bycatch and International Concern Over the State of the Oceans, Bycatch and Sea Turtles).

13. In relation to the five countries directly involved in the present dispute, a recent report by the FAO indicates that 90 per cent of the bycatch is discarded in India, Malaysia, Pakistan and the United States, while 50 per cent is discarded in Thailand (Teutscher, 1995b: Table 6).

*Implications of Utilization of Bycatch:*

14. Over the last few years, technologies have been developed to utilize fishes which were formerly regarded as "trash fish" (Clucas, 1997c:32). Indeed, as world fisheries production reached a plateau - despite tremendous advances in technology and capital investment in modern vessels, gear and advanced electronics, competition for fisheries resources became "increasingly acute" (Alverson and Hughes, 1995:14), and as a result, there were countless initiatives to utilize more of what was caught during fishing operations. For example, in 1981 the FAO together with the International Development Research Centre sponsored an international technical consultation "Fish By-Catch ... Bonus from the Sea", which resulted in a 163-page proceedings of technical information and recommendations on exploiting more bycatch (IDRC, 1982).

15. There are numerous "success stories" of technological advancements and consequent increases in utilization of bycatch. The marketing and consumption of what were considered to be "trash fish" in Southeast Asia, using technologies promoted by the Southeast Asian Fisheries Development Center, in Bangkok (SEAFDEC), is a clear example (Clucas, 1997a:12). It has been reported that, in some instances, very little of the bycatch from the Thai shrimp fishery is now discarded at sea (Kungsuwan, 1996), and recent descriptions of the fishes utilized from trawling activities in both Thailand and Malaysia indicate that they are removing virtually everything which gets into the nets (Chee, 1997; Clucas, 1997c:32-33).

16. Clearly, utilization of bycatch - and avoiding the tremendous wastage involved in discards - is now a major priority in fishery policy around the world (Teutscher, 1995a), yet, there are many diverse issues which complicate the implementation of policies to reduce discards. Ironically, one of the factors which favors more efficient bycatch utilization is the demise of inshore fisheries (Bostock and Ryder, 1995:47). Clucas (1997b:65) identified this phenomenon in the trawl fishery for finfish in Malaysia: "As 'traditional' food fish sources become increasingly under pressure because of scarcity of stock and growing human populations more unusual species will be taken into the [human] food chain and change from being discarded bycatch to incidental catch". In those cases where effective at-sea bycatch collection procedures have developed, there has regularly been a decrease in inshore harvests, frequently related to conflicts with mechanized trawlers. Two clear examples are India (Bostock and Ryder, 1995:47) and Gambia (Jallow, 1995:32). Other prime examples of this phenomenon are Cameroon (Eyabi-Eyabi, 1995:22) and Mozambique (Kelleher and Mussa, 1995:66), where artisanal fisheries are no longer lucrative, and the fishers have turned to collecting bycatch from shrimp trawlers.

17. In other words, in these cases of "efficient bycatch utilization" what were once self-sufficient inshore fishers, have now been reduced to the role of bycatch collectors, dependent on discards, or low-value sales, of what are regarded as "trash fish" from other fisheries. As the phenomenon takes place within national borders, it is seen as progress and efficiency: if the producers of bycatch were instead from one nation and the artisanal fishermen, converted to "trash fish" collectors, were from another nation, the relationship would be perceived in totally different light, and with considerable alarm.

18. Another question that needs to be considered is just what the bycatch is used for. For example, during the 1990's in Thailand, the bycatch which has been used "has usually ended up at fishmeal factories...as an important ingredient for animal feed" (Kungsuwan, 1995:87-88). At the same time, a significant (but unknown) part of the utilized bycatch in Viet Nam is used for animal food or as fertilizer for agriculture (Tuoc, 1995:97). Nearly 85 per cent of the utilized bycatch in Cuba is destined for animal feed (García-Rodríguez, 1995:25). This pattern is repeated on a world level, and it estimated that a third of the production from modern fisheries is destined for use as fishmeal or other secondary products. As a matter of course, this involves the export of fishmeal and oil from the "Third World" to be used as animal feed and fertilizer in the "First World". Needless to say, many people concerned with food security in the poorer countries are deeply alarmed by this mercantile arrangement of "the poor feeding the rich" (e.g., Kent, 1980; 1983; 1984; 1985; 1986; 1987; 1989; 1994; McGoodwin, 1990). This is to say nothing of ecological and social costs of processing and transporting animal protein to be used as animal feeds (e.g., Folke and Kautsky, 1989; Barraclough and Finger-Stich, 1995).

19. At one level, the extensive utilization of bycatch could be used to argue that fishing is more efficient, because there are fewer discards. However, both the ecological and the sociological consequences of this form of intensive exploitation are likely to be disastrous. Indeed, publications representing the small-scale fisheries (which constitutes the vast majority of the world's fishers), leave little doubt about the problems generated by trawling activities and near complete utilization of their bycatch, particularly in

Southeast Asia (e.g., Pauly, 1988; 1995; Pauly and Neal, 1985; Pauly and Chua, 1988; Mathew, 1990).

20. Pronouncements of the FAO, based on regional fisheries meetings, make this point very clear: "It was recognized however that there are particular problems associated with the use of shrimp bycatch. The catch consists of a large number of small fish of many species, which are being caught at maturity or as juveniles, which makes conventional methods of utilization problematical." (FAO, 1997a:11). "It should be noted that the fuller utilization of incidental catches and the consequent decline in discards does not necessarily indicate an improvement in fisheries conservation of the ecological impact of the fishery. In some cases this may lead to increased pressure on some stocks of species and to increases in unidentified species mixes in reported landings" (FAO, 1997a:12). Clucas (1997c:47) discusses several critical points relevant to this issue, showing that much more is involved in conserving marine resources than just utilizing everything that is caught.

21. "The expert consultations leading up to the adoption of the Code of Conduct for Responsible Fisheries gave definitive priority status to the avoidance of fish that might be subsequently discarded and only as the last resort to marketing and utilization issues. The rational behind this was that little is known about the effects of removal of the discards on the ecosystem and if a market is generated it is going to be difficult to reverse the situation." (see FAO, 1994).

*Implications of Taking Bycatch:*

22. Independently of whether or not bycatch is utilized, or discarded, the simple act of taking it has both ecological and social implications. Even critiques from a strictly economic stand point, have conceded that lessening incidental capture reduces costs to those fishers who depend on the species taken as bycatch in other fisheries, and this "benefits the traditional harvesters". (Smith, 1995).

23. The ecological impacts of taking bycatch are not well understood, but are usually thought to be substantial (Andrew and Pepperell, 1992). "If large quantities of bycatch are taken important parts of the marine ecosystem may be affected. If the taking of bycatch removes a fish habitat such as corals, sponges and seaweed, this may also affect fish populations". (Prado, 1997:41).

24. Many authors have explained that the gravity of the bycatch problem is a symptom of the contemporary dilemma with overfishing (e.g., Romine, 1995): "One of the major contributing factors to the significance of the bycatch problem is systematic overfishing" (Murawski, 1995:7); "The easiest solution to discard problems involving overexploited species may be a reduction in fishing effort". (Alverson and Hughes, 1995:27). "The single action that will provide the greatest improvement to the bycatch and discard problem in certain fisheries is the reduction of these effort levels. Without such control, other solutions to the bycatch and discard problem will be less effective, and real success in efforts to better manage the ocean's resources will be more difficult to attain". (Everett, 1995:280).

25. The importance of reducing bycatch and minimizing ecological impacts from fishing operations have been emphasized by a long list of people, in diverse occasions and in diverse fora (e.g., Andrew and Pepperell, 1992; Alverson et al., 1994; R. Bin Ali, 1995b; R. Alverson, 1995; Alverson and Hughes, 1995; Dilday, 1995; Fairley, 1995;

FAO, 1995; 1997a; Laist, 1995; Murawski, 1995; Olsen, 1995; Prado and Rahman, 1995; 1996; Romine, 1995; Kungsuwan, 1996; Everett, 1997; Norse, 1997a; Prado, 1997).

26. This has led to the conclusion that managing fisheries, protecting marine organisms and ecosystems cannot be done by just considering one species at a time, out of context with other species and the marine environment: "The commonly referred to 'ecosystem approach' to fishery management is now necessitating that research extends beyond the emphasis on target species and single species approaches to stock assessment, and that rather more emphasis be given to determine optimal relationships among populations in the same ecosystem". (Everett, 1997:47). Species that are components of bycatch, need to be managed and conserved by resolving the bycatch problem, together with other more conventional conservation activities.

*Avoidance and Exclusion of Bycatch:*

27. The reduction of bycatch has been given priority status by various specialists and agencies, both national and international. In the parlance of fisheries biology and management, this means using fishing gear and techniques which are more "selective", and today this is one of the great challenges before modern fisheries (see, for example, Andrew and Pepperell, 1992; FAO, 1994; 1995; 1997a; Fairley, 1995; Prado and Rahman, 1995; 1996; Wray, 1995; Clucas, 1997c).

28. Aside from the technological and scientific challenges, there are other basic matters that must be resolved. For example, during the FAO/INFOFISH/SEAFDEC Workshop on Research in Selectivity of Fishing Gear and Methods in South East Asia and Selective Shrimp Fishing, fisheries experts from Southeast and South Asia observed that "in general, research in fishing technology, including fishing gear selectivity, was not given priority". With special reference to shrimp fisheries, they recommended that: there should be modifications to some gear to reduce bycatch; traditional fishing methods should be studied to improve resource conservation; and "state authorities should implement suggestions made by the researchers" (Prado and Rahman, 1995:24-25). (As usual, people with technical expertise provide basic information, but are rarely part of the decision making process for national policy, so it is not surprising to see the level of frustration expressed in this last statement. This situation is seen by the fact that numerous biologists, conservationists and fisheries officers - many of them from the countries involved in the present dispute - have for decades been trying to and promote more selective fishing and the use of TEDs, often with negligible results at the policy making level - see Annex II).

29. One of the most succinct summaries of the discussion on bycatch comes from two, forward-looking members of the fishing industry: "The merits of a fisherman can no longer be measured solely by how much he catches, but also on what he does not". (Paine and Gruver, 1995).

*Environmental Impacts of Bottom Trawling:*

30. For more than 600 years, bottom trawling has been claimed to be deleterious to fishers and fisheries, but there have been few systematic studies on this complex issue (McGoodwin, 1990). "As an efficient but unselective fishing method, this [bottom trawling] has led to the capture of numerous small sized species as well as juveniles of the larger species taken by other fishery sectors". "Many bycatch species are exploited at a small size and the yield of the resource could increase if [they could be] exploited at a larger species size which may also increase the landed value". (FAO, 1997a:7).

31. One of the earliest signs of effects of trawling is changes in the species composition and/or size composition of the organisms captured in the nets. Sainsbury (1987; 1989), working in Northwestern Australia, reported that as a trawl fishery developed in time, the occurrence of sponges and other emergent organisms that anchor to the sea floor decreased. At the same time, those species of fishes which associate with dense emergent organisms also declined in abundance. Routinely, as in Sainsbury's study, the fishes which decrease in numbers are of commercial value.

32. Nichols (1989) showed that with increased shrimp trawling in the Gulf of Mexico, some species of fishes dropped dramatically in abundance; Atlantic croaker, for example, dropped to 20 per cent of what they were in the 1970s. Furthermore, mean weight per individual for these species followed the same sharp decline, and instead of being composed of several age classes, by the mid 1980s the catch was mainly first year fish. These are both clear signs of intensified mortality - in this case attributed to bycatch problems.

33. There are few systematic studies of the effects of trawling, especially in tropical fisheries stocks, but where there is information, it shows that fishes preferred for food by people decrease, while fishes not normally consumed increase. Chan and Liew (1986) did a detailed study off the coast of Terengganu, Malaysia, comparing the fishes caught in trawls with what was known of the fish fauna 18 years before trawling was introduced. They found that fishes of the family Leiognathidae (food fishes), dropped from 12.79 per cent to 2.70 per cent of the biomass. In addition, their analysis of the trophic structure of the fish assemblages sampled indicated that they were relatively simple; this may also be an effect of the ecological impacts of 18 years of bottom trawling. Pauly and Neal (1985) reported similar changes in fish assemblages after shrimp trawling in other areas of Southeast Asia.

34. To a great extent, these ecological changes are attributed to mortality of bycatch. However, there are other, less evident but pernicious effects of bottom trawling. Norse (1997a) reported on the results of an international workshop on bottom trawling, in which it was concluded that this form of fishing "is the most important source of human-caused physical disturbance on the world's continental shelves". The participants determined that this disturbance results, among other things, in the crushing of marine animals and their habitats, greatly reducing the complexity of the sea floor; furthermore, trawling can cause major changes in biogeochemistry, water clarity, and other abiotic features. The reduction in biological and textural diversity is a major deterrent in the survival and recruitment of countless marine organisms, including many species that are commercially important.

35. Of those detailed investigations on the physical effects of bottom trawling, that reported by Auster et. al. (1996) is most remarkable. These authors explained that although it is widely known that the use of "mobile fishing gear" (which includes

bottom trawls and dredges) alters sea floor habitats, few studies have attempted to quantify these effects. They used a remotely operated vehicle (ROV) to obtain video images of the sea bed in the Gulf of Maine. Indices of bottom cover were calculated for transects inside an area that had been closed to mobile fishing gear for 10 years, as well as for other transects just outside the closed area. In addition, they compared images of a second area taken before trawling occurred there, and then six years later after the bottom had been exposed to trawling. The evidence clearly shows, both visually and statistically, that these gear greatly reduce the diversity of organisms living on the sea bed, as well as the textural complexity of the bottom. The authors explained how deterioration in sea floor complexity directly affects the survival of juvenile target species and hence, productivity from the fisheries point of view. Thus, effects of fishing gear must be evaluated not simply in terms of the removal of target and non-target species, but also taking into account other impacts on the environment.

36. Although there is a clear need for systematic studies comparing trawled and un-trawled sea bottoms, Auster et. al., (1996:197) argue that in some fishing grounds "no sufficiently large areas exist that can act as true non-impacted reference sites". Concluding that habitat-based management should take into account the impacts of mobile fishing gear, they explain: "Clearly, mobile gear provide efficient ways to harvest living marine resources in the short-term, but economic efficiency may have an ecological price that requires restriction of the activity in select areas".

*The Relevance of Shrimp Trawling to Bycatch Problems:*

37. Of the various types of bottom trawling, shrimp trawling is one of the best known. This is not only because of the high monetary value of the target species - shrimp and prawns - but also because of the relatively high environmental impact of shrimp trawling, as indicated especially by the amount of bycatch and discards that it produces. Shrimp fisheries are estimated to contribute some 1.8 million tons of landed catch, or about 2.3 per cent of the total of annual marine catch. At the same time, it has been estimated that shrimp fisheries produce 9.5 million tons of discards, or 35 per cent of the annual world total (Alverson et al., 1994; Teutscher, 1995b:11; Clucas, 1997a:7). Hence, 2.3 per cent of total marine production results in 35 per cent of the total discards. (Since nearly half the weight of a shrimp is "head", and this part of the animal is usually discarded before consumption, if shrimp with "heads" were included in the calculations for landed catch, the contribution of food for human consumption will be considerably less than indicated by the above figures.)

38. Considering the way in which shrimp trawlers operate, it is not difficult to understand why they produce so much bycatch. Take for example a typical "twin trawler" from Malaysia (R. Bin Ali, 1995b). It is equipped with two trawl nets, each about 13 meters wide. If the boat steams at 1.25 knots while trawling, and one trawling session lasts for 3 hours, during one trawl (also called "tow" or "drag") the boat would advance nearly 7 km. With both nets open, the total width covered would be about 26 meters, giving an area of 175,500 square meters of sea floor that would be dragged during one trawl. With an average of 4 trawls a day and 20 days a month of active fishing, one single shrimp trawler would scrape and drag 168 square kilometers of sea floor in a year. (Ali [1997:5] reported trawling speeds of 2.5 to 3.0 knots and nets that were 18.0 and 23.9 m wide; using these higher values, the calculated area covered

would be 744 square kilometers per year per boat.) When thousands of such trawlers are operating, the area impacted is enormous.

39. In shrimp trawl fisheries the catch is separated into shrimp and prawns (the "target species") and bycatch; the latter can be proportioned into: "food fish" and "trash fish". "Food fish" are usually sold directly for human consumption, either fresh or preserved, for example by salting and drying. Those fishes separated as "trash fish" have no conventional market for human food, so their commercial value is low or non existent. When they are utilized, "trash fish" species are normally processed into a secondary product, such as fishmeal or fish oil, and then employed in animal foods or agricultural fertilizers. Since the monetary value of bycatch can be less than a twentieth that of bycatch (Clucas, 1997c:6), there is often little economic incentive for marketing non-target species.

40. The proportion of "trash fish" in the catch varies depending on place, time, fishery and other factors. For example, a recent report from the Department of Fisheries, Thailand (Kungsuwan, 1996: Tables 3 and 4) shows that 75 per cent of the production from all fishing activities in the Gulf of Thailand (excluding shrimp culture) was "true trash fish", while in the Andaman Sea 76 per cent was "true trash fish". As usual, the proportion of "trash fish" produced from shrimp trawling is much higher than for the other fisheries. In the Gulf of Thailand, 82 per cent of the catch from shrimp trawling was "true trash fish", while in the Andaman Sea the "true trash fish" component was 85 per cent of the catch of shrimp trawlers.

41. Of the different types of shrimp fisheries, it is the industrialized tropical fishery that is most typically characterized as highly destructive to marine resources, with relatively high levels of discards (e.g., Andrew and Pepperell, 1992; Teutscher, 1995b:12; Clucas, 1997a:7). This has been documented in many nations (Alverson et. al., 1994), including: Cameroon (Eyabi-Eyabi, 1995:20); India (Bostock and Ryder, 1995:41 ff.); Malaysia (R. Bin Ali, 1995b); Nigeria (Akande and Tobor, 1995:72); Suriname (Lieveld, 1995: Tables 1, 4 and 5); Tanzania (Mgawe, 1995:81); and Thailand (Kungsuwan, 1995:87-88);

42. A comparison between two Asian fisheries may help illuminate the gravity of the problem. Annual discards from just the fleet based at Vishakapatnam (East coast of India) are estimated to be between 99,000 and 130,000 metric tons (Gordon, 1990). A number of explanations have been offered for the fact that so much bycatch is discarded, in a land where food, especially protein, is needed by so many people; the main reasons point to the fact that there is little financial incentive to sort, store, transport, handle, and sell most types of bycatch (Bostock and Ryder, 1995:43-45). Yet, it is remarkable that in India, where costs of labor are remarkably low, there is little financial incentive to market bycatch, while in Thailand and Malaysia, where operational costs are considerably higher, a much greater proportion, or virtually all, bycatch is utilized. Two questions arise: Is the efficiency of handling and marketing low value bycatch that much greater in Southeast Asia, despite higher labor and operating costs? or, Is fisheries production from Southeast Asia meager in relation to the Bay of Bengal, resulting in bycatch which would not normally be economically viable, being attractive for a lack of more lucrative alternatives? Indeed, in Thailand it has been stated that "the quality of by-catch and true trash fish is low and unsuitable for human consumption". (see Kungsuwan, 1995:88).

43. Recent information from the FAO (1997b:86) shows that in the Gulf of Thailand demersal fish stocks are now just one tenth of what they were 30 years ago, when trawling began in this area; nearly 70 per cent of the catch today is small, non-edible species of low commercial value and juveniles of species that would be of commercial importance if they were larger. The Gulf of Thailand has been called an "underwater desert" (Mathew, 1990:84), and the intense depletion of marine resources there has become a classic example of overexploitation (Pauly, 1998; 1995; Pauly and Chua, 1988). Hence, in the above case, apparent "economic efficiency" is nothing more than a manifestation of the serial depletion of fisheries resources.

44. Indeed, the concept of "trash fish" - a term incongruous with ecological processes - is evolving as fisheries resources become less available to burgeoning human populations: what was once discarded as worthless is now sought as a source of nutrients. Pauly (1995:287) discussed how this loaded term came about, and explained that it was a creation of the shrimp trawling industry.

45. As stated earlier, there is a long, and growing, list of publications on fisheries that have emphasized the pressing need to reduce bycatch destruction, and it is a widely accepted fact that shrimp trawling is by far one of the most destructive forms of fishing (e.g., Andrew and Pepperell, 1992; Alverson et. al., 1994; Teutscher, 1995a:3; 1995b; Clucas, 1997a; 1997b; Clucas and James, 1997; FAO, 1997a:11).

*The Social Impacts of Shrimp Trawling:*

46. Because shrimp trawling targets highly valued shrimp, there is high motivation to harvest as much and as fast as possible. This sort of competition for a common resource has led to "overcapitalization" of shrimp fleets globally (with the notable exception of Australia). The fact that there are more boats and gear than economically or ecologically warranted by the productive capacity of the fishery, is a further impulse for overfishing. Since shrimp are most abundant in coastal waters - especially in the tropics, fishing intensity for shrimp is greatest in inshore waters. As these same coastal waters are the traditional grounds of small-scale fishers, shrimp trawling logically leads to serious conflicts. The situation is further complicated as the trawlers fish ever-more intensely in response to declining shrimp stocks, resulting in an upward spiral of conflicts in coastal waters (e.g., Mathew, 1990; McGoodwin, 1990; Pauly, 1995).

47. Conflicts between small-scale fishers and modernized/industrialized/ motorized fishers - notably shrimp trawls - are widely documented, and include many nations: e.g., Cameroon (Eyabi-Eyabi, 1995:20, 23); Gambia (Jallow, 1995:32); India (McGoodwin, 1990:130; Debnath, 1994); Indonesia (Mathew, 1990; McGoodwin, 1990); Malaysia (Mathew, 1990); Mexico (McGoodwin, 1990); North Yeman (McGoodwin, 1990:127); Suriname (Lieveld, 1995:80); Thailand (Mathew, 1990; Yamamoto, 1994); Venezuela (Guada, pers. com.); and Viet Nam (Tuoc, 1995:97). Pauly, one of the most respected fisheries biologists in Southeast Asia, has been discussing the problems of conflicts with trawlers in this region for years (Pauly, 1988; 1995; Pauly and Neal, 1985; Pauly and Chua, 1988), and as he has mentioned, there is a voluminous literature on the subject.

48. The pattern in India, for example, is typical of the development of shrimp fisheries in the Tropics. "The mainstay of the Indian fishing industry in economic terms is penaeid shrimp which also forms a major component of the marine products exports

from India". (Pillai, 1995). Yet, there are numerous indicators that the main east coast trawler fleet in India is much larger than what the resource base can maintain, resulting in calamitous environmental as well as social and economic events: "In general, as prawn catches have declined as a result of uncontrolled (and often heavily and centrally subsidized) open access, the income derived from bycatch *per se* becomes proportionately more important to the small-scale operators commonly found around the coasts of India". "Considerable evidence exists that traditional fisheries are increasingly under threat from overfishing and that prawn trawling is much to blame". (Bostock and Ryder, 1995:41-42).

49. There is overwhelming evidence in Southeast Asia that shows that increased fishing effort - notably for shrimp - is to fuel "increasing needs for exports" (Tuoc, 1995). Elsewhere, the same pattern is repeated; in Gambia, where 87 per cent of the licensed industrial fleet in 1992 was foreign, shrimp, soles and cuttlefish were the main target species for export (Jallow, 1995:29-31). In Nigeria the shrimp fishery is also export oriented (Akande and Tobor, 1995:70-71), and in Suriname the fishery is not only for export, but mainly in foreign hands (Lieveld, 1995:77).

50. Not surprisingly, the lure of export earnings has resulted in overcapitalized shrimping fleets, which generally exert severe pressures on fisheries stocks, typically resulting in decreased harvests and rates of capture (presented as "Capture Per Unit Effort" or "CPUE" in studies of fisheries). Information consistent with this scenario comes from many nations, including Cameroon (Eyabi-Eyabi, 1995: Tables 3 and 4), Nigeria (Akande and Tobor, 1995:70, Table 1) and Tanzania (Mgawe, 1995:82). Pauly (1988; 1995; Pauly and Neal, 1985; Pauly and Chua, 1988) has explained the same problem in Southeast Asia.

51. As described above, on a global level shrimp trawling produces at least 15 times as much discard as food product. Clearly, the relative benefits of shrimp fishing for human food, must be viewed in the context of the ecological costs from discards, bycatch and environmental destruction. Examined more carefully, within a social context, it must be appreciated that the vast majority of shrimp production in the tropics is destined for export to industrialized nations.

52. Hence, the production of shrimp not only entails a relatively high environmental cost, especially when compared to the direct nutritional benefits for humans, but these benefits are not destined for the people and ecosystems who pay the high costs. This is a classic case of one society bearing the costs of another society's benefits.

53. But the social implications are even more complex. What is generally hidden from view and rarely discussed, is the fact that while certain members of the exporting nation reap considerable financial benefit from these commercial activities, there are far more people in the exporting country who not only do not benefit, but whose resource base is depleted and whose already precarious way of life is further complicated and debilitated (Bailey, 1985:1986; 1988a; 1988b; 1988c; 1988d; 1989; Bailey and Zerner, 1988; Bailey and Jentoft, 1990; Bailey et al., 1986; Mathew, 1990).

*Concern about Bottom Trawling, Particularly Shrimp Trawling:*

54. Considering the above discussion, it is to be expected that there is tremendous concern about bottom trawling, particularly shrimp trawling. This concern has been expressed by specialists from different disciplines, for a variety of reasons.

55. Fisheries managers have pointed out the complexities of understanding and managing fisheries impacted by this type of activity. Bycatch from shrimp trawling yields mainly large numbers of small-sized fishes - individuals that have not yet reached maturity (see section above on Environmental Impacts of Bottom Trawling). However, fish harvesting is usually directed at individuals above a certain minimum size, to allow the animals to grow so that the yield from the fishery will be more productive. Concentrating exploitation on small, immature fish is known by fisheries biologists as "growth overfishing", and it is responsible for "considerable economic waste" (Murawski, 1995:7). However, the complications of managing fisheries impacted by bottom trawlers is even more complex because of the mixed species composition of the catch. "While trawling has increased the catch of shrimp and fish, increases of fishing effort has turned bycatch and discard issues into primarily a multi-species fishery exploitation problem. There may be a large number of species in the catch from these fisheries but the actual quantities of each species may be low making it necessary to understand more fully the nature and composition of the individual components and their interactions of a full assessment of the impact of the fishery is to be made. In essence the entirety of species, coastal and marine habitats appear to be under heavy exploitation but the impacts on sustainable use of resources are unknown". (FAO, 1997a:8). Given that there is a long litany of failed, single species fisheries, for which adequate information has been available to implement effective management (e.g., Ludwig et. al., 1993), the challenges of managing mixed species fisheries, concentrated on "undersized" individuals, are tremendous.

56. Fisheries managers, marine biologists and conservationists have also warned about the large scale environmental impacts from bycatch and alteration of the sea floor (see sections above on Environmental Impacts of Bottom Trawling and The Relevance of Shrimp Trawling to Bycatch Problems). As Norse (1997b) described, "Bottom trawling is scouring continental shelf seabeds from the poles to the tropics". Again, the consequences of these impacts are poorly understood.

57. Conservationists, development specialists and social scientists have tried to alert decision makers in the fishing industry, commercial sector, government authorities, and multilateral agencies of the social risks and dangers of this form of exploitation (see section above on The Social Impacts of Shrimp Trawling). As ever, the difficulty is counterbalancing the head-long drive of profit-oriented activities which extract common resources with the long-term needs of society and the environment (Utting, 1995).

58. In summary, countless problems are attributed to bottom trawling - particularly shrimp trawling, starting with the fact that this is a highly unselective form of extracting renewable resources.

*Calls to Ban Bottom Trawling:*

59. As explained above (section on "Avoidance and Exclusion of Bycatch"), one of the greatest challenges before modern fisheries is to develop and implement selective fishing. The concern is global: for example, experts from the Marine Fishery Resources Development and Management Department, in Malaysia, have described the trawl as "a very destructive gear" and have explained that there is a great need to both reduce this destructiveness and to "strictly enforce the present legislation." (R. Bin Ali, 1995b). Similar sentiments have been expressed by officials from the Department of Fisheries in Thailand (Kungsuwan, 1996). Other enlightened fisheries administrators have warned

that: "Unless species and size selectivity of fishing techniques are improved, tough new rules will place additional requirements on existing fisheries or fisheries may be closed all together" and "Once articulated, achieving our bycatch goals may indeed require that some fisheries as we know them will cease to exist." (Murawski, 1995:5 and 9; see also Clucas, 1997c:52).

60. Obviously, bottom trawling is the antithesis of selective fishing, and given the innumerable negative impacts of this form of resource extraction, it is to be expected that there have been many initiatives to prohibit trawling. For example, although infringements are common for lack of enforcement (Mathew, 1990; Pauly, 1995), trawling is legally banned in most of Indonesia (Mathew, 1990) along the Kerala coast of India during the monsoon season (SAMUDRA, 1994:316; Pillai in Prado and Rahman, 1995:10) and in several areas in Thailand (Kungsuwan, 1996). Not surprisingly, "in the trawl fisheries of the Gulf of Thailand there is now an outline proposal for a drastic reduction in capacity (FAO, 1996)". It has been estimated that a reduction of trawler effort by 30 to 40 per cent would result in a 132 per cent increase in trawler catch and a 147 per cent increase in value (Everett, 1997:47, 54-55).

61. Of those technologies introduced into the Third World in an effort to increase fisheries productivity, the bottom (or otter board) trawl is a prime example, and because of the extraordinarily high export value of shrimp and prawn products, shrimp trawling provides one of the clearest examples of unintended (and often unspoken) environmental and social consequences of development (as described in various sections above). Numerous writers have explained that fishing is a way of life and the resource base for millions of small scale fishers - people who have little if any political clout and few economic resources; thus, fisheries resources must be managed for the common good - not just for the elite and transnational export interests (SAMUDRA, 1994). Hence, people who have analyzed the impacts of these activities have argued that "No effective fisheries management practices have been applied to trawl fisheries. Monitoring, surveillance and policing have consistently failed to protect resources and the marine environment, or the livelihoods of fishing communities. The battle for fish should be about securing and sustaining livelihoods for fishing communities around the world, and ensuring that important food supplies are maintained. In the countries of the South, more than 100 million of the world's poorest people struggle to survive against an onslaught of Western technology, unleashed by commercial interests and consumer demand in the North". (O'Riordan, 1994).

62. In this light it is important to consider the results of the conference "The Struggles of Fishworkers: New Concerns for Support", which was attended by some 100 people representing 31 countries, including 7 Asian nations, among them India and Thailand. The attendees, including fishworkers, scientists, national and international policy makers, focused on the complex issues involving fisheries, as well as the many and diverse peoples who depend on them. In concluding the week-long meeting, they emitted a Declaration, in which they called for, *inter alia*, a ban on bottom trawling in tropical waters (SAMUDRA, 1994:321).

63. While banning bottom trawling will not be easy (e.g., R. Bin Ali, 1995b), nor will it occur quickly, there is an ever-growing appreciation of the environmental and social dangers of this form of fishing. Just as international pressure swelled, resulting in a ban on the use of cyanide and dynamite for fish extraction, as well as a UN

moratorium on the use of high seas drift nets (Alverson and Hughes, 1995:14; Dilday, 1995:303), there is certain to be continued and greater calls to prohibit bottom trawling.

*Alternate Methods for Harvesting Shrimp and Prawns:*

64. Shrimp and prawns do not have to be caught in trawls. Certainly, Indonesian fishermen have been harvesting large numbers of shrimp for decades, without bottom trawls; pawn production from gill nets in 1986 was more than 900,000 tons (Mathew, 1990:26). The statistics presented by Kungsuwan (1996: Tables 3 and 4) clearly show that in Thailand, there are several ways to catch shrimp - other than trawling - that are productive and result in little or no bycatch. These include: acetes scoop nets, set bag nets, mullet gill nets, scoop nets, seines and stationary gear. It was reported that in the Andaman sea, set bag nets produced 33,946 tons of shrimp in 1993, out of a total of 55, 251 tons (61 per cent of the total): yet no bycatch at all was reported for this technique.

65. There is growing international recognition of the need to employ traditional fishing methods - and not just for shrimp (e.g., McGoodwin, 1990; FAO, 1995; Prado and Rahman, 1995:24-25). Indeed, using trawls to catch shrimp - in addition to causing countless environmental and social problems, as mentioned earlier - has definite drawbacks for the shrimp industry. It is noteworthy that the "highest quality [of shrimp] are normally caught from shrimp gill nets" - not in the industrialized trawls in Thailand (Kungsuwan, 1995:87).

*Importance of Selective Fishing Gear and Bycatch Exclusion Devices:*

66. Until bottom trawling is banned, practical means must be found to reduce the destructiveness of the gear. One of the first places to start is by making it more selective, so that non-target species are less severely impacted. Given the nature of bottom trawls, the simplest way to increase fishing selectivity is by incorporating Bycatch Excluder Devices (BEDs) in the nets (known also as "Bycatch Reduction Devices", or "BRDs").

67. As with other aspects of fisheries management and gear design, there are many questions that need to be worked out before excluder devices can be designed, tested, and finally offered to the industry. To stimulate more work and collaboration on this problem, the FAO has published a 150-page compilation of references on gear selectivity (Prado, 1992). One of the major questions that needs - urgently - to be answered and resolved is: "to what extent can the quantities of by-catch be reduced through activities such as the deployment of exclusion devices, the use of passive gear?" (Bostock and Ryder, 1995:41). Hence, fisheries experts have "...recognized a need for research into the selectivity of fishing gear particularly of trawls used in tropical industrial fisheries". (FAO, 1997a:8, 14).

68. From research already carried out in some areas, it has been established that bycatch exclusion devices, in addition to reducing bycatch, wastage and environmental damage, can provide direct benefits to the fisherman by:

- reducing the time and effort needed to sort the catch (Clucas, 1997a:10; Prado, 1997:39);
- increasing the value of the catch, by reducing damage from bycatch, and increasing efficiency in handling and quality and value of the

primary product (Clucas, 1997:10; Prado, 1997:39): for example, in Gambia, shrimp trawlers consider bycatch a problem for it may damage the shrimp, thus lowering the quality of the catch (Jallow, 1995:30);

- increasing the efficiency of fishing by reducing distortion to the gear from the bycatch (Clucas, 1997a:10; Prado, 1997:30).

These points, now being promoted by fisheries experts at the FAO, were described in 1982 when early models of TEDs were tested (Easeley, 1982).

*Specialized BEDs - The TED:*

69. It is widely recognized by fisheries specialists and conservationists that the capture of endangered species in fishing gear presents special problems for fisheries, and sea turtles are routinely discussed in this light (e.g., Easeley, 1982; National Research Council, 1990; Andrew and Pepperell, 1992; Alverson et al., 1994; FAO, 1994 Dilday, 1995; Everett, 1995; 1997; Hall 1995; Laist, 1995; Romine, 1995; FAO, 1997a; Prado 1997:25).

70. Turtles are caught and drown in different types of fishing gear, but it is often not easy to remove these risks, short of banning the fishery. High seas drift nets are a case in point. This gear was shown to be highly unselective, and a major source of mortality for diverse forms of marine life - including sea turtles and other endangered species; mounting international concern resulted in the United Nations General Assembly adopting, by consensus, a global moratorium on all large-scale pelagic driftnet fishing on the high seas (Alverson and Hughes, 1995:14; Dilday, 1995:302-303). Yet, turtles continue to drown in other fishing gear, such as gill nets, long lines and trawls. In the case of the first two, there is little that has been developed which can be done to abate mortality; reducing bycatch depends on fishers attending the gear at short intervals to remove captured turtles before they drown. However, in the case of trawls, considerable time, effort and resources have been invested over the past two decades in developing specialized BEDs - known variably as "trawl efficiency devices", "trawl excluder devices", "turtle excluder devices" or "TEDs". The TED is simply a BED adapted to exclude sea turtles from trawl nets.

71. Often fishers argue that turtle exclusion is not necessary because they see few turtles in their nets. However, fisheries biologists take a different perspective, for they must consider not only single boats, but also entire fleets operating in a country or region. Hence, at a FAO meeting on bycatch problems "...it was noted that examination of the magnitude of total discards can miss catches of special concern that are associated with particular fishing gears and locations. The occurrence of animals, such as reptiles [viz. marine turtles], mammals and birds is often incidental or rare but, over the entire fishery their numbers can be significant". (FAO, 1997a:6).

72. For example, only one turtle was caught in TED trials off the west coast of Peninsular Malaysia (Ali, 1997), and the data yield a CPUE estimate of 0.032258 (turtles caught per hour of trawling), which appears to be a low value. However, this value can be used to calculate the number of turtles caught per boat per year (based on trawl effort data in R. Bin Ali, 1995b), and the estimate is 92 turtles per boat per year. Even if this yearly estimate were off by as much as factor of 10, and only 9 turtles were

caught per boat per year, when a fleet of thousands of trawlers is taken into account, the yearly total could be several thousands of turtles caught in trawls per year.

73. TED designs which have been tested and certified by the NMFS have been shown - when properly installed and used - to exclude at least 97 per cent of the sea turtles that enter the net. The value of TEDs, however, goes beyond their function in saving marine turtles from drowning. Excluder devices are designed to exclude bycatch from trawls; not only do TEDs exclude sea turtles, but they are also effective at keeping other kinds of animals and debris out of trawl nets. Indeed, the "Georgia Jumper" - one of the more popular TEDs - was designed by shrimpers in the State of Georgia to exclude large jellyfish (known as "cannonballs") from their nets.

74. An analysis of TEDs done in 1982, using one of the first models, identified several benefits for shrimpers, including bycatch exclusion, reduced sorting and handling time of the catch, potential reduction in fuel usage, and improved dynamics of trawl operation (Easeley, 1982). Now that TEDs have been greatly refined, many former operational problems have been solved.

75. TEDs, depending on the model, can be very effective at excluding bycatch, thereby making shrimp trawls more selective and helping them to comply with one of the most pressing priorities in fisheries today. For example, studies on bycatch reduction have found that a decrease of more than 70 per cent of red snappers (Lutijanidae) in the 0 and 1 year age classes was achieved with certain TEDs (Graham, 1995; Harrington and Vendetti, 1995). These fish - if allowed to grow - would be of considerable commercial importance, but their removal as yearlings in the bycatch is not only unprofitable, but has resulted in the decimation of red snapper stocks in the Gulf of Mexico.

76. At the FAO-organized Expert Consultation on the Code of Conduct for Responsible Fishing, it was concluded that "in tropical shrimp fishing, the use of Turtle Excluder Devices has not only reduced the by-catch of turtles but further work in similar devices had increased the selectivity of the fishing gear and reduced the number of discards." (FAO, 1994:8). Prado, after reviewing gear modifications, stated that "the reduction of fish bycatch has, in many cases, to be combined with a turtle excluder". He concluded that "…results are, in many cases, excellent with up to 90 to 100 per cent escape of juveniles or 85 per cent escape of flatfish" (1997:29-31). Thus, at a FAO meeting on bycatch, turtle exclusion devices were included in the list of 12 "successful introductions of efficient selective fishing gear and harvesting practices" (FAO, 1997a:10).

77. Developed over the past two decades in the southeast shrimp fishery of the United States, TEDs have attracted interest elsewhere. Dr. E. G. Silas, former Director of the Central Marine Fisheries Research Institute, Cochin, India, recognized the value of TEDs for reducing mortality in sea turtles in Indian waters, and in 1983 he proposed testing and using TEDs in Indian trawlers (Silas et. al., 1983a; 1983b). Other fisheries specialists and conservationists in India have made similar recommendations (e.g., James et. al., 1989; Department of Fisheries et. al., 1996; Mohanty-Hejmadi, 1996; Sarkar et. al., 1996; Behera, 1997c; Pandav et. al., 1997). In 1995 it was reported that "Experiments are being undertaken by the Central Institute of Fisheries Technology in collaboration with the Marine Products Export Development Authority, Cochin, on the Turtle Excluder Device". (Pillai, 1995).

78. The Marine Fishery Resources Development and Management Department of Malaysia has carried out work, mostly on the east coast of Peninsular Malaysia, to increase selectivity of shrimp trawls. This included tests with bycatch excluder devices (BEDs), which were a "modified version of the US Turtle Excluder device (TED)". The work was conducted in 1986, so the BED would have been based on the early model of the NMFS TED, which was a rigid cage. On the basis of these tests, done over 10 years ago, it was concluded that "BED is not suitable in Malaysian waters." (R. Bin Ali, 1995a; 1995b). However, there were operational problems with the early model of the TED, and during the intervening decade, the gear has been greatly modified and improved, making present-day TEDs much more efficient and easier to use.

79. Specialists from Malaysia have shown that there are clear needs for excluder devices. Studies carried out in Sabah found that "Research on shrimp trawler impacts on the mortality of adult sea turtles in the area has been identified as one of the most urgent aspects to be investigated." Hence, it was concluded that "similar device [TED] should be introduced in Malaysia" (Suliansa et. al., 1996). Furthermore, work done off the east coast of Peninsular Malaysia has emphasized the urgent need to reduce the destructiveness of trawling by using devices and techniques to improve selectivity: it is noteworthy that the possibility of banning trawls was even contemplated - although it was thought to be "almost impossible" (R. Bin Ali, 1995:13).

80. Recently, the Thai Turtle Free Device ("TTFD"), a modified "Super Shooter" (which in turn was developed from the "Georgia Jumper"), was tested off the western coast of Peninsular Malaysia, and it was "found to be suitable for the use by Malaysian fishermen" (Ali, 1997). Similar tests in Philippines (Dickson, 1997) and Thailand (Bundit et. al., 1997) also found that the TTFD TED performed adequately. Recent publications by the FAO have explained the value of trials being undertaken in Thai waters to test turtle excluder devices and bycatch reduction, as well as the need to expand this work to other countries (Everett (1997:55-56); and the Southeast Asian Fisheries Development Center in Bangkok has been promoting TED testing in the Southeast Asian region (SEAFDEC, 1996; 1997a; 1997b; 1997c).

81. Most of the work on TEDs in Southeast Asia has evaluated the rates of retention for shrimp and food fish, and there has been little attention paid to bycatch exclusion. Given the urgent need to reduce overfishing and to reverse the trend of intense, unselective fisheries in the region - especially from trawling, TEDs can serve an invaluable role in paving the way to more selective fisheries.

*Mechanisms for Implementing Selective Fishing:*

82. In general, there have been few incentives for "clean fishing" (i.e., using fishing gear and techniques which are least likely to result in bycatch and other environmental problems), but this is now changing (Murawski, 1995:6-7). According to the FAO: "In contrast to the modest successes recorded in developed countries with reducing discards, it was observed that in developing countries the problem of discards, notably from shrimp trawlers, was generally ignored." (FAO, 1997a:8). Although "the history of research regarding selectivity/bycatch reduction dates back almost a century...", "as far as developing countries are concerned, their participation in research has been mainly limited to the transfer of European or North American technology and testing it under conditions in tropical waters (often without enough consideration to local conditions)".

"It should also be pointed out that, up to now, research and implementation of the results on selectivity and bycatch reduction in commercial fisheries has begun, in general, after the introduction of a new regulation. Recently a precautionary approach has been recommended with calls for changes in fishing practices to ensure better selectivity and a reduction of bycatch when a known risk of depleting stocks in any given fishery is thought to exist, even though it has not yet been scientifically proven". (Prado, 1997:26-27).

83. Unilateral decisions to reduce bycatch have been taken by several states. For example, it is illegal to discard at sea in Norway, and all fish caught must be landed. This has resulted in the use of separator grid technologies in the shrimp fishery, which are now compulsory. (Olsen, 1995; Clucas, 1997a:14; 1997c). Likewise, square mesh windows, designed to reduce capture of juvenile fishes, are compulsory for certain finfish fisheries in European waters (Prado, 1997:28). Canada and Iceland have also instituted bans for discarding most fish species at sea. The logic behind banning discards is to force fishers to be more selective, so that they will fill their quotas with the most fish that are legal and lucrative (Clucas, 1997c:47-49)

84. Alverson and Hughes (1995:13-14) explained that although the need to solve bycatch problems has been known in fisheries biology for many years, the problem of bycatch has recently become a significant national policy issue in the United States, as in some other countries, due especially to public interest in endangered, charismatic animals - namely whales, dolphins, sea birds and sea turtles. Catalyzed by concerns over these "flagship species", most fisheries have today been scrutinized for their relationship with bycatch. In response to public demand, relayed by government representations, the United Nations General Assembly adopted, by consensus, a resolution on bycatch and discards in 1994, and this issue is now clearly on the international agenda (Dilday, 1995:304; Clucas, 1997a:1-3).

85. While acknowledging "that multilateral, negotiated approaches to fishery bycatch and discard issues are preferable to unilateral pronouncements" (Dilday, 1995:305), "US officials have supported restricting the imports of fishery products from sources which fail to incorporate bycatch reduction so as not to penalize fishers in the US who have modified their fishing" (Murawski, 1995:6-7). Dilday (1995:305) described US diplomatic involvement in fisheries bycatch issues, concluding that "because of the importance of fisheries to many nations, international bycatch policy should minimize social and ecological conflict, be independent of ideological differences, and be based on sound conservation principals".

86. As Everett, from the FAO Department of Fisheries summarized: "Stringent regulations and harsh penalties will not do the whole job of reducing [bycatch or] discards, especially when enforcement is underfunded and/or inept. However good research and statistics, along with a combination of a carrot, a stick, and education, could well be a productive approach" (Everett, 1997:56). Clearly, if answers to seemingly simple biological and fisheries questions are illusive, implementing selective fishing is a complex challenge for many sectors of different societies. What is very clear, however, is that there is great urgency in implementing effective mechanisms for assuring selective fishing, and reducing overfishing - on a global level.

*International Accords Regarding Bycatch:*

87. Over the last few years the issue of bycatch has become a major concern at both national and global proportions (e.g., Alverson and Hughes, 1995:13; Dilday, 1995; Olsen, 1995). Reviews of the international accords, treaties, resolutions and initiatives to reduce bycatch and wastage in fisheries are discussed in numerous publications, notably diverse reports of the Food and Agriculture Organization of the United Nations, such as Everett (1995; 1997), Clucas (1997a; 1997c), Prado (1997), and (FAO, 1997a:1). On the basis of these studies, a few of the more salient international accords are summarized below.

88. UN Resolution (AIC.2149.I.50.Rev 1), entitled "Fisheries by-catch and discards and their impact on the sustainable use of the world's living marine resources" emphasizes that the issue: "warrants serious attention by the international community and a continued and effective response is necessary to ensure the long-term and sustainable development of fisheries" (Earth Negotiations Bulletin, 1995).

Other international resolutions expressing concern for the same issue include:

- UN General Assembly Resolutions 49/116 and 49/118 of December 1994;
- Resolution 50/25 of 5 December 1995;
- Rome Consensus on World Fisheries, March 1995;
- United Nations Agreement for the Conservation and Management of Straddling Fish Stocks and Highly Migratory Fish Stocks, August 1995;
- Kyoto Declaration and Plan of Action, from the International Conference on the Sustainable Contribution of Fisheries to Food Security, December 1995.

89. As explained by the FAO (1997a:2-4), it is important to appreciate that "the conservation and management provisions of the Agreement for the Conservation and Management of Straddling Fish Stocks and Highly Migratory Fish Stocks have been negotiated to implement the UN Convention on the Law of the Sea". As a result, there are "obligations, new to international fisheries law, regarding the conservation and management of straddling and highly migratory fish stock fisheries". States must:

- assess the impacts of fishing … on target stocks and species belonging to the same ecosystem or dependent upon or associated with the target stocks [5 (d)];
- protect biodiversity in the marine environment [5 (g)];
- minimize pollution, waste, discards, catch by lost or abandoned gear, catch of non-target species, both fish and non-fish species … and impacts on associated or dependent species, in particular endangered species [5 (f)];
- implement the development and use of selective fishing gear and techniques [5 (f)];
- develop data collection and research programmes to assess the impact of fishing on non-target and associated or dependent species and their environment, and adopt plans which are necessary to ensure the con-

servation of such species and to protect habitats of special concern [6.3 [d]);

- be more cautious when information is uncertain, unreliable or inadequate. The absence of adequate scientific information shall not be used as a reason for postponing or failing to take conservation and management measures [6.2].

90. The Code of Conduct for Responsible Fisheries (FAO, 1995) - adopted unanimously by the 28th Session of the FAO Conference on 31 October 1995 (Everett, 1997:45), further supports these concepts:

- "... where proper selective and environmentally safe fishing gear and practices exist, they should be recognized and accorded a priority in establishing conservation and management measures for fisheries" [6.6];
- phasing out of fishing gears and practices inconsistent with responsible fishing [7.6.4];
- "States should take appropriate measures to minimize waste, discards, catch by lost or abandoned gear, catch of non-target species, both fish and non-fish species, and negative impacts on associated or dependent species, in particular endangered species" and "...should promote to the extent practicable, the development and use of selective and environmentally safe gear and techniques." [7.6.9];
- "... encourage the development and implementation of technologies and operational methods that reduce discards. The use of fishing gear and practices that lead to the discarding of catch should be discouraged and the use of fishing gear and practices that increase survival rates of escaping fish should be promoted" [8.4.5];
- "Research on the environmental and social impacts of fishing gear and, in particular, on the impact of such gear on biodiversity and coastal fishing communities should be promoted." [8.4.8]
- "... should require that fishing gear, methods and practices, to the extent practicable, are sufficiently selective so as to minimize waste, discards, catch of non-target species ... impacts on associated or dependent species ..." [8.5.1];
- "... should carry out studies on selectivity of fishing gear, the environmental impact of fishing gear on target species and on the behaviour of target and non-target species in relation to such fishing gear as an aid for management decisions and with a view to minimizing non-utilized catches as well as safeguarding the biodiversity of ecosystems and the aquatic habitat." [12.10];

91. The Kyoto Declaration and Plan of Action (1995) called, *inter alia*, to "Promote fisheries through research and development aiming at: ... (iii) reduction of discard mortality; (iv) development and use of selective environmentally safe and cost effective fishing gear and techniques"; [Declaration 15]. The Plan of Action includes points such as: "... increase efforts to estimate the quantity of fish, marine mammals, sea birds, sea turtles and other sea life which are incidentally caught and discarded in fishing

operations; assess the effect on the populations or species; take action to minimize waste and discards including, to the extent practicable, the development and use of selective, environmentally safe and cost effective fishing gear and techniques; and exchange information on methods and technologies to minimize waste and discards". [7].

92. The World Food Summit (1996) established accords related to this topic, including: "The resource base for food, agriculture, fisheries and forestry is under stress and is threatened by problems such as desertifiction, deforestation, overfishing, overcapacity and discards in fisheries, losses of biodiversity,..." [24]. Flowing from the United Nations Convention on the Law of the Sea of 10 December 1982, the UN Agreement on Straddling Fish Stocks and Highly Migratory Fish Stocks, the FAO Agreement to Promote Compliance with International Conservation and Management Measures by Fishing Vessels on the High Seas, the World Food Summit Plan of Action further develops these concepts:

> "Implement sustainable fisheries management and practices, in particular the Code of Conduct for Responsible Fisheries, to address a responsible and sustainable utilization and conservation of fisheries resources in order to optimize the long-term sustainable contribution of fisheries resources to food security ... minimizing wastes in fisheries, reducing excess fishing capacity and applying the precautionary approach in accordance with the UN agreement on Straddling Fish Stocks and Highly Migratory Fish Stocks and Code of Conduct for Responsible Fisheries..." [d];

In this light, Sr. Joel Prado, of the Fishery Industry Division of FAO, has explained: "In line with the United Nations Convention on the Law of the Sea (1982) and Chapter 17 of Agenda 21, the 1995 UN Agreement Relating to the Conservation and Management of Stocks and Highly Migratory Fish Stocks (U.N. 1995) specifically refers to the problems of insufficiently selective gear and lack of sufficient co-operation between States". (Prado, 1997:25).

*International Concern Over the State of the Oceans, Including Bycatch and Sea Turtles:*

93. This concern for the state of the world's oceans, and more particularly the issues of devastated marine resources, overfishing, bycatch, and the environmental and social consequences of these problems is not limited to the rhetoric of governments and multinational organizations. There is considerable anxiety and grave concern in non-governmental groups and civilian associations. Unshackled by the pressures of international diplomacy, the statements of these concerned citizen groups, and people who depend directly on the resources in question, are not only germane, clear and succinct, but also more direct. In 1992 a 25-point Declaration was endorsed by a consortium of 104 organizations, representing millions of people in two dozen countries - including development organizations, environmental organizations, fishing communities, fishing companies, and even a canning company. It was explained that "even the most comprehensive bycatch strategies will only be partial solutions if broader overfishing and structural issues in fisheries are not addressed." "Overfishing, waste, and discards leading to ecosystem degradation and collapse are tied, in large part, to over-capacity, non-selective technologies and the lack of cooperative systems of

management, control, and enforcement based on strong conservation principles and objectives. Driven often by short term economic objectives and trade, these conditions drive an extremely destructive cycle that if allowed to continue into the future, will result in more social dislocation and environmental destruction". (Romine, 1995).

94. The Declaration, which specifically mentions sea turtles, makes it perfectly clear that "[m]any countries have pursued policies designed to maximize export earnings and fisheries production, often under pressure to service foreign debt, and often to the detriment of fish stocks, marine biodiversity, and coastal communities." [4]; and "[r]ising demand in industrialized countries for high-value species of fish is driving destructive fisheries practices worldwide, including shrimp trawl and aquaculture, with negative impacts on coastal wetlands, mangroves, marine biodiversity, and coastal fishing communities." [22]. Focusing on the mild language of intergovernmental accords, this Declaration states "[t]hough all relevant mechanisms or instruments should be viewed as opportunities to advance these issues, we would like to emphasize that codes of conduct, resolutions, declarations, or other agreements that are voluntary in nature are unacceptable substitutes for legally binding agreements." [7], and "[a]t a minimum, international agreements .... must contain provisions that require, rather than merely promote or encourage, the use of selective gears and techniques." [11].

95. Between the 2 and 7 of June 1994, nearly 100 people, from 31 nations, gathered in Cebu, Philippines to celebrate the Tenth Anniversary of the International Conference of Fishworkers and their Supporters. The Cebu Conference "The Struggles of Fishworkers: New Concerns for Support" resulted in a published proceedings of 345 pages, including a fourteen-page Declaration. What makes this conference remarkable is the integration of social and environmental issues, and the clarity with which they perceived the way in which the health of a society depends on the health of the environment. Among the recommendations were:

- "promote and facilitate greater awareness on coastal environmental issues affecting fishworker communities as well as help to develop [and] nurture strategies for a sustainable future";
- "provide international advocacy for appropriate action against coastal degradation and ... document and publicize examples of successful coastal environment management";
- "monitor relevant developments concerning negotiations and treaties for the protection of the environment at the international level and inform fishworkers' organizations of these developments";
- "launch an international campaign to achieve a complete ban on bottom trawling in tropical waters...";
- "facilitate continued discussion amongst fishworkers' organizations and help draft and elaborate a general set of agreed criteria against which to measure the social and ecological impacts of fishing technology to determine the acceptability of various technologies";
- "monitor the evolving situation of the fishworkers with regard to the impacts of international trade, structural adjustments, and other aspects of international economic policies (especially as they affect food security in certain countries) and promote the exchange of information

on these questions among the fishworkers' organizations of different countries".

96. Another, just publicized, global initiative is "Troubled Waters: A Call for Action"; this statement, organized by the Marine Conservation Biology Institute, has been endorsed by more than 1,600 scientists, from 65 nations. It expresses concern about the state of the oceans and calls for immediate action to reverse the trends in widespread destruction to marine species and ecosystems. Among the threats of greatest importance which were pointed out were overfishing and bottom trawls. The plight of endangered sea turtles, drowning in shrimp trawls and the need for TEDs, was not mentioned in the one page statement, for it was assumed that this was general knowledge (Norse, 1997b).

97. Resolutions for the 17th Annual Symposium on Sea Turtle Biology and Conservation, attended by more than 700 people from more than 30 nations, have recently expressed concern about: implementation of the FAO Code of Conduct for Responsible Fisheries, the status of the Interamerican Convention for the Protection and Conservation of Sea Turtles, incidental mortality sea turtles in shrimping operations in the United States, and the conservation activities for sea turtles in India (Wyneken, 1997).

98. Several other recent non-governmental undertakings have focused specifically on the issue of endangered sea turtles, the use of TEDs and questions of the present dispute:

- A Statement of Scientists, to date signed by more than 260 people from 31 countries, has emphasized the endangered status of marine turtles and the need to use TEDs to reduce mortality in shrimp trawling (Sierra Club Legal Defense Fund, 1997);
- A "TEDs Today" campaign in India had accumulated 104 signatures as of 11 November 1997, endorsing the need to provide protection for sea turtles by using TEDs in shrimp trawlers (Helpin Herps, 1997);
- An Amicus Brief on the present dispute before the WTO, prepared by the Foundation for International Environmental Law and Development (FIELD, 1997), representing the World Wide Fund for Nature (WWF) International, presented a series of arguments, seeking to "demonstrate the utility of a formal right of intervention for non-governmental organizations in disputes before the WTO". After presenting conservation information, the Amicus presents a detailed analysis of "Law and Policy", and concluded that "the measures under dispute relate to conservation, are necessary, and are not arbitrary or unjustifiable";
- A second Amicus Brief was prepared by the Center for International Environmental Law (CIEL, 1997), in collaboration with the Center for Marine Conservation (Washington, D. C.), the Red Nacional de Acción Ecológica (Chile), The Environmental Foundation, Ltd. (Sri Lanka), and The Philippine Ecological Network. It is preceded by a "Motion to Submit Amicus Brief" which argues that "Acceptance of the amicus brief enhances public participation in the WTO and improves the WTO dispute settlement process". This Amicus provides a second analysis of biological and technical matters, followed by a de-

tailed analysis of "Legal Arguments", similarly supporting the need and legal basis for protecting sea turtles by using TEDs.

99. While many of these initiatives have been undertaken in 1997, it is important to realize that the international concern for the status of sea turtles and the use of TEDs is not new. For example, a Resolution urging maximum size limits, protection of habitat and TED's was passed unanimously at General Assembly of the 17th Session of the IUCN, in San José, Costa Rica, 1-10 February 1988. The members of the General Assembly of the International Union for the Conservation of Nature (now World Conservation Union) urged the United States to implement "federal regulations requiring the use of TEDs needed to prevent the capture and drowning of the critically endangered Kemp's ridley sea turtle or any other species of sea turtle." They further urged "member governments to enact and enforce national legislation to increase the conservation of sea turtles", *inter alia*, "[w]here sea turtles are present, require use of TEDs by shrimp trawlers, and control all other fishing methods as needed to minimize incidental catch, particularly off the nesting beaches during the breeding season." (Canin, 1989).

100. It is important to emphasize that the widespread, international manifestation of concern about the state of the oceans, destructive fishing operations, bottom trawling, shrimp trawling, endangered sea turtles and the use of TEDs is not some isolated social phenomenon. It is part of a burgeoning civilian concern about the social and environmental damages caused by modern fisheries practices. A case in point is a global civilian movement in response to the world shrimp industry. The documentation of intense environmental and social problems caused by industrial shrimp farming is vast and growing, and includes the work of the United Nations Research Institute of Social Development (Barraclough and Finger-Stich, 1995), citizen action groups (e.g., Quarto, 1992; Ahmed, 1997) and environmental scientists (e.g., Goss 1997). It is noteworthy that although the industry has characterized these civil movements as "extremist", the leaders of diverse national organizations include national heroes and Gandhians who espouse non-violence - despite the way in which the industry has treated them (Ahmed, 1997).

*The Need for International Collaboration:*

101. The complexities of protecting and managing migratory animals are tremendous, and have been recognized and acknowledged in different fora. For example, the officer in charge of selective fishing issues in the FAO wrote: "Regarding the management of the exploitation of shared resources or migratory stocks, a difficulty may result from the migration of growing fish [and other animals] to foreign waters. Such a situation requires that the management measures are taken not only at a national level but also at a regional level. Very selective and efficient fishing methods at a given time could affect future fish populations in the long term". (Prado, 1997:42).

102. Dilday (1995:303), from the US Department of State summarized the conundrum, between the need for international collaboration on the one side, and the exigency to catalyze action promoting changes in fisheries on the other: "[a]s in the case of the tuna/dolphin situation, the threat and imposition of US embargoes have helped encourage some countries to devote greater attention to sea turtle protection in the wider Caribbean. However, the Department of State recognizes that this approach may not be viable over the long term. Therefore, we are currently engaged in discussions with other

countries to establish a multilateral regional convention for the protection and conservation of sea turtles."

*Conclusions and Implications of the Above Discussion:*

103. The state of the world's oceans is of grave concern, at national, regional and international levels; most fisheries stocks have been depleted or are being harvested at maximum yield, and untold species - including many that are endangered - are confronted by unrelenting pressures. Yet, intensity of fishing effort only seems to increase, and modern fishing methods are notoriously unselective, impacting far more than the species that are being targeted for human use. One of the clearest manifestations of this dilemma is shown by the statistics on bycatch. The effects of intense, unselective fishing - producing millions of tons of bycatch every year - are multifarious and ponderous. These practices seriously afflict fisheries stocks, the marine environment and coastal societies, both at present and for the future.

104. One of the most destructive of modern fishing practices is bottom trawling, particularly shrimp trawling, for it produces vast amounts of bycatch - most of which is discarded - and alters the ocean floor, reducing the quality of habitats. In addition to direct impacts on fisheries of commercial importance, the bycatch of shrimp trawlers includes countless other species of ecological and conservation importance: endangered species of sea turtles are among these.

105. Marine turtles are internationally regarded as endangered because many populations are greatly depleted from former times, and environments critical to their survival have been destroyed and contaminated - routinely at the hand of Man. Because they have complex life cycles, are slow to mature, and live for decades, these animals present tremendous challenges in terms of conservation; there is no simple prescription for conserving turtles or their habitats, but what is clear is that an interdisciplinary, integrated approach is absolutely essential. This means providing protection at all stages of the complex life cycle, in different environments and over extended periods of time. This simple fact means that by providing adequate protection for marine turtles, a multitude of animals, plants and environments must be considered and protected: conserving marine turtles leads to protecting a tremendous area of marine ecosystems. Put another way, marine turtles cannot be conserved if the marine environments in which they live are in jeopardy.

106. An animal that is applied as a symbol with which to protect many other species and ecosystems, is known as a "flagship species". The relevance of marine turtles to global conservation transcends issues of protecting endangered species and biological diversity, for it also bears directly on global fisheries matters. Because the most critical life history stages of sea turtles are those animals that are reproducing, or close to reproducing, and because it is those animals that are most at risk in fishing operations conserving sea turtles means dealing adequately with the bycatch issue. However, it is not easy to bring about changes in methods and attitudes in the fisheries industry, to convince them to modify gear, making it more selective, and to employ responsible operating procedures. Gear that is widely acknowledged to be among the most destructive (shrimp trawls) can be simply adapted (using TEDs) in order to conserve sea turtles; at the same time this small modification will serve both practically and ideologically as an invaluable step in developing responsible fisheries.

107. In this context, sea turtles have the potential to function as flagship species for solving much larger bycatch problems. Accomplishing this would not only save sea turtles, but it would help preserve other diverse marine organisms and marine environments. The success of these feats will be measured by a growing number of coastal peoples around the world whose livelihoods and very culture depend intimately on the availability of inshore marine resources.

108. In many respects, this deed would be "coming full circle", with technology providing a simple means for the turtle - an ancient religious and mythological symbol - to serve as savior in facilitating the resolution of a global dilemma.

DOCUMENTS APPENDED TO THIS ANNEX:

Canin, J., (1989), *Greenpeace guest editorial: IUCN Resolution*, Marine Turtle Newsletter, 44:1-4.

CIEL (Center for International Environmental Law), (1997), *Amicus Brief to the Panel on United States - Import Prohibition of Certain Shrimp and Shrimp Imports*, Center for Marine Conservation, Red Nacional de Acción Ecológica, The Environmental Foundation Ltd., and The Philippine Ecological Network, (vi), iii + 39 p.

FIELD (Foundation for International Environmental Law and Development), (1997), *WWF Amicus Brief to WTO Shrimp-Turtle Dispute*, World Wide Fund for Nature; Gland, Switzerland, 31 p.

Helpin Herps, (1997), *TEDs today: Kachab's story*, Helpin Herps; Ahmedabad, 9 p.

Norse, E. A., (1997b), *Troubled Waters: A Call for Action*, Marine Conservation Biology Institute; Redmond, Washington, 11 p.

Romine, T., *Perspectives on the global fisheries crisis*, in: T. Wray (technical editor), *Solving Bycatch: Considerations for Today and Tomorrow*, University of Alaska Sea Grant College Program; Fairbanks, Alaska, pp. 61-69.

SAMUDRA, (1994), *The Cebu Conference, Proceedings,* International Collective in Support of Fishworkers; Madras, India, 346 p.

Sierra Club Legal Defense Fund, (1997), Statement of Scientists, 12 p.

Wyneken, J., (1997), Resolutions of the 17th Annual Symposium on Sea Turtles Biology and Conservation, 4-8 March 1997, Orlando, Florida, US, 9 p.

## Appendix 2

*TRANSFER OF TED TECHNOLOGY*

By Dr. J. Frazier

1. It is with some distress that I have read repeated criticisms that there have been no, incompetent, or inadequate attempts to transfer technology on TEDs to fishermen, fisheries officers, other authorities, conservationists and other concerned people outside of the United States. Having interacted with the gear specialists of the National Marine Fisheries Service (NMFS) responsible for the development of TEDs, I can assert from both professional and personal experience that they have consistently made considerable efforts for close to two decades to share their information with people interested in sea turtle conservation and reducing incidental mortality of turtles and other bycatch. A public presentation on the first results of their early work was given in November 1979, at the World Conference on Sea Turtle Conservation, attended by more than 300 participants from 40 different nations (McVae and Seidel, 1982). Publications explaining their work, gear modifications used and other details, have appeared for close to 20 years in international journals, such as *International Council for Exploration of the Sea* (Watson and Seidel, 1980) and the *Marine Turtle Newsletter* (Mrosovsky, 1982; Oravetz, 1984; Mitchell, 1991), as well as in regional fishery journals, such as *Australian Fisheries* (Oravetz and Grant, 1986). These specialists have also been participating for years in international meetings, such as the Annual Symposium on Sea Turtle Biology and Conservation (which is attended by hundreds of people, from dozens of countries), where TED specialists make public presentations on their work and take part in formal and informal discussions with other sea turtle biologists and conservationists (e.g., Christian and Harrington, 1988; Oravetz, 1988; Kendall, 1989; Klima et. al., 1989; Mitchell et. al., 1989; Mitchell et. al., 1990; Klima et. al., 1991; Oravetz, 1991).

2. In 1985, while I was working in the People's Republic of China, I sent a request to Mr. Chuck Oravetz, Protected Species Management Branch, NMFS, asking for information on TEDs, so that I could give it to colleagues in China. On receiving a large package of manuals and other materials, these were distributed to various people involved in coastal fisheries in China. In more recent years, while working on TEDs with students in Mexico (Olguin, 1996; Olguin et. al., 1996), requests for technical advice, reports and manuals, videos and other materials relevant to the design, installation, use, and evaluation of TEDs have always been fulfilled: the response of the specialists in the Pascagoula Laboratory of NMFS has always been helpful and friendly. From repeated discussions about TEDs and problems of bycatch with other colleagues in Latin America (e.g., Brazil and Costa Rica), it is clear that this sharing of information and readiness to assist in matters related to TEDs and bycatch reduction has been a constant feature of the NMFS specialists.

3. Since none of the delegations involved in the present dispute seem to appreciate the amount of effort and dedication, or the long history, of this attempt to transfer TED technology as widely as possible, a selection of supporting documents is being annexed (with the time constraints involved in preparing this report, the materials that are included are what could be acquired at very short notice).

4. The appended documents clearly show that there have been countless efforts to make TED technology available to fishers, fisheries officers, NGO's, and other organizations in various nations (documentation from nearly two dozen countries is included herein). There has been correspondence between NMFS specialists and leading sea turtle biologists in Australia, Canada, France, India, Japan, Malaysia and Philippines, some of which dates back to the early 1980's. In addition, they have conducted more than 40 workshops held outside the United States, each of which has involved not only expenses in travel, communications and materials, but time and effort in planning and execution.

5. Having worked with the NMFS specialists, I can testify to their high level of interest, competence and commitment in sharing information and technology, instrumental in the reduction of mortality of sea turtles in fishing activities. I find absolutely no justification for characterizing the TED technology transfer programme, or the specialists responsible for it, as unconcerned, incompetent, or having ulterior motives to protect the domestic fishery for shrimp in the United States: the transparency, frankness and dedication with which they have been disseminating information on TEDs and other gear modifications for nearly two decades belies any such claims.

6. Finally, it must be emphasized that this desire to reduce destruction of endangered species and other bycatch, by assisting in the transfer of technology, is shared by other specialists from other agencies, for this attitude is central to a professional ethic. For example Ms. Julie Robins of the Queensland Department of Primary Industries, Australia, has also consistently provided helpful advice and materials to us in Mexico, while we have been working to gather more information on the effects of TEDs and how best to use them in Campeche.

7. This point is further supported by a perusal of the voluminous literature on bycatch, generated by academics, fisheries officers and gear technicians, in which descriptions - often in considerable detail - of experiments, gear modification and other innovations are publicly presented and discussed. For example, an international workshop on bycatch problems held in September, 1995 in Seattle, Washington, resulted in a published proceedings of 322 pages and 50 chapters (Wray, 1995). The reports, circulars and other publications produced by the Food and Agriculture Organization on the problem of bycatch (e.g., Clucas, 1997c; Clucas and James, 1997; FAO, 1994; 1995; 1997a; Prado, 1992), as well as meetings such as the SEAFDEC Regional Workshop on Responsible Fishing (24-27 June 1997), are further evidence of the intent to share experiences and information that will facilitate the development of more selective fishing gear and techniques, and in this way provide better protection for the world's marine resources. This approach is the antithesis of a profit-oriented venture, for although the information presented in these workshops and publications derives from work made possible from considerable amounts of private and state funding, state-of-the-art descriptions on methods for reducing bycatch problems are available to anyone who reads the reports, despite their institutional affiliation.

8. In summary, there are a number of specialists who have dedicated their professional careers to finding ways to improve modern fishing activities, making them more selective (and thus, less destructive) and allowing fishers to be more responsible. Advances of this nature are regarded as assets to humanity, and for this reason, these

specialists are eager to share their information and skills with as wide a public as possible.

FORMAL MATERIALS APPENDED:

Chronological listing of TED technology transfer workshops: 5 p.

Mitchell, J. F., J. W. Watson, D. G. Foster and R. E. Caylor, (1995), *The Turtle Excluder Device (TED): A Guide to Better Performance*, US Department of Commerce; National Oceanographic and Atmospheric Administration; National Marine Fisheries Service; Southeast Fisheries Science Center, Mississippi Laboratories, Pascagoula, Mississippi. NMFS-SEFSC-366, 35 p.

Mitchell, J. F., J. W. Watson, D. G. Foster and R. E. Caylor, ( 1995), *El Excluidor de Tortugas (TED): Un Guía para Mejorar su Funcionamiento,* U.S. Department of Commerce; National Oceanographic and Atmospheric Administration; National Marine Fisheries Service; Southeast Fisheries Science Center, Mississippi Laboratories, Pascagoula, Mississippi. NMFS-SEFSC-366, 34 p.

Mitchell, J. F., J. W. Watson, D. G. Foster and R. E. Caylor, (1995), *Tái-liêu hu'ó'ng dàn cách xú'-dung bô phân loc rùa biể'n môt cách hu'u hiêu*, U.S. Department of Commerce; National Oceanographic and Atmospheric Administration; National Marine Fisheries Service; Southeast Fisheries Science Center, Mississippi Laboratories, Pascagoula, Mississippi. NMFS-SEFSC-366, 35 p.

Pelatihan Petugas Perikanan Dalam Rangka Pembuatan Konstruksi Dan Penggunnan TED (Turtle Excluder Device) Tanggal 14 S/D 19 Oktober 1996 Di Tegal (Jawa Tengah), (1996), Direktorat Bina Produski, Direktorat Jenderal Perikanan, Indonesia, 8 p.

H.E. Montri Darnpaiboon, (1996), Opening Address, Workshop on the Use of Turtle Free Devices in Shrimp Trawlers, 2 p.

H.E. Deputy Minister, (1996), The Report Address, Workshop on the Use of Turtle Free Devices in Shrimp Trawl Net, 3 p.

Thai Turtle Free Device, 13 p.

TED Regulations Summary Card: Single Grid Hard TEDs n. d. U.S. Department of Commerce; National Oceanographic and Atmospheric Administration; National Marine Fisheries Service; Southeast Fisheries Science Center, Mississippi Laboratories, Pascagoula, Mississippi. 2 p.

Tarejeta Resumen de Reglamentos de Tortuga (TED): TED Parilla Sensilla Rigida. n. d. U.S. Department of Commerce; National Oceanographic and Atmospheric Administration; National Marine Fisheries Service; Southeast Fisheries Science Center, Mississippi Laboratories, Pascagoula, Mississippi. 2 p.

Báng Tóm-Lu'o'c Nhû'g DiêuL*ê*, Áp D*u*ng Cho Nhû'g B*ô*-Ph*ân* L*o*c Rùa (TED). LO*A*I VÎ SÃT CÚ'NG. n. d. U.S. Department of Commerce; National Oceanographic and Atmospheric Administration; National Marine Fisheries Service; Southeast Fisheries Science Center, Mississippi Laboratories, Pascagoula, Mississippi. 2 p.

Seidel, W. R., (1997), *Foreign TED technology transfer to India and Bangladesh: Trip report*, Wilber R. Seidel, David Bernhart and Jack Forrester, May 2-14, 1997, United States Department of Commerce, National Oceanic and Atmospheric Administration, National Marine Fisheries Service, Southeast Fisheries Center, Pascagoula, 5 p.

CORRESPONDENCE APPENDED:

*Australia:*

February 1982. C. J. Limpus to J. W. Watson, 1 p.

1 August 1983. C. A. Oravetz to C. Limpus, 1 p.

29 August 1983. C. A. Oravetz to C. Limpus, 1 p.
28 June 1984. A. Mager to C. Limpus, 1 p.
27 November 1985. C. A. Oravetz to C. J. Grant, 1 + 10 p.
26 February 1986. C. A. Oravetz to C. J. Grant, 1 p.
9 April 1986. C. J. Grant to C. A. Oravetz, 1 p.
21 May 1986. C. A. Oravetz to C. J. Grant, 1 p.
24 August 1987. W. D. Mitchell to P. W. Raymond, 1 + 2 p.
15 September 1987. C. A. Oravetz to D. Mitchell, 1 p.
24 March 1988. C. A. Oravetz to G. Goeden, 1 + 1 + 6 p.
5 February 1992. T. Tucker to C. A. Oravetz, 2 p.
24 March 1992. C. A. Oravetz to T Tucker, 2 p.
28 June 1996. J. F. Mitchell to J. McGilvray, 1 p.

*Bangladesh:*

9 June 1997. Powel to SEC STATE, 6 p.

*Canada:*

21 May 1986. J. W. Watson to W. H. L. Allsopp, 2 p.
29 May 1986. C. A. Oravetz to W. H. L. Allsopp, 2 p.
16 July 1995. J. F. Mitchell to J. J. Ryan, 1 p.
6 December 1995. J. F. Mitchell to N. Mrosovsky, 1 p.

*Colombia:*

14 July 1995. J. F. Mitchell to G. Piacenza, 1 p.
2 October 1995. J. F. Mitchell to P. Thiriez, 1 p.

*Costa Rica:*

21 May 1997. W. R. Seidel to J. Campos M., 2 p.

*France:*

6 November 1984. C. A. Oravetz to J. Fretey, 1 p.

*India:*

23 November 1982. J. C. Sawhney to J. W. Watson, 1 p.
14 December 1982. C. S. Kar to J. W. Watson, 1 p.
2 August 1991. Lorton to AM EMBASSY New Delhi, 2 p.
2 August 1991. Lorton to AM EMBASSY New Delhi, 1 p.
27 February 1992. Clark to SEC. STATE, 1 p.
30 July 1992. R. Ganapathy to P. Williams, 1 p.
13 August 1992. R. Ganapathy to "J. Oravitz", 1 p.
26 August 1992. C. A. Oravetz to R. Ganapathy, 2 p.
28 August 1992. R. Ganapathy to C. A. Oravetz, 1 p.
14 November 1994. B. Patnaik to R. Schmitten, 2 p.
9 January 1995. R. A. Schmitten to B. Patnaik, 1 p.
24 January 1995. M. K. Ahmed to R. A. Schmitten, 1 p.
15 March 1995. R. A. Schmitten to M. K. Ahmed, 2 p.
26 December 1995. R. A. Schmitten to H. S. Sarkar, 1 p.

30 December 1995. H. S. Sarkar to R. A. Schmitten, 1 p.
5 January 1996. Daley to SEC. STATE, 1 p.
29 March 1996. Wisner to SEC STATE, 2 p.
4 April 1996. Christopher to AM EMBASSY New Delhi, 1 p.
23 April 1996. W. R. Seidel to D. Roychowdhury, 2 p.
5 September 1996. W. R. Seidel to H. S. Sarkar, 2 p.
5 September 1996. W. R. Seidel to D. Roychowdhury, 2 p.
5 September 1997. B. Pradeep Kumar to W. R. Seidel, 1 p.

*Indonesia:*

24 August 1982. G. S. Posner to file, 5 p.
24 August 1982. C. A. Oravetz to L. Ogren, 1 p.
9 September 1982. W. R. Seidel to G. S. Posner, 1 p.
26 November 1982. Telegram from AM EMBASSY Jakarta, 1 p.
28 April 1983. C. A. Oravetz to E. C. Bricklemeyer, Jr., 1 + 5 p.
17 June 1983. W. R. Seidel to G. S. Posner, 2 p.
21 March 1985. C. A. Oravetz to Gomal, 1 p.

*Italy:*

30 November 1995. J. F. Mitchell to G. Gerosa, 1 p.

*Japan:*

1982 ?. S. Fuwa to J. W. Watson, 1 p.
15 November 1982. H. Enomoto to J. Watson, 1 p.
22 January 1996. J. F. Mitchell to K. Horikoshi, 1 p.

*Malaysia:*

26 February 1982, E. O. Moll to W. Seidel, 1 p.
25 March 1984. Chan Eng Heng to C. A. Oravetz, 1 p.
2 April 1984. C. A. Oravetz to Chan Eng Heng, 1 p.
26 March 1984. C. Leh to C. A. Oravetz, 1 p.
10 April 1984. C. A. Oravetz to C. Leh, 1 p.
20 July 1984. C. Leh to C. A. Oravetz, 1 p.
22 February 1985. C. A. Oravetz to Chan Eng Heng, 1 p.
2 August 1985. Ch'ng Kim Looi to C. A. Oravetz, 1 p.
27 August 1985. C. A. Oravetz to Ch'Ng Kim Looi, 1 p.
4 June 1996. A. Ali to Director NMFS, 1 p.

*Mexico:*

5 May 1994. J. F. Mitchell to J. Flores O., 1 p.

*Morocco:*

23 June 1996. J. F. Mitchell to Ministere des Peches Maritimes, 1 p.

*Netherlands:*

15 November 1982. A. J. Zwinenberg to J. W. Watson, 1 p.
22 November 1982. J. H duPon to J. W. Watson, 1 p.

*Philippines:*

2 September 1986. D. F. Ladra to C. A. Oravetz, 1 p.
15 September 1986. C. A. Oravetz to D. F. Ladra, 1 p.

*Saudi Arabia:*

26 June 1996. J. F. Mitchell to M Al Faiz, 2 p.

*South Africa:*

11 November 1982. G. R. Hughes to J. W. Watson, 1 p.
1 August 1983. C. A. Oravetz to G. R. Hughes, 1 p.
9 September 1983. G. R. Hughes to C. A. Oravetz, 2 p.

*Switzerland (IUCN):*

29 July 1986 A. J. Calio to K. R. Miller, 1 p.

*Taiwan:*

8 February 1996. J. F. Mitchell to I-Juinn Cheng, 1 p.

*Thailand:*

24 April 1992. Danuch Boonyaprapatsorn to J. Mortimer, 1 p.
17 September 1992. J. A. Mortimer to C. Oravetz, 1 p.
14 January 1993. C. A. Oravetz to Danuch Boonyaprapatsorn, 1 p.
19 January 1993. C. A. Oravetz to Danuch Boonyaprapatsorn, 1 p.

*Turkey:*

1 April 1997. J. F. Mitchell to E. Tasavak, 1 p.

*United Kingdom:*

1 April 1997. J. F. Mitchell to B. J. Godley, 1 p.

*Venezuela:*

5 May 1993. J. F. Mitchell to L. Ravago C., 1 p.
9 April 1996. J. F. Mitchell to R. C. Ward, 1 p.

*Yemen:*

18 January 1996. J. F. Mitchell to S. Wilson, 1 p.

# ANNEX III

*LITERATURE AND OTHER SOURCES CITED BY THE EXPERTS*

**Cited by Dr. S. Eckert:**

Aguilar, R., J. Mas, X. Pastor, (1992), *Impact of Spanish Swordfish Longline Fisheries on the Loggerhead Sea Turtle Caretta Caretta Population in the Western Mediterranean*, pp. 1-6, in Richardson, J.I. and T.H. Richardson (Compilers), 1995, Proceedings of the Twelfth Annual Workshop on Sea Turtle Biology and Conservation, NOAA Tech. Memo. NMFS-SEFSC-361, 274 pp.

Aguilar, R., J. Mas, X. Pastor, (1993), *Sea Turtles and Surface Longline Fishery*, Greenpeace International Mediterranean Sea Project.

Ali, A. Alwi, S.S.S., Ananpongsuk, S., (1997), *Experiments on the Use of Turtle Excluder Devices (TEDs) in Malaysian Waters*, presentation from The Regional Workshop on Responsible Fishing, 24-27 June 1997, Bangkok, Thailand, 11 pp.

Amelang, M.A., (1994), *Battling Bycatch Saving Snapper*, Texas Shores (winter):23-28.

Andrews, H., (1993), *Olive Ridleys Threatened in India: Letters Needed*, Marine Turtle Newsletter, 61:5-6.

Argano, R.A.B.F., (1983), *Status of Western Mediterranean Sea Turtles*, Rapp. Comm. int. Mer Medit. 28(5):233-235.

Balazs, G.H., (1976), *Green Turtle Migrations in the Hawaiian Archipelago*, Biol. Conserv. 9:125-140.

Balazs, G.H., (1994), *Homeward Bound: Satellite Tracking of Hawaiian Green Turtles From Nesting Beaches to Foraging Pastures*, Proceedings of the Thirteenth Annual Symposium on Sea Turtle Biology and Conservation, NOAA Tech. Memo. NMFS-SEFSC-341, 278 pp.

Balazs, G.H., P. Craig, B.R. Winton, R.K. Miya, (1994), *Satellite Telemetry of Green Turtles Nesting at French Frigate Shoals, Hawaii, and Rose Atoll, American Samoa*, Proceedings of the Fourteenth Annual Symposium on Sea Turtle Biology and Conservation, NOAA Tech. Memo. NMFS-SEFSC-351, 306 pp.

Balazs, G.H. and Pooley, S.G., (1994), *Research Plan to Assess Marine Turtle Hooking Mortality: Results of an Expert Workshop Held in Honolulu*, Hawaii, November 16-18, 1993, NOAA Tech. Memo. NOAA-TM-NMFS-SWFSC-201, 166 pp.

Bell, R. and J. I. Richardson, (1978), *An Analysis of Tag Recoveries From Loggerhead Sea Turtles (Caretta Caretta) Nesting on Little Cumberland Island, GA.*, in: Proc FL & Interregional Conf on S.Turtles, 1976, Jensen Beach FL (G.E. Henderson, ed.) Fla Mar Res Publ 33:20-24.

Bhaskar, S., (1985), *Mass Nesting by Leatherbacks in Irian Jaya*, WWF Monthly Report, January.

Bowen, B. W., F.A. Abreu-Grobois, G.H. Balzas, N. Kamezaki, C.J. Limpus and R.J. Ferl, (1995), *Trans-Pacific Migrations of the Loggerhead Turtle (Caretta Caretta) Demonstrated With Mitochondrial DNA Markers*, Proc. Natl. Acad. Sci. 92:3731-3734.

Bowen, B., J.C. Avise, J.I. Richardson, A.B. Meylan, D. Margaritoulis and S.R. Hopkins-Murphy, (1993), *Population Structure of Loggerhead Turtles (Caretta Caretta) in the Northwestern Atlantic Ocean and Mediterranean Sea*, Conservation Biology 7(4):834-844

Bustard, H.R., (1979), *Population Dynamics of Sea Turtles*, in: Turtles: Perspectives and Research. M. Harless and H. Morlock (eds.), New York: John Wiley and Sons, Inc.

Chaloupka, M.Y. and J.A. Musick, (1996), *Age, Growth and Population Dynamics*, pp. 233-276, in: Biology of Sea Turtles, P.L. Lutz and J.A. Musick (eds.), CRC Press Inc. New York.

Chan, E.H., (1991), *Sea Turtles*, pp. 120-134, in: The State of Nature Conservation in Malaysia, R. Kiew (ed.), Malaysian Nature Society, Kuala Lumpur, Malaysia, 238 p.

Chan, E.H. and H.C. Liew, (1996), *Decline of the Leatherback Population in Terengganu, Malaysia, 1956-1995*, Chelon. Cons. and Biol. 2(2):196-203.

Chan, E.H. and H.C. Liew, (1996), *A Management Plan for the Green and Hawksbill Turtle Populations of the Sabah Turtle Islands*, Rpt to Sabah Parks, 26 p.

Chan, E.H., H.C. Liew, and Mazlan, A.G., (1988), *The Incidental Capture of Sea Turtles in Fishing Gear in Terengganu, Malaysia*, Biological Conservation 43(1988):1-7.

Chantrapornsyl, S., (1997), *Status of Marine Turtles in Thailand*, Country Report for Thailand presented at the Northern Indian Ocean Sea Turtle Workshop and Strategic Planning Session on Jan. 13-18, 1997 in Bhubaneswar, Orissa, India.

Chua, T.H., (1988a), *Nesting Population and Frequency of Visits in Dermochelys Coriacea in Malaysia*, J. Herp, 22(2):192-207.

Chua, T.H., (1988b), *On the Road to Local Extinction: the Leatherback Turtle (Dermochelys Coriacea) in Terengganu, Malaysia*, Proc. 11th Annl Sem. Malaysian Soc. Mar. Sci. 1988:153-158.

Cliffton, K., D.O. Cornejo, and R.S. Felger, (1982), *Sea Turtles of the Pacific Coast of Mexico*, in: K.A. Bjorndal (ed.), Biology and Conservation of Sea Turtles, Smithsonian Institution Press, Wash, D.C., p. 199-209.

Crouse, D.T., L.B. Crowder, and H. Caswell, (1987), *A Stage-Based Population Model for Loggerhead Sea Turtles and Implications for Conservation*, Ecology 68:1412-1423.

Crouse, D.T., M. Donnelly, M.J. Bean, A. Clark, W.R. Irvin, C.E. Williams, (1992), *The TED Experience: Claims and Reality*, Center for Marine Conservation, Environmental Defense Fund, and National Wildlife Federation, 17 p.

Crowder, L.B., S.R. Hopkins-Murphy, J.A. Royle, (1995), *Effects of Turtle Excluder Devices (TEDs) on Loggerhead Sea Turtle Strandings With Implications For Conservation*, Copeia 1995(4):773-779.

Das, B.B., (1998), (in press), *Present Status of Gahirmatha Beach in Bhitara Knika Sanctuary, Orissa*, Marine Turtle Newsletter 79:1-2.

Dash, M.C. and C.S. Kar, (1990), *The Turtle Paradise Gahirmata*, Interprint, New Dehli, India, p. 295.

Dayton, P.K., S.F. Thrush, M.T. Agardy, R. J. Hofman, (1995), *Environmental Effects of Marine Fishing*, Aquatic Conservation: Marine and Freshwater Ecosystems 5:205-232.

de Silva, G.S., (1987), T*he Leatherback and the Olive Ridley in Sabah Waters*, Sarawak Mus. J. 58:115-123.

de Silva, G.S., (1982), *The Status of Sea Turtle Populations in East Malaysia and the South China Sea*, pp. 327-337, in: Bjorndal, K.A. (ed.), Biology and Conservation of Sea Turtles, Smithsonian Inst. Press, Wash. D.C.

Dodd, C.K. Jr., (1988), *Synopsis of the Biological Data on the Loggerhead Sea Turtle, Caretta Caretta (Linnaeus 1758)*, U.S Fish Wildl. Serv. Biol. Rep. pp. 110.

Dredge, M.C.L. and N. Trainor, (1994), *The Potential for Interactions Between Trawling and Turtles in the Queensland East Coast Trawl Fishery*, pp. 136-141, in: James (Compiler), Proc. Austral. Marine Turtle Conservation Workshop, Gold Coast, 14-17. Nov. 1990. Qld Dept. Environ. Heritage and Austral. Nature Cons. Agency.

Easley, J.E., (1982), *A Preliminary Estimation of the Pay-Off to Investing in a Turtle Excluder Device for Shrimp Trawls*, Final Report prepared for MONITOR, Int'I and CEE in cooperation with NMFS, unpub.

Eckert, K.L., (1993), *The Biology and Status of Marine Turtles in the North Pacific Ocean*, NOAA Tech. Memo., NOAA-TM-NMFS-SWFSC-186, 156 pp.

Eckert, S.A., (1997) in press, *Perspectives on the Use of Satellite Telemetry and Other Electronic Technologies for the Study of Marine Turtles, With Reference to the First Year Long Tracking of Leatherback Sea Turtles*, Proceedings of the Eighteenth Symposium on Sea Turtle Biology and Conservation, NOAA Tech. Memo., NMFS-SEFSC-XXX.

Eckert, S.A., E.H. Chan, H.C. Liew, K. Eckert, (1996), *Shallow Water Diving by Leatherback Turtles in the South China Sea*, Chelon. Cons. and Biol. 2(2):237-243.

Eckert, S. and L. Sarti M., (1997), *Distant Fisheries Implicated in the Loss of the World's Largest Leatherback Nesting Population*, Marine Turtle Newsletter 78:2-7.

Frazer, N., (1983), *Survivorship of Adult Female Loggerhead Sea Turtles, Caretta Caretta, Nesting on Little Cumberland Island, GA, USA*, Herpetologica 39(4):436-447.

Frazer, N.B., (1992), *Sea Turtle Conservation and Halfway Technology*, Cons. Biol. 6(2):1-8.

Frazer, N.B. and J.I. Richardson, (1985a), *Annual Variation in Clutch Size and Frequency For Loggerhead Turtles, Caretta Caretta, Nesting at Little Cumberland Island, Georgia, USA*, Herpetologica, 41(3):246-251.

Frazer, N.B. and J.I. Richardson, (1985b), *Seasonal Variation in Clutch Size For Loggerhead Sea Turtles, Caretta Caretta, Nesting on Little Cumberland Georgia, USA*, Copeia, 1985(4):1083-1085.

Frazer, N.B. and J.I. Richardson, (1986), *The Relationship of Clutch Size and Frequency to Body Size in Loggerhead Turtles, Caretta Caretta*, J. Herp, 20(1):81-84.

Groombridge, B. and R. Luxmoore, (1989), *The Green Turtle and Hawksbill (Reptilia: Cheloniidae) World Status, Exploitation and Trade*, Secretariat of the Conv. on Int'l Trade in Endangered Species of Wild Fauna and Flora, pp 601.

Harris, A.N. and I.R. Poiner, (1990), *By-catch of the Prawn Fishery of Torres Strait: Composition and Partioning of the Discards Into Components that Float or Sink*, Aust. J. Mar. Freshwater Res. 41:37-52.

Henwood, T.A. and W.E. Stuntz, (1987), *Analysis of Sea Turtle Captures and Mortalities During Commercial Shrimp Trawling*, Fish. Bull. 85(4):813-817.

Henwood, T.A., W. Stunz. and N. Thompson, (1992), *Evaluation of U.S. Turtle Protective Measures Under Existing TED Regulations, Including Estimates of Shrimp Trawler Related Mortality in the Wider Caribbean*, NOAA, Tech. Memo., NMFS-SEFSC-303. 14 pp.

Hill, G., (1991), *Villagers in Thailand Protect Turtle Eggs, Bring Conservation Home*, Marine Turtle Newsletter, 53:8-9.

Hill, G., (1992), *The Sustainable Sea Turtle*, Marine Turtle Newsletter, 58:2-5.

Hillestad, H.O., J.I. Richardson, and G.K. Williamson, (1978), *Incidental Capture of Sea Turtles by Shrimp Trawlermen in Georgia*, Proc Ann Conf S E Assoc Fish and Wildl Agencies 32:167-178

Hillestad, H.O., J.I. Richardson, C. McVea Jr., J.M. Watson Jr., (1979), *Worldwide Incidental Capture of Sea Turtles*, pp. 489-495, in: K.A. Bjorndal (Editor), Biology and Conservation of Sea Turtles, Smithsonian Institution Press, Washington D.C.

Hoekert, W.I.J. and A.D. Schouten, (1996), *Is the Suriname Olive Ridley on the Eve of Extinction? First Census Data for Olive Ridleys, Green Turtles and Leatherbacks Since 1989*, Marine Turtle Newsletter 75:1-4.

Hughes, G.R., (1974), *The Sea Turtles of South-East Africa I. Status, Morphology and Distributions*, Oceanographic Research Institute Investig. report 35:130 p.

Johannes, R.E., (1986), *A Review of Information on the Subsistence Use of Green and Hawksbill Sea Turtles on Islands Under U.S. Jurisdiction in the Western Pacific Ocean*, National Marine Fisheries Service, SWR-86-2, Honolulu, 41 pp.

Keinath, J.A.a.J.A.M., (1990), *Dermochelys Coriacea (Leatherback Sea Turtle) Migration*, Herp Review 21(4):92.

Kolinski, S., (1991), *Outer Islands Turtle Project: Stage I, Final Report on the Olimaro Atoll Fieldwork*, 22 pp.

Kraemer, J.E. and J.I. Richardson, (1979), *Volumetric Reduction in Nest Contents of Loggerhead Sea Turtles (Caretta Caretta) (Reptilia, Testudines, Cheloniidae) on the Georgia Coast*, J. Herp, 13(3):255-260.

Liew, H.C., Chan, E.H., Luschi, P. and Papi, F., (1995), *Satellite Tracking Data on Malaysian Green Turtle Migration*, Rend. Fis. Acc. Lincei 6:239-246.

Limpus, C.J., (1995), *Myths, Reality and Limitation of Green Turtle Census Data*, pp. 170-173, in: Keinath, J.A., D.E. Barnard, J.A. Musick, B.A. Bell (eds.), Proceedings of the Fifteenth Annual Symposium on Sea Turtle Biology and Conservation, 355 pp.

Limpus, C.J., J. Miller, C.J. Parmenter, D. Reimer, N. McLachlan, R. Webb, (1992), *Migration of Green (Chelonia Mydas) and Loggerhead (Caretta Caretta) Turtles To and From Eastern Australian Rookeries*, Wildl. Res., 19:347 pp.

Limpus, C.J. and. N. Nicholls, (1988), *The Southern Oscillation Regulates the Annual Numbers of Green Turtles (Chelonia Mydas) Breeding Around Northern Australia*, Aust. Wildl. Res. 15:157-161.

Luschi, P., Papi, F., Liew, H.C., Chan, E.H. and Bonadonna, F., (1996), *Long-Distance Migration and Homing After Displacement in the Green Turtle (Chelonia Mydas): a Satellite Tracking Study*, J. Comp. Physiol. A 178:447-452.

Maley, C., M. Murphy, and S. Kent, (1994), *Georgia Sea Turtle Stranding and Salvage Network: 1979-1993*, pp. 249-254, in: Bjorndal, K.A., A.B. Bolten, D.A. Johnson, P.J. Eliazar, Proceedings of the Fourteenth Annual Symposium on Sea Turtle Biology and Conservation, NOAA, Tech. Memo., NMFS-SEFSC-351, 306 pp.

Marquez, M.R., R.A. Byles, P. Burchfield, M. Sanchez, P.J. Diaz F., M.A. Carrasco A., A.S. Leo P., and C. Jimenez O., (1996), *Good News! Rising Numbers of Kemp's Ridleys Nest at Rancho Nuevo, Tamaulipas, México*, Marine Turtle Newsletter 73:2-5.

Marquez, M.R., C. Penaflores, and J. Vasconcelos, (1996), *Olive Ridley Turtles (Lepidochelys Olivacea) Show Signs of Recovery at La Escobilla, Oaxaca*, Marine Turtle Newsletter 73:2-5.

Meylan, A., et. al., (1997 draft), *Biology and Status of the Hawkbill in the Caribbean*, IUCN/SSC Marine Turtle Specialist Group, Washington, DC, USA.

Meylan, A.B., (1982), *Sea Turtle Migration - Evidence from Tag Returns*, in: Bjorndal K.A. (ed.), Biology and Conservation of Sea Turtles, Smithsonian Institution Press, Wash, D.C., p. 91-100.

Mitchell, J.F., J.W. Watson, D.G. Foster, R.E. Caylor, (1995), *The Turtle Excluder Device (TED): a Guide to Better Performance*, NOAA, Tech. Memo., NMFS-SEFSC-366.

Mohanty-Hejmadi, P., (1994), *Latest Word on the Talachua Jetty, Orissa, India*, Marine Turtle Newsletter 67:1

Morreale, S.J., E.A. Standora, (1990), *Occurrence, Movement and Behaviour of the Kemp's Ridley and Other Sea Turtles in New York Waters*, Okeanos Ocean Research Foundation Annual Report, April 1989-April 1990.

Mortimer, J.A.a.C.A., (1987), *Reproduction and Migrations of the Ascension Island Green Turtle Chelonia Mydas*, Copeia 1:103-113.

Mrosovsky, N., S.R. Hopkins-Murphy, J.I. Richardson, (1984), *Sex Ratio of Sea Turtles: Seasonal Changes*, Science 225:739-741.

Murphy, T.M. and S.R. Hopkins-Murphy, (1989), *Sea Turtle and Shrimp Fishing Interactions: A Summary and Critique of Relevant Information*, Center for Marine Conservation, 52 pp.

Murphy, T.M. and S.R. Hopkins-Murphy, (1984), *Sea Turtle and Shrimp Fishing Interactions: A Summary and Critique of Relevant Information*, Wash. D.C.: Center for Marine Conservation, 60 pp.

Musick, J.A. and C.J. Limpus, (1996), *Habitat Utilization and Migration in Juvenile Sea Turtles*, in: Biology of sea turtles, P.-L. Lutz and J.A. Musick (eds), CRC Press Inc., New York, p. 137-164.

National Marine Fisheries Service and U.S. Fish and Wildlife Service, (1996a draft), *Recovery Plan for U.S. Pacific Populations of the Green Turtle (Chelonia Mydas)*, National Marine Fisheries Service, Silver Spring, MD., 73 pp.

National Marine Fisheries Service and U.S. Fish and Wildlife Service, (1996b draft), *Recovery Plan for U.S. Pacific Populations of the East Pacific Green Turtle (Chelonia Mydas)*, National Marine Fisheries Service, Silver Spring, MD., 51 pp.

National Marine Fisheries Service and U.S. Fish and Wildlife Service, (1996c draft), *Recovery Plan for U.S. Pacific Populations of the Olive Ridley Turtle (Lepidochelys Olivacea)*, National Marine Fisheries Service, Silver Spring, MD., 42 pp.

National Marine Fisheries Service and U.S. Fish and Wildlife Service, (1996d draft), *Recovery Plan for U.S. Pacific Populations of the Loggerhead Turtle (Caretta Caretta)*, National Marine Fisheries Service, Silver Spring, MD., 49 pp.

National Marine Fisheries Service and U.S. Fish and Wildlife Service, (1996e draft), *Recovery Plan for U.S. Pacific Populations of the Hawksbill Turtle (Eretmochelys Imbricata)*, National Marine Fisheries Service, Silver Spring, MD., 72 pp.

National Marine Fisheries Service and U.S. Fish and Wildlife Service, (1996f draft), *Recovery Plan for U.S. Pacific Populations of the Leatherback Turtle (Dermochelys Coriacea)*, National Marine Fisheries Service, Silver Spring, MD., 51 pp.

National Marine Fisheries Service and U.S. Fish and Wildlife Service, (1993), *Recovery Plan for Hawksbill Turtles in the U.S. Caribbean Sea, Atlantic Ocean, and Gulf of Mexico*, National Marine Fisheries Service, St. Petersburg, Florida, 47 pp.

National Marine Fisheries Service and U.S. Fish and Wildlife Service, (1992), *Recovery Plans for Leatherback Turtles in the U.S. Caribbean, Atlantic and Gulf of Mexico*, National Marine Fisheries Service, Washington D.C., 52 pp.

National Marine Fisheries Service and U.S. Fish and Wildlife Service, (1991a), *Recovery Plan for U.S. Population of Loggerhead Turtle, National Marine Fisheries Service*, Washington, D.C., 56 pp.

National Marine Fisheries Service and U.S. Fish and Wildlife Service, (1991b), *Recovery Plan for U.S. Population of Atlantic Green Turtle*, National Marine Fisheries Service, Washington, D.C., 52 pp.

National Marine Fisheries Service and U.S. Fish and Wildlife Service, (1992), *Recovery Plan for the Kemp's Ridley Sea Turtle (Lepidochelys Olivacea)*, National Marine Fisheries Service, St. Petersburg, Florida, 40 pp.

National Research Council, (1990), *Decline of the Sea Turtles: Causes and Prevention*, National Academy Press, Washington D.C., 259 pp.

Ogren, L.H., Watson, J.W. and Wickham, D.A. (1977), *Loggerhead Sea Turtles, Caretta Caretta, Encountering Shrimp Trawls*, Mar. Fish. Rev. 39(11):15-17.

Pandav, B. and B.C. Choudhury, (1995), *A note on the Occurance of Sub-Adult Olive Ridley Turtles Along the Gahirmatha Coast*, Marine Turtle Newsletter, 71:15-17.

Poiner, I.R., R.C. Buckworth, and A.N.M Harris, (1990), *Incidental Capture and Mortality of Sea*

*Turtles in Australia's Northern Prawn Fishery*, Aust. J. Mar. Freshwater Res., 41:97-110.

Pritchard, P.C.H., (1973), *International Migrations of South American Sea Turtles (Cheloniidae and Dermochelyidae)*, Anim Behav 21:18-27.

Pritchard, P.C.H., (1981a), *Marine Turtles of the South Pacific*, p. 253, in: Bjorndal, K.A. (ed.), Biology and Conservation of Sea Turtles, Smithsonian Institution Press, Wash. D.C., 583 pp.

Pritchard, P.C.H., (1981b), *Marine Turtles of Micronesia*, p. 263, in: Bjorndal, K.A. (ed.), Biology and Conservation of Sea Turtles, Smithsonian Institution Press, Wash. D.C., 583 pp.

Pritchard, P.C.H., (1982), *Nesting of the Leatherback Turtle, Dermochelys Coriacea in Pacific Mexico, with a New Estimate of the World Population Status*, Copeia 4:741-747.

Renaud, M., G. Gitschlag, E. Klima, A. Shah, D. Koi, and J. Nance, (1991), *Evaluation of the Impacts of Turtle Excluder Devices (TED's) on Shrimp Catch Rates in Coastal Waters of the United States Along the Gulf of Mexico and Atlantic, September 1989 through August 1990*, NOAA, Tech. Memo., NMFS-SEFC-288.

Renaud, M., G. Gitschlag, E. Klima, A. Shah, J. Nance, C. Caillouet, A. Zein-Eldin, D. Koi and F. Patella, (1990), *Evaluation of the Impacts of Turtle Excluder Devices (TED's) on Shrimp Catch Rates in Coastal Waters of the United States Along the Gulf of Mexico and South Atlantic, March 1988 through July 1989*, NOAA, Tech. Memo., NMFS-SEFC-254.

Richardson, J.I., (1978), *Results of a Hatchery for Incubating Loggerhead Sea Turtle (Caretta Caretta) Eggs on Little Cumberland Island, Georgia*, Florida Marine Research Publ. 33:15.

Richardson, J.I., (1982), *A Population Model for Adult Female Loggerhead Sea Turtles (Caretta Caretta) Nesting in Georgia*, Ph.D. Dissertation, Univ. Georgia, Athens, Georgia, 233 p.

Richardson, J.I., (1992), *An Investigation of Survivorship, Mortality, and Recruitment of Adult Female Loggerhead Sea Turtles Nesting at Cumberland Island National Seashore, Georgia (1987-1991)*, Final Report, Georgia Sea Turtle Cooperative, University of Georgia, Athens, 35 p.

Richardson, J.I., T.H. Richardson and M.W. Dix, (1976), *Population Estimates for Nesting-Female Loggerhead Sea Turtles (Caretta Caretta) in the St. Andrews Sound Area of Southeastern Georgia, USA*, Florida Marine Research Pub No. 33:34-38.

Richardson, T.H., J.I. Richardson, C. Ruckdeschel and M.W. Dix, (1976), *Remigration Patterns of Loggerhead Sea Turtles (Caretta Caretta) Nesting on Little Cumberland and Cumberland Islands*, Georgia, Florida Marine Research Pub. No. 33:39-44.

Ross, J.P., (1996), *Caution Urged in the Interpretation of Trends at Nesting Beaches*, Marine Turtle Newsletter 74:9-10.

Sarti, L.M., S.A. Eckert, N. Garcia T. and A.R. Barragin, (1996), *Decline of the World's Largest Nesting Assemblage of Leatherback Turtles*, Marine Turtles Newsletter 74:2-4.

Senalak, S. and Sujittosakul, T., (1997), *Post-Evaluation of Thai Turtle Free Devices (TTFDs) Use With Shrimp Trawlers in East Coast of the Gulf of Thailand*, Tech. Paper No. 4, Dept. of Fisheries, Kasetglang, Chatuchak, Phaholyothin Road, Bangkok 10900, Thailand, 16 pp.

Shaver, D., (1996), *Head-started Kemp's ridley Turtles Nest in Texas*, Marine Turtle Newsletter, 74:5-7

Shoop, C.R., Kenney, R.D., (1992), *Seasonal Distribution and Abundances of Loggerhead and Leatherback Sea Turtles in Waters of the Northeastern United States*, Herpetological Monographs 1991(6): 67 p.

Spotila, J.R., A.E. Dunham, A.J. Leslie, A.C. Steyermark, P.T. Plotkin, and F.V. Paladino, (1996), *Worldwide Population Decline of Dermochelys coriacea: Are Leatherback Turtles Going Extinct?*, Chel. Cons. Biol. 2(2):209-222.

Stabenau, E.K., T.A. Heming, J.F. Mitchell, (1991), *Respiratory, Acid-Base and Ionic Status of Kemp's Ridley Sea Turtles (Lepidochelys Kempi) Subjected to Trawling*, Comp. Biochem. Physiol. 99A(1/2):107-111.

Stark, M., (1993), *Field Survey of Leatherback Nesting Beaches in the Bird's Head Region, Irian Jaya, Is Renewed*, Marine Turtle Newsletter, 60:1-4.

Stinson, M.L., (1984), *Biology of Sea Turtles in San Diego Bay, California and in the Northeastern Pacific Ocean*, MS Thesis, San Diego State University.

Stoneburner, D.L., J.I. Richardson and G.K. Williamson, (1982), *Observations on the Movement of Hatchling Sea Turtles Caretta-Caretta*, Copeia 1982(4):963-965.

Stoneburner, D.L. and J.I. Richardson, (1981), *Observations on the Role of Temperature in Loggerhead Turtle Nest Site Selection*, Copeia 1:238-241.

Taylor, B.L., (1993), *Population Viability Analysis for the Little Cumberland Island Loggerhead Turtle Population*, Unpub Draft Report.

Van Buskirk, J.a.C., L.B., (1994), *Life-History Variation in Marine Turtles*, Copeia 1994(1):66-81.

Wetherall, J.A., G.H. Balazs, R.A. Tokunaga and Marian Y.Y. Yong, (1993), *Bycatch of Marine Turtles in North Pacific High-Seas Driftnet Fisheries and Impacts on the Stocks*, Bull. of the N. Pacific Commission, 53(III):519-538 .

Witzell, W.N., (1983), *Synopsis of Biological Data on the Hawksbill Turtle*, Eretmochelys Imbricata (Linnaeus, 1766), FAO Fisheries Synopsis No. 137.

**Cited by Dr. J. Frazier:**

Ackerman, R.A., (1997), *The nest environment and the embrionic development of sea turtles*, in: P.L. Lutz and J. A. Musick (eds.), The Biology of Sea Turtles, CRC Press, New York, pp. 83-106.

Ahmed, F., (1997), *In defense of land and livelihood: Coastal communities and the shrimp industry in Asia*, in: Consumers' Association of Penang, CUSO, Inter pares, Sierra Club of Canada, Quebec, Canada, 34 pp.

Akande, G. and J. Tobor, (1995), *Utilization of by-catch of shrimp in Nigeria*, in: F. Teutscher (technical secretary), Report and Proceedings, TCDC Workshop, Utilization of By-Catch from Shrimp Trawlers, Nose Bé, Madagascar, 6-8 June 1995, Government of Madagascar, United Nations Development Programme, Food and Agriculture Organization, pp. 70-76.

Ali, A., S.S.S. Alwi and Suppachai A., (1997), *Experiments on the use of turtle excluder devices (TEDs) in Malaysian waters*, in: Regional Workshop on Responsible Fishing, Bangkok, Thailand, 24-27 June 1997, SEAFDEC/RESF/97/WP.7, 11 pp.

Ali, R.B., (1995a), *The progress of selectivity studies in Malaysia*, in: J. Prado and F. A. Rahman (eds.), FAO/INFOFISH/SEAFDEC, Workshop on Research in the Selectivity of Fishing Gear and Methods in South East Asia and Selective Shrimp Fishing, Chendering, Malaysia, 28-30 May 1995, FAO Fisheries Circular No. 902, Food and Agriculture Organization of the United Nations, Rome, p. 5.

Ali, R.B., (1995b), *Shrimp trawl fishing methods in Malaysia*, in: J. Prado and F.A. Rahman (eds.), FAO/INFOFISH/SEAFDEC, Workshop on Research in the Selectivity of Fishing Gear and Methods in South East Asia and Selective Shrimp Fishing, Chendering, Malaysia, 28-30 May 1995, FAO Fisheries Circular No. 902, Food and Agriculture Organization of the United Nations, Rome, pp. 11-13.

Alverson, D.L., M.H. Freeberg, S.A. Murawski and J.G. Pope, (1994), *A global assessment of fisheries bycatch and discards*, in: FAO Fisheries Technical Paper 339, Food and Agriculture Organization of the United Nations, Rome, xxi + 236 pp.

Alverson, D.L. and S.E. Hughes, (1995), *Bycatch: From emotion to effective natural resource management*, in: T. Wray (technical editor), Solving Bycatch: Considerations for Today and Tommorrow, University of Alaska Sea Grant College Program, Fairbanks, Alaska, pp. 13-28.

Alverson, R., (1995), *Introduction*, in: T. Wray (technical editor), Solving Bycatch: Considerations for Today and Tommorrow, University of Alaska Sea Grant College Program, Fairbanks, Alaska, p. 3.

Andrew, N.L. and J.G. Pepperell, (1992), *The by-catch of shrimp trawl fisheries*, in: A.D. Ansell and R.N. Gibson (eds.), Oceanography and Marine Biology, Annual Review, 30:527-565.

Anon, (1982), *Migratory turtle threatened*, Statesman, 7 December 1982.

Anon, (1985), *Saving the ridley turtles*, Statesman, 20 April 1985.

Anon, (1986), *Rockets or ridleys?* Oryx, 20(4).

Anon, (1992), *Orissa jetty poses threat to sanctuary*, The Telegraph, 29 December 1992.

Anon, (1996), *Endangered turtles struggle to survive*, Statesman, 9 January 1996.

Anon, (1997a), *A breeding ground which has turned turtle*, Pioneer, 7 February 1997.

Anon, (1997b), *Over 5,000 olive ridleys, 10 dolphins die in 3 months*, Sun Times, 23 March 1997.

Anon, (1997c), *Mass killing of turtles in Orissa*, Asian Age, 24 March 1997.

Anon, (1997d), *Dead turtles found in Gahirmatha*, Telegraph, 24 March 1997.

Anon, (1997e), *High mortality of young turtles worries experts*, Indian Express, 4 April 1997.

Anon, (1997f), *Govt curbs to help Ridley turtle*, Pioneer, 10 June 1997.

Anon, (1997g), *Orissa plan to save sea turtles*, Indian Express, 10 November 1997.

Anon, (1997h), *Scientists, greens call for protection of olive ridley turtles,* Sun Times, 10 November 1997.

Anon, (1997i), *Shrinking rookery of turtles causes concern*, Times of India, 10 November 1997.

Anon, (1997j), *Gahirmatha*, Indian Express, 12 November 1997.

Arauz, R., (1990), *The importance of testing TED efficiency in Costa Rica*, in: T. H. Richardson, J. I. Richardson and M. Donnelly (compilers), Proceedings of the Tenth Annual Symposium on Sea Turtle Biology and Conservation, U.S. Department of Commerce, National Oceanographic and Atmospheric Administration, National Marine Fisheries Service, Southeast Fisheries Center, Miami, Florida, NMFS-SEFSC-278, pp. 51-53.

Arauz, R., (1996a), *A description of the Central American shrimp fisheries with estimates of incidental capture and mortality of sea turtles*, in: J.A. Keinath, D.E. Barnard, J.A. Musick and B.A. Bell (compilers), Proceedings of the Fifteenth Annual Symposium on Sea Turtle Biology and Conservation, U.S. Department of Commerce, National Oceanographic and Atmospheric Administration, National Marine Fisheries

Service, Southeast Fisheries Science Center, Miami, Florida, NMFS-SEFSC-387, pp. 5-9.

Arauz, R., (1996b), *Size of turtles captured along the western coast of Costa Rica during commercial shrimp operations*, Sea Turtle Restoration Project, Tibás, Costa Rica, 3 pp.

Arauz, R., (1997), *Letter to J. Frazier*, 17 December 1997, 1 p.

Arauz, R., R. Vargas, I. Naranjo and C. Gamboa, (1997a), *Analysis of the incidental capture and mortality of sea turtles in the shrimp fleet of Pacific Coasta Rica*, Sea Turtle Restoration Project, Tibás, Costa Rica, 5 pp.

Arauz, R., I. Naranjo, R. Rojas and R. Vargas, (1997b), *Evaluation of the Supper Shooter and Seymour turtle excluder devices with different deflector bar spacing in the shrimp fishery of Pacific Costa Rica*, Sea Turtle Restoration Project, Tibás, Costa Rica, 13 pp.

Asrar [*ne* Firdous], F.F., (1995?), *Marine turtles of Pakistan*, Sind Wildlife Management Department, Karachi, 5 pp.

Auster, P.J., R.J. Malatesta, R.W. Langton, L. Watling, P.C. Valentine, C.L.S. Donaldson, E.W. Langton, A.N. Shepard and I.G. Babb, (1996), *The impacts of mobile fishing gear on seafloor habitats in the Gulf of Maine (Northwest Atlantic): Implications for conservation of fish populations*, Reviews in Fisheries Science, 4(2):185-202.

Bailey, C., (1985), *The blue revolution: the impact of technological innovation on Third-World fisheries*, The Rural Sociologist, 5(4): 259-266.

Bailey, C., (1986), *Government protection of traditional resource use rights - the case of Indonesian fisheries*, in: D.C. Korten (ed.), Community Management: Asian Experience and Perspectives, Kumarin Press, West Hartford, Conn, pp. 292-308.

Bailey, C., (1988a), *The social consequences of tropical shrimp mariculture development*, Ocean & Shoreline Management, 11:31-44.

Bailey, C., (1988b), *Optimal development of Third World Fisheries*, in: M.A. Morris (ed.), North-South Perspectives on Marine Policy, Westview Press, Boulder, Colorado, pp.105-128.

Bailey, C., (1988c), *The political economy of fisheries development in the Third World*, Agricultural and Human Values, 5(1&2):35-48.

Bailey, C., (1988d), *The political economy of marine fisheries development in Indonesia*, Indonesia, 46:25-38.

Bailey, C., (1989), *Social issues in Third World fisheries development*, in: J.S. Thomas, L. Maril and E.P. Durrenberger (eds.), Marine Resource Utilization: A Conference on Social Science Issues, University of South Alabama Publication Services, Mobile, Alabama, pp. 137-143.

Bailey, C., D. Cycon and M. Morris, (1986), *Fisheries development in the Third World: The role of International agencies*, World Development, 14(10/11):1269-1275.

Bailey, C. and C. Zerner, (1988), *Community-based fisheries management institutions in Indonesia*, Marine Anthropological Studies, 5(1):1-17.

Bailey, C. and S. Jentoft, (1990), *Hard choices in fisheries development*, Marine Policy, 14(4):333-344.

Bailley, J. and B. Groombridge, (1996), *IUCN Red List of Threatened Animals*, IUCN, Gland, Switzerland.

Balazs, G.H., (1980), *Synopsis of biological data on the green turtle in the Hawaiian Islands*, U. S. Department of Commerce, National Oceanic and Atmospheric Administration, National Marine Fisheries Service, Southwest Fisheries Science Center, NOAA Technical Memorandum NMFS-SWFSC-7, 141 pp. (cited by K.L. Eckert, (1993), *The biology and population status of marine turtles in the north Pacific Ocean*, U.S. Department of Commerce, National Oceanic and Atmospheric Administration, National Marine Fisheries Service, Southwest Fisheries Science Center, NOAA Technical Memorandum NMFS-SWFSC-186, viii + 156.).

Balazs, G.H., (1982), *Driftnets catch leatherback turtles*, Oryx, 16(5):428-430.

Balazs, G.H., (1985), *Impact of ocean debris on marine turtles: entanglement and ingestion*, in: R.S. Shomura and H.O. Yoshida (eds.), Proceedings of the Workshop on the Fate and Impact of Marine Debris, U.S. Department of Commerce, National Oceanic and Atmospheric Administration, National Marine Fisheries Service, Southwest Fisheries Science Center, NOAA Technical Memorandum NMFS-SWFSC-54, pp. 387-429.

Balazs, G.H., (1994), *Homeward bound: Satellite tracking of Hawaiian green turtles from nesting beaches to foraging pastures*, in: B.A. Schroeder and B.E. Witherington (compilers), Proceedings of the Thirteenth Annual Symposium on Sea Turtle Biology and Conservation, U.S. Department of Commerce, National Oceanographic and Atmospheric Administration, National Marine Fisheries Service, Southeast Fisheries Center, Miami, Florida, NMFS-SEFSC-341 pp.

Balazs, G.H. and J.A. Wetherall, (1991), *Assessing impacts of North Pacific high-seas driftnet fisheries on marine turtles: Progress and problems*, presented at: North Pacific Driftnet Scientific Review Meeting; Sidney, British Columbia, Canada, 11-14 June 1991, 15 pp.

Balazs, G.H., P. Craig, B.R. Winßton and R.K. Miya, (1994), *Satellite telemetry of green turtles nesting at French Frigate shoals, Hawaii, and Rose Atoll, American Samoa*, in: K.A. Bjorndal, A.B. Bolten, D.A. Johnson and P.J. Eliazar (compilers), (1994), Proceedings of the Fourteenth Annual Symposium on Sea Turtle Biology and Conservation, U.S. Department of Commerce, National Oceanographic and Atmospheric Administration, National Marine Fisheries Service, Southeast Fisheries Center, Miami, Florida, NMFS-SEFSC-351, pp. 184-187.

Balzas, G.H., D.M. Ellis, W.G. Gilmartin and L.K. Katahira, (1997), *Use of satellite telemetry to determine the migratory routes and resident foraging habitats of nesting hawksbill turtles: A case study in the Hawaiian Islands*, in: The International Workshop on the Management of Marine urtles, 3-4 February 1997, Kuta, Bali, Indonesia, 10 p.

Balzas, G.H. and D.M. Ellis, in press, *Satellite telemetry of migrant male and female green turtles breeding in the Hawaiian Islands*, In: Proceedings of the Sixteenth Annual Symposium on Sea Turtle Biology and Conservation, U.S. Department of Commerce, National Oceanographic and Atmospheric Administration, National Marine Fisheries Service, Southeast Fisheries Center, Miami, Florida, NMFS-SEFSC.

Balzas, G.H, L.K. Katahira and D.M. Ellis, in press, *Satellite tracking of hawksbill turtles nesting in the Hawaiian Islands*, in: Proceedings of the Sixteenth Annual Symposium on Sea Turtle Biology and Conservation, U.S. Department of Commerce, National Oceanographic and Atmospheric Administration, National Marine Fisheries Service, Southeast Fisheries Center, Miami, Florida, NMFS-SEFSC.

Barraclough, S. and A. Finger-Stich, (1995), *Some ecological and social implications of commercial shrimp farming in Asia*, United Nations Research Institute for Social Development, Draft report, 55 pp.

Behera, C., (1997a), Ref. No. TED/PS-97, date 20.3.97, *Survey & video recording of mass killing of olive ridley sea turtles in the Gahirmatha coast by Project Swarajya on 18th & 19th of March '97* (The survey and video recording of mass killing of olive ridley sea turtles in the Gahirmatha beach under the Bhitarkanika Wildlife Sanctuary on 18th & 19th of March '97 by Project Swarajya, Cuttack: A Brief Report, Project Swarajya, Cuttack, Orissa, India.), 5 pp.

Behera, C., (1997b), *Letter to J. Frazier*, 7.4.1997, 1 p.

Behera, C., (1997c), *Letter to Earth Island Institute*, 8.4.97, 2 pp.

Bjorndal, K.A., (1997), *Foraging ecology and nutrition of sea turtles*, in: P.L. Lutz and J.A. Musick (eds.), *The Biology of Sea Turtles*, CRC Press, New York, pp. 199-231.

Bjorndal, K.A. and Zug G.R., (1995), *Growth and age of sea turtles*, in: K.A. Bjorndal (ed.), *Biology and Conservation of Sea Turtles*, (revised edition), Smithsonian Institution Press, Washington, D.C., pp. 599-600.

Bolten, A.B. and G.H. Balazs, (1995), *Biology of the early pelagic stage - the "lost year"*, in: K.A. Bjorndal (ed.), *Biology and Conservation of Sea Turtles* (revised edition), Smithsonian Institution Press, Washington, D.C. pp. 579-581.

Bostock, T. and J. Ryder, (1995), *By-catch usage in India: An NRI/ODA BOBP project experience*, in: F. Teutscher (technical secretary), Report and Proceedings, TCDC Workshop, Utilization of By-Catch from Shrimp Trawlers, Nose Bé, Madagascar, 6-8 June 1995, Government of Madagascar, United Nations Development Programme, Food and Agriculture Organization, pp. 40-50.

Bowen, B.W., (1995), *Molecular genetic studies of marine turtles*, in: K.A. Bjorndal (ed.), *Biology and Conservation of Sea Turtles* (revised edition), Smithsonian Institution Press, Washington, D.C. pp. 585-587.

Bowen, B.W. and S.A. Karl, (1997), *Population genetics, phyogeography, and molecular evolution*, in: P.L. Lutz and J.A. Musick (eds.), *The Biology of Sea Turtles*. CRC Press, New York, pp. 29-50.

Brongersma, L., (1972), *European Atlantic turtles*, Zool, Verhand, Leiden, 121:1-318.

Bundit, C., Yuttana, T., Supachai, A., Somboon, S., Lertchai, P., Peera Aosomboon and A. Ali, (1996), *The experiments on turtle excluder devices (TEDs) for shrimp trawl nets in Thailand*, Regional Workshop on Responsible Fishing, Bangkok, Thailand, 24-27 June 1997, SEAFDEC/RESF/97/WP.6. 43 pp.

Canin, J., (1989), *Greenpeace guest editorial: IUCN Resolution*, Marine Turtle Newsletter, 44:1-4.

Carr, A., M.H. Carr and A.B. Meylan, (1978), *The ecology and migrations of sea turtles*, 7, *The West Caribbean green turtle colony*, Bulletin American Museum Natural History, 162(1):1-46.

Chaloupka, M.Y. and J.A. Musick, (1997), *Age, growth, and population dynamics*, in: P.L. Lutz and J.A. Musick (eds.), *The Biology of Sea Turtles*, CRC Press, New York, pp. 233-276.

Chan, E.H., (1991), *Sea turtles*, in: R. Kiew (ed.), The State of Nature Conservation in Malaysia, Malayan Nature Society, Kuala Lumpur, pp. 120-134.

Chan, E.-H. and H.-C. Liew, (1986), *Characteristics of an exploited tropical shallow-water demersal fish community in Malaysia*, in: J.L. Maclean, L.B. Dizon and L.V. Hosillos (eds.), *Proceedings of the First Asian Fisheries Forum*, 26-31 May 1986, Manila, Asian Fisheries Society, pp. 349-352.

Chan, E.H. and H.C. Liew, (1996a), *Decline of the leatherback population in Terengganu*, Malaysia, 1956-1995, Chelonian Conservation and Biology, 2(2):196-203.

Chan, E.H. and H.C. Liew, (1996b), *A management plan for the green and hawksbill turtle populations of the Sabah turtle islands*, A Report to Sabah Parks.

Chan, E H., H.C. Liew and A.G. Mazlan, (1988), *The incidental capture of sea turtles in fishing gear in Terengganu*, Malaysia, Biological Conservation 43:1-7.

Chee, P.-E., (1997), *A review of the bycatch and discards in the fisheries of Southeast Asia*, in: I.J. Clucas and D.G. James (eds.), (19979, *Papers presented at the technical consultation on Reduction of Wastage in Fisheries*, Tokyo, Japan, 28 October - 1 November 1996, FAO Fisheries Report, No. 547, Supplement, Rome, FAO, pp. 257-270.

Choudhury, B.C., in press, *Country Report: India*, Proceedings of the Northern Indian Ocean Sea Turtle Workshop and Strategic Planning Session, Bhubaneshwar, Orissa, India, 13-18 January 1997.

Christian, P.A. and D.L. Harrington, (1988), *Soft turtle excluder device (TED) testing at Cape Canaveral, Florida*, in: B.A. Schroeder (compiler), Proceedings of the Eighth Annual Workshop on Sea Turtle Biology and Conservation, U.S. Department of Commerce, National Oceanographic and Atmospheric Administration, National Marine Fisheries Service, Southeast Fisheries Center, Miami, Florida, NOAA Tec. Mem. NMFS-SEFC-214, pp.7-10.

CIEL (Center for International Environmental Law), (1997), *Amicus Brief to the Panel on United States - Import Prohibition of Certain Shrimp and Shrimp Imports*, Center for Marine Conservation, Red Nacional de Acción Ecológica, The Environmental Foundation Ltd., and The Philippine Ecological Network, (vi), iii + 39 pp.

Clifton, K., D.O. Cornejo and R.S. Felger, (1982), *Sea turtles of the Pacific coast of Mexico*, in: K.A. Bjorndal (ed.), *Biology and Conservation of Sea Turtles*, Smithsonian Institution Press, Washington, D.C. pp. 199-209.

Clucas, I.J., (1997a), *Reduction of fish wastage - an introduction*, in: I.J. Clucas and D.G. James (eds.), (1997), *Papers presented at the technical consultation on Reduction of Wastage in Fisheries*, Tokyo, Japan, 28 October-1 November 1996, FAO Fisheries Report, No. 547, Supplement, Rome, FAO, pp. 1-14.

Clucas, I.J., (1997b), *The utilisation of bycatch/discards*, in: I.J. Clucas and D.G. James (eds.), 1997, Papers presented at the technical consultation on Reduction of Wastage in Fisheries, Tokyo, Japan, 28 October-1 November 1996, FAO Fisheries Report, No. 547, Supplement, Rome, FAO, pp. 59-67.

Clucas, I., (1997c), *A study of the options for utilization of bycatch and discards for marine capture fisheries*, FAO Fisheries Circular, No. 928, Rome, FAO, 59 pp.

Clucas, I.J. and D.G. James (eds.), (1997), *Papers presented at the technical consultation on Reduction of Wastage in Fisheries*, Tokyo, Japan, 28 October-1 November 1996, FAO Fisheries Report, No. 547, Supplement, Rome, FAO, 338 pp.

Cornelius, S.E., (1982), *Status of sea turtles along the Pacific coast of middle America*, in: K.A. Bjorndal (ed.), Biology and Conservation of Sea Turtles (revised edition), Smithsonian Institution Press, Washington, D.C. pp. 211-219.

Crowder, L.B., D.T. Crouse, S.S. Heppell and T.H. Martin, (1994), *Predicting the impact of turtle excluder devices on loggerhead sea turtle populations*, Ecological Applications 4(3):437-445.

Crowder, L.B., S.R. Hopkins-Murphy and J.A. Royle, (1995), *Effects of turtle excluder devices (TEDs) on loggerhead sea turtle strandings with implications for conservation*, Copeia, 1995(4):773-779.

Crouse, D., (1996), *Message sent to "readers of CTURTLE*, subject: Malaysian headstarting announcement, 4 November 1996, Center for Marine Conservation, Washington, D.C. 3 pp.

Crouse, D.T., L.B. Crowder and H. Caswell, (1987), *A stage-based population model for loggerhead sea turtles and implications for conservation*, Ecology, 63(5): 1412-1423.

Crouse, D.T. and N.B. Frazer, (1995), *Population models and structure*, in: K.A. Bjorndal (ed.), *Biology and Conservation of Sea Turtles* (revised edition), Smithsonian Institution Press, Washington, D.C. pp. 601-603.

Dash, M.C. and C.S. Kar, *The Turtle Paradice: Gahirmatha*, Interprint, New Delhi, 295 pp.

Debnath, H., (1994), Country Report - India. *In:* SAMUDRA. *The Cebu Conference, Proceedings.* International Collective in Suport of Fishworkers; Madras, India. pp. 232-241.

DENR (Department of Environment and Natural Resources, The Philippines) and WRI (World Resources Institute, United States), (1997), *Conservation and Sustainable use of coastal and marine biological diversity - The way forward, A view from Southeast Asia*, Recommendions from the southease Asia Regional Workshop on Marine Biodiversity and the Convention on Biolgocial Diversity, October 24-25, 1996, Subic Bay, the Phillippines, To the Thrid Meeting of the Subsidiary Body on scientific, Technical, and Technological Adivce (SBSTTA), September 1-5, 1997, Montreal, Canada, 10 pp.

Department of Fisheries, Government of Orissa and Project Swarajya, (1997), *Workshop on Turtle Excluder Device*, 11-14 November 1996, Paradip, A report, pag. var.

Dickson, J.O., (1997), *Study on turtle excluder and by-catch reduction devices in the Philippines*, Regional Workshop on Responsible Fishing, Bangkok, Thailand, 24-27 June 1997, SEAFDEC/RESF/97/WP.6, 22 pp.

Dilday, W.E., (1995), *U.S. diplomatic involvement in fisheries bycatch issues*, in: T. Wray (technical editor), Solving Bycatch: Considerations for Today and Tommorrow, University of Alaska Sea Grant College Program, Fairbanks, Alaska, pp. 301-305.

di Silva, G.S., (1982), *The status of sea turtle population in East Malaysia and the South China Sea*, in: K.A. Bjorndal (ed.), Biology and Conservation of Sea Turtles, Smithsonian Institution Press, Washington, D.C., pp. 327-337.

Dodd, C.K., (1988), *Synopsis of the biological data on the loggerhead sea turtle, Caretta caretta* (Linnaeus, 1758), U.S. Fish and Wildlife Service, Biological Report 88(14), 110 pp.

Donnelly, M., (1994), *Sea turtle mariculture: A review of relevant information for conservation and commerce,* Center for Marine Conservation, Washington, D.C., 113 pp.

Dutton, P.H., G.H. Balazs and A.E. Dizon, in press, *Genetic stock identification of sea turtles caught in the Hawaii-based pelatic longline fishery*, in: Proceedings of the 17th Annual Sea Turtle Symposium.

Earth Negotiations Bulletin, (1995), Resolution (AIC.2149.I.50.Rev 1) of the UN General Assembly Conference on Straddling Fish Stocks and Highly Migratory Fish Stocks: entitled *Fisheries by-catch and discards and their impact on the sustainable use of the world's living marine resources* (cited by Bostock, T. and J. Ryder (1995), *By-catch usage in India: An NRI/ODA BOBP project experience*, in: F. Teutscher (technical secretary), Report and Proceedings, TCDC Workshop, Utilization of By-Catch from Shrimp Trawlers; Nose Bé, Madagascar, 6-8 June 1995, Government of Madagascar, United Nations Development Programme, Food and Agriculture Organization, p. 40).

Easeley, J.E., (1982), *A preliminary estimate of the payoff to investing in a turtle excluder device for shrimp trawls*, Final report prepared for Monitor International and The Center for Environmental Education, 16 pp.

Eckert, K.L., (1993), *The biology and population status of marine turtles in the north Pacific Ocean*, U.S. Department of Commerce, National Oceanic and Atmospheric Administration, National Marine Fisheries Service, Southwest Fisheries Science Center, NOAA Technical Memorandum NMFS-SWFSC-186, viii + 156.

Eckert, K.L., (1995), *Anthropogenic threats to sea turtles*, in: K.A. Bjorndal (ed.) (1995), Biology and Conservation of Sea Turtles (revised edition), Smithsonian Institution Press, Washington, D. C., pp. 611-612.

Eckert, S.A. and L. Sarti M., (1997), *Distant fisheries implicate in the loss of the world's largest leatherback nesting population*, Marine Turtle Newsletter 78:2-7.

Emerson, D.K., (1980), *Rethinking artisanal fisheries development: Western concepts, Asian experiences*, Staff working paper No. 423, The World Bank, Washington, D.C., (cited in: C. Bailey, (1985), *The blue revolution: the impact of technological innovation on Third-World fisheries*, The Rural Sociologist, 5(4):259-266.)

Europa, (1997), *The Europa World Year Book*, (1997), Volume II Kazakstan - Zimbabwe, Europa Publications, London.

Everett, G.V., (1995), *Fisheries bycatch and discards: A report from FAO*, in: T. Wray (technical editor), Solving Bycatch: Considerations for Today and Tommorrow, University of Alaska Sea Grant College Program, Fairbanks, Alaska, pp. 279-283.

Everett, G.V., (1997), *Actions to reduce wastage through fisheries management*, in: I.J. Clucas and D.G. James (eds.), Papers presented at the technical consultation on Reduction of Wastage in Fisheries, Tokyo, Japan, 28 October - 1 November 1996, FAO Fisheries Report No. 547, Supplement, Rome, FAO, pp. 45-58.

Eyabi-Eyabi, G., (1995), *Utilization of by-catch from shrimp trawlers in Cameroon*, in: F. Teutscher (technical secretary), Report and Proceedings, TCDC Workshop, Utilization of By-Catch from Shrimp Trawlers, Nose Bé, Madagascar, 6-8 June 1995, Government of Madagascar, United Nations Development Programme, Food and Agriculture Organization, pp. 19-24.

Fairley, S. (ed.), (1995), *Overfishing: Causes and consequences*, The Ecologist 25(2/3): 41-128.

FAO, (1994), *Report of the Expert Consultation on the Code of Conduct for Responsible Fishing - Fishing Operations*, Sidney, British Colombia, Canada, 6-11 June 1994, FAO Fisheries Report No. 506, Food and Agriculture Organization of the United Nations, Rome, 16 pp.

FAO, (1995), *Code of Conduct for Responsible Fisheries*, Food and Agriculture Organization of the United Nations, Rome, 41 pp.

FAO, (1997a), *Report of the Technical Consultation on Reduction of Wastage in Fisheries*, Tokyo, Japan, 28 October - 1 November 1996, FAO Fisheries Report No. 547, Food and Agriculture Organization of the United Nations, Rome, 27 pp.

FAO, (1997b), *Review of the state of world fisheries and aquaculture*, Food and Agriculture Organization of the United Nations, Rome.

FIELD (Foundation for International Environmental Law and Development), (1997), *WWF Amicus Brief to WTO Shrimp-Turtle Dispute*, World Wide Fund for Nature, Gland, Switzerland, 31 pp.

Firdous, F., (1989), *Dead turtles on Karachi coast*, typescript, Sind Wildlife Management Board, Karachi, Pakistan.

Firdous, F., (1991), *A turtle's journey from Pakistan (Karachi) to India (Gujarat)*, Marine Turtle Newsletter 53:18-19.

Firdous, F., in press. *Marine turtle conservation in Pakistan*, Proceedings of the Northern Indian Ocean Sea Turtle Workshop and Strategic Planning Session Bhubaneshwar, Orissa, India, 13-18 January 1997.

Folke, C. and N. Kautsky, (1989), *The role of ecosystems for a sustainable development of aquaculture*, Ambio, 18(4):234-243.

Fraser, T.M., Jr., (1960), *Rusembilan: A Malay Fishing Village in Southern Thailand*, Cornell University Press, Ithaca, New York.

Frazier, J., (1980), *Exploitation of marine turtles in the Indian Ocean*, Human Ecology, 8(4):329-370.

Frazier, J., (1982), *Status of sea turtles in the central western Indian Ocean*, in: K.A. Bjorndal (ed.) (1982), Biology and Conservation of Sea Turtles, Smithsonian Institution Press, Washington, D.C., pp. 385-398.

Frazier, J., (1997a), *Guest Editorial: Inter-American Convention for the Protection and Conservation of Sea Turtles*, Marine Turtle Newsletter, 78:7-13.

Frazier, J., (1997b), *Sustainable development: modern elixir or sack dress?*, Environmental Conservation, 24(2):182-193.

Frith, R., (1946), *Malay Fishermen: Their Pesant Economy*, Kegan Paul, Trench, Trubner & Co., Ltd., London.

García-Rodríguez, E., *Utilization of shrimp by-catch in Cuba*, in: F. Teutscher (technical secretary), Report and Proceedings, TCDC Workshop, Utilization of By-Catch from Shrimp Trawlers, Nose Bé, Madagascar, 6-8 June 1995, Government of Madagascar, United Nations Development Programme, Food and Agriculture Organization, pp. 25-28.

Gates, C.E., R.A. Valverde, C.L. Mo, A.C. Cháves, J. Ballesteros and J. Peskin, (1996), *Estimating arribada size using a modified instantaneous count procedure*, Journal of Agricultural, Biological, and Environmental Statistics, 1(3):275-287.

George, R.H., (1997), *Health problems and diseases of sea turtles*, in: P.L. Lutz and J.A. Musick (eds.), The Biology of Sea Turtles, CRC Press, New York, pp. 363-385.

Gibbons, D., (1976), *Public policy towards fisheries development in Peninsular Malaysia: A critical review emphasizing Penang and Kedah*, in: L.J. Fredericks (ed.), Proceedings of the Seminar on the Development of Fisheries Sector in Malaysia, Kuala Lumpur (cited by Mathew, S., (1990), *Fishing Legislation and Gear Conflicts in Asian*

*Countries*, SAMUDRA, International Collective in Support of Fishworkers, Madras, India, No. 1, 124 pp.)

Ginsberg, J., (1981), *The status of sea turtles in Tarutao National Park, Satun, Thailand*, Tigerpaper (FAO), 8(2):27-29.

Gordon, A., (1990), *By-catch from Indian Shrimp Trawlers in the Bay of Bengal, The Potential for Improved Utilization*, Report on work undertaken in India between September 1988 and October 1989, (cited by T. Bostock and J. Ryder (1995), *By-catch usage in India: An NRI/ODA BOBP project experience*, in: F. Teutscher (technical secretary), Report and Proceedings, TCDC Workshop, Utilization of By-Catch from Shrimp Trawlers, Nose Bé, Madagascar, 6-8 June 1995, Government of Madagascar, United Nations Development Programme, Food and Agriculture Organization, p. 42).

Goss, J., (1997), *Conflict and resistance in Indian shrimp aquaculture*, Third World Resurgence, No. 84:2-3.

Graham, G.L., (1995), *Finfish bycatch from the southeastern shrimp fishery*, in: T. Wray (technical editor), Solving Bycatch: Considerations for Today and Tommorrow, University of Alaska Sea Grant College Program, Fairbanks, Alaska, pp. 115-119.

Groombridge, B., (1989), *Aerial survey of the Baluchistan coast (Pakistan)*, Marine Turtle Newsletter, 46:6-9.

Groombridge, B., A.M. Kabraji and A.L. Rao, (1988), *Marine turtles in Baluchistan (Pakistan)*, Marine Turtle Newsletter, 42:1-2.

Guinea, M.L. and S. Whiting, (1997), *Sea turtle deaths coincide with trawling activities in Northern Australia*, Marine Turtle Newsletter, 77:11-14.

Hall, M.A., (1995), *Strategic issues in managing fishery bycatches*, in: T. Wray (technical editor), Solving Bycatch: Considerations for Today and Tommorrow, University of Alaska Sea Grant College Program, Fairbanks, Alaska, pp. 29-32.

Harrington, D.L. and R.A. Vendetti, Jr., (1995), *Shrimp trawl bycatch reduction in the southestern United States*, in: T. Wray (technical editor), Solving Bycatch: Considerations for Today and Tommorrow, University of Alaska Sea Grant College Program, Fairbanks, Alaska, pp. 12-135.

Harris, A.N. and I.R. Poiner, (1990), *By-catch of the prawn fishery of Torrews Strait; Composition and partitioning of discards into components that float or sink*, Aust. J. Mar. Freshwater Res, 41:37-52.

Helpin Herps, (1997), *TEDs today: Kachab's story*, Helpin Herps, Ahmedabad, 9 pp.

Henwood, T.A. and W.E. Stuntz, (1987), *Analysis of sea turtle captures and mortalities during commercial shrimp trawling*, Fisheries Bulletin 85(4):813-817.

Heppell, S.S., L.B. Crowder and D.T. Crouse, (1996a), *Models to evaluate headstarting as a management tool for long-lived turtles*, Ecological Applications, 6(2):556-565.

Heppell, S.S., C.J. Limpus, D.T. Crouse, N.B. Frazer and L.B. Crowder, (1996b), *Population model analysis for the loggerhead sea turtle, Caretta caretta, in Queensland*, Wildlife Research, 23:143-159.

Hill, G., (1992), *The sustainable sea turtle*, Marine Turtle Newsletter, 58:2-5.

Hillestad, H.O., J.I. Richardson, C. McVae, Jr. and J.M. Watson, Jr., (1982), *Worldwide incidental capture of sea turtles*, in: K.A. Bjorndal (ed.), (1982), Biology and Conservation of Sea Turtles, Smithsonian Institution Press, Washington, D.C., pp. 489-495.

Hillman, J.C. and T. Gebremariam, (1996), *The status of sea turtle conservation in Eritrea*, in: S.L. Humphrey and R.V. Salm (eds.), *Status of sea turtle conservation in the western Indian Ocean*, Regional Seas Reports and Studies, UNEP, Nairobi, Kenya, No. 165, pp. 41-56.

Hilmi, A.H., (1997), *Shrimp trawl net (modified) in Malaysia*, Southeast Asian Fisheries Development Center and Marine Fishery Resources, Kuala Terengganu, Malaysia, 13 pp.

Hirth, H.F., (1997), *Synopsis of the biological data on the green turtle Chelonia mydas (Linnaeus 1758)*, U.S. Department of the Interior, Fish and Wildlife Service, Washington, D.C. Biological Report 97 (1), v + 120 pp.

Howell, K.M. and C. Mbindo, (1996), *The status of sea turtle conservation in Tanzania*, in: S.L. Humphrey and R.V. Salm (eds.), *Status of sea turtle conservation in the western Indian Ocean*, Regional Seas Reports and Studies, UNEP, Nairobi, Kenya, No. 165, pp. 73-80.

IDRC (International Development Research Centre), (1982), *Fish By-Catch...Bonus from the Sea*, International Development Research Centre, Ottawa, Canada, 163 pp.

IUCN (World Conservation Union), (1995), *A Global Strategy for the Conservation of Marine Turtles*, IUCN/Species Survival Commission, Cambridge, UK, 26 pp.

IUCN (World Conservation Union), (1996), *A Marine Turtle Conservation Strategy and Action Plan for the Western Indian Ocean,* IUCN/Species Survival Commission, Cambridge, UK, 24 pp.

IUCN (World Conservation Union), in press, *A Marine Turtle Conservation Strategy and Action Plan for the Northern Indian Ocean*, IUCN/Species Survival Commission, Cambridge, UK.

Jackson, J.B.C., (1997), *Reefs since Columbus*, Coral Reefs, 16.

Jallow, A.M., (1995), *Recent positive and negative experiences on the utilization of shrimp by-catch in the Gambia*, in: F. Teutscher (technical secretary), Report and Proceedings, TCDC Workshop, Utilization of By-Catch from Shrimp Trawlers, Nose Bé, Madagascar, 6-8 June 1995, Government of Madagascar, United Nations Development Programme, Food and Agriculture Organization, pp. 29-35.

James, P.S.B.R., M. Rajagopalan, S.S. Dan, A.B. Fernando and V. Selvaraj, (1989), *On the mortality and stranding of marine mammals and turtles at Gahirmatha, Orissa from 1983 to 1987*, Journal of the Marine Biological Association of India, 31(1 & 2): 28-35.

James, P.S.B.R., M. Rajagopalan, S.S. Dan, A.B. Fernando and V. Selvaraj, (1991), *Observations on mass nesting of the olive ridley Lepidochelys olivacea at Gahirmatha, Orissa during the 1987 season*, Journal of the Marine Biological Association of India, 33(1 & 2): 69-75.

Kabraji, A.M. and F. Firdous, (1984), *Conservation of Turtles: Hawksbay and Sandspit, Pakistan*, World Wildlife Fund Project 1451, World Wildlife Fund International and Sind Wildlife Management Board, Karachi, v + 52 pp.

Kaplan, R.D., (1994), *The coming of anarchy*, Atlantic Monthly, February 1994:44-76.

Kar, C.S. and S. Bhaskar, (1982), *Status of sea turtles in the eastern Indian Ocean*, in: K.A. Bjorndal (ed.), (1982), *Biology and Conservation of Sea Turtles*, Smithsonian Institution Press, Washington, D. C., pp. 365-372.

Kelleher, V. and A. Mussa, (1995), *Retention of by-catch for human consumption: The Mozambique experience*, in: F. Teutscher (technical secretary), Report and Proceedings, TCDC Workshop, Utilization of By-Catch from Shrimp Trawlers, Nose Bé, Madagascar, 6-8 June 1995, Government of Madagascar, United Nations Development Programme, Food and Agriculture Organization, pp. 60-69.

Kendall, D., (1989), *Fishing characteristics of the Morrison soft TED*, in: S.A. Eckert, K.L. Eckert and T.H. Richardson (compilers), Proceedings of the Ninth Annual Workshop on Sea Turtle Conservation and Biology, U.S. Department of Commerce, National Oceanographic and Atmospheric Administration, National Marine Fisheries Service, Southeast Fisheries Center, Miami, Florida, NMFS-SEFC-232, pp. 77-79.

Kennelly, S.J. and M.K. Broadhurst, (1995), *Fishermen and scientists solving bycatch problems: Examples from Australia and possibilities for the northeastern Unites States*, in: T. Wray (technical editor), Solving Bycatch: Considerations for Today and Tommorrow, University of Alaska Sea Grant College Program, Fairbanks, Alaska, pp. 121-128.

Kent, G., (1980), *Waste and malnutrition at sea*, Food Monitor, 17:4-8.

Kent, G., (1983), *The pattern of fish trade*, ICLARM Newsletter, April 1983, pp. 12-13.

Kent, G., (1984), *National fishery policies and the alleviation of malnutrition in the Philippines and Thailand*, FAO Fisheries Circular No.777FIIU/C777, United Nations Development Programme, Food and Agriculture Organization, Rome, v + 31 pp.

Kent, G., (1985), *Fisheries and undernutrition*, Ecology of Food and Nutrition, 46:281-294.

Kent, G., (1986), *The industrialization of fisheries*, Peasant Studies, 13(2):133-143.

Kent, G., (1987), *Fish and nutrition in India*, Food Policy, 12(2):161-175.

Kent, G., (1989), *Overselling fisheries trade: The European Community and the Third World*, Unpublished manuscript, 16 + 2 pp.

Kent, G., (1994), *Fisheries, nutrition, and nutrition rights*, Unpublished manuscript, 21 pp.

King, F.W., (1982), *Historical review of the decline of the green turtle and the hawksbill*, K.A. Bjorndal (ed.), (1982), Biology and Conservation of Sea Turtles, Smithsonian Institution Press, Washington, D. C., pp. 183-188.

Klima, E., M. Renauld and G. Gitschlang, (1989), *Evaluation of commercial use of TEDs*, in: S.A. Eckert, K.L. Eckert and T.H. Richardson (compilers), Proceedings of the Ninth Annual Workshop on Sea Turtle Conservation and Biology, U.S. Department of Commerce, National Oceanographic and Atmospheric Administration, National Marine Fisheries Service, Southeast Fisheries Center, Miami, Florida, NMFS-SEFC-232, p. 81.

Klima, E., G. Gitschlang and M. Renauld, (1992), *Evaluation of commercial use of turtle excluder devices (TEDs) in the Gulf of Mexico and South Atlantic*, in: Salmon, M. and J. Wyneken (compilers), Proceedings of the Eleventh Annual Workshop on Sea Turtle Biology and Conservation, U.S. Department of Commerce, National Oceanographic and Atmospheric Administration, National Marine Fisheries Service, Southeast Fisheries Center, Miami, Florida, NOAA Tec. Mem. NMFS-SEFSC-302, p. 68.

Kungsuwan, A., (1995), *Utilization of by-catch from shrimp trawlers in Thailand*, in: F. Teutscher (technical secretary), Report and Proceedings, TCDC Workshop, Utilization of By-Catch from Shrimp Trawlers, Nose Bé, Madagascar, 6-8 June 1995, Government of Madagascar, United Nations Development Programme, Food and Agriculture Organization, pp. 87-94.

Kungsuwan, A., (1996), *Regulations, practices and statistics with regard to by-catch in the shrimp industries in Thailand*, Paper prepared for FAO (55.08FT), 13 pp.

Laist, D.W., (1995), *Marine debris entanglement and ghost fishing: A cryptic and significant type of bycatch?* in: T. Wray (technical editor), Solving Bycatch: Considerations for Today and Tommorrow, University of Alaska Sea Grant College Program, Fairbanks, Alaska, pp. 33-39.

Leh, C.M.U., (1989), *The green turtle, Chelonia mydas (L.) in Sarawak: Is there a future?* in: S.M. Phang, A. Sasekumar and S. Vickineswary (eds.), Proceedings 12th Annual Seminar of the Malaysian Society of Marine Seciences, Kuala Lumpur, Malaysia: 219-227.

Lekagul, B., and D. Daman, (1977), *Sea turtles*, Conservation News (Assoc. Cons. Wild., Bangkok), 1977:5.

Leong, T.S. and K.T. Siow, (1980), *Sea turtles in the east coast of Peninsular Malaysia and their economic importance*, in: T.E. Chua and J.K. Charles (eds.), Coastal Resources of East Coast Peninsular Malaysia, Universiti Sains Malaysia, pp. 319-346 (cited by E.H. Chan and H.C. Liew, (1996b), *Decline of the leatherback population in Terengganu, Malaysia, 1956-1995*, Chelonian Conservation and Biology, 2(2):196).

Lieveld, R., (1995), *Utilization of shrimp by-catch in Suriname*, in: F. Teutscher (technical secretary), Report and Proceedings, TCDC Workshop, Utilization of By-Catch from Shrimp Trawlers, Nose Bé, Madagascar, 6-8 June 1995, Government of Madagascar, United Nations Development Programme, Food and Agriculture Organization, pp. 77-80.

Liew, H.C., in press, *Country Report for Malaysia*, Proceedings of the Northern Indian Ocean Sea Turtle Workshop and Strategic Planning Session, Bhubaneshwar, Orissa, India, 13-18 January 1997.

Liew, H.C., E.H. Chan, F. Papi and P. Luschi, (1995a), *Long distance migration of green turtles from Redang Island: The need for regional cooperation in sea turtle conservation*, in: B. Devaux (technical director), Proceedings International Congress of Chelonian Conservation, Gonfaron, France, Editions SOPTOM, pp. 73-75.

Liew, H.C., E.H. Chan, P. Luschi and F. Papi, (1995), *Satellite tracking data on Malaysian green turtle migration*, Rend. Fis. Acc. Lincei, 9 (6): 239-246.

Limpus, C.J., (1982), *The status of Australian sea turtle populations*, in: K.A. Bjorndal (ed.), (1982), Biology and Conservation of Sea Turtles, Smithsonian Institution Press, Washington, D.C., pp. 297-303.

Limpus, C.J., (1994), *Current declines in South East Asian turtle populations*, in: B.A. Schroeder and B.E. Witherington (compilers), Proceedings of the Thirteenth Annual Symposium on Sea Turtle Biology and Conservation, U.S. Department of Commerce, National Oceanographic and Atmospheric Administration, National Marine Fisheries Service, Southeast Fisheries Center, Miami, Florida, NMFS-SEFSC-341, pp. 89-92.

Limpus, C.J. (1995), *Global overview of the status of marine turtles: A 1995 viewpoint*, in: K.A. Bjorndal (ed.), (1995), Biology and Conservation of Sea Turtles (revised edition), Smithsonian Institution Press, Washington, D.C., pp. 605-609.

Limpus, C.J. and N. Nicholls, (1988), *The southern oscillation regulates the annual numbers of green turtles (Chelonia mydas) breeding around northern Australia*, Australian Journal Wildlife Research, 15:157-161.

Limpus, C.J. and D. Reimer, (1994), *The loggerhead turtle, Caretta caretta, in Queensland: a population in decline*, in: R. James (compiler), Proceedings of the Australian Marine Turtle Conservation Workshop, Queensland Department of Environment and Heritage and Australian Nature Conservation Agency, Canbera, pp. 39-59.

Ludwig, D., R. Hilborn, and C. Walters, (1993), *Uncertainty, resource exploitation, and conservation: Lessons from history*, Science, 260:17, 36.

Lutcavage, M.E. and P.L. Lutz, (1991), *Voluntary diving metabolism and ventilation in the loggerhead sea turtle*, Journal of Experimental Marine Biology and Ecology, 147:287-296.

Lutcavage, M.E., P. Plotkin, B. Witherington and P.L. Lutz, (1997), *Human impacts on sea turtle survival*, in: P.L. Lutz and J.A. Musick (eds.), The Biology of Sea Turtles, CRC Press, New York, pp. 387-409.

Manger, V. and R. Chapman, (1996), *The status of marine turtle conservation in Mauritius*, in: S.L. Humphrey and R.V. Salm (eds.), Status of sea turtle conservation in the western Indian Ocean, Regional Seas Reports and Studies, UNEP, Nairobi, Kenya, No. 165, pp. 121-124.

Marcano, L.A. and J.J. Alio M., (1994), *Impacto de la pesca de arrastre sobre las poplaciones de tortugas marinas en la region oriental de Venezuela*, Informe Técnico FONAIAP, Cumaná, Venezuela, 8 pp.

Marcovaldi, M.A. and A. Filippini, (1991), *Trans-Atlantic Movement by a juvenile hawksbill turtle*, Marine Turtle Newsletter, 59:3.

Matchima Chanswangpuwana, (1996), *Small trawlers blamed for sea turtle losses*, Thai newspaper, 11 March 1996.

Mathew, S., (1990), *Fishing Legislation and Gear Conflicts in Asian Countries,* SAMUDRA, International Collective in Support of Fishworkers, Madras, India, No. 1, 124 pp.

McGoodwin, J.R., (1990), *Crisis in the World's Fisheries: People, Problems, and Politics*, Stanford University Press, Stanford, California, ix + 235.

Meylan, A., (1982a), *Sea turtle migration - evidence from tag returns*, in: K.A. Bjorndal (ed.), (1982), Biology and Conservation of Sea Turtles, Smithsonian Institution Press, Washington, D.C., pp. 91-100.

Meylan, A., (1982b), Estimating population size in sea turtles, in: K.A. Bjorndal (ed.), (1982), *Biology and Conservation of Sea Turtles*, Smithsonian Institution Press, Washington, D.C., pp. 135-138.

Meylan, A., *et al*, in prep, *Status of the Caribbean Hawksbill*, IUCN/SSC.

Mgawe, Y., (1995), *Recent positive and negative experiences in Tanzania with regard to utilization of shrimp by-catch*, in: F. Teutscher (technical secretary), Report and Proceedings, TCDC Workshop, Utilization of ByCatch from Shrimp Trawlers, Nose Bé, Madagascar, 6-8 June 1995, Government of Madagascar, United Nations Development Programme, Food and Agriculture Organization, Rome, pp. 81-88.

Miller, J.D., (1997), *Reproduction in sea turtles*, in: P.L. Lutz and J.A. Musick (eds.), The Biology of Sea Turtles,CRC Press, New York, pp. 51-81.

Milne, R.S. and D.K. Mauzy, (1986), *Malaysia: Tradition, Modernity, and Islam*, Westview Press, London.

Mishra, A., (1997), *Coast a graveyard for Ridley, dolphin, The Asian Age*, 29 March 1997.

Mitchell, J.F., (1991), *Turtle excluder device(TED) technology transfer to Latin American shrimp fisheries*, Marine Turtle Newsletter, 56:5-7.

Mitchell, R.R. Lohoefener and J. Watson, (1989), *A method for evaluating the exclusion of juvenile sea turtles from turtle excluder devices (TEDs)*, in: S.A. Eckert, K.L. Eckert and T.H. Richardson (compilers), Proceedings of the Ninth Annual Workshop on Sea Turtle Conservation and Biology, U.S. Department of Commerce, National Oceanographic and Atmospheric Administration, National Marine Fisheries Service, Southeast Fisheries Center, Miami, Florida, NMFS-SEFC-232, pp. 115-117.

Mitchell, J.F., J.W. Watson, W.R. Seidel and A K. Shah, (1990), *An alternative protocol for the qualification of new turtle excluder devices (TEDs)*, in: T.H.

Richardson, J.I. Richardson and M. Donnelly (compilers), Proceedings of the Tenth Annual Symposium on Sea Turtle Biology and Conservation, U.S. Department of Commerce; National Oceanographic and Atmospheric Administration, National Marine Fisheries Service, Southeast Fisheries Center, Miami, Florida, NMFS-SEFSC-278, pp. 47-50.

Mohanty-Hejmadi, P. and G. Sahoo, (1994), *Biology of the olive ridleys of Gahirmatha*, Orissa, India, in: K.A. Bjorndal, A.B. Bolten, D.A. Johnson and P.J. Eliazar (compilers), (1994), Proceedings of the Fourteenth Annual Symposium on Sea Turtle Biology and Conservation, U.S. Department of Commerce, National Oceanographic and Atmospheric Administration, National Marine Fisheries Service, Southeast Fisheries Center, Miami, Florida, NMFS-SEFSC-351, xiv + 306 pp + appendix II.

Mohanty-Hejmadi, P. (Chair), (1996), *Sea turtles*, in: D. Obura, A. Hangakoon, H. Jayewardene and G. Stone (eds.), Integrating Marine Conservation in the Indian Ocean: 1996 and Beyond, Summary and Working Group Reports, 28 November- 1 December 1995, Mombasa, Kenya, Indian Icean Conservation Program, pp. 21-24.

Mortimer, J. A., (1990), *Marine turtle conservation in Malaysia*, in: T.H. Richardson, J.I. Richardson and M. Donnelly (compilers), Proceedings of the Tenth Annual Symposium on Sea Turtle Biology and Conservation, U.S. Department of Commerce, National Oceanographic and Atmospheric Administration, National Marine Fisheries Service, Southeast Fisheries Center, Miami, Florida, NMFS-SEFSC-278, pp. 21-24.

Mortimer, J.A., (1995), *Headstarting as a management tool*, in: K.A. Bjorndal (ed.), (1995), Biology and Conservation of Sea Turtles (revised edition), Smithsonian Institution Press, Washington, D.C., pp. 613-615.

Mrosovsky, N., (1982), *Editorial*, Marine Turtle Newsletter, 22:1-2.

Murawski, S.A., (1995), *Meeting the challenges of bycatch: New Rules and new tools*, in: T. Wray (technical editor), Solving Bycatch: Considerations for Today and Tommorrow, University of Alaska Sea Grant College Program, Fairbanks, Alaska, pp. 5-11.

Murphy, T.M. and S.R. Hopkins-Murphy, (1989), *Sea turtle & shrimp fishing interactions: A summary and critique of relevant information*, Center for Marine Conservation, Washington, D.C., iii + 52 pp.

Musick, J.A. and C.J. Limpus, (1997), *Habitat utilization and migration in juvenile sea turtles*, in: P.L. Lutz and J.A. Musick (eds.), The Biology of Sea Turtles, CRC Press, New York, pp. 137-163.

National Research Council, (1990), *Decline of the Sea Turtles: Causes and Prevention*, National Academy Press, Washington, D.C.

Nakahara, J. and R.A. Witton, (1971), *Developent and conflict in Thailand*, Southeast Asia Program, Department of Asian Studies, Cornell Univeristy, Ithaca, New York, Data Paper:80.

Nichols, S., (1989), *The bycatch issue*, in: D. Burrage (compiler), Proceedings of a Mississippi Sea Grant advisory service workshop, 12 April 1989, Mississippi State

University, Division of Agriculture, Forestry and Veterinary Medicine, Department of Information Services, pp. 40-45.

Norse, E.A., (1997a), *Bottom trawling: The unseen worldwide plowing of the seabed*, Scientific Newsletter from New England Biolabs 8(2):8-9.

Norse, E.A., (1997b), *Troubled Waters: A Call for Action*, Marine Conservation Biology Institute, Redmond, Washington, 11 pp.

Olguin P., José Gabriel, (1996), *Análisis de los Dipositivos Excluidores de Tortugas (DET) Tipo Morrison y su impacto sobre las Capturas de la flota Camaronera de Ciudad del Carmen, Campeche*, Unpublished Masters degree thesis, Departamento de Recursos del Mar, Centro de Investigaciones y de Estudios Avanzados del IPN, Unidad Mérida.

Olguin P., G.J. Frazier and J.C. Seijo (1996), *The impact of TEDs on the shrimp fishery in Campeche, Mexico*, in: J.A. Keinath, D.E. Barnard, J.A. Musick and B A. Bell (compilers), Proceedings of the Fifteenth Annual Symposium on Sea Turtle Biology and Conservation. U.S. Department of Commerce, National Oceanographic and Atmospheric Administration, National Marine Fisheries Service, Southeast Fisheries Center, Miami, Florida, NMFS-SEFSC-388, pp. 226-229.

Olsen, V.J., (1995), *Ways in which Norway is solving the bycatch problem*, in: T. Wray (technical editor), Solving Bycatch: Considerations for Today and Tommorrow, University of Alaska Sea Grant College Program, Fairbanks, Alaska, 289-291.

Oravetz, C.A., (1984), *Trawling efficiency device (TED) technology transfer program*, Marine Turtle Newsletter, 27:6-7.

Oravetz, C.A., (1988), *Status of federal regulations to reduce the incidental capture and mortality of sea turtles from shrimp trawling*, in: B.A. Schroeder (compiler), Proceedings of the Eighth Annual Workshop on Sea Turtle Biology and Conservation, U.S. Department of Commerce, National Oceanographic and Atmospheric Administration, National Marine Fisheries Service, Southeast Fisheries Center, Miami, Florida, NOAA Tec. Mem. NMFS-SEFC-214, pp. 75-77.

Oravetz, C.A., (1992), *The status of revisions to the TED regulations and implementation of Public Law 101-162 (the sea turtle conservation/shrimp embargo bill)*, in: Salmon, M. and J. Wyneken (compilers), Proceedings of the Eleventh Annual Workshop on Sea Turtle Biology and Conservation, U.S. Department of Commerce, National Oceanographic and Atmospheric Administration, National Marine Fisheries Service, Southeast Fisheries Center, Miami, Florida, NOAA Tec. Mem. NMFS-SEFSC-302, pp. 87-89.

Oravetz, C.A., and C.J. Grant, (1986), *Trawl efficiency device shows promise*, Australian Fisheries. February, 37-40.

O'Riordan, B., (1994), *Tangled webs of chaos adrift*, New Scientist, 20 August 1994, 1939:44-45.

Oruç, A.F. Demirayak and G. Sat, (1997), *Trawl fisheries in the eastern Mediterranean and it's impact on sea turtles*, The Society for the Protection of Nature, Istanbul, Turkey, 30 pp.

Paine, B.C. and J. Gruver, (1995), *Bycatch reduction: Achieving new objectives by innovative footrope and net configuration*, in: T. Wray (technical editor), Solving Bycatch: Considerations for Today and Tommorrow, University of Alaska Sea Grant College Program, Fairbanks, Alaska, p. 87.

Panda, P., (1997), *Dash urges new plan to save turtles*, Asian Age, 10 November 1997.

Pandav, B., B.C. Choudhury and C.S. Kar, (1997), *Olive Ridley Sea Turtle (Lepidochelys olivacea) and its Nesting Habitats Along the Orissa Coast, India: A Status Survey* (revised edition), Wildlife Insitute of India, Dehra Dun, (iv) + 48 pp.

Papi, F., H.C. Liew, P. Luschi and E.H. Chan, (1995), *Long-range migratory travel of a green turtle tracked by satellite: Evidence of navigational ability in the open sea*, Marine Biology, 12:171-175.

Pauly, D., (1988), *Fisheries research and the demersal fisheries of southeast Asia*, in: J.A. Gulland (ed.), Fish Population Dynamics, John Wiley & Sons Ltd.; London, pp. 329-348.

Pauly, D., (1995), *Fleet-operational, economic, and cultural determinants of bycatch uses in Southeast Asia*, in: T. Wray (technical editor), Solving Bycatch: Considerations for Today and Tommorrow, University of Alaska Sea Grant College Program, Fairbanks, Alaska, pp. 285-288.

Pauly, D. and Chua Thia Eng, (1988), *The overfishing of marine resources: Socioeconomic background in southeast Asia*, Ambio, 17(3):200-206.

Pauly D. and R. Neal, (1985), *Shrimp vs. Fish in Southeast Asian fisheries: The biological, technological and social problems*, in: Recursos Pesqueros Potenciales de México: La Pesca Acompañante del Camarón. Programa Universitario de Alimentos, Instituto de Ciencias del Mar y Limnología, Insituto Nacional de la Pesca, UNAM, México, D.F., pp. 487-510.

Phasuk, B., (1982), *Sea turtle conservation in Thailand*, Thai Fish, Gaz, 35(2):171-177.

Phillips, H.P., (1965), Thai Peasant Personality: *The Patterning of Interpersonal Behavior in the Village of Bang Chan*, University of California Press, Berkeley.

Pillai, N.S., (1995), *On-going research activities on selective shrimp trawling in India.* in: J. Prado and F.A. Rahman (eds.), FAO/INFOFISH/SEAFDEC, Workshop on Research in the Selectivity of Fishing Gear and Methods in South East Asia and Selective Shrimp Fishing, Chendering, Malaysia, 28-30 May 1995, FAO Fisheries Circular No. 902, Food and Agriculture Organization of the United Nations, Rome, pp. 13-15.

Pitman, R.L., (1990), *Pelagic distribution and biology of sea turtles in the eastern tropical Pacific*, in: T.H. Richardson, J.I. Richardson and M. Donnelly (compilers), Proceedings of the Tenth Annual Workshop on Sea Turtle Biology and Conservation, U.S. Department of Commerce, National Oceanographic and Atmospheric Administration, National Marine Fisheries Service, Southeast Fisheries Center, Miami, Florida, NOAA Tec. Mem. NMFS-SEFC-278, pp. 143-148.

Plotkin, P.T., R.A. Byles, D.C. Rostal and D.W. Owens, (1995), *Independent versus socially facilitated oceanic migrations of the olive ridley*, Lepidochelys olivacea, Marine Biology 122:137-143.

Plotkin, P.T., D.C. Rostal, R.A. Byles and D.W. Owens, (1997), *Reproductive and developmental synchrony in female*, Lepidochelys olivacea, Journal of Herpetology 31(1):17-22.

Poiner, I. and A. Harris, (1994), *The incidental capture and mortality of sea turtles in Australia's northern prawn fishery*, in: R. James (compiler), Proceedings of the Australian Marine Turtle Conservation Workshop, Queensland Department of Environment and Heritage and Australian Nature Conservation Agency, Canbera, pp. 127-135.

Polunin, N.V.C. and N.S. Nuitja, (1982), *Sea turtle populations of Indonesia and Thailand*, in: K.A. Bjorndal (ed.), (1982), Biology and Conservation of Sea Turtles, Smithsonian Institution Press, Washington, D.C., pp. 353-362.

Prado, J., (1992), *List of references on the selectivity of various fishing gears and methods: Research in this field*, FAO Fisheries Circular No. 850, Food and Agriculture Organization of the United Nations, Rome, iii + 150 pp.

Prado, J., (1997), *Technical measures for bycatch reduction*, in: I.J. Clucas and D.G. James (eds.), (1997), Papers presented at the technical consultation on Reduction of Wastage in Fisheries, Tokyo, Japan, 28 October-1 November 1996, FAO Fisheries Report, No. 547, Supplement, Rome, FAO, pp. 25-44.

Prado, J. and F.A. Rahman, (1995), FAO/INFOFISH/SEAFDEC, *Workshop on Research in the Selectivity of Fishing Gear and Methods in South East Asia and Selective Shrimp Fishing*, Chendering, Malaysia, 28-30 May 1995, FAO Fisheries Circular No. 902, Food and Agriculture Organization of the United Nations, Rome, iii + 29 pp.

Prado, J. and F.A. Rahman, (1996), *FAO/China Society of Fisheries Experts and Industry*, Consultation on Selective Fishing for Responsible Exploitation of the Marine Resources in Asia, Bejing, China, 12-17 October 1995, FAO Fisheries Report No. 545, Food and Agriculture Organization of the United Nations, Rome, v + 24 pp.

Pritchard, P.C.H. and R. Marquéz M., (1973), *Kemp's ridley turtle or Atlantic ridley Lepidochelys kempi*, IUCN Monograph, Marine Turtle Series No. 2, Morges, Switzerland, 30 pp.

Pritchard, P.C.H. and P. Trebbau, (1984), *The Turtles of Venezuela*, Society for the Study of Amphibians and Reptiles, 404 pp.

Pultz, S., D. O'Daniel, S. Krueger, H. McSharry and G. Balazs, (submitted), *Marine turtle study on the Island of Tinian*, Commonwealth of the North Mariana Islands, Micronesia.

Quarto, A., (1992), *Fishers among the mangroves*, Cultural Survival Quarterly, Winter 1992, pp. 12-15.

Rai, S., (1997), *Trawlers leave a trail of turtles' death*, Hindustan Times, 10 February 1997.

Renaud, M., G. Gitschlag, E. Klima, A. Shah, D. Koi and J. Nance, (1993), *Loss of shrimp by turtle excluder devices (TEDs) in coastal waters of the United States*, North Carolina to Texas: March 1988- August 1990, Fisheries Bulletin, 91:129-137.

Robins, J.B., (1995), *Estimated catch and mortality of sea turtles from the east coast otter trawl fishery of Queensland, Australia*, Biological Conservation, 75:157-167.

Robins-Troeger, J.B., R.C. Buckworth and M.C.L. Dredge, (1995), *Development of a trawl efficiency device (TED) for Australian prawn fisheries*, II Field evaluations of the AusTED, Fisheries Research, 22:107-117.

Robins, J.B., R.C. Buckworth, R.P. Mounsey and M.C.L. Dredge, (1997), *Development and application of AusTED in the Australian Trawl Industry*, Queensland Department of Primary Industries, Fisheries research & Development Corporation, Project No. 93/231.07 53, pp. + IV Appendices.

Romine, T., *Perspectives on the global fisheries crisis*, in: T. Wray (technical editor), Solving Bycatch: Considerations for Today and Tomorrow, University of Alaska Sea Grant College Program, Fairbanks, Alaska, pp. 61-69.

Ross, J.P., (1982), *Historical decline of loggerhead, ridley, and leatherback sea turtles*, in: K.A. Bjorndal (ed.), (1982), Biology and Conservation of Sea Turtles, Smithsonian Institution Press, Washington, D.C., pp. 189-195.

SAMUDRA, (1994), *The Cebu Conference, Proceedings,* International Collective in Support of Fishworkers, Madras, India, 346 pp.

Sarker, H.S., P. Mohanty-Hejmadi, W.R. Seidel, H. Lingham, K.P. Philip, C. Behera, R.S. Mishra, J. Ramesh, T.K. Patnaik, (1996), *Recommendations of the training-cum-demonstration workshop on turtle excluder device (TED) held at Paradeep, Orissa*, from 11-14 November 1996, Department of Fisheries, Government of Orissa & Project Swarajya, Cuttack, Orissa, 8 pp.

SEAFDEC, (1996), *TED gained Thai fishermen's acceptance*, SEAFDEC Newsletter July-September, pp. 11, 15.

SEAFDEC, (1997a), *Workshop on TED in Malaysia*, SEAFDEC Newsletter January-March 20(1):10

SEAFDEC, (1997b), *TED research in Malaysia proves another theory*, SEAFDEC Newsletter January-March 20(1).

SEAFDEC, (1997c), *TD promotes TED's in the region*, SEAFDEC World Wide Web page.

Seidel, W.R. and C. McVae, R., (1982), *Development of a sea turtle excluder shrimp trawl for the southeast U.S. penaeid shrimp fishery*, in: K.A. Bjorndal (ed.), (1982), Biology and Conservation of Sea Turtles, Smithsonian Institution Press, Washington, D.C., pp. 497-502.

Settle, S., (1995), *Status of nesting populations of sea turtles in Thailand and their conservation*, Marine Turtle Newsletter, 68:8-13.

Shaver, D.J., (1994), *Sea turtle strandings along the Texas coast reach alarming levels*, Marine Turtle Newsletter, 66:8-9.

Shaver, D.J., (1995), *Sea turtle strandings along the Texas coast again cause concern*, Marine Turtle Newsletter, 70:2-4.

Sierra Club Legal Defense Fund, (1997), *Statement of Scientists*, 12 pp.

Silas, E.G., (1984), *Observations on turtles at sea and in the Lakshadweep*, Central Marine Fisheries Researcy Institute Bulletin 35:59-61.

Silas, E.G., M. Rajagopalan and A. Bastian Fernando, (1983a), *Sea turtles of India - Need for a crash programme on conservation and effective management of the resource*, Marine Fisheries Information Service, (Special issue on management and conservation: Sea Turtles), 50:1-12.

Silas, E.G., M. Rajagopalan, A. Bastian Fernando and S.S. Dan, (1983b), *Marine turtle conservation and management: A survey of the situation in Orissa 1981/82 and 1982/83*, Marine Fisheries Information Service, (Special issue on management and conservation Sea Turtles), 50:13-23.

Silas, E.G., M. Rajagopalan and S.S. Dan, (1983c), *Marine turtle conservation and management: A survey of the situation in West Bengal 1981/82 and 1982/83, Marine Fisheries Information Service*, (Special issue on management and conservation Sea Turtles), 50:54-32.

Silas, E.G., M. Rajagopalan, S.S. Dan and A. Bastian Fernando, (1984), *Observations on the mass nesting and immediate postmass nesting influxes of the olive ridley Lepidochelys olivacea* at Gahirmatha, Orissa-1984 season, Central Marine Fisheries Researcy Institute Bulletin 35:76-82.

Silas, E.G., M. Rajagopalan, S.S. Dan and A. Bastian Fernando, (1985), *On the large and mini arribadas of the olive ridley Lepidochelys olivacea* at Gahirmatha, Orissa during the 1985 season, Marine Fisheries Information Service, 64:1-19.

Siow K.T. and E.O. Moll, (1982), *Status and conservation of estuarine and sea turtles in West Malaysian waters*, in: K.A. Bjorndal (ed.), (1982), Biology and Conservation of Sea Turtles, Smithsonian Institution Press, Washington, D.C., pp. 339-347.

Smith, A.R., (1997), *Selectivity in its wider context*, in: I.J. Clucas and D.G. James (eds.), (1997) Papers presented at the technical consultation on Reduction of Wastage in Fisheries, Tokyo, Japan, 28 October-1 November 1996, FAO Fisheries Report, No. 547, Supplement. Rome, FAO, pp. 15-23.

Smith, T.P., (1995), *Solving the bycatch problem: An economic perspecive*, in: T. Wray (technical editor), Solving Bycatch: Considerations for Today and Tommorrow, University of Alaska Sea Grant College Program, Fairbanks, Alaska, pp. 53-59.

Spring, C.S., (1982), *Status of marine turtle populations in Papua New Guinea*, in: K.A. Bjorndal (ed.), (1982), Biology and Conservation of Sea Turtles, Smithsonian Institution Press, Washington, D.C., pp. 281-291.

Sridhar, V., (1997a), *Threatened habitat: Olive ridley turtles on the Orissa coast need protection*, Frontline (New Delhi), 16 May 1997, pp. 66-69.

Sridhar, V., (1997b), *Tracking the olive ridley*, Frontline (New Delhi), 16 May 1997, pp. 70-71.

Stabenau, E.K., T.A. Heming and J F. Mitchell, (1991), *Respiratory, acid-base and ionic status of Kemp's ridley sea turtles* (*Lepidochelys kempi*) subjected to trawling, Comparative biochemistry and Physiology 99A, No. 1/2:107-111.

Stancyk, S.E., (1982), *Non-human predators of sea turtles and their control*, in: K.A. Bjorndal (ed.), (1982), Biology and Conservation of Sea Turtles, Smithsonian Institution Press, Washington, D.C., pp. 139-152.

Steiner, T., (1994), *Shrimpers implicated as strandings soar in USA*, Marine Turtle Newsletter, 67:2-5.

Stuart, E. and M. Cartin, (1994), *Conservation of sea turtles at two national parks on the Andaman sea coast of Thailand*, Marine Turtle Newsletter, 67:6-8.

Suliansa, M.S., P. Basintal and N.L. Chan, (1996), *Impacts of fishery related activities on sea turtles*, Paper presented at the National Seminar/Workshop on Marine Turtles and Terrapin Management, 22-23 October 1996, Cherating, Malaysia, 6 pp.

Supot C., (1997), *Status of marine turtles in Thailand*, Country Report presented at Northern Indian Ocean Workshop on Sea Turtles, Bhubaneshwar, India, January 1997.

Teutscher, F., (technical secretary), (1995a), *Report and Proceedings*, TCDC Worksh, Utilization of By-Catch from Shrimp Trawlers, Nose Bé, Madagascar, 6-8 June 1995, Government of Madagascar, United Nations Development Programme, Food and Agriculture Organization, 97 pp.

Teutscher, F., (1995b), *By-catch in tropical shrimp fisheries*, in: F. Teutscher (technical secretary), Report and Proceedings, TCDC Workshop, Utilization of By-Catch from Shrimp Trawlers, Nose Bé, Madagascar, 6-8 June 1995, Government of Madagascar, United Nations Development Programme, Food and Agriculture Organization, pp. 11-18.

TEWG (Turtle Expert Working Group), (1996), *Kemp's ridley sea turtle* (*Lepidochelys kempii*) status report, 28 June 1996, Unpublished manuscript, (deposited at Center for Marine Conservation, Washington, D.C.), 49 pp.

Tucker, A.D., J.B. Robins and D.P. McPhee, (1997), *Adopting turtle excluder devices in Australia and the United States: What are the differences in technology transfer, promotion, and acceptance?* Coastal Management, 25:405-421.

Tuoc, P., (1985), *Shrimp resource and reasonable utilization of by-catch from shrimp trawlers*, in: F. Teutscher (technical secretary), Report and Proceedings, TCDC Workshop, Utilization of By-Catch from Shrimp Trawlers, Nose Bé, Madagascar, 6-8 June 1995, Government of Madagascar, United Nations Development Programme, Food and Agriculture Organization, pp. 95-97.

Utting, P., (project co-ordinator), (1995), *States in Disarray: The Social Effects of Globalization*, United Nations Research Institute for Social Development (UNRISD) and Banson, Geneva & London, 172 pp.

Van Buskirk, J. and L. B. Crowder, (1994), *Life-history variation in marine turtles*, Copeia, 1994:66-81.

Walakkamon Lamwitwatkit, (1996), *Trawlers are behind sea turtle decline*, The Nation (Bangkok), 13 March 1996.

Wamukoya, G.M., F. Kaloki and C. Mbindo, (1996), *The status of sea turtle conservation in Kenya*, in: S.L. Humphrey and R.V. Salm (eds.), Status of sea turtle conservation in the western Indian Ocean, Regional Seas Reports and Studies, UNEP, Nairobi, Kenya, No. 165, pp. 57-72.

Watson, J.W. and W.R. Seidel, (1980), *Evaluation of techniques to decrease sea turtle mortalities in the southeastern United States shrimp fishery*, International Council for Exploration of the Seas, C.M., B 31:1-8.

Weber, M., D. Crouse, R. Irvin and S. Iudicello, (1995), *Delay and Denial: A political history of sea turtles and shrimp fishing*, Center for Marine Conservation, Washington, D.C., 46 pp.

West, B., (1995), *Turtle turmoil in India*, Earth Island Journal, Spring 1995, p. 8.

Witzell, W.N., (1994), *The origin, evolution and demise of the U.S. Sea Turtle Fisheries*, Marine Fisheries Review, 56(4):8-23.

World Bank, (1997), *World Development Indicators*, The World Bank, Washington, D.C.

World Conference on Sea Turtle Conservation, (1982), *Sea turtle conservation strategy*, Action plan for the conservation of sea turtles, Action projects, in: K.A. Bjorndal (ed.), (1982), Biology and Conservation of Sea Turtles, Smithsonian Institution Press, Washington, D.C., pp. 567-583.

Wray, T., (technical editor), (1995), *Solving Bycatch: Considerations for Today and Tommorrow*, University of Alaska Sea Grant College Program, Fairbanks, Alaska, ix + 322 pp.

Wright, A., (1984), *Letter to Shri. J. B. Patnaik*, Hon'ble Chief Minister of Orissa, 2 pp.

Wyneken, J., (1997), *Resolutions of the 17th Annual Symposium on Sea Turtles Biology and Conservation*, 4-8 March 1997, Orlando, Florida, USA, 9 pp.

Yamamoto, T., (1994), *Fishing rights and licences, A new fishery law may help*, SAMUDRA 10 & 11:29-30.

**Cited by Mr. M. Guinea:**

Broderick et. al., (1994), *Genetic Studies of the Hawksbill Turtle Eretmochelys Imbricata: Evidence for Multiple Stocks in Australian Waters*, Pacific Conservation Biology, Vol. 1 No. 2, p. 123-131.

Carr, A., (1973), *So Excellent a Fish*, Anchor Press.

Chaloupka, M.Y. and Musick, J.A., (1997), *Age, Growth and Population Dynamics*, in: Lutz, P.L. and J.A. Musick (ed.), The Biology of Sea Turtles. CRC Press pp 234-276.

Chan, E.H., H.C. Liew and A.G. Mazlan, (1987), *The Incidental Capture of Sea Turtles in Fishing Gear in Terengganu, Malaysia*, Biological Conservation, 1-7.

Chatto, R., M. Guinea and S. Conway, (1995), *Sea Turtles Killed by Flotsam in Northern Australia*, Marine Turtle Newsletter, 69:17-8.

Chokesanguan, B., Y. Theparoonrat, S. Ananpongsuk, A. Siriraksophon, L. Podapol, P. Aosomboon, and A. Ali, (1996), *The Experiments on Turtle Excluder Devices (TEDs) for Shrimp Trawl Nets in Thailand.*

Crouse, D.T., L.B. Crowder, H. Caswell, (1987), *A Stage-Based Model for Loggerhead Sea Turtles and Implications for Conservation*, Ecology, 68(5):1412-1423.

Davis, T.A. and Bedi, R., (1978), *Mass Slaughter of Sea Turtles*, Hamadryad, p. 8.

Eckert, S.A. and Sarti, L., (1997), *Distant Fisheries Implicated in the Loss of the World's Largest Leatherback Nesting Population*, Marine Turtle Newsletter, 78:2-7.

Frazier, J., (1980), *Exploitation of Marine Turtles in the Indian Ocean*, Human Ecology, 8(4):329-370,.

Grand, J. and Beissinger, S.R., (1997), *When Relocation of Loggerhead Sea Turtle (Caretta Caretta) Nests Becomes a Useful Strategy*, Journal of Herpetology, 31(3):428-434.

Guinea, M.L. and Chatto, R., (1992), *Sea Turtles Killed in Australian Shark Fin Fishery*, Marine Turtle Newsletter, 57:5-6.

Guinea, M.L., (1993), *The Sea Turtles of Fiji*, SPREP Reports and Studies Series, No. 65.

Heppell et. al., (1996), *Population Model Analysis for the Loggerhead Sea Turtle Caretta Caretta, in Queensland*, Wildlife Research, 23:143-59.

IUCN (World Conservation Union), (1995), Integrating Marine Conservation in the Indian Ocean: 1996 and Beyond, Summary and Working Group Reports, November 28-December 1, 1995, Mombasa, Kenya.

IUCN/SSC Marine Turtle Specialist Group, (1995a), A Global Strategy for the Conservation of Marine Turtles.

Johannes, R E. and MacFarlane, J.W., (1991), *Traditional Fishing in the Torres Strait Islands*, pp. 53-71, CSIRO Division of Fisheries.

Kar, C.S. and Bhaskar, S., (1992), *Status of Sea Turtles in the Eastern Indian Ocean*, in Biology and Conservation of Sea Turtles, K.A. Bjorndal ed.

Liew H.-C., (1997), *Marine Turtle Research and Management in Malaysia*, in: Proceedings of Workshop on Marine Turtle Research and Management in Indonesia, Jember, East Java, November 1996, pp. 101-110.

Limpus, C.J., (1997), *Marine Turtle populations of Southeast Asia and the Western Pacific Region: Distribution and Status*, in: Proceedings of the Workshop on Marine

Turtle Research and Management in Indonesia, Jember, East Java, November 1996, pp. 37- 72.

Limpus, C.J., (1997a), *The Marine Turtle Life Cycle*, in Proceedings of the Workshop on Marine Turtle Research and Management in Indonesia, Jember, East Java, Indonesia, November 1996, pp. 185-6.

Limpus, C.J. and Reed, P.C., (1985), *Green Sea Trutles Stranded by Cyclone Kathy on the South-Western Coast of the Gulf of Carpentaria*, Aust Wildl. Res., 12:523-33.

Lohmann, K.J., B.E. Witherington, C.M.F. Lohmann and M. Solomon, (1997), *Orientation, Navigation, and Natal Beach Homing in Sea Turtles*, in: Lutz, P.L. and J.A. Musick, The Biology of Sea Turtles, CRC Press.

Lutcavage, M.E., P. Plotkin, B. Witherington, and P.L. Lutz, (1997), *Human Impacts on Sea Turtle Survival*, in: P.L. Lutz and J.A. Musick (ed.), The Biology of Sea Turtles, pp. 387-409.

Marine Turtle Newsletter, *Hurricane Pauline Destroyed 40 Million Sea Turtle Eggs in the Oaxacan Beach of Mazunte*, (1997), No. 78, p. 26.

Marquez, R., (1990), *Sea Turtles of the World*, FAO Species Catalogue, p. 48,.

Monanunsap, S., (1997), *Marine Turtle Research and Management in Thailand*, in: Proceedings of the Workshop on Marine Turtle Research and Management in Indonesia, Jember, East Java, November 1996, pp. 139-149.

Mortimer, J.A., (1995), *Teaching Critical Concepts for the Conservation of Sea Turtles*, Marine Turtle Newsletter, 71:1-4. (Attachment 30).

Mounsey, R., (1995), *The Australian Trawl Efficiency Device (AusTED) in the Northern Prawn Fishery (NPF)*, FAO Workshop on Selective Shrimp Trawling With Selective Devices, 24-26 July 1997, Darwin NT Australia.

National Research Council, National Academy of Sciences, (1990), *Decline of the Sea Turtles - Causes and Prevention.*

Paterson, P., (1979), *Shark Meshing Takes a Heavy Toll of Harmless Marine Animals*, Australian Fisheries, 38(10):17-23.

Poiner I.R., R.C. Buckworth, and A.N. Harris, (1990), *Incidental Capture and Mortality of Sea Turtles in Australia's Northern Prawn Fishery*, Aust. J. Mar. Freshwater Res. 41:97-110.

Pritchard, P., (1997), *Evolution, Phylogeny and Current Status*, in: P.L. Lutz and J.A. Musick (ed.), The Biology of Sea Turtles, p. 16.

Robins, J. and Campbell M., (1997), *History of BRD Development in Australia*, FAO Workshop on Selective Shrimp Trawling With Selective Devices, 24-26 July 1997, Darwin NT Australia.

Robins, J., (1995), *Estimated Catch and Mortality of Sea Turtles From the East Coast Otter Trawl Fishery of Queensland, Australia*, Biological Conservation, 74:157-167.

Sachse, M. and Wallner, B., (in press), *Marine Turtle Bycatch in the Northern Prawn Fishery - Scale of the Problem and Developing Solutions*, in: Proceedings of the Workshop on Marine Turtle Conservation and Management in Northern Australia, 3-4 June 1997.

Satapathy Rajaram, The Times of India News Service, per Frazier J., 17 November 1997.

Stanley W., (1996), *US Net Ban to Prawn Industry*, Northern Territory News, May 6, 1996.

Steiner, T., (1994), *International Implementation of TEDs Law, PL. 101-162, by the U.S. Government: Fact or Science Fiction*, Proceedings of the Thirteenth Annual Symposium on Sea Turtle Biology and Conservation, NOAA, Technical Memorandum, NMFS -SEFSC-341: pp. 171-181.

*The Status of Major Sea Turtle Populations in Malaysia*, (http://www.upmt.edu.my/seatru/mals3.htm),.

*Threats to Sea Turtles*, (http://www.opmt.edu.my/seatru/cons2.htm).

Travis, W., (1967), *The Voice of the Turtle*, George Allen and Unwin, London.

Verbal presentation by India at FAO Responsible Fishing Workshop Darwin, NT, Australia, 24-26 July 1997.

WWF, Marine Turtles of Pakistan.

**Cited by Mr. H.-C. Liew:**

M. Coyne, (16-06-97), *Some good and bad news for Kem*p's, CTURTLE List (Internet Source).

D. Crouse, (20-05-96), *TEDs Action Alert*, CTURTLE List (Internet Source).

Limpus C.J., (1997), *Marine Turtle Populations of Southeast Asia and the Western Pacific Region: Distribution and Status*, Yus R. N., R.L. Irwansyah, R. Ounsted, S. Troeng and A. Abdullah (eds). Proc. Of the Workshop on Marine Turtle research and Management in Indonesia, Jember, East Java. Nov. 1996, Wetlands International/PHPA/Environment Australia, Bogor.:37-73.

T. Steiner, (29-07-97), *Are TEDs coming off*, CTURTLE List (Internet Source).

T. Steiner, (19-11-97), *Re: Kemp's at Rancho Nuevo*, CTURTLE List (Internet Source).

Suliansa M.S., P. Basintal and N.L. Chan, (in press), *Impacts of Fishery Related Activities on Sea Turtles*, Paper presented at the National Seminar/Workshop on Marine Turtle and Terrapin Management, 22-23 October 1996, Cherating, Malaysia.

**Cited by Dr. I. Poiner:**

Anonymous, (1997), *Interim Advice to the Minister for the Environment from the Endangered Species Scientific Subcommittee (ESSS) on a Public Nomination to Schedule 3 of the Endangered Species Protection Act 1992* (ESP Act). (*Note* - the nomination was for the incidental catch (bycatch) of sea turtles during coastal otter-trawl fishing operations in Australian waters north of 28$^0$S to be declared a key threatening process of sea turtles).

Bowen, B.W., Abreu-Grobois, F.A., Blazas, G.H., Kamezaki, N., Limpus, C. and Ferk, R.J., (1995), *Trans-Pacific Migrations of the Loggerhead Turtle (Caretta caretta) Demonstrated with Mitochondrial DNA Markers*, Proceedings of the National Academy of Sciences, U.S.A. 92:3731.

Broderick, D., Moritz, C., Millar, J.D., Guinea, M., Prince, R.I.T. and Limpus, C., (1994), *Genetic Studies of the Hawksbill Turtle, Eretmochelys imbricata: Evidence for Multiple Stocks in Australian Waters*, Pacific Conservation Biology 1:123.

Brewer, D.T., Eayrs, J. and Rawlinson, N.J.F., (1995), *Bycatch Reduction Devices Show Promise in the NPF*, Australian Fisheries 54:24-26.

Brewer, D.T., Eayrs, J., Rawlinson, N.J.F., Salini, J.P., Farmer, M., Blaber, S.J.M., Ramm, D.C., Cartwright, I. And Poiner, I.R., (1997), *Recent Advancements in Environmentally Friendly Trawl Gear Research in Australia*, Proceedings of the 2nd World Fisheries Congress.

Caillouet, C.W., Shaver, D.J., Teas, W.G., Nance, J.M., Revera, D.B. and Cannon, A.C., (1995), *Relationship Between Sea Turtle Stranding Rates and Shrimp Fishing Intensities in the Northwestern Gulf of Mexico: 1986-1989 versus 1990-1993*, Fisheries Bulletin 94:237-249.

Chaloupka, M.Y. and Limpus, C.J. (MS), *Heuristic Simulation Modelling of Trawl Fishery Impacts on Southern Great Barrier Reef Loggerhead Population Dynamics*, Fisheries Bulletin.

Chaloupka, M.Y. and Musick, J.A., (1997), *Age, Growth and Population Dynamics*, in: The Biology of Sea Turtles, Lutz, P.L and Musick, J.A. Eds., CRC Press Boca Raton, USA, p. 233-276.

Chan, E.H., Liew, H.C. and Maslan, A.G., (1987), *The Incidental Capture of Sea Turtles in Fishing Gear in Terengganu, Malaysia*, Biological Conservation 43:1-7.

Chark, L.H., (1997), *Country Paper - Malaysia*, Proceedings of the Workshop on Marine Turtle Research and Management in Indonesia, Jember, East Java, Indonesia, November 1996, p. 101-110.

Crouse, D.T., L.B. Crowder, & H. Caswell, (1987), *A Stage Based Population Model for Loggerhead Sea Turtles and Implications for Conservation*, Ecology 68:1412-1423.

Crowder, L.B., Crouse, D.T., Heppell, S.S. and Martin T.H., (1994), *Predicting the Impact of Turtle Excluder Devices on Loggerhead Sea Turtle Populations*, Ecological Applications 4:437-445.

Henwood, T.A. and W.E. Stuntz, (1987), *Analysis of Sea Turtles Captures and Mortalities During Commercial Shrimp Trawling*, Fisheries Bulletin, U.S. 85:813-817.

Henwood, T.A., Stuntz, W.E. and Thompson, (1992), *Evaluation of U.S. Turtle Protective Measures Under Existing TED Regulations, Including Estimates of Shrimp Trawler Related Mortality in the Wider Caribbean*, NOAA Technical Memorandum NMFS-SEFSC-303.

Heppell, S.S., Limpus, C.J., Crouse, D.T., Frazer, N.B. and Crowder, L.B., (1995), *Population Model Analysis for the Loggerhead sea Turtle, Caretta caretta, in Queensland*, Australian Wildlife Research, 23:143-154

Limpus, C., (1997), *Marine Turtle Population of South East Asia and the Western Pacific Region: Distribution and Status*, Proceedings of the Workshop on Marine Turtle Research and Management in Indonesia, Jember, East Java, Indonesia, November 1996.

Lutcavage, M.E., Plotkin, P., Witherinton, B. and Lutz, P., (1997), *Human impacts on sea turtle survival*, in: The Biology of Sea Turtles, Lutz, P.L and Musick, J.A. Eds., CRC Press Boca Raton, USA, p. 387-409.

Monanunsap, S., (1997), *Country paper - Thailand*, Proceedings of the Workshop on Marine Turtle Research and Management in Indonesia. Jember, East Java, Indonesia, November 1996, p. 139-149.

Poiner, I.R. and Harris, A.N.M., (1996), *Incidental Capture, Direct Mortality and Delayed Mortality of Sea Turtles in Australia's Northern Prawn Fishery*, Marine Biology 125:813-825.

Robins, J.B., (1995), *Estimated Catch and Mortality of Sea Turtles form the East Coast Otter Trawl Fishery of Queensland, Australia*, Biological Conservation 74:157-167.

Robins-Troeger, J.B., Buckworth, R.C. and Dredge, M.C.l., (1995), *Development of a Trawl Efficiency Device (TED) for Australian Prawn Fisheries. II. Field evaluations of the AusTED*. Fisheries Research 22:107-117.

Settle, S., (1995), *Status of Nesting Populations of Sea Turtles in Thailand and their Conservation*. Marine Turtle Newsletter 68:8-13.

Somers, I., (1994), *Modelling Loggerhead Turtle Populations*, in: Proceedings of the Marine Turtle Conservation Workshop, James, R., Compiler, Australian National Parks and Wildlife Service, Canberra, p. 142-153.

Tucker, A.D., McPhee, D.P., and Robbins, J.B., (1997), *Adopting Turtle Excluder Devices in Australia and the United States: What Are the Differences in Technology Transfer, Promotion and Acceptance?* Coastal Management 25:404-421.

# ANNEX IV

*TRANSCRIPT OF THE MEETING WITH EXPERTS HELD ON 21 AND 22 JANUARY 1998*

## First day - 21 January 1998

### Chairman

1. I would like to welcome the scientific experts as well as the parties to this meeting. Let me start by informing you that the proceedings are going to be recorded. Therefore, when taking the floor, representatives, experts are requested to use the microphones and to speak slowly and clearly. A transcript will be made of this meeting and it is the intention of the Panel to attach the transcript to the Panel Report as part of the record. At this stage I would like first of all to thank the experts very sincerely for the effort they have already put in and the very hard work that they have put in over a very short period of time to respond to the request from the Panel for them to give advice and to the answers to the questions that we have put to them. As you know, we are operating under very stringent time constraints and we have to produce reports within certain time frames and this puts enormous pressure on all persons involved in these proceedings. But I would like to say a special word of thanks to the experts who have come out of the blue to assist in this process.

2. The purpose of this meeting is really to allow the experts to expand on their written reports and to discuss amongst themselves in front of us for the benefit of the Panel. The documents which have been produced are very substantive and obviously its not a matter of repeating them all, but really more of highlighting the main points, commenting as appropriate on colleagues reports, so that the Panel can be as fully informed as possible regarding sea turtle conservation problems so that we can be in a better position to assess the controversial issues underlying the facts of this case.

3. Now in this regard the parties will be given an opportunity during this meeting to seek clarification regarding the reports of the experts and to express their views on them. It is not the purpose of the meeting though to hear further argumentation or new evidence which the parties did not submit by the time of the second meeting of the Panel which was held in September 1997. Similarly, we do not intend to have formal statements by the parties, the purpose of this meeting is to hear the experts and to put questions to the experts including though from scientific experts of the parties. But parties will of course be allowed to address matters raised by the experts and the Panel expects the parties to put all their questions in the context of this meeting and to seek replies from the experts within this meeting.

4. The Panel considers that by the end of the meeting tomorrow there will have been sufficient time for the parties to make all the necessary comments even if they have already missed some of the deadlines in the past, the opportunity is now to get their points across and to get answers from the experts. As I said at the beginning, this will be a recorded proceeding, so to the answers will be written and will be in the record. Therefore, the Panel does not intent to prolong the process beyond the end of this meeting tomorrow. We see this as the final point at which comments on comments and comments are going to have to come to an end but it is really an expert process that

we are in rather than any sort of continuation of the previous argumentation that we heard from the parties.

5. Experts can if they want react to what has been said by the parties and priority will be given to the experts and therefore parties will be asked to limit their interventions to questions and comments related to the issues raised by the experts. The Panel will not take account of interventions outside this framework. I want to stress that the proceedings are confidential, everything which is being said in this room is subject to the rules of the Dispute Settlement Understanding and the Code of Conduct.

6. I would also like to explain how the Panel intends to proceed in actually handling this meeting today and tomorrow. We propose first to invite statements by the experts focusing on their main points, their main arguments, main areas of contention and also, if necessary, where they see problems between their own and their colleagues reports. I propose that we have that process initially in alphabetical order and after the statements to allow the experts then a second round to make comments on each others presentations and to develop the discussion and argumentation.

7. When this is concluded, the parties to the dispute will be given an opportunity to put their questions and comments and again we would want to take that in series starting with the complaining parties in the order that we established in the earlier meetings, that is to say, Thailand, India, Pakistan and Malaysia followed by the United States. After this process we would then give the floor back to each expert again to give their final statement, their responses to the parties and their conclusions. Now, that is roughly the outline of how we expect it to go, of course as the discussion develops I would expect that the Panel will wish to interject questions and the parties may also wish to develop a freer discussion as it goes along.

8. But I think we have to keep in mind the time frame which is basically this afternoon and tomorrow morning and we would hope to be in a position to conclude this meeting by the end of the morning. Bearing in mind that there are ten speakers potentially and that we will have more than one round from at least half of them, I think it would be helpful to try and keep the interventions to the point and as brief as possible. Having said that, I don't wish to limit the experts in any way in what they want to say. I think that they are well aware of the issue that is before us, the terms of reference of the Panel, they have seen all the documentation in the dispute and I think really that it should be for them to present their reports in the way that they see best. That said I would like to now give the floor to the experts in alphabetical order and that means that I start with Dr. Eckert.

**Dr. Eckert**

9. Thank you Mr. Chairperson. My name is Scott Eckert and my current position is a senior research biologist at the Hubbs-Sea World Research Institute. I think, as you have probably all gathered from the information that we as a group of scientist have provided to you, the issues relative to sea turtle biology are not an easy issue to understand. Those of us who have been working with turtles for many years feel like we have barely scratched the surface of what we understand about the biology of these creatures. Much of the information available today about these creatures is limited to anecdotal information or very limited reports and so if you see confusion in some of the various documents and even disagreements in some of the documents, it often comes

because there is not a ready set of reference materials you can turn to out there that tells you everything you ever wanted to know about the biology of a turtle.

10. And I think in our discussion as the day progresses you will see maybe some of those distinctions may get clarified once we have had a chance to chat with each other about our various opinions. My responses to the questions and I am going to limit this presentation to a very short summary of the points I tried to point out in my particular responses. I understand later that we will have some more time for more detail and if there are issues that I can present then in more detail with backing factual information I will do so.

11. The issue as I see it, we see turtle biology today and we see turtle populations in general is that virtually all sea turtle population are in trouble. There is ample evidence to indicate that all species are in decline with the possible exception of the Australian flatback (*Natator depressus*) because it is an endemic species to Australia and has not had the same sort of perturbations that we have seen from other populations. But on a global level, all sea turtle populations have exhibited decline, all sea turtle species have exhibited decline in their population to the point where we need to be worried about them. In a general sense, most of the problems faced by sea turtle populations or sea turtle species today are anthropogenic. While there are large numbers of various sources of mortality and various sources of problems that populations face, the so-called natural problems, natural threats, have been dealt with by the biology of the animals. The leatherback is the oldest of the species and it is about 120 million years old, that predates virtually every mammal on the planet. Therefore you can realize that these animals are finely tuned to the environments in which they live. Thus, the perturbations that have caused the declines have been primarily due to man's influence on these environments and on the species themselves. In my opinion, incidental take is the single most destructive threat faced by sea turtle populations in modern times.

12. There have been other threats, such as direct take which is a historically much longer term threat over the last maybe, 200 to 400 years, but in modern times, in the last 25 years, again this is my opinion but it is based on about 20 years of working with these creatures, incidental take is the most significant problem faced by all sea turtle species. There are other forms of challenges to the populations, such as habitat degradation is an issue in some countries and some areas, but when you read in our discussions that we feel that there are variations in the threats faced by sea turtles, you must realize that there are variations, there are quite a few different possible threats faced by sea turtle populations but the most significant ones are the incidental take of sea turtles by fishing industries.

13. The other point that I want to make is that of population status and stocks and we can have more discussion about this later. It is my opinion and my belief, again based on the years that I have been working with sea turtles, that at this time based on our current data available to us on the biology of sea turtles that we cannot consider individual stocks as individual management units and this is primarily because we do not know the full range of each of these stocks. Now there are some wonderful techniques coming on line that have allowed us to begin to solve some of those issues but it will be many many years until we can adequately say we know that this particular individual stock can be treated as independent management unit. I will go into more detail on that again as we bring the discussion back up. The other issue is conservation programmes. Conservation programmes must be specifically tailored to address the

primary threat faced by the species and I do not think that there is any question among any of us on that particular issue. Which means that if bycatch is a primary reason for species to decline you must address bycatch. If nesting beach perturbations have been a problem, rather that the habitat degradation, the illegal or the legal harvest of eggs or of nesting females, those must be addressed specifically. I do not believe that it is possible to mitigate incidental take in fisheries if that is your problem by simply trying to enhance production on a nesting beach. The data that we have so far to date suggests that this is simply is not a valid mitigation measure. You must take a multifaceted approach to all of your conservation. Conservation must address the problems in order of priority and the problems in order of impact on the species itself. I think that that summarizes my comments for today, thank you.

**Chairman**

14. Thank you very much. Perhaps I could now invite Dr. Frazier to give his opening statement.

**Dr. Frazier**

15. Mr. Chairman, distinguished members of the Panel, distinguished delegates, I would like to reciprocate the thanks, I think that it is extremely important that science be used to the fullest of its capabilities in the resolution of disputes when it concerns resources which are important to peoples and the development of countries. I realize that this is not a simple process, it has not been simple for me and I do not think that it has been simple for my colleagues. I'm sure it has complicated the lives of many people, nonetheless, I am grateful that we have been given the chance.

16. I am a biologist, I am trained in biology, I am trained in ecology. Those who have looked at my submission will see that I have made an effort to venture out into another discipline, the discipline which is to some of us in biology, is part of biology, but usually is described as a social science. You have read more about sea turtles, you will hear more about sea turtles, during the course of today and tomorrow than you will ever want to hear, I am sure. And I will do my best not to belabour more sea turtle biology, I think that the experts on either side of me can do that perfectly well; I would like to draw attention to something which I feel has been left out of this discussion. Why is there trade? Trade is for people, and trade must be done for the best number of people in a society. I am deeply concerned that the social aspects involved in this have not been included. I see us from a perspective of someone who has worked and spent their life studying turtles and dealing with different problems of conservation of sea turtles, and more recently fisheries issues, and I see, I perceive in a way we are very close to an exercise which could be described as rearranging the deck chairs on the Titanic. The Titanic was a large ship which was sunk in the North Atlantic, and to rearrange the deck chairs on a ship which is about to sink is a useless venture. The trade issue, I desperately hope, can be put into a social context. What we have in conservation biology is what is called a flagship species, a sea turtle is a charismatic animal. What we see here today is because sea turtles are charismatic. If this was involving stone fish or indeed sharks, other species of marine resources which one could equally argue are in desperate need of conservation, issues which in fact may have great value to societies of the countries here, I doubt very much that this would have occurred. It is because sea turtles are charismatic that political action can be focused on. It is with this philosophy

that I have addressed the question, hoping that using sea turtles as charismatic species, as flagships, very deep problems, environmental problems, fisheries problems can be resolved. It is my feeling that trade must benefit the largest number of people in a country. I am deeply concerned by the little I have been able to learn in the short time available about the way the shrimp industry functions. I am not convinced that the shrimp industry functions to help the largest number of people in the producing societies. I realize that I am taking this discussion away from the focus of the main points but nonetheless, I feel that, unless the root problems of a dispute, of a conflict in environment, in society are resolved, we are dangerously close to rearranging deck chairs on the Titanic.

**Chairman**

17. Thank you very much. Perhaps I could now invite Dr. Guinea to make his opening statement.

**Mr. Guinea**

18. Thank you Mr. Chairman. Ladies and gentlemen thank you for the opportunity for me to highlight some of the aspects of my submission. I would like to thank the Chairman, Mr. Cartland and members of the Panel and would also like to take the opportunity to thank Ms. Cossy for organizing so well. I would also like to thank my colleagues for the stimulating presentations and the truthfulness of their discussions. I have been involved with sea turtle research since 1970 as a volunteer and over the last couple of decades as a lecturer at universities and so my presentation is based mainly on observations and discussions through scientific literature with colleagues, particularly in Australia. Shrimp trawling in the USA has been responsible for killing numerous sea turtles, there is no doubt about that and that is not a subject that we are arguing about. US legislation requiring TEDs on all shrimp trawl nets is believed to have reduced this mortality, the USA restrictions on imported shrimp is based on reasoning if the demographic units of sea turtles that inhabit the Gulf of Mexico and the Caribbean Sea are depleted by present day trawling, then all sea turtles are threatened by shrimp trawling. The proposed solution to this problem is the forced implementation of TEDs for all shrimp trawl fleets in countries that export shrimp to the USA. During reading the material, I was looking for several aspects, several things in the submissions, the information I was looking for was the size of other fisheries and their respective effort in the impact on sea turtles, so this is other fisheries going on in conjunction with trawl fisheries. Statistics on sea turtle mortality by other fishing gear, for example gill nets existing shrimp management measures, protected areas for shrimp breeding grounds, nursery areas, protected areas rich in biodiversity, distance offshore and minimum depth limitations. I was also looking for gear limitations, size of vessels, types and numbers of nets and the economic trawl time durations for different shrimp species and these were not provided. Fishing activity, for example diurnal and nocturnal trawling restrictions and seasonal closures were also not provided.

19. Other points for consideration. I was looking at the embargo that had focused not on the product, but rather, how it was caught and the aspirations that all sea turtles would benefit once this threatening process is reduced. There is no indication or milestones or checks to ascertain if the embargo has had the desired effect in the affected countries. The questions that need to be considered. We are looking at sea

turtle survival by measuring mortality and we should be looking for surrogate indicators of sea turtle mortality, things such as trawling effort and catch rates of turtles in trawl nets. Has the embargo reduced sea turtle mortality from trawling in those countries that did not comply with the TED requirements on all shrimp trawl nets? Did shrimp prices in the USA increase to entice countries to comply with TED requirements so as to gain access to a more lucrative market for their products? And were other markets found for shrimp that were banned from the USA market? Were shrimp or shrimp products transshipped through third party countries to the USA? And has the embargo had the desired effect? TEDs are just one option in the responsible management of a fishery. If the cause of the decline of a demographic unit is shrimp trawling, then the use of TEDs will assist in the recovery of the species. If, however, the breeding unit is threatened by excessive egg harvesting, then increase in hatchling survivorship should be the priority of management measures. If gill nets are the problem, then there are many options available to modify nets and their deployment to reduce the negative impacts on sea turtles. Data on sea turtle mortality and trawl fisheries are relatively easy to obtain, replicate and analyze. By their presence offshore trawlers are easily implicated in sea turtle strandings. Data on sea turtle mortality in gill nets are not so forthcoming and gill nets are not so readily implicated in the deaths of sea turtles. I am concerned that TEDs will be seen as the panacea to prevent sea turtle extinction. Other management options have to be employed as sea turtles are just one component of the by-catch. Restrictions on areas, seasons and fishing effort of trawls are needed to protect shrimp stocks, their habitats and other marine species which are less charismatic than marine turtles for example sea snakes. Thank you Mr. Chairman.

**Chairman**

20. Thank you very much. Perhaps I could now invite Dr. Liew to make his opening statement.

**Mr. Liew**

21. Thank you Mr. Chairman. Just to clarify, I am not Dr. but just Mr. Thanks again ladies and gentlemen. What I want to say here is there has been some confusion as to what constitutes a population in sea turtles. Some may define, for example, you are going to say the green turtle population in the world is facing problems, or the loggerhead population in the world is facing problems, but can we solve the problem by treating this as a global population? I think the way to manage sea turtles is we have to identify each individual population unit or breeding unit. Breeding units of loggerheads in the United States is different from the breeding units of loggerheads in Australia and each breeding unit or population unit has got its own problems. It is difficult for us to say if shrimp trawling harms loggerheads in the States, the same process would harm loggerheads in Australia and the same process would harm loggerheads in Oman. The Oman loggerhead population is still the largest population, but can we give a blanket coverage? So the similar situation applies for all the other species of sea turtles. We have to identify breeding units, we have to identify what are the actual threats for each of these breeding units and then tackle from there and thus work up priorities and handle them one by one. So to give a global consensus or issue saying that shrimp trawlers is the most important problem, then it would take the focus away from other

problems that may be affecting that particular breeding unit. So I think, that is a point I wish to make in this first statement. Thank you Mr. Chairman.

**Chairman**

22. Thank you very much. Finally, perhaps I can ask Dr. Poiner, if he would make his opening statement.

**Dr. Poiner**

23. Thanks Mr. Chairman. My background, I come from probably a little bit different than the other four experts in the sense that my background is in dealing with the impacts of fishing on ecosystems and in particular looking at the impacts of prawn trawling, as well as shrimp trawling, but being an Australian we tend to refer to them as prawns, on the system, including the impacts on turtle populations. Indeed, it is a significant issue worldwide. I think in my opening statement, I'd like to mention from a technical point of view, summarize what the assessment process, that we go through in making decisions about the status of some of these stocks, because I think that its quite important that people may be not as technically involved, understand some of the problems associated with that process. So to put it simply, firstly, we look at biological and ecological data on life history and habitats of a population. Secondly we look at estimates of natural and anthropogenic rates of mortality by age or size on the population and use all that information, usually in modeling studies using mathematical models, to come up with estimates of the status of the stock and then following up often estimates of the chances of recovery of that stock following different, using different management measures. I think, be it turtles or be it southern blue fin tuna or be it many different marine populations and probably terrestrial populations too. Often there is general agreement, and I think what we are following here, there is a general agreement about the status of the stocks and that for sea turtles you have the status that they are fairly low population levels. However, you usually find that differences in terms of looking at recovery or under different management regimes and I think that is what you will find, both in terms of the cases being put by the experts and by the parties, that really we are trying to predict the future, when we are dealing with a great deal of uncertainty about the information and it is how we deal with that uncertainty generally results in different outcomes or different predictions. The other thing that I think is important to know is that this is a interactive process. It is not a set process and all the time more information more data comes in, so the process is repeated and hopefully gets a little bit more certain. I think that some of the uncertainty that often arises, and I think has arisen in this process is uncertainty about the identification of a stock. We have already heard two experts, one placing a lot of emphasis on the identification of breeding unit, I would tend to concur with that, another saying that we need to take a more global perspective. I think that there is often inter-annual fluctuations in many of the things, many of the information and I think how you deal with those fluctuations often has an impact on your outcomes. There are always logistical and jurisdictional problems that always create other uncertainties and dealing with such long-lived animals as turtles that there is simply difficulties in detecting trends in populations. How we deal with the uncertainty in our population estimates often leads to different predictions. I think that we need to be aware of it and I think what we will find and

what we need to discuss today is not so much the status of the stock but looking at what is the likelihood of recovery using different management tools.

24. The other thing, just before I finish, I'd like to make a comment on because I, having been involved heavily in the introduction of TEDs and other bycatch reduction devices, certainly in Australian fisheries, I think there has been a little bit of, we need a little bit more elaboration on the introduction of some of those devises into a fishery. I think that it is important and I don't think that it is argued anywhere now that the properly selected and installed TEDs are very effective at reducing turtle catches and turtle mortalities. That's a fairly easily demonstrated thing, it's a fairly straightforward simple process of doing it, I can elaborate on that later. However, TED performance in a commercial fishery is a different issue and that's an issue of understanding the fishery and understanding the area where the fishery is being undertaken. And in understanding the fishery, that's both biophysical issues but also socio-economic issues and the introduction of TEDs via these indoor fisheries is not a simple process. It is a process that will often take, well from the Australian experience, it's is probably going to take us about six to eight years to do. And I think that's an important point and the other issue is that, be it TEDs or be it area closures or be it seasonal closures or be it a whole variety of management techniques, monitoring enforcement will always be an issue in the fishery. And I think I'll leave my opening comments at that point. Thanks Mr. Chairman.

**Chairman**

25. Thank you very much. I think those initial statements already point the way to further discussion on some issues and I think that perhaps, as we go into the second round, I think Dr. Eckert mentioned population status and stocks as something that he would like to come back to, and I think that we have already seen that there is some discussion there against the global approach as opposed to the breeding unit approach. I think perhaps you might want to take the opportunity of the second round to take us a little further into that subject. Dr. Eckert you have the floor.

**Dr. Eckert**

26. Thank you for the opportunity to visit the issue of stocks. Let me begin by saying that I am actually in complete agreement with my colleagues relative to the need to define what individual stock boundaries are. And that progress is being made in that particular direction. The advent of DNA fingerprinting or mtDNA, as it's referred to mitochondrial DNA, the linking of females to their native beaches is an excellent means by which we can begin to understand stocks. The increasing use of satellite telemetry to actually monitor the movement patterns of females away from their home stock is also excellent. All of these lead us down the path to being able to define stocks in terms of how we have traditionally measured them and that is based on the number of females annually nesting in a nesting beach. We are also improving our ability to estimate what percentage of the at least female population is represented by those nesting females on the beach. Where I have some concerns, is that an issue that has been defined and fairly well agreed upon, I think, by all the scientific panel, is that we need to address specific issues that are threatening the sea turtle populations. However, our ability to define the stock boundaries is still too immature to be able to do that. Now, what that means for us is the following. If we have a sea turtle population nesting in country X, I try not to use

a specific country because this is just a model, but if we have a sea turtle population nesting in country X, and we have that population distributing to, say, 15 other countries of various regional distances from that nesting beach, we are then faced with saying OK, countries 1 through 10 have shrimp trawling and they have a high incidental take, countries 10 through 11 through 15 have gill net fleets and they're taking turtles in that fleet. Now, how do we, from a management perspective, apportion if we are not aware of the gill netting problem as a possible source of mortality, so for example if we only know where 10 of the 15 resident populations live, and we are seeing a population decline on our beach, who do we blame? And, what I'd have to say about that is right now, we simply do not have enough data to be able to tell you where the stocks in the world today go when they leave their nesting beaches. The other issue is that of juvenile foraging habitats in juveniles. The amount of information that we have on where juveniles reside, and juveniles will move through various habitats and various areas, they are not fixed on one particular regional jurisdiction, we know less about, much less about than we know about even with females. And in my own research, what I begun to realize is the more we look, the more range the stocks inhabit and the more overlaps there are between stocks, so your particular beach that you are monitoring the population on, on the foraging grounds it may overlap with 10 other populations.

27. So we have got to be very very aware of these issues if we are going to address the problem in a manner that is most applicable to the populations. Let me just briefly show you some examples of what I mean by this discussion. I am going to switch over to this microphone. Can everybody hear that needs to hear? Those two issues that we need to be aware of when we are talking about stocks, the one issue is what of the stock ranges. Where are these animals actually going after they leave their nesting beaches? Or where were these juveniles residing and how were they moving around between those areas? What I've argued is that we really don't know from most populations what is the full extent of their range or where these populations will move. What I've also argued is that we're getting there and in maybe another 10 years, we will be able to define those issues for you very well. There is a tremendous amount of very good work going on in Australia right now with this and the United States is also beginning to do quite a bit of work in gathering DNA tissue samples from turtles to be able to piece them back to their natal beaches, at least for nesting females.

28. But we have a very long way to go before we are going to be able to do that adequately. Now, as an example, there are some populations in which we understand a little bit more about the juveniles. One of the loggerhead populations in the Atlantic and the Pacific, and what we have found from those is that they make trans-Pacific or trans-Atlantic migrations and they will reside in developmental habitats on the other side of the ocean where they will remain for a number of years. In the case of the Atlantic, loggerheads breeding on the Carolina Coast, the Georgia Coast, the Florida Coast, all will move over towards the Azores on the other side of the Atlantic where they will grow up for a while and then they will swim back. In the Pacific we see the same thing. Stocks that are hatched in Japan are actually developing and growing off the coast of Baja and off the coast of California in that they will then migrate back to Japan. So you see right there we have a very very long distance between where these populations are actually residing and yet they would be identified as Japanese loggerheads, if we take a strict stock basis. That's the only species we can say that about. We cannot say that about any other species with certainty.

29. The other issue then becomes one of, OK, given that we don't know where these things go, how are we going to assign jurisdiction to them from a regional perspective? Now, a lot of my research over the years has focused on satellite telemetry as a methodology for understanding the movements and the habitats of the animals. I work predominantly with leatherback sea turtles and so let me bring up a few things about leatherbacks that we have determined over the last few years.

30. [See graphs 1 and 2, Appendix 1] With leatherbacks, the paradigm for understanding leatherbacks used to be that they move north and south, they nest in the tropics, they nest and then they move into the North Pacific or the North Atlantic waters where they will feed and then they will migrate back. That was based on tag returns. Tag returns data we have is the point they were tagged on this particular beach, they were recovered usually as a dead animal at some other point. It was considered pretty much a migration, point A to point B. However, when satellite telemetry came on line, and I began to use satellite telemetry to understand the movement patterns of leatherheads in particular, what we have found is that leatherbounds are not just making north-south migrations but they are likely making circum-oceanic migrations, they are making regular forays around the perimeter of the oceans. These two data sets, this upper one here was leatherbacks that were tracked out of the country of Trinidad in the Southern Caribbean off the coast of Venezuela here. I tracked three turtles, one of the transmitters was entangled in a gill net and damaged and so it failed early, the other two transmitters gave us the first perspective that leatherbacks may be doing something other than just simply making north-south migrations which is what we had from tag data. Then this animal moved up into the north Atlantic, it spent about a month and a half here and then it migrated down to the coast of Africa. This animal moved across the Atlantic up into the Bay of Biscay, then it too moved down the coast of Africa. Now, some significant issues are these two animals left within a week of each other in their northern habitats to get down to the southern habitats. Not only did these animals know where they were, they also knew what time of year it was, and where they had to get to. In Mexico this is a project which is ongoing right now, I am currently tracking leatherbacks off the Pacific Coast of Mexico. The animals have moved south here to the coast of Chile. The "El Niño" has caused some problems down here when they got into some warm water, and you can see that some of them have made divergences out away from there. What does this tell us about movements and how can I say that it is not that they are simply making north-south movements based on this.

31. Well, my hypothesis is this. Here, off the African coast at the time of year when the turtles appear, there is a tremendous amount of upwelling, that means coastal production has risen quite a bit and there is a lot of food for leatherbacks to eat. Same thing goes in these two northern habitats at the time of year they are here. Basically, what this species appears to be doing is following sources of food. They know that food is going to be prevalent down here in the early parts of the year so they migrate down to there and they are driven by that particular pattern. Here in Mexico, these animals have spent three to six months reproducing, probably feeding very little, they head for the first closest they can find where there is going to be food available. For the leatherbacks that means jellyfish. That's here at the coast of Chile and Peru. These are areas very famous for their fisheries. Where do they go from here? The hypothesis that I have proposed is that leatherbacks make this kind of migratory patterns in both the Pacific and ... [tape turnover] ... split the Pacific down the middle like this particular mapping

programme doesn't allow me ship the Pacific over to centre its focus. These are the animals that we tracked south. I'm hypothesizing that they move out across the Pacific after they feed here and they come up into this northern Pacific area here and then make their way back around in a circular pattern in the Pacific. That's very much the pattern we have already documented for the Atlantic. The reason I 'm proposing that they go from here up to here is that we know in this area that the drift net fleets were catching large numbers of leatherbacks in the mid 1980s. These leatherbacks' subsequent data, genetic data, has indicated that incidentally caught leatherbacks from the Hawaiian long lined fleets here, exhibit the signature familiar with those that we would see from Mexico and Costa Rica. So therefore, these animals simply have to be getting up here somehow and this appears to be the route that they are taking.

32. Now, in the case of Malaysia and the large nesting colony down here in Irian Jaya, in Indonesia, there's also DNA evidence and a single tag return from Malaysia to "Hawaii", we haven't exactly been able to sort out what that means, but that clearly indicates that that animal moved into the north Pacific. There is DNA evidence indicating that Irian Jaya turtles from here have stranded on the California coast as well as been encountered up in this area. So I think that the hypothesis that these animals are making multi-jurisdictional migratory movements around the perimeter of the ocean to take opportunities for good feeding is very very real. Now, my point of belabouring this whole issue to you is that the only reason we knew or we are beginning to discover that these turtles were making these kind of movements is with the advent of the most recent technologies and satellite telemetry and DNA. The number of sea turtles of all species that have ever been tracked by satellite, probably numbers less than 50, with many data anything other than just a few weeks of information. Yet, we are trying to say that we can define the stocks of sea turtles based on these very few studies so that we can then address the particular threats that are perturbing these individual stocks and I am arguing that we simply do not have the data to allow for that yet. Now, there is a practicality issue and that practicality issue is: is it practical to say well, since we can't identify stocks, therefore we need to address the threats on a global level and what I argue is yes, that is exactly the situation. We know that it has been well demonstrated that turtle populations were severely damaged by shrimp trawling in at least one country of the world. That's why I think it is prudent to make the same argument that if shrimp trawling is as destructive to sea turtle populations in that country, then it is likely destructive to sea turtle populations elsewhere in the world and this is where I'm probably going to have some disagreement with my colleagues. But the bottom line is the way a shrimp trawler fleet operates perturbs the environment and if there are turtles present, and that is a significant question, if there are turtles present, I would argue that they will be drowned by shrimp fleets or shrimp fleet activities.

33. There has also been some discussion, at least in the comments I received the other day, relative to jurisdictional aspects and this falls very much within the same parameters as understanding stocks. You have to understand jurisdiction, and as I understand it, if you don't have jurisdiction, you don't have the ability to introduce this sort of regulations. I want to show you this briefly [see graph 3, Appendix 1]. Remember there is very little data on green turtle movements from Malaysia or Thailand in the case of the Pacific which is the area that I am most familiar with. There have been some satellite tracking studies and there is some DNA evidence being gathered. There is no data to indicate that green turtles have ever been recovered from

Guam or the Northern Mariana Islands that I'm aware of. Maybe my colleagues would know something else. However, the fact that there is no evidence for that doesn't mean that it doesn't exist and I know that's a really strange and backwards way of approaching it, but that's simply the issue. There has not been enough research done to indicate rather there is jurisdictional overlap with these populations. I argue that there is jurisdictional overlap with leatherbacks and I think I have demonstrated that and it is being demonstrated by DNA evidence as well and there is possibly jurisdictional overlap with green turtle populations here. Twenty seven hundred kilometres is well within the range of post-nesting migrations of female green turtles for the western Pacific. So those are the issues that I wanted to point out briefly and I am sure that that'll stimulate a little bit more discussion and maybe we'll come to some consensus as to where, as a scientific community, we all fall in on this particular issue.

**Chairman**

34. Thank you very much Dr. Eckert. In continuing the round, I don't know whether Dr. Frazier wishes to jump in on this question of the population stocks which we have now got into or whether you would like to come back a little bit later on to talk perhaps about the Titanic and the deckchairs at a later stage. Otherwise, I could go to one of the other experts who also flag this subject and hear perhaps a slightly different perspective on the issue we have just been discussing.

**Dr. Frazier**

35. I think what I am hearing is people speaking to the same issue, but using different ways to get to it. A concern which Dr. Eckert mentions about no information is not negative information, is fundamental to science and this same concern is well expressed in the FAO Code of Conduct for Responsible Fisheries. If you don't know something, there is not a reason not to protect it. I think that is a very simple issue. To fine tune, to describe in more detail what a breeding stock is, and where it lives, and what countries have rights to it will take us many years, and I think all parties here would agree that when they're on the high seas, then they are common resources to the world community, not in anyone's jurisdiction, but in fact in everyone's jurisdiction. I think the complication here is at different levels, it is political and it's biological.

**Chairman**

36. Thank you. Dr. Guinea you certainly mentioned the breeding units and perhaps you would like to go on with that.

**Mr. Guinea**

37. Yes, thank you Mr. Chairman. The fundamental unit of conservation is the breeding unit from my perspective. We measure the populations of sea turtles by the number of nesting females. Very few studies have produced estimates of population size from other than nesting females. A few feeding ground studies in limited areas will usually present densities or a biomass per hectare or square kilometre, but the unit of population size is traditionally the number of females that nest in a particular year or because of some species having high fluctuations from year to year in their nesting populations maybe over a number of years, a decade or even longer to get an indication

of the yearly fluctuations in population size and also population fluctuations associated with cyclical events such as the "El Niño" or the southern oscillation event.

38. So the breeding unit is what we measure. We measure the number of females on a particular breeding beach, or in a particular locality, whether it's one island or several islands and that becomes the unit. I should say that a lot of work has been done with tagging sea turtles. There are large numbers of sea turtles carrying tags around the oceans of the world. Dr. Eckert has indicated new technologies that have come onto line. These include mitochondrial DNA studies whereby the maternal lineage is determined for a nesting population, which indicates that because the mitochondria are not carried in the sperm and are not transferred to the ovum, therefore each individual carries the mitochondria from its mother and therefore, because of the characteristics of that mitochondria, the DNA finger print can be established for a breeding unit. It might be one island. It might be several islands. Sea turtles will move either on a yearly basis, in some areas. In some areas, they may even move on a nightly basis between islands, if one island isn't particularly satisfactory. So, the tagging studies are some of the most basic studies of sea turtles. Mitochondrial DNA studies support tagging studies. If mitochondrial DNA studies were in conflict with tagging studies, then they would not have progressed, regardless of the theory associated with them. Latest technology, looking at satellite telemetry. Again, if satellite telemetry did not agree with tagging studies and mitochondrial studies, it wouldn't be accepted and this, as Dr. Eckert has indicated, is a new technology. There are probably fewer than 50 sea turtles carrying satellite tags as he mentioned. There are also other means of looking at the migratory routes of sea turtles. A thing such as temperature depth datalogue is attached to sea turtles, whereby the depth to which they dive, the temperature of the waters through which they move. This information can be carried with the turtle and when it returns to its feeding ground or nesting beach, then a map can be produced of where the turtle actually went or at least the limitations of where the turtle has been during its nesting migrations.

39. In Australia, the breeding units of turtles that are involved with shrimp trawls. I should also point out that the leatherback sea turtle is not a species that is negatively impacted by shrimp trawling, but the loggerhead populations in Australia are nominated as being affected by shrimp trawling as are the Australian flatback sea turtles. These turtles do move from feeding grounds to breeding grounds and back to feeding grounds on a regular basis. With work in Queensland, where turtles are being satellite tagged as well as using depth-temperature dataloggers as well as using mitochondrial DNA as well as using physical tags, turtles can be monitored throughout the year. The laparoscopic investigation, this is internal investigation, can determine when they are about to breed and almost the day when the turtle leaves its feeding ground can be nominated. It can be tracked to its nesting ground. Researchers find her on the nesting beach. The number of nesting events can be recorded and then the turtle can be tracked back to its feeding ground again. So, with some populations, you can define where most of the population is residing. Admittedly there are some populations, some loggerheads, that will move to New Caledonia from Queensland, for either feeding or breeding. Loggerhead turtles that feed on the southern Great Barrier Reef are known to migrate to New Caledonia to breed and then return at the end of the breeding season to exactly the same reef on the southern Great Barrier Reef. Similarly, sea turtles found feeding in New Caledonia move into Queensland for nesting.

40. So, the concept of breeding units can be established. I think we have a number of countries in very close proximity to each other. If you are looking at the turtles or the species that are involved with shrimp trawling. And we could nominate those as being loggerheads, the Australian flatback is not one of those listed in the dispute, the olive ridley sea turtle, also the hawksbill turtle and the green turtle to some extent. Their movements are fairly well known for some countries. Just because we don't know the movement of every turtle from a population in every country, there is no reason to say that we should disregard the idea of breeding units. The breeding unit is the only tool we have to say whether our numbers are increasing or decreasing and because of that I would stress again the need to use the paradigm of a breeding unit as a conservation unit and this is very important for those species that are affected by shrimp trawling.

**Mr. Liew**

41. Thank you again. [referring to graph 4, Appendix 2] There are two things when you talk about movements of turtles. One is the hatchling - that means those that have just emerged from the nest - so they also will move in the oceans and hatchlings are oceanic. That means that once they have emerged from the nest they will run straight into the sea and they will swim offshore and the prevailing currents will then carry them. And some of them, we don't know how many, will be carried into the ocean and they will circulate the ocean. So, for example if they are hatchlings that come from Terengganu in Malaysia, currents will then carry them and if the currents are flushing up and down [indicating the South China Sea] then they will follow the currents and be flushed up and down. Some of the hatchlings will make their way to the open oceans and promptly they will be carried into the open ocean. But you must remember, the hatchlings are very small, they are pelagic, they will remain very near the surface and they will be moving around and probably going a few times [around the Pacific Ocean gyres], we don't know. And for 5 [to] 7 years or even more until they grow up to a size of about a dinner plate. So during this period, they are more or less dispersed, this is the dispersion phase which most scientists agree to, but you must remember that during this phase they are really pelagic, shrimp trawlers are of no threat to them.

42. So even though you find juveniles coming here [pointing at the Californian/Mexican coast, graph 5, Appendix 2] they are still pelagic, there is very little chance that they get caught in shrimp trawlers. But they may be caught in gill nets, drift nets and so on. So, if you are talking about the loggerheads that nest here [pointing at Japan], the juveniles occur here [pointing at the Californian/Mexican coast] but eventually, when they decide to settle into their feeding grounds, they probably will try to make their way back to somewhere nearer this location [pointing at the coast off China]. So that is the pelagic phase. So, once they have completed the pelagic phase, they would then try to settle, especially for the loggerheads, the greens, the hawksbills and olive ridleys, they would settle and have already benthic habitat, that means they remain feeding close to the sea floor. That is the time when shrimp trawlers will impact them. But usually, by that time they would be settling closer to where the nesting grounds are. You are talking about a distance of nearly 10,000 km [referring to the distance across the Pacific Ocean], so that is why in general you find feeding grounds and nesting grounds to be in a close region, not feeding grounds here [pointing at the Californian/Mexican coast] and then nesting grounds there [pointing at Japan]. So, like the breeding unit in Hawaii, you will find that they will probably be feeding in the

region along that area [indicating the region around Hawaii]. The breeding unit of loggerheads in Japan will be feeding around there. The adults will be feeding around there and, in fact, satellite telemetry studies by the Fisheries Department in Japan have found that their loggerheads move to the coast of China to feed and there is where the feeding grounds are, not here [pointing at the Californian/Mexican coast].

43. Similarly for Australia, feeding grounds are around there [indicating the northeastern Australian region] and for this part and there [indicating the northwestern Australian region] for that region. It is very unlikely for turtles nesting here [pointing at the eastern Australian coast] to be feeding there [pointing at the northwestern Australian region]. To add to this point, I think that Mr. Guinea has already mentioned that Colin Limpus, in Australia, has made studies using laparoscopy to look at the abdominal cavity of female adults in their feeding grounds. And by looking, using the tube and a light they could see what is inside the abdominal cavity. And they found green turtles when they are feeding, the abdominal cavity is filled with food because they feed on sea grass and all that. And when they found that the females are about to breed, that means, about to make their migration to the nesting ground, the big follicles would have already formed and they would take quite a large amount of area in the abdominal cavity and there is very little food left in the gut. So, which means for a female to make their migration to the nesting ground, they will have to accumulate a lot of energy stores in their fat. So that is why you find turtles spending 3, 4 or 5 years before they will make their migration to breed, because they need to gather up enough or sufficient energy stores to make the migration.

44. So, in our work in Terrenganu, we have been tagging turtles for quite a number of years and every turtle that comes to the beach, we tag them, so we will know when the turtle first nests until the last day that she nests. So we will know exactly when was the first day she nested until the very last day. And some of them have nested 10 times. And every time there is a nesting interval of about 10 days, so you are talking about 100 days interval at the nesting ground. We have also satellite-tracked these turtles, the very same turtles, back to their feeding grounds. They would swim straight across the open ocean, they don't stop to feed and they would swim something like almost a month continuously before they reside back at their feeding ground. So you are talking about a turtle when they are ready to breed they will have to swim from their feeding ground, taking them one month, to their nesting ground. At the nesting ground they don't feed because the abdominal cavity is all full with eggs. There is no way they can feed and we have observed turtles, we have put ultra-sonic tags, we follow them, see what they do, we dive and observe what they are doing and most of the time the green turtles will be just sitting at the bottom and then waiting for the next nesting. They don't feed. So you are talking about 1 month to travel there and spending at least 2 months at the nesting site and then another month to go back to their feeding ground. So something like about 4 months without feeding. So, if you are talking about a loggerhead that is feeding here [pointing at the Californian/Mexican coast] and travelling 10,000 km to nest there [pointing at Japan] and then having to travel another 10,000 km to go back, it is very unlikely. So whatever loggerheads that are found here [pointing at the Californian Mexican coast] are probably just the pelagic phase and they will try to move back to areas very close to the nesting ground, because if you are talking about swimming 10,000 km, the swim itself will take at least 5 to 6 months without feeding and

loggerheads, we are talking about loggerheads in the open Pacific Ocean, it is not very likely.

45. Sometimes you may find strays that may not make it back to the west [referring to the Western Pacific]. Those strays will probably not be able to nest because it is just too distant. So, that is why I would say, if you are talking about breeding units, they will be quite isolated. There is a certain range. You cannot talk about breeding unit as here to there [pointing from the Californian coast to Western Pacific]. You're not talking about that kind of range - you are talking about this kind of a range [indicating the regional areas as marked], beyond that I think it would be very hard for them to survive. Now, coming back to Scott Eckert's leatherbacks, where he tracked them going south and he hypothesized that they would go across to here [pointing at the West Pacific] and come here [pointing at the Northern East Pacific]. Well, there is also another hypothesis. They could go from here directly to there. The numbers they could track is how many? 5, 10? Out of a total population of [Dr. Eckert's answer not audible]. OK, right, so I mean, I was thinking some of them may go south, some of them may go north, I don't know. But, going round the Pacific Ocean is just a hypothesis and yet to be proven. Perhaps it may be so, if he considers that all of them go south. But then we have also to remember the leatherbacks that are going in this Ocean are in very deep waters, totally not affected by shrimp trawling. Only high seas drift nets or gill nets or long lines will catch them. Trawling in Malaysia will not catch their turtles.

**Chairman**

46. Thank you. That brings us back to Dr. Poiner.

**Dr. Poiner**

47. Thanks Mr. Chairman. I'd like to raise two issues. I too think it is critically important that you focus on a breeding unit when deliberating and deciding on management measures. I also think it is very important that we are careful in not assuming that the process operating for one species of turtle will be the same process as operating for all species of turtle and I think the contrast from the information available for leatherbacks versus, say green turtles in and around the West Pacific is a good example to show that there are differences and I think there should be a great deal of care. Similarly, I think there should be a great deal of care in interpreting the impacts of fishing on different species in different areas. So, for example, Dr. Eckert mentioned that there is clear evidence that the US shrimp fisheries have had an impact on several species and I agree that there is clear evidence. But I also think, in determining the impact of a fishery on a breeding unit or globally, whatever perspective you take, you need to remember really that in making that assessment, the first thing you do is measure the catch rate of the turtles, in this case of the turtle species, and catch rates are usually relatively low in the sense that the number of turtles captured per number of trawls. Then you need to multiply that figure by the total effort, how much trawling in the overall fishery, to get a total number of individuals that are caught and then you need to make an assessment of what is the impact of that total number at whatever size on the population.

48. Now, fisheries vary tremendously and I think that the shrimp fisheries vary tremendously around the world in terms of the nature, distribution and level of effort. So, for example, where the incidental capture rate has been measured, and that has been

in the southern US fisheries and the Australian fisheries, there is very little difference in terms of the catch rate, i.e. the number of times a shrimp trawl actually captures, say, a loggerhead turtle. However there is a significant difference in terms of the effort in the two fisheries. So, for example in the east coast Australian fishery and the Northern Australian fishery, the effort levels are much lower than in the Gulf of Mexico fisheries. Hence, the total number captured will be much less. So then you need to make an assessment of what is the level of impact. Now, I must make it clear I'm not arguing that in saying those Australian fisheries that shrimp trawling is not a significant source of mortality, but you would need to be very careful in arguing that just because you demonstrate, in this case, that the impact of fishing in the Southern Gulf, in the Gulf of Mexico in the other US fisheries has had an impact on species is the major source of mortality anthropogenic on species of turtles there. You have got to be very careful in making that assumption that therefore it will be the major source of mortality in other areas. So, for example, especially as we know in those other areas, there has been and continues to be significant source of mortality, be it direct harvest or be it egg harvests.

**Chairman**

49. Some new points have come out. Do the experts want to carry on and take those up? Or, Dr. Eckert, you are looking thoughtful.

**Dr. Eckert**

50. Yes, I guess I'm in a position to decide if we want to argue specific points or if I should try to back up a little bit, and think in terms of the overall thesis. I guess maybe what I can do is illustrate this issue a little bit with an example. One of Liew's comments relative to the loggerhead (*Caretta caretta*) and its distribution around the ocean basins is interesting. Off the coast of Mexico, where these animals are in their developmental habitat, Mexican shrimpers are indeed catching juvenile loggerheads and what I am trying to point out with continually revisiting this point that we need to be aware of the entire stock range of these species when we are trying to apply conservation, is that in situations like that, where the developmental habitats may occur in other countries' jurisdictions, you may see it in a distant country's nesting population. A case in point for that is on the US Atlantic coast, we have two distinct genetic loggerhead populations, those that nest in the Carolina and Georgia and those that nest in Florida. The Florida population appears relatively stable whereas the Carolina population and the Georgia population have declined very significantly. It appears that one of the reasons for that is that the juveniles of those populations forage in two different locations. The juveniles from the Carolina and Georgia forage in Carolina and Georgia and a little bit down in to Florida in shipping areas, whereas those that are coming from the Florida population are foraging out of the Bahamas where there is no shipping. And this has defined why there has been two very different reflections on the nesting beaches. So, my point, that I want to stress over again, is that we need to understand those particular stock issues before going to try to manage stocks on regional basis. One of the arguments that was put forth in some documentation that we received is that the Malaysian green turtle populations nesting in the Turtle Islands are recovering and therefore shrimping is not having an impact on those populations. Well, we have now heard quite a bit of documentation that green turtles do not forage where they necessarily feed and what probably hasn't been pointed out is that often, it isn't the

nesting females that are impacted by fisheries, but rather the juveniles and the foraging females. Part of that comes from the way that these animals behave. As Liew pointed out, reproductive females, with the exception of the leatherback, do not feed during the nesting season and they tend to just hang out on the bottom often that will be in hard bottom areas where they are more secure. There has been some work done on diving behaviour in hawksbills and tracking work with hawksbills and green turtles that seemed to indicate that. And so, in the case of that particular argument - the fact that the population may be going up, indicates that it is not being impacted by shrimp fishing in the Turtle Islands - doesn't stand up. What you need to be looking at in that case is what are the juvenile populations and the resident female populations and resident mature populations, what is happening to them on their natal grounds. Again we have to get back to understanding what these stocks are, where these stocks go and before we are going to properly be able to talk in terms of stock management and that is simply my point.

**Chairman**

51. Dr. Frazier, do you have any further comments at this stage?

**Dr. Frazier**

52. I guess, briefly I basically am in agreement with both sides of the argument. I think that we are trying to fine tune a complex issue. I think we are all in agreement that we need to manage a stock, the question is what is that stock? and where does that stock reside. In the case of Australia, there are many years of studies; in the case of the US there are many years of studies and there is a reasonably good idea of where stocks go. In most cases, we don't have that information. That takes us to this problem of no information is not negative information. The description that Liew gave distinguishing what leatherbacks do and what the hard-shelled turtles do, I find correct. The problem is: where can we actually say we know a stock well enough to be able to say all of the different means of protecting that stock throughout decades of maturity, of the animal developing to maturity, and then decades of living after that to its full reproductive potential? In most cases I don't believe we have that information. I agree that we must prioritize conservation activities, I am not convinced that we should have an either/or approach and look for the major, the most important and only do that. Sea turtle conservation strategies for decades have tried to impress upon the need for integrated activities, I think all the people here have argued that you need to protect eggs and you need to protect turtles in the oceans. Doing one and not the other is not enough. I am a bit confused as to why sometimes, some of the submissions seem to focus on the most important, I don't think that's the argument. I think the argument is integrating conservation, so that it takes into account all the distinct aspects of this very complicated animal. And in that respect we then come into what are the pragmatic ways to address some of those threats. And that then becomes a more political issue, that's outside the hands of biologists. In conservation biology, what we look for often are ways for users to pay for the way they are exploiting resources. There is a concept there of user pays.

53. Now on trade issues, this is not my training, but in trade issues I would say that that means incorporating the externalities into the cost of the product. So that the consumer then pays for the product. So that the product is both environmentally and

socially acceptable to the producer. That's simply my way of seeing things, I don't see contention here, I see that we are viewing, I think Buddha made a statement once that three blind men describing an elephant would describe it in different terms. One a column, one a large wall and the other a fan and I certainly don't consider myself an expert, I am specialist, but I have great deal to learn about turtles although I spent 30 years learning about them. So I think we are probing here, there is something extremely complex that we are trying to grapple with, which is a great challenge to conserve.

**Chairman**

54. Thank you very much. Dr. Guinea, I think just to take that on a little bit. Dr. Poiner mentioned earlier that he thought we should be talking about the likelihood of recovery using different management tools. I am not sure whether those who were advocating the integrated approach mean we should use management tools all the time, or whether we should sort of try and prioritize it or identify different tools for different populations. I wonder if perhaps you could develop it a little further because I think in your original written proposals you talked about the importance of having nationally developed conservation programmes with a national flavour and I think that perhaps in that context it would be useful to hear whether you could develop the points a little bit more.

**Mr. Guinea**

55. Yes, in my original submission I was talking about countries developing ownerships of technologies and using technology appropriate to that country. This is part of the concept of responsible fishing. The individual countries have an idea of the resources they are taking from the sea, they know what is marketable, they know where the profit lies, whether the profit is in shrimp, whether the profit is in small fish, so in fact whether the bycatchers are one of the components of the profitability of the fishery. In that regard, the countries know what the target species are. By importing technologies, something that works in the USA or Australia or works in the other country that may be imposing a technology, the ownership of that technology stays with the exporting country until the receiving country has modified it to the fishery - modified it to their existing social, cultural and financial arrangements. This modification process gives the country an ownership and this also builds up a concept of, rather than importing something that is good for conservation of the species that is in our waters, this is now something that we are doing, we have modified a technology for our present conditions. This may involve a modification to the design, a change in the net. I was very impressed when I saw the Thai Turtle-Free Device. It didn't resemble the Georgia Jumpers or the USA TEDs on which probably it had its origins and it was something that was definitely Thai looking. It had an elegance that you could associate with Thai and the Thai people. The technologists that demonstrated it showed it with a national pride. This was our TED. We have a similar situation in Australia where we have the AusTED and our AusTED doesn't resemble a number of TEDs that you can commercially buy from America, but our AusTED is flexible. So it is not a rigid TED, it is not a soft TED, it is a flexible TED made of plastic coated stainless steel cables. It has cross members which are different to other TED designs. and trials in Australian waters have indicated that the fishing fleet are happy with it. Although more refinement, more experimentation is required, there is a general feeling that, yes, this is something that we

have developed, that has come from CSIRO, has come from various fishing organizations. ... [end of tape]

**Dr. Poiner**

56. ... the issue I was raising is in terms of the way you will introduce a bycatch reduction device, call it TED or whatever, and how you use that tool in fishery. You can do it in different ways. One way is to do a certification approach, that has been used and then you focus a lot on certifying reperformance of that device. The other you take, is an agreement on specific targets and then let the industry or whoever develop ways of meeting those targets and then you focus on monitoring of performance and reaching that target rather than certification. In different fisheries and different conditions we will use those different approaches.

**Chairman**

57. Thank you very much. Dr. Frazier would you like to continue on that one?

**Dr. Frazier**

58. I think the lessons to be learned from the Australian fisheries are profound. The Australian fisheries are what are called "closed entry". There is a limited number of vessels which can go and shrimp. Unfortunately that model of managing fisheries is not common. If other countries could have done what Australia has done, we would all be much better off today. The people responsible for developing TEDs in the US had originally planned on voluntary compliance, and there was a long period of trying to make that work. The fishery is over-capitalized, there are too many people fishing, as in many countries, as in most countries, and in the end the only way to make it work, was through certification - was to go the other road. That was not the original intention, in terms of what I understand, although perhaps Dr. Eckert who has worked in that area more than I have, could clarify - my understanding was the original intention was voluntary compliance. But because it is an open-entry fishery, it means it is a free-for-all. And therefore, it is not only a national sense of ownership, it is more of a personal sense of responsibility toward the fishery. This is what we lack on a world basis now. With a few exceptions, and Australia is one of those exceptions.

**Chairman**

59. There are others, are there?

**Dr. Eckert**

60. New Zealand.

**Dr. Frazier**

61. Well, the ITQs [individual transferable quotas] are not working there, I don't think.

**Dr. Poiner**

62. One comment: limited entry does not necessarily equate to reduced effort, I think that should be the point. It just means limited entry is used often to either manage

over-capitalization rather than effort-reductions. So for example, one example I am very familiar with in the Australian Northern Prawn Fishery where a halving in the number of participants does not mean a halving of the effort. And the effort for a variety of reasons is now approaching the same levels with half that number of participants. So you should be very careful in that. Because you get into issues of efficiency of the fleet. The argument I was raising here was that I think the important issue when dealing with the management of fisheries, be it the management of the stock being targeted or the management of the impact of those fisheries, you need to be very careful and you need to be very clear in terms of the nature of the fishery and what the management objectives of that fishery are.

**Chairman**

63. On the same point, Dr. Eckert.

**Dr. Eckert**

64. Just a brief comment. My understanding, and I can be corrected by my Australian colleagues, but the Australian fishery is sociologically quite different from what we saw in the United States. In the United States shrimp fishermen are generally independent owner-operators. I was in the south-east during a lot of this bru-ha-ha, so I understand a lot of what went on in the application of TEDs, and one of the great problems that occurred there was that these independent operators-owners do not have an umbrella spokesperson or any kind of an organization under which they work cooperatively. So when approaches were made to them to voluntarily adopt things, you basically had to go to each boat, to each owner, to each little parish in Louisiana, and say "will you please use TEDs and here's why." From an environmental education perspective, which is often a good way of introducing these sorts of issues, because it has been my experience that shrimp fishermen care more about the environment that they are working in, than just about any people I know. They are very sensitive to what is going on out there. But you need to introduce the issue of turtles to them. The reason it was such a dismal failure in the United States was simply that it was too big a task. In Australia, it is a relatively young fishery, it appears that they have tremendous cooperation, government to industry and industry as an industry, instead of a bunch of individual guys out there fishing. So, when you talk about the approaches that transpired into actually introducing TEDs or BRDs (bycatch reduction devices) into the fleet, it has been a much more pleasant task, and this is why Australia can talk in terms of voluntary, probably getting good cooperation on voluntary introduction, whereas in the United States, despite very valiant attempts, it was an absolute failure. It is also one of the reasons why the application of TED regulations in the United States was so slow in coming. There has often been discussion that application of TEDs took 10 or 15 years in the United States. Well, this is often why. They went down a lot of blind-ends before they finally found the scenario that worked. And I would have to say that that has only been at most 5 years, it really hasn't been that long before an effective way of getting TEDs put into place has occurred.

**Chairman**

65. Thank you. I am sorry Dr. Liew, I have kept you waiting a long time. You have got some new subjects to raise.

**Mr. Liew**

66. Before that, I just want to ask a question. Should not the voluntary option be given first, before you force somebody? Should not the fishermen or the country be given the voluntary option?

67. I would just raise some points that I have noticed in some of the other experts' deliberations. This is about protecting eggs or adults and about using reproductive values to say that it is more important to protect adults than to protect the eggs. A healthy population needs individuals in all stages of development, not just eggs or just the adults. It would be detrimental to turtle populations to say that we should protect the adults and allow rampant egg harvest to continue in countries, especially when commercial egg harvest is still a very major threat. We need to learn from the Malaysian leatherback situation, the Sarawak green turtle experience, we need to learn from them. Where they have failed to protect the eggs in the early stages, and the population is now in decline. In the US egg harvest is now probably not a problem, but mortality in adults or mortality of adults in shrimp trawl is. So, to conserve their turtles, they need to convince the public that the adults must be protected, because their eggs are already well-protected. They must now convince properly their public that adults must be protected because they have a high reproductive value. Some of the experts cite the work of Crouse that the reproductive value of an egg is 1, and the reproductive value of a breeding adult would be 584. I would like to note that the unit that is used here is in numbers, 1 egg to 584 for the female or breeding adult. Can we use numbers to equate an egg to an adult? In ecological modeling, we have to standardize the unit and we have to standardize in energy units or in biomass, biomass means in weight. So a turtle egg only weighs about 40 grammes, while a young adult female will weigh 60 kg, which is about 1,500 times the biomass of an egg. So when we standardize reproductive value in terms of biomass, not in terms of numbers, then the reproductive value of an egg is 1 and that of a young adult is 0.4. So using reproductive values is just how you interpret it, but I feel we should interpret in terms of biomass rather than in numbers because we cannot equate an egg that small, with an adult. It is true that the mortality of adults has a very instantaneous impact on the status of a population. Almost immediately you will be able to see the decline of the number of nestings. But the impact on eggs or hatchling mortality will not be obvious until decades later, many years later. By that time it will be too late to take remedial action because the population has virtually collapsed. That's what has happened to the leatherbacks in Malaysia, and [green turtles] in Sarawak. It is like a case of trying to determine which virus is more deadly, the Ebola virus or the AIDS virus. The Ebola virus is a very contagious virus, spreads very rapidly and it kills in a matter of days. But because of that you are able to identify it, isolate it and then take action. The AIDS virus, and its transmission is more discreet, it will take many, many years before you detect it. By that time millions of people are infected. You have to be very careful when you talk about protecting adults or protecting eggs. I think both have to be handled with equal priority. Not just one.

**Chairman**

68. Do other experts want to take on those points?

**Dr. Eckert**

69. Just a couple of points. Liew's point taking an example from Malaysia is very good on a number of fronts, not just for the problems sustained by the Malaysians with their leatherbacks which was really, I consider it, through no fault of their own, there was simply no scientific knowledge at the time to suggest that the 10 per cent egg buy-back that they were executing in Malaysia was not going to be adequate to restore the population. And also having worked in Malaysia for some time I have to say that Malaysia has one of the best conservation programmes for marine turtles anywhere in the world. They have really taken hold of the situation relative to the conservation of their nesting stocks, and done very, very well. It's been a very admirable effort.

70. A quick comment about the reproductive value point that Liew was bringing up. The reproductive value curves, the references they are making to that, is the value of the individual towards supporting the population reproductively. The only time that you would want to use a terminology such as caloric value or something along those lines is that would be more of a fisheries biomass term relative to harvesting the egg or the adult. If you were going to harvest an adult, how much of a protein yield are you going to get? So the reproductive curve is based on the ability of the individual to support the stability of a population. That's why that value is expressed as it is. The models that were done for that are arguably difficult to work with. They are based on loggerheads, and much of the data is on declining population for loggerheads. That's why you see such a wide range. When we say it takes 1,000 to 10,000 eggs to yield 1 adult, it is because of the lack of precision in a lot of those estimates. But what is clear is qualitatively, that it takes a whole lot of production of eggs, because of the high mortality and small size classes to get one adult. That's why we use what seem to be a very broad range of numbers. There is probably nothing to suggest that those numbers aren't within the ball park for all species because we see very similar reproductive strategies across all species. Reproduction in marine turtles is very conservative and so those numbers are probably not so far off for the other species as well. And as Liew well pointed out, we definitely need to take a balanced approach to all of this. The example that I gave in my report of the leatherbacks in Mexico is a very good one. In Malaysia they had an almost 100 per cent egg harvest for many, many years and probably until the mid-1980s didn't have a lot of at-sea mortality, that we are aware of, that we can quantify. There may have been some trawling mortality that Chan and Liew have documented very well but there was also the high-seas driftnet fishery that kicked in in the early 1980s. So that population decline was probably due primarily to the egg taking and it took 40-50 years to actually see it start being reflected in a distinctive manner on the population.

71. In Mexico we have a different situation. The Mexicans have done extraordinarily well at protecting their beaches, they have the marines out there, camped out on the beach to protect their nesting females and their eggs and they have severely limited mortality for upwards of 15 years and maybe a little longer on leatherbacks. Yet we have seen in excess of 90 per cent decline in that population in 10 years. The primary reason for that is that we weren't taking a whole population approach to our conservation. We didn't know that the Chileans or the Chilean and the Peruvian gill-net fisheries were taking large numbers of leatherbacks. And we didn't figure that out until last year when we put satellite transmitters on them. So it is a classic example of being blind-sided from the other direction. It wasn't the egg-take issue, it was the high-seas

take. Again it hammers home this point, that you have to manage these populations in a holistic sense, that you have to understand all the sources of mortality and you have to deal with those. Now the conservative approach relative to shrimp fishing is if you have mortality associated with shrimp fishing that you have to fix it. It's the bottom line. How you want to approach that? You have heard quite a bit of variation and I am sure that you are going to have to wrestle with that on your own, but the bottom line is that if you've got a problem, you've got to fix it.

**Chairman**

72. Thank you very much. Do any of the other experts want to take on these points at this time?

**Dr. Frazier**

73. In my comments to the Panel, I tried to, in the best terms I could, to simplify this aspect of the concept of the breeding value. This is a magic number, it is not something you go out and measure. It is a way of synthesizing, in one number, many different aspects in the ecology of an animal. To try and visualize very simply in a column of numbers, this animal represents more in the reproduction and maintenance to the population than this animal in this stage. It is an abstraction, the fact that hatchlings are 1 and breeding females are 584, that can be changed. The hatchlings can be 0.5 if we like. 1 is used simply because that's the unit to start with. It's simply a matter of convenience. The end number will vary from population to population, and will certainly vary within a population through time, depending on how those ecological processes are operating. The reason for doing this is to simplify many different things that are happening in the ecology of an animal, to very simply come up with a list and say this is where there is more importance in maintaining the population. I don't think any sea turtle biologist would recommend omitting protection on all stages. This gets us back to this integrated approach. The way perhaps to use these numbers is, if I protect a handful of eggs, or if I protect one large animal just about to breed, where will I have more value in my population? Although I have lots of eggs here that could potentially become breeders or have an animal here which is just one. By the odds of biology (and biology is not a pure science, its a science of statistics and stochastic processes) this handful of eggs is not anywhere near the value of this one animal by the chances. So if I have the opportunity to protect this animal, my instantaneous response to the population is likely to be much greater than protecting these eggs. This does not mean I should ignore the eggs, it simply means that I should not be deceived into protecting large numbers of eggs is going to give me an immediate response and necessarily going to protect the population. This again takes out of biology into the social sciences. We see this a great deal in Mexico. Scott has mentioned that. There is a big impact politically in protecting eggs because politicians can go to the beach and have their pictures taken, they can be displayed in local newspapers and they can be seen protecting turtles. It's very visual, it's charismatic and that leads us to a danger in focusing and in omitting the other aspect which is not visible to us, and that's what happens in the ocean. At no point in my submissions, and I don't think in anyone here, would anyone want to omit protection of the different life stages. That's not an issue, we want to integrate it. The breeding value is simply an abstraction to try and focus where an individual may have

more value. One egg does not have as much value stochastically as one individual which is near to breeding or indeed breeding. That's simply the matter.

**Chairman**

74. Thank you. Dr. Poiner.

**Dr. Poiner**

75. The issue of a reproductive value, again I would agree with Dr. Frazier that I don't think there is a lot of argument about the reproductive value of an egg versus a mature female for example. However, I think that in making an assessment of the impact of an activity there is the other part of the equation that needs to be taken into consideration, that's the relative mortality rates on those different stages. And that's invariably done under modeling, in modeling studies, and then you get into, what some would argue into the lap of the gods, because you are starting to make some of the assumptions, and what you find when you actually look at the modeling studies, the differences that are often predicted usually relate to different levels of mortality on different stages fed into the models. Hence the important issue is that there are two bits of data, you need not just the reproductive value data in terms of making those assessments. But I would agree with Dr. Frazier that the important issue here is that you need to focus on the whole population, all sources of mortality and obviously in any management situation, in any population stock, given that you probably won't be able to deal with all of them, you deal with the bigger ones or the most important ones first. Hence it is important to know what they are, and where they're acting and at what stage of the population they're acting.

**Chairman**

76. Thank you. Dr. Eckert

**Dr. Eckert**

77. From a management perspective I often argue with resource managers on this. Using these value curves and saying that approximately 500 eggs equal 1 adult turtle, what that also suggests from a conservation management perspective is that you should be able to afford that much more effort to protecting those juveniles and adults. I often hear from managers that it is so expensive to protect juveniles and adults because we have to do fishery modifications, we have to whatever and yet, those adults are worth 500 times more than an egg on a beach. So if you're going to protect your animals you should be allocating your resources in a similar manner and in a world of limited resources, you don't have enough money to do everything, and that's understood. So when you look at these things, you say "OK, how much is it going to cost to protect those eggs on the beach? Yes, I have to do that". And I also have to realize that I get more conservation bank from my buck by protecting the adults as well. So you need to balance it, but also be aware that, yes, it is more expensive to go out there and protect those juveniles and adults, but you're getting a lot more return for that value that you're putting into that conservation effort.

**Chairman**

78. Thank you very much. Dr.Guinea you had a point on this?

**Mr. Guinea**

79. Yes, thank you. I'll just make it a comment here. This magic figure of 584 does raise some problems in that it tends to bind us into a set way of thinking. The figure 584 has been produced for computer synthesis. This figure enables certain numbers in certain columns to add up to a certain prescribed number at the end. In the Australian studies of loggerheads, the figure, instead of 584, was somewhere between 200 and 400. And so that's within the same species, be it two different reproductive units or demographic units. So this will change from breeding unit to breeding unit, but its use is just to make rows and columns, add up to suitable numbers. Now whether it is actually viable in the field, in real life, is another point altogether. A conservative approach is that anything that is impacting negatively on any of the stages of the sea turtle life-cycle should in fact be addressed. Now I have mentioned this already. if it's a death through incidental capture in gill nets that should be addressed. If it's a problem of excessive harvesting, then that should be addressed. There are a few advantages in having shore-based conservation activities. These advantages come from community involvement, in that more and more people become involved in the conservation process. If you're going to have your conservation process restricted to the back decks of trawling vessels some kilometres off the coast, the community is not involved in that process. The community doesn't see the process going on, and they may be led to believe that "Yes, sea turtles are secure because we have TEDs on the nets on the vessels that are operating off-shore". I think a better all-encompassing approach is to have the community at the village, state or parish level involved with protecting their turtle beach and having resources put into that to focus on sea turtles and the state of the oceans but not to the exclusion of protecting sea turtles at sea and from various forms of mortality, be it shrimp trawlers or gill nets or whatever.

**Chairman**

80. Thank you very much. Dr. Liew.

**Mr. Liew**

81. In general I agree that we have to take care of both, but I brought this point up because there were some statements saying that protecting adults is more important than protecting eggs. We have to look at both, and not only look at both, we have to look at situations, populations. Some populations, you find that eggs are not the problem, you don't really need to protect them, because they are already well-protected. That's why you have to concentrate on the adults. But there are certain other populations where egg harvesting is the problem. So that is where you have to, and in these countries they usually have very limited financial resources for conservation. All conservations have very limited resources for some reason and that is why they have to concentrate more on the eggs because they are really having problems with the eggs. They don't really get enough quota for protection because they are still harvested, legally or illegally or whatever, or even in cases where you have problems of predation so that is where you find that you need to channel your attention to protection of the eggs. And if, of course, adults also have problems definitely you need to. But every population you have to weigh the situation and see which is of more priority and where you should channel your resources.

**Chairman**

82. Thank you very much. We had an extended discussion from the experts. Of course we'd be happy to go on with that, but I think it might be more efficient if we interrupted it at this stage and allowed the parties, each in turn, to make their comments and put their questions for the experts and I think once we have heard those five interventions that would be a suitable point at which to break for tonight so that the experts can then have time to reflect and come back tomorrow morning with their round of responses. As I indicated earlier we propose the parties to follow the order which had been established in our earlier meetings, which is to say to begin first with the complaining parties, in the order of Thailand, India, Pakistan and Malaysia and then to turn finally to the United States. So perhaps I could invite the Ambassador of Thailand to give his comments and questions. You have the floor.

**The Ambassador of Thailand**

83. Mr. Chairman, I really appreciate the chance to appear before you again and to witness this very interesting conversation this afternoon. I must say from the outset that as you know I am no expert in shrimp and turtle apart from a great lover of turtles and of a fond eater of shrimps. So I find this discussion this afternoon extremely educational and interesting. It reminds me of the first morning that we brought this case to you Mr. Chairman We were very concerned and very worried about the time and effort that we should put in. But I think that it is more than compensated by the knowledge that we have gained today. Well, I'd like to say given the fact that I am no expert on this, and given the complexity of the matters at hand, and given the fact that we have a very high quality discussion by the experts this afternoon and they also show a high degree of professionalism and professional ethics, I have not much to say this afternoon. But I would certainly like to reflect upon what has been said so far by the five experts and I shall come back to you tomorrow. I would like to consult with my expert back home. I simply would like to say that, number one is to thank the experts for their input because you have worked hard to answer all these questions raised by the Panel, and we have made our comments to your responses and I think that I don't want to repeat them here today or tomorrow. Secondly, I must say that we appreciate not only your effort but we have learned a great deal from what you have said in your written responses and from your intervention this afternoon. I only hope that we would have a better understanding of this very complex matter so that both the conservation and the enforcement could be better done to the benefit of all. I think I will leave it at that, I thank Mr. Guinea for pointing to the Thai TED. I think it looks better than our Thai financial flu which is floating around over there!

**Chairman**

84. Thank you Mr. Ambassador. Perhaps I could now invite the representative of India to put questions and comments on behalf of his delegation.

**The representative of India**

85. The issue we are looking at today is sea turtle conservation problems and that is the purpose of this meeting and before I express any comments or views on this, I would like to take this opportunity to thank you and the experts for having provided us and my delegation especially with such an enlightening experience and of course to say

that, since that this is the first meeting that we are having in the New Year to wish all of you a very happy and prosperous New Year. Having said that Mr. Chairman, our delegation has no specific question to put to the experts. We have heard with a lot of interest the view that sea turtle conservation has to be looked at in a holistic manner, in an integrated manner. It is something that we ourselves are very much committed to and have worked at actively towards promoting in our own way and I think I should just stop there and let the work carry on. Thank you.

**Chairman**

86. Thank you very much. Perhaps I could now turn to the representative of Pakistan.

**The representative of Pakistan**

87. Thank you Mr. Chairman and I am extremely grateful to you for this opportunity and my delegation owes a debt of gratitude to the worthy experts for their very enlightening comments. In fact for me this is the first lesson in marine biology and certainly I need a little more time to reflect on what they said, but I greatly appreciate the kind of very knowledgeable comment they made on various issues. Thank you Mr. Chairman.

**Chairman**

88. Perhaps I could now turn to the representative of Malaysia and invite him to make whatever comments or questions he might have.

**The representative of Malaysia**

89. Mr. Chairman, thank you very much. I, like the rest of my colleagues around the table, would like to thank you Mr. Chairman, members of the panel and our distinguished experts. I too do not profess to be a turtle expert, being a trade man, I found these discussions extremely enlightening. One thing I definitely learnt is that there is no single prescription to an illness, it all depends on the degree of the illness. I would like to take the example of having the flu. If it is a simple flu, you just take a Panadol, but if it is a bad case of flu, then you go for antibiotic or maybe even a jab. The point that I am trying to say is that one thing I learnt today is that conservation takes many different aspects and methods of conserving turtles. Mr. Chairman, Malaysia has already put in its questions in writing yesterday.

**Chairman**

90. On that point you are referring to the questions that were included in the written comments on the reports that we had from the experts. Perhaps we could invite the experts tomorrow to address those points.

**The representative of Malaysia**

91. Sure, Sir, and we would also like to reserve our right in the event that we would like to come back to any further questions.

**Chairman**

92. I think that concludes the points from the complaining parties, although I note that there may well be the possibility of further questions tomorrow, additional to the ones that have already been put forward by Malaysia. There will no doubt be time for those, if anything further eventuates. Can I now turn to the United States and ask if they have comments and questions that they wish to put forward?

**The representative of the United States**

93. I first want to thank the Panel for again coming to Geneva for this very difficult case. I want to thank also the Panel and the parties and the experts for trying to accommodate our scheduling requests and I know that our delegation spoke to all of the parties and they all agreed to our request. Unfortunately, we still couldn't get it right it quite right, Mr. Balton was not available to come, he sends his regrets. Of course I'd like to thank the experts. They did an outstanding job of a massive amount of information and a very limited amount of time. I think they've done Ph.D thesis in a few weeks.

94. Just a preliminary comment on the procedure. Pakistan presented all new facts, basically responding on their own respect to the questions and Malaysia in its brief also presented new facts. It was a new conservation programme involving different coloured boats and different exclusion zones which wasn't present in their prior briefs. We are not commenting on that, we understand that there is not the time for new information but we would ask if that is something that the Panel wants to consider, that we of course be given a chance to respond to it. We also have developed a list of questions which I could read to you now, or else Mr. Andersen was suggesting that we could also type them up very quickly and fax them tonight if that would be more convenient or I could do both.

**Chairman**

95. I think if you have them available in writing, I think it would help everybody and save our time now. If you could just read them out, they would then be read into the record and then tomorrow they could just be answered. If we could have the written version tonight, that would be helpful for the experts to prepare their answers.

**The representative of the United States**

96. There's been some dispute among the experts about the recoveries of various populations and even about whether one can define various populations. Our question about that is, leaving aside the specific populations and in particular the Malaysian Sabah Turtle Island populations which is much discussed, aren't there other sea turtle populations found in each of the complainants waters that are members of populations which are not yet showing signs of recovery? Further, if such sea turtles suffer incidental mortality in shrimp trawl nets, wouldn't this contribute to the endangerment of sea turtles?

97. This is a question, referring to Mr. Guinea's response and also to the other experts as well. Mr. Guinea performed a calculation based on the reproductive values of sea turtles and concluded that the annual mortality of 5,000 sea turtles from Gahirmatha was "relatively minor". It was not clear to us reading that, whether that was intended to be an analysis of threats to Gahirmatha or merely a hypothetical example. In any event,

could the other experts comment on whether shrimp trawling on that level would be relatively minor, shrimp trawling mortality would be relatively minor off the coast India?

98. All the experts have noted various causes of sea turtle mortality, including mortality on the beaches and due to incidental mortality in shrimping and various fishing operations. Our question is: does the existence of all of these threats to sea turtles make it more important or less important to prevent sea turtle mortality in shrimp nets? In other words, I think we have to go to the analogy used by Mr. Liew and also by Malaysia. If the patient comes in with a heart condition and a kidney condition and a lung condition and the doctor says we should treat all three because the patient is seriously ill, is it appropriate to say well don't bother treating the heart condition because there is also two other serious conditions.

99. I think I have heard the answer to this, but it is important to clarify. Do the experts agree that TEDs, when, properly installed and used, reduce the mortality of sea turtles in shrimp trawl nets? Related question: if all the world's shrimp trawl fleets used TEDs, would this contribute to the reduction in the threat to sea turtles? Note that we are not asking whether TEDs would be sufficient, but whether they would contribute to sea turtle conservation, whether it would help. We are also not asking a sociological question about how TEDs should come about to be used, about whether it should be voluntary or mandatory, but just the scientific question, that if TEDs were used properly would it help sea turtle conservation.

100. This is a question to Dr. Eckert: there is a comment in your answer that seasonal migrations would not be expected in regions with warm waters. I think there is some confusion about what that meant. I think it would be helpful if that statement could be clarified. Question to Mr. Poiner. In his statements he noted that 6-8 years would be helpful for the adoption of TEDs. We have also heard talk that the Thai TED is very effective and in fact beautiful and apparently was adopted in just a matter of months or for about a year. We would just like the experts to discuss that. Question to all the experts, Mr. Liew in particular: there has been a lot of talk about beach conservation versus conservation of adult turtles. Our question is would the use of TEDs exclude the adoption of beach conservation programmes. Is there some reason why a country can't do both? Question to all the experts: both Dr. Poiner and Mr. Guinea mentioned time and area closures as helpful approaches to sea turtle conservation. Could the other experts comment on this and in particular address whether sea turtle mortality remains a problem in areas where and during times when shrimp trawling is not banned?

101. Follow-up question. I believe Mr. Poiner noted that there was contemporaneous monitoring going on in Australia which helped these bans and whether that same monitoring is used in any of the complainant countries. Follow-up question to that is also about "hot spots", whether we have enough science to really select all of the hot spots where sea turtles and shrimp trawling might interact. Mr. Chairman, I hope that would be most of my questions but I hope that we would be able to reserve our rights to ask a few more questions tomorrow because we've heard a lot today.

**Chairman**

102. Thank you. I note then that there will be the possibility of further questions tomorrow from at least three of the participants. Meeting adjourned until 9.30 am. tomorrow.

## Second day - 22 January 1998

**Mr. Chairman**

103. Last night, just before we closed the meeting, the US asked to have the opportunity to respond to any material that was contained in the comments from the parties on the expert's reports. Any material that was either further argumentation or new evidence that had not been produced at the previous meeting because we had at that time closed off the process. I would just like to recall in this context the opening remark I made at the beginning of the session yesterday, which was to the effect that it's not the purpose of this meeting to hear further argumentation or new evidence, that the process was really intended for hearing the experts, and questions and comments to the experts and I added that the Panel will not take account of interventions outside this framework. That also was intended to apply to the documents submitted prior to this meeting as well. In other words, to the extent that they fall outside this framework, they will not be taken into account by the Panel for arriving at our conclusions. So, for that purpose we don't see that there should be a need to respond to it at this stage.

**The representative of the United States**

104. Thank you Mr. Chairman we are certainly comfortable with that, we were just then expecting none of these new arguments would be reflected in the descriptive part of the Panel's Report. Is that correct?

**Mr. Chairman**

105. No, that is not quite. The documents have already been submitted and everything that would be here will actually appear as part of the record. What I'm talking about is what we're actually going to take account of, as opposed to what we are not going to take account of, and that fact will be mentioned in the descriptive part. Is that sufficient?

**The representative of the United States**

106. That's fine, thank you.

**The representative of Malaysia**

107. Mr. Chairman thank you very much for giving us the floor. We have just heard what you have just stated and we will certainly adhere to that decision. But just for the record, yesterday the US had stated that Malaysia had in our comments introduced the new facts and I think we would like to be given the opportunity to respond to that. Can we do that now or later?

**Mr. Chairman**

108. You mean you wish to point to the document to which bits you consider are or are not. By all means, please do.

**The representative of Malaysia**

109. Malaysia's comments on the "zoning of trawling activities in Malaysia" as per paragraph 1 of our comments on responses of experts [Section V, paragraphs 5.313-316] is not a new effect. The comments are an amplification of what we had stated

earlier in our submission, i.e. Malaysia's second submission, answers to questions posed by the Panel to the Parties, in answer to question 27, paragraph 10.7 to 10.8 at page 14 and is a response to Annexes I and II of Mr. Frazier. Thank you.

**Chairman**

110. Thank you. The Panel takes note of that remark. Passing on, perhaps we can now go back to the questions that we were last night gathering from the parties to put to the experts this morning. We had some questions that were included in the Malaysian document. These are the ones after page 20 headed "Questions to the Experts". The first four were for Dr. Eckert and the other six were for all experts. We also had questions from the United States which have since been confirmed and circulated in writing, I hope everybody has those. There are eight of those questions. There were two other parties last night who indicated that they might possibly have questions this morning, can I inquire whether that is so on or not. Malaysia?

**The representative of Malaysia**

111. Not at this point Sir.

**Chairman**

112. Can I ask the Ambassador of Thailand whether he is likely to have any questions this morning?

**The Ambassador of Thailand**

113. I am working on one or two questions, Mr. Chairman, and I will let you know as soon as possible.

**Chairman**

114. Thank you. Very well, in that case we will proceed to ask the experts to respond to the questions that are already there, that's to say the ones that are in the Malaysian document and the US questions and, as yesterday perhaps, I can give the floor in alphabetical order to the experts to respond to these. You have the floor Dr. Eckert.

**Dr. Eckert**

115. Thank you. I guess I'm starting here with the questions from the Malaysian Delegation.[678] In answering to the first question about the hypothesis of migrations relative to joint jurisdiction by the United States and the country of Malaysia, I have presented the data that I have used to construct that hypothesis yesterday during the presentation. I feel very strongly that the hypothesis is very well supported actually by the scientific evidence available. There may be some question as to its publication status and whether it is in press, some of it is in press currently and I have to say that the information is so recent - this tracking study in the Pacific is currently ongoing - and it will probably be a matter of at least two years before that project is in a position to publish that information. So, you will need to take the information as I present it as a

[678] See Appendix 1 to this Annex.

scientific expert as it stands. As I said before I do believe that hypothesis is quite well supported. The other issue I presented yesterday was that there is a potential for cross jurisdictional relationship between Malaysia and the US in the green turtle populations as well. Guam and the Northern Mariana Islands do have green turtle populations foraging and nesting. There is actually a nice little nesting population in Tinian of green turtles who are well within the migratory distances travelled by green turtle females post-nesting and that certainly does not even include juvenile foraging habitats or juvenile migrations which we know so much less about. So I think there is good solid evidence to propose that there is a possible joint jurisdiction between Malaysian leatherback and Malaysian green turtles stocks. That's the basis of that answer.

116. The answer relative to rates of turtles strandings where TEDs are currently required. I don't have a lot of information on that. Probably the best study to date that I am aware of is that by Crowder et. al., showing that in actual use, if I remember correctly, there was a 44 per cent reduction in strandings due to the use of TEDs in shrimp nets. Relative to the relationship between turtle strandings and shrimping activities in the reports, such as that on sea turtles that has been described here, you have to remember that it is something of an ongoing discussion on that information. The information at this point can really be considered quantitatively factual. What they are basically seeing is that their strandings do continue and the question is why are those continuing. Is it an enforcement issue, is it an issue of TED design, is it an issue of closure areas, is it an issue of pulse fishing - this is one of the things that Jack Frazier described in his report. There is also some possibilities, there haven't been a lot of tests done on a CPUE basis so there is some question that there may be continued strandings simply due to the fact that populations are getting larger out there. The fact that turtle excluder devices have gone into effect have meant that some of these populations are showing a relatively nice response and if you have efficiency of 97 per cent and you have 3 per cent of the turtles still getting captured, which is what TEDs are supposed to do, 3 per cent may represent a larger number in real numbers just based on that fact there are more turtles out there to catch. So there is a number of things ongoing in the debate, that's why it is posted on something like CURTLE which is a discussion network for sea turtle biologists.

117. In question number 3 relative to the leatherback population on St. Croix. The St. Croix project was indeed a nesting beach project whose goal was to try to enhance the leatherback population nesting at St. Croix, to the use of conservation measures on the beach, including egg relocation and active protection on the beach. This is a programme that my wife and I started back in 1981/1982 and one of the reasons that this programme was undertaken is that there was an identified source of mortality. There was an issue of possible beach development and then there was an issue of identified mortality of eggs due to poaching and, even more significantly, due to loss of the nests due to erosion. In the first season down there, we documented 65 per cent of the eggs were lost annually simply to natural erosive processes. So, our response as a conservation measure on that beach, was simply to relocate eggs to safer areas and thereby boost egg production substantially over what had been historical levels. Now, there is the current nesting population size, which is somewhere in the neighbourhood of a 100 females, and one of the questions says, would you say protecting nesting females on the nesting beaches and protecting eggs undergoing incubation had contributed towards the build-up of the nesting population in St. Croix? At this point, it

is still too early to say. The population has been showing a slow but sure increase over the last few years and we are very encouraged that it may be providing support to the population. After all we have been doubling egg production on that beach since about 1982, so that has been a significant increase in the number of turtles being put into the sea.

118. Question 4 is actually a comment not a question so I will leave it at that. Do you want me to get into all the expert questions as well here? I will just race through them. In your expert opinion would trade prohibition on the import of shrimps to the US save sea turtles from shrimp trawlers and extinction? [Question 5 by Malaysia] Certainly. I think it would cause a net benefit to sea turtles. Any time you can reduce the number of turtles killed in shrimp trawlers you are going to benefit the populations, its relative to the trade prohibition. Let me just briefly describe a situation that I witnessed in Trinidad, a country in which I maintained an ongoing research programme for about the last five years. I am going to have a difficult time with the factual information here because, again, I am just pulling this off from my own experience and memory, I am sure this can be documented. A couple of years ago Trinidad was embargoed for failure to maintain shrimp trawler TEDs in their shrimp trawler fleet. The effect in Trinidad was extraordinary. I was down there just after this embargo had gone into place and the price of shrimp had dropped out of the market. The local market in which you could barely buy shrimp in previous years was flooded with shrimp and the value had gone way, way down. Clearly the impact to the shrimp fishery had been economically very significant. The response by the fisheries management agency in Trinidad was also extraordinary. In previous years, there was a bit of a jurisdictional split, turtles were jurisdictionally managed by their Wildlife Section under the Department of Agriculture and the Fisheries Department is a separate department and they had virtually ignored any of the requests from the Wildlife Section to support sea turtle conservation or minimise take in the fishery. Subsequent to the embargo the Fisheries Department immediately called the Wildlife Section and requested a biologist to come with them and advise them on what they should be doing. So Wildlife sent one of their sea turtles biologists over to work with both the shrimping fleet and the Fisheries Department and TEDs were put into place in a matter of months and it was an extraordinarily fast turnaround. So, relative to the effectiveness of the embargo in supporting the conservation of green turtles, my experience is that it was extremely effective in Trinidad and it was just a matter really of the Fisheries Department recognizing the need for this and taking steps to have the process occur and believe me, it did not take very long at all for them to get out there and start making sure that these devices were being utilized.

**Chairman**

119. Can I just confirm that your answer to that question is that a US trade prohibition would by itself, on its own, without any other measures, save sea turtles from shrimp trawlers and extinction? I just wondered whether that was the question you were really answering.

**Dr. Eckert**

120. Yes, I'm sorry I didn't see the "by itself" and in response to that, no. Certainly, what we have talked about extensively yesterday is that you need to take a multiple

approach to the conservation of turtles addressing specific problems. I guess what I was interpreting this to mean was that, would it help to save sea turtles and the answer to that question would be, yes it would, as opposed to by itself, no it would not.

121. "What is the acceptable recognized method of determining population size of breeding units? [Question 6 by Malaysia] I am not sure that there is a complete consensus on this, but what I have stated in my response to the Panel was that the general consensus among biologists, at least among the biologists that I have spoken to and worked with, are that you need to monitor the population for a number of years. You need to monitor the number of nesting female for a number of years before you will be able to determine the trend. What I have suggested is that the time period needs to be approximately 3 migration cycles. The average re-migration cycle is defined as the number of years that the average female within a nesting aggregation takes between nestings. Now, in Australia, if I understand Colin Limpus' work, that is often 5 to 7 years, in the Caribbean where I have substantially more experience, it is 2 to 3 years. So it can vary depending on the individual region as to how long you need to monitor that population. It also depends somewhat on the species, in that olive ridleys and Kemp's ridleys often have annual nesting events and, thus, the annual average re-migration rate can be a single year thereby, (by the way I am using the calculations), 3 years might be adequate to indicate a trend for those nesting populations. Having said that, you have to realize there is a tremendous amount of variation in this depending on other environmental external factors, such as southern oscillations. Colin Limpus' work on green turtles has specifically pointed that out that the El Niño or the southern oscillation in Australia has a large impact on the re-migration rate of those animals and that their re-migration rate can change based on what's going on out there in their particular world, particularly relative to food availability. That is actually somewhat significant over the last few years, it is going to be interesting to see what has happened in the last 10 years in the green turtle populations of the Western Pacific because we have seen an increase in the rate of Southern oscillation events over the last 10 years. That may very well explain issues relative to a shifting, there may be a shifting in the re-migration intervals and in those populations. The best folks to speak to that are obviously the Australians who work on the species and have been able to document this very well.

122. "Please tell us your views of the concept of unit stocks or populations of breeding units and sea turtles". [Question 7 by Malaysia] We have worked this pretty heavily over the last day or so. There is no question, in my opinion, that the identification of unit stocks is an extraordinarily important management tool for marine turtles. It will be the tool by which we can apply proper management to sea turtle populations in the future. As I was the Chairman of the US Pacific Sea Turtle Recovery Team, that developed the recovery plans for the Pacific for the United States, and in those plans, we were all in uniform agreement that one of our top priorities is to see the stock ranges of all sea turtle nesting aggregations identified. However, what I would also like to say, is that currently we do not have enough information on those stocks and on those stock ranges to use it as a management tool. It is simply a goal that we are working very hard towards obtaining and it will be a number of years before I feel that it is adequately documented to become a useful management tool. This is why I have advocated an approach more of, when you see a problem with the sea turtle population due to, say, incidental take in this case, that you address that problem irrespective of individual stock, quantities of individual stock status. We simply do not have enough

information on individual stock status to warrant the approach that says we do it stock by stock. So, if turtles are taken in shrimp trawling, I feel very strongly that you must address that issue immediately and not wait another 10 or 20 years until you can identify whether it's important to that particular population or not. There is enough evidence out there on the impact of incidental take on turtle populations, in populations that have been better studied, to indicate that the problem probably exists globally. "When studies on a particular sea turtle population are made, will the results applied to populations being studied?" [Question 8 by Malaysia] I think I have just covered that question as well. "Would you say that there are sea turtle populations in the world that are quite healthy?" [question 9 by Malaysia] I have a very difficult time saying that. Based on my experience it would be very difficult to say that there is any population of sea turtles that is quite healthy. You have to sort of look at the historical context of a question like this and the question sort of comes back to, do you want to back to 200 years, 500 years or 1 million years, as to how you answer a question like that. If you go back a million years obviously no, if you go back 10 years, there is some encouragement in a few populations that there may be something other than remnant populations. Otherwise I cannot be encouraged with our current status, even in the last 30 years that we see any population that could be considered healthy.

123. Would I agree that "loggerheads are the most vulnerable to shrimp trawling?" [Question 10 by Malaysia] The question "are they most vulnerable", all sea turtle populations are vulnerable to shrimp trawling. In the United States there has been some discussion about whether leatherbacks can be subject to shrimp trawling. In the United States and the coast of Georgia, North Carolina, there were large numbers of leatherbacks killed in the shrimp trawler a number of years ago and that number seems to fluctuate quite a bit probably based on what the migratory pathways the leatherbacks are on at the time. Basically, my feeling is that if you have a habitat in which any species of sea turtle and shrimp trawling occur you will have significant mortality of sea turtle populations. I think this is the way in which this thing has to be examined. If there are turtles there and shrimp trawling there, there will probably be mortality to the sea turtle populations. Thank you.

**Mr. Chairman**

124. Do you wish to address the US questions as well?

**Dr. Eckert**

125. Let's look at question 1.[679] I think a lot of this has been pointed out fairly clearly in some of our previous discussions and previous answers. Jack Frazier has brought up Indian Ocean turtle populations and the declines in some of those, I hope I am not speaking out of term for Jack. Certainly, the leatherback turtle population of Malaysia is not in recovery. The green turtle and hawksbill peninsular populations, I believe, are also in decline for the hawksbill of Malaysia. I am not sure what the status is of turtles in Thailand other than what we have written down. I am going to pass on with that question, it's probably more than I can try to answer at this time. I am going to let Mr.

[679] See Appendix 2 to this Annex.

Guinea deal with Question 2 because it is really addressed more towards him. I have stated in my response that I think that the annual documented mortality of 5,000 turtles nesting at Gahirmatha is not minor. It probably represents quite a bit more than that. I think that the Murphy's study on what percentage of the turtles actually make it to shore after being killed in a drowning incident suggest the number is probably substantially higher than 5,000. But shy of getting into a numbers game on this thing, which I am not really equipped to do right here, I don't want to go any further than that. Question 3, "... does existence of all these threats to turtles make it more important or less important regarding turtle mortality in shrimp trawlers?" I guess, what you have to say about this is, I get back to this point. Mortality in shrimp trawling is a documented fact in a number of areas and in other areas it simply isn't documented. There are a few areas where it simply isn't documented. In those areas where it is documented, we obviously need to address the shrimp induced mortality on turtles. Areas where it is not documented, we need to use our best judgement to indicate rather there are turtles and trawlers working in the same habitats and if there are, one has to assume that mortality is going to be associated with that. That's my own opinion on that. "Do experts agree that TEDs that have been properly installed and used reduce the mortality of sea turtles in shrimp trawl nets?" [question 4 by the United States] Yes, I don't think there is any question there. "If all the world shrimp fleets used TEDs would it contribute to reduction, to the threat of sea turtles?" [question 5 by the United States] Yes, in my opinion it would. Any time you can introduce something that reduces the mortality of wild turtle populations, which are in trouble obviously, it is going to help.

126. Time and area closures: this is more of a management type question and it's a difficult one to answer, just simply from a science perspective, it is one that managers need to address but there have been problems with time and area closures in the US experience that I am familiar with. Primarily, I think that one of the most significant sources for the problem are that if you are using a time closure or a time and area closure; we are closing a particular area for a certain time. Very often it is difficult to respond to the turtles changing in their patterns, of either movements or migrations. We saw this in the US when, for example, leatherbacks started moving in closer to the coast than they had in previous years. During times of the year when turtles normally would not necessarily have been an issue in those waters, the management agencies had a difficult time responding by putting the regulations into place, by banning shrimping in the area. So, unless you close an area pretty much all the time, which is often very unpalatable to the fishing industry, using a time and area closure is often very cumbersome. I think in the case of the US, and I don't want to try to speak for the Fishery Services on this because this is their business, but it does seem to me that after a number of years of experience of trying to do time and area closures they realized that it was far simpler, from both an enforcement perspective and a management perspective, to simply require turtle excluder devices all the time so that they didn't have to try to deal with the vagrancies of the biology of the animals which we well pointed out that we don't understand very well. It also meant that they did not have to be confusing the fishing industry with closures on, closures off, closures on and continuous monitoring of what was going on out there relative to the turtle take. I think time and area closures can be a very very difficult from a management perspective and not necessarily well received by the fishing industry because it puts them in a source of confusion to know whether they will be able to fish or not. Most significantly when they are done they cannot be static they have to be plastic. All of a sudden you have got turtles in the water,

you must call up the fleet and tell them to shut down. If you are not willing to do that, then time and area closures will not be effective for turtle populations, they simply move around too much.

127. Let's go to Question 7, "could Dr. Eckert please elaborate on his statement of 'seasonal migrations will not be expected in regions of warm waters'". I made that statement because in the discussion on migration in sea turtle populations. What we see, and it is based partly on my experience on the US West Coast and what I know about information from the US East Coast. One of the primary things that we look at, when we look at the presence or absence of turtles particularly on the West Coast, is water temperatures. There have been some nice studies done that indicate in the West Coast that turtles follow the 18 degree isotherm, at least the hard-shelled turtles, what we call the Thecate turtles, which are the greens, hawksbills, loggerheads. When the water temperature comes up to 18 degrees, turtles start moving in. Some satellite tracking studies I have done on an eastern specific green turtle male, which is actually quite unique (not a lot of work has been done with male turtles), showed that that animal very much preferred water temperatures at 22 degrees and he seemed to move to make sure that he was within 22 degrees. He was vertically in the water column, or horizontally, depending on his location. This was tracked up the US West Coast. My statement relative to that is that temperature can be an indicator of either biological factors that the animals are moving for, or simply physiologically what the animal needs. So that is the primary reason for turtles moving. My reason for saying that I did not expect to see that kind of behaviour in countries of the Western Pacific particularly is due to lack of knowledge about temperature structure there. I feel that I don't believe that they have those kind of temperatures they get down into areas in which the turtles will move out. My colleagues from there, particularly Liew from Malaysia, could probably answer best on that one. That is how that statement was generated, I guess I was suggesting that, what I had seen, was true for turtles in areas where you have temperature fluctuations. Leatherbacks, on the other hand, are not quite as temperature prone. Leatherbacks have been seen swimming around icebergs, they can deal with very very cold waters and are considered a north temperate species in distribution. Some of my satellite data is beginning to indicate that they are far more cosmopolitan than we ever realized before. However, on the coast of California and the West Coast of the United States, we do see a relationship between temperature and the distribution of leatherbacks probably based on water mass movements. When our temperatures get above about 16 degrees we see leatherbacks start moving into Californian waters, but they are coming from off shore and what they are usually following is often water masses that are coming in. So there is some suggestion that it may be not necessarily temperature related but water mass movement related. Based on what my satellite tracking data shows, what is probably driving things, that an overall desire to move for leatherbacks is based on food availability and where that food is going to occur. So, I guess what I would do is make a statement that temperature does seem to affect the seasonal migrations and movements of turtles in habitats in which they see those kind of temperatures and this is irrespective of nesting females who have their own thing going relative to the nesting season.

**The representative of the United States**

128. Mr. Chairman, I just want to clarify the question. The season migration we are talking about here is not the same thing as what Dr. Liew was talking about, when the

turtles have one place to nest and one place to feed and they go back and forth. They are different things, is that right?

**Dr. Eckert**

129. Thank you. Yes, that is exactly what I am trying to point out. We need to separate the kind of migration that I was talking about here which is seasonal migrations, from reproductive migrations. This refers very much more to say, juveniles or non-breeding females or non-breeding males relative to migration. Now, on reproductive migrations yes, that has been much better defined. There are these reproductive migrations and you have to realize that most of our research has been very myopic when it comes to sea turtles. We have looked at reproductive females, it is sort of the equivalent to martians studying humans by studying them in the maternity ward. It has left big gaps in our understanding about the biology of these creatures and we are having to address those issues now, because what we are finding is that the other 99 per cent of their lives are significant to the overall biology of the species. So, yes, I am primarily addressing non-reproductive migrations. One final note about reproductive migrations is that males also seem to exhibit reproductive migrations though they are much more poorly defined. "The adoption by TEDs of shrimp trawling would take between 6 to 8 years, could experts comment on this point?" [question 8 by the United States] Yes, I have some experience in the history of how they were put in the United States, just having been in Georgia for ten years during some of the early years of the implementation of the use of TEDs. A lot of the problems were simply problems of introduction. I think a lot of those problems have been solved and I would say that 6 to 8 years may be a little longer than is absolutely necessary but, as we talked about before, a lot of this depends on the sociological factors associated with the particular industry. In Australia, they seem to have a very good cooperative relationship with a relatively small industry. In the United States, you had independent fisherman working in their own boats and their own areas and a very large fleet, certainly the number of vessels operating there were numbering in the thousands, in Australia it is numbering in the hundreds. So, there are a lot of those factors that have to be brought into play: of how easy it is to work with the fisherman, how easy it is to teach them how to use these and I would have to say that if Mr. Guinea feels it would take 6 to 8 years in Australia, it very well might. Although Mr. Poiner certainly has more expertise there than I would. But, in the US the long duration that it took to introduce was mainly because it was the first time that anybody tried to put something like that into place with a fleet of that size and there was simply a long learning process on how to introduce it. I think that in the last few years they found that the optimum way was simply to require it and go from there, it has been a lot more effective. So, I will turn it over to Jack. Thank you.

**Dr. Frazier**

130. I will start with Malaysia then. Just passing very quickly over the first questions directed to Scott. The question of jurisdiction, although this is not directed to me, I feel that this concept is very important. When turtles are on the high seas outside the EEZs of any country, they are on the high seas in the commons, in the world commons, and I think that is one of the reasons why sea turtle biologists often speak of this as a global resource because at that point any nation can have an impact on it. Clearly, they are not under the impact of trawlers out there, trawlers do not work in the high seas, but they

are a global commons when they are in that part of their life stage. As a concept in conservation biology, when you have a charismatic flagship species like this; my hope is that it will draw nations together to collaborate in the conservation of these shared resources, whether it is in shrimp trawling or high sea drift netting, long lining or whatever. Just that point to me is very important as a strategy in conservation.

131. The first question [by Malaysia] to all experts. Using TEDs won't grow more hair on my head, I won't have more girlfriends, it won't solve the problems of poverty and suffering on the planet. But using TEDs will contribute, if they are correctly done, to reducing sea turtle mortality and will be part of an integrated approach to conserving a very complex resource. I don't think it is useful for us to go to extremes and say what is the greatest, what is the smallest, by itself will it do this. I don't believe we can effectively conserve a complex resource by limiting our vision to something like this. It would be the same as human health, you would not raise a child by just giving it rice, you have to give it other sources of food, you have to give it love, education and so forth. So, the rice is necessary but it is not sufficient alone. By itself, it is not enough but I do not understand why we should consider that by itself.

132. The question of population size, breeding units or management stocks [question 6 by Malaysia], I tried to address that in my comments. It is a source of discussion because we are just beginning to understand this with sea turtles. If they were white rats or squirrels or lizards on a wall it would be much easier for us to manage them because we could understand these animals with much simpler investigation. With animals which take decades to reach maturity, which live for long periods, to maintain their populations must breed for long periods, which move about the world's oceans, some of them more than others, it is very, very difficult to understand just what a breeding unit is. To determine the population size in normal population biology means everything that is part of a breeding unit, a management stock from the very smallest animals to the very largest animals; I tried to address this in my comments, and I hope I have been clear. The trouble with sea turtle biology is that most, all of our work is limited to the beaches because it is easier to get to beaches. Biologists will be constantly complaining that we do not have enough funds to do what we need to do. If you have to work on the high seas it is much more expensive, it's much more complex but that's where the turtles spend 99 per cent of their lives. Most of what we know about sea turtles is from what they do on beaches. Therefore most of what we can do in terms of estimating population size is what happens on beaches. This is why we see graphs of egg production or graphs of numbers of nests or graphs of number of females. That's where we have the best idea of what's happening. This is not a complete idea; it is an index of what is happening. In that respect we must be very careful, because the number of eggs produced on a beach represents a number of phenomena which are subject to variation. The number of eggs in a single clutch will vary from female to female. Each female will lay a number of clutches in a season, that number of clutches will vary between females, between species, between populations and indeed between years ... [tape turnover] ... This is then an indicator of the number of females that nested in that year, but it has to be looked at as a very sloppy indicator. You cannot just take one number and divide it by the number of eggs to get to the exact number of females that nested in that year.

133. Indeed, if you could note a number of females that nested on a beach, all the females that nested on a beach in a single year, that only tells you the number of females that nested in that year. That doesn't tell you the number of females in the population,

nor is it simple to take that number and estimate the total number of females in the population. The numbers of females every year can vary, there has been some very dramatic changes in numbers of females nesting in a single year from work done in Australia. There is an island called Raine Island, my colleagues from Australia can, I am sure, explain this much better than I can, but in Raine Island they cannot count the number of turtles in a season for a number of reasons. The first reason is that it is a remote area and it is difficult to get to; the second is that the density of turtles is so great that it is almost physically impossible to count them. It is like Gahirmata in India, or some of the nesting beaches in Central America. It is physically impossible to count the turtles, there are so many. As I recall in some years they have had in a single night in excess of 10,000 turtles in a single night, and then the next year the greatest number of turtles nesting in a single night, several hundred, I believe. So, what has happened? Why are the turtles doing this? Does it mean they have all gone extinct? No, these are tremendous fluctuations. In Australia, they have good information which shows this is relevant to the southern oscillation and there seems to be a relationship to food availability. In other areas we are much more ignorant, we do not know what is happening. We still have these fluctuations. I have tried to address this also, I have tried to include scientific references which deal with this. Green turtles are famous for this but other species also show this. So it is very very difficult with our information to be able to estimate what is the size of a population. With long-term data, Scott Eckert prefers to use an indication of generation times, or maturation times, or re-migration times to give an index of what length of time we need to monitor. There are other people who would simply say we need 10 or 20 years. The point is we need many years of information with these long-lived animals, and this in fact is not something unique to sea turtles, it is something that in biology we have begun to realize that problems of scale are tremendously important. If we are going to understand biological phenomena, we are going to need to understand the tremendous fluctuations that happen in the living world. So I am not sure whether I have done anything more than confuse you with this, I'm sorry if I have done that because I myself am confused, this is very complex. We need to have better information here, clearly we need it, but at the moment at least I consider myself to be terribly ignorant with this topic.

134. "Please tell us your views about the concept of unit stocks or populations or breeding units of sea turtles". [question 7 by Malaysia] Well, this touches back on what I have just been mentioning and what I would add here is something which, especially in fisheries biology, I believe now is an international accord. Certainly, I hope it becomes much much more talked about, and this is the precautionary approach. This is well described in the FAO Code of Conduct for Responsible Fisheries. In simple terms, the precautionary approach is, if we don't know enough we have to be careful. Especially if we are managing resources which are shared by many different people and on which generations of people will depend. The history of the world shows us that, we, as a species, independent of which nationality, have not been careful. The status of fishery stock shows us that we are in a desperate situation. We have to be more careful with the way we manage fishery stocks. Sea turtles are impacted by the way we manage fishery stocks. That is my concept on it. As I mentioned in one of the letters I wrote to the Secretary, if this was as simple as rocket science we could give you straight answers. It's not as simple as rocket science, it's much more complex. "When studies of any particular sea turtle population are made with the results applied to the population study or whether you as a scientist generalize your data, for all sea turtles irrespective of the

species...". [question 8 by Malaysia] No, I would not generalize to all species nor to all populations. Indeed, I would say the data I have found are relevant to this population for the time when I was studying it. That is careful science. However, if I don't know enough from another population or from another period or from another species and my level of ignorance forces me to admit that I don't know and I'm forced to take a decision to protect that species, I then have to start grabbing the best information I can find, and I then grab at the closest I can find which is comparable. If that means that I don't know enough about migrations and I have to go to another ocean basin to say, well, I know that this species in another ocean basin does this, I will therefore assume it is not that different in this ocean basin. I will use that as my best approach for management until I have better information.

135. "Notwithstanding the status listings, would you not say that there are sea turtle populations in the world which are quite healthy and which have benefitted from long-term conservation programmes started some 30 years ago?" [question 9 by Malaysia] Definitely, any conservation programmes, especially if they started 30 years ago, would have benefitted sea turtles. What worries me is "quite healthy". I am not sure what "quite healthy" means. As a global phenomenon we have seen that there have been declines of sea turtles populations around the world, that is why they are listed in IUCN and CITES as endangered species. This is not a trivial observation, it is a global observation. If a few years ago someone had asked me where are the healthiest populations of sea turtles, I would have turned to my colleagues in Australia and said, they have them in Raine Island. But now I am terribly depressed to know that even those populations are declining. Colin Limpus, whom you have heard cited numerous times during these proceedings, has shown that populations in Australia which were enormous, are now in decline. The reason they are in decline evidently is that when they migrate out of Australia into other waters of neighbouring countries, they are subjected to very high mortality, in some cases a direct mortality. So I would prefer to put, instead of "quite healthy", "at a lesser degree of risk". I am not comfortable with "quite healthy".

136. "Which species are most vulnerable to trawling?" [Question 10 by Malaysia] Certainly, the information which is available from the US shows very clearly that loggerhead and Kemp's ridley are highly susceptible to trawling. Those are the species which are most abundant in those waters. Where the behaviour of a turtle means that it will share time in the water in areas where shrimp occur or shrimp trawlers occur, it makes that turtle obviously subject to being caught in trawlers. My information is that in Surinam (where I have never worked and I must be clear here), there seems to be some confusion at some point. I am not responding to this information with my own personal experience. I am responding as a scientist reviewing information that I can gather. I have not worked in Surinam, the information I have from reading this scientific information is that indeed green turtles and olive ridley's are subject to capture, and at some degree of importance in Surinam. We do not have good data from Gahirmatha. Colleagues who work on that beach, and this number has been bantered around quite a bit, have shown that there is a large number of turtles which are stranded in Gahirmatha. There is some question as to whether that is in gill nets or trawlers or some other type of fishing activity. No one has done a study, those data don't exist. However, the simplest explanation that I see and my colleagues, for example, colleagues from the Wildlife Institute of India, see that a significant number of those animals are being drowned in

shrimp trawlers. We have no data, no study has been done and that takes me back to the precautionary approach. To say that I don't know cannot mean the problem does not exist. We have to be very careful, not to do that because that will simply make it more difficult to solve the problem. I would say that our lack of information makes it very difficult to know whether outside of areas where there have been long-term studies, whether other species are highly susceptible. I would certainly say that in Surinam, other species other than loggerhead and Kemp's ridley are susceptible from the data I have read, and the indications that have come from Orissa indicate that olive ridley is heavily affected there. Along the Pacific Coast of Central America, there are good data that olive ridleys are captured in very large numbers; the estimates for just the country of Costa Rica were 20,000 turtles a year captured in shrimp trawlers. In other countries north of Costa Rica there is less information and less study, but the numbers appear to be very significant. I am confused by a lack of information, but the snippets, the pieces of information I see from the people who work in Sabah make me very worried that there seems to be some kind of interaction between green turtles and trawling in the south. The reason I say this is indeed in this submission by Malaysia, the last page, which is a study done by Mohammed Suliansa. He ends by saying that there is a need for study of accidental capture of turtles in trawl nets and that there is a need to educate the trawl operators. My guess, I would need to speak to him, my guess is that he is concerned, and the reason that he is concerned, that he has manifested here, is that there is a problem. I remember in one of the submissions, that there are data which show that there are strandings of turtles when trawling begins in Sabah. The same phenomenon has been well documented in the US, in Texas and Louisiana especially, that when trawling begins in Sabah, strandings begin. The number of turtles which are documented is very small, and a large number of the turtles which were documented, there was a large number of those turtles for which the cause of drowning was not known. I don't have the report in front of me but, as I recall, a very significant percentage of the drownings, of the sources of mortality that could be determined, were from trawling and those were green turtles. So I am very concerned that we don't know, but certainly the people who are working in Sabah seem to be indicating that there is a very high potential for a problem. So, again my long elaborated comment which hasn't provided you with a dogmatic yes or no, again I am manifesting my ignorance. We don't have enough information but I would say, yes, other species are subject and we have to be careful. The lack of information cannot be used to prove that there is a lack of a phenomenon. If we can do studies, if someone can do a study and show that so much effort of trawling has produced so many turtles, then we can make a comparison. Without that information we are blind. I think I'll finish here.

137. I am going now to the questions provided last night. "Are other sea turtles found in each of the complainants waters that the members of population are not yet showing signs of recovery?" [question 1 by the United States] The issue of recovery has been deliberated. Again we must be very careful, we are dealing with complex animals that have these long periods of time to mature, which have long life cycles. To understand them we need long-term data. A short-term study will not give us the information we need. There are two populations which in voluminous proceedings have been discussed as having recovered and I am told to leave them aside, well at least the Sabah population aside. Under the instructions here that would leave me with Gahirmatha. I don't know what's happening at Gahirmatha. Obviously large numbers of turtles are nesting at Gahirmatha, at Devi and Rushikula. There are three mass nesting areas in

Orissa that have been discovered so far. One has to be very careful, I address this in my comments, with numbers, especially from mass nesting areas. I mentioned previously the difficulty that the Australian biologists have in counting green turtles on Raine Island. With olive ridleys in mass nesting situations, this is even worse. There can be tens of thousands of animals on a beach in a single night. It is physically impossible to have a good count. I really sincerely wish that everyone here could see this. It is a phenomenon which makes you understand why sea turtle biologists are as crazy as we are. It is something that renews your faith in the world to see this, it is phenomenal.

138. In order to estimate what's happening with the population, you need long-term data. If you are going to use numbers those numbers have to be something that you have to have confidence in. If you are estimating numbers, you need to have what are called confidence intervals around those numbers. I can count everyone in this room right now and produce what is called an exact estimate. But if there were so many people in the room that I could not count them and I had to do a statistical procedure of counting, a sample of them, I would have to be careful to be scientifically rigorous. I would have to have this done in such a way that there were confidence intervals around that number. This has been a major source of difficulty with the mass nesting populations. Statistics for these numbers are very sloppy and there have been attempts now on a beach in Costa Rica, called Nancite, to try different ways of estimating mass nesting populations. One is to use a transect down the beach and to count over a period of days at a fixed interval, the numbers of turtles that are in the transect. Another is to use what is called quadrat (a square area on the beach) and count the number of turtles in that quadrat. Then you have enough transects and enough quadrats to produce an average and then a variation around that average which gives you a confidence interval. Unfortunately, these two methods don't always give the same estimates and we are now a little bit confused about what we should do, because on some beaches people have been using transects and on other beaches people have been using quadrats and we are not sure how to compare these data. My colleagues at the Wildlife Institute of India are very concerned about getting counts from Gahirmatha which have confidence intervals. I spoke with some length with Bivash Pandav who is the graduate student who is doing this study. We have discussed some of the pros and cons about the widths and lengths of transects and I am confident that he is a remarkably dedicated man and I am sure he will be getting very good data from Gahirmatha which will provide confidence intervals. We need long-term data by the same institution on beaches. Gahirmatha was monitored by the Forest Department of Orissa, the Central Marine Fisheries Institute for some years, by other institutions, and every institution will have its own way of counting. So it is very difficult to know just what's happened at Gahirmatha. I would be pessimistic to say that I don't want that population to be in recovery, or to be growing or to be at least stable, but I don't know that, I can't say that because I don't understand enough about the way the numbers have been derived and I don't see confidence intervals around those estimates. So I would be careful about saying anything about Gahirmatha at the moment. Sorry for such a long talk, but they are such complex animals. Yes, "if they suffer mortality ..." [question 1 by the United States] clearly, that is what we have been trying to explain. Any source of mortality, especially directed at the animals which have been able to survive this long period of maturation, is very very costly for the population. I'm not saying that eggs are not important, I'm simply saying that those animals that have managed to have the good luck or good sense to do the

right things for 10 or 20 years, those are now very valuable to the population. If we loose them, it is a very costly loss for maintaining the population.

139. This magic number of 5,000 turtles stranding in Gahirmatha [question 2 by the United States]. Firstly, let's be very clear that 5,000 is a number of strandings, it's not mortality. We don't know how many died but certainly many, many more than 5,000. How many more I can't say, 10,000, 15,000, I can't say. But certainly if 5,000 were counted dead on the beach, the number that died would be many many more. We need to know how long they float, we need to know what the currents were, we need to know what the winds were. The only people that, as far as I know, have looked at this in a systematic way are researchers from South Carolina and I have provided a synopsis of that in my comments to show some of the problems of trying to interpret stranding data in terms of mortality. So, let's be clear that this is not mortality, this is stranding. I am worried by that number. I realize that large numbers of turtles nest at Gahirmatha, but a continual mortality of in excess of 5,000 animals (some number we don't know) worries me and I would not be comfortable to call it minor or relatively minor.

140. The third question [by the United States], "does existence of all these threats make it more or less important to prevent sea turtles mortality in shrimp trawlers?" Evidently, I haven't been clear, I would have thought that my comments had made it clear that the more sources of mortality we have, the more risks these animals are under, the more we have to use every possible means to reduce mortality. Liew in his comments, at some point said that it's necessary to reduce all sources of mortality. Again we don't know enough. If I could sit here very cooly and say, "Gentlemen, this population is this big, the sources of mortality are here, its rates of recruitment are this, this source of mortality is therefore unimportant and we can ignore it", if I could do that, it would be a different sort of situation, but I cannot. I don't have that information, I don't believe anyone does. The fourth question [by the United States], "do the experts agree that TEDs when properly installed and used reduce the mortality of sea turtles?" I thought that was clear, yes. I thought as far I understand there is a consensus that if they're installed and used properly they reduce mortality. I have tried to address this also in the Annex. [Annex 1 to the report] A TED is not a piece of magic, it's simply, a BED "a bycatch excluder device". Now fisheries biologists don't use that [term] so much, they use more BRD which is a bycatch reduction device, but it is simply a way of removing some part of what is caught in the net from the net. In the fisheries biology discussions you will often see discussions of the need for fisheries techniques to be more selective. More selective means, I'm going to target this species because I want to catch it, because I want to eat it, because I want to sell it. Therefore everything else that could be affected by my fishing activities has to be left out of it. A BED is a way of making a trawl more selective, perhaps less unselective. A TED is a modified BED, a modified BRD, which is designed to remove sea turtles from a trawl net. It's very simple, it's a sort of filter, I'm sure you have seen drawings of them, the grid TED, the one you developed in Thailand, the Thai Turtle Free Device or the Georgia Jumper or the Super Shooter or the AusTED, simply acts as a filter. It permits small things, like prawns and fish, to pass through and large things like a turtle can't pass through and is pushed up. If it is a top-shooter it goes up through the top; if it is a bottom-shooter, it goes through the bottom. The concept of a TED is very simple. There are problems, people need to learn how to use them as with any kind of equipment. There was a question in here, does the level of education affect the way a fisherman works.

Fishermen may not have a formal education; they may not have doctorates, but fishermen are people who have a tremendous amount of practical experience, if they are professional fisherman. They are people who, I think, most of us here respect greatly when we work with them. So, I don't think formal education is a matter of concern. These are people who learn by experience. If the fisherman is shown how the instrument works with a gear technician and given time to work with it, I don't see any reason why he can't learn how to use it. He has to learn how to use it, definitely, but he also has to learn to use his winches, he has to learn how to use all the instruments he uses on his boat. It's part of the equipment.

141. "If all the world's shrimp trawlers use TEDs would this contribute to the reduction to the threat to the sea turtles ...?" [question 5 by the United States] Again, I would have thought that at least my own comments have made this clear. I would like to explain perhaps why I have troubled you all with yet more papers, with an Annex on bycatch. To me this issue is a bycatch issue. When we are talking about turtles caught in shrimp trawls, we are talking about a bycatch problem. They are there because they are bycatch. Therefore, the whole issue of bycatch is relevant, it fits within that complex of problems. As I have tried to indicate in my written comments, a TED is a BED, it's a modified bycatch excluder device which is designed to remove turtles. Depending on the design of the TED, you can also remove other unwanted elements from the trawl nets, and that can include, depending on the way you design your TED, that can include other species of animals which are being negatively impacted by shrimp trawling. My strategy as a conservation biologist now takes me outside of biology and technical aspects into the realm of dealing with people and indeed impacting political decisions. My vision as a conservation biologist is that TEDs could be an important first step in showing fishermen that they have to be more selective. So, I would take question 5 [by the United States] and say that this focus is too narrow for me. I would say that TEDs indeed, not only are important for reducing catch of sea turtles, but for dealing with this very, very grave problem we have with bycatch and showing the way to open up methods for getting fishermen to be more selective. Bottom trawls are notoriously damaging to the environment, the history of bottom trawling in tropical countries is a very sad history. I have mentioned in the Annex that there are civil movements, there are organizations of fishermen from the Third World, from developing countries who are calling for a ban on bottom trawlers. This is a very, very serious situation. These people feel that their lives have been impacted negatively by bottom trawling; their gear has been destroyed, their sources of livelihood have been destroyed by bottom trawling. I know that fisheries officers in many countries, not publicly but among themselves, would be much happier to get rid of bottom trawling. It's not going to happen quickly, if it happens at all, but certainly one way to move towards making this very damaging fishing technique less damaging is to start implementing more selective ways of fishing. One of those is to get TEDs in the nets and show the fishermen that they can't continue this way, you have got to be more selective. I was talking with Liew yesterday, I am in total agreement with him. They are fishing with nets that are so closed, the mesh sizes are so closed that virtually nothing gets through. I am surprised they can even advance in the water, it is like they have a tube which is almost closed. They are catching all the larvae, this can't go on indefinitely. We have seen that FAO and I believe, Thai fisheries experts, have estimated that the demersal stocks in the Gulf of Thailand are now 10 per cent of what they were when trawling began 30 years ago. We are in a desperate situation and this is much bigger than sea turtles, we are seeing the tip of the iceberg. I

am very clear, this is the tip of the iceberg. If we can deal with sea turtles in such a way that it will give us momentum to solve these other bycatch problems, I think this will be a major contribution to fisheries management. The sixth question [by the United States]: will prizes be given out?

**Mr. Chairman**

142. Only if you get to the end!

**Dr. Frazier**

143. "Dr. Poiner and Mr. Guinea mentioned time and area closures are helpful ..." [question 6 by the United States] Yes, that's definitely true; they are helpful. Do we have enough knowledge to identify potential "hot spots." Again, I sincerely believe that the way Australians manage their fisheries is something we should all learn from. Ian Poiner and I had a discussion on record yesterday; he clarified that effort is essential, that simply limited entry doesn't have all the answers and later on we discussed this further. I am still convinced that the Australians are way ahead of the rest of us, they have, Ian was explaining to me, 120 vessels in the northern prawn trawling area and 1,100 to 1,200 licences in the eastern fishery, not all of which are fishing. If we could only deal with such a small number of vessels, it would be much easier to manage. I don't believe any of us here, any of the countries assembled here, has a fishing management programme as well set up as that. We are dealing with thousands of vessels. I will let him explain to you what they are doing, it's marvelous. They are going to be able to monitor where the vessels are, on real time, to be able to actually communicate with them. They can do magnificent things in that fishery. We were talking here about, I believe, another situation, other fisheries which are extremely large. I don't see how we can possibly pretend to enforce time and area closures without tremendous amounts of investment in vessels which will be out there looking for this. The indications I see in FAO documents, written by or about, for example, some of the Malaysian fisheries officers, lead me to believe that they are very concerned with area closures, with the zoning. There is one report by Hilmi, which I mentioned in the Annex here, there is another report from Ali, the way they are expressed I see concern that they are not confident that they are getting exclusion from that 5 kilometres. At one point it says, I believe, fishing will go on unless enforcement vessels are seen: why would you stop fishing if an enforcement came along, unless you were doing something that was against the law. If you were in the right place and an enforcement vessels comes along, what difference should it make to you. We know classically that area closures in fisheries with large numbers of vessels are very, very difficult. I know that Thailand also has excellent laws. The laws in both Malaysia and Thailand, I believe are very well thought out to provide area closures, zoning. I am not convinced that the trawlers are respecting this. Everything I read makes me think the opposite. I see that there is concern indeed in some of the documentation, which I believe was provided in Thailand. There is a discussion of why are the trawlers coming into the coastal areas. It's normal, it's human nature as Daniel Pauly has pointed out - this man is one of deans of fisheries biology in South East Asia.

144. In general shrimp are coastal species, shrimp and prawns occur along the coast. Ian Poiner was explaining to me yesterday, in Australia, they target them, he can explain it much better than I can. They do terrestrial phenomena for nutrients, nutrients come

from terrestrial phenomena, nutrients coming down rivers in catchment areas. This means that they will be in coastal areas, where those nutrients are most concentrated. Certain sorts of habitats such as sea grass and types of bottom, will not be long distances from the coast in general. That means that if you want to catch prawns you have to come close. When you come close, you come inside the zones where they have been to told to stay out. When you do that you cause conflicts with a small-scale coastal fisherman. The documentation of conflicts, of civil strife, caused by trawling in the tropics especially in South East Asia, there are libraries full of this. There are grave, grave social problems caused by trawling, by trawlers coming inside these coastal areas. The laws are very well thought out, but I don't see the trawlers are respecting them. There is such a pressure to get prawns from the coastal area and they are coming inside. I cannot provide you with studies, I don't believe such studies exist. What I see in the FAO documentation and in the reports of the experts from these different countries make me very concerned that they are also very worried about infringements in coastal areas.

145. The time closures, unless we are talking about long periods of time, will often produce what is called "pulse fishing": I will allow you to fish this period and that period and then this period you cannot fish. By human nature the most likely thing is the effort which Ian Poiner talked about yesterday. The effort will increase just before the closure, so that I can catch as much as possible before they stop me and the moment they let me start again the effort will be very, very intense. This may mean then that all the animals that were not impacted during the time closure are subjected to a very, very intense effort just before and just after. So, time closure has to be looked at with great care if it's really going to work, simply legislating a time closure and pretending it's working is not necessarily going to work.

146. "Do we have enough knowledge to identify potential hot spots?" [Question 6 by the United States] No, we don't. This seventh question has been dealt with. Then I will finish with TEDs which will take 6 to 8 years [to implement]. Australia has been working through voluntary implementation which I have tried to explain in my written submission, which I firmly believe is the best way to go: to work with the fisherman, in terms of community based conservation. However, where you have fisheries which are extremely large and in my opinion outside of normal control, where the fisheries department is unable to develop this sort of contact where you have a limited fishery, it's a tremendous problem to develop rapport with the fisherman and get voluntary compliance. I would much prefer voluntary compliance, there is no question in my mind at all about that. But if you can't do it, what will we do? Will we just wait? How long will we wait? Will we wait until resources are so diminished that there is nothing left to save? I know that Dr. Silas from the Cochin Central Marine Fisheries Research Institute, years ago, in 1983, proposed adopting TEDs at least in Orissa. Dr. Silas is, he is no longer Director of the Institute, but he is a very dynamic person with tremendous vision. Other fisheries officers, other people concerned with conservation of marine resources followed this up with other suggestions. It's not easy, I know this, but nothing has happened so far. How long can we wait? How much destruction of these resources on which many coastal peoples depend, can we tolerate? Something has to be done to tell these trawlers "you cannot continue like this, you have got to be more selective, you've got to take care of these resources, they are not your resources." These resources, if we are talking about the trawling, are national resources, they do not belong to the

trawling community. They belong to the nation and I am deeply concerned - this is why I have gone into great detail with the social aspects - that other people who have a right to these resources have also access. In South East Asia there are large communities of people who for generations used types of fishing which are selective. They have done this for God knows how long, and now those people have been marginalized by a technology ... [end of tape] ... which is very, very destructive. I believe trawling in this way is socially unjust and I am very concerned about it. I would say there is great reason to make trawling as selective as possible, as fast as possible. I would prefer that it be voluntary and if we can't do that then, something has to be done, such as in Thailand where it was legislated and quickly done in a matter of months.

**Chairman**

147. Thank you very much, Dr. Frazier. Dr. Guinea?

**Mr. Guinea**

148. Thank you Mr. Chairman. In reply to the questions posed by Malaysia, those questions which were directed to Dr. Eckert have been adequately explained by him or answered by him. I do not wish to comment on the first four questions. The questions directed to all the experts, "in your expert opinion, would trade prohibition on the import of shrimp to the US by itself save sea turtles from shrimp trawlers and extinction?" [question 1 by Malaysia] I have addressed this before in my opening remarks and also in my written submission. As I was going through the submissions by the various parties I was looking for some index or some measure of reduction of fishing effort resulting from the embargo. Some of the documents are still fairly recent but the figures indicated that the exports from the affected countries to the USA decreased. This simply meant that the product going into America was reduced. I was looking for some measure to say that the product that was not allowed into America, was being dumped or was the trawl fishery suffering; were there boats remaining in port because they could not comply with the US embargo? Nowhere in the document was there any evidence to suggest that the fishing fleet had been reduced, that there were hardships being accounted on the trawl fisheries and in discussions at other meetings it was indicated that the product was making its way to other markets. This was expressed as a concern in my submission by some of the fishery officers in Australia. So if there is no reduction in fishing effort, then the same number of vessels are going to sea for the same number of days, towing the same number of nets and, should they be encountering turtles, they will be encountering the same number of turtles and regardless of where the product is going. In this regard I see the US are saying "we do not want to eat a product that has not been caught in a particular way". Now that does not affect the number of turtles that are surviving, it is a preference for a market or for a way a product is being prepared. So if you are looking for some measure of the success of an embargo, you will be looking for a thing such as positive outcome in terms of the numbers of sea turtles that are surviving on the trawling grounds. I have yet to see numbers to demonstrate that after some years of TEDs being used in the Gulf of Mexico, Caribbean sea fisheries, that the turtle numbers have actually increased on those fields. We have figures relating to a decrease in the number of turtles washing ashore, that is referred to as a "stranding", that you would be looking for some positive measure to say "yes, if 5,000 turtles were not killed this year then the population of that trawl field should have

increased by at least 5,000". If the TEDs have been installed for 5 years then it is 5 times 5 and we are looking at 25,000 turtles increasing in a population. That sort of data just has not been presented - that is a concern.

149. Also looking at the embargo, there is no indication of milestones or checkpoints as to how the success of the embargo was likely to be planned. There seems to be an adoption that once a TED is installed then the turtles will be saved from extinction. I think that if you are going to put some form of an embargo in place you will be keeping regular checks of what is happening not only with your own population on the feeding grounds but also what is happening on the population of sea turtles in the affected countries. That does not seem to be happening either. There may be a need to develop surrogate measures of sea turtle survivorship or sea turtle mortality. This may be best directed towards some sort of measure of fishing effort presented in a standard format in either head rope lengths, number of boats or something in that nature, and there seems to be a mixture of measures by which effort is mentioned. In some countries we simply have a measure of the number of vessels that are involved with a fishery - whether that is 2,000 vessels or 3,000 vessels - but that still does not give an indication of how long each tow is, how many days they are at sea and what is their likely capture of sea turtles. There is a general lack of information provided in the submissions in this regard. The other point that I was looking for was did shrimp prices increase in the USA as a result of the embargo? What incentives are there for the affected countries to coerce their fleets to bring about the implementation of TEDs - indicating that "yes, you can get more money for your product if you are using a TED". In fact, the information provided with the submissions indicated that the costs of shrimps actually decreased after the implementation of the embargo. In fact, it decreased by about 9 dollars to 8 dollars or something in that order per kilo. So those figures indicate that the market was not maintained; it was not a profitable market awaiting countries that are implementing the use of TEDs. There are also other questions. I have addressed the fact that other markets were found for the shrimp products. It has also been suggested, and the US has challenged this, that some shrimp or shrimp products could be transshipped through third party countries. Now, whether this does or does not occur, it could surely be a valid case for environmentally labelling products as to the country of origin and method of capture, etc. I shall just state the point again that TEDs or turtle-excluded devices are just one of the options that should be or could be imposed in the responsible management of a fishery. I think that might suffice for question 5 [by Malaysia].

150. "What is the acceptable recognized method of determining the population size of breeding units of sea turtles especially in the assessment of population trends?" [question 2 by Malaysia] From the literature there appears to be no case of a sea turtle nesting in one country and then nesting in another country. We talk about migrating to a nesting beach and that nesting beach has a geographic location and then that geographic location becomes the centre of the breeding unit. That may in fact be one beach, it may be a number of islands, it may be a geographic location covering several hundred square kilometres. This is actually fundamental to all the other aspects of sea turtle biology. We talk about using mitochondrial DNA to look at philopatry - or the return of individuals to their nesting beaches. If a turtle is nesting in one country and then moves to another country and then moves to another country to nest, if those countries are at a distance, then all the mitochondrial DNA work should be thrown out the window. The basis of the mitochondrial DNA is that there is only migration between breeding units at a rate

of less than two females per generation and that means that in the lifespan of a sea turtle, which may be some decades, no more than two females will move from one breeding unit to another breeding unit. That is fundamental. So the breeding units become the focus of your conservation measures. If one breeding unit is wiped out, through any number of reasons, it will not be replenished by neighbouring breeding units because the sea turtles exhibit a strong returning to a geographic locality for breeding. Therefore by assessing the number of females on a breeding ground you can assess the status of your breeding population. All of the life tablework that has been produced, the growth models are in fact based on female sea turtles. So when we talk the magic number of 584, we are talking about 584 females. We do not talk about the number of males. Therefore we use a philopatrical breeding area as the unit for assessing sea turtle populations - either the relevant numbers, the relative importance, the changes from year to year and also seasonal declines over time or in fact increase over time.

151. Question 7 [by Malaysia], I have also raised this point of stocks and breeding units. I prefer not to talk about stocks, I prefer to talk about breeding units. Stocks tend to be a very value-loaded concept where historically in fisheries they tend to be able to determine all the parameters of the stock. With a breeding unit, the concept, on the other hand looks at the means of assessing the numbers of nesting females. And you can actually live with the situation of not knowing where all the individuals are at any one time of that breeding unit, as long as there is an assessable number that is returning annually or over a period of time to the breeding area. With the concept of stocks regularly on a feeding ground, it is likely that you will have more than one breeding unit of sea turtles present and it is important to address the composition of the feeding ground as regards to the breeding unit composition. As an example, if there are two breeding units on a feeding ground, at the rookery, one of those breeding units might be suffering very heavy egg harvesting, natural mortality or commercial harvesting of their products. The other breeding unit may not suffer those consequences on the nesting beaches. In order to prioritize your conservation activities, if you can identify that, not only is a population being negatively impacted on a feeding ground but is also suffering heavy mortality on the rookery, then that breeding unit can be ranked as being more worthy of conservation effort than a breeding unit that may be suffering some mortality on the feeding ground, but the rookeries and nesting areas are still intact. In terms of being able to prioritize your research activities, your conservation activities, you can then nominate very clearly that you are going to address a particular aspect of one breeding unit of sea turtle and you are going to address particular points regarding its life cycle and its conservation. This also brings about the fact that, as far as funding organizations can go and also managers and funding agencies, you can produce stronger and more focused arguments to protect, as a matter of priority, selective breeding units. This could be a case for funding organizations to identify projects, give them a better chance of success and also it would bring the researchers into more accountability for actually producing what they set out to do. I think this business of accountability, of research funds and the conservation dollar is very important. I think I shall leave question 7 at that, thank you.

152. Now in question 8 [by Malaysia], "when studies on any particular sea turtle population are made, would the results apply to the population being studied or would you generalize the data for all sea turtles irrespective of the species or where they

occur?" There are fundamental dangers in generalizing. There are fundamental dangers just as there are in generalizing about countries. There is fundamental dangers in generalizing not only about what a species does, not only about its growth rate, not only about where it lives, but not only where it occurs on the feeding grounds. There is also dangers in generalizing about fisheries because a generalization can lead people to think a fishery the world over is the same. Therefore the way a net is operated in Australia is similar to the way a net is operated in the USA or regions where nets are operated. So there is a danger and I find this in the report saying "shrimp trawling in the USA versus shrimp trawling in Malaysia". I am not aware in either country whether the shrimp trawling is exclusive of sea grass beds or whether shrimp trawling is conducted up to the shoreline, or whether shrimp trawling is conducted at night or whether shrimp trawling is conducted in all seasons of the year. We have this generalization that shrimp trawling *per se*, regardless of any other management implication or procedure used by the fishers themselves, is then transferred immediately to another country. I think this is a danger in itself of generalizing in trawl fisheries. Because sea turtles and trawls are the focus of this talk, I think that it is a justification for my wandering into a fisheries area. So just to reiterate, it is very important to exercise caution in interpretation of sea turtle data and also fisheries data.

153. Question 9 [by Malaysia], "notwithstanding the status listed of sea turtles provided in the IUCN etc. would you not say there are sea turtle populations in the world which are quite healthy and which benefit from long-term conservation programmes that started some 30 years ago?" I think all sea turtles benefit from conservation programmes which started 30 years ago. There is a few milestones in these conservation programmes where fundamental research, such as the longevity of different tags that have been applied to sea turtles, the effectiveness of different tags. It was only a few decades ago where we were talking about particular species of sea turtles nesting only once in their life. The reason for those misconceptions was the fact the tags which were applied to those turtles fell off in about 10 years and so therefore we had so few tag recoveries, we were led to the idea that they nest during only one season and there were many options built on those assumptions. Now over the last 20 years, having changed from Monel metal to Inconel to Titanium we realize now that the turtle tags can remain far longer, possibly as long as the turtle. So now the whole focus of these early management options have been changed. That brings about an increase in benefit to all sea turtles - not just those turtles that were tagged on the Great Barrier Reef or not just those turtles that were tagged in Southern USA. Sea turtle researchers in other countries do not have to follow the same path; they do not have to make the same mistakes over and over again in doing the fundamental research. If you are looking for areas that were quite healthy, there is good documentation from South Africa where species numbers have increased. I should also point out that in a number of countries, Australia included, sea turtles were not actually protected until about the 1960s and prior to that there were active turtle soup factories. Turtles were harvested and turned into soup and exported to whoever wanted to eat turtle soup. It was only in the 1960s that conservation efforts came in. So that is still less than one generation time for a green turtle which was the target of the turtle soup factories. In that regard, having removed the commercialization from sea turtles of Australia and remove the cash value of the turtle, those turtles have enjoyed a degree of protection for the last 30 years. There has been a move for cash value of sea turtles in neighbouring countries, from where the Australian breeding units move, and this is a cause of concern. There has

been a general realization that in some areas sea turtles are negatively impacted by prawn trawlers or shrimp trawlers. The overall conservation measures provided in Australia are trying to build a secure foundation for sea turtle biology - for sea turtle conservation. Realizing the time frame, then we are hopeful that in years to come we have good news of sea turtle numbers in scientific literature rather than bad news of decreasing numbers and the like.

154. Question 10 [by Malaysia] talks about loggerheads being the most dominant species followed by Kemp's ridleys. In response to that question I would like to know whether the composition of the catch in shrimp trawls in the USA is a true reflection of the distribution and abundance of sea turtles on the feeding grounds in the Gulf of Mexico and the Caribbean sea. It would appear from the Australian studies that not all sea turtles are impacted to the same extent. Not all sea turtles suffer the same mortality. Some species seem to be more resilient to being dragged in a prawn trawler. Others, by their particular behaviours, may be more susceptible to capture. It has been suggested in some of the literature that green turtles, being quicker, can outswim the approaching trawler net. Loggerhead sea turtles, being less agile, less inclined to swim, are more prone to being captured in trawl nets. So there are a few questions that have to be sorted out. One is whether you have a true sample of your feeding population being presented in the shrimp trawl bycatch or whether you have particular species which through the course of their nature or energetics or may be even feeding biology are more prone to being caught in a shrimp trawl. In that regard you may find that loggerhead sea turtles may be far more prone to capture because they are more reluctant to swim out of the way of trawlers. That is a supposition and you have to do a lot of work with trawl and experiment with loggerheads in a trawl net environment. However, there has been some suggestion that this is in fact the case.

155. If I could just turn to the questions posed by the United States - the first question refers to the status in the complainant's country, in the complainant's waters. There are members of populations which are not yet showing signs of recovery. "If such sea turtles suffer incidental mortality in shrimp trawl nets would this not contribute to the endangerment of sea turtles?" [Question 1 by the United States] As I just mentioned in my last response, some of the sea turtles are more prone to being caught in shrimp trawls and other sea turtles seem to be less prone to capture in shrimp trawls. Seeing that on the Panel of Experts we have Mr. Liew,who is far more familiar with Malaysia than I am, I would like to leave some of the aspects of this answer to Mr. Liew. I would also mention that some of the population in Malaysia, possibly the leatherbacks in Terengganu, may still not be recovering; but then, they may not be affected by shrimp trawling either. So again, I reiterate the problem of generalizations.

156. In Question 2 [by the United States], which was directed to me, I produced in my response a calculation, to which I would like to thank the United States for allowing me to expand on this aspect of my submission. The reproductive value figures that I mentioned yesterday are a mathematical abstraction, and are in fact modeling which have been used to indicate the relative worth of an adult female loggerhead in the south east United States of America. This figure has a great deal of plasticity, as indicated by the much lower values of between 200 and 400 in Australian populations of the same species. This value of 584 is the most widely quoted value in submissions and also in the masterly works provided by the National Academy of Sciences in *the Decline of Sea Turtles*. Due to the lack of reproductive values for other species, the figure of 584 has

been used as an implement to argue the worth of adult sea turtles in other species. However, as an instrument, it is like a two-edge sword that can be used to predict the survivorship of eggs to adults and the subsequent recruitment. It is in this context that I have used it to illustrate the possible recruitment to the Gahirmatha olive ridley population. A nesting population estimated to be 500,000 females would produce approximately 50 million eggs and this figure comes actually from the submissions. In a season, using Crouse's figures for loggerheads, the recruitment would be possibly 85,000 female adults. A mortality of 5,000 female adults represents less than 1 per cent of the estimated nesting population and should those 5,000 die before reproducing, it would be less than 6 per cent of the year's new recruits. Should the reproductive value of Gahirmatha olive ridleys be 200, as it is for some of the breeding units of the Australian loggerheads, then the recruitment would be in the order of 250,000 individuals in one generation's time. So sea turtle reproductive strategies are an exercise in numbers. To the casual observer the loss of 5,000 individuals would be a reason for concern but when the nesting population is estimated to be in the order of 600,000 animals, then this loss is relatively minor. The concern should be not for the absolute number, but rather the proportion of a breeding unit that is adversely affected. Within the various submissions I found figures of one million turtle eggs being taken to market or 400,000 eggs lost to natural causes. This should be viewed in relation to the total number of eggs deposited by the breeding unit in one generation, which may be for them some decades. Although these numbers are large, sea turtle biology is all about a numbers game. You have to look at the egg production in a generation by a breeding unit to ascertain whether that is an effective or substantial number or whether that is relatively minor.

157. Question 3 [by the United States]: "all the experts have noticed various causes of sea turtle mortality including mortality on the beaches and due to incidental mortality in shrimping and fishing operations. Does the existence of all these threats to sea turtles make it more important or less important to prevent sea turtle mortality in shrimp trawlers?" If you use the paradigm of a breeding unit then you have to address this on a case-by-case basis rather than a gross generalization. It is the case-by-case basis that is important. Only on this case-by-case basis can you actually achieve something. If you take on conservation of sea turtles of the world as your prime objective, then you are unlikely to succeed. However, if everybody is working on a case-by-case basis, the total of the conservation effort may well in fact result in the conservation of the sea turtles of the world. So, in answer to question 3, you have to look at this on a case-by-case basis.

158. In question 4 [by the United States]: "do the experts agree that TEDs when probably installed and used reduce mortality of sea turtles in shrimp trawl nets?" I would think that there needs to be more information provided with this question. We are talking about TEDs properly installed. I would go further to say, if the TED is properly designed for that fishery and if the TED is properly installed and properly used, then it will reduce the mortality of a trawl fishery. To explain this: if a country or a fleet bought a TED off the shelf from a producer and used that TED blindly, thinking that "yes, this will be the answer to all their problems", then they are unlikely to be successful. If they are going to look at the use of a TED, the TED should be designed for those fishing areas and this may in fact involve several designs operating within a country. Selected areas may be looking at a TED specifically designed for the sea turtle population that is likely to be encountered in that trawl field. This may involve narrow-

grated TEDs. It may involve larger TEDs. It would depend on the sea turtles that are present on that feeding ground and the level of trawl activity. Again, the size of the sea turtles is also important. Also the species of sea turtles. In fact some work has gone into the AusTED, in recognition of the fact that the flatback sea turtles are one of the most commonly caught sea turtles in the Australian trawl fishery. There are in fact no data available for how flatback sea turtles behave in trawl nets or how they respond to TEDs. Therefore, there is an argument for countries to develop a TED for their trawl fishery based on the species of sea turtles that are present.

159. There appears to be no data available for olive ridley sea turtles in TEDs from the USA. Olive ridley sea turtles are a component of the feeding grounds in the countries concerned. So I shall go further to say that a TED, if it was properly designed and installed and used in a proper manner then it will go some way to reducing sea turtle mortality. If the United States figures are still a decrease of 40 per cent in strandings by the use of their TEDs which were properly used, properly designed and in their fishery, you could not say that they were going to have a complete reduction of sea turtle mortality. It will go some way to reducing the sea turtle mortality in the trawl fishery or the shrimp trawl fishery.

160. Question 5 [by the United States]: "if all the world's shrimp trawling fleets used TEDs would this contribute to the reduction to the threat of sea turtles?" The answer to that, we need to look at what is meant by the world's shrimp trawling fleets. Is it the desire for the United States to comment on the temperate water shrimp trawler fleets or should we restrict their answers to the tropical water shrimp trawl fleets? Of course, by exclusion the temperate water shrimp trawl fleet tend to have little or no impact or implied impact with sea turtles. So the question should be whether the use of TEDs would contribute to sea turtle conservation and I think my last answer would indicate that properly designed TEDs, properly installed TEDs would go some way to reducing sea turtle mortality. Until we get better data from the United States as to the effectiveness of their TEDs, I would be hesitant to say that they will go all the way to achieving their 97 per cent reduction in sea turtle strandings.

161. Question 6 [by the United States]: I shall leave the full discourse of time and area closures to Dr. Poiner, if I may. But I will make some comments. "Could the experts comment on this and in particular address whether sea turtle mortality could also occur in areas during times where shrimp trawling is not banned?" Now I have some confusion over this. Sea turtle mortality occurs throughout the sea turtles' life; whether trawls are present or not. It is my experience dealing with stranded sea turtles that when we encounter a dead turtle we tend to look for someone to blame, rather than for something to blame. I have encountered this in parts of Timor Sea where, during particular spring tides, sea turtles that are slow at moving off the beaches are caught on the reef flat and succumb to the heat during the day. Those turtles may then wash up on beaches in the area. Part of my work then is trying to assess whether this sea turtle died of natural causes, whether it be through a misadventure of tardy nest preparation and being caught by the heat of the day - succumbed to the heat during the low tide. So we have developed a stranding or a means of assessing strandings as to whether this a likely impact of a natural cause or whether this has been an impact of subsistence fishermen in the area who have moved in and taken a turtle or has it succumbed to fishing operations in the area. So I think when we are looking at sea turtle mortality we have to improve our intelligence as to what was the nature of the mortality. There are a few things that

can be used to ascertain whether this animal drowned, was dropped onto a sorting deck, caught in a gill net, has been through a drum winch, been adversely affected by humans removing flesh or eggs or whatever. So the intelligence associated with assessing the mortality is very important. So saying, "we looked at a number of turtles and it would appear they were carrying eggs, they were unsuccessful nesters and were caught by the tide, they succumbed to the heat during the day," rather than saying "we saw 30 dead turtles and therefore there must be a subsistence fishing fleet in the area who have been killing turtles." I think this is very important to ascertain the cause of the mortality rather than just saying "yes, there is a mortality". I was looking for something like that in the report that there was 5,000 turtles washing ashore in Gahirmatha. Where was the intelligence of this? It is very easy to point at a vessel offshore and say, yes, it has come from that vessel. But when you are dealing with 600,000 animals trying to nest in one year you are likely to have a very high mortality from natural causes - just sheer natural causes. Even on islands like Raine Island where in excess of 10,000 turtles may nest a night, over the course of the nesting season there will be hundreds of dead turtles on the beach. There will be turtles that are caught by the tide, turtles who have just come to the end of their life and turtles that have expired while nesting. Where you have large numbers of turtles, you have large natural mortalities. This is something that should be looked at when we are talking about "does mortality occur in the absence of shrimp trawling?" Mortality occurs throughout the turtles life and it may be excessive on some of the nesting beaches or larger in non-nesting turtles and may be females are more prone to this sort of mortality than are males.

162. "Do we have enough knowledge to identify all potential hot spots where sea turtles and shrimps interact?" [question 6 by the United States] I think the idea of looking at the concept of hot spots, these areas where sea turtles will be feeding and by closures of areas likely to encounter sea turtles, you have gone a long way to excluding sea turtles from the trawl fishery. In some of the areas in Northern Australia olive ridley sea turtles feed in very shallow water, feeding on mollusc. They are not actually feeding on the shrimp. They just happen to be in the same area as the shrimp and they feed on shellfish and the like. By having closures in those areas, those turtles would be protected from shrimp trawlers. I think I shall leave Dr. Pointer to say more about that. Question 7 [by the United States], seeing it is directed to Dr. Eckert, I shall leave that question. In question 8 [by the United States], I would like to indicate that it was Dr. Pointer that noted that the adoption of TEDs by a shrimp trawl fleet would take 6 to 8 years. However, I am happy to comment as best I can as to the implementation of TEDs and I welcome Dr. Pointer's opinion as well. I cannot speak for Thailand as to how it produced such an elegant and effective TED within a matter of months. I congratulate Thailand for doing so, but the means by which they did it are best known to Thailand and I would encourage Thailand, to produce some of their documents on the means of developing turtle free TEDs.

163. Australia has been trying to develop trawler efficiency devices, that still goes by the acronyms as TED but has a different complexion to it. The trawler efficiency devices, as they are referred to in Australia, look at making the trawls more efficient. They also incorporate such added extras, as fish eyes, for juvenile fish that are associated as a bycatch with shrimp trawls. They are being developed in sub-tropical as well as tropical waters. They are not driven solely by turtle excluding pressures. They are in fact designed, if I am correct, the underlying assumptions for the trawler

efficiency devices, is to sustain fisheries whether they are being commercial fisheries or recreational fisheries and to maintain the profitability of fisheries to prevent fisheries succumbing to financial hardship and also to maintain the viability of fisheries. So there is a cause of concern if shrimp trawlers are seen in the locality where there is a large recreational fishing. The recreational fishers are too keen to point their fingers at the trawling operations offshore. And therefore the trawlers have a responsibility to be able to answer these charges and say "yes, we will adopt trawl efficiency devices so that the juveniles of the fin-fish species of the recreational anglers or the professional fisherman wish to catch are not being harmed by the trawl fishery". So there is a trawl efficiency device that also serves as a turtle excluding device, but I think the thrust of Australia has been ... [tape turnover] ... the efficiency of the trawl, the responsibility, to make it a responsible fishery and to reduce conflict between the shrimp fishery and other fisheries operating in the area. I would like to conclude there and thank you for listening.

**Mr. Chairman**

164. Thank you very much. I do not particularly wish to put any sort of restriction on the two remaining experts, but given the time I would want to ask them to be as economical as possible in their answers with regard to the remaining time available to us. Perhaps at new points or where they have different views and try to avoid repeating where the material has already been covered.

**Mr. Liew**

165. Thank you Mr. Chairman. I will skip quite a number of the questions because I think they have been quite well answered by the other colleagues of mine. What I will I do is I will answer the US questions first concerning question 4 on TEDs. I would like to sort of expand it a bit and talk about trawling TEDs and bycatches in relation to trawls that are in use in the US and trawls that are in use in the complainant countries. I agree with Jack here that trawls are very destructive to the environment. It is a very destructive form of fishing and it catches everything in its path: from large animals - like sea turtles, large fish, sharks, rays, large groupers, sometimes tunas (Scombrids), they all get caught in the trawl, pomfrets, bream, all the way down to the very small fish which are the juveniles of those large commercially important fish. In addition to that, you get crabs, prawns and a whole lot of other invertebrates that are on the sea bottom. Apart from this process of dragging, the trawl device on the sea bed, it sort of scrapes the bottom many times and you may have a productive bottom and it eventually ends up like a desert. So, as Frazier has mentioned, there has been some call to ban the device in some countries but very few have really taken up the ban. Notwithstanding that, if you compare trawling in Malaysia or in the other complainant countries and trawling in the US, for example in Malaysia, when a licence is issued for trawling there is no distinction as to whether it can only catch fish or you can only catch prawns. If they are fishing in an area where there are prawns, then all they do is change the cod-end to a smaller meshed cod-end to catch the prawns. If they are fishing in an area where there are no prawns then they go for the fish and they change the cod-end to a larger mesh so that the smaller trash escapes. Almost all the catch from these trawlers are landed: the large commercially important fishes: the prawns and the trash fish. The trash fish refers to the small fish of the commercially important ones. All this is to provide the badly needed protein in these developing countries - that is why they catch and use

everything. The larger fish are important so they are sold in markets, the trash fish they convert to fishmeal or animal feed and then the prawns are also sold in markets and if they fetch a good price then they are exported for the country's foreign earnings. Thus, for many of these trawlers the earnings they get from prawns is only a component of the total earnings.

166. This graph [graph 6, Appendix 2] shows you different years [pointing at the x-axis], the largest column is the trash fish component - that means the young, small fish which they use to convert into fishmeal. This component [middle "fish" column] is the larger, commercially important fish that they sell in the market. This component is the prawn [indicating the right column]. So every year the prawn is this [indicating the right columns]. So, when you put a TED on a trawler like this, ...as you know the TED gets rid of the larger fish. So you put a TED here and this will reduce [pointing at the fish column] - they are talking about losing some of the commercially important fish. This will remain in the bycatch [pointing at the trash fish column] - OK the trash fish in this trawler is the bycatch and will still be there - you do not handle the bycatch. You lose the larger fish. There is a difference in the US shrimp trawlers: this [indicating the prawns column] is what they want and all this [indicating the fish and trash fish columns] they throw away. Their bycatch is the fish and the trash fish because they only want the prawns. So I think that is the difference that we have to be aware of when we talk about putting TEDs on fish trawlers. So we have to look at this problem along the perspective of the fishermen. You are going to introduce a device to fishermen and you want them to comply. You cannot expect them to use a device and find they lose profits in terms of the large fish. When you talk about it [referring to TEDs] being an efficient device which gets rid of bycatch, in this case it is not the bycatch that it has got rid of, it's the larger fish - that is the bycatch that the US are talking about in their shrimp trawler that are excluded with the turtles. Yes, it gets rid of turtles.

**Chairman**

167. Can I just ask a question. Does the Thai TED take care of this problem or is this something which suffers from the same...

**Mr. Liew**

168. Well, the Thai TED is similar - it is just a similar device. It also gets rid of the large fish. Because, I mean, logically you look at the design of a TED - all the large animals are got rid of and all the small ones get into the net. Even though the Thai TED is similar, depending on the size of the grid, it would depend on the size of the animals that there are ejected. Even for the Thai TED, they have used it but are the fishermen happy with it? If you look at the most recent reports I think they are not too happy because they are losing fish.

**The Ambassador of Thailand**

169. Mr. Chairman, I am very sorry but I would just like to ask permission, but I can make certain qualifications as far as the Thai TED is concerned or you would like me to wait until the experts finish their answers to questions. In order not to leave any misunderstanding on this perception about the Thai TEDs. I want simply to say that the Thai TEDs is the response to an embargo imposed by the United States and then we would like to solve these trade problems. That is why the Fishery Department of

Thailand has modified in the shortest possible time-frame without having to go through scientific experiment. Of course an elegant TED, as put by one expert. But the effectiveness, I am not quite sure because once we have put in place we still have to monitor and I think it would take many more years before we can say about the effectiveness of this Thai TED. Thank you very much.

**Mr. Liew**

170. It seems that they have problem. It is good if there is a TED device, if there is some kind of device that would get rid of turtles but then retain the big fish, the commercially important fish, and similarly get rid of all the trash, but still retain the prawns. We still have not been able to get that kind of device and I think this is the reason why the complainant countries have been quite reluctant to introduce TEDs in their trawlers because they still find this kind of dilemma. I think it is time here for research to be done to really work and find out whether we can improve on a device that would help save the turtles but still retain the big fish and the prawns. I would like here to sort of jump to question 8 of the US about how long it takes to adopt the TED. How long will the US be able to help us develop a device that the local fishermen will accept. If they can find a device that is suitable that would be the kind of time-frame and then introduce it to local fish trawlers. The local fish trawlers will be very glad to have a device that would exclude turtles, exclude the small trash fish and retain the big fish and prawns. I will appeal to the US with all their expertise and funding to help and find good solutions to this.

171. I would then like to jump to the question by the Malaysian submission. The first question: "would trade prohibition on the imports of shrimps to the US by itself save turtles from shrimp trawlers?" If the question is would TEDs save turtles, as what Frazier has interpreted it has, I would say yes, TEDs would save turtles. But would a trade embargo save turtles, I would say no and I would agree with Scott, by itself it would not. But by virtue of this case being brought up in the WTO dispute, it has put attention on many governments to the plight of turtles, irrespective of the outcome. This itself is a plus for turtle conservation. However, a shrimp embargo may undermine the efforts of turtle conservation and the protection of costal habitats especially in Malaysia. How is that possible? Because with the threat of an embargo it will carry a message that shrimp trawlers are the single most important cause of decline of sea turtles. Together with that message, it will also say that it is OK to continue with the present level of egg harvest, or even increase the level of egg harvest, because shrimp trawlers are the problem, not the egg harvest. Together with that message, it may also go with the message that it is OK to continue with the hunting of turtles for meat, because shrimp trawlers are the problem, not hunting. I mean you look at the irony of the situation of the shrimp trawler: he stops or is caught because he did not have a TED on his boat, even though he did not have any dead turtles. Just because he did not have a TED he is stopped and he is penalized. At the same moment a boat passes by, with 20 or 30 turtles going to the slaughterhouse. This situation is happening in Costa Rica where they allow slaughter of turtles but they use TEDs. They slaughter turtles for cosmetic [products] - this is happening in Bali, in Indonesia, where slaughtering is still rampant. It is very ironical. Another point is that it will also give the message that TED is more effective in protecting turtles at sea than closed areas as what we have in Malaysia for trawling. Trawl fishermen will then use this to fight for the lifting of zoning. They say "we have

TEDs and we protect with environmentally friendly device so why can we not come in and fish in a nearby zone". They may use this as a case. Another point is that TEDs are not required if you do not export your prawns to the US - this is what the embargo is going to be. It will leave that kind of a message: TEDs are not required if you do not export your prawns to the US. So trawlers who do not export their prawns to the US will argue that they need not use TEDs. It is already happening. We have reports from fishermen from places who say "we do not export our prawns to the US, why should we use TEDs?" This creates a serious obstacle to the Fisheries Department, to the turtle conservationists who are presently experimenting with TEDs to try to introduce to these fishermen. We do not want to give them that message that if you do not export your prawns to the US, you do not need TEDs. We are still working on trying to find a suitable TED to introduce to them. Another point is when affected countries see they cannot sell their prawns to the US, they look for other markets, like Michael Guinea pointed out. Instead of using TEDs to save turtles, the fishermen would instead just look for other markets for their prawns. The purpose of the embargo will be defeated. They will sell their prawns to countries that are exempted from the embargo, like Japan or Singapore. These countries will repackage it with other prawns from aquaculture and ship it to the US. I feel that embargo is not the solution. It may create more problems to turtle conservation. I agree TEDs will help but you have to design a TED or produce a TED that is acceptable to the fishermen. You have to get them to accept and not force it on them. Fishermen are proud people - you force them and they will not do it. If there is an option of other markets, then they will just look for other markets.

172. I will go to the second question of the Malaysian submission. My other colleagues have brought up something about population sizes and long-term monitoring before you can detect whether a population has recovered or not. So they mention that you require very long periods of population monitoring because there is very high fluctuations and then you need many, many years before you can really say that the population is recovering. There are populations that I have here that show signs of recovery. Probably most of you have seen this [graph 7, Appendix 2]. This is the leatherbacks in St. Croix - quite a few years data and there appears to be an increasing trend and they are recovering. I am not saying they have recovered but they are in the process - the recovering process. This is the leatherbacks in South Africa. It has a very long dataset, ... many years, you can see the trend - they are recovering. Similarly, the green turtles of the Sabah islands [graph 8, Appendix 2]. There has been a decline but then they are recovering. If you talk about wide fluctuations, it is there, but if you follow the trend, they are recovering. So the efforts of these conservationists - they have spent many years working on this and getting the populations to recover and they are showing signs of recovering. You just cannot step in and say it has not recovered. How would they feel? They would feel they have not done something that is good. We have to recognize that they have done a good job. We have to recognize that the population is recovering. By the same token, it is very slow for us to recognize the populations are recovering but it is very quick for us to recognize that the population is declining. Why? In 5 years you find out the populations are going down very quickly and you jump up - it is declining! Why do you not give it 20 years. By that time it is too late. Recognition has actually been given to this population. They have been given awards for the fact that they have worked very hard to recover these populations and we have to recognize that it is so. Not only just recognize that, but it gives us hope. There are many populations that are down and we are using the recovering populations as examples that if you do

conservation work properly, nesting conservation, there is a hope that your population will recover. For us, in Terengganu, our leatherbacks are very, very low and there have been talks in the state about forgetting the nesting beach and develop it for tourism for hotels. We are standing firm and we say "there is a chance that we can recover populations, look at this population [referring to graph 7]." We are using these as examples that populations are recovering.

173. Something that Jack Frazier submitted is the TED technology transfer. Yes, the US have worked very hard to try and transfer the technology of TEDs to many countries. But if you look at the amount of transfer of technology to the complainant countries I think it is nothing more than just the complainant countries requesting for the information about TEDs. I do not know whether you call it technology transfer or not, or it is just for getting information. For example, in Thailand - I was going through the letters to see what actually transpired - Thailand initiated a request for information about TEDs in 24 April 1992. The US did not respond until January 1993. In both cases it was just sending information, requesting for information and sending the information. There was no offer by the US to run training workshops or join research on TEDs or anything like that. It was not until September 1996 that one workshop was held in Thailand and that was after the embargo. In Malaysia also all the correspondences are just request for information. To Pakistan there was nothing. To India, the first correspondence was in 1982 - it was a request for information on TEDs and in August 1992, India...

**The representative of the United States**

174. I do not know what this is in response to. This is not a question, this is a recitation of which apparently appears to be from the various briefs of the complainants and I think this is inappropriate. We have been holding our fire, but this is now getting out of control.

**Chairman**

175. I wonder if we could just try and keep to the questions as they are framed and move along because we are now getting very short on time and we still have one other speaker.

**Mr. Liew**

176. Basically, what I am trying to say here is that use of TEDs cannot be applied straight away. You cannot take from one country and straight away apply to another nation. There has to be some kind of work done to see its suitability. I feel that the US has not really come out to work with the complaining countries to transfer their technology.

**Chairman**

177. Could we just keep to the scientific aspects of the question because that is getting more into the subject matter of the dispute and away from the scientific facts which is really the purpose of the expert process. I am sorry to interrupt you but perhaps we could try and deal with the scientific bits because time is getting a little bit short.

**Mr. Liew**

178. Well, basically, OK. I will then end by saying I am a turtle biologist. I am just as concerned about conserving sea turtles as turtle biologists in other countries. I have written, we, in Malaysia have written, for information about TEDs and we have also suggested to our Fisheries Department to try and work and develop TEDs. But, all in all, I just hope that TEDs should be introduced in a more friendly, cooperative manner. I do not think that trying to get people to comply with TEDs by an embargo would solve the problem and I shall end here. Thank you.

**Chairman**

179. Mr. Poiner, there is not a lot of time left. We have now got some questions that have been put forward by Thailand and these have been circulated in writing [see Appendix 1]. Necessarily, the answers are going to be rather brief because of the remaining time. In addition to the other questions perhaps I could ask you to look at those and then I will give the other experts also an opportunity to say something briefly on those as well.

**The representative of the United States**

180. Mr. Chairman, before we go to the Thai questions, I would ask that you look at the first two on the second page [questions 2 and 3 by Thailand, Appendix 1] which are really not a question. It is not a scientific question but just ask the experts whether they know something about Thailand - it is not really a scientific question and the second question is not really a scientific question either. I guess the second question would be "are they effective?" and premises falls "are the experts aware that Thai TEDs have not been found effective?" when there is a scientific study showing that they are effective. So you cannot ask a question, with a false premise. I would ask that these questions be struck or re-phrased.

**Chairman**

181. I can certainly see the point on those first two questions but the third one on time is one that bears on something that we have already been discussing. I do not think that any of these, because they are in fact bearing on matters which have been extensively covered already, actually require very much time in the answers at any rate. So perhaps the experts could bear that in mind. Mr. Poiner would you like to continue please.

**Mr. Poiner**

182. Thank you. I will start with the Malaysian questions and in the interest of time I will try to be as brief as possible. Turning to the first question to all experts relating to the trade prohibition, I think there is really two aspects to this. The first is the trade issue, in the sense that if a country is not exporting to the US, then a prohibition would have little effect. Australia is a good example of that. Very little of the product goes into the US and unless there is subsequent indirect impacts on the market in terms of realigning where the product is eventually going, that would have very little impact. There is also a biological perspective on this in terms of the use of TEDs. I think I shall try and briefly summarize what my view on this would be. My professional view is that

I think that the current data on the incidental capture of sea turtles in shrimp trawl fisheries offers an estimate of trawl induced mortality and allows comparisons with other sources mortalities. For some species and some breeding units, I think that current data does not give a clear indication about the effects of these mortalities on the turtle populations, apart from probably some of the US examples. But the evidence does suggest that it is an important source of mortality for many species and breeding units. Given that, I think we have heard about the precautionary principle and I think that is a valid principle in terms of managing these sorts of issues. I think there is a need to reduce the capture of turtles in trawls, but I would emphasize that needs to be part of a wider programme to reduce all sorts of mortalities and that part of that programme is identifying the source of mortality for the breeding unit that you want to manage. Finally, the use of TEDs is one of several possible measures that could be used to reduce turtle captures in trawls.

183. I will now move on to the second question from Malaysia in relation to acceptable recognized methods of determining population sizes. We have heard a lot about this and I can generally concur. I just want to make the point that there are three issues that are critical here. One is the determination of what is being called breeding unit and there are methods that relate to things like genetic methods, tagging methods and a variety of others. Then, there are other ways of measuring trends in populations, because the key to this is determining the trend in a population. Most of these revolve around breeding females at beaches and the important issue there is to be able to be detect trends over long periods of time. Those periods of time are a combination of the life history of the animal being studied and for these turtles that is a long period of time - 10, 20 or 30 years is not unexpected. There is also the factor of the biophysical events that impact on those populations and the best example we have all heard of is the impacts of the "El Niño" phenomenon in the West Pacific populations. The important issue is identifying the breeding unit and then having statistically robust estimates of the population that you can use to detect trends over the appropriate time-frames. Our methods will be improved, they will change and that is part of the process. Moving on to question 3, I will just simply say that I think the concept of a breeding unit is a key and critical concept. That is what we need to focus on in developing management strategies for these animals. Question 4, in general I agree with most of my colleagues - great care should be taken in generalizing any data outside the areas studied but it really does depend on the study and depend on the question being asked. Jack's answer to this was a very good one in the sense that if you are studying green turtles in the Atlantic and show that they do migrate, I think it is a reasonable assumption to help you frame a question for Pacific green turtles that they are also likely to migrate. It can be done but should be done with great care and then should be followed up by studies to get the data specific to that population.

184. Moving on to question 5, that there are sea turtle populations which are quite healthy, I too would have to question the use of the word "healthy". I think that is a fairly difficult word to define in terms of a population study. I think there are a few examples of breeding units which either have not shown the drastic declines of many populations - probably a reasonable example of that is the Raine Island population. I should have made the note that I too think that these questions need to be framed in terms of time-frames and the time-frame that I have assumed in this is about the 20- or 30-year period for such data. Assuming that sort of time-frame that we are looking at,

then I think there are a few examples of populations that have not shown drastic declines and the South African one is a good example of populations that are probably increasing. But I think for most stocks there is a general agreement that populations are at low levels and I think that there is still debate about the nature of recovery and if recovery is occurring in those populations.

185. Moving on to question 6 of the Malaysian submission: what species are the dominant species impacted by trawling. This, like a lot of things that we have heard today and yesterday, this really does depend on the fishery and the distribution of the turtles in respect to that fishery. We do have 4 fisheries where we have very good data looking at what species and where the important species are impacted, coming from the US and Australia. In the US, in one of those fisheries, it is loggerhead that is certainly the major species being impacted or was impacted and that is the Southern Atlantic in terms of the Gulf of Mexico - loggerheads and Kemp's ridleys. However in Australia, for example, the Northern Prawn Fishery, it is flatbacks and olive ridleys which are the key species impacted and on the Queensland Eastcoast it is loggerheads and green turtles. So the point I am making is, it really does depend on the fishery. I think some care is needed in making global generalization based on data from one area.

186. Moving on to the United States questions: the simple answer [to question 1] is yes. Yes, although I think, and my colleagues have expanded to some extent, but I think these sorts of questions -it's over-simplifying a very complex issue and I think that in dealing with these issues, one needs to be quite careful and quite specific to the fishery or to the breeding unit or to the species that you are addressing. I think we have spent quite a bit of time on that. I guess in terms of this, the questions themselves are a bit of an over-simplification of the situation.

187. Moving on to question 2, some of my colleagues have referred to the numbers games. I note that really what we are talking about here is interpreting complex data and data from a variety of sources basically using modeling techniques. I think, in using modeling techniques, they are essential and they are probably one of the few tools that we have to really look at predictions of the impacts of management measures over long time periods. However, in using those modeling techniques, we need to be very careful in terms of making very clear about our assumptions because, as I said yesterday, assumptions being made in our models and how we deal with some of the uncertainty in our models.

188. I think what you will find is that tools are very good but if we do not clearly state those assumptions and those uncertainties then it is very difficult to interpret the outcomes. I will use the example of Crouse and Crowder models which demonstrate that the impacts of trawling on sub-adult and adults potentially do have a major impact on the population. Similar models by other people, for example, Somers in Australia, where a slight modification of things like egg and hatchling stage mortality rates come up with a somewhat different picture. Then more recently, studies by Chaloupka and others, who use different sorts of modeling approaches and somewhat different assumptions, come up with indications of the importance of managing to control for egg mortalities. The point I am making here is that these are very valuable, very useful tools. However, we should be careful in terms of over-simplifying some of the numbers that are used in these tools and we have a bit of an example of it here. Moving on to question 3. Again I think the simple question here depends on the breeding unit and the source of mortality in terms of determining the relative importance of minimizing

mortalities from shrimp trawling. Again I think we have had quite a lot of discussion about that and I do not need to say much more. Moving on to question 4. Again, properly installed and used, yes, TEDs are very effective eliminating turtles from a trawl. However, in my answer to question ... [end of the tape] ... if you have a properly installed TED in a trawl and a turtle enters that trawl, there is a very very high probability that that turtle will leave that trawl without being caught in the cod end. Moving onto question 5, I think my answer to one of the Malaysian questions and I won't repeat it, basically what I would say is that the current data does demonstrate that for many breeding units the incidental capture, not for all but for many breeding units of some species, the incidental capture of turtles in shrimp trawls is an important source of mortality. The data, apart from one or two populations, does not give a clear indication about the effects of these mortalities on the breeding units or the populations, or the stocks themselves. However, again, I think that it's rather prudent to reduce the capture of turtles in trawls but again not in isolation of other measures to reduce other sources of mortalities. By themselves, I doubt whether that would effectively conserve these populations.

189. I think I will move on now to question 6, time and area closure. I would like to spend a few minutes on this Mr. Chairman. A little bit of comment on approaches to fisheries management: there are generally two approaches, what we term input controls and output controls. Without going into great detail, shrimp fisheries are generally managed on input controls simply because of their short life period. Most shrimps you are talking about, one or two years max. and because of the variability in terms of the natural variability in the catch from environmental processes. What this means is that things like total allowable catches and ITQ management systems really don't work for shrimp fisheries and I can't think of an example where they are applied. What that means is that they generally use import control measures and they will range from things like gear restrictions and gear modifications. These are commonly used in, if I'm correct, the Gulf of Mexico, together with other management measures such as area and time closures. Now I think again we should be very careful of generalizing about some of the measures used for one or two fisheries to all fisheries and it's not correct to suggest that area and time closures are important and very useful and very effective measures used in fisheries management particularly for species like shrimp. They generally use the things like the protection of critical habitat. For example, many species of tiger prawns, which are very important species in the Pacific, as juveniles only live in sea grass communities. Hence, if you are going to manage that fishery, you have to manage the sea grass community. Similarly, for many of the white shrimp only live in mangroves. So, often you will find in this part of fisheries management you'll have permanent closures of shallow water areas that are supporting for example sea grass communities. They are also used to enhance the value of the catch, so you'll tend to have time closures to maximize the return on the size of the products. So for example, you'll find that there'll be what's called pre-season monitoring of the size of the catch so as to maximize the value of the catch when it's caught. Because, for example, the Japanese market like shrimp about this big and the difference between the returns on a shrimp that big and that big are quite large, so time closures we use for that. Time closures are also used to enhance recruitment. For example, you get periods when the fishery is shut down around breeding times actually to enhance, for example, egg production. They are also being used to minimise interactions between fisheries. One of the two examples I can think of is Indonesia with the in-shore traditional and artisanal

fisheries being separated from the larger industrial trawl fisheries. Similarly in Northern Australia, in Torres Strait; you get a similar example in Papua New Guinea. These are well and commonly used techniques and management tools in many fisheries. In that, they offer an opportunity to be useful in terms of turtle management of the incidental catch of turtles. So I can think of two examples of this that I am well aware of, both directly and indirectly. An indirect example would be probably in the Northern Australian prawn trawl fishery for example, the lower catch rate of green turtles compared to the East Coast prawn trawl fishery, probably can be explained simply because of a permanent closure of shallow water in the Northern prawn fishery to sea grass communities. The closure has driven the fleet, if that's the correct word, further off shore than say the corresponding East Coast prawn trawl fishery. Another more direct example is in a place called Mon Repos, near Bundaberg on the East Coast of Australia where it is a loggerhead nesting area. Seasonal closure of trawling off shore which is in place now, I think will be effective in terms of reducing the trawl catch of those breeding females as they migrate to that beach. I don't think we should exclude area and time closures as a potential tool for the management of this issue. However, like all these things it will depend on a variety of other things particularly the nature of the fishery, the nature of the socio-economic issues surrounding the fishery and all those sorts of things.

190. Do we have enough knowledge about hot spots? [question 6 by the United States] No we don't. For some breeding units we do, for some areas we do, again these generally come from places like for example in Australia, where we can identify different catch rates of turtles in different areas of the fishery, both in relation to the feeding and breeding areas. But, generally that information is not available. I will skip question 7 because that is addressed to Dr. Eckert. The final one, the adoption of TEDs by shrimp trawling fleets [question 8 by the United States]. In my comments yesterday, I used the example of the introduction of bycatch reduction devices, including TEDs, in the Australian shrimp trawl fisheries to demonstrate that this is not necessarily a quick process, because in many of the documents surrounding the case is that this is an issue of a matter of months. The example I used in Australia where it is probably going to take 6 to 8 years (I'm not saying that it will take 6 to 8 years in every area), but I think that by the same token it's somewhat naive to think this can be done in a matter of months. I say that because really, the introduction of these sorts of devices in the fishery is really a three stage process. The first process is the identification of the device that potentially will do the job for you and doing the job depends on what you want to exclude. For example, I note that the earlier comments about elimination of trash but retention of large fish that my colleague Mr. Liew made. There are two types of bycatch reduction devices. There are types that work on basically mechanical means and that's often the TEDs: they're actually rigid structures in the net that a large object like a turtle will hit and be forced out of the net. There's also other devices that work on the relative swimming ability of the animals being caught. So these are often used to eliminate the trash species, so basically there's things called square-mesh panels, fish eyes, a whole variety of things that now basically work on the assumption that fish can generally swim a lot better than prawns, so the fish move down the net and swim out these holes. There are also devices that use a combination of these things. For example, you might want to eliminate large animals plus so some of the trash. So really you need to identify what you are trying to do and then select your device. Now, the device will need to be modified for the individual characteristics of the fisheries and by that I mean it relates

both to the types of nets being used, the types of vessels being used, the types of fishing strategies being used but also relates to issues in terms of types of environments being fished. So, for example, in some areas of shrimp fishing, where there is a large community of animals that live on the bottom, particularly sponges, they tend to clog a lot of the rigid TEDs; so again you need to develop ways of overcoming those sorts of problems. You really need to identify the device and demonstrate that it is effective and that's what we have been talking about in terms of properly installed TEDs to eliminate turtles. That's only one part of a three stage process. The next stage is the extension of that gear or gears into the fishery which is really similar to most agricultural fisheries or whatever processes where you want to change the behaviour of a group of people, be it fisherman or farmer; it generally involves an extension process and the length of that really does again depend on the particular nature of the fishery. What I'd think is the final part of the process is what I call the formulation of the use of the gear to the management plan or the way the fisheries are managed. That's when you get into the issues of whether you are doing a regulatory approach, i.e. compulsory introduction, or are you doing as what I talked about, a target approach. So, you are setting a target and how you achieve that target is really up to the fishery. I think it is important to realize that this is not simply a process of demonstrating this device will eliminate turtles, it's a process of demonstrating that in the extension and then the capture of that information and formulation of that information into the management plans that govern those fisheries. Mr. Chairman I will try to deal with questions raised by Thailand although it might be more efficient to rotate through and I can read this, as well as my other colleagues.

**Chairman**

191. Yes, perhaps I can just say that since the time is now reached almost one o'clock, I think I would like to give the experts each at least one last opportunity to say whatever few brief summary words they want to, or add any other points they would like to at this stage. Perhaps they could, in doing so, add any brief answers that they may have on those Thai questions and incorporate that together. We've had, I think, all the questions and points from the parties and I don't intend, unless there's any reason to do so, to offer the floor to the parties again and perhaps we can just go into the final round and, as I say, include the answers as far as possible. But, please try and be as brief as you can. Dr. Eckert.

**Dr. Eckert**

192. I will try to break my typical mould here and I'll go through this promptly. Let me deal with the questions first [questions by Thailand], just briefly. The first four questions and the first three questions deal with the application of TEDs in a fishery. From my own experience, what I can say is, having worked with shrimp fishermen on the Georgia Coast for a number of years before moving to California, TEDs are not difficult to operate, they are a very simple device. However, as Dr. Poiner pointed out, fine tuning or modification of the basic design is very important to the individual fishery. I know there has been tremendous work done on that. In the United States they instituted a programme of TEDs certification, by which shrimpers can develop their own TEDs and bring them to a certification programme and get them certified as being a viable TED, that would work in the kind of environments that they were working in.

That apparently has been very effective and quite creative developments in efficient TEDs. "Mandating TEDs requirements is not guaranteed that sea turtle mortality will be reduced?" Like all laws and regulations I don't know any of us that actually drive the speed limit either. The enforcement of a regulation is only as good as its enforcement. However, if one shrimper uses the TED, the turtle mortality will be reduced. I think we are all in agreement that TEDs reduce the take of sea turtles and so if one person follows the law, it's going to be in that game for the sea turtle populations. On the second page relative to the first two questions [question 2 and 3 by Thailand]. The answer to the first question, no, I was not aware of any developments in the TED, the same thing for the second question, I am not aware of any expert testing the TEDs other than there was one brief report included in our briefings provided. Relative to the last question, it would depend on the situation, the country, the fishery and so on and so on. I'm probably not in a good position to speak to that.

193. Final comments, you have heard a lot of testimony in the last day and a half about sea turtles. The take-home message is that global sea turtle populations are in trouble. I think we are all in agreement with that. There seems to be a message that TEDs reduce mortality in sea turtles and that shrimp fisheries often, if not always, provide a source of mortality to sea turtle populations. I think we are all very clear on that. You heard some discussion about the biology of the animals and where we agree and disagree and how we are trying to play the numbers games and trying to understand what is going on out there. All that stuff is reflective on more of a management decision that has to made as to how are your resource management dollars best spent and how are your resources towards conserving sea turtles best spent. You have heard from us that we could probably go on for another three or four or five days on that same issue. It would be up to the individual countries as to how they approach that. But, I think that we are all in agreement that you need to take a balanced approach to the conservation of your turtles. You need to address them in the water as well as on the land and all aspects of their life histories and so that is what I have for my conclusion. Thank you.

**Chairman**

194. Thank you very much indeed. Doctor Frazier.

**Dr. Frazier**

195. Thank you for your patience with us. The first page of questions from Thailand, I know that Arauz from Costa Rica has been working with TEDs with the fishermen in Costa Rica and he has told me that he does not think it's difficult - you have to work with the fishermen. I have worked with Gabriel Olguin in Campeche in Mexico, and Gabriel is convinced that it is not that difficult in Mexico to use TEDs. It's a matter of will, I think. If the fisherman wants to do it, he can learn to do it. It is like any kind of gear, it has to be learnt. I have said that before, it is not simply a matter of sticking it in the net and it's magically going to work. Other colleagues have mentioned the need for training and I am in total agreement with that. But it is not difficult to use properly, I don't believe it is difficult to use properly. "TED requirements are very easy to evade and many shrimpers ...". Well, there are two parts to the question. Are TED requirements easy to evade? Yes, all requirements are easy to evade. Drug import requirements are easy to evade, gun requirements are easy to evade, all requirements are easy to evade, it depends on the will of the person. The second part of the question, well

perhaps Liew mentioned that if people are against them they won't use them. It depends on the shrimpers. This is why Ian pointed out the need for extension. Clearly the shrimpers must be working with the fisheries people. Part 3, "TED requirements are not easily enforced". Again I think that's a re-phrasing of the earlier question. Any requirements can be evaded. Perhaps to put this in context one needs to look at this with other sorts of requirements. It is my impression that area closures, I tried to mention before, I believe area and time closures are very useful, and I believe there are excellent laws that exist that address those issues. However, depending on the characteristics of the fishery, as Ian pointed out, those might not be effective and it may be easier to put TEDs into shrimp trawl nets. Another reason which I tried to explain before is, I see this not so much as a technical problem, but as a social problem in biological conservation. To try and impress upon trawlers they must be more selective, they must use their gear better. They should go towards a step to reducing this tremendous destruction that is caused by bottom trawling. The fourth question "mandating TED requirements does not guarantee that sea turtle mortality is reduced". Definitely not. We can mandate everything we like and nothing will happen unless there is a response by society. We can mandate against drugs, we can mandate against poverty, that won't get rid of it. But, if we don't make some effort to impress society, what are our options? Do we sit and wait? I don't know. This is a political question really, I don't see this as a biological question. It is a very relevant question.

196. "Are the experts aware that Thailand was unable to develop the TEDs within the short 4 month period provided by the US measures?" Again, I think this is really to be answered by a Thai fisheries expert who was involved in this. This is not something I have been involved in. I do know that Thailand made a major effort to send fisheries experts, I believe to the NMFS laboratory in Pascagoula [Mississippi, USA], if I'm wrong I can be corrected. I'm very certain they sent their fisheries people to Mexico, to see designs that were in use in another country outside the US. I believe Thailand made a major effort to learn from other experiences and to adapt this. That's about all I can say on that question. "Are the experts aware that the Thai TEDs are not found effective in actual use?" I know of very little about this, I have tried to assemble the information I can get. There is a fisheries expert at Bandit at SEAFDEC. If it's necessary I'll find it. There is one report published in the proceedings of a regional meeting where an expert from Thailand reported having testing TEDs, the Thai Turtle Free Device, and that clearly shows that, as far as he was concerned, it was functioning. I have looked through that report quite carefully and my impression is that he was convinced that it was working well, that it would be usable in Thai waters. Now, that same reply seemed to come from another report from Malaysia published in the same meeting and another report coming from the Philippines, I have cited those in the Annex on bycatch. So, my impression is that fisheries experts in three countries in South East Asia feel that the Thai Turtle Free Device is useful. Perhaps, implicit in this question is a submission I think that came with Thailand about an analysis which was done this year. I don't remember the author's name. Now, this showed that there was a tremendous loss of economic value from the use of the Thai Turtle Free Device. The difficulty I have in interpreting that, is that the analysis was done based on 1995, I believe, when the Thai Turtle Free Device was not used and then the next year when the device was used. So, in the first instance we are comparing between two years as well as, with or without Turtle Free Device. So, we have several complications in interpreting the data. What concerns me for many reasons is, if I look at production of prawn from Thailand over

those years, I see a decline. Firstly, it concerns me that there is a decline and that's general throughout most regions, there has been a decline. But it also concerns me in interpreting the data because if there is a decline then it means comparing one year and then a later year, I can't tell whether anything I've changed in my fishery is due to that change or to the decline which is in the background. So, I have difficulty in interpreting that data.

197. Finally, "do experts believe that four months is sufficient time to ... all steps necessary?" It is a very short time, I would much rather see more time. Other experts have expressed reasons why. I think that Thailand has shown that with political will, these things can be done quickly. I would much rather see more time for many reasons. I believe, however, that in many countries the fisheries experts have been expressing a need to do this for years. There is an FAO document, which I have cited in the Annex, where fisheries experts concluded that they are really not being listened to. Excuse me if I overstep my role, but please make sure that your fisheries people get this support, they need it, this is imperative. So, I would like to say that this is very frustrating, that there is so much to discuss and so little time. In general, I don't have any contentions with the generality of the comments, there are a few fine things that I think we could discuss further. The focus of the comments of other colleagues, I am in agreement with. As I said, there are fine points which I would prefer to discuss further. Michael mentioned something which, I believe, is valid and that is the value of these environmentally friendly shrimp, what's happened to that? Now, something which I was not able to include for lack of time, there is an attempt now, curiously by the organization which pushed this through the courts, the Earth Island Institute, to make shrimp caught in trawls which have TEDs more valuable, "turtle friendly shrimp", and make it marketable, economically more useful. So, I believe that there is every reason why the countries represented here should make use of that. Sell their shrimp at a higher value, make the consumers assume these social and ecologic costs which are now externalized. I don't see any reason why they shouldn't be doing this. Again this is outside my purview, I am not an economist, but I don't see why they shouldn't. As I said this is very frustrating, we have opened such a tremendous number of Pandora's boxes. This could go on for years and we are quite capable, but I better shut up.

**Chairman**

198. Thank you very much. Mr Guinea perhaps you can be equally brief.

**Mr. Guinea**

199. Thank you Mr. Chairman. I will address the first three questions (a), (b) and (c) [question 1 by Thailand]. These three questions are all related to the willingness of fishermen or boat operators to accept TED technology and, associated with, there this is also the trust that is generated by the sea turtle experts in saying that you need to use TEDs to protect sea turtles. Now, that trust component is a very difficult thing to generate externally. Trust is far better generated internally within a country, if a country has made a commitment and believes that what they are doing is the correct thing, then this trust will flow through. When we are looking at generating trust you can look at the long-term goals of survival of sea turtles, where that may be an element of generating trust or you may be looking at short-term goals, such as producing more value for a product. However, if the fisheries are unwilling to adopt TED technology, then all these

problems associated with implementation, enforcement and non-compliance will continue. So it's generally a matter of generating trust within a country. Mandating a TEDs requirement, there's no guarantees in biology. I think nobody's going to give you the guarantee that TEDs are going to be the sole answer to sea turtle conservation. They may make a contribution to sea turtle conservation and that contribution may vary from country to country, from breeding unit to breeding unit and also from species to species, but there is no guarantee. I was also going to make one comment relating to Dr. Eckert, to his example of speed limits. I would just like the record to show that I do drive at the speed limit and not otherwise. On the second page the first two questions [questions 2 and 3 by Thailand] I believe we are not dealing with those. Relating to the third question [question 4 by Thailand], I believe that 4 months is insufficient time to have a technology developed, not only from the physical but also developing a trust within the fishery that this technology is for their betterment. I would not like to put a time-limit on the development of TEDs. I think TEDs are going to be in those areas even in the United States, I imagine, they will undergo refinement, improvement, modifications. We've already seen things such as the soft TEDs removed from some areas. There's arguments over top shooting and bottom shooting TEDs, so I think TED technology is not going to be static, but I think if a country is going to implement TEDs, then it should be done on a basis where the operators of the vessels adopt the use of the TEDs for either the betterment of the fishery or their own financial gain or for some goal. So, the implementation of the TEDs should really take as long as required.

**Chairman**

200. Thank you very much indeed. Any final words Mr. Liew?

**Mr. Liew**

201. Thank you. I'll try to make it short for fear of overstepping my bounds. Actually I'm in total agreement with what Jack Frazier has said, so most of the things that he said is similar to my views. There are a few things that I want to raise, some slight changes. Basically, it is in the Thai TED where he did mention about the recent report in 1997. I agree using 1995 data and comparing it with 1997 data, it is hard to accept, but I suppose for Thailand that was the only data they had. What should have been done was to have some trawlers without the TEDs and some trawlers with the TEDs, operating in more or less the same area and then you compare them and that would give you a much better indication as to whether it works or whether it doesn't work. Nonetheless, if you look at the indepth report, they also mention things like operating costs and they found that with TEDs the costs of operation seem to have increased, in terms of usage of fuel and all that. Those things you can take but not so much on the catch rate, you can't compare between 1995 and 1997. In general, to close, I'm really sort of not against TEDs neither am I against turtles, God forbid. The problem is the incidental capture of turtles in trawlers. They do exist and TED is a possible solution. The complainant countries have, I don't know whether I am overstepping my bounds here, but the complainant countries have been sort of slow in addressing the problem. I mean it took them something like 15 years or so before they started looking at TEDs. This was probably because of the apprehension they have of using TEDs on the kind of trawlers they have, which target fish and prawns. So there is this apprehension. So, I mean the US here will be in the best possible position because of the expertise to come in to help

develop a much more suitable technical TED. They may start with a simple TED but it has to be done with proper research and studies, not trying to get all the fishermen to use it and then they start to complain about it because it doesn't work, they are loosing a catch and all that kind of thing. You find that they don't comply and then it is very hard to convince them to accept TED usage. It has to be done in a way where the fisherman sort of accept the device. It has to be done that way. I think I'll end with that, thank you very much.

**Chairman**

202. Thank you very much. Dr. Poiner.

**Dr. Poiner**

203. Thanks Mr. Chairman. Firstly, just addressing the questions of Thailand. Again briefly in terms of [question 1 (a)], I think it really does depend on the implementation process and the attitude of the fishers in terms of how difficult or otherwise TED use with time is in the fishery. In terms of the other questions that TED requirements are easy to evade, yes, again if fishermen want to evade something, they will tend to work out a way of evading it. Similarly, in terms of where TEDs are required, again evasion you can do it again. It highlights the need to have the support of the operators, in this case the fishermen, in terms of the use of gear modifications like TEDs, if they are going to be incorporated in the fishery. "TED requirements are not easily enforced." Many, if not most requirements of fishers at sea are difficult to enforce and will always be an issue and always expensive, so the answer is yes. "Mandating TED requirements does not guarantee that sea turtle mortality will be reduced." I will agree with that. Mandating TEDs will not ensure sea turtle mortality will be reduced, however, appropriately and properly implemented regimes that could or may or may not include TEDs could help in terms of reducing turtle mortalities. In terms of the other questions, I was not aware of the first two points, so I will say the answer is no, I am not aware of it. Do I believe that 4 months is sufficient time? Definitely not. I don't think 4 months is sufficient time to effectively implement those sorts of changes in any fisheries, let alone the fisheries like the complex trawl fisheries in a place like Thailand. In terms of final points, again I will just make the final point that I too, like many of my colleagues, have the view that the turtle stocks, many if not most turtle stocks are severely depleted, in low numbers and I think it's very important that we do something about it and doing something about it means trying to eliminate some of these anthropogenic mortalities. Also it's clear for many populations and many species that incidental capture in trawl fisheries is an important source of mortality and I think that we need to reduce it. However, we should not make what I think would be a fatal assumption that just reducing that source of mortality would be the solution for the species. I think that reduction needs to be in the context of a wider programme to reduce all the important source of mortalities because we really at this point cannot distinguish between them for many of the populations. And I finally make the comment that I have made several times is that the use of TEDs is only one measure, but only one measure, of several that are available, that may be useful in terms of reducing full capture of sea turtles. Thanks Mr. Chairman.

**Chairman**

204. Well thank you very much. I think at this stage I would like to express my thanks to all the experts. They've given us both yesterday afternoon and today as well as in writing before that the benefit of their wisdom and I certainly think they have helped very considerably the work of this Panel by giving us a very good picture of the scientific and technical background to the problems of sea turtle conservation and sea turtle behaviour. So, I would really like to express my very warm thanks to them for that. I think that concludes our work today and I would like to thank everyone for participating and in particular our experts who have been so helpful and so patient with us and with our questions.

Thank you very much indeed.

## Appendix 1

*QUESTIONS BY THE PARTIES AT THE MEETING WITH THE EXPERTS*

*Questions by Malaysia*

**To Dr. Eckert:**

1. You have formulated a hypothesis for the migration of leatherback to justify US jurisdiction over the sea turtles stocks of Malaysia, Thailand and Indonesia. What hypothesis can you propose to justify US jurisdiction over the sea turtle stocks of India and Pakistan?

2. You have not provided answers to the question "Are you aware of data on the rate of turtle stranding in areas where TEDs are currently required or on the relationship between turtle stranding and shrimping activities in areas where TEDs are required?" Data released to the CTURTLE List through the internet has actually shown that turtles still strand in large numbers even as recently as 1997 in areas where TEDs are required.

3. You have worked on the leatherback population of St. Croix. What were the major conservation measures taken there? Would you say that the population there is showing signs of recovery? What was the nesting population size when you were working there in the mid-1980s? What is the current nesting population size? Would you say that protecting the nesting females on the nesting beaches, and protecting the eggs undergoing incubation have contributed towards the build-up of the nesting population in St. Croix?

4. Malaysia has submitted rebuttals to some of the points raised by you in your responses to the questions from the Panel. We would like to have your comments in writing.

**To all the experts:**

5. In you expert opinion would trade prohibition on the import of shrimp to the United States by itself save the sea turtles from shrimp trawlers and extinction?

6. What is the acceptable recognized method of determining the population size of breeding units of sea turtles, especially in assessments of population trends?

7. Please tell us your views about the concept of unit stocks or populations or breeding units of sea turtles.

8. When studies on any particular sea turtle population are made, would the results apply to the population being studied, or would you as a scientist, generalize your data for all sea turtles, irrespective of the species or where they occur?

9. Notwithstanding the status listings of sea turtles provided in the IUCN Red Data Book and CITES, would you not say that there are sea turtle populations in the world which are quite healthy and which have benefited from long term conservation programmes started some 30 years ago?

10. Data provided by Henwood and Stuntz, 1987 and numerous other reports of turtle mortalities in shrimp trawls, as well as stranding data show that loggerheads are the predominant species impacted followed by Kemp's ridleys. Based on all scientific evidence available, and the feeding habits of loggerheads would you agree that the

loggerhead turtle is the species which is most vulnerable to shrimp trawling, followed by Kemp's ridleys and these species are found in the U.S. and not in Malaysia.

*Questions by the United States*

1. There appears to be some disagreement over whether sea turtles should be analyzed in terms of specific populations of nesting sea turtles, and whether there is sufficient evidence to conclude that certain populations of nesting sea turtles have stabilized. Leaving aside these specific populations - in particular the Malaysian Sabah Turtle Islands population - aren't there other sea turtles found in each of the Complainants' waters that are members of populations which are not yet showing signs of recovery? If such sea turtles suffer incidental mortality in shrimp trawl nets, wouldn't this contribute to the endangerment of sea turtles?

2. Mr. Guinea has performed a calculation, based on the reproductive values of sea turtles, and concludes that an annual mortality of 5,000 sea turtles nesting at Gahirmatha is "relatively minor". It was unclear to us whether this was merely an example explaining how "reproductive values" affect conservation analyses, or whether Mr. Guinea meant this as a definitive opinion that shrimp trawling off Gahirmatha is not a concern. Could the other experts also comment on this matter?

3. All of the experts have noted various causes of sea turtle mortality, including mortality on the beaches, and due to incidental mortality in shrimping and fishing operations. Does the existence of all of these threats to sea turtles make it more important, or less important, to prevent sea turtle mortality in shrimp trawl nets?

4. Do the experts agree that TEDs, when properly installed and used, reduce the mortality of sea turtles in shrimp trawl nets?

5. If all the world's shrimp trawling fleets used TEDs, would this contribute to the reduction to the threat to sea turtles? Note: We are not asking whether the use of TEDs would be sufficient to conserve sea turtles, but whether the use of TEDs would contribute to sea turtle conservation. We are also not asking the separate, sociological question of the best way (such as the adoption of regulations or the promotion of voluntary use) to encourage shrimp fishermen to use TEDs.

6. Both Dr. Poiner and Mr. Guinea mention time and area closures as a helpful approaches to sea turtle conservation. Could the experts comment on this, and in particular, address whether sea turtle mortality could also occur in areas where, and during times when, shrimp trawling is not banned. Do we have enough knowledge to identify all potential "hot spots" where sea turtles and shrimp fisheries interact?

7. Could Dr. Eckert please elaborate on his statement that seasonal migrations would not be expected in regions with warm waters?

8. Mr. Guinea noted that the adoption of TEDs by a shrimp trawling fleet would take 6-8 years. Could the experts comment on this point, particularly in light of Mr. Guinea's comment that Thailand modified existing technology to create an elegant and effective TED within a matter of months?

*Questions by Thailand*

1. Several of the experts have commented on the high number of turtle strandings that occur in the United States where and when TEDs are required. Do the experts agree

that this evidence demonstrates any or all of the following: (a) even after years of implementation, TEDs are difficult to use properly; (b) TEDs requirements are easy to evade and many shrimpers in areas where TEDs are required believe that reasons exist to evade the requirements; (c) TEDs requirements are not easily enforced; and/or (d) mandating a TEDs requirement does not guarantee that sea turtle mortality will be reduced?

2. Although Thailand was able to quickly modify an existing TEDs design in order to receive certification from the United States, are the experts aware that Thailand was unable to develop the TEDs within the short-four-month time period provided by the U.S. measures?

3. Are the experts aware that the Thai TEDs has not been found effective in actual use?

4. Do the experts believe that four months is sufficient time to select and modify gear, train shrimper, and take all other steps necessary to implement a TEDs requirement?

# Appendix 2
# Graphic 1: Dr. S. Eckert
# 21 January 1998

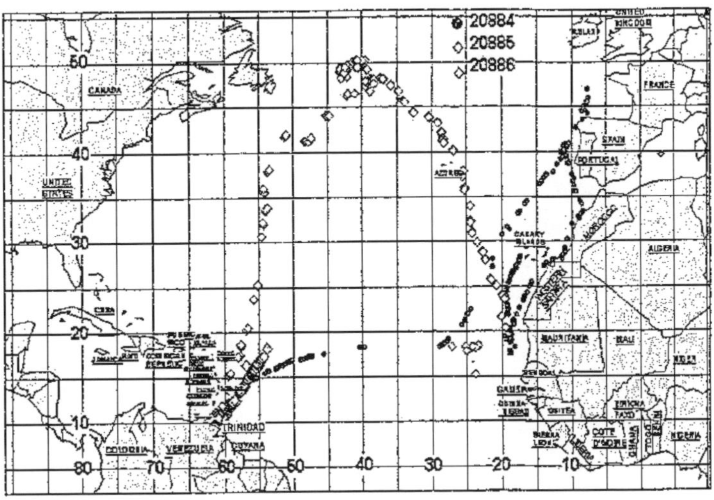


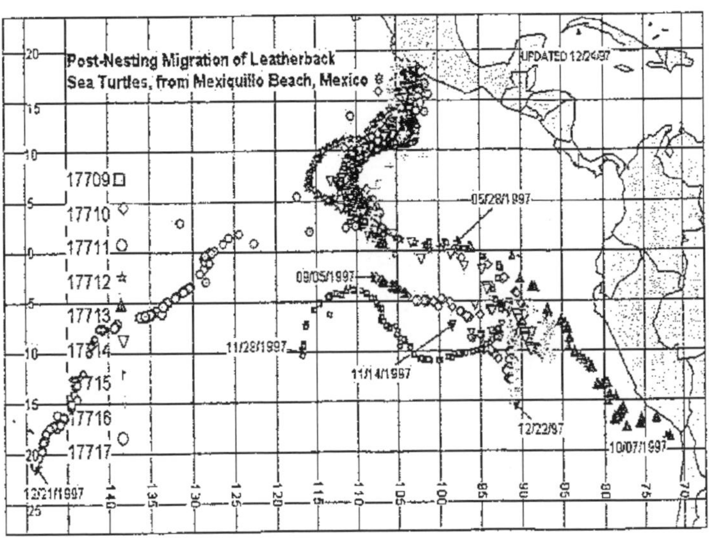

## Graph 2: Dr. S. Eckert
## 21 January 1998

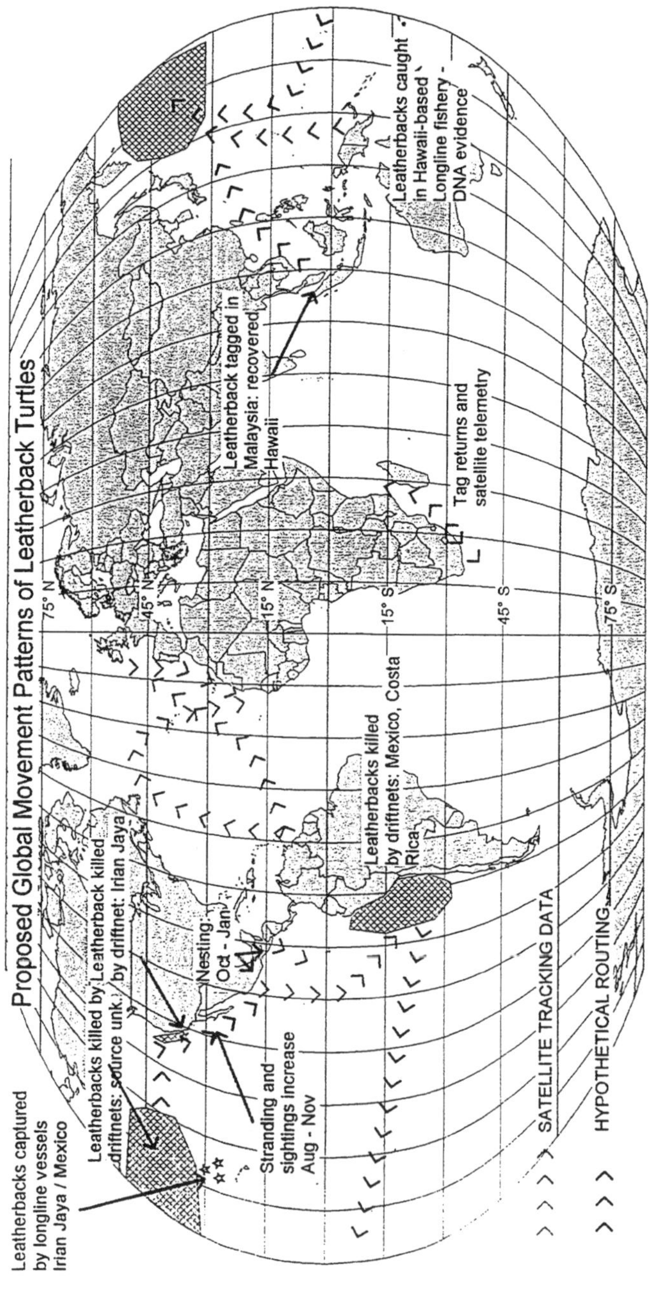

**Graph 3: Dr. S. Eckert**
**21 January 1998**

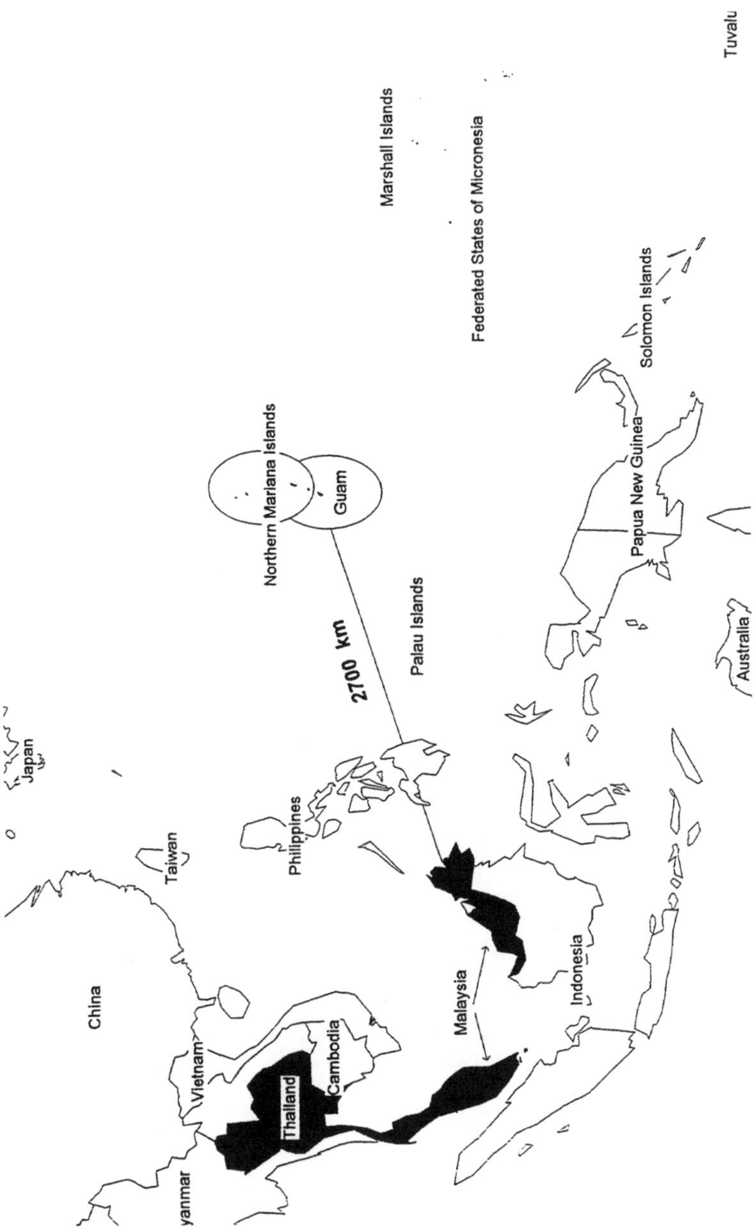

**Graph 4: Mr. H.-C. Liew**
**21 January 1998**

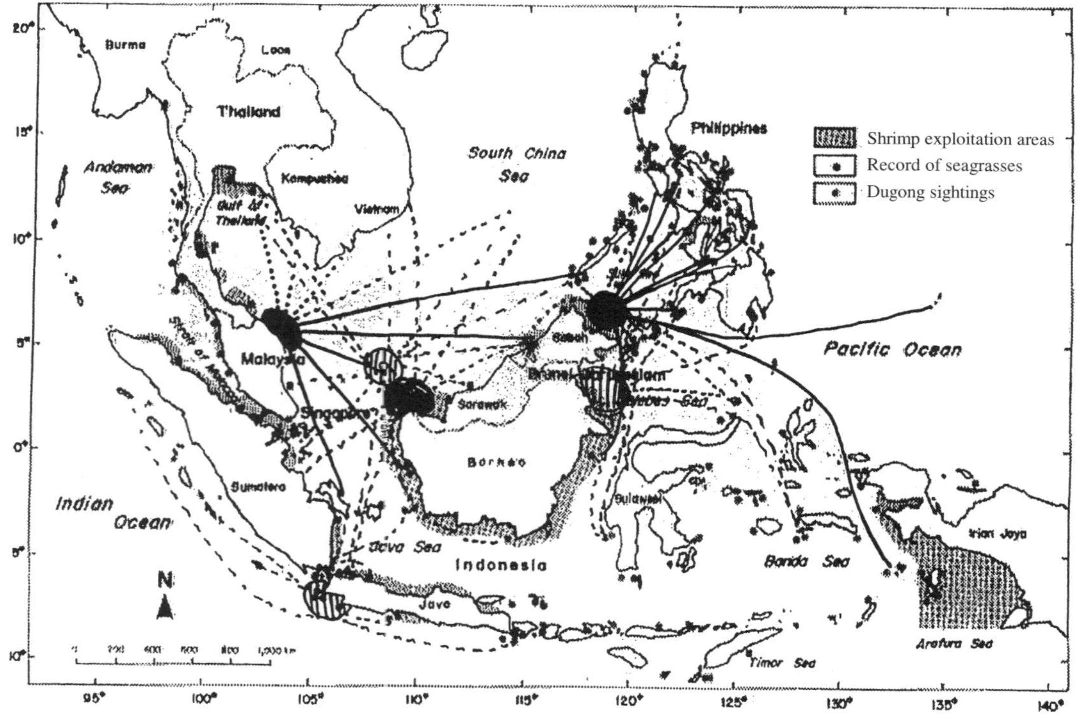


Sea-grass distribution in the ASEAN

**Nesting location of breeding/population units:**

Malaysian

Indonesian

**Graph 5: Mr. H.-C. Liew**
**21 January 1998**

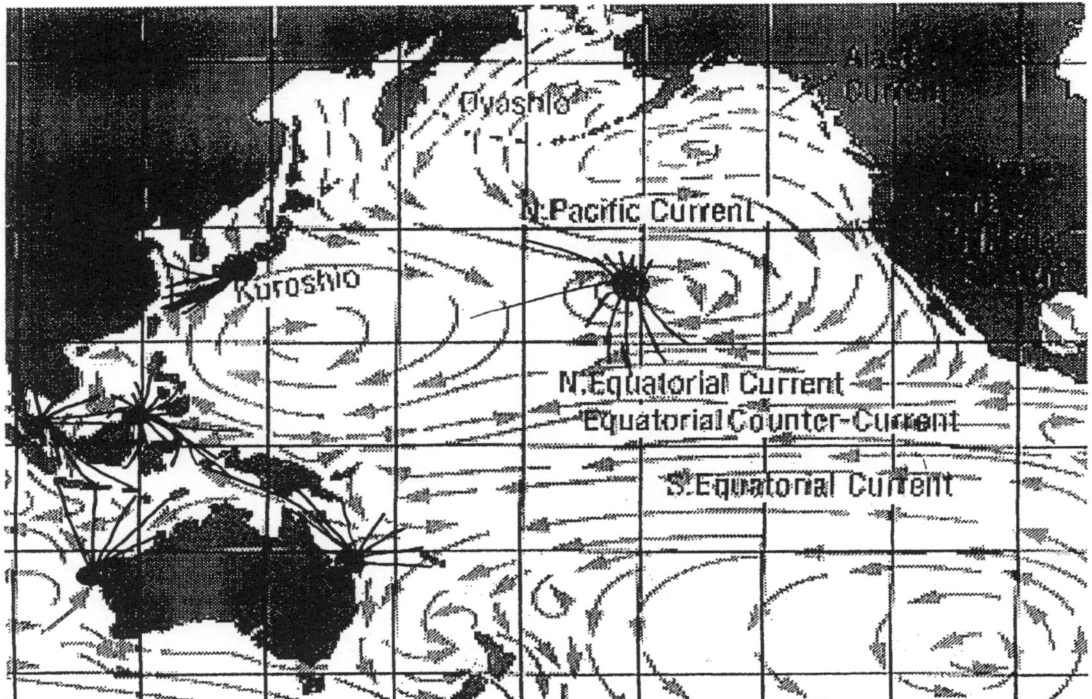


**Ocean currents of the Pacific during the northern winter**

## Graph 6: Mr. H.-C. Liew
## 22 January 1998

**PENDARATAN PUKAT TUNDA, 1991-1995**
*(Trawl Landings, 1991-1995)*
**SEMENANJUNG MALAYSIA**
*(Peninsular Malaysia)*

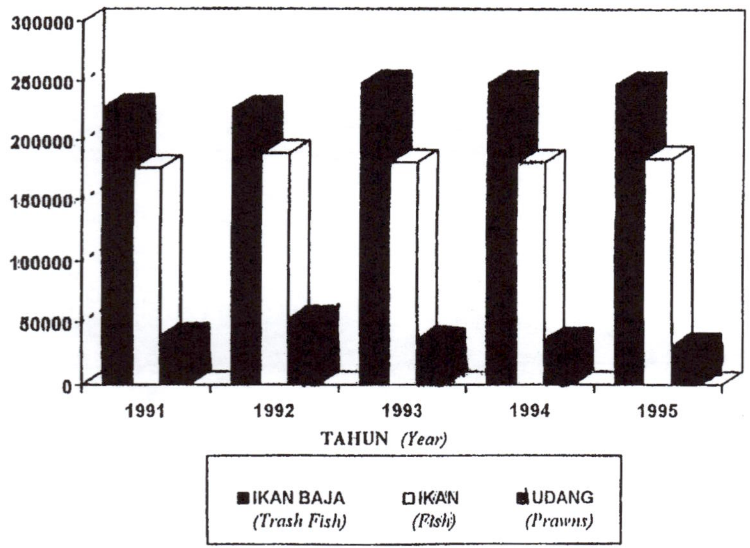


**Taken from: Annual Fisheries Statistics 1995, Dept. of Fisheries Malaysia**

# Graph 7: Mr. H.-C. Liew
## 22 January 1998

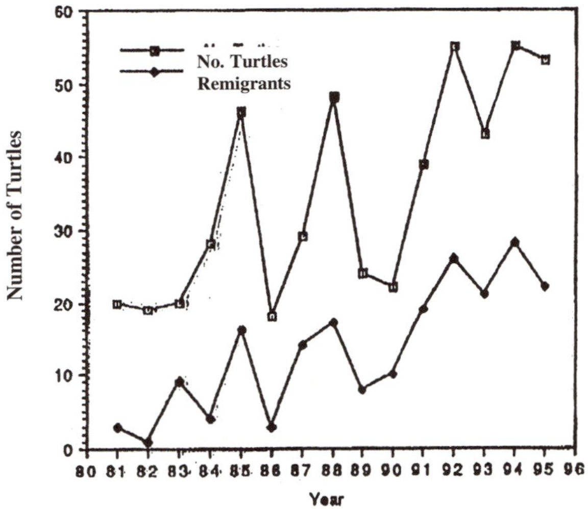


**Annual number of leatherback turtles and remigrants, Sandy Point, St. Croix, from 1981 to 1995.**
(Taken from Boulon R.H., P.H. Dutton and D.L. McDonald, 1996. Leatherback Turtles (*Dermochelys coriacea*) on St. Croix, U.S. Virgin Islands: Fifteen Years of Conservation. Chelonian Conservation and Biology, 2(2): 141-147.)

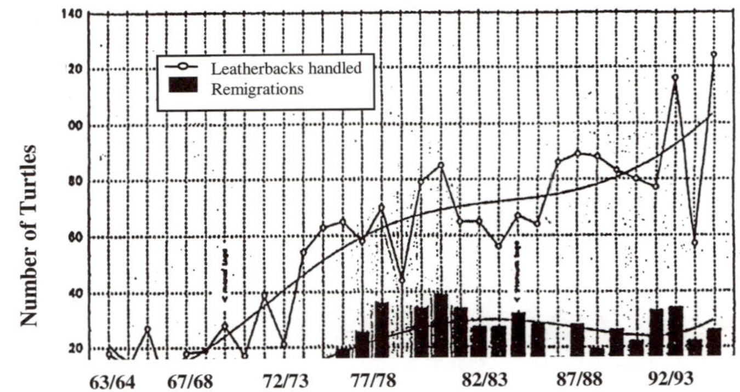


**Tongaland leatherback nesting population numbers and remigrations.**
(Taken from Hughes, G.R. 1996. Nesting of the leatherback (*Dermochelys corlacea*) in Tongaland, KwaZulu-Natal, South Africa, 1963-1995. Chelonian Conservation and Biology, 2(2): 153-158)

Graph 8: Mr. H.-C. Liew
22 January 1998

## Green Turtle nesting in the Sabah Turtle Islands, Malaysia

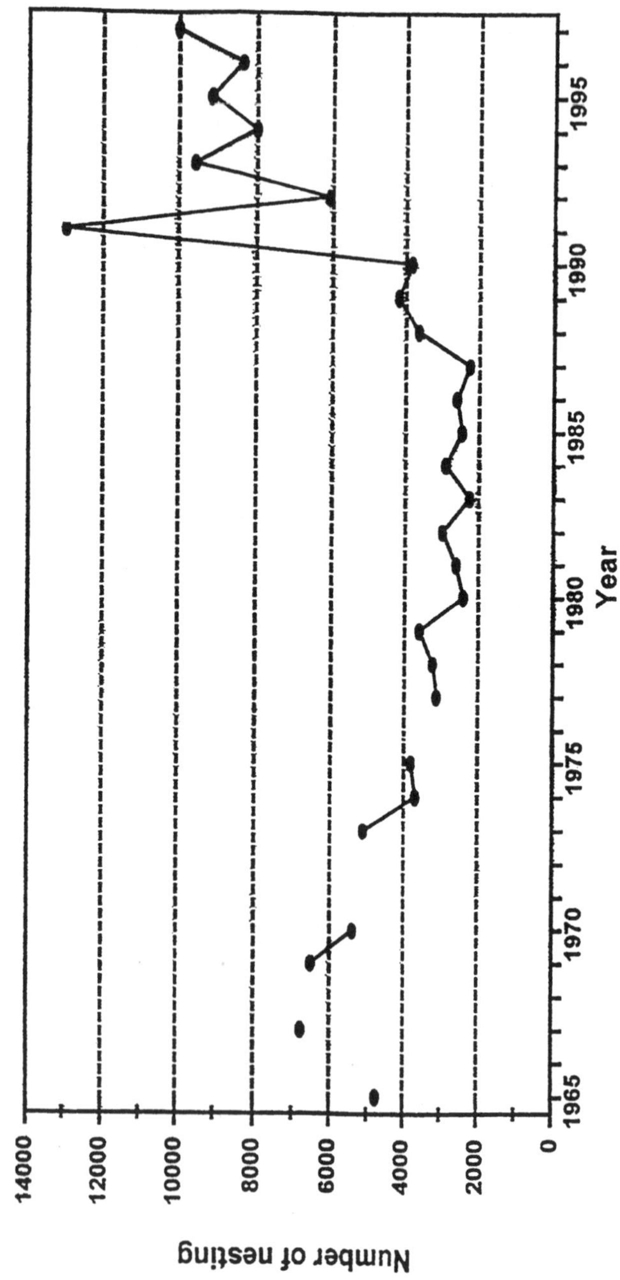